THE ECONOMICS OF AIRPORT OPERATIONS

ADVANCES IN AIRLINE ECONOMICS

Series Editor: James H. Peoples

Recent Volumes:

Volume 1: Competition Policy and Anti-Trust, Darin Lee

Volume 2: The Economics of Airline Institutions, Operations and Marketing, Darin Lee

Volume 3: Pricing Behaviour and Non-Price Characteristics in the Airline Industry, James H. Peoples

Volume 4: The Economics of International Airline Transport, James H. Peoples

Volume 5: Airline Efficiency, John D. Bitzan, James H. Peoples, and Wesley W. Wilson

ADVANCES IN AIRLINE ECONOMICS VOLUME 6

THE ECONOMICS OF AIRPORT OPERATIONS

EDITED BY

JOHN D. BITZAN

North Dakota State University, Fargo, ND, USA

JAMES H. PEOPLES

University of Wisconsin-Milwaukee, Milwaukee, WI, USA

emerald PUBLISHING

United Kingdom – North America – Japan
India – Malaysia – China

Emerald Publishing Limited
Howard House, Wagon Lane, Bingley BD16 1WA, UK

First edition 2017

British Library Cataloguing in Publication Data
A catalogue record for this book is available from the British Library

ISBN: 978-1-78714-498-9 (Print)
ISBN: 978-1-78714-497-2 (Online)
ISBN: 978-1-78714-949-6 (Epub)

ISSN: 2212-1609 (Series)

CONTENTS

LIST OF CONTRIBUTORS

Margaret Arblaster	Institute of Transport Studies, Monash University, Melbourne, Victoria, Australia
Paolo Beria	Department of Architecture and Urban Studies, Polotecnoco di Milano, Milano, Italy
John D. Bitzan	Department of Management and Marketing, North Dakota State University, Fargo, ND, USA
Anna Bottasso	Dipartimento di Economia, Universita di Genova, Genova, Italy
Valentina Bracaglia	Sapienza Universita di Roma, Roma, Italy
Mike Brown	Greater Toronto Airports Authority, Toronto AMF, Ontario, Canada
Jeffrey P. Cohen	School of Business, University of Connecticut, Storrs, CT, USA
Maurizio Conti	European Commission, Joint Research Center, Ispra (VA), Italy
Tiziana D'Alfonso	Department of Computer, Control and Management Engineering, Sapienza University of Rome, Roma, Italy
Xavier Fageda	Department of Econometrics, Statistics and Applied Economics, Faculty of Economics and Business, University of Barcelona, Barcelona, Spain
Ricardo Flores-Fillol	Department d'Economia and CREIP, University Rovira i Virgili, Avinguda de la Universitat 1 Reus, Reus, Spain

Xiaowen Fu	Institute of Transport and Logistics Studies, University of Sydney, Sydney, NSW, Australia
Soraya Hidalgo-Gallego	Facultad de Ciencias Económicas y Empresariales, Santander, Spain
Katsuya Hihara	The University of Tokyo, GraSPP, Tokyo, Japan
Finn Jørgensen	Nord University, Business School, Bodø, Norway
Tay T. R. Koo	School of Aviation, Faculty of Science, University of New South Wales, Sydney, NSW, Australia
Antonio Laurino	Department of Architecture and Urban Studies Polotecnoco di Milano, Milano, Italy
Valeriano Martínez-San Román	Facultad de Ciencias Económicas y Empresariales, Santander, Spain
Terje A. Mathisen	Nord University, Business School, Bodø, Norway
Marquise J. McGraw	U.S. Consumer Financial Protection Bureau, Washington, DC, USA
Ramón Núñez-Sánchez	Facultad de Ciencias Económicas y Empresariales, Santander, Spain
Andreas Papatheodorou	Department of Business Administration, University of Aegean, Chios, Greece; School of Aviation, Faculty of Science, University of New South Wales, Sydney, NSW, Australia
Pål A. Pedersen	Nord University, Business School, Bodø, Norway
James H. Peoples	Department of Economics, University of Wisconsin-Milwaukee, Milwaukee, WI, USA

Maria Nadia Postorino Department of Civil Energy, Environment and Materials Engineering, University of Mediterranea of Reggio Calabria, Localita Feo di Vito, Calabria, Italy

Héctor Rodríguez-Déniz Department of Transportation Science, KTH Royal Institute of Technology, Stockholm, Sweden

Georgina Santos School of Geography and Planning, Cardiff University, Wales, UK

Gisle Solvoll Nord University, Business School, Bodø, Norway

Pere Suau-Sanchez Cranfield University, Centre of Air Transportation Management, Bedfordshire, UK

Augusto Voltes-Dorta University of Edinburgh Business School, Edinburgh, UK

Hangjun Yang University of International Business and Economics, Beijing, China

EDITORIAL MEMBERS

ABOUT THE EDITORS

John D. Bitzan is Professor of Management at North Dakota State University. Over a 25 year period, he has performed research related to a variety of transportation issues, including costs, energy, intermodal competition, investment, industry structure, pricing, profitability, and regulation. Moreover, his research has examined a variety of modes, including air, motor, public transit, rail, and water carriers. He has performed research for the U.S. Army Corps of Engineers (as an independent reviewer), the U.S. Department of Agriculture, and the U.S. Federal Railroad Administration. He is Associate Editor of Advances in Airline Economics and of the Journal of the Transportation Research Forum.

James H. Peoples is Professor of Economics at the University of Wisconsin-Milwaukee. His current research interests include analysis of production efficiency for different modes of freight transportation. He has served as president of the *National Economic Association* and president of the *Transportation and Public Utilities Group*. He currently serves as series editor of *Advances in Airline Economics*. Other editorial responsibilities include serving as editorial board member of *Transport* Policy, as well as editorial board member of *Open Economics*. He previously served as associate editor of the *Review of Black Political Economy*.

CHAPTER 1

INTRODUCTION

John D. Bitzan and James H. Peoples

Airports serve an essential role in domestic and international travel, facilitating the origination, termination, and connections of air flights. Airport services enhance regional, national, and global connections, increasing the mobility of people worldwide and enhancing local and regional economies. Although, there is a large amount of literature that examines airline costs and productivity, consumer welfare from air travel, and the influence of economic regulation of airline services, there is much less literature that examines airports. This is important, as airport operations play a critical role in influencing airline travel. This volume examines the role that airports play in economic development and land values, the regulation and economic efficiency of airports, airport pricing and competition, and the role played by airports in influencing airline operations and networks.

It is well known that air travel allows businesses to efficiently transport products and people over long distances, and enhances connections and mobility of people worldwide. For businesses, access to airport service lowers the costs of obtaining resources and of selling products in other locations. This, in turn, enhances their competitiveness in other markets. Moreover, air service also enables firms from other locations to more easily access regional markets, thereby enhancing price competition and benefitting consumers. The important role that airports play in influencing regional economies and land values is one area explored in this book.

In addition, the book focuses on the crucial role of airports in the scope of airline services. Because airline efficiency, pricing, and networks are influenced

The Economics of Airport Operations
Advances in Airline Economics, Volume 6, 1–14

ISSN: 2212-1609/doi:10.1108/S2212-160920170000006001

by airport operations, a full understanding of air services requires an understanding of airport issues, such as regulation, efficiency, pricing, capacity decisions, and competition. This is especially important given major changes that have occurred in the way airports are operated. Since the mid-1980s, as part of a broader move toward privatization, many airports throughout the world have been privatized (Poole & Edwards, 2016). According to the U.S. Government Accountability Office, 450 airports worldwide have been at least partially privatized (U.S. Government Accountability Office (GAO), 2014). Moreover, these airports are increasingly relying on non-aeronautical services, such as car rentals, retail sales, and food sales for large portions of their revenues. As a result, it is important for governments to carefully consider new regulatory alternatives to traditional methods, such as rate of return regulation and price cap regulation. This book examines changes in airport business models and various approaches to government oversight in light of these changes. Further, the book examines airport efficiency, airport pricing, airport competition, and airport–airline relationships. Chapters in this book volume contribute to our understanding of the economic impact of airport operations by using contemporary empirical methods grounded in transportation economic theory.

Chapter contributions can be grouped into four categories: (1) chapters examining the changing nature of airport operations and implications for the role of government; (2) chapters examining the efficiency, structure, and pricing of airport services; (3) chapters that directly examine the effects of airport operations on local and regional economies; and (4) chapters examining airport competition and the role airports play in influencing airline operations and networks. Chapters examining the changing nature of airport operations discuss a new approach to regulation called "light-handed" regulation, the implications of increased non-aeronautical revenues for regulation of airport pricing, the impact of privatization strategy on airport efficiency, and innovative commercial arrangements that have been made between airports and airlines. Theory suggests that regulation can introduce market distortions that hamper efficiency, choice of operating structure, and pricing of services. The increased commercialization of airports suggests several potential benefits from these new more market-based approaches to airport oversight. Further explorations of these market outcomes are examined in the second set of chapters. These chapters include analysis of social welfare implications of various airport fees and the ability of airlines to pass-on airport fees, the cost structure of airports, and a discussion of a new approach to examining airport policy debates, called new geographical economics. Such analyses are significant, in part, because they contribute to our understanding the potential and limitations airports face as economic drivers. The third group of chapters reveals how well airport operations have enhanced regional and economic growth by examining the effect of this service on cities, land values, as well as considering the potential of airport endogeneity by examining airport dependency from an economic geography perspective. The final group of chapters explores airline–airport interactions, and how these interactions influence economic efficiency and the welfare of society.

In sum, this volume provides a nuanced and thorough analysis of the economic impact of airport operations.

THE CHANGING NATURE OF AIRPORT OPERATIONS AND THE ROLE OF GOVERNMENT

As mentioned above, airports are increasingly operated as commercial entities. Worldwide, many airports have been privatized. According to Young (2014), over $6.2 billion in airport revenues were generated by for-profit airport groups in 2009, with the largest fully privatized airports in Copenhagen, Denmark and Brussels, Belgium (Young, 2014). Moreover, although most U.S. airports are not privatized, almost 40% of the largest 100 airports are managed by port or airport authorities (Young, 2014). Thus, airports are operated much more like businesses than like government entities (Young, 2014). Airports rely heavily on non-aeronautical revenues for growth and survival, including generating revenues from rents paid by concession tenants (food shops, restaurants, etc.), parking fees, rental car operations, rental of airport land, and advertising (Airports Council International, 2013). According to the Airports Council International, more than 45% of U.S. airport revenues were generated from non-aeronautical sources, such as parking and ground transportation, rental cars, retail shops, and food and beverages (Airports Council International, 2016).[1]

In the context of these changes that have taken place, the initial chapter by Margaret Arblaster examines a different approach to regulation, called "light-handed regulation." Arblaster suggests that the consideration of the appropriate form of regulation for airports has increased in importance due to their increasing commercialization. She notes that traditional regulatory approaches for airports have included things like rate of return regulation and price cap regulation. However, as is well known, these types of regulations lead to various problems, such as inefficiency, overcapitalization, and a lack of innovation. Arblaster discusses an alternative approach, called "light-handed regulation," where the government allows free negotiation of prices between airports and airlines, with the threat of regulatory intervention should the airport abuse its market power. Arblaster reviews the experiences of Australia and New Zealand, where "light-handed regulation" has involved required information disclosure and sometimes negotiate-arbitrate regulation. She finds that the effectiveness of "light-handed regulation" depends on three important factors: (1) how credible is the threat of stronger regulatory intervention if poor performance is identified? (2) how much transparency is provided to airport users under the regulatory approach (more transparency decreases the likelihood of poor performance)? and (3) how high are administrative and compliance costs associated with the regulatory approach? In the cases of Australia and New Zealand, she finds an important tradeoff: While New Zealand's new enhanced information disclosure requirement is likely to be more effective in preventing an abuse of monopoly power by airports, it also imposes a high regulatory burden.

Just as the changing nature of airport operations may present opportunities for less prescriptive forms of regulation, it may also change the way airport services are priced. Through a review of the relevant literature, Tiziana D'Alfanso and Valentina Bracaglia show that the increased use of non-aeronautical services (concessions) for airport revenues has important implications for the pricing of airport services. The authors point out that the implications of increased revenues from concessions on the pricing of aeronautical services depend on whether the complementary relationship between concession services and aeronautical services runs one way or two ways, and whether the overall demand for concession services is independent of traveling. Through reviewing the literature, the authors show that if the demand for concession services increase when aeronautical charges decrease, but the demand for aeronautical services is unaffected by concession charges, then having concession revenues tends to put downward pressure on aeronautical charges. This is because airports can attract more passengers to their airports through the reduced aeronautical charges, therefore increasing concession sales. On the other hand, when the complementary relationship between concessions and aeronautical services is "two-sided," this can exert upward pressure on aeronautical charges. For example, if a passenger needs to rent a car at their destination, a lower car rental price can increase the demand for air service to that destination, increasing the aeronautical charge. The authors also point out that when more of the demand for concession services is independent of traveling (e.g., you would consume food whether traveling or not), the difference between profit maximizing and social welfare maximizing prices for aeronautical services is reduced. Based on a review of literature in this area, the authors find: (1) there is no generalized finding on either of these issues (two-sided complementarity and welfare neutrality), (2) the two may be interrelated, and (3) these should be examined on a case by case basis, as they are often determined by the type, ownership, and size of airport. Moreover, these issues have very important implications for the desired nature of airport regulation. For example, if the complementary relationship between concessions and aeronautical services is "one-sided" (demand for aeronautical services is unaffected by concessions prices) and demand for concession services is independent of traveling, then the need for economic regulation of airport pricing may be limited. This suggests an important area for future research.

As highlighted Soraya Hidalgo-Gallego, Valeriano Martínez-San Román, and Ramón Núñez-Sánchez, the motivations for privatizing airports worldwide vary widely. One motivation that has been highlighted by many researchers in the airport industry and in other industries is the potential for private entities to improve efficiency over government involvement. Hidalgo-Gallego, Martinez-San Roman, and Nunez-Sanchez measure the change in allocative efficiency that occurred for Spanish airports from 2009 to 2014, in the period just prior to their partial privatization. The authors note the Spanish government's efforts to privatize Aena, a firm that manages 46 airports throughout Spain, ranging from those in Madrid and Barcelona that each handles about 40 million passengers per year to small airports that handle less than 500,000 passengers per year. As described by Hidalgo-Gallego et al., the initial focus of privatization by the Spanish government was to privatize the largest airports (Madrid and Barcelona) and encourage decentralized airport management. However, the newly elected government in 2012 changed the privatization plan to include partial privatization of the whole system, with a focus on improving the smaller regional airports. In evaluating the changing allocative efficiency during this pre-privatization period (2009–2014), the authors find several interesting results. First, they find an improvement in allocative efficiency as a result of the move toward privatization. Second, they find important differences between the periods coinciding with changes in government philosophy regarding privatization. During the first period, when the focus was on privatizing the largest airports, there were big improvements in allocative efficiency. During the second period, when the focus was on partially privatizing the entire system, allocative efficiency did not improve. Interestingly, when allocative efficiency change is broken down by airport group, it is shown that there were large improvements in allocative efficiency for the large airports when they were the primary target of privatization, while the allocative efficiency of these airports decreased when the focus of privatization shifted toward the entire system. These results suggest that the success of privatization in improving airport efficiency depends on the way that airports are privatized. The results may also be interpreted as showing an important benefit from managing airports individually, rather than as a group.

As the increasing commercialization of airports has created opportunities for new forms of regulation, has changed the way that airport services are priced, and has resulted in many privatized entities, it has also resulted in new opportunities for various cooperative relationships between airlines and airports. In Chapter 5, Xiaowen Fu and Hangjun Yang note there are major financial challenges for airports now, with requirements that many be free from government subsidy at the same time that there is a demand for more services. This, along with other changes in the industry has resulted in airlines and airports engaging in a number of innovative commercial arrangements. Fu and Yang review the literature on airport–airline arrangements, identifying common types of arrangements, methods used to assess the impacts of such arrangements, and findings of recent studies regarding their effects. Some interesting airport–airline arrangements identified by Fu and Yang include (but are not limited to): (1) airlines being designated as "signatory airline" at an airport, where they pay residual airport costs (after subtracting other airport revenues from costs), but also maintain more control of airport operations and may realize lower charges, (2) direct airline investment in terminal facilities, allowing them to control such facilities, (3) long-term usage contracts, allowing airlines to lock-in favorable terms, (4) airport issued bonds backed by airlines, allowing airlines to have exclusive or near-exclusive use of specific facilities, (5) sharing of airport non-aeronautical revenues with airlines as an incentive to generate more traffic, (6) load factor guarantees, where airports guarantee a certain load factor on new services provided by an airline, (7) airport–airline consortiums, where groups of airlines jointly finance various airport facilities, (8) information sharing and joint marketing by airlines and airports, and (9) various incentive programs given by airports to encourage traffic growth. Fu and Yang identify several potential benefits of these arrangements, such as internalizing the positive externality between non-aeronautical services and aeronautical services, increasing service quality, enabling more investment in capacity, allowing sharing of risks between airlines and airports, and increasing airport traffic. However, they also note that these arrangements lead to concerns over their ability to harm competition. Fu and Yang note that the overall economic impacts of these types of arrangements vary depending on market structure and the type of arrangement. They suggest that although these arrangements should be assessed on a case by case basis, they are likely to be more beneficial to society with more competition in the airline or airport sector and with more transparency on the nature of the airport–airline arrangements. Fu and Yang suggest that only limited empirical research has been carried out in this area. As government fiscal pressures increase and airports become increasingly commercialized, this is certainly an important area for future research.

One of the particularly interesting types of airport–airline arrangements identified by Fu and Yang is the risk-sharing relationship, where the airport guarantees a certain load factor to the airline to attract service. In Chapter 6, Katsuya Hihara examines an airport–airline relationship between All Nippon Airways and the Noto Airport in Japan. This airport is in a less populated area of Japan and was built in 2003 to provide better access to Tokyo, which was previously a 7 hour trip without air service. The new airport has been able to provide twice a day service to Tokyo through a load factor guarantee arrangement between All Nippon Airways and the airport. The load factor guarantee arrangement is particularly innovative and effective in that it is structured so that risks of low traffic and the gains of high traffic are shared by the airline and the airport. In many of these contracts, the risks of the low traffic are shared by the airport, but the gains from the high traffic are not shared by the airport. The All Nippon Airways-Noto arrangement is set up so that the airport pays the airline when the traffic is low and the airline pays the airport when the traffic is high. Hihara highlights several benefits of this arrangement, such as enhancing the efforts of the airport and the airline to achieve the common load factor goal, the signed commitment by the airline to serve the airport for at least a year ensuring continued service, and the ability for the arrangement to be adjusted to achieve a stable load factor goal. He also proposes a framework to assess the risk-sharing balance between the airport and airline in this type of arrangement, and he examines this type of arrangement using contract and principal agent theories. Hihara shows that if this type of arrangement is designed the right way, it can increase the effort levels and the benefits to both airline and airports. Moreover, it can ensure continued air service to low traffic density areas without requiring government subsidies.

EFFICIENCY, STRUCTURE AND PRICING OF AIRPORT SERVICES

While airports worldwide are becoming increasingly commercialized entities, and often various airport–airline arrangements exist, there are still parts of the world where airports are primarily government owned and where airport charges are closely regulated. In Chapter 7 of this volume, Gisle Solvoll and Terje Mathisen examine airport charges in Norway, where the state-owned company Avinor operates most of the airports. Using data on Avinor operated airports, they estimate the marginal cost for each passenger and air traffic movement, and examine the changes in charges that would occur if the current charges were changed to be based on marginal costs. They find that a switch to marginal cost pricing would result in lower charges per air traffic movement and higher charges per passenger in Norway. Moreover, they also find that revenues would be substantially reduced for Avinor. Solvoll and Mathisen extend their analysis to examine social welfare implications of using marginal cost pricing and making up revenue losses with general taxation. They find that there is a social welfare gain from marginal cost pricing when the costs of general taxation are zero, but there is a social welfare loss from marginal cost pricing when the costs of general taxation are 20%. The authors also demonstrate the changes in per passenger changes and air traffic movement charges that would occur if a Ramsey approach to pricing were used, where rural airports are charged higher fees than more heavily used airports. They note, however, that this type of approach would be difficult to implement in Norway, where the Ministry of Transport has directed that charges be the same for all airports. Solvoll and Mathisen provide an interesting analysis of airport charges that might be applied to airports elsewhere.

In the changing airport environment discussed earlier, an understanding of airport costs is crucial. As Anna Bottasso and Maurizio Conti (Chapter 8) point out, a wide range of policy and management issues require a detailed understanding of airport costs. For example, while new approaches to regulation such as "light-handed regulation" are being considered worldwide, the main rationale for regulation of airports is based on the idea that they are natural monopolies – i.e., they meet the condition of cost subadditivity. Understanding airport costs are also crucial in regional decisions involving airport expansion or building new airports, and in decisions on creating specialized airports. In addition, whether airports are private or public, intelligent pricing decisions depend on an understanding of costs, as do decisions on mixing aeronautical with non-aeronautical services and international services with domestic services. However, as Bottasso and Conti point out, even though these and several other policy issues rely heavily on understanding cost structure, more attention in the literature has been devoted to efficiency determinants, using data envelopment analysis (DEA). They suggest that more research is needed that identifies cost structure using an econometric approach. In a comprehensive study, Bottasso and Conti examine the importance of carefully measuring inputs and outputs in estimating airport costs, and identify measures of multi-output scale and scope economies and their relationships and the methodological issues associated with trying to identify cost subadditivity. They also discuss the merits of using flexible functional forms, and review the empirical literature on airport costs. Bottasso and Conti's review yields several important findings, including: (1) a consensus on scale economies in airports does not exist, though a broader consensus might be reached by more studies using airport fixed effects and variable cost functions or input distance functions, (2) there is very little evidence on economies of scope for airports, (3) the translog cost function should be abandoned in favor of more flexible forms that allow the inclusion of zero outputs, and (4) given the increased commercialization of the industry, more attention needs to be given to the potential endogeneity of outputs. They also suggest that an area of future research (in addition to those above) may be to extend airport cost analysis to consider externalities. Bottasso and Conti's chapter is an important read for anyone considering an analysis of airport costs. Moreover, given the important unresolved issues they identify, and their important policy implications, there is much room for more research in this area in the future.

Accurately depicting airport cost structure is critical to understanding fee determination of airlines because of airlines' abilities or lack thereof to pass-on airport costs to passengers in the form of higher fares and fees. In Chapter 9, Terje A. Mathisen, Finn Jørgensen, Pål A. Pedersen, and Georgina Santos examine airline carriers' abilities to "pass-on" airport costs to passengers using an economic model of supply and passenger demand that allows for airport managerial objective heterogeneity and airline market (route) structure heterogeneity. Airport fees are determined given airport managerial objectives that include profit maximization, passenger welfare maximization, and management utility maximization. Airline pass-on rates influenced by airport fees are determined for monopolistic and duopoly airline market (route) structures. Within this theoretical framework, the authors observe a wide range of potential pass-on rates. The lowest rates arise for a monopoly airline market structure with a linear passenger demand function where 50% of the airport fees are passed on to passengers, while the highest rates arise for a monopoly airline structure with a power demand function where over 100% of fees are passed on. These authors apply their model using information from small and mid-sized Norwegian airports, which allows for examining the influence of managerial objectives on passenger fares. Their findings show that airport fees can vary widely depending on the objectives of the airport authority, market structure, airline and airport costs, and demand. They conclude that the decision making process on airport fees should include consideration of passenger demand and airline market structure.

The preceding chapters note the significance of airport performance and pricing as determinants of passenger demand. Passenger demand for airport service, however, is not limited to these determinants as the theory of economic geography suggests that the physical landscape of a location promotes economic activity that can facilitate air transport demand. Within the economic geography literature, these natural resources are called "first nature causes" of regional economic activity. This literature observes that regional economic activity is also influenced by factors associated with human actions and economic incentives such as economies of scale and transport costs, known as "second nature causes" (Gonzalez-Val & Pueyo, 2010). In Chapter 10 in this volume, Tay Koo and Andreas Papatheodorou focus on the "second nature" component of geographical economics, which is identified as new geographical economics (NGE), to frame the airport policy debates on issues such as the decision to invest in an airport system that serves a region using a single hub or relying on several airports. The analysis of this chapter is rich with examples revealing the benefits of using NGE to help guide the policy discussion on airport development and provides a path toward future research opportunities for deriving empirically testable hypothesis on airport operations.

AIRPORT EFFECTS ON LOCAL AND REGIONAL ECONOMIES

While regional and local amenities affect airport operations, these amenities on airport operations, these amenities are not exogenous since airports also influence a locality's amenities by promoting local and regional economic development (Kasarda & Appold, 2014). In Chapter 11, Marquise McGraw contributes to the literature on airport influence on local economies by examining the role of airports as sources of employment and population growth. His approach provides a more precise analysis of airports' local economic effects by considering the possibility of airport economic impact heterogeneity. His chapter's research design includes analysis spanning the 110 years recent history of aviation in the United States, starting in 1900. He applies a synthetic control empirical approach to compare employment and population growth across localities. The benefit derived from using this empirical methodology, in part, is it allows examination of airports' heterogeneous influences on local labor markets. His findings suggest that when controlling for airport heterogeneity, airport operations contribute to local employment and population growth ranging from 0.2 to 0.6 percent annually. In addition, he finds airports benefit cities more when they are in close proximity to major research universities, are near state capitals, and when they are located in temperate areas. In contrast, his findings did not reveal appreciable differences in impacts across regions or by type of airport governance. He interprets these results to suggest that while investment in airport infrastructure can promote local employment growth, the full benefits may not be realized without robust amounts of human capital developed by universities or in other ways to enhance the economic impact of airport infrastructure investment.

In addition to benefitting local economic development by promoting employment growth, airport operations can also contribute to the development of local economies by increasing the value of commercial property. In Chapter 12, Mike Brown and Jeffrey Cohen examine commercial property values located near Canada's two largest international airports at Toronto, Ontario, and Vancouver, BC. As noted in previous chapters, international air transport plays a vital role in the competitiveness of businesses in a globalized economy. Gains from the degree of connectivity an airport experiences, coupled with local business proximity to these airports, are reflected not only in local business performance but also in property values. The authors of this chapter empirically test this hypothesis and introduce a broader classification of aviation-dependent property to included hotels and corporate headquarters as examples commercial property that might be value-sensitive to location near airports. Their findings reveal the enhancement of commercial property value attributable to proximity to these international airports varies according to land use, with the greatest effects on commercial property occupied by aviation-dependent occupants. The authors note, though, that the description of such business should be broadened to include "non-aviation" related property that benefits from airport operations, even though their business is not directly related to aviation operations. The authors interpret these findings to suggest that regional competitiveness can be enhanced by accommodating "aviation-dependent" business to locate near airports even if their core business is not classified as "aviation-related" in the traditional use of this term.

AIRPORT OPERATIONS AND AIRPORT CONNECTIVITY

Chapters in the preceding three sections of this volume explore the changing nature of airports, examine efficiency and pricing issues, and reveal the significance of airports as determinants of local and regional economic development.

Complementing the work presented in these chapters, other research emphasizes the importance of airline connectivity in taking full advantage of the economic benefits of efficient and affordable airport services (Arvis & Shepherd, 2011; Morphet & Bottini, 2014).[2] The three remaining chapters examine different aspects of airport operations and airline connectivity in contributing to a complete analysis of the economic role of airports in the aviation industry.

In Chapter 13, Xavier Fageda and Ricardo Flores-Fillol examine the relationship between an airline's network structure and airport congestion by focusing on the relative advantages and disadvantages of hub and spoke networks and point-to-point services and by analyzing the effectiveness of slot-constraint regimes. The authors' theoretical framework allows for the comparison of two symmetric networks. Within this theoretical framework, the authors provide conditions in which congestion would be more profitable for either network, highlighting the importance of including empirical analysis to examine the issue of airport heterogeneity with regards to congestion. Their empirical findings show some evidence suggesting air carriers using a hub and spoke network are less reactive to delays compared to air carriers using fully connected configurations. They also find that airline companies operating in slot-constrained airports seem to react to higher levels of congestion by using larger aircraft at lower frequencies. Based on these findings policy recommendations are provided suggesting that slot constraints or other policies promoting direct connections at non-hub airports may present the appropriate incentive for airline companies in reducing airport traffic congestion.

Including secondary airports as part of an air carrier's network presents an additional option for addressing airport congestion. Widespread use of these airports grew with the stepped-up entry of low cost carriers (LCCs) following airline service liberalization policies in the late 1970s. In Chapter 14, Paolo Beria, Antonio Laurino, and Maria Nadia Postorino present a detailed analysis of improved accessibility and connectivity levels attributable to the use of secondary airports by LCCs. Their analysis includes a categorization of LCC – airport relationships into three themes: the LCC's relation with secondary and primary regional airports, the balance of power between LCCs and dominated and non-dominated airports, and LCC's relationship with airports that may or may not serve as the main base of the carrier. The framework for their analysis is based on a dynamic model of annual passengers carried at an airport and the geographic proximity to surrounding airports. Applying their model to 16 representative EU airports over a 10-year time span, the authors conclude that the relationship between LCCs and airports depend heavily on the role of the airport in its catchment area. Their concluding comments include the observation that the sole presence of LCC does not guarantee growing passenger demand, despite the opportunity of passengers to receive low fares. In addition, airports sharing catchment areas with other airports place themselves at risk, due to the mobility of LCCs, even if the area served by the airport experiences growth and provides access to a large pool of potential passengers. Such information provides valuable insights for airports negotiating the terms for a profitable relationship with LCCs.

Chapter 15 of this volume continues the analysis of connectivity by observing the increasingly important role of Gulf carriers and their airport connections in other regions. Pere Suau-Sanchez, Augusto Voltes-Dorta, and Héctor Rodríguez-Déniz identify these carriers as super connectors because they have developed a network that provides passengers with greater travel options, and lower fares compared to incumbent carriers. The authors observe that where the real airport competition occurs in connecting traffic, the Middle Eastern hubs, such as Dubai, Doha, and Abu Dhabi, and Istanbul have gained market share at the expense of European hubs. They suggest that one reason European hubs may be losing connecting shares in long-haul markets is due to capacity and noise related operational restrictions, and the need to open secondary hubs. However, Suau-Sanchez et al., also find that despite the fact that Middle East hubs are leaders in connectivity in quantitative terms, they lag behind in terms of connecting times and geographical efficiency. They suggest that European and Asian hubs should capitalize on their strengths in terms of the passenger experience in marketing their services. The authors also identify a potential opportunity for airline hubs – the idea of "self-connectivity," where flight transfers are booked by passengers when the flights are not coordinated by the airlines. Although this is often thought of in the context of connecting short-haul flights between LCCs, the authors note that self-connections are supported by London Gatwick and Milano Malpesa airports. In using a unique data set that combines supply data (airline schedules and seat capacity) with demand data (actual passengers making connections) they find significant potential for self-connectivity at major hubs throughout the world. They suggest that this may be an important revenue generator in the future. In addition to their in-depth exploration of hub competition and connectivity, an important contribution by the authors of this chapter is in providing detailed measures of the quantity and quality of connectivity and potential connectivity. These important measures are likely to play an important role in future analyses of airport competition. Moreover, the airline connectivity findings unveil a new dimension of aviation competition, which enhances consumer (passenger) welfare.

SUMMARY AND CONCLUDING OBSERVATIONS

While airports have traditionally been thought of as natural monopoly type, government run entities, the chapters in this book demonstrate the changing nature of airports and the wide variety of airport issues that have important implications for the economic futures of regions, nations, and the world. The chapters of this book examine four important areas of airport issues in this new environment. The first set explores how the role of government might change when airports are increasingly run like for-profit businesses. Questions addressed in the first set of chapters include: (1) "are there alternative forms of regulation that might allow airports to perform better in the newly dynamic environment?" (2) "does the increased reliance on non-aeronautical revenues by airports suggest that airport price regulation should change?" (3) "can airport privatization increase efficiency, and does it matter how privatization occurs?" and (4) "are there commercial relationships between airlines and airports that may be beneficial for consumers?" The second set of chapters examines pricing, cost, and efficiency issues of airports. Questions addressed in this second set include: (1) "when airports are regulated, what is the best way to set prices?" (2) "what does airport cost structure suggest about appropriate airport pricing decisions, airport expansion decisions, decisions regarding the appropriate mix of services, and other decisions?" (3) "what portion of airport charges are passed on to passengers and how should it affect airport fees?" and (4) "is there an alternative way to understand the spatial effects of airport investment and policy?" The third set of chapters examines the effects of airports on regional economies, addressing two questions: (1) "what impacts do airports have on regional employment and population?" and (2) "how are commercially property values affected by proximity to an airport?" Finally, the last set of chapters addresses airport operations and airport connectivity. The chapters address the questions of: (1) "how do different types of air carriers react to delays, and what are the implications for dealing with congestion?" (2) "how has accessibility of local economies to other markets been enhanced by relationships between low cost carriers and their airports?" and "how is airport connectivity measured, and what does it suggest about the competitiveness of hubs worldwide?"

The chapters in this volume explore these questions in detail using state of the art economic theory and empirical methods. They provide significant insight into the state of the airport industry, its changes, and future areas of research. The volume is sure to provide researchers and those interested in the industry with new insights into airport issues, a better understanding of the state of knowledge regarding airport issues, and new techniques and ideas for further examination of airport issues.

NOTES

1. Airports Council International, *2015 ACI-NA Concessions Benchmarking Survey – Summary Results*, April 2016.
2. Morphet and Bottini (2014) define connectivity as an overall measure of the level of service—frequency of flights, reliability, and diversity of destinations—available to end users.

REFERENCES

Airports Council International. (2013). *AirportInfo: Non-Aeronautical Revenue*. September.

Airports Council International. 2015 (2016). ACI-NA Concessions Benchmarking Survey – Summary Results, April.

Arvis, J.-F., & Shepherd, B. (2011). The Air Connectivity Index Measuring Integration in the Global Air Transport Network, The World Bank Poverty Reduction and Economic Management Network International Trade Department, Policy Research Working Paper 5722.

Gonzalez, R., & Pueyo, F. (2010). *First nature vs. second nature causes: Industry location and growth in the presence of an open-access renewable resource*. Retrieved from http://www.ieb.ub.edu/aplicacio/fitxers/WS10Gonzalez.pdf

Kasarda, J., & Appold, S. (2014). Planning a competitive aerotropolis. In J. Peoples, (Ed.), *The economics of international airline transport* (pp. 281–308). Bingley, UK: Emerald Group Publishing.

Morphet, H., & Bottini, C. (2014). *Air connectivity: Why it matters and how to support growth*. https://www.pwc.com/gx/en/capital-projects-infrastructure/pdf/pwc-air-connectivity.pdf

Poole Jr., R. W., & Edwards, C. (2016). Privatizing U.S. Airports. Tax and Budget Bulletin No. 76, Cato Institute.

U.S. Government Accountability Office. (2014). Airport Privatization: Limited Interest Despite FAA's Pilot Program. GAO Highlights, GAO-15-42. November.

Young, S. (2014). Airport management: Facilitating the business of air transportation. In D. Prokop (Ed.), *The business of transportation* (Vol. 2). Santa Barbara, CA: Praeger.

CHAPTER 2

LIGHT-HANDED REGULATION OF AIRPORT SERVICES: AN ALTERNATIVE APPROACH TO DIRECT REGULATION?

Margaret Arblaster

ABSTRACT

The concept of light-handed regulation, including light-handed approaches to the regulation of airport services, is discussed. The rationale for the economic regulation of airport services and the traditional approaches used for economic regulation of airport charges are summarized. The evolution of international practice of light-handed regulation is outlined, including the experience with minimal regulation across monopoly industries in New Zealand and the acceptance of "negotiated settlements" in utility industries in North America. General reasons for moving to light-handed regulation of airports include the disadvantages of the price cap approach in practice and the benefits of facilitating greater negotiation between airports and users. Comparisons are made between alternative approaches to light-handed regulation of airport services, including price and quality of service monitoring, information disclosure regulation and negotiate-arbitrate regulation, approaches that have been applied to airport services in Australia and New Zealand. The role and nature of the incentives under each approach are discussed. The chapter concludes that whether light-handed regulation provides

The Economics of Airport Operations
Advances in Airline Economics, Volume 6, 15–47

ISSN: 2212-1609/doi:10.1108/S2212-160920170000006002

a suitable alternative approach to direct regulation depends on the market circumstances and the design characteristics of the light-handed approach.

Keywords: Light-handed regulation; airport; price cap regulation; incentive regulation

JEL Classifications: L510; L930; R480

INTRODUCTION

The concept of light-handed regulation, including light-handed approaches to the regulation of airport services, has been widely lauded and attracted the attention of governments, policy makers, and airport stakeholders. What is light-handed regulation? Why should it be considered? Who has done it? What is the experience with it? What issues need to be considered in applying a light-handed approach to regulation of airport services? This chapter addresses these questions in the context of economic regulation of airport services.

What is "Light-Handed" Regulation?

In the relatively limited literature on "light-handed regulation," the term "light-handed regulation" is typically discussed without being explicitly defined. In a discussion on the effectiveness of "light-handed" regulation of telecommunications in New Zealand, Blanchard (1994) refers to the government selection of "a "light-handed" regulatory alternative, which had the objective of encouraging rather than specifically requiring the dominant carrier to act in a competitive manner" (p. 156). Schultz (1999) study of light-handed regulation, which was in the context of a regulatory framework proposed for Westcoast Energy Inc. in Canada, considers that:

> It is plain that it (light-handed regulation) is a relative term since it implies something lighter than the traditional approach to regulation. It is, however, still a form of regulation. It is not deregulation. … (T)he acceptance of negotiated agreements is a critical breakthrough in the evolution of light-handed regulation. (Schultz, 1999, p. 388)

Schultz's interpretation of the term "light-handed regulation" emphasizes the regulator's ability to accept negotiated outcomes rather than being involved in directly determining prices and other terms and conditions. Forsyth (2008) describes light-handed regulation of airports in Australia and New Zealand where "prices are not explicitly regulated, but regulation could be imposed if performance is considered to be poor" (p. 65). Yang and Fu

(2015), who have modeled light-handed airport regulation, identify the distinctive feature of light-handed regulation as involving ex post regulation in contrast to other regulatory regimes, such as price cap regulation, which are ex ante regulation. They note that under light-handed regulation, government intervention, if any, is based on the actual airport performance assessed in regulatory reviews.

Carpenter and Lapuerta (1999) refer to the intended "light-handed" regulation of British Gas "where prices were to be updated automatically on an annual basis by a mathematical formula that accounted for inflation and for target improvements in efficiency" (p. 479). Their discussion of "light-handed regulation" goes onto identifying that the regulation, which was initially thought would be "light-handed," turned out to be quite interventionist and burdensome to administer and to comply with. Price cap regulation, as practiced in the United Kingdom and subsequently introduced in some other jurisdictions, was initially referred to as "light-handed" regulation. However, it is now generally referred to as "incentive regulation."

The Glossary developed by the Body of Knowledge on Infrastructure Regulation,[1] defines "light-handed regulation" as regulation that:

> Allows the firm discretion in how it meets regulatory targets. Regulation that is not intrusive, in contrast to command and control or even cost of service regulation. This process is designed to reduce information requirements and high compliance costs, while introducing clear incentives for good performance. (BoKIR, 2017)

This definition emphasizes the degree of regulatory intrusion and compliance costs associated with the form of regulation. However, as this definition identifies "regulatory targets" it may include some ex ante approaches to economic regulation, such as some price cap approaches.

Based on discussions on light-handed regulation in the literature, and the significant experience of light-handed regulation in Australia and New Zealand, light-handed regulation is defined in this chapter as follows:

> Light-handed regulation is a form of ex post regulation where the regulated firm determines its prices and service quality based on negotiation without regulatory intervention unless specific circumstances arise, such as the outcome of a regulatory review that has assessed market performance.

Under light-handed regulation, the prospect of possible intervention by a regulator, or the introduction of stronger regulation from a regulatory review, provide incentives for "good performance" by a firm. An important aspect of light-handed regulation is that it is expected to be less interventionist or intrusive into the affairs of regulated entities, and involve relatively low costs of compliance and greater flexibility for the regulated firm than conventional ex ante approaches to regulation.

Examples of Light-Handed Regulation of Airports

In an airport context, Australia and New Zealand have had a relatively long history of light-handed regulation, which includes the use of information disclosure regulation, price and quality of service monitoring and negotiate-arbitrate regulation. Light-handed regulation was first applied to major airports in New Zealand in the late 1980s. A light-handed approach to regulation was also applied to major Australian airports after removal of price caps in 2002. A distinguishing feature of the major airports in Australia and New Zealand is that they are regarded as having a high degree of market power due to the geographical distances between them and the poor substitutability of other modes of transport, particularly in relation to domestic air transport (see, e.g., Australian Productivity Commission, 2006, 2011, New Zealand, Commerce Amendment Bill, 2008. Explanatory Note).

In Europe, there are examples where direct regulatory approaches have been modified to become more light-handed, such as through allowing negotiation of the terms and conditions for airline access to airport services with a "fall-back" to regulation in the event of non-agreement, or subject to final regulatory endorsement. The economic regulation of airports in some European cities, such as Copenhagen, Dusseldorf and London (Gatwick), provide examples of this type of approach. Since 2008, the regulatory framework applying to Copenhagen airport has been based on the development of a charges agreement between the airport and airlines (including on service levels for selected services) with fall back to regulation if agreement is not reached. Additionally, Copenhagen Airport is required to provide airlines with sufficient material to ensure an equitable and transparent process to negotiate from (Copenhagen Airports, 2009). Düsseldorf airport has had an agreed negotiating framework developed between the airport and major airlines and representatives of smaller airlines, which includes an explicit price cap formula since 2004. If unable to reach agreement there would be regulation under the Luftverkehrs-Gesetz, the airport would have to seek approval of charges from the relevant transport authority (ICAO, 2013; Oxera, 2013). In 2014, Gatwick Airport moved from a price determined by the regulator, the CAA, to relying on the development of specific commitments on the level of charges and quality over 7 years through negotiations with the airlines (CAA, 2016).

The Government in Ireland has foreshadowed a possible change to airport charges regulation. The National Aviation Policy statement released in August 2015 identifies that the Irish model of regulation is more interventionist than is required by the 2009 EU Airport Charges Directive (Ireland, Department of Transport, Tourism, and Sport, 2015). The Policy notes that the price cap regime has experienced some difficulties since it commenced in 2001, including appeals and/or legal challenges.

Structure of the Chapter

The chapter begins with a discussion on the rationale for economic regulation of airports. The section "Traditional Approaches to the Economic Regulation of Airports" provides a summary of the traditional approaches used for economic regulation of airport charges. The evolution of light-handed regulation is outlined in the section "The Evolution of Light-Handed Regulation." The section "General Reasons for Moving to Light-Handed Regulation of Airports" discusses some general reasons for moving to light-handed regulation of airports. The section "Comparison of Light-Handed Approaches to Regulation of Airport Services in Australia and New Zealand" compares the characteristics of the light-handed approaches to regulation that have been applied to airport services in Australia and New Zealand. The section "The Design of Light-Handed Regulation" discusses important aspects of the design of light-handed regulation of airport services and compares the design characteristics under alternative approaches to light-handed regulation. The chapter concludes with an assessment of particular approaches to light-handed regulation of airport services.

REGULATION OF AIRPORT SERVICES – THE RATIONALE

As part of aviation infrastructure, airports play an important role in the productivity of airline services and in the accessibility for passengers and freight to airline services. Where there is significant market power associated with airport services, the potential for inefficient airport performance arises.

The structure of airport markets implies that there are impediments to competition. In some markets, airports have been characterized as natural monopolies in that there are significant economies of scale and scope over the relevant range of output so that it is often only economic to have one major airport supply a particular city market. There are significant barriers to new airport entry as it takes several decades to plan, environmentally review, and construct a new airport especially near a major metropolitan area (Oum & Fu, 2008). Further, the lead times required to expand airport capacity are typically long, and periods of rapid growth in air traffic can create shortages of capacity increasing airport pricing power. In some locations, an airport has a significant ability to attract large numbers of passengers due to the airport's attractiveness as a point of departure/arrival and on its usefulness as a hub for connecting passengers, which enhances its ability to set aeronautical prices. A major transfer (connecting) hub, such as London's Heathrow Airport, has been considered to have some ability to set prices above the competitive level (UK Department for Transport, 2009).

Common ownership of airports is a further factor limiting potential competitive influences in some cases. The breakup of the three London Airports (Heathrow, Gatwick, and Stanstead) and Edinburgh owned by BAA (British Airports Authority) into separately owned entities commencing in 2009 is an example of a policy designed to increase competition between airports (UK Competition and Markets Authority, 2016).

In circumstance where an airport has monopoly power, economic regulation of airport services may be introduced with the key objective being to promote economic efficiency and to protect the interests of current and future users. Not all services provided at airports need to be regulated. Airports are multi-product firms with two main sides[2] to their business: an aeronautical[3] side and a non-aeronautical[4] side. It is in the provision of aeronautical services that airports have been regarded as having relatively high market power and therefore these are the charges which are generally subject to some type of regulation or scrutiny. In comparison, the provision of non-aeronautical services is generally subject to greater competitive influences because there is greater substitutability in service provision.

Historically airports have been government owned and operated and therefore subject to government controls on their operations. The trend over the last few decades has been for airports to be operated on a more commercial basis independent from government, either as corporatized, partially privatized or fully privatized entities. The greater freedom available to airports to pursue profit opportunities under different governance arrangements, particularly in privatized organizational structures, heightens the issue of the economic regulation of airports.

Increasingly, there is recognition that the existence of impediments to competition in airport services does not imply that airports are not subject to competitive influences. There are a wide variety of factors influencing the degree of market power that an airport holds, and consequently whether economic regulation of airports should be considered (see e.g., CAA, 2011; Copenhagen Economics, 2012; Forsyth, Gillen, Müller, & Niemeier, 2010; IATA, 2013; Starkie, 2008, 2010). In some geographic regions, it is economically feasible to have a few major airports: London, New York, and Paris are notable examples. Alternative, or secondary, airports may be considered to exercise some degree of competitive constraint on major airports in some regions. In Western Europe, for example, there is a relatively dense coverage of airports and, as a result, there can be some degree of substitution of one airport for another. The London airports, and the airports in Amsterdam (Schiphol), Brussels, and Copenhagen, are examples of airports in Europe where a large proportion of passengers are within 2 hours' drive of another airport. Additionally, at these airports alternative transport modes, such as high-speed rail, may be a good substitute for short-haul trips.

Airlines may have countervailing buyer power at an airport providing a further constraint on airport market power. The ability of an airline to switch to an alternative airport is a crucial underpinning required for the exercise of countervailing power (Button, 2010). Button (2010) argues that the ability to switch airports depends not simply on the availability of alternative airports, but also on the business model of the airline concerned. Where an airline has very significant costs of moving services to another airport, even if there is adequate capacity available at an alternative airport, they may have limited bargaining power. Airlines that operate on a low cost carrier mode, involving relatively fewer sunk costs at an airport compared to a full service carrier, are likely to have greater bargaining ability because they are not tied to a particular geographic market (and hence airport).

The institutional structure that an airport operates under is a further factor affecting the approach to economic regulation. The approach to economic regulation needs to take into account the governance and institutional context in which an airport operates. In North America airports tend not to be privatized and operate under governance arrangements which limit the incentive to take advantage of any significant market power that they may have (Morrison & Winston, 2008).

For many airports, competitive influences on airport prices imply that economic regulation is either not warranted, or that "lighter" or less intrusive regulation is appropriate. Starkie (2008) has raised the issue of the appropriateness of traditional approaches to regulation of airports involving direct controls on prices, such as price caps and rate of return regulation. He supports the use of lighter handed approaches or no regulation at all. In contrast, Biggar (2011) views the major purpose of economic regulation of airports as the protection and promotion of sunk complementary investments by airport users, rather than the consequent misallocation of resources from the potential use of market power by airports. He argues that if this is a primary purpose of airport regulation, then control of prices is important for users in order to prevent price shocks.

In summary, airports operate in different market circumstances which implies that the degree of market power that an airports has, and whether economic regulation is warranted, needs to be assessed on a case-by-case basis. Further, markets change over time so the degree of market power an airport holds can change. Not all airports are regulated, or if regulated continue to need to be regulated over time.

TRADITIONAL APPROACHES TO THE ECONOMIC REGULATION OF AIRPORTS

A variety of approaches to economic regulation has been applied to airports. Traditional approaches involve direct regulation of prices upfront, i.e., regulatory determinations are made on an ex ante basis. Direct regulatory approaches include price caps regulation, rate of return regulation, and cost of service approaches to regulation.

Rate of Return Regulation and Cost-based Regulation

Rate of return regulation has applied to airports in some European cities, including the main airports in Brussels, Frankfurt, Munich, Berlin (Tegel), Rome (Fiumicino), Milan (Malpensa), Amsterdam (Schiphol), and Athens (Steer Davies Gleave, 2013). Under rate of return regulation, the regulator typically sets charges based on the reasonable costs incurred in providing the service including an allowable rate of return on the airport's regulated asset base. Cost-based approaches to regulation are similar to rate of return regulation. Under these approaches prices are regulated so that the regulated firm can expect to earn a reasonable rate of return on its regulated investments. Rate of return regulation is often criticized because the approach provides an incentive for "gold-plating" of assets (where rates are based on a rate of return on capital there is an incentive to grow the asset base) and does not provide an incentive for cost efficiency (as cost savings cannot be kept as profit by the company) (see discussion in Carpenter & Lapuerta, 1999 for example).

Price Cap Regulation

Price cap regulation is a dominant approach to economic regulation of airports where there is a high degree of management discretion, in particular in the case of privatized and corporatized airports (ICAO, 2013). The price cap approach to regulation was developed in the UK in the 1980s and generally applied to newly privatized entities.

Price caps have been a popular form of "incentive regulation" in that they are a flexible form of regulation, which can be adapted to the firm's environment (Sappington & Weisman, 2010). Price caps encourage a firm to realize efficiencies with a view to ultimately passing the benefit onto users. Price caps were seen as a preferable form of regulation to traditional cost-based forms of regulation as they gave incentives to the newly privatized firms to pursue cost efficiencies through the possibility of retaining profits achieved within the price cap period. Further, under a price cap there is more flexibility to adjust specific prices to reflect new developments or competition (Sappington & Weisman, 2010). The level of the price cap for the next period is typically reviewed by the regulator before the end of the price cap period.

Under a price cap approach the overall level of prices is constrained over a period of time to an upper limit often linked to inflation minus a productivity factor, such as CPI – X or RPI – X.[5] There are incentives for cost efficiency because the regulated firm is able to keep the gains from cost reduction which may be passed on to users at the next price review. In the context of regulation of airports, an airport operating under a price cap has flexibility to set prices within groups of services as long as the overall cap is complied with.

Price cap regulation has been applied to airport charges at a number of newly privatized airports. The application of price caps to the former BAA airports of Heathrow, Gatwick, and Stansted airports following privatization in 1987 are a well-known example with a long history. Price caps were also applied to Australian airports following privatization beginning in 1997, to privatized airports in Mexico from 1995, and more recently, India has applied price caps to its airports where privatization began in 2006 (ICAO, 2013). Although not privatized, the government of Ireland applied price caps to Ireland's three major airports in 2001 following corporatization (CAR, 2001).

Variations to Direct Regulatory Approaches

Within the broad approaches to direct regulation of airport charges there are variations to the technical specification of the price control and the degree of regulator intervention in the price determination process. For example, additional variants of the broad approaches of regulation, include "sliding scale regulation" and "earnings sharing regulation." "Earnings sharing regulation" typically specifies a range of earnings around a target rate of return on investment so that the firm is authorized to keep all earnings within a range but outside the range must share earnings with its customers. In an airport context the level of charges is typically negatively related to passenger growth over a given period of time (OECD/ITF, 2010). Under "sliding scale regulation" adjustment is made to reflect the financial impact of unanticipated events beyond the control of the firm which have a pronounced effect on the firm and which are not otherwise accounted for (Niemeier, 2002).

Governance Arrangements Involving "Checks" and "Balances" – Airports in the US

In the US, airports which receive federal funding under the National Plan of Integrated Airport Systems are required to comply with obligations in funding contracts (called "grant assurances"), such as an obligation to ensure fees are fair and reasonable and not in excess of the cost of providing the facilities and services efficiently at the airport (FAA, 2017). The reasonableness of airport fees charged to airlines can be reviewed by the Department of Transportation if a complaint is received or there is a request for a determination and a finding of a significant dispute. In general, the U.S. Department of Transportation relies on airport operators, users and the market to ensure compliance with the applicable legal requirements, however, direct intervention is available if needed.

THE EVOLUTION OF LIGHT-HANDED REGULATION

Experience of light-handed regulation of airports, where prices are not directly determined by regulation unless specific circumstances arise, is more limited than that of price caps and primarily confined to Australia and New Zealand (Forsyth, 2008). In New Zealand, light-handed regulation was adopted as a general approach to economic regulation in the late 1980s. There is some experience of the application of light-handed regulation to utility industries in North America, where regulators allow negotiated settlements of prices in energy industries, and in some other utility industries.

Introduction of Light-Handed Regulation in New Zealand (late 1980s)

General reforms to New Zealand's economy were undertaken during the period 1984–1989. Utilities were generally converted from statutory monopolies under state ownership to corporatized or privatized entities and restructured so that the monopoly elements were separated from the more contestable elements of the industries (Rebstock, 2004). During this process, New Zealand was transformed from a heavily regulated economy to one of the lightest regulated western economies (Patterson, 2004). New Zealand relied on general competition laws to deal with both the terms of interconnection and conduct generally, unlike other countries where interconnection to natural monopoly elements in network industries was governed by a regulatory framework. The reliance on general competition law, with the threat that more heavy-handed regulation could be introduced if necessary, was known as "light-handed" regulation.

Corporatized electricity lines networks were covered by "light-handed" regulation involving mandatory information disclosure requirements with no regulator (Bertram & Twaddle, 2005). The approach to electricity deregulation was described as "unusually radical in the extent to which it relied upon self-regulation to curb monopolistic behaviour" (Bertram & Twaddle, 2005, p. 282). The New Zealand government also relied on general competition laws and court processes in deregulating its telecommunications industry (Blanchard, 1994a). Although it was recognized that there were natural monopoly elements in parts of the industry, it was expected that technological advances would allow sustainable and effective competition to develop without government intervention to promote competition (Blanchard, 1994a). Further, there were concerns that "heavy-handed regulations" in the interconnection context could result in outcomes that are no better, or possibly worse, than those under light-handed regulation.

A similar approach was also applied to the regulation of the three major international airports in New Zealand. Until legislative changes were implemented in 2008, regulation of airports in New Zealand was under an industry specific framework administered by the Minister of Transport. Regulation of was based on a statutory requirement under the *Airports Authorities Act 1966* (AAA) for the major airports to disclose information and to consult airline users before setting charges. These provisions require airports to disclose specified financial information relating to aeronautical activities but are not specific or prescriptive in relation to the principles for the preparation of the disclosed information. Every substantial customer has to be consulted before fixing or altering charges, and larger customers consulted on capital expenditure plans at least every 5 years; airports, however, had the power to set charges as they see fit. The consultation provisions under the AAA are complimented by the threat of price control under the *Commerce Act 1986* (the Commerce Act), part IV.

Light-Handed Regulation in the Utility Sector in North America (1980s onwards)

The acceptance of negotiated outcomes between a utility and by some, or all, of the interested parties by a regulatory commission in the energy sector in North America has been characterized as a form of light-handed regulation. Rather than formal litigation, rate cases are settled by negotiation with the agreement subsequently considered and typically approved by the regulatory commission (Doucet & Littlechild, 2006). Referred to as "negotiated settlements," their use has become widespread in rate making cases in the energy sector since the 1980s as well as being used in a wide variety of contexts in other industries, such as the water and telecommunication sectors (Doucet & Littlechild, 2006). During the 1990s negotiated settlements largely superseded conventional processes in the energy sector of regulation by litigation.

Review of experience of negotiated settlements in the energy sector by Doucet and Littlechild (2006) and Littlechild (2009a) indicate that the approach was seen to have a number of advantages in addition to providing a quicker, less costly and more convenient way of dealing with a regulatory load. Among the other benefits are the flexibility and creative responsiveness of alternative processes available under negotiated settlements; the achievement of results that better serve the needs of the parties; and the enhancement of community involvement in the dispute resolution process. Doucet and Littlechild (2006) describe the role of the regulator under these processes as still critical but as changing to be one that is more like "enabling the market to work" (p. 275).

Schultz (1999) examines light-handed regulation in the context of gas pipeline tolls and tariffs. He reviews the Framework for Light-Handed Regulation proposed by Westcoast Energy Inc. (Westcoast) in Canada to replace cost of service regulation. Under the Framework prices and terms of service would be set through negotiations between individual shippers and Westcoast. This would be subject to requirements for fair dealing and subject to regulatory oversight by the National Energy Board (NEB) through a complaint mechanism. Under the Framework Westcoast was required to provide shippers with periodic summary information on contracts by area. The parties could obtain the assistance of a mediator in resolving differences, which potentially could proceed to formal adjudication. Schultz (1999) considers the approach captures well-developed conceptions of fairness while at the same time supporting a market-based approach to regulation.

The Introduction of Light-Handed Regulation of Airports in Australia (2002)

The Australian Government introduced light-handed regulation involving price and quality of service monitoring following removal of price caps in 2002. The Government intended that the new regulatory framework would encourage airport operators and their customers to negotiate directly, and resolve prices without Government involvement. A particular concern under the price cap approach was the way in which a provision to accommodate new investment had led to greater regulatory intervention than had been anticipated at the time of privatizing the airports (Arblaster, 2014). This, combined with the effect of a dramatic fall in demand for aviation services in 2001, led an independent review of the airport regulatory framework to recommend removal of price caps on airport services (Productivity Commission, 2002).

Price caps on the largest airports were replaced by price monitoring by the Australian Competition and Consumer Commission (ACCC), an independent federal authority responsible for the implementation of competition policy. Additionally, the government threatened that stronger regulation could be invoked if airports abused their market power (Arblaster, 2014). Price monitoring was performed under a statutory provision that allowed the ACCC to collect information related to the prices, profits, and costs of aeronautical services and to make annual public reports summarizing the information collected. Monitoring of indicators of the quality of airport services complemented price monitoring. It was the first time in Australia that this type of regulation had been applied to services regarded as having natural monopoly characteristics.[6]

In addition to price caps and price monitoring of airport services, airports in Australia can potentially be covered by negotiate-arbitrate regulation under a National Access regime introduced in 1995 (Arblaster, 2016). Negotiate-arbitrate regulation under the national economy-wide access regulation can be applied to infrastructure services with monopoly characteristics if specified conditions are met.[7] There are four cases where airport users have sought to apply negotiate-arbitrate provisions under this legislation to airport services. From 1997 to 2002 an airport specific access regulation additionally applied to airport services at newly privatized airport services (s.192 of the *Airports Act 1996 (Cth)*). The airport specific framework potentially covered a broader range of airport services and had fewer appeal processes than the national access framework. Two applications were made to have airport services covered by the airport specific regulation.

Changes to Light-Handed Regulation in New Zealand (2000s)

Concerns about increasing prices in the electricity industry under New Zealand's light-handed approach to regulation arose in the early 2000s. In 2001, the New Zealand Commerce Commission (NZCC) became responsible for the information disclosure regulation in the electricity industry and was given powers to regulate electricity prices in the event that prices (or revenue) breached "threshold" levels set by the Minister. Despite the disclosure of high monopoly prices, direct control of electricity prices was not introduced during the period (Bertram & Twaddle, 2005).

Using the annual financial information disclosed by electricity distribution networks, combined with information from company annual reports and other public sources, Bertram and Twaddle (2005) review price–cost margins in New Zealand's lines (transmission and distribution) businesses since deregulation in comparison to outcomes expected under rate of return regulation. They find increases in price–cost margins in real terms between 1995 and 2002 with compounded excess earnings of the lines industry estimated to represent roughly an 8% premium over the weighted average cost of capital.

In the telecommunications industry, a local loop interconnection dispute between a new entrant, Clear Communications (Clear), and the incumbent telecommunications provider, Telecom, developed in the early 1990s. The dispute ended up in substantial court processes, including an appeal on the New Zealand Court of Appeal decision to the Privy Council in England (Blanchard, 1994b). The New Zealand court processes considered that Telecom's interconnection offer to Clear had the purpose of preventing and restricting Clear's endeavors to enter the central business district calling market (Blanchard, 1994b). However, the Court determined that it had no jurisdiction to direct the negotiations nor the terms for interconnection. The Court was adamant that the parties must return to negotiations and cautioned that if negotiations proved unsuccessful the government would have no choice but to regulate the industry more heavily than at present (Blanchard, 1994b).

Failure of telecommunications companies to reach agreement on the terms of interconnection led to increasing concern by the government (Given, 2010). The Telecommunications Act 2001 created a telecommunications-specific access regime administered by a Commissioner. The New Zealand Commerce Commission (NZCC) was given new powers to enforce the Act and to cost and monitor Telecom's expanded public service obligations (Given, 2010).

In 1998 high airport charges led to a public inquiry into airport charges (see Arblaster, 2014). The Inquiry took 4 years to complete and did not lead to unanimous recommendations with a majority recommendation for regulation of Auckland Airport and a minority recommendation not to do this. In May 2003, the Government's decision was that price controls would not apply. A study by Domney, Wilson, and Chen (2005) using data envelopment analysis found that Auckland Airport, with significant market power, had consistently increased profitability, while not showing a corresponding increase in efficiency.

Following a review of New Zealand's competition law in 2007, new provisions relating to economic regulation were introduced into the Commerce Act and passed as the *Commerce Amendment Act 2008* (the Amendments). The Amendments provide for a broader range of regulatory tools under the Commerce Act so that "fit-for-purpose" regulatory instruments[8] can be applied to regulated goods or services and different types of regulation can be applied in different industry circumstances with a consistent set of principles applying across industries. Under the amended New Zealand framework there is the potential to adopt other regulatory tools following a recommendation from an inquiry and a direction from the Government (NZCC, 2008). For example, if agreements cannot be reached or disputes not be resolved the application of another regulatory measure, such as negotiate-arbitrate regulation, could be considered.

Under the Amendments the NZCC sets price and quality controls for some electricity network and distribution businesses.[9] The controls restrict the revenue these businesses can earn, or the maximum average prices, they can charge and can include requirements on the quality of the services provided. In addition, electricity line businesses are covered by information disclosure regulation involving input methodologies. Transportation of gas by pipeline is regulated in markets where there is little or no competition, and where there is little or no likelihood of a substantial increase in competition (NZCC, 2017).

New Zealand's three main airports are now covered by a new form of information disclosure regulation under the Amendments to the Commerce Act. The Amendments relating to information disclosure require the airports to disclose a wider range of information.[10] In a similar way to the regulation of the energy industries, detailed rules, called "input methodologies," prescribe how the information disclosed should be compiled for the value of assets, treatment of taxation and allocation of costs. The methodologies do not apply to price setting. The provisions in the *Airports Authorities Act*, which allows airports to set charges as they see fit, still apply. The NZCC is expected to monitor and analyze information supplied by the airports and following this publish a summary and analysis of the information[11] and to report to the Minister in 2012 on the effectiveness of the regulation.[12]

GENERAL REASONS FOR MOVING TO LIGHT-HANDED REGULATION OF AIRPORTS

Two main reasons for favoring light-handed regulation of airport services are the difficulties experienced with traditional approaches to regulation, such as price cap regulation, and the potential benefits identified by allowing greater negotiation of airport services.

Difficulties Experienced with Price Cap Regulation of Airport Services

Increased Complexity and Regulatory Intervention Over Time

While price cap regulation started out to be a relatively simple approach, overtime it has become increasingly complex and burdensome. Carpenter and Lapuerta (1999) illustrate the problems of price cap regulation using the experience of British Gas. Initially, price caps were developed to be a comparatively simple approach compared to traditional rate of return regulation as practiced in the United States.[13] They were seen as involving less reliance on cost-based information, less intrusive and simpler to administer than cost-based rate of return regulation.

Littlechild (2010) has argued that the process of setting prices under price cap approaches to regulation has become extremely costly and time consuming, is not adequately reflecting customer and company circumstances nor facilitating innovation. Further, he considers that the UK process has become more complicated in terms of the calculations involved and the incentive mechanisms incorporated (Littlechild, 2009b). In the airport context, Starkie (2008) and Gillen (2011) have argued that the traditional price cap approach to regulation has become heavy handed and can be problematic.

Examples of the complexities that have been introduced into price cap regulation include measures to take into account quality of service explicitly in the price cap through financial incentives and conditional provisions, including provisions for variations in revenue allowances associated with the achievement of milestones relating to completion of large-scale investments, such as new terminals and other specified capital works (Arblaster, 2010). While the increased technical complexity of price caps can improve the performance of regulation for users, it is likely to increase the administrative costs of regulation for the regulator and the industry. Additionally, in some countries, such as Ireland, there has been a high incidence of appeals and judicial reviews of price cap determinations.

Australian experience with price cap regulation of airport services in the late 1990s and early 2000s provides another example where this form of regulation resulted in a higher degree of regulatory intervention than had been anticipated at the outset (Australian Productivity Commission, 2002).

Risk and Uncertainty

The adoption of a price cap approach to economic regulation can pose challenges for the management of risk and uncertainty. Under price cap regulation the rate of change of overall price increases is fixed for a period of time, typically 5 years. Unless specific provisions are incorporated in the price cap design, such as a sliding scale provision, the occurrence of substantial unforeseen changes in demand or the cost of providing airport services can make the determination of an appropriate price cap problematic and cause significant risks to the airport operator. The experiences of price cap regulation in Australia and in Ireland are illustrative this issue.

In Australia, there was a dramatic fall in demand for aviation services shortly after price caps had been applied to newly privatized airports (Arblaster, 2014; Forsyth, 2008). In October 2001, Ansett Australia, a major Australian domestic airline carrier, ceased operation coinciding with a global reduction in demand associated with the September 11 terrorist attacks in the United States and followed by the severe acute respiratory syndrome (SARS) epidemic in 2002. Substantial reductions in demand put pressure on smaller airports and the sustainability of price cap regulation.[14]

In 2009, the Commission for Aviation Regulation in Ireland (CAR, 2009) was required to determine the level of the next price cap for Dublin Airport in the context of the onset of the global financial crisis and considerable uncertainty on the timing of the opening of the second passenger terminal and its associated costs (CAR, 2009). The determination of a CPI − X price cap for Dublin airport in 2009 was particularly challenging at a time of rapidly changing economic circumstances and the proposed large scale and contentious terminal expansion (Arblaster, 2010).

The Benefits of Greater Negotiation of Airport Services

Weighed against the difficulties of administering price cap regulation are the potential benefits seen from less interventionist light-handed approaches to regulation that allow greater scope for negotiation between airport operators.

Reduced regulatory intervention through greater scope for negotiation has advantages in terms of the cost of regulation. The challenges for regulators in dealing with issues of information asymmetry and regulatory gaming and the scope for regulatory error are reduced when there is less regulation. In situations where there are a small number of large airline users of an airport, they are highly likely to have a good understanding of the airport business, and therefore potentially be able to negotiate effectively with an airport operator.

Greater scope for negotiation can be seen to have benefits in its own right. Negotiation of prices allows for the development of arrangements that are better tailored to the needs of airlines and their passengers. The use of bilateral contracts can provide a framework for the provision of greater diversify in the services offered to airlines facilitating innovation in airline marketing strategies and promoting competition. Negotiation between London Gatwick Airport and the airlines using the airport led to the development of a longer time period of agreement to align with investment horizons, rather than the shorter fixed terms established under conventional price cap regulation (CAA, 2016). This greater flexibility is expected to facilitate efficient investment, more tailored to the needs of airlines.

Through negotiation with less regulatory intervention the development of improved airport–airline relations can develop. Light-handed approaches are considered to promote more mature and constructive relationships in contrast to the adversarial relationships that often tend to develop through the intervention of the regulator under direct regulatory approaches (CAA, 2016). Despite this benefit negotiations may not always be easy. Smaller airlines and network airlines making limited or occasional use of a particular airport are likely to have difficulty devoting sufficient time to review relevant performance data and other information carefully. In these circumstances the difficulties of negotiation may be alleviated by representative associations of airlines undertaking negotiations on behalf of member airlines and relevant information presented in readily accessible formats.

COMPARISON OF LIGHT-HANDED APPROACHES TO REGULATION OF AIRPORT SERVICES IN AUSTRALIA AND NEW ZEALAND

The approaches to light-handed regulation of airport services used in Australia and New Zealand can be categorized into broad groups; information disclosure regulation, price, and quality of service monitoring and negotiate-arbitrate regulation.

Information Disclosure and Price and Quality of Service Monitoring Regulation

Information disclosure regulation and price monitoring have three key design elements in common: information requirements, reporting arrangements, and a threat of stronger regulation. Neither of these approaches involves direct determination of prices nor quality of service by the regulator. Under these approaches any restraint on airports' pricing decisions is indirect, namely through moral suasion, providing customers with additional information that they otherwise would not have had, and the threat of stricter forms of regulation being introduced if performance is adverse.

New Zealand has used information disclosure regulation under two approaches, a "minimalist" approach from the late 1980s to 2008 and an "enhanced" approach from 2010 onwards. Australia has used price and quality of service monitoring of airport services from 2002 onwards. In terms of the degree of regulatory intervention, these three approaches are on a continuum with the first ("minimalist") information disclosure regulation being the least interventionist approach; price and quality of service monitoring involving an intermediate degree of regulatory intervention; and "enhanced" information disclosure regulation being the most interventionist approach (Arblaster, 2014). The latter two approaches have been administered by an independent regulatory agency with broad economy-wide responsibilities for administration of competition policy as well as economic regulation.

Negotiate-Arbitrate Regulation

Negotiate-arbitrate regulation has been applied to airports in Australia in two forms; under a general national access framework applicable to "bottleneck"[15] infrastructure and under an airport specific access framework. In 20 years of experience to 2017 there have been six cases where airport users have sought to have airport services in Australia covered by negotiate-arbitrate regulation (Arblaster, 2016).

Although negotiate-arbitrate regulation has not been applied to airport services in New Zealand legislative provisions in the amended *Commerce Act 1986* contain this form of regulation which could be applied to airport services.[16]

Summary

Table 1 covers the two different approaches to Information Disclosure regulation in New Zealand, price and quality of service monitoring in Australia, and the two different forms of negotiate-arbitrate regulation as applied to airport services in Australia.

Reviews of Light-handed Regulation of Airport Services in Australia and New Zealand in the Literature

The literature on light-handed regulation of airport services is not extensive and largely confined to experience in Australia and New Zealand.

Table 1. Key Characteristics/Features of Light-Handed Regulation of Airport Services in Australia and New Zealand.

Regulatory Framework	Key Features of the Regulation
New Zealand	
Information disclosure regulation – minimalist approach[a] Applies from the late 1980s to 2008	Airports are required to disclose specified financial information relating to aeronautical activities but no independent regulator. There are consultation requirements before fixing or altering charges and major capital expenditure plans. Threat of stronger price regulation under the Commerce Act.
Enhanced information disclosure[b] 2008 onwards	Regulation administered by the Commerce Commission (NZCC). A wide range of information is required to be disclosed under detailed rules.[c] Airports must consult on relevant elements in their price setting methodologies when determining their charges but are free to determine charges. The NZCC is required to monitor and analyze information and to report publicly on it.
Australia	
Price and quality of Service monitoring[d] 2002 onwards	Airports are required to disclose limited information to the Australian Competition and Consumer Commission (ACCC) which is published annually.[e] Threat of stronger regulation if airport performance is poor. Periodic independent reviews of the regulatory framework.
Negotiate-arbitrate regulation – national general access approach[f] 1995 onwards	Negotiate-arbitrate regulation can be applied if certain criteria are met. The process can be lengthy and costly (prior to 2010). If the legislation applies (i.e. the service is "declared") there is a right to negotiation and arbitration by the ACCC if negotiations fail. Appeal processes exist at each stage in the process.
Negotiate-arbitrate regulation – airport-specific approach[g] 1996–2002	Streamlined processes for applying negotiate-arbitrate regulation to airport services. If negotiate-arbitrate regulation applies then there is a right to negotiation and arbitration by the ACCC if negotiations fail. Appeals of decisions are restricted to the arbitration stage of the process.

Source: Derived from the statutory sources by the author.

[a]This regulation was applied through the *Airports Authorities Act 1966*.

[b]This regulation was applied through the *Commerce Act 1986* as amended in 2008.

[c]The Commerce Act 1986, s.53C(2).

[d]The regulatory function of price monitoring is contained in Part VIIA, *Competition and Consumer Act 2010*, previously named the *Trade Practices Act 1975*. Quality of service monitoring regulation is contained in Part 8 of the Airports Act 1996.

[e]The regulation is contained in Part VIIA of the *Competition and Consumer Act 2010* (CCA), (s.95ZA to s.95ZG of the CCA) called the prices surveillance part of the Act, and includes three forms of regulation; prices surveillance, price monitoring and price inquiries. This regulation is a general provision which can potentially apply to any industry.

[f]Part IIIA, Competition and Consumer Act 2010 (Cth).

[g]Part XIII, Airports Act 1986 (Cth).

In an examination of light-handed regulation in Australia and New Zealand, Forsyth (2008) considers that under light-handed regulation, prices have been somewhat above what they might have been under tighter regulation, but well below monopoly levels. Schuster (2009) discusses the experience of negotiations on airport charges at Sydney Airport under light-handed regulation. He concludes that contractual relationships in an environment of informal regulation provide sound, and arguably superior, outcomes to formal price regulation.

A review of the experience of privatization and "light-handed" regulation of Sydney Airport by O'Donnell, Glennie, O'Keefe, and Kwon (2011) considers that the "light-handed" model of regulation has not provided an effective regulatory framework, and that stronger regulation that goes beyond monitoring is arguably required. Littlechild (2012) examines Australia's approach to airport regulation. He considers that in general light-handed regulation has worked well in Australia but the adoption of independent dispute resolution processes would lead to the alleviation of some airline concerns about regulation.

Yang and Fu (2015) examine light-handed regulation of airports using a model of the behaviors of a welfare-maximizing regulator, a profit-maximizing airport, and competing airlines in a multistage game. Their model is broadly based on the characteristics of airport regulation in Australia and New Zealand post-privatization of major airports and the presence of demand uncertainty. The model is used to compare no regulation, price cap regulation and "light-handed" regulation. In their model, "light-handed" regulation involves no ex ante direct regulation but a threat of regulation. The threat of regulation is modeled as a "penalty" with a probability of occurrence. The penalty is the extra cost or lost profit when the government reintroduces price cap regulation, or imposes fines. In their model higher airport charges will increase the airport's revenue but increase the chance of a penalty from the regulator. Additionally, higher service quality always comes with a higher airport charge.

Through examining eight scenarios, Yang and Fu find that overall, neither price cap regulation nor light-handed regulation dominates in terms of welfare, airport charges or service quality. The relative performance of the two types of regulation depends on many factors. They favor light-handed regulation because it is likely to offer more flexibility than price cap regulation, and more likely to lead to higher welfare. Yang and Fu (2015) findings follow directly from their analytical results, including the use of some simplifying assumptions. They note that the model specifications may affect the relevance of the analytical results.

Arblaster (2014) examines the experience of light-handed regulation of airports in Australia and New Zealand from the point of view of whether it has achieved the stated objectives associated with its introduction in each country and makes an assessment based on the findings of independent reviews of the regulation in each country. She identifies the important role that the design of light-handed regulation plays in determining the achievement of stated objectives and that there appears to be an apparent trade-off in the achievement of objectives with different approaches to light-handed regulation.

THE DESIGN OF LIGHT-HANDED REGULATION

The effectiveness of light-handed regulation of airports with substantial market power depends on the incentives associated with the regulatory approach, which in turn depends on the design of light-handed regulation.

Threat of a Stronger Regulatory Measure, or Regulatory Intervention, Under Light-handed Regulation

A key characteristic of light-handed regulation of airports in Australia and New Zealand is the threat of the introduction of a stronger regulatory measure or regulatory intervention if adverse performance is identified. In particular, the existence of a credible threat (i.e., high likelihood or probability) of regulatory intervention has been the important issue in practice.

The importance of the credibility of a threat of a stronger regulatory measure has been raised in reviews of light-handed regulation of airports in Australia. For example, a second independent review of light-handed regulation of airports in Australia observed:

> Fundamental to the effectiveness of the light handed approach is the credible threat of sanction for airports that abuse their market power. (Australian Productivity Commission, 2011, p. XXXV)

Similarly, the New Zealand Commerce Commission has identified the importance of a credible threat of stronger regulation:

> (t)he threat of further regulation incentivizes suppliers to ensure their performance is consistent with desired outcomes from workably competitive markets (NZCC, 2013, p. 16)

Given that light-handed regulation does not involve direct determination of the regulated firm's prices and quality of service in advance, a credible threat of a stronger regulatory action or regulatory intervention if poor performance is identified, is a mechanism providing an incentive for good economic outcomes. The degree of regulatory commitment to invoking a stronger regulatory action is affected by the institutional features, such as the characteristics of the stronger measure, or measures, that could be used and the likelihood that a stronger regulatory measure would be implemented.

Information Disclosure Regulation and Price and Quality of Service Monitoring
The type of stronger regulatory action that would take place if poor performance is identified is one dimension of this issue. Under the "minimalist" information disclosure regulation in New Zealand, and price monitoring in Australia, the stronger regulatory action has been the introduction of price controls. In both cases, the relevant price controls that were already in legislation involved outdated approaches to price regulation not consistent with modern approaches to regulation of privatized entities.[17]

In New Zealand, as a result of amendments to the Commerce Act in 2008, there are a variety of new types of price control regulation, including negotiate-arbitrate regulation. As a result, the enhanced information disclosure regulation in New Zealand is supported by a range of alternative regulatory measures that could be invoked if required.

In Australia, government philosophies and the process for invoking the stronger regulation have adversely influenced the credibility of a threat of a stronger regulatory measure. A political decision is involved to invoke stronger regulation so the prevailing government philosophy, and the potential for the decision to be influenced by political lobbying, affects the view of the likelihood of a stronger regulatory measure being invoked. In the 1990s in New Zealand, the government philosophy was strongly non-interventionist so it was considered unlikely that the government would invoke a stronger regulatory measure. Under the initial information disclosure regime in New Zealand the threat of price control was effectively only a political tool because at that time the government was seen as unlikely to introduce price controls (Bollard & Pickford, 1995; Small, 2000).

If a stronger regulatory measure requires new legislation to be developed and then implemented, it is likely to be a lengthy process and subject to uncertainty of implementation. The availability of specialist regulatory skills and the information required for price determination is a further factor affecting the credibility of an alternative stronger regulatory measure.[18] In Australia, the threat of stronger regulation is further weakened by the airlines view which has not supported the reintroduction of price controls (Australian Productivity Commission, 2006, 2011).

Negotiate-Arbitrate Regulation
Under negotiate-arbitrate regulation, the stronger regulatory action that is invoked if negotiation does not result in an agreed outcome is an independent determination through arbitration of the disputed terms and conditions on which services are supplied. Once a service is covered by negotiate-arbitrate regulation then there is effectively an "inbuilt" threat of a stronger regulatory measure through the possibility of an arbitration. As there is no further need for intervention by a government, or a regulatory process required to invoke an arbitration, the credibility of a threat of a stronger measure is likely to be stronger than information disclosure regulation or price and quality of service monitoring.

Australian experience, under both the national process and the airport specific process, has been that where negotiate-arbitrate regulation has been applied to an airport service negotiated outcomes have resulted and there has been no need for a regulatory determination through arbitration (Arblaster, 2016).[19]

Transparency of Airport Performance under Light-handed Regulation

The ability of light-handed regulation to provide transparency on airport performance, and therefore identify adverse performance, such as excessive prices, poor quality or denied access to services, contributes to its effectiveness. The extent to which the regulatory approach provides transparency of airport performance affects the probability of a stronger regulatory action or regulatory intervention.

Information Disclosure Regulation and Price and Quality of Service Monitoring

The initial (minimalist) information disclosure regulation in New Zealand required limited information to be disclosed without specifying the format for information disclosure. In order to resolve concerns raised by airlines about airport pricing, the New Zealand government initiated an independent inquiry under the Commerce Act in 1998. The inquiry was required to assess whether there would be a net benefit associated with introducing price controls on New Zealand's three major airports. Given the limited information available the Inquiry had to acquire a large amount of additional data and develop assessment methodologies. Analysis on the performance of the three major airports took place over a 4 year timeframe.[20] The inquiry found that Auckland and Wellington airports had performed with inefficiencies and earned excessive profits. While the majority of inquiry commissioners considered that there would be a net benefit from the introduction of price controls for at least Auckland airport, a minority of commissioners disagreed due to a different view on pricing methodologies (NZCC, 2002). The result of the inquiry was therefore inconclusive and the government did not implement price controls.

The information requirements under the enhanced information regulation implemented in New Zealand in 2010 has required airports to disclose a wide range of information, including historical financial and quality of service information, forecast revenue requirements and pricing methodologies. Additionally, the airports are required to use prescribed formats for information and "input methodologies" for reporting historical information of key variables, such as asset valuations, cost allocations, regulatory tax treatment, and cost of capital.

Under the enhanced information disclosure regulation the New Zealand Commerce Commission has been able to make assessments of the performance of each airport and assess the extent to which the new regulation is influencing the pricing decisions of individual airports.[21] The Commerce Commission has been able to reach definitive conclusions. For example, they reported that the information disclosure provisions has limited excessive profits and led to improvements in the way Auckland Airport structured its prices (NZCC, 2013).

Enhanced information disclosure regulation has influenced airport behavior in New Zealand over time. This is illustrated by the experience of Wellington Airport. In 2013, the NZCC reported that information disclosure regulation had limited the ability of Wellington Airport to extract excessive profits although they were unable to conclude on efficiency of operational expenditure, investment efficiency, or sharing the benefits of efficiency gains given the short length of time the regulation had been in place. However, in 2015 the NZCC reported that Wellington Airport had made adjustments to their pricing approach suggesting that information disclosure regulation is limiting excessive profits from specified services (NZCC, 2015).

Both price and quality of service monitoring in Australia are not designed to enable a detailed assessment of the airports' performance but rather to track trends in airport prices, costs, profitability, and quality of service over time. Price monitoring is undertaken by developing a set of indicators based on historical accounting information at the beginning of a period and tracking these forward. As time passes adjustments have had to be made to the indicators because of changed market circumstances, changed accounting standards or other factors, such as a changes in the definition of aeronautical services. Assessment of information provided by quality of service indicators needs to take into account that airports may not have complete control of the quality of service provided because of the involvement of other parties, such as customs and immigration officials and airline staffing of check in desks. Given the limitations of the data obtained, monitoring results cannot be used to establish whether or not an airport has exercised its market power to earn monopoly profits (ACCC, 2016).

The independent reviews of airport regulation by the Australian Productivity Commission have not used information from price and quality of service monitoring to make definitive conclusions on airport performance under light-handed regulation. The approaches adopted to assess the airports performance have been largely based on qualitative evidence, or the absence of positive findings.

Negotiate-arbitrate Regulation (Dispute Resolution Approach)

Negotiation and arbitration processes are normally confidential so that they do not generate public information about airport performance. Under negotiate-arbitrate regulation the incentive for good airport performance relies on airport users identifying adverse performance and resolving issues through negotiation and threat of an arbitration in negotiation processes. Generally, airports supply airport users with information on a confidential basis during the negotiating process. The effectiveness of negotiations with airport operators will depend on the information available to airlines and other users.

Regulatory Compliance Costs of Alternative Approaches

The regulatory compliance costs are an additional factor that will affect the incentive to achieve efficient airport performance. The compliance burden and degree of intrusion into the regulated airport under light-handed regulation will affect the costs of regulation to the airport and the administration of the regulation.

Information Disclosure Regulation and Price and Quality of Service Monitoring

The initial information disclosure regulation in New Zealand involved minimal compliance requirements on airports and low-administrative costs for the Government. Enhanced information disclosure requires the disclosure of extensive additional information in addition to that required under the initial (minimalist) approach. The New Zealand Commerce Commission undertook a thorough and robust process to develop the enhanced information disclosure information requirements which took place over a 2 year period. In comparison to the earlier information disclosure approach, and the monitoring approach in Australia, enhance information disclosure is resource intensive for the industry and for the regulator to administer (Arblaster, 2014).

The information requirements for price monitoring under the Australian regulatory framework are restricted to historical information in a format which is largely consistent with statutory reporting requirements, and which is not prescriptive with respect to methodological issues, such as cost allocations and asset valuation. The Productivity Commission has found that compliance costs for the monitoring program are low (Australian Productivity Commission, 2011, Finding 10.1). Australia's price monitoring has the benefit of limited regulatory intervention in airport operations and relatively low-administrative and compliance costs in comparison to the previous price cap regulation.

Negotiate-arbitrate Regulation

Australian experience has shown that regulatory design plays a critical role in influencing the costs associated with the declaration (or coverage) process for negotiate-arbitrate regulation (Arblaster, 2016). The costs of using the national generic provisions in negotiate-arbitrate regulation were quite high prior to amendments of the regulation in 2006 and 2010, especially in terms of the length of the processes and restricting appeals associated with declaration processes (ACCC, 2013). The airport specific framework in operation prior to 2002 had more streamlined processes for applying negotiate-arbitrate regulation resulting in shorter lead times and lower costs of using the provision.

Summary of Design Characteristics that Contribute to the Effectiveness of Different Types of Light-handed Regulation

Table 2 summarizes the extent to which different general approaches to light-handed regulation of airport services are likely to contain the attributes of an effective regulatory approach likely to promote efficient performance based on the experience of light-handed regulation of privatized airports in Australia and New Zealand.

Table 2. Summary of Design Characteristics Affecting the Effectiveness of Light-Handed Approaches to Regulation of Airport Services.

Regulatory Regime	Mechanism for Stronger Regulation if Airport Performance is Poor	Transparency of Airport Performance	Regulatory Burden on Airport
Information disclosure (minimalist approach)	The single form of price regulation available in legislation was generally considered to be an outdated approach. The likelihood that regulation would be introduced if performance is poor was low	Information available for assessment of performance under information disclosure regulation was inadequate	Minimal
Information disclosure regulation (enhanced approach)	A range regulatory of measures is available in legislation. The likelihood that regulation will be introduced if performance is poor is uncertain	Information available permits an assessment of airport performance	High regulatory burden
Price and Quality of Service Monitoring	The price control mechanism available in legislation is generally not considered suitable. The likelihood that it will be introduced if performance is poor has been low	Information is not sufficient to assess whether an airport has used its market power.	Low
Negotiate-arbitrate regulation (dispute resolution approach)	The likelihood of invoking negotiate-arbitrate regulation depends on the criteria for application of the regulation. Threat of independent dispute resolution (arbitration) is credible once the regulation applies	As the processes are confidential the effectiveness of negotiations will depend on the availability of suitable information provided by the airport to its users	Design of the regulation affects the time and costs involved in using the process

Source: Derived by the author based on research in Arblaster (2014 and 2016).

In general information disclosure regulation and monitoring rely on the availability of suitable stronger regulatory measures if airport performance is poor and on the likelihood that a stronger measure will be invoked, factors which will vary depending on the jurisdiction. The levels of transparency provided by minimalist approaches, such as the early information disclosure regulation in New Zealand and price monitoring in Australia, are low. The degree of transparency provided to airport users under negotiate-arbitrate negotiation will depend on the circumstances. Negotiations may not be effective if airport users do not have access to relevant information. Enhanced information disclosure regulation has a relatively high regulatory burden compared to a minimalist approach and compared to monitoring. The regulatory burden associated with negotiate-arbitrate regulation depends on the design characteristics of the framework.

CONCLUSIONS ON LIGHT-HANDED REGULATION OF AIRPORT SERVICES

Light-handed regulation applied to airports aims to be less intrusive into the affairs of the regulatory entity and to allow greater opportunity for negotiation in comparison to direct regulatory approaches, as well as providing some protection against the misuse of market power. Light-handed regulation has also been seen as a way to avoid some of the problems arising from price cap regulation.

Australia and New Zealand are two countries which have applied light-handed regulation to airports which have significant market power. A variety of approaches to light-handed regulation of airports have been used, with information disclosure regulation and price and quality of service monitoring being the main approaches. In addition, two forms of negotiate-arbitrate regulation have also been applied to some airport services.

While it is not clear what the general effects of the regulation on airport efficiency have been, the experience of light-handed regulation of airports, and also in some utility industries, has shown that the form of the regulation and its design are very important in determining whether the regulation is considered effective. In New Zealand, information disclosure regulation involving the application of a minimalist approach to monopoly industries, including airports, energy networks and telecommunications, was not sustainable and there was reversion to stronger regulatory approaches.

Three elements of light-handed regulation that affect its effectiveness as an approach, in circumstances where an airport has significant market power, are whether there is a credible threat of a stronger regulatory measure if poor performance is identified, the degree of transparency under the regulatory approach and the regulatory compliance and administrative costs involved in the approach used.

Information disclosure regulation involving minimal information requirements applying to New Zealand airports prior to 2010, and price and quality of service monitoring applying to Australian airports since 2002, have not involved a "credible" threat of a stronger regulatory intervention if concerns of adverse airport performance arise, nor provided sufficient information to evaluate airport performance.

Enhanced information disclosure regulation, involving extensive information has led to the disclosure of sufficient information to enable the New Zealand Commerce Commission to evaluate airport performance. Additionally, through a legislative framework involving a variety of alternative stronger regulatory measures, as well as robust review provisions, it seems likely the threat of a stronger measure in the event of adverse performance would be credible. The experience to date suggests that this approach is likely to provide an effective restraint on pricing airport services. However, the information and reporting requirements are substantial compared to other light-handed approaches. It is not clear to what extent "enhanced" information disclosure regulation is any less burdensome from a compliance point of view than direct regulatory approaches, such as price cap regulation.

A dispute resolution approach to regulation, such as negotiate-arbitrate regulation, has the advantage of narrowing regulation to unresolved issues in dispute. It is flexible in that it can cover a variety of circumstances, price and non-price issues. An advantage which the approach has is that a credible threat of stronger regulation is "inbuilt" through the availability of independent dispute resolution, such as an arbitration, and does not require deliberate intervention through the application of a separate regulatory measure. Experience in Australia has shown that, depending on the design of this form of regulation, the processes under the regulation can be very time consuming and costly and the applicability of the regulation very limited. The introduction of time constraints on the processes involved in negotiate-arbitrate regulation has improved the functioning of the approach.

A further important consideration with dispute resolution approaches, such as negotiate-arbitrate regulation, is the market characteristics. The potential of a negotiate-arbitrate approach to achieve efficient outcomes depends on effective competition in the airport user/airline market (Arblaster, 2016). A single dominant airline (or airport user) negotiating with a monopoly supplier of airport services could have the incentive to establish high airport prices involving a sharing of monopoly rents. Alternatively, if there is not effective competition among airport users, any benefits achieved from increasing airport users' bargaining power through application of negotiate-arbitrate regulation are not likely to be passed on to final consumers.

In short, whether light-handed regulation provides a suitable alternative approach to direct regulation depends on the market circumstances and the design characteristics of the light-handed approach. Further research on the experience of negotiated settlements in North American utility industries, and the regulatory approaches at some European airports which allow for greater negotiation, could provide further insights on the design light-handed regulation.

NOTES

1. The Body of Knowledge on Infrastructure Regulation (BoKIR) was developed by Public Utility Research Center, at the University of Florida, in collaboration with the University of Toulouse, the Pontificia Universidad Catolica, the World Bank and a panel of international expert. See http://regulationbodyofknowledge.org/. Accessed on January 6, 2017.
2. Alternative splits in airport services also exist, such as airside, terminal, and landside.
3. Aeronautical services generally comprise landing, take off, boarding, disembarking, parking planes, baggage transport, and security.
4. 'Non-aeronautical' services include car parking and rents for shops and offices used at airports.
5. CPI stands for consumer price index and RPI stands for the retail price index while X is the expected efficiency gains by the company.
6. This observation is based on the author's experience as a senior manager in the ACCC from 1995 to 2010.
7. The regulation was applied through a declaration (coverage) process (Part IIIA of the *Competition and Consumer Act 2010 (Cth) (CCA)*).
8. The Government can impose one or more of the various regulatory instruments under Part 4 after considering a recommendation from the NZCC following an inquiry into particular services under of the *Commerce Act 1986* (NZCC, 2008).
9. See NZCC (2017) and New Zealand Ministry of Business, Innovation, and Employment (2015).
10. The *Commerce Act 1986*, s.53C(2).
11. *Commerce Act 1986*, s.53B(2)(b).
12. See the *Commerce Act 1986*, s.52A.
13. Traditional approaches to rate of return regulation involved time intensive and lengthy regulatory hearings resulting in complex and administratively expensive regulation.
14. The price caps contained some features which reduced airports exposure to risk, such as provision for under and over-recovery between periods for unused parts of the cap and passing back excess revenue where the price cap had been exceeded. In the year following the removal of price caps there were significant increases in passenger numbers at most airports.
15. 'Bottleneck' infrastructure refers to essential infrastructure which has natural monopoly characteristics. Examples include rail tracks, electricity wires, telecommunication lines, port facilities, gas pipelines, and airports.
16. In New Zealand negotiate-arbitrate regulation potentially could be applied to airport services if the Government in New Zealand decided to invoke legislative provisions in the Commerce Act (s.53C(2)), *New Zealand Commerce Act 1986*. A recommendation from an independent inquiry is likely to precede a decision of this kind.
17. The approach to price control in the New Zealand legislation prior to 2008 was not generally considered to be suitable to the industry circumstances. There was only one form of price control already in legislation (Part IV, Commerce Act) which was considered a heavy-handed and inappropriate approach in the airport context. Similarly,

there are problems associated the existing legislative provisions for price controls in Australian legislation (Arblaster, 2017).

18. It was claimed that these skills were not readily available in New Zealand in the early 1990s (Small, 2000).

19. There have not been any completed arbitrations under negotiate-arbitrate regulation applied to airport services. One arbitration was commenced but not completed.

20. The Inquiry was initially required to report by 14 December 1999 but later extended to 27 August 2002 (NZCC, 2008).

21. These reviews have been completed in reasonable timeframes (around 12 months).

REFERENCES

Arblaster, M. (2010). A comparison of the approaches adopted to regulating airports in Ireland and New Zealand. Paper presented to the 12th world conference of the transport research society, Lisbon, 11–15 July, 2010. Retrieved from http://www.wctrs-society.com/wp/wp-content/uploads/abstracts/lisbon/selected/01527.pdf

Arblaster, M. (2014). The design of light-handed regulation of airports: Lessons from experience in Australia and New Zealand. *Journal of Air Transport Management*, *38*, 27–35.

Arblaster, M. (2016). Negotiate-arbitrate regulation of airport services: Twenty years of experience in Australia. *Journal of Air Transport Management*, *51*, 27–38.

Arblaster, M. (2017). Regulation in the face of uncertainty: The case of Australia. *Journal of Air Transport Management*, Article in Press.

Australian Competition and Consumer Commission (ACCC). (2013). Productivity commission review of the national access regime. Submission on the Issues Paper, February. LINK. Accessed on March 4, 2015. Retrieved from http://www.pc.gov.au/inquiries/completed/access-regime/submissions/submissions-test/submission-counter/sub016-access-regime.pdf

Australian Competition and Consumer Commission (ACCC). (2016). Airport monitoring report 2014-2015. Retrieved from https://www.accc.gov.au/publications/airport-monitoring-reports/airport-monitoring-report-2014-15. Accessed May 20, 2016.

Australian Government, Productivity Commission. (2002). Price regulation of airport services, Report no. 17, AustInfo Canberra.

Australian Government, Productivity Commission. (2006). Review of price regulation of airport services, Report no. 40, Canberra.

Australian Government, Productivity Commission. (2011). Economic regulation of airport services, Inquiry Report no.57, Canberra.

Bertram, G., & Twaddle, D. (2005). Price-cost margins and profit in New Zealand electricity distribution networks since 1994: The cost of light handed regulation. *Journal of Regulatory Economics*, *27*(3), 281–307.

Biggar, D. (2011). Why regulate airports? A re-examination of the rationale for airport regulation? *Journal of Transport Economics and Policy*, available online 2 November.

Blanchard, C. (1994a). Telecommunications regulation in New Zealand: How effective is 'light-handed' regulation? *Telecommunications Policy*, *18*(2), 154–164.

Blanchard, C. (1994b). Telecommunications regulation in New Zealand: The court of appeal's decision in clear communications v telecom corporation. *Telecommunications Policy*, *18*(9), 725–733.

Body of Knowledge on Infrastructure Regulation (BoKIR). (2017). Glossary. Retrieved from http://regulationbodyofknowledge.org/glossary/l/light-handed-regulation. Accessed on January 6, 2017.

Bollard, A. E., & Pickford, M. (1995). New Zealand's 'light-handed' approach to utility regulation. *Agenda*, *2*(4), 411–422.

Button, K. (2010). Countervailing power to airport monopolies. In P. Forsyth, D. Gillen, J. Müller, & H.-M. Niemeier (Eds.), *Airport competition – The European Experience*. Ashgate Publishing.

Carpenter, P., & Lapuerta, C. (1999). A critique of light-handed regulation: The case of British gas February 1999. *Northwestern Journal of International Law & Business*, *19*(3), 479–497.

Copenhagen Airports. (2009). Announcement to the NADAC OMX Copenhagen, 2009/6, 14 September. Retrieved from https://www.cph.dk/globalassets/om-cph/investor/fondsborsmeddelelser/2009/cphstockannouncementcharges_uk_final.pdf. Accessed April 17, 2016.

Copenhagen Economics. (2012). Airport Competition in Europe. Report prepared for the Airports Council International (ACI Europe). June. Authors: Martin Hvidt Thelle, Torben Thorø Pederse and Frederik Harhoff. Retrieved from http://www.moodiereport.com/pdf/Copenhagen_Economics_Study_Airport_Competition_2012.pdf. Accessed on January 12, 2016.

Domney, M. D., Wilson, I. M., & Chen, E. (2005). Natural monopoly privatization under different regulatory regimes: A comparison of New Zealand and Australian airports. *International Journal of Public Sector Management*, *18*(3), 274–292.

Doucet, J., & Littlechild, S. (2006). Negotiated settlements: The development of legal and economic thinking. *Utilities Policy*, *14*, 266–277.

Forsyth, P. (2008). Airport policy in Australia and New Zealand: Privatization, light-handed regulation, and performance. In C. Winston & G. de Rus (Eds.), *Aviation infrastructure performance: A study in comparative political economy* (pp. 65–99). Washington, DC: Brookings Institution Press.

Forsyth, P., Gillen, D., Müller, J., Niemeier, H.-M. (Eds.). (2010). *Airport competition – The European experience*. Aldershot: Ashgate Publishing.

Gillen, D. (2011). The evolution of airport ownership and governance. *Journal of Air Transport Management*, *17*, 3–13.

Given, J. (2010). Take your partners: Public private interplay in Australian and New Zealand plans for next generation broadband. *Telecommunications Policy*, *34*, 540–549.

IATA. (2013). Airport Competition, Economics briefing no. 11, James Wlitshire. Retrieved from http://www.iata.org/whatwedo/Documents/economics/airport-competition.pdf. Accessed on March 23, 2015.

ICAO. (2013). Commercialization and Privatization of Airports and Air Navigation Services Providers. Working Paper ATConf/6-WP/6, Worldwide Air Transport Conference (ATConf), Sixth Meeting, Montréal, 18 to 22 March 2013, Case Studies. Retrieved from http://www.icao.int/sustainability/Pages/Eap_ER_Databases_CaseStudies_ANSPs.aspx. Accessed on January 16, 2017.

Ireland, Commission for Aviation Regulation (CAR). (2001). CP2/2001: Economic regulation of airport charges in Ireland, February. Retrieved from http://www.aviationreg.ie/_fileupload/Image/PR_AC1_Pub2_CP2_2001%20_Consultation_on_Airport_Charges.pdf. Accessed on May 16, 2016.

Ireland, Commission for Aviation Regulation (CAR). (2009). CP3/2009. Maximum level of airport charges at Dublin Airport, draft determination, June. Retrieved from http://www.aviationreg.ie/_fileupload/2009_07_06_draft_determination_redacted_version.pdf. Accessed on January 7, 2016.

Ireland, Department of Transport, Tourism and Sport. (2015). A national aviation policy for Ireland, August. Retrieved from http://www.dttas.ie/sites/default/files/publications/aviation/english/national-aviation-policy-ireland/national-aviation-policy-ireland.pdf. Accessed on March 4, 2016.

Littlechild, S. (2009a). The bird in hand: Stipulated settlements in the Florida electricity sector. *Utilities Policy*, *17*, 276–287.

Littlechild, S. (2009b). RPI-X Regulation: Ofgem's RPI-X@20 review and the scope for more customer involvement in network. A publication of the Australian Competition and consumer commission for the utility regulators forum, Issue 34 December 2009. Ofgem's website Retrieved from http://www.ofgem.gov.uk/Networks/rpix20/publications/Pages/Publications.aspx. Accessed on March 6, 2016.

Littlechild, S. (2010). German airport regulation: Framework agreements, civil law and EU Directive. Paper? 9 October, 2010.

Littlechild, S. (2012). Australian airport regulation: Exploring the frontier. *Journal of Air Transport Management*, *20*, 50–62.

Morrison, S., & Winston, C. (2008). Delayed! U.S. aviation infrastructure policy. In C. Winston & G. de Rus (Eds.), *Aviation infrastructure performance: A study in comparative political economy* (pp. 7–35). Washington, DC: Brookings Institution Press.

New Zealand, Commerce Amendment Bill. (2008). Explanatory note.

New Zealand Commerce Commission (NZCC). (2002). Part IV Inquiry into Airfield Activities at Auckland, Wellington, and Christchurch International Airports, Final Report, 1 August.

New Zealand Commerce Commission (NZCC). (2008). Regulatory Provisions of the Commerce Act 1986, Discussion Paper, 19 December Retrieved from http://www.comcom.govt.nz/assets/Imported-from-old-site/industryregulation/ContentFiles/Documents/comcom-regulatory-provisionofcommerceactdiscussionpaper.pdf. Accessed on May 28, 2016.

New Zealand Commerce Commission (NZCC). (2013). Final report to the Ministers of Commerce and Transport on how effectively information disclosure regulation is promoting the purpose of Part 4 for Auckland Airport, Section 56G of the Commerce Act 1986, 31 July. Retrieved from http://www.comcom.govt.nz/regulated-industries/airports/section-56g-reports/. Accessed on July 3, 2016.

New Zealand Commerce Commission (NZCC). (2015). Summary and analysis of Wellington airport's third price setting event, 30 June. Retrieved from http://www.comcom.govt.nz/regulated-industries/airports/airport-services-media-releases/detail/2015/commission-releases-final-report-on-wellington-airports-revised-pricing. Accessed on July 3, 2016.

New Zealand Commerce Commission (NZCC). (2017). Retrieved from http://www.comcom.govt.nz/regulated-industries/electricity/electricity-role/ and http://www.comcom.govt.nz/regulated-industries/gas-pipelines/gas-default-price-quality-path/initial-default-price-quality-path/. Accessed on January 5, 2017.

New Zealand, Ministry of Business, Innovation and Employment. (2015). Chronology of New Zealand Electricity Reforms. Retrieved from http://www.mbie.govt.nz/info-services/sectors-industries/energy/electricity-market/electricity-industry/chronology-of-new-zealand-electricity-reform/chronology-of-nz-electricity-reform.pdf. Accessed on January 10, 2017.

Niemeier, H.-M. (2002). Regulation of airports: The case of Hamburg Airport – A view from the perspective of regional policy. *Journal of Air Transport Management*, *8*, 37–48.

O'Donnell, M., Glennie, M., O'Keefe, P., & Kwon, S.-H. (2011). Privatisation and 'light-handed' regulation: Sydney Airport. *The Economic and Labour Relations Review*, *22*(1), 65–80.

OECD/ITF. (2010). Airport regulation, investment and the development of regulation, International Transport Forum.

Oum, T., & Fu, X. (2008). Impact of Airports on Airline Competition: Focus on Airport Performance and Airport-Airline Vertical Relations. OECD/ITF Joint Transport Research Centre Discussion, 2008–17, OECD, September 2008. Retrieved from http://www.internationaltransportforum.org/jtrc/DiscussionPapers/DP200817.pdf

Oxera. (2013). Regulatory regimes at airports: an international comparison, Prepared for Gatwick Airport, January 23. Q5-050-LGW51 Downloaded 22 February 2016. Retrieved from http://www.oxera.com/Latest-Thinking/Publications/Reports/2013/Regulatory-regimes-at-airports-an-international-c.aspx

Patterson, R. (2004). Utility Regulation In New Zealand: From Light-handed to Many-Handed, Partner, Minter Ellison, Sydney. Paper prepared for the Australian Competition and Consumer Commission Regulatory Conference, 30 July. Retrieved from https://www.accc.gov.au/system/files/Session%203_%20New%20Zealand%20-%20Ross%20Patterson%20paper.pdf. Accessed on January 5, 2017.

Rebstock, P. (2004). The New Zealand Experience in Utility Regulation. Chair, Commerce Commission New Zealand. Paper prepared for the Australian Competition and Consumer Commission Regulatory Conference, 30 July. Retrieved from http://www.accc.gov.au/system/

files/Session%203_New%20Zealand%20Experience%20-%20Paula%20Rebstock%20%28paper%29%20-%20The%20New%20Zealand%20Experience%20in%20Utility%20Regulation.pdf. Accessed on January 6, 2017.

Sappington, D. E. M., & Weisman, D. L. (2010). Price cap regulation: what have we learned from 25 years of experience in the telecommunications industry? *Journal of Regulatory Economics*, *38*, 227–257.

Schultz, N. (1999). Light-handed regulation. *Alberta Law Review*, *37*(2), 387–418.

Schuster, D. (2009). Australia's approach to airport charges: The Sydney Airport experience. *Journal of Air Transport Management*, *15*(3), 121–126.

Small, J. (2000). In Georgina Lawrence (Ed.), Overview of Utility Regulation in New Zealand in Utility Regulation 2000 series (Vol. 5, pp. 20–25). Centre for the Study of Regulated Industries.

Starkie, D. (2008). *Aviation markets, IEA, studies in competition and regulatory reform*. Aldershot: Ashgate Publishing Company.

Starkie, D. (2010). The airport industry in a competitive environment: A United Kingdom perspective. In P. Forsyth, D. Gillen, J. Müller, & H.-M. Niemeier (Eds.), *Airport competition – The European experience*. Aldershot: Ashgate Publishing.

Steer Davies Gleave. (2013). Evaluation of Directive 2009/12/EC on airport charges, Final Report, Prepared for DG Move, Rue de Mot, Brussels, Belgium. September.

UK Department for Transport. (2009). Reforming the Framework for the Economic Regulation of UK Airports, March. Retrieved from https://www.gatwickairport.com/globalassets/publicationfiles/business_and_community/regulation/economic_regulation/doc5-dftregulatoryframeworkconsultation.pdf. Accessed on 4 April, 2016.

United Kingdom, Civil Aviation Authority (CAA). (2011). Guidance on the assessment of airport market power, April. LINK. Accessed on June 5, 2016.

United Kingdom, Civil Aviation Authority (CAA). (2016). CAP 1387 and CAP 1437. Economic Regulation: A Review of Gatwick Airport Limited's Commitments Framework, A consultation document and Update. Retrieved from http://publicapps.caa.co.uk/modalapplication.aspx?appid=11&mode=detail&id=7487 and http://publicapps.caa.co.uk/docs/33/CAP%201387%20March%202016.pdf. Accessed on June 15 and August 2, 2016.

United Kingdom, Competition and Markets Authority. (2016). BAA Airports: Evaluation of the Competition Commission's 2009 Market Investigation Remedies, 16 May. Retrieved from https://assets.publishing.service.gov.uk/media/57399d43ed915d152d00000b/evaluation_of_baa__market_investigation_remedies.pdf. Accessed on August 5, 2016.

United States. Department of Transport, Federal Aviation Authority (FAA). (2017). FAA website. Retrieved from http://www.faa.gov/airports/planning_capacity/npias/. Accessed on April 12, 2016.

Yang, H., & Fu, X. (2015). A comparison of price-cap and light-handed airport regulation with demand uncertainty. *Transportation Research Part B*, *73*, 122–132.

CHAPTER 3

TWO-SIDEDNESS AND WELFARE NEUTRALITY IN AIRPORT CONCESSIONS

Tiziana D'Alfonso and Valentina Bracaglia

ABSTRACT

Airport economics literature has recently included the supply of concession services among the factors that might affect airport pricing. In particular, there is only little empirical analysis on whether: (i) the supply of airport concession services can stimulate the demand for travel (two-side complementarity) and (ii) the demand for airport concession services is independent of traveling activities (welfare neutrality). In this chapter, we survey papers that have addressed two-side complementarity and welfare neutrality in airport concessions. Our goal is to discuss the different assumptions that have shaped the models and to collect evidences, facts and empirical findings that may support analytical hypotheses. We argue that the notions of two-side complementarity and welfare neutrality might be interrelated – especially when airports invest in concessions in the area accessible to non-passengers. Welfare gains should be assessed on a case by case basis, depending on the type of airport in terms of ownership, size (and the relative mass of connecting passengers compared to origin–destination passengers), and the source of concession revenues. Our arguments might be particularly relevant to policy makers who need to understand (i) whether the supply of concessions reduces or increases the benefits of airport (aviation) price regulation and

The Economics of Airport Operations
Advances in Airline Economics, Volume 6, 49–68

ISSN: 2212-1609/doi:10.1108/S2212-160920170000006003

(ii) whether the effective control of market power may require the regulation of the prices of both the businesses.

Keywords: Airport pricing; concessions; welfare neutrality; complementarity

JEL classifications: L93; L1

INTRODUCTION

The growing importance of revenues from non-aviation activities is acknowledged as one of the most striking and consistent trends in the airport sector over the last 30 years (Czerny, Guiomard, & Zhang, 2016; Halpern & Graham, 2013). Aviation activities are associated with the operation of runways, aircraft parking, and terminals, whereas concessions or non-aviation activities include retailing inside and outside passenger terminals, car rentals, car parking, advertising as well as any rental within airport land other than terminals. On average, airports worldwide derive as much revenues from concession activities as from aviation ones (ACI, 2012), owing partly to prevailing regulation mechanisms which leave concession activities unregulated (Jones, Vieho, & Marks, 1993; Starkie, 2001), and partly to locational rents enjoyed in relation to passengers (Forsyth, 2003). For instance, the percentage of non-aviation revenues approaches 40% at airports in Latin America, Europe, and Africa, while it is almost 50% at airports in North America and Asia (ACI, 2012).

The airport economics literature has recently included the supply of concession services among the factors that might affect airport (congestion) pricing. This literature argues that airports may curb their market power and restrain the aviation charge that they impose to airlines in order to boost traffic and expand revenues from concessions. If this is true, the need for heavy-handed airport regulation would be alleviated (Starkie, 2002). Insightful reviews of this literature are provided by Zhang and Czerny (2012) and Czerny Guiomard, et al. (2016), who concentrate on airport market power and the need for airport regulation, as well as on the role that non-aviation revenues may have in financing capacity investments.

In particular, Zhang and Czerny (2012) in their interpretive review of recent research on airports and airlines economics and policy, highlights that there is only little empirical analysis on whether: (i) airport concession services can change the passenger quantity and (ii) airport concession services contribute to welfare. These issues are critical for two reasons. First, concessions may play a role when evaluating price regulation (if concessions can change the passenger quantity, airports may use their market power to ask for higher aviation charges than absent the non-aviation business). Second, whether concessions are welfare neutral or not would reduce or increase the difference between the private and public aviation charges.

Thus, rather than replicating the above-mentioned reviews, we concentrate on two key open questions:

i. to what extent the supply of airport concession services can stimulate the demand for travel (*two-side complementarity*);
ii. to what extent the demand for airport concession services is independent of traveling activities (*welfare neutrality*).

We survey analytical papers within the airport economics literature that have addressed, since 1997, two-sidedness and welfare neutrality in airport concessions. Our goal is to discuss the different assumptions that have shaped the models and to collect evidences, facts and empirical findings that may support analytical hypotheses. We argue that the notions of two-sidedness and welfare neutrality might be interrelated – especially when airports invest in concessions in the area accessible to non-passengers. Welfare gains should be assessed on a case by case basis, depending on the type of airport in terms of ownership, size (and the relative mass of connecting passengers compared to origin–destination passengers), and the source of concession revenues.

Our arguments might be particularly relevant to policy makers who need to understand: (i) whether the supply of concessions reduces or increases the benefits of airport (aviation) price regulation and (ii) whether the effective control of market power may require the regulation of the prices of both the businesses.

We organize the rest of the paper around the two open questions identified (see the sections "Two-sidedness in Airport Concessions" and "Welfare Neutrality in Airport Concessions") and we conclude with a summary that makes explicit the relationship between two-sidedness and welfare neutrality in airport concessions (see the section "The Relationship between Two-Sidedness and Welfare Neutrality in Airport Concessions"). The section "Concluding Remarks and Avenues for Future Research" provides some concluding remarks.

TWO-SIDEDNESS IN AIRPORT CONCESSIONS

Since airports possess a significant amount of monopoly power, infrastructure charges of privatized airports are often subject to economic regulation. However, since concession operations depend greatly on the passenger throughput, airports may curb their market power and restrain the aviation charge they impose to airlines in order to boost traffic and expand revenues from concessions. If this is true, the need for heavy-handed airport regulation might be alleviated (Starkie, 2002).

Starkie (2002)'s conjecture has been investigated under two distinct assumptions on the nature of the demand complementarity between aviation and non-aviation services, that is whether the passenger quantity is independent or not of airport concession prices.

On the one hand, some contributions assume that passenger demand for air ticket is independent of the price of concession services (*one-side complementarity*). This may be the case because buying the air tickets and concession services can be separated in time (D'Alfonso, Jiang, & Wan, 2013; Oum, Zhang, & Zhang, 2004; Wan, Jiang, & Zhang, 2015; Yang & Zhang, 2011; Zhang & Zhang, 1997, 2003, 2010). These papers suppose that passengers make two separate decisions. First, they book their flight, based on their (perceived full) price; second, after arriving at the airport, they make decisions on purchasing concession goods. Zhang and Zhang (1997, 2003, 2010) and Oum et al. (2004) model profit from concessions as a fixed add-on profit per passenger. D'Alfonso et al. (2013), Wan et al. (2015), and Yang and Zhang (2011) consider a stochastic framework in which the demand for concession services is derived from the probability that their valuation for the good is greater than the price they are charged for the services. The literature on one-side complementarity finds that the non-aviation business unambiguously exerts a downward pressure on the private aviation charge, and confirms Starkie's conjecture.

On the other hand, the second strand of the literature assumes that consumers may make decisions about buying the flight and non-aviation services simultaneously rather than independently (*two-side complementarity*). In this case, passenger quantity increases as the price for concession services decreases. Indeed, a reduction in the price for concession services can be considered as an increase in airport "quality," which enhances consumer surplus and thus stimulates travel demand (Czerny & Lindsey, 2014). Since only passengers can buy concession services, the demand for the latter is a subset of the demand for flights. Hence, lowering the price for concessions increases revenues by a larger amount than lowering the aviation charge. As a result, the non-aviation business may exert upward pressure on the private monopolistic aviation charge.

The argument behind two-side complementarity is that the issue of the time-separation has been moderated over time by the e-commerce advancement that allows the airports to increasingly advertise their concession services online (Bracaglia, D'Alfonso, & Nastasi, 2014). Furthermore, many passengers, in particular business travelers, are frequent flyers, which are likely aware of the surplus associated with concession services, such as car rental or car parking (Czerny, 2013).

Bracaglia et al. (2014), Czerny (2006, 2013), and Flores-Fillol, Iozzi, and Valletti (2015) introduce two-sidedness in airport business on the basis of different assumptions. Czerny (2006, 2013) assumes that individuals consume aviation and non-aviation services together, even if what they are willing to pay for the flight is lower than the ticket price, provided that the combined willingness to pay for flying and consuming concession services exceeds the ticket price plus the price of non-aviation services. Czerny (2006) focuses on price cap regulation of a monopolistic airport, while Czerny (2013) compares the behavior of private versus public monopolistic airports. Flores-Fillol et al. (2015) assume that passengers may account for a certain portion of the surplus that they expect to obtain from the consumption of the retail good once at the airport, depending on their degree of foresight. They explicitly model market structure of airlines and retailers that operate in a monopolistic airport. The airport decides the number of concessionaires, which then compete on quantities in a Salop circle with exogenous transportation cost – i.e., degree of substitutability between the products supplied by different retailers.[1] In Bracaglia et al. (2014) whether travelers decide to travel accounting (also) for the surplus they would gain from concession consumption depends on e-commerce strategies of airports, since the interaction of purchasing decisions is induced by the observability of concession prices at the time of the ticket purchase. Bracaglia et al. (2014) focus on airport competition and investigate whether airports have an incentive to induce two-side complementarity between airport businesses strategically through e-commerce.

In general, airports are often referred to as two-sided platforms (see also D'Alfonso & Nastasi, 2014; Gillen, 2011; Gillen & Mantin, 2012), but whether airports can be considered as two-sided is an empirical question.

Baron and Wass (1996) examine and discuss the shopping behavior of international passengers in a UK regional airport. The study relies on an on-site passenger survey, which reveals that, while there is evidence of impulse purchasing brought about by affective responses to the airport context, passengers plan much of the browsing and purchasing in advance of the airport visit and they see it as a component of the trip/holiday. Geuens, Vantomme, and Brengman (2004) examine the shopping behavior of a sample of Belgian travelers leaving from Bruxelles airport and they report that 40% of travelers preplan purchases at the airport. Flores-Fillol et al. (2015) add that, according to a recent report by Mintel (2013), 16% of German leisure travelers anticipate airport shopping, while the percentage is 18% for British ones. These evidences may support the argument that passengers are unlikely unaware of the surplus associated with concession services, which shape the models of Czerny (2006, 2013) and Flores-Fillol et al. (2015).

Evidence also shows that e-commerce is a growing trend in airport management. This evidence might support the argument in Bracaglia et al. (2014). Schiphol Group, for instance, attributes the 15.5% and 5% increase in 2011 in long and short stay parking, respectively, to the growing number of reservations via the web (Schiphol Group, 2011). Similarly, starting from 2010, car parking booking at Paris Orly can be made online up to 6 months in advance and 50,000 customers used this service in 2010 (Groupe ADP, 2010). Airport Direct Travel (ADT) provides e-commerce platforms specifically geared to increase revenues to several airports, e.g., Birmingham, Manchester, Belfast, Geneve, Glasgow, Leeds, London Luton or Stockholm Skavsta. ADT has recognized that "[...] there has been a clear shift in people purchasing their travel online over the past decade and identifying the departure airport as a highly regarded and trusted source of information." Consequently, the platform *CarParkREZ* has been developed in order to help airport managers to meticulously plan and execute their pre-book parking strategy. SITA (2013) mentions that 45% of airports surveyed plans to offer the ability to pay for ancillary services, such as parking, through their mobile apps during the next 3 years, taking the total to 63% by the end of 2016.

In fact, there are not univocal empirical evidences on the nature of complementarity between aviation and commercial services. Choo (2014) finds a negative relationship between the aviation charge and the share of concession revenues of US airports, which supports the assumption of one-side complementarity. Bilotkach, Clougherty, Mueller, and Zhang (2012) do not detect any significant relationship between the aviation charge and commercial revenues on a sample of European airports. Van Dender (2007) finds that per-passenger concession revenues at US airports are declining in air passenger quantity. This finding is consistent with the concept that concession prices can change the passenger demand: if the airport manages to increase the passenger quantity reducing concession prices, the per-passenger concession revenues of the infrastructure will decrease (see also Czerny, Shi, & Zhang, 2016). However, the result could also be due to the fact that higher passengers' traffic comes with lower airfare, and, therefore, when traffic increases the airport is attracting more low-income passengers, which are unlikely to spend money on concessions. More recently, Ivaldi, Sokullu, and Toru (2015) find that passengers fly more if the price of the representative commercial product (i.e., daily parking fee) goes down. That is to say that the airport can affect the number of transactions between airlines and passengers by changing its pricing structure. In parallel but independent work, Czerny, Shi et al. (2016) show that a one-dollar increase in the daily car rental price reduces passenger demand at 199 US airports by more than 0.36%.

Understanding the nature (one-side or two-side) of airport business is relevant for competition and welfare analyses. In this sense, Ivaldi et al. (2015), though finding empirical evidence of the two-sided nature of airport business, show that airports in the US do not internalize the externalities between the two sides of their business when choosing their prices. In fact, they simulate the pricing of a monopolist airport and make a comparison with the actual pricing behavior of airports and they find that the airports adopt (different) one-sided pricing schemes: they set profit-maximizing prices for daily parking and Ramsey prices for aviation services to airlines. Furthermore, they compute the social welfare under the assumption that a monopolist profit-maximizing airport is setting the prices fully accounting for the two-sidedness of its activities and they compare it with the actual social welfare. They find that the results are airport dependent: for some airports, two-sided pricing would increase the welfare while for others it would not. In such a case, they advocate the need of single till regulation, in which landing fees and non-aviation prices are globally price capped. Similarly, a major implication of Czerny, Shi, et al. (2016)'s findings is that, for the case of airports, the effective control of market power may require regulation of both prices for aviation and non-aviation businesses.

WELFARE NEUTRALITY IN AIRPORT CONCESSIONS

It has been argued that the consumption of concessions at the airport might not be welfare enhancing. This is the case when individuals would derive the same surplus from buying concessions whether they travel or not, i.e., when the aggregate demand for concessions within and outside the airport land is independent of traveling activities.

In this paragraph, we argue that:

a. the substitutability between concession goods at airport and goods elsewhere has increased over time; airports have become tourism and leisure destinations, which attract demand without a direct correlation with the possession of an airline ticket. Consequently, if individuals do not travel they have either the opportunity to buy the concession services at the airport or outside the airport;
b. the value of concession services at the airport might be higher to travelers than to non-travelers. In other words, the welfare associated with the consumption of concession services may depend on whether individuals travel or not.

The Substitutability between Concession Goods at Airport and Goods Elsewhere

Nowadays, airports invest in non-aviation activities that lay outside the traditional boundary of services complementary to the airside. They extend their offerings to new target groups, in addition to the traditional captive audience of origin, destination, and transit passengers (Doganis, 1992; Poungias, 2009). These include the employees of airport authorities, airlines, and other air service providers, local residents all around the airport,[2] as well as meeter-and-greeters, strollers and half-day trippers, motivated to shop by the international flair, the exciting atmosphere and the variety of offerings that are supplied at the airport (Jarach, 2001; Sulzmaier, 200). Such strategies are becoming prevalent as airports are actively pursuing initiatives for de-risking their aviation and (passenger-dependent) non-aviation businesses (Poungias, 2009; Reiss, 2007). For instance, between 1998 and 2008, operating revenues derived from rent of land and non-passenger terminal facilities grew by 58% at large hubs, 24% at medium hubs, 43% at small hubs, and 54% at non-hubs in the US (Kramer, 2010).

With the spread of out-of-town retail followed to the third wave of shopping decentralization, the expansion of airport retail has been openly criticized for the impact that it may have on nearby shopping centers in the last 20 years (Fernie, 1995; Jarach, 2005; Levitt, 1980). Today, many commercially run airports have evolved into real *airport cities* (Kasarda, 2008; The Economist, 2013, 2015a; The New York Times, 2010), integrated real estate developments whose clustering functions expand in the landside property zone of the airport. According to Euromonitor International, similarly to a traditional metropolis and its outlying suburbs, the airport is becoming the focus of a sprawl of businesses – hotels, convention, trade, and exhibition facilities, corporate offices, and retail complexes along with culture, entertainment and recreation centers. The implication is that airport shops will no longer be solely for duty-free gifts and indulgences. Instead, industry players will have to diversify their travel retail product mix to appeal (also) to the workers and residents of the surrounding city (Euromonitor International, 2006).

In Europe, Schiphol actively promotes the concept of an airport city (Adey, 2006). Conceived as a *civic amenity*, with more than 5,300 square meters of shopping, dining, and entertainment arcades before passport control, it attracts city residents along with approximately 58,000 people who work in the airport business district (Morrison, 2009). Schiphol group appears keen to export the concept of airport cities to locations, such as Cairo International Airport, where there are plans to include an international airport hospital that will compete in the regional market for medical treatments and operations (Morrison, 2009). The new major project "The Circle" at the Zurich airport is another prominent example (Orth, Frei, & Weidmann, 2015). It is 12 minutes from the city center and it is already Switzerland's second biggest shopping center by revenues, with the highest sales in terms of square meters. In 2013, the Circle attracted 68,000 air travelers and 55,000 non-travelers (20,000 commuters, 10,000 visitors, 25,000 employees on site) daily (Orth et al., 2015). Athens has already completed many undertakings in its particular airport city: it has a large IKEA and Kotsovolos Megastore (Kasarda, 2008). Fraport is extensively developing and marketing attractive commercial spaces in direct proximity of the Frankfurt airport (such as Monchhof site or Gataway gardens). The airport of Munich has attracted more tourists than Ludwig's castle Neuschwanstein and it is Bavaria's tourist attraction number one (Sulzmaier, 2001).

In a similar vein, other numerous projects demonstrate the popularity of the airport city concept in Australia (Freestone & Baker, 2010), Canada (Business Vancouver, 2015; The Province, 2015), China (Poungias, 2009), Hong Kong or Taiwan (Wang & Hong, 2011).

These evidences certainly support the argument that the substitutability between concession goods at airport and goods elsewhere has increased over time and travelers as well as non-travelers shop at airports nowadays.

Travelers reach the airport since their primary intent is to fly and, once at the facility, they may purchase concession services. On the other hand, some non-travelers also reach the airport to make use of concessions, simply because they know that there are stores there. The open question is: does the utility from non-aviation good consumption depend on whether individuals travel or not?

Traveler and Non-traveler Surplus in Concessions Consumption

Czerny (2009, 2013) distinguishes between two categories of concession services: *car rental-type services* – which include car rental, car parking, hotel reservation or business offices – and *food and beverage-type services* – which include retail services as clothes and footwear, food and beverages, cigarettes, alcohol, cosmetics or electrical appliances. The author argues that the demand for *food and beverage* inside and outside the airport area is independent of traveling activities, since individuals will eat and drink whether they travel or stay at home. In other words, the total welfare associated with the consumption of airport food and beverage (sum of consumer surplus and airport profit) may materialize outside the airport area when individuals do not travel. The supply of these concession services may, therefore, be considered as welfare neutral from the social viewpoint. As opposite, the aggregate demand for *car rentals* (sum of car rental demands inside and outside the airport area) depends on traveling, therefore airport car-rental business is unlikely to be welfare neutral. This is because *car rentals* are normally not used when individuals decide to stay at home where they have their private car available.

In fact, Czerny (2013) does explicitly consider the substitutability between retail services at airport and retail services elsewhere, but he imposes an exogenous surplus parameter. In his model, individuals may be better or worse off buying retail services outside the airport area. The reason for this ambiguity is based on the observation that airport retail prices may be high or low relative to prices charged outside the airport area due, for instance, to locational rents or tax discounts, respectively.

D'Alfonso et al. (2013) argue that every type of concession service might elicit extra-value to travelers. This happens because airports are unique retailing environments, which can make travelers react in unusual ways and to behave unlike general shoppers. Thus, in their setting, the total welfare associated with the consumption of concession services is higher compared to what would occur outside the airport area if individuals decide to stay at home. Different authors emphasize the specificities of airport shopping that may convert browsers at airports into impulsive customers with a higher willingness to pay than normal (Crawford & Meleware, 2003; Davies, 1995; Dube & Menon, 2000;

Entwistle, 2007; Geuens et al., 2004; Huang & Kuai, 2006; Lin and Chen, 2013; Lu, 2014; Omar & Kent, 2001; Perng, Chow, & Liao, 2010; Vlitos Rowe, 1999). The motivations are almost inherent to traveling activities and arise as one starts the trip:

i. the 'I'm on my holidays syndrome';
ii. confusion – information overload by the retailers can serve to reduce cognitive effects and stimulate purchasing behavior;
iii. exclusivity – many products are developed exclusively for the travel retail channel of distribution, inducing purchases;
iv. disposal of foreign currency;
v. fear – for some people, traveling causes fear or feelings of insecurity, leading them to search for comforting behaviors from shopping;
vi. waiting time – waiting travelers shop because they are bored and seek entertainment in shopping;
vii. captivity – travelers constitute a captive group with a high disposable income but little time to dispose of it in the high street as they are constrained at the facility, since their primary intent is to fly (see also The Economist, 2015b; The New York Times, 2011);
viii. symbolic act – shopping at the airport might become a ritual that gives expression to the consumers' self-presentation and self-fashioning: authenticity is not necessarily what they are looking for, hyperreality and hypersignification can become a more plausible version of reality, as the disneyfication of urban and suburban shopping malls and town centers shows (Sulzmaier, 2001).

In order to take into account these specificities, D'Alfonso et al. (2013) include a fixed portion of the surplus from concession services in the social welfare function. This reconciles two approaches in the literature: if the portion is equal to 1, all of the surplus from concession activities is counted into social welfare (Oum et al., 2004; Wan et al., 2015; Yang & Zhang, 2011; Zhang & Zhang, 1997, 2003, 2010); if the portion is equal to 0, the surplus from concession activities is excluded (Czerny, 2013).

The assumption of welfare neutrality in concessions is critical in airport economics.

When an unregulated private airport has profitable concession operations, its aviation charge is closer to the social optimum compared to the case in which there are no concession activities, or if aviation and concession activities are treated separately. At the same time, a private airport would charge a higher price than the socially optimal level (Zhang & Zhang, 2003). However, the welfare contribution of airports must be discounted to account for the welfare that is independent of traveling activities. This can reduce the difference between the private and public aviation charges. Czerny (2013) shows that the public and private aviation charges can be the same when a part of concessions are welfare neutral.

We note that the hypothesis of a hierarchical structure of demands for aviation and non-aviation goods, i.e., consumers can buy one good (concession goods) only if they buy another as well (the flight) shapes all papers that we have reviewed so far.

D'Alfonso, Bracaglia, and Wan (2014, 2015) remove the assumption of a hierarchical structure of demands and recognize in their model that the demand for non-aviation products might not be a subset of the demand for flights because non-travelers can buy concession services from the airport. The authors model explicitly the surplus that non-travelers derive from their outside option (e.g., downtown shopping), or, equivalently, the extra-surplus gained by travelers, compared to non-travelers, from consuming aviation and non-aviation services together. In their framework, while some individuals are willing to buy airport concession services irrespectively of traveling, some others derive a positive surplus from consuming non-aviation services only if they travel. The latter constitute an *induced demand* for concession services, which increases with the extra-surplus elicited by travel-related motivations. This modeling implicitly assumes that concessions are not welfare neutral. Again, the extra-surplus gained by travelers from consuming aviation and non-aviation services together is an exogenous surplus parameter in D'Alfonso et al. (2014, 2015), although it should be endogenous in a complete framework.

In a parallel but independent work, Kidokoro, Lin, and Zhang (2016) incorporate both travelers and non-travelers in a general-equilibrium model that includes consumers, airlines, an airport as well as shops outside of the airport in the city center that involve in perfect competition with shops at the airport. The authors endogenously determine the size of the airport's non-aviation services provided by shops given constraints in capacity, that is, shop space is usually limited and can only be increased by investment.[3] However, as the airport commercial rent is set to be an increasing function of passenger quantity only, it explicitly assumes that non-travelers will not purchase at the airport and hence fails to capture the key feature of an airport city.

If the structure of demands for aviation and non-aviation goods is not hierarchical, the non-aviation business may not unambiguously exert downward pressure on the private aviation charge (D'Alfonso et al., 2015). The assumption of welfare neutrality of concession services for travelers again is critical in this framework: as the extra-surplus from non-aviation services consumption elicited by travel-related motivations increases, price elasticity of the demand for non-aviation goods reduces. Thus, the marginal benefit from aviation price reduction further decreases.

THE RELATIONSHIP BETWEEN TWO-SIDEDNESS AND WELFARE NEUTRALITY IN AIRPORT CONCESSIONS

In this section, we argue that the notions of two-sidedness and welfare neutrality might be interrelated.

Bracaglia et al. (2014) and Czerny (2013) assume that the concessions that might stimulate the demand for travels tend to be welfare enhancing, while the opposite is not necessary true. In their modeling, they explicitly distinguish between car rental-type and food and beverage-type services. As noted, according to Czerny (2013), car rental-type services are generally welfare enhancing. Bracaglia et al. (2014) share this assumption and both the papers assume that a reduction in the price of car rental-type services increases passengers' quantity. Similarly, both the papers assume that the price of food and beverage-type services is not set strategically by the airport so as to increase passengers' quantity. For such services, the welfare contribution of airports is partly discounted to account for the welfare that is independent of traveling activities.

Czerny (2013) assumes that travelers are conscious about the surplus associated to car rental-type services and whether they are better-off buying retail services inside or outside the airport area, in Bracaglia et al. (2014), whether individuals decide to travel accounting (also) for the surplus they would gain from car rental-type services depends on e-commerce strategies of airports. This is because the interaction of purchasing decisions is induced by the observability of both prices at the time of the ticket purchase. In other words, whether two-side complementarity between aviation services and car rental-type services arises is the result of a strategic decision of airports.

Passengers are usually willing to buy car rental-type services before departure since these services might complement the travel, i.e., travel might not occur if those services are not available. This is why airports are interested in offering them online at the time of the ticket purchase in order to stimulate the demand for flights and gain advantages when they compete. Take the example of a traveler that is interested in car reservation, while planning a fly-and-drive trip (or that needs to reach the final destination when landing in a secondary airport). If she finds out that the air ticket price is higher than what she is willing to pay, she may still decide to travel if she is offered a very convenient car rental rate at the time of ticket purchase (Bracaglia et al., 2014). On the contrary, she might not buy the ticket if she would have to wait until the day of departure (or the arrival at the destination airport) to be informed about the car rental rate. The same might happen if she would have to incur high searching costs to get this information (Bracaglia et al., 2014). A similar logic can be applied taking the example of car parking. As opposite, purchases of food and beverage-type services are usually related to instant needs since do not complement the travel. Thus, airports are not interested in web-market these services in order to stimulate demand for travel.

Reasonably, car rental-type services, i.e., those services that strictly complement the travel, are welfare enhancing and they are an example of two-side complementarity, at least for frequent fliers or business travelers. In a similar vein, we remark that car rental and car parking services are supplied landside, i.e., in the area accessible to non-passengers, therefore, if we accept that their price affects passengers demand we are implicitly sharing the idea that they are welfare enhancing when purchased by travelers.

Conversely, some concession services elicit extra-surplus simply because they are consumed within the unique retailing environments that are the airport. Most of these purchases are related to instant needs, e.g., the need to eat and drink, or psychological issues linked with the travel process, e.g., exclusivity. This is the case of food and beverage-type services, which do not strictly complement the travel, i.e., travel might occur even if those service are not available, but may elicit extra-surplus.[4] Whether the supply of such services stimulates demand for flights depends on whether a reduction of prices increases the incentives to travel. We argue this is more likely to happen for connecting passengers who are aware of the waiting time they have to spend at the connecting hub.

Established that two-sidedness and welfare neutrality are likely to be dependent on the type of concession service, we turn our attention to the importance of the different types of non-aviation activities of airports.

Results from the 2012 Concessions Benchmarking Survey (ACI, 2012) highlight some differences in concessions. Fig. 1 shows how the importance of non-aviation activities vary among regions.

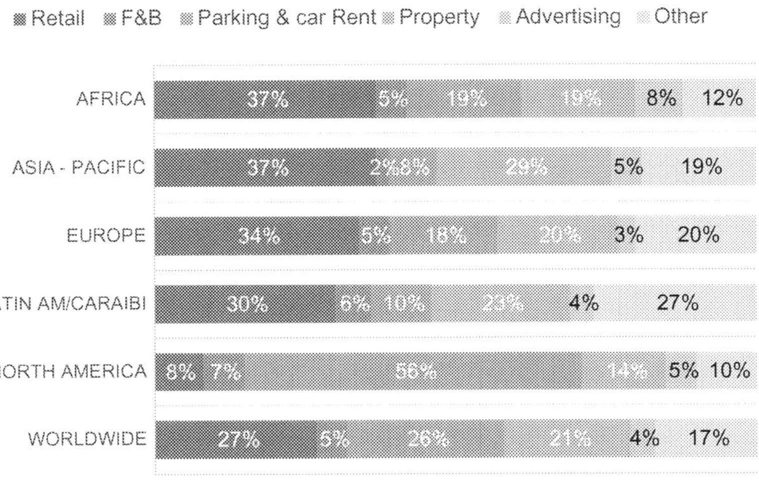

Fig. 1. Importance of non-aviation activities by regions. *Source:* 2012 ACI-NA Concessions Benchmarking Survey.

Parking and car rental are definitively the most important source of non-aviation revenues for airports in North America, where distances are more spread out and public transport connections are less smooth. The story is consistent with the findings on two-sidedness of Czerny, Shi, et al. (2016) and Ivaldi et al. (2015) on a sample of US airports.

Retail and food and beverage are more important at larger airports, that usually are hubs where people spend time shopping during connection (Fig. 2). As opposite, parking and car rental are more important at smaller and medium airports (less the 15 million passengers). Smaller airports are often located far from the city center and connection by public transport is less smooth. Moreover, the percentage of origin–destination passengers at smaller airports is higher than that of connecting passengers. Thus, parking and car rental are required and it is seen as a complement to the travel. Roughly, two-sidedness (and the associated welfare gains) does matter at smaller and medium airports. It is not surprising, then, that in its negotiations with some airports Ryanair asks for parking revenue sharing as a condition to serve them, within its co-operation with the leading airport parking company Better Choice for Parking (BCP).

Generally speaking, one major implication of our arguments is that whether pricing under a two-sided market structure would increase the welfare should be assessed on a case by case basis, depending on the type of airport in terms of ownership, size (and the relative mass of connecting passengers compared to origin–destination passengers) and the structure of concession revenues.

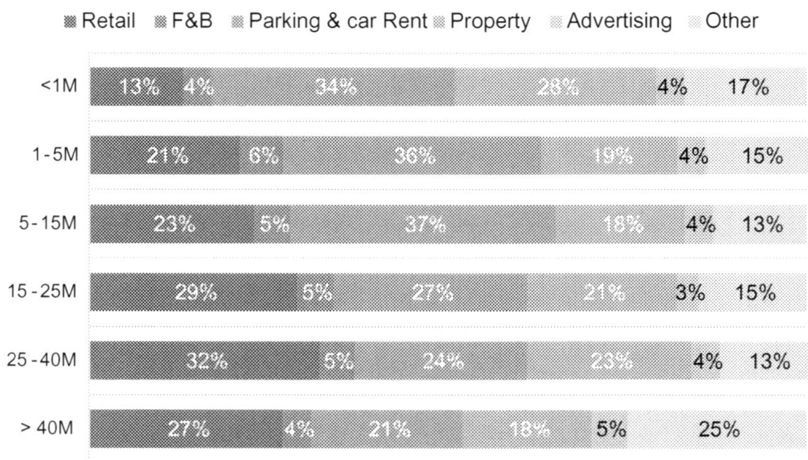

Fig. 2. Importance of non-aviation activities by the size of the airport. *Source:* 2012 ACI-NA Concessions Benchmarking Survey.

CONCLUDING REMARKS AND AVENUES FOR FUTURE RESEARCH

In this chapter, we have discussed two key open questions in the debate around the economics of airport pricing:

i. to what extent the supply of airport concession services can stimulate the demand for travel (*two-side complementarity*);
ii. to what extent the demand for airport concession services is independent of traveling activities (*welfare neutrality*).

The first issue is critical since when a reduction in the prices for concession services stimulates travel demand the non-aviation business may exert upward pressure on the private aviation charge. The second issue is critical since social welfare must be discounted to account for the welfare that is independent of traveling activities. This can reduce the difference between the private and public aviation charges.

We have surveyed analytical papers within airport economics literature that have addressed, since 1997, two-sidedness and welfare neutrality in airport concessions. We have discussed the different assumptions that have shaped the models and we have provided evidences, facts, and empirical findings that may support analytical hypotheses.

We argue that there are not univocal empirical evidences on the nature of complementarity between aviation and commercial services. Furthermore, we argue that the notions of two-sidedness and welfare neutrality might be interrelated, especially as airports invest in concessions landside, in the area accessible to non-passengers.

If traveling occurs only when some concession services are available, this clearly illustrates the relevance of two-side complementarity. Reasonably, car rental-type services, i.e., those services that strictly complement the travel, are welfare enhancing and an example of two-side complementarity, at least for frequent fliers or business travelers. Furthermore, car rental and car parking services are supplied landside, i.e., in the area accessible to non-passengers: if we accept that their price affects passengers demand, we are implicitly sharing the idea that they are welfare enhancing when purchased by travelers.

Conversely, some concession services elicit extra-surplus simply because they are consumed within unique retailing environments that make travelers react in unusual ways. Most of these purchases are related to instant needs, e.g., the need to eat and drink, or psychological issues linked with the travel process, as feelings of anxiety, stress or excitement, which make passengers react in unusual ways, or impulsively. This is the case of food and beverage-type of services, which do not strictly complement the travel. Whether the supply of such services stimulates demand for flights depends on whether a reduction of prices increases the incentives of traveling. This is more likely to happen for connecting passengers who are aware of the waiting time at the connecting hub.

Data show that retail and food and beverage are more important at larger airports, which usually are hubs where people spend time shopping during connections. As opposite, parking and car rental are more important at smaller and medium airports (less the 15 million passengers). Smaller airports are often located far from the city center and connections by public transport are less smooth. Moreover, the percentage of origin–destination passengers at smaller airports is higher than that of connecting passengers. Thus, parking and car rental are required and it is seen as a complement to the travel.

Our discussion raises avenues for further research. First, whether two-sidedness and welfare neutrality are interrelated is an empirical question. Empirical papers shall clarify whether the answer depends on the type of airport in terms of size (and the relative mass of connecting passengers compared to origin–destination passengers) and the source of concession revenues (i.e., car rental-type services and food and beverage-type of services). Accordingly, different regulation schemes could be implemented for small airports or big airports to internalize the effects of concessions' supply on airport pricing.

Second, the degree of complementarity between aviation and non-aviation services could be affected by the airport – for instance, through the choice of the type of retailers in the terminal or in the surrounding land parcels, as well as creating a unique environment able to convert travelers into customers.[5] In this framework, the airport might have incentives to stimulate passenger foresight in order to exploit the benefit of the supply of concession services on demand for aviation services. Consistently, theoretical studies shall incorporate airport's strategic choice of concessions' variety in order to investigate whether such strategies enhance consumer surplus.

NOTES

1. The airport economics literature generally assumes that concessions are awarded to private operators and perfect competition among the bidders allows the airport to capture all rents (e.g., through take-it-or-leave-it offers). Then, the price for concessions, i.e., the rent, is set to maximize commercial profits. All papers reviewed in this survey, other than Flores-Fillol et al. (2015), adopt this assumption. In reality, there are different degrees to which an airport authority becomes directly involved in operating the concessions available within its spaces. The reader may refer to Kim and Shin (2001) for a useful taxonomy of vertical relationships between airports and retailers.
2. For instance, Frankfurt Airport with 75,000 people working on the airport land is one of the largest regional places of work in Germany. More importantly, 60% of airport employees live within approximately 35 kilometers from the airport. An increasing number of airports employs more than 50,000 daily workers, which would make them metropolitan central cities by the U.S. census definition (Kasarda, 2008).
3. Flores-Fillol et al. (2015) assume unit demand for non-aviation services and they do not impose constraints in airport capacity. Substitutability between goods sold at

airport and those sold elsewhere is not considered in Flores-Fillol et al. (2015). Finally, people who do not fly cannot purchase concession goods.

4. As noted by an anonymous referee, this may be the case of *gourmet* airport restaurants.

5. Crawford and Meleware (2003), for instance, describe different strategies in order to increase the surplus that browsers may obtain from airport purchases. See also Davies (1995) for a spectrum of primary activities and their typical complementary retail opportunities.

ACKNOWLEDGMENTS

We thank Achim Czerny, Ricardo Flores-Fillol and Anming Zhang for constructive comments on first drafts of this chapter. We also express our gratitude to David Gillen, Robin Lindsey, Yulai Wan and Changmin Jiang for fruitful discussions on airport concessions through years.

REFERENCES

ACI. (2012). 2012 ACI-NA concessions benchmarking survey. Montreal, QC: Airports Council International (ACI).

Adey, P. (2006). Airports and air-mindedness: Spacing, timing and using the Liverpool Airport, 1929–1939. *Social and Cultural Geography*, *7*, 343–363.

Baron, S., & Wass, K. (1996). Towards an understanding of airport shopping behaviour. *International Review of Retail, Distribution and Consumer Research*, *6*(3), 301–322.

Bilotkach, V., Clougherty, J. A., Mueller, J., & Zhang, A. (2012). Regulation, privatization, and airport charges: Panel data evidence from European airports. *Journal of Regulatory Economics*, *42*(1), 73–94.

Bracaglia, V., D'Alfonso, T., & Nastasi, A. (2014). Competition between multiproduct airports. *Economics of Transportation*, *3*(4), 270–281.

Business Vancouver. (2015). Richmond's McArthurGlen mall named world's best outlet centre. Retrieved from https://www.biv.com/article/2015/11/richmonds-mcarthurglen-mall-named-worlds-best-outl/.

Choo, Y. Y. (2014). Factors affecting aeronautical charges at major US airports. *Transportation Research Part A: Policy and Practice*, *62*, 54–62.

Crawford, G., & Meleware, T. C. (2003). The importance of impulse purchasing behaviour in the international airport environment. *Journal of Consumer Behaviour*, *3*(1), 85–98.

Czerny, A. I. (2006). Price-cap regulation of airports: single-till versus dual-till. *Journal of Regulatory Economics*, *30*(1), 85–97.

Czerny, A. I. (2009). Airport pricing and concession revenues. WHU – Working Paper Series in Economics, WP 09/05.

Czerny, A. I. (2013). Public versus private airport behavior when concession revenues exist. *Economics of Transportation*, *2*, 38–46.

Czerny, A. I., Guiomard, C., & Zhang, A. (2016). Single-till versus dual-till regulation of airports: Where do academics and regulators (dis)agree? *Journal of Transport Economics and Policy (JTEP)*, *50*(4), 350–368.

Czerny, A. I., & Lindsey, R. (2014). Multiproduct pricing with core goods and side goods. Mimeo, University of British Columbia.

Czerny, A. I., Shi, Z., & Zhang, A. (2016). Can market power be controlled by regulation of core prices alone? An empirical analysis of airport demand and car rental price. *Transportation Research Part A: Policy and Practice*, *91*, 260–272.

D'Alfonso, T., Bracaglia, V., & Wan, Y. (2014). Multiproduct facility pricing with outside demand for side services. Paper presented at the Center for Transportation Studies Seminar Series, Sauder School of Business, University of British Columbia, December 2014.

D'Alfonso, T., Bracaglia, V., & Wan, Y. (2015). Airport cities and multiproduct pricing. Department of Computer, Control and Management Engineering Working Papers Series, No. 2015-14.

D'Alfonso, T., Jiang, C., & Wan, Y. (2013). Airport pricing, concession revenues and passenger types. *Journal of Transport Economics and Policy*, *47*(1), 71–89.

D'Alfonso, T., & Nastasi, A. (2014). Airport–Airline interaction: Some food for thought. *Transport Reviews*, *34*(6), 730–748.

Davies, G. (1995). Bringing stores to shoppers-not shoppers to stores. *International Journal of Retail & Distribution Management*, *23*(1), 18–23.

Doganis, R. (1992). *The airport business*. New York, NY: Routledge.

Dube, L., Menon, K. (2000). Ensuring greater satisfaction by engineering salesperson response to customer emotions. *Journal of Retailing*, *76*, 285–308.

Entwistle, M. (2007). Customer service and airport retail: Stimulate passenger spending. *Journal of Airport Management*, *1*(2), 151–157.

Euromonitor International. (2006). Airports as malls: Everyday beauty brands enter travel retail. Retrieved from http://www.marketresearchworld.net/content/view/830/77/.

Fernie. (1995). The coming of the fourth wave: New forms of retail out of town development. *International Journal of Retail & Distribution Management*, *23*(1), 4–11.

Flores-Fillol, R., Iozzi, A., & Valletti, T. (2015). Platform pricing and consumer foresight: The case of airports. CEIS Tor Vergata Research Paper Series, 3(2), n. 335.

Forsyth, P. (2003). Regulation under stress: Developments in Australian airport policy. *Journal of Air Transport Management*, *9*, 25–35.

Freestone, R., & Baker, D. (2010). Challenges in land use planning around Australian airports. *Journal of Air Transport Management*, *16*(5), 264–271.

Geuens, M., Vantomme, D., & Brengman, M. (2004). Developing a typology of airport shoppers. *Tourism Management*, *25*(5), 615–622.

Gillen, D. (2011). The evolution of airport governance and ownership. *Journal of Air Transport Management*, *17*(1), 3–13.

Gillen, D., & Mantin, B. (2012). Transportation infrastructure management: One and two sided market approaches. *Journal of Transport Economics and Policy*, *47*(2), 207–227.

Groupe ADP. (2010). Report on activities and sustainable growth.

Halpern, N., & Graham, A. (2013). *Airport marketing*. New York, NY: Routledge.

Huang, W. H., & Kuai, L. (2006). The in-flight shopper. *Journal of air transport management*, *12*(4), 207–211.

Ivaldi, M., Sokullu, S., & Toru, T. (2015). Airport prices in a two-sided market setting: Major US airports. CEPR Discussion Paper No. DP10658.

Jarach, D. (2001). The evolution of airport management practices: Towards a multi-point, multi-service, marketing-driven firm. *Journal of Air Transport Management*, *7*(2), 119–125.

Jarach, D. (2005). *Airport marketing*. Burlington: Ashgate Publishing.

Jones, I., Vieho, I., & Marks, P. (1993). The economics of airports slot. *Fiscal Studies*, *14*, 37–57.

Kasarda, J. D. (2008). Shopping in the airport city and aerotropolis. *Research Review*, *15*(2), 50–56.

Kidokoro, Y., Lin, M. H., & Zhang, A. (2016). A general equilibrium analysis of airport pricing, capacity and regulation. *Journal of Urban Economics*, *96*, 142–155.

Kim, H. B., & Shin, J. H. (2001). A contextual investigation of the operation and management of airport concessions. *Tourism Management*, *22*(2), 149–155.

Kramer, L. S. (2010). Airport Revenue Diversification (Vol. 19). Transportation Research Board. Retrieved from http://onlinepubs.trb.org/onlinepubs/acrp/acrp_syn_019.pdf

Levitt, T. (1980). Marketing success through differentiation — Of anything. *Harvard Business Review, 58*, 83–91.

Lin, Y. H., & Chen, C. F. (2013). Passengers' shopping motivations and commercial activities at airports – The moderating effects of time pressure and impulse buying tendency. *Tourism Management, 36*, 426–434.

Lu, J. L. (2014). Investigating factors that influence passengers' shopping intensions at airports — Evidence from Taiwan. *Journal of Airport Transport Management, 35*, 72–77.

Mintel. (2013). Airport retailing — Europe. Retrieved from http://reports.mintel.com/display/643273/?__cc = 1#. Accessed on March 2013.

Morrison, W. G. (2009). Real estate, factory outlets and bricks: A note on non-aviation activities at commercial airports. *Journal of Air Transport Management, 15*(3), 112–115.

Omar, O. & Kent, A. (2001). International airport influences on impulsive shopping: Trait and normative approach. *International Journal of Retail & Distribution Management, 29*(5), 226–235.

Orth, H., Frei, O., & Weidmann, U. (2015). Effects of non-aviation activities at airports on the public transport access system: A case study of Zurich Airport. *Journal of Air Transport Management, 42*, 37–46.

Oum, T. H., Zhang, A., & Zhang, Y. (2004). Alternative forms of economic regulation and their efficiency implications for airports. *Journal of Transport Economics and Policy, 38*(2), 217–246.

Perng, S. W., Chow, C. C., & Liao, W. C. (2010). Analysis of shopping preference and satisfaction with airport retailing products. *Journal of Air Transport Management, 16*(5), 279–283.

Poungias, P. (2009). Airport city developments: An airport investor's perspective. *Journal of Airport Management, 4*(1), 14–22.

Reiss, B. (2007). Maximising non-aviation revenue for airports: Developing airport cities to optimise real estate and capitalise on land development opportunities. *Journal of Airport Management, 1*(3), 284–293.

Schiphol Group. (2011). Annual Report to Investors 2011.

SITA. (2013). Airport IT Trends Survey 2013. SITA, Brussels.

Starkie, D. (2001). Reforming UK airport regulation. *Journal of Transport Economics and Policy, 35*, 119–135.

Starkie, D. (2002). Airport regulation and competition. *Journal of Air Transport Management, 8*, 63–72.

Sulzmaier, S. (2001). *Consumer Oriented Business Design: The Case of Airport Management; with 108 Tables*. Springer.

The Economist. (2013). *What is an aerotropolis?* December 11, 2013.

The Economist. (2015a). *Aerotropolitan ambitions*. March 14, 2015.

The Economist. (2015b). *Flying High. Why Buying airports has taken off*. June 6, 2015.

The New York Times. (2010). *The aerotropolis*. December 10, 2010.

The New York Times. (2011). *The airport experience now includes shopping for the family*. August 1, 2011.

The Province. (2015). *New Vancouver airport outlet mall announces list of 46 retailers*, looking to hire 600. May 13, 2015.

Van Dender, K. (2007). Determinants of fares and operating revenues at US airports. *Journal of Urban Economics, 62*, 317–336.

Vlitos Rowe, I. (Ed.). (1999). *The future of duty-free retailing: Developments and trends in Europe and the Middle East*. London: Financial Times Retail and Consumer Publishing.

Wan, Y., Jiang, C., & Zhang, A. (2015). Airport congestion pricing and terminal investment: Effects of terminal congestion, passenger types, and concessions. *Transportation Research Part B: Methodological, 82*, 91–113.

Wang, K. J., & Hong, W. C. (2011). Competitive advantage analysis and strategy formulation of airport city development—The case of Taiwan. *Transport Policy, 18*(1), 276–288.

Yang, H., & Zhang, A. (2011). Price-cap regulation of congestion airports. *Journal of Regulatory Economics, 39*(3), 293–312.

Zhang, A., & Czerny, A. I. (2012). Airports and airlines economics and policy: An interpretive review of recent research. *Economics of Transportation*, *1*(1-2), 15–34.
Zhang, A., & Zhang, Y. (1997). Concession revenue and optimal airport pricing. *Transportation Research Part E: Logistics and Transportation Review*, *33*(4), 287–296.
Zhang, A., & Zhang, Y. (2003). Airport charges and capacity expansion: Effects of concessions and privatization. *Journal of Urban Economics*, *53*(1), 54–75.
Zhang, A., & Zhang, Y. (2010). Airport capacity and congestion pricing with both aviation and commercial operations. *Transportation Research Part B*, *44*(3), 404–413.

CHAPTER 4

ESTIMATION OF ALLOCATIVE EFFICIENCY IN AIRPORTS FOR A PRE-PRIVATIZATION PERIOD

Soraya Hidalgo-Gallego, Valeriano Martínez-San Román and Ramón Núñez-Sánchez

ABSTRACT

In this chapter, we estimate the allocative efficiency of Spanish airports in the pre-privatization period from 2009 until 2014. The estimation of an input-oriented distance system of equations allows us to calculate different allocative efficiency measures using two approaches. The results show that allocative inefficiencies exist for Spanish airports during this period. Moreover, in breaking down allocative efficiency changes by periods coinciding with different government strategies of privatization, we find important differences. In the initial period, when the government encouraged decentralized management of airports and privatization of the largest airports, allocative efficiency improved (from 2009 to 2012). In the second period, however, when the government focused on centralized airport management and privatization of the system as a whole (from 2012 to 2014), inefficiencies slightly increased again.

Keywords: Airport privatization; Spanish airports; allocative efficiency; distance functions

JEL classifications: D24; L33; L93

The Economics of Airport Operations
Advances in Airline Economics, Volume 6, 69–95

ISSN: 2212-1609/doi:10.1108/S2212-160920170000006004

INTRODUCTION

Airport deregulation has become one of the most interesting topics for transport policymakers and academicians to consider in recent years. Traditionally, airports were considered as local natural monopolies in their catchment areas. In this sense, most regions had only one airport, usually operated by the central or local government. However, several facts, such as the building of new airports, the emergence of low cost carriers, the improvement of ground transport, and the privatization of some airports have dramatically changed the airport industry. In this context, airport efficiency and productivity have been considered as the cornerstone in airport management.

Airport privatization is a relatively recent phenomenon given that the first experience took place in The United Kingdom in 1987, when the British government sold BAA to private investors. After that, other countries such as Australia and New Zealand continued this process in different ways. More recently, some of the most important airports in continental Europe have been partially or totally privatized. In fact, 13% of European airports were owned by mixed public–private shareholders and 9% were fully privatized in 2010 (ACI, 2010). In the case of partially privatized airports, most of the governments have retained golden shares in order to give them veto powers over any major corporate action.

Motivations for partial or full airport privatization are diverse. Some reasons for privatization include financial difficulties realized by governments and a resulting inability to fund the large airport's infrastructure investments, privatization processes as a source of revenue to cover or reduce budgetary deficits, consideration of airports as commercial entities rather than public utilities, and pressures from private entities to involve private participation in airport management (ICAO, 2012). Some empirical studies show that fiscal constraints and market attractiveness promote private participation. On the other hand, integrated governance models and large market shares by network carriers prevent the presence of private ownership. Regarding the decision on the degree of private participation, it appears to be pragmatic rather than ideological (Albalate, Bel, & Fageda, 2014).

Literature related to transport economics points out the improvement of airport efficiency as another motivation for private involvement in this industry. In this sense, Oum, Yan, and Yu (2008) examine the effects of different forms of ownership on airport cost efficiency using a sample of airports around the world. Their most relevant empirical findings show that airports either controlled by majority private firms or autonomous public corporations are more efficient than those operated by a mixed firm with government majority ownership. Moreover, airports owned/operated by a mixed firm with government majority ownership have significantly lower efficiency in multiple airport markets than in single airport markets.

The Spanish airport system has been recently partially privatized in February 2015. The importance of airport privatization may be especially relevant in Spain for different reasons. On the one hand, Spanish airport competitiveness is relevant for the Spanish economy given the importance of the tourism sector. On the other hand, the most important airports are owned by a single operator (Aena). Unlike other airport systems of similar size, the Spanish airport system has been characterized by the high centralization in airport management, which barely take into account the heterogeneity among Spanish airports. Thus, the funding mechanism of airport investments is made through a common fund, where cross-subsidies are present among airports (Núñez-Sánchez, 2015).

In this chapter, we estimate the allocative efficiency for Spanish airports. Then we evaluate the evolution of allocative efficiency in the pre-privatization period from 2009 until 2014. The estimation of an input-oriented distance system of equations allows us to calculate different allocative efficiency measures. This chapter contributes to the airport benchmarking literature in two ways. First, a stochastic frontier approach is used to estimate two different allocative efficiency measures by means of an input-oriented distance function. Almost all existing academic contributions in the field of airport efficiency have focused on technical or cost efficiencies (Liebert & Niemeier, 2013). However, to the best of our knowledge, there is no previous literature that specifically studies the airport allocative inefficiency. The only exception is Barros and Sampaio (2004) who study allocative efficiency for Portuguese airports using a non-parametric approach based on data envelopment analysis (DEA). Second, we evaluate whether the privatization agenda has affected allocative efficiency among the Spanish airports. In this sense, our research differs from Oum et al. (2008), as we study a pre-privatization period for the Spanish context in which the public-owned single operator, Aena, and the Spanish Ministry of Transport implemented different actions in order to improve Spanish airports' performance. As it has been remarked in the literature (ICAO, 2012), this aspect is crucial in order to ensure the success in any privatization process.

The results show that allocative inefficiencies exist for Spanish airports during this period. Inefficiency indices became closer to the optimal level in the first stage of the pre-privatization process (2009–2012), when the proposal of new airport regulation tried to encourage decentralized management of airports. However, after 2012, when the newly elected Spanish government ensured that the centralized management model of Aena would remain unchanged, allocative inefficiencies slightly increased again.

The chapter is structured as follows. In the "The Spanish Airport System" section, we undertake an analysis of the performance for the Spanish airport system and the schedule of the privatization process. Subsequently, in the "Methodology" section, we describe the methodology employed for the estimation of two different allocative measures: error component and parametric approaches. In the "Econometric Specification and Data" section, the econometric specification and data are presented. The "Results" section describes the main results. Finally, the "Conclusions" section summarizes the main findings and discusses the policy implications.

THE SPANISH AIRPORT SYSTEM

Taxonomy of Spanish Airports

Aena is a public firm, dependent on the Ministry of Transport, which manages 46 Spanish airports and two heliports of national interest on a centralized basis. In addition, Aena, through its subsidiary Aena International, operates the infrastructure management of 16 airports in four countries (United Kingdom, Mexico, Jamaica, and Colombia). Overall, Aena moved more than 195 million passengers in 2014, accounting for the largest network of jointly managed airports in the world.

Centralized management implies that Aena and the Ministry of Transport make all the relevant decisions regarding airports, including investments, charges, development of retail activities, and the allocation of slots, check-in counters, and gates to airlines. In addition, this centralized system softens competition among airports in attracting new airline services. Moreover, any financial losses are compensated through a cross-subsidy system (Fageda & Voltes-Dorta, 2012).

Aena classifies the Spanish airports into five groups according to the levels of traffic and the aeronautical charges. Madrid and Barcelona airports, with more than 41 and 37 million passengers in 2014, respectively, fit in Group 1. Group 2 includes airports specialized in tourism, with traffic levels generally higher than 10 million passengers per year. Group 3 comprises those airports located in large cities or tourist destinations that generally move between 1 and 4 million passengers yearly. Finally, airports based in smaller tourist destinations or medium-size cities that move between 0.5 and 1 million passengers, and regional airports with traffic levels lower than 0.5 million passengers are included in Groups 4 and 5, respectively. Table 1 shows the Spanish airports classified into the aforementioned five groups.

Fig. 1 plots the spatial situation of the 41 Spanish airports covered in this study. We can observe at the first glance the importance of tourism. In fact, 11 airports are located in the Canary and Balearic Islands. There are 15 airports situated in coastal cities, and Madrid, Seville and Granada, principal touristic cities, have important airports.

Fig. 2 plots the volume of passengers in 2014 and its evolution from 2009 to 2014 for the Spanish airports. On the one hand, the size of the bubbles represents the volume of passengers carried in 2014, from less than 0.5 million to more than 15 million. On the other hand, the bubble color accounts for the cumulative annual growth rate. Light gray colors denote negative rates, and

Table 1. Spanish Airport Classification.

Group	Airports
Group 1	Madrid (MAD); Barcelona (BCN)
Group 2	Alicante (ALC); Gran Canaria (LPA); Tenerife Sur (TFS); Málaga (AGP); Palma de Mallorca (PMI)
Group 3	Bilbao (BIO); Fuerteventura (FUE); Girona (GRO); Ibiza (IBZ); Lanzarote (ACE); Menorca (MAH); Santiago (SCQ); Sevilla (SVQ); Tenerife Norte (TFN); Valencia (VLC)
Group 4	Almería (LEI); Asturias (OVD); Coruña (LCG); Granada-Jaén (GRX); Jerez (XRY); La Palma (SPC); Murcia (MUV); Reus (REU); Santander (SDR); Vigo (VGO); Zaragoza (ZAZ)
Group 5	Albacete (ABC); Badajoz (BJZ); Burgos (RGS); El Hierro (VDE); La Gomera (GMZ); León (LEN); Logroño (RJL); Melilla (MLN); Salamanca (SLM); San Sebastián (EAS); Pamplona (PNA); Vitoria (VIT); Valladolid (VLL)

Source: Own elaboration based on AENA's data.

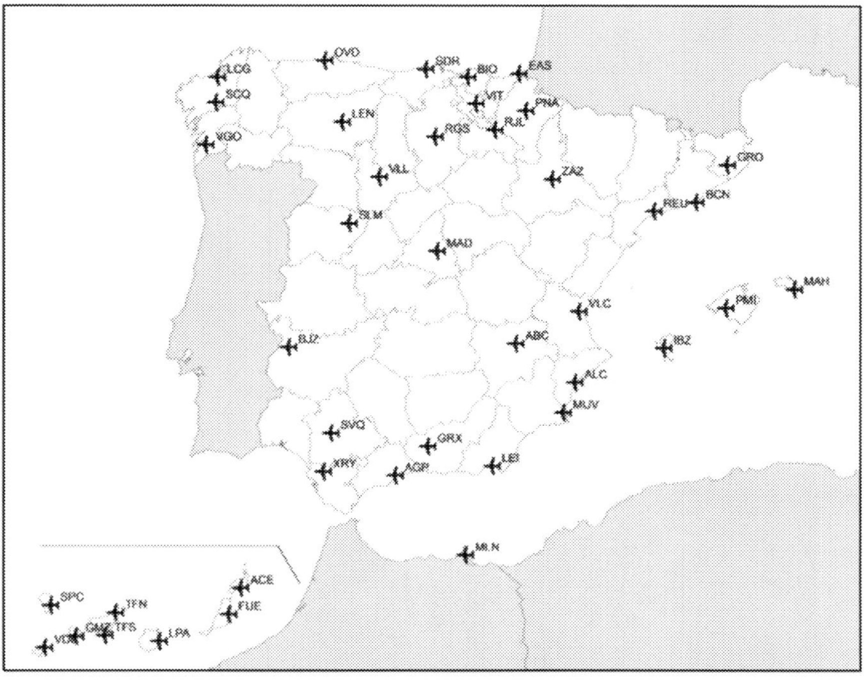

Fig. 1. Spanish Airport System. *Source:* Own elaboration based on AENA's data.

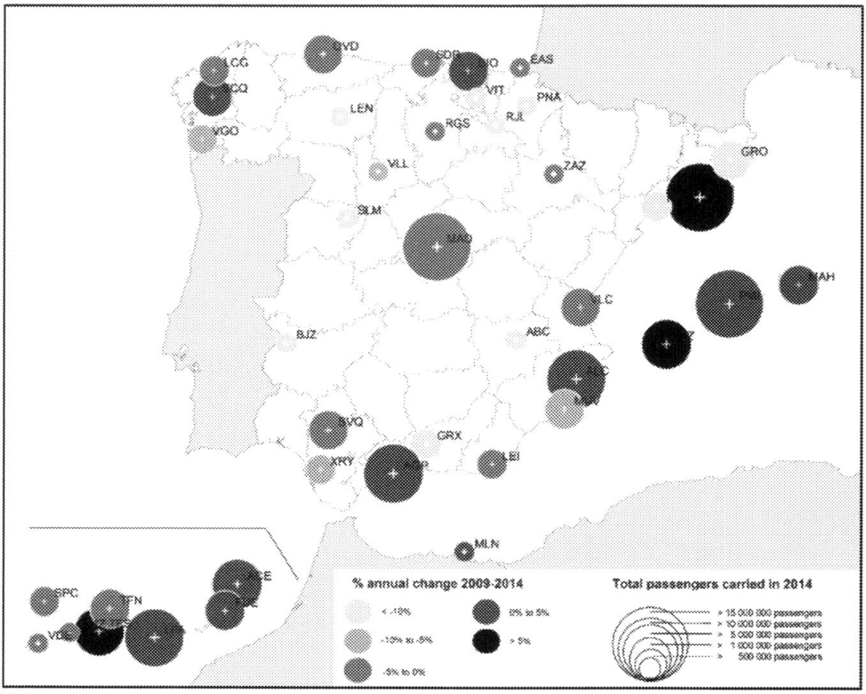

Fig. 2. Passenger Volumes and Dynamics of the Spanish Airports. *Source:* Own elaboration based on AENA's data.

dark gray and black colors symbolize positive growth rates in passenger volumes. Regarding the volume of passengers, the major airports are Madrid, Barcelona, and Palma de Mallorca, followed by other airports located on the Mediterranean coast (Málaga and Alicante) and on the Islands (Gran Canaria, Ibiza, and Tenerife Sur). On the other side, the smallest airports in terms of passenger volumes are located in interior zones.

Regarding passenger dynamics, only 13 airports have seen their traffic volumes increase in comparison to 2009. Moreover, 11 of them are located on the Mediterranean coast and the islands. Only Bilbao and Vigo do not correspond with this pattern (they are located on the North and Atlantic coasts, respectively). The more dynamic airports during the period analyzed were Barcelona (6.5% per year), Ibiza (6.3% yearly), and Tenerife Sur (5.2% per year). On the other side, Albacete lost a 37% per year, followed by Vitoria (29.3% per year), and León (24.6% per year). In general terms, the airports that lost more passenger volume were the smaller and landlocked ones.

When it comes to airport finance, the 41 airports generated 476.4 million Euros in earnings after taxes in 2014. This is up from 2009, when earnings after

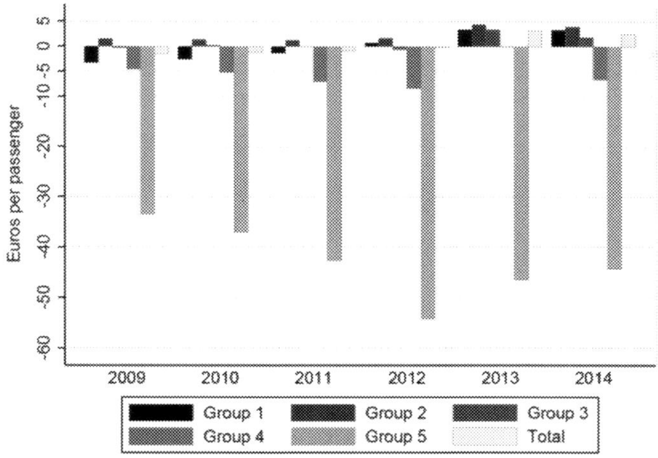

Fig. 3. Earning after Taxes Per Passenger. *Source:* Own elaboration based on AENA's data.

taxes were negative 299 million Euros. During the period 2009–2014, the Spanish airport system as a whole has improved its profits tremendously. Despite this aggregate positive result, only 14 airports realized profits in 2014 – Group 1, Group 2 and most airports from Group 3–, that is, the larger ones. These 14 airports with positive profits are an improvement from 2009, when only nine had positive earnings.

Fig. 3 shows the earnings after taxes for the five groups of airports and for the system as a whole. We can see a positive evolution at the aggregate level and for Groups 1, 2, and 3. These groups change from having losses in 2009 to profits by 2012. However, for Groups 4 and 5, the evolution has not been so successful. All airports in Groups 4 and 5 accounted for losses. In some cases, like Albacete and Vitoria, these losses amounted 1,334 and 940 Euros per passenger in 2014, respectively.

Privatization Schedule

In 2009, in order to face the economic recession, the Spanish Government placed a strategic priority on improving Aena, the single publicly-owned firm. One of its main aims has been to ensure high levels of safety and quality, while improving airport competitiveness by means of reducing operational costs. From its creation, different policies of cost reduction and productivity improvements were applied since 2009. In 2010, due to the critical situation of the Spanish economy and with the aim of reducing fiscal deficits and public debt,

Table 2. Airport Privatization Schedule 2009–2015.

Period	Facts
–2009	The Spanish government invested 17,000 million € from 2000 to 2010 in airport infrastructure. Aena's total debt amounted to 12,000 million € in 2009
2010–2011	The Spanish government started a privatization schedule creating Aena Aeropuertos. Creation of concession societies for Madrid and Barcelona airports
2012–2014	Auction for a concession of Madrid and Barcelona is canceled by the new Spanish government. Airport efficiency plan aims to improve the performance of regional airports
2015–	In February 2015 Aena Aeropuertos is partially sold through public offering

Source: Own elaboration.

the central government implemented different policies. The privatization of Spanish airports was one of them.

In June 2011, Aena Aeropuertos was created with the aim of selling 49% of its capital to private investors. At the same time, the government authorized the creation of concession societies for the hub airports of Madrid-Barajas and Barcelona-El Prat, in order to privatize 90% of their capital. The new airport regulation tried to encourage decentralized management of airports. However, although the aim was to sell 49% of Aena Aeropuertos to private investors, this never occurred as the capital of this new firm remained completely public (Núñez-Sánchez, 2015).

In January 2012, the newly elected Spanish government canceled the auction for the concession of both airports given that the former privatization schedule was incompatible with its proposed airport management model. According to the new government, the centralized management model of Aena should remain unchanged. Instead, an airport efficiency plan was presented to improve the performance of regional airports in June 2012. The three main aims of this plan were setting schedules to the demand for flights, matching services to needs, and enhancing the mobility of workers (Aena, 2012). Finally, 49% of Aena Aeropuertos was sold through a public offering in February 2015, while the Spanish government maintained 51% of total shares (Table 2).

METHODOLOGY

Definition of Distance Function

According to the neoclassical theory of production, the objectives of any firm are either cost minimization or profit maximization. Some firms, especially those that are publicly-owned or monopolies, may fail to fulfill these objectives due to various factors such as: lack of motivation defined as X-inefficiency

(Leibenstein, 1966), unobservable factors related to inputs, such as quality (Timmer, 1971), technological differences (Stigler, 1976), or management problems (Farrell, 1957). In many cases, various inefficiencies appear. In assessing efficiency, there are different types to consider. Technical efficiency is when a firm is able to achieve the maximum amount of output given a specific amount of inputs and given a technology. On the other hand, allocative efficiency implies that the relative proportions of inputs used by a firm in the production process are optimal given their market prices. This means that the marginal rate of technical substitution between any pair of inputs must be equal to the ratio of their respective market prices.

As we mentioned in a previous section, we estimate an allocative efficiency measure using a stochastic frontier model. Specifically, we apply an input-oriented distance function (Atkinson & Primont, 2002; Färe & Grosskopf, 1990). This function is defined as the maximum scalar by which all inputs can be proportionally divided yielding the same level of output (Coelli, Rao, O'Donnell, & Battese, 2005). Formally, the input distance function is defined on the input set, $L(\vec{q}_{it})$, as:

$$D_I(\vec{x}_{it}, \vec{q}_{it}) = max\{\rho: (\vec{x}_{it}/\rho) \in L(\vec{q}_{it})\} \tag{1}$$

where the input set $L(\vec{q}_{it})$ represents the set of all input vectors, $\vec{x}_{it}$, that can produce the output vector, $\vec{q}_{it}$ (Coelli et al., 2005).

Since the distance function value is unknown, it is commonly assumed that its value is equal to one, i.e., it is assumed technical efficiency (Baños-Pino, Fernández-Blanco, & Rodríguez-Álvarez, 2002). Therefore, technical inefficiencies are collected in the error term as deviations from the optimal behavior or frontier. Moreover, due to the duality of the distance function with the cost function, applying Shephard's (1953) Lemma to the distance function, the optimal input cost share equations are obtained (Färe & Grosskopf, 1990). Then, allocative efficiency can be measured using two different, but related approaches: the error components approach and the parametric approach (Atkinson & Cornwell, 1994).

$$\frac{\partial D_I(\vec{x}_{it}, \vec{q}_{it})}{\partial x_{jit}} = \frac{w^s_{jit}}{C(\vec{q}_{it}, \vec{w}^s_{it})} \tag{2}$$

and thus

$$\frac{\partial lnD_I(\vec{x}_{it}, \vec{q}_{it})}{\partial lnx_{jit}} = \frac{\partial D_I(\vec{x}_{it}, \vec{q}_{it})}{\partial x_{jit}} \frac{x_{jit}}{D_I(\vec{x}_{it}, \vec{q}_{it})} = x_{jit}\frac{w^s_{jit}}{C(\vec{q}_{it}, \vec{w}^s_{it})} \tag{3}$$

Following Rodríguez-Álvarez, Fernández-Blanco, and Lovell (2004), we estimate the following system of equations formed by an input-oriented distance function (4) (Shephard, 1953, 1970) and its associated input share Eq. (5).

$$lnD_I = lnD_I(\vec{x}_{it}, \vec{q}_{it}) + v_{it} + u_{it}, \ i = 1, 2, \ldots, N; t = 2, \ldots, N \tag{4}$$

$$\frac{x_{jit} w_{jit}}{C_{it}} = \frac{\partial lnD_I(\vec{x}_{it}, \vec{q}_{it})}{\partial lnx_{jit}} + v_{jit} + A_{jit} \tag{5}$$

where $D_I(\vec{x}_{it}, \vec{q}_{it})$ is the input-oriented distance function, $\vec{x}_{it}$ is the vector of input, $\vec{q}_{it}$ is the vector of outputs, i relates to the $i - th$ airport and t relates to the time period. The error components v_{it} and v_{jit} represent the random disturbance identically, independent and normally distributed with zero mean; u_{it} represents technical efficiency and finally, terms A_{jit} contain allocative inefficiencies, represented by the difference between actual and stochastic input cost shares once random disturbances are discounted. One of the most important advantages of using an input distance function to measure inefficiencies is that it allows us to separate technical and allocative efficiency in a multiproduct context, since the terms u_{it} and A_{jit} are independent (Rodríguez-Álvarez et al., 2004).

After the estimation of the system (4) and (5), two different, but closely related, measures of allocative efficiency can be obtained by the approaches mentioned before.

Parametric Approach

Economic theory shows that a firm minimizes its costs when the marginal rate of technical substitution between a pair of inputs is equal to the ratio of their prices. However, in practice firms do not always minimize their cost. When using a parametric approach, it is not necessary to assume that firms minimize their real costs; it is enough if they minimize their shadow costs. This implies that the marginal rate of technical substitution is equal to the ratio of the shadow prices of the inputs (w^s) instead of their market prices (w). In this sense, we allow the possibility for firms to be allocative inefficient. Then, when the shadow price ratio coincides with the market price ratio, the firm is allocative efficient. On the other hand, if both ratios differ, it means that inputs are not optimally allocated.

Following Färe and Grosskopf (1990), shadow prices (w^s) can be obtained from the input-oriented distance function by applying the dual Shephard's Lemma (6):

$$\frac{\dfrac{\partial D_I(\vec{x}_{it}, \vec{q}_{it})}{\partial x_{jit}}}{\dfrac{\partial D_I(\vec{x}_{it}, \vec{q}_{it})}{\partial x_{rit}}} = \frac{w^s_{jit}}{w^s_{rit}} \tag{6}$$

In order to study the magnitude and direction of such deviations, a relationship between shadow price and actual price ratios is introduced by means of parametric price corrections (7):

$$\frac{w^s_{jit}}{w^s_{rit}} = k_{jr}\frac{w_{jit}}{w_{rit}} \tag{7}$$

So, if $k_{jr} = 1$, there is allocative efficiency; if $k_{jr} > 1$, input j is under-utilized relative to input r; and if $k_{jr} < 1$, input j is over-utilized relative to input r.

Finally, these indices (k_{jr}) can be calculated by comparing actual and optimal input cost shares as Eq. (8) shows:

$$k_{jr} = \frac{S_{rit}\hat{S}_{jit}}{S_{jit}\hat{S}_{rit}} \tag{8}$$

where S_{rit} and S_{jit} are the actual cost shares of inputs r and j, respectively; and $\hat{S}_{rit}$ and $\hat{S}_{jit}$ are the optimal cost shares of inputs r and j which are obtained by the estimation of the system (4) and (5).

Error Component Approach

The error component approach estimates allocative efficiency from the disturbances of the input cost share equations which are formed by the white noise (v_{jit}) and the inefficiency term (A_{jit}). Since the white noise is normally distributed with zero mean, if the mean of the composed error term is different from zero, this deviation is assumed to be allocative inefficiency in the use of that input. Then, the means of the terms A_{jit} (a_j) are interpreted as a measure of systematic allocative inefficiency. Therefore, if inefficiencies in an allocative way exist, a_j should be different from zero. If a_j is positive, the input j is being over-utilized with regard to the other inputs. If a_j is equal to zero, the input j is being used in the optimal proportion, and finally, if a_j is negative, the input j is being under-utilized.

We calculate these indices as Eq. (9) shows:

$$a_j = mean(S_{jit}) - mean(\hat{S}_{jit}) \tag{9}$$

where S_{jit} is the actual cost share of input j and $\hat{S}_{jit}$ is the optimal cost share of input j which is obtained by the estimation of the system (4) and (5).

The main shortcoming of this approach is that allocative inefficiencies can be only estimated at the sample mean. Since the errors of the estimated share equations ($\hat{v}_{jit}$) have zero mean, and thus systematic efficiency, (a_j) can be separated from those without imposing additional assumptions over the distribution of the allocative inefficiency terms (A_{jit}). Thus, with the error component approach, we only obtain a measure of the inefficiency in the use of each input for the whole sample; we are unable to analyze the evolution of inefficiency or differences among airports. On the other hand, there is another important difference with the parametric approach: the parametric approach assumes a multiplicative relationship between prices and shadow prices, while the error components approach implies an additive one.

ECONOMETRIC SPECIFICATION AND DATA

Econometric Specification

For the specification of the stochastic frontier distance function, we chose a translog, which is a second order flexible functional form linear in the parameters. So, the resulting system of equations to estimate is the following one:

$$\begin{aligned}\ln 1 = {} & \beta_i + \sum_{r=1}^{R} \beta_r \ln x_{rit} + \sum_{m=1}^{M} \beta_m \ln q_{mit} + \frac{1}{2}\sum_{r=1}^{R}\sum_{j=1}^{R} \beta_{rj} \ln x_{rit} \ln x_{jit} \\ & + \frac{1}{2}\sum_{m=1}^{M}\sum_{n=1}^{M} \beta_{mn} \ln q_{mit} \ln q_{nit} + \frac{1}{2}\sum_{r=1}^{R}\sum_{m=1}^{M} \beta_{rm} \ln x_{rit} \ln x_{mit} + v_{it} + u_{it}\end{aligned} \tag{10}$$

$$\frac{x_{rit} w_{rit}}{C_{it}} = \beta_r + \sum_{r=1}^{R} \beta_{rj} \ln x_{rit} + \sum_{m=1}^{M} \beta_{mn} \ln q_{mit} + v_{rit} + A_{rit} \tag{11}$$

where x_r is the $r - th$ input, q_m is the $q - th$ output, i relates to the $i - th$ airport and t relates to the time period. The error components v_{it} and v_{jit} represent random disturbances identically, independent and normally distributed with zero mean; while u_{it} and A_{jit} represent technical and allocative inefficiencies, respectively.

Homogeneity of degree one of the distance function in variable inputs is enforced and variables are divided by their geometric means, so first-order coefficients can be interpreted as elasticities at the sample mean.

Finally, in order to estimate allocative inefficiencies by the parametric approach, from the parameters estimated in (10) and (11) we calculate the indices k_{jr} as follows:

$$k_{jr} = \frac{x_{rit} w_{rit}\left[\beta_j + \sum_{r=1}^{R} \beta_{rj} \ln x_{rit} + \sum_{m=1}^{M} \beta_{jm} \ln q_{mit}\right]}{x_{jit} w_{jit}\left[\beta_r + \sum_{r=1}^{R} \beta_{rj} \ln x_{rit} + \sum_{m=1}^{M} \beta_{rm} \ln q_{mit}\right]} \tag{12}$$

Data

As we have mentioned in the "The Spanish Airport System" section, Aena manages 46 Spanish airports and two heliports of national interest. In this study, however, we have excluded the two heliports and five airports that are very small or do not operate regular flights (Córdoba, Madrid-Cuatro Vientos, Son Bonet, and Huesca). Then, the data used in this chapter are composed of information on 41 Spanish airports for the period 2009–2014. This is a balanced data set with 246 observations. Financial and traffic data were obtained from Aena, while other statistical information was gathered from the Spanish Statistical Office (INE).

As seen in the "Methodology" section, to estimate airports' distance frontier we need to know inputs and outputs. We describe airport activities using two outputs: *Work Load Units* (q_{WLU}) and commercial revenues (q_{COM}). Although one of the most commonly used output measures in airport literature is aircraft total movements (q_{ATM}) (Malighetti, Martini, Paleari, & Redondi, 2007; Oum, Yu, & Fu, 2003; Pels, Nijkamp, & Rietveld, 2003), in this chapter it has not been included to avoid multicollinearity problems in the estimation because of its correlation with the variable q_{WLU} (0.9909). With respect to the outputs included in the analysis, the variable *work load units* (*wlu*) (Barros & Dieke, 2008) combines passenger and cargo traffic outputs representing a proxy for the units of aeronautical services provided by airports. This variable was introduced in airport literature as a measure of output in the early 1980s and one unit can be defined as a passenger or as 100 kilograms of cargo (Salazar de la Cruz, 2013). Commercial revenues (q_{COM}) approximate the level of commercial activity developed by an airport. Because it is objectively very difficult to describe commercial activities in physical terms due to the heterogeneity of these activities and the lack of price information, it is common to find studies in airport literature that use physical variables with operating or financial ones to approximate airports' outputs (Abrate and Erbetta, 2010; Barros, 2008; Barros and Dieke, 2008; Oum et al., 2008; Pacheco and Fernández, 2003; Sarkis, 2000).

On the input side, Aena does not publish information about the physical units of inputs used in airports' operations. In this sense, one of the main problems in empirical studies is the lack of relevant statistical information, so authors have to approximate some variables that are crucial for the analysis. On the other hand, there is no consensus in literature about which is the best way to approximate airport inputs, so authors usually base their choices on two criteria: the previous literature and the data available (Barros, 2008). In our case, Aena publishes information about input cost but not about their amount or prices, so input quantities have to be approximated. It is common in literature to approximate input variables by their costs (Barros & Dieke, 2008; Curi, Gitto, & Mancuso, 2008; Hooper & Hensher, 1997; Martin & Roman,

2001; Yu, Hsu, Chang, & Lee, 2008), but this assumes that input prices are unit and do not vary over the time, which it could seem quite unrealistic. Thus, it would be desirable that input variables be collected in some way to capture the evolution of their prices. Therefore, we build the prices of the inputs for the Spanish airports based on previous literature. Then by dividing input costs by their respective prices, we are able to obtain a measure of inputs in which price evolution is considered.

In this analysis, three variable inputs are considered: labor (x_L), capital (x_C), and intermediate consumptions (x_{IC}). Regarding labor, the most common measure used is the number of employees (Barros, 2008; Oum & Yu, 2004; Tovar & Martín-Cejas, 2010). The problem is, as we said before, that Aena's reports only provide information about labor cost but not about the number of employees. So, we have approximated it by dividing labor cost (published by Aena) by the price of labor. As there is no information about the wages paid by Aena to its workers, we build the price of labor following Bottasso and Conti (2012). In this way, the price of labor is obtained by the Annual Labor Cost Survey (Encuesta Anual de Costes Laborales) published by the Spanish Statistical Office (INE) as the average wage paid to the employees in activities related to warehousing and transport in Spain, in which airport activities are included. Because of this wage is a national average, it has been weighted by a ratio between regional and national general labor cost per worker, in order to collect differences in labor cost among Spanish regions. Once the price of labor is obtained, we are able to get an approximation of the number of employees.

With respect to the capital variable, it is very common to use physical units, such as terminal size, number of gates, or runaway area to approximate airport capital (Barros, 2008; Fung, Wan, Van Hui, & Law, 2008; Oum et al., 2003). However, such measures present an important shortcoming; they show limited variability over the time. Other proxies to capital are the accounting value of fixed assets or the amortization expenses (Barros & Dieke, 2008; Barros & Sampaio, 2004). It is assumed that the more accounting value of fixed assets or the more expense in amortization, the more capital. However, these measures do not take into account the effect of changes in prices. In order to collect the variability in the prices of capital, we build an index in which the evolution of building prices in public works, the depreciation of airports' capital and the evolution of long-term interest rates are gathered (Bottasso & Conti, 2012). Then, a capital variable is calculated by dividing the capital expense by this index. Specifically, the index (r) is, as Eq. (13) shows: a building index price (bip) of public works (obtained from the reports of Confederación Nacional de la Construcción, SEOPAN) is multiplied by the sum of long-term interest rate ($rate$) plus the depreciation rate (dep). Depreciation rate is calculated as the annual depreciation expenditures of each airport over their fixed assets. We follow the procedure proposed by the OECD (2001) which measures the price of capital at a macroeconomic level, based on the perpetual inventory method devised by Jorgenson and Griliches (1967).

Table 3. Descriptive Statistics of the Variables.

Variable	Units	Mean	St. Dev	Min	Max
X_L	Workers	235.6	273.4	13	1713
X_C	Millions of constant Euros year 2011	150.2	391.2	3.3	2877.1
X_{CI}	Millions of constant Euros year 2011	24.6	56.7	0.9	311.46
q_{WLU}	Passenger and hundred tons	4,880,243	9,607,788	1211	5.36E+07
q_{COM}	Millions of constant Euros year 2011	16.1	34.8	1.00E−05	211.38
ratcargpax	Tons per passenger	66.1	528.4	1.33E−05	5960.8
$g1$	Dummy group one	0.05	0.22	0	1
$g2$	Dummy group two	0.12	0.33	0	1
$g3$	Dummy group three	0.24	0.43	0	1
$g4$	Dummy group four	0.27	0.45	0	1
$g5$	Dummy group five	0.31	0.46	0	1

Source: Own elaboration.

$$r_{it} = \left[bip_{it}\left(rate_{it} + dep_{it}\right)\right]*100 \tag{13}$$

Finally, intermediate consumptions are commonly approximated by their expenses. Again, the effect of prices is not taken into account, so we deflated intermediate consumption expenses by a purchasing power parity index at a regional level proposed by Costa, García, López, and Raymong (2015).[1]

Moreover, we include control variables that could affect the heterogeneity of the distance frontier across airports or groups of airports. The ratio between cargo and passengers (*ratcarpax*) as a way to include the differences in airports' traffic composition. Airport group dummy variables are included to collect the unobserved heterogeneity among groups. In Table 3 some descriptive statistics of the variables are shown.

RESULTS

Input-Oriented Distance Function

Table 4 displays the estimation of the system of Eqs. (10) and (11) using two different methodologies and four specifications. In models 1 and 3, we estimate the distance system by means of an Iterated Seemingly Unrelated Regression. Estimations in models 2 and 4 use a Three-Stage Least Square estimator to

Table 4. Estimates of the Distance Frontier System.

Regressor	Model 1		Model 2		Model 3		Model 4	
	SUR		3SLS		SUR		3SLS	
	Coeff.	Std. Error	Coeff.	Std. Error	Coeff.	Std. Error	Coeff.	Std. Error
constant	0.236	0.023***	0.237	0.026***	−1.274	0.255***	−1.373	0.294***
ln x_L	0.272	0.002***	0.265	0.002***	0.271	0.002***	0.265	0.002***
ln x_C	0.328	0.003***	0.336	0.032***	0.328	0.003***	0.336	0.003***
ln x_{IC}	0.400	0.002***	0.399	0.002***	0.400	0.002***	0.399	0.002***
ln q_{WLU}	−0.247	0.055***	−0.198	0.066***	−0.171	0.055***	−0.125	0.065*
ln q_{COM}	−0.287	0.048***	−0.34	0.059***	−0.192	0.048***	−0.207	0.060***
ln x_L ln x_L	0.169	0.003***	0.166	0.004***	0.167	0.003***	0.165	0.004***
ln x_C ln x_C	0.166	0.006***	0.167	0.006***	0.163	0.006***	0.164	0.006***
ln x_{IC} ln x_{IC}	0.200	0.004***	0.196	0.004***	0.200	0.003***	0.197	0.004***
ln q_{WLU} ln q_{WLU}	0.091	0.038**	−0.044	0.070	0.036	0.037	−0.038	0.066
ln q_{COM} ln q_{COM}	0.330	0.014**	−0.122	0.072*	0.006	0.014	−0.085	0.067
ln x_L ln x_C	−0.067	0.004***	−0.068	0.004***	−0.065	0.004***	−0.066	0.004***
ln x_L ln x_{IC}	−0.102	0.003***	−0.098	0.003***	−0.103	0.003***	−0.099	0.003***
ln x_C ln x_{IC}	−0.098	0.003***	−0.098	0.003***	−0.098	0.003***	−0.098	0.004***
ln x_L ln q_{WLU}	0.009	0.003***	0.007	0.004**	0.008	0.003***	0.008	0.004**
ln x_L ln q_{COM}	−0.006	0.003**	−0.005	0.003	−0.006	0.003**	−0.005	0.003
ln x_C ln q_{WLU}	−0.015	0.004***	−0.015	0.006***	−0.015	0.004***	−0.015	0.006***
ln x_C ln q_{COM}	0.007	0.004*	0.008	0.005	0.008	0.004**	0.009	0.005*
ln x_{IC} ln q_{WLU}	0.006	0.002***	0.008	0.003**	0.006	0.002***	0.008	0.003**
ln x_{IC} ln q_{COM}	−0.002	0.002	−0.003	0.003	−0.002	0.002	−0.003	0.003
ln q_{WLU} ln q_{COM}	−0.129	0.025***	0.022	0.071	−0.053	0.027*	0.036	0.066
ln ratcarpax	−0.032	0.005***	−0.026	0.006***	−0.03	0.005***	−0.028	0.006***
$g2$					0.0845	0.132***	0.806	0.148***
$g3$					1.278	0.195***	1.309	0.222***
$g4$					1.472	0.257***	1.562	0.294***
$g5$					1.671	0.301***	1.837	0.347***
Equation	R^2	Std. Error	R^2	Std. Error	R^2	Std. Error	R^2	Std. Error
Distance	–	0.257	–	0.260	–	0.236	–	0.238
Labor	0.890	0.029	0.910	0.026	0.890	0.029	0.910	0.026
Capital	0.740	0.043	0.780	0.040	0.740	0.043	0.780	0.040
Obs	246		205		246		205	

Notes: *, **, and *** denote parameters significant at 10%, 5%, and 1%, respectively.

take into account the possibility of endogeneity among input variables using the same variables lagged one period as instruments. Moreover, models 3 and 4 include dummy variables for the above-mentioned groups of airports to capture the unobservable heterogeneity among them. All the estimations fulfill the expected theoretical properties of the distance function regarding the regularity conditions. That is, the distance function is non-decreasing and quasi-concave in inputs (x_L, x_C, and x_{IC}) and decreasing in outputs (q_{WLU} and q_{COM}) at the sample mean. To find the most appropriate econometric specification to characterize Spanish airports' technology we run three tests (Table 5). First, we test the translog functional form estimated in Table 4 against the widely used Cobb-Douglas function by means of a joint significance test of the second order coefficients. The null hypothesis states that all second order coefficients are equal to zero; that is, the Cobb-Douglas function is preferred. Secondly, there is a possibility that airport managers choose productive factors following criteria other than cost minimization. This being the case, input quantity variables could be endogenous. We run a Hausman over-identification test on models 1 and 3 to test for endogeneity among input variables. Finally, a joint significance test of airport group fixed effects is carried out to test for unobserved heterogeneity among groups. As Table 5 shows, these tests reject the null hypotheses of a Cobb-Douglas function, non-endogeneity of inputs, and pooled model estimation, pointing to model 4 as the most appropriate one to characterize Spanish airport technology. Nonetheless, there are not significant differences among the four models, so the results obtained are robust to different specifications and econometric techniques.

First-order estimates of input and output variables in model 4 have the expected signs and report statistically significant coefficients. Group dummies indicate that there are performance differences across groups of airports. Finally, we control for traffic composition by including the logarithm of the ratio between cargo and passengers as a proxy. We conduct additional robustness estimations to ensure that the results for model 4 are robust to the inclusion of different variables. Model 4a in Table A1 in the appendix reports

Table 5. Models' Test.

Test	Null Hypothesis	Model 1	Model 2	Model 3	Model 4
Cobb-Douglas vs. Translog	H_0: Cobb-Douglas	5704*** (0.000)	3839.6*** (0.000)	5718.8*** (0.000)	3932.8*** (0.000)
Endogeneity test (Haussman test)	H_0: Exogeneity of inputs	12.02*** (0.007)		15.51*** (0.001)	
Pooled vs. Fixed effects	H_0: Pooled			35.11*** (0.000)	39.67*** (0.000)

Notes: *, **, and *** denote parameters significant at 10%, 5%, and 1%, respectively.

the distance function when the regional consumption price index is included instead of the regional ppp index to compute intermediate consumptions. Model 4b estimates the distance function using the ratio between cargo and work load unit instead of cargo per passenger as the traffic composition control variable. Finally, model 4c includes both the cpi index and the ratio cargo per wlu. There is not significant variation in the results, and the estimated coefficients are slightly larger or smaller depending on the variable considered.

From the estimation of the system (10) and (11), it is possible to obtain two alternative measures of allocative inefficiencies. On the one hand, from a parametric approach we can compute allocative efficiency indices for input pairs. That is, we can analyze whether an input is over-utilized or under-utilized relative to any other particular input. On the other hand, following an error component approach we obtain systematic allocative efficiency indices that capture whether the actual use of a particular input is equal to the optimal. The sections "Allocative Inefficiency through the Parametric Approach" and "Allocative Inefficiency through the Error Component Approach" discuss the results for allocative efficiency through the parametric and error components approaches, respectively.

Allocative Inefficiency through the Parametric Approach

We can obtain relative indices of allocative inefficiency for each observation from the parameters estimated in Eqs. (10) and (11) following the expression (12). These parametric indices show relative inefficiencies for each pair of inputs. Table 6 presents the results for these indices for the whole period, the period 2009–2011, and the period 2012–2014. A coefficient smaller than 1 means that the first input is over-utilized relative to the other input. When values are greater than 1, the first input is under-utilized. Finally, a coefficient equal to 1 implies that the use of the pair of inputs is allocative efficient. The

Table 6. Inefficiency Indices by Pair of Inputs (Parametric Approach).

Variable	2009–2014		2009–2011 (P_1)		2012–2014 (P_2)		Diff. (P_1–P_2)
	Coeff.	Std. Error	Coeff.	Std. Error	Coeff.	Std. Error	z-stat
Labor-Capital	0.9759	0.0158	0.9525	0.0211**	0.9985	0.0176	−1.6766**
Labor-Interm. consumption	0.9813	0.0096*	0.9764	0.0120*	0.9798	0.0098**	−0.2199
Capital-Interm. consumption	1.0474	0.0136***	1.0682	0.0203***	1.0063	0.0144*	2.4910***

Notes: *, **, and *** denote parameters significant at 10%, 5%, and 1%, respectively. The Null hypothesis for periods (P_1) and (P_2) is H_0: Coefficient = 1. The Null hypothesis for the difference between periods ($P_1 - P_2$) is H_0: (Coeff. P_1) − (Coeff. P_2) ≤ 0.

last column displays the z-statistic of the difference between coefficients in the first subperiod (2009–2011) and second subperiod (2012–2014) to analyze whether there is a significant change in allocative efficiency after the change in the privatization strategy. Overall, results suggest that the Spanish airport system as a whole over-utilizes labor and underuses capital relative to intermediate consumptions. We also observe that labor is over-utilized relative to the capital but it is not statistically significant. For the first subperiod indices suggest the existence of inefficiencies since all of them are statistically different from one. For the second subperiod, however, coefficients are closer to 1.

Additionally, we are interested in the analysis of efficiency differences between subperiods. Furthermore, we want to test whether these differences are significant and coefficients tend to efficiency. Results from the last column of Table 6 suggest that there is a significant difference between periods for labor vs. capital and capital vs. intermediate consumptions pairs. In both cases, the relative use of these pairs of inputs moves toward allocative efficiency, although only labor relative to capital achieves efficiency.

Fig. 4 shows the evolution of the allocative inefficiency indices for the Spanish airport system. Although, in general terms, allocative efficiency in the Spanish airport system has improved during the pre-privatization period, some insights are worth mentioning. At the beginning of the period, we can identify important imbalances in the use of inputs. In particular, labor is over-utilized relative to capital and intermediate consumptions, while capital is under-utilized relative to intermediate consumptions. Up to 2011, there is an effort to

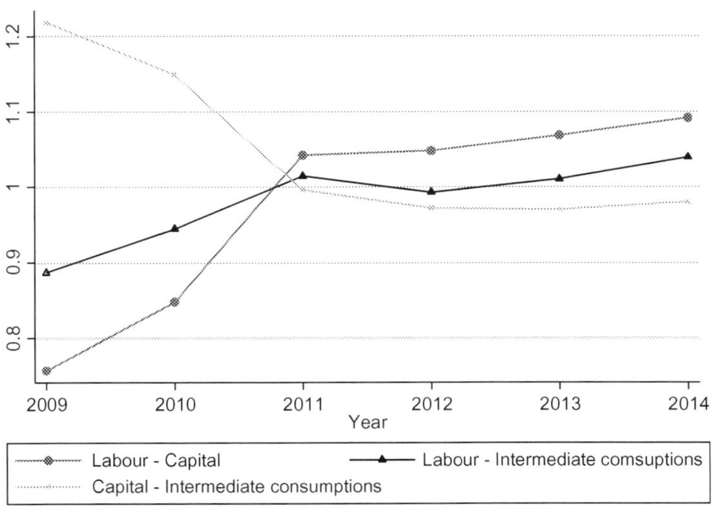

Fig. 4. Evolution of the Allocative Efficiency for Each Pair of Inputs. *Source:* Own elaboration.

reduce input pair inefficiency and achieve allocative efficiency among them. As we will analyze later on, this movement towards allocative efficiency is driven by the two biggest airports (Madrid and Barcelona, Group 1) – the ones with major imbalances in the first years of the analysis. This evolution is in line with the first attempt of privatization proposed by the Spanish Government in 2010, when the objective was to privatize these two airports. Thus, the most intensive efforts in cost reduction and efficiency were made in those particular airports. The second period, from 2012 onwards, is characterized by a change in the privatization proposal made by the newly elected government. The new strategy aims to partially privatize the whole airport system, instead of some particular airports. Additionally, in June 2012 the Spanish Ministry of Transports implemented an airport efficiency plan targeting the smaller or non-profitable airports with the objective of reducing economic losses by 50%. As a result, although total costs declined notably since 2012, it has not a significant effect on allocative efficiency. Moreover, Fig. 4 shows an increase in allocative inefficiency between labor and intermediate consumptions and between labor and capital. In both cases, labor is under-utilized at the end of the period.

Another interesting finding is performance differences among groups of airports. Figs. 5–7 show the group-specific evolution of the parametric indices for allocative inefficiency. Results show that airports in Group 1, Madrid and Barcelona, present the highest levels of allocative inefficiencies between

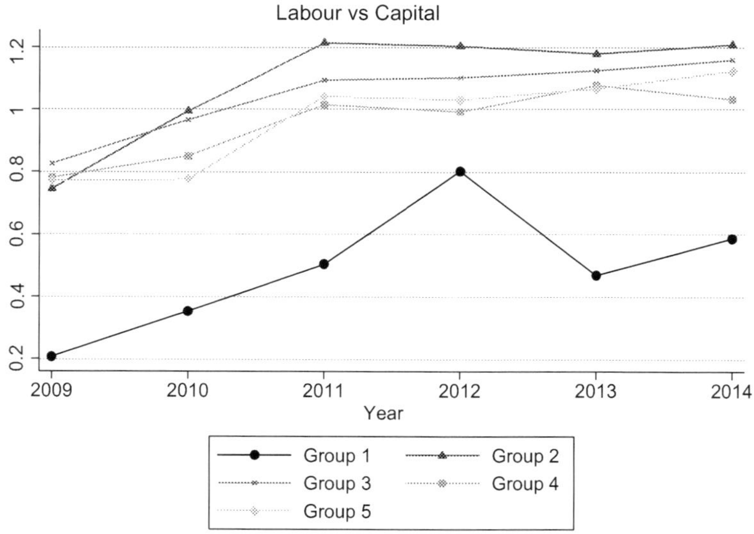

Fig. 5. Specific-Group Evolution of Allocative Efficiency Labor–Capital. *Source:* Own elaboration.

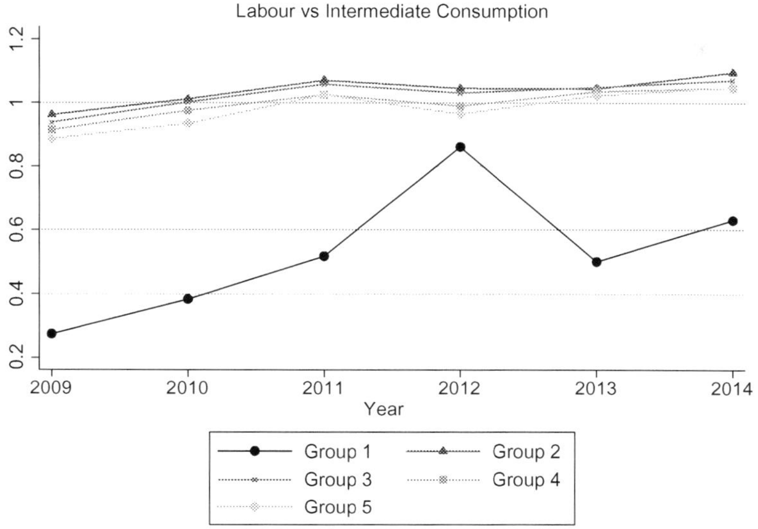

Fig. 6. Specific-Group Evolution Efficiency Labor–Intermediate Consumption. *Source:* Own elaboration.

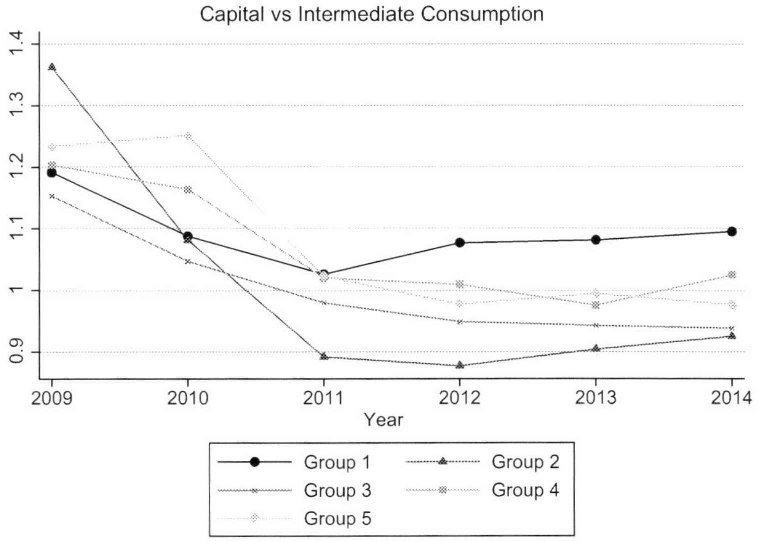

Fig. 7. Specific-Group Evolution of Allocative Efficiency Capital–Intermediate Consumption. *Source:* Own elaboration.

input pairs. These inefficiencies are especially high for labor relative to the other two inputs. In both cases, labor is over-utilized. The rest of the airport groups are closer to the allocative efficiency than Group 1; in particular for the pairs labor vs. capital and labor vs. intermediate consumptions.

By groups, we can identify the same evolution as in the aggregate case. That is, allocative inefficiencies at the beginning of the period (especially relevant is the under-utilization of capital relative to the other two inputs). There is a movement towards allocative efficiency up to 2011/2012, and finally, we observe mixed evidence between groups for the last 3 years.

Regarding labor–capital and labor–intermediate consumption allocative efficiency, all groups of airports overuse labor at the beginning of the period. Moreover, Group 1 is far away from efficiency and constantly overuses labor for the whole period. The rest of groups are closer to one, especially for the case of labor–intermediate consumption. From 2009 to 2012, Spanish airports experience a trend towards allocative efficiency for these two pairs of inputs. This result implies a reallocation of inputs from labor to capital and intermediate consumption that could be explained by two facts: (1) the strong infrastructure investment in airport facilities from 2000 and (2) a higher degree of externalization of some airport services. From 2012, however, there are not additional gains in allocative efficiency. Furthermore, allocative inefficiencies arise again – especially in the case of Group 1, which partially retraces its steps. This result matches the two privatization proposals. For the first subperiod, when the proposal is to privatize Madrid and Barcelona airports, there is a more intense effort towards allocative efficiency in these airports (Group 1). From 2012, when the first privatization proposal is discarded in favor of privatizing the whole system, Group 1 experiences an increase in allocative inefficiency

Finally, capital is under-utilized relative to intermediate consumption in 2009 and across all groups of airports. The strong infrastructure investments from 2000 fostered significant efficiency gains between these two inputs up to 2011. Afterwards, the evolution of this index differs between groups: capital remains under-utilized in Group 1, it is over-utilized in Groups 2 and 3, and it is close to the optimum level for Groups 4 and 5.

Two main findings arising from the previous analysis. First, the allocative inefficiency of the Spanish airport system is driven mainly by the two biggest airports, Madrid and Barcelona (Group 1). While the rest of airport groups are performing reasonably well in terms of allocative efficiency, Madrid and Barcelona remain very inefficient despite their good performance in the first half of the period, when they were at the core of the privatization schedule. Second, there is room to further reduce airport costs by improving allocative efficiency. However, since efficiency indices among input pairs differ across groups – some groups present over-utilization of a particular input while others are underusing it – , it requires different policies for each group of airports.

Table 7. Systematic Allocative Efficiencies.

Variable	2009–2014		2009–2011 (P_1)		2012–2014 (P_2)		Diff. ($P_1 - P_2$)
	Coeff.	Std. Error	Coeff.	Std. Error	Coeff.	Std. Error	z-stat
Labor	0.055	0.0018***	0.0093	0.030***	0.0051	0.0021**	−1.667
Capital	−0.0066	0.0028**	−0.0109	0.0043**	−0.0011	0.0043	−1.6209*
Interm. consumption	0.001	0.0017	0.0015	0.0024	−0.0039	0.0030	1.4262*

Notes: *, **, and *** denote parameters significant at 10%, 5%, and 1%, respectively. The Null hypothesis for periods (P_1) and (P_2) is H_0: Coefficient = 1. The Null hypothesis for the difference between periods ($P_1 - P_2$) is H_0: (Coeff. P_1) − (Coeff. P_2) ≤ 0.

Allocative Inefficiency through the Error Component Approach

Table 7 displays the indices for systematic inefficiencies obtained by the error components approach. Coefficients greater than 0 imply that the actual cost share of a particular input is higher than the optimal one (i.e., the input is overused). Coefficients smaller than 0 imply that inputs are under-utilized. Finally, a coefficient equal to 0 implies that the use of that input is allocative efficient.

All coefficients are different from zero, except for intermediate consumptions for all groups. In particular, results suggest that although Spanish airports are allocative efficient in the use of intermediate consumptions at the sample mean, labor is inefficiently overused and capital is under-used. Some interesting results arise in disaggregating by subperiods. First, although labor is still over-utilized in the second subperiod, it is closer to efficiency. Second, capital goes from being under-utilized in the first subperiod to efficiency in the second subperiod. Third, the use of intermediate consumptions remains allocative efficient throughout both periods.

CONCLUSIONS

This chapter adds to the empirical literature on airport allocative efficiency. We have analyzed Spanish airport performance during a pre-privatization process. Three facts make the Spanish experience interesting from a policy-making point of view. First, Aena is the world's largest airport operator. It manages 46 airports and two heliports in Spain and 16 airports in the United Kingdom, Colombia, México, and Jamaica. Second, Aena's management system is based on a centralized management model, which implies that Aena and the Ministry of Transport make all the relevant decisions regarding airports, softening competition among airports and establishing a cross-subsidy system to compensate airport financial losses. Third, the privatization strategy followed by the

Spanish government is a singular case in the world. After a first attempt of privatizing particular airports (Madrid and Barcelona) in 2010, the Spanish government opted in favor of partially privatizing the whole airport system in 2012. We argue that this change in the privatization strategy, as well as the strong infrastructure investment in airport facilities from 2000 have had relevant implications for the evolution of allocative efficiency.

We have estimated allocative efficiency in the pre-privatization period, 2009–2014, by means of an input-oriented distance system of equations. This methodology allowed us to obtain two different measures of allocative efficiency using an error component approach and a parametric procedure. Our results suggest that Spanish airports are more efficient in 2014 than they were in 2009. From the error component approach, we conclude that Spanish airports have achieved allocative efficiency in the use of capital and intermediate consumption. Labor is still over-utilized. When examining the relative efficiencies by pair of inputs, we find a movement towards a more efficient allocation of resources. This trend is especially intense for the first years of the period. Some relevant insights arise in focusing at airport groups. Madrid and Barcelona were the most allocative inefficient airports and the ones that improved efficiency the most up to 2012.

Our results raise interesting policy implications. First, the privatization strategy plays an important role when it comes to allocative efficiency. Further efforts towards cost reduction and efficiency are made in those airports targeted to be privatized. For the Spanish case, this is especially clear. When Madrid and Barcelona were at the core of the privatization process – until 2012–, they performed notably well, reducing inefficiencies. Afterwards, with the new privatization strategy shifted toward cost reducing efforts at less profitable and smaller airports, the performance at Madrid and Barcelona declined. Second, there is room for cost reduction by improving allocative efficiency. Our estimates suggest that allocative inefficiencies differ across groups of airports. Thus, cost reducing and productivity improvement policies should be individually oriented to take into account airport heterogeneity.

NOTE

1. These authors calculate this index fusing two indirect approaches. Specifically, the first one is a macroeconomic estimation of the relation between PPP and GPD with EU data (Eurostat), then this relation is used to make predictions with Spanish regions data (INE). The second one is a microeconomic estimation in which PPP is measured as regional effects of an equation of the total expense of the Spanish households. Then, they weight these two measures to obtain the final index. Finally, the temporal evolution of these indices is based on the evolution of consumption price index (INE, several years).

REFERENCES

Abrate, G., & Erbetta, F. (2010). Efficiency and patterns of service mix in airport companies: An input distance function approach. *Transportation Research Part E: Logistics and Transportation Review*, *46*(5), 693–708.

ACI. (2010). The Ownership of Europe's airports. Brussels: ACI Europe, Airports Council International. Retrieved from https://www.aci-europe.org/component/downloads/downloads/1457.html

Albalate, D., Bel, G., & Fageda, X. (2014). Beyond pure public and pure private management models: Partial privatization in the European Airport Industry. *International Public Management Journal*, *17*(3), 308–327.

Atkinson, S. E., & Cornwell, C. (1994). Parametric estimation of technical and allocative inefficiency with panel data. *International Economic Review*, *35*, 231–243.

Atkinson, S. E., & Primont, D. (2002). Stochastic estimation of firm technology, inefficiency, and productivity growth using shadow cost and distance functions. *Journal of Econometrics*, *108*(2), 203–225.

Baños-Pino, J., Fernández-Blanco, V., & Rodríguez-Álvarez, A. (2002). The allocative efficiency measure by means of a distance function: The case of Spanish public railways. *European Journal of Operational Research*, *137*(1), 191–205.

Barros, C. P. (2008). Technical change and productivity growth in airports: A case study. *Transportation Research Part A: Policy and Practice*, *42*(5), 818–832.

Barros, C. P., & Dieke, P. U. (2008). Measuring the economic efficiency of airports: A Simar–Wilson methodology analysis. *Transportation Research Part E: Logistics and Transportation Review*, *44*(6), 1039–1051.

Barros, C. P., & Sampaio, A. (2004). Technical and allocative efficiency in airports. *International Journal of Transport Economics/Rivista internazionale di economia dei trasporti*, *31*(3), 355–377.

Bottasso, A., & Conti, M. (2012). The cost structure of the UK airport industry. *Journal of Transport Economics and Policy (JTEP)*, *46*(3), 313–332.

Coelli, T. J., Rao, D. S. P., O'Donnell, C. J., & Battese, G. E. (2005). *An introduction to efficiency and productivity analysis*. New York: Springer Science & Business Media.

Costa, A., García, J., López, X., & Raymong, J. L. (2015). Estimación de las paridades de poder adquisitivo para las comunidades autónomas españolas. Reuniones de estudios regionales. Reus 2015. Retrieved from http://www.reunionesdeestudiosregionales.org/Reus2015/htdocs/pdf/p1402.pdf.

Curi, C., Gitto, S., & Mancuso, P. (2008). An application of data envelopment analysis (DEA) to measure the efficiency of the Italian airports after the privatisation. *L'industria*, *29*(4), 689–712.

Fageda, X., & Voltes-Dorta, A. (2012). *Efficiency and profitability of Spanish airports: A composite non-standard profit function approach*. Universitat de Barcelona.

Färe, R., & Grosskopf, S. (1990). A distance function approach to price efficiency. *Journal of Public Economics*, *43*(1), 123–126.

Farrell, M. J. (1957). The measurement of productive efficiency. *Journal of the Royal Statistical Society: Series A (General)*, *120*(3), 253–290.

Fung, M. K. Y., Wan, K. K. H., Van Hui, Y., & Law, J. S. (2008). Productivity changes in Chinese airports 1995–2004. *Transportation Research Part E: Logistics and Transportation Review*, *44*(3), 521–542.

Hooper, P. G., & Hensher, D. A. (1997). Measuring total factor productivity of airports – An index number approach. *Transportation Research Part E: Logistics and Transportation Review*, *33*(4), 249–259.

ICAO. (2012). *Manual on privatization in the provision of airports and air navigation services*.

Jorgenson, D. W., & Griliches, Z. (1967). The explanation of productivity change. *The Review of Economic Studies*, *34*(3), 249–283.

Leibenstein, H. (1966). Allocative efficiency vs. "X-efficiency". *The American Economic Review*, *56*(3), 392–415.

Liebert, V., & Niemeier, H. M. (2013). A survey of empirical research on the productivity and efficiency measurement of airports. *Journal of Transport Economics and Policy (JTEP)*, *47*(2), 157–189.

Malighetti, P., Martini, G., Paleari, S., & Redondi, R. (2007). An empirical investigation on the efficiency, capacity and ownership of Italian airports. *Rivista di Politica Economica*, *97*(1), 157–188.

Martín, J. C., & Roman, C. (2001). An application of DEA to measure the efficiency of Spanish airports prior to privatization. *Journal of Air Transport Management*, *7*(3), 149–157.

Núñez-Sánchez, R. (2015). Regional public support to airlines and airports: An unsolved puzzle. *Transportation Research Part E: Logistics and Transportation Review*, *76*, 93–107.

OECD. (2001). Measuring capital OECD manual: Measurement of capital stocks, consumption of fixed capital and capital services. Organization for Economic Cooperation and Development, Paris.

Oum, T. H., Yan, J., & Yu, C. (2008). Ownership forms matter for airport efficiency: A stochastic frontier investigation of worldwide airports. *Journal of Urban Economics*, *64*(2), 422–435.

Oum, T. H., & Yu, C. (2004). Measuring airports' operating efficiency: A summary of the 2003 ATRS global airport benchmarking report. *Transportation Research Part E: Logistics and Transportation Review*, *40*(6), 515–532.

Oum, T. H., Yu, C., & Fu, X. (2003). A comparative analysis of productivity performance of the world's major airports: Summary report of the ATRS global airport benchmarking research report-2002. *Journal of Air Transport Management*, *9*(5), 285–297.

Pacheco, R. R., & Fernandes, E. (2003). Managerial efficiency of Brazilian airports. *Transportation Research Part A: Policy and Practice*, *37*(8), 667–680.

Pels, E., Nijkamp, P., & Rietveld, P. (2003). Inefficiencies and scale economies of European airport operations. *Transportation Research Part E: Logistics and Transportation Review*, *39*(5), 341–361.

Rodríguez-Álvarez, A., Fernández-Blanco, V., & Lovell, C. K. (2004). Allocative inefficiency and its cost: The case of Spanish public hospitals. *International Journal of Production Economics*, *92*(2), 99–111.

Salazar de la Cruz, F. (2013). Industria aeroportuaria. Círculo Rojo Ed., Seville, Spain.

Sarkis, J. (2000). An analysis of the operational efficiency of major airports in the United States. *Journal of Operations Management*, *18*(3), 335–351.

Shephard, R. W. (1953). *Cost and production functions*. Princeton, NJ: Princeton University Press.

Shephard, R. W. (1970). *Theory of cost and production functions*. Princeton, NJ: Princeton University Press.

Stigler, G. J. (1976). The existence of X-efficiency. *The American Economic Review*, *66*(1), 213–216.

Timmer, C. P. (1971). Using a probabilistic frontier production function to measure technical efficiency. *The Journal of Political Economy*, *79*(4), 776–794.

Tovar, B., & Martín-Cejas, R. R. (2010). Technical efficiency and productivity changes in Spanish airports: A parametric distance functions approach. *Transportation Research Part E: Logistics and Transportation Review*, *46*(2), 249–260.

Yu, M. M., Hsu, S. H., Chang, C. C., & Lee, D. H. (2008). Productivity growth of Taiwan's major domestic airports in the presence of aircraft noise. *Transportation Research Part E: Logistics and Transportation Review*, *44*(3), 543–554.

APPENDIX

Table A1. Additional Robustness Estimation for Model 4.

Regressor	Model 4		Model 4a		Model 4b		Model 4c	
	Coeff.	Std. Error	Coeff.	Std. Error	Coeff.	Std. Error	Coeff.	Std. Error
Constant	−1.373	0.290***	−1.347	0.293***	−1.190	0.285***	−1.190	0.285***
ln x_L	0.265	0.002***	0.265	0.002***	0.264	0.002***	0.264	0.002***
ln x_c	0.336	0.003***	0.336	0.003***	0.335	0.002***	0.335	0.002***
ln x_{IC}	0.399	0.002***	0.399	0.002***	–	–	–	–
ln x_{IC2}	–	–	–	–	0.401	0.002***	0.401	0.002***
ln q_{WLU}	−0.125	0.065*	−0.126	0.065*	−0.194	0.064***	−0.194	0.064***
ln q_{COM}	−0.207	0.06***	−0.209	0.06***	−0.183	0.06***	−0.185	0.06***
ln x_L ln x_L	0.165	0.004***	0.165	0.004***	0.166	0.006***	0.166	0.006***
ln x_C ln x_C	0.164	0.006***	0.164	0.006***	0.178	0.005***	0.178	0.005***
ln x_{IC} ln x_{IC}	0.197	0.004***	0.197	0.004***	0.195	0.006***	0.195	0.006***
ln q_{WLU} ln q_{WLU}	−0.038	0.066	−0.031	0.066	−0.063	0.063	−0.056	0.064
ln q_{COM} ln q_{COM}	−0.085	0.067	−0.077	0.067	−0.081	0.065	−0.075	0.065
ln x_L ln x_C	−0.066	0.004***	−0.066	0.004***	−0.074	0.004***	−0.074	0.004***
ln x_L ln x_{IC}	−0.099	0.003***	−0.099	0.003***	−0.092	0.005***	−0.092	0.005
ln x_C ln x_{IC}	−0.098	0.004***	−0.098	0.004***	−0.103	0.004***	−0.103	0.004***
ln x_L ln q_{WLU}	0.008	0.004**	0.008	0.004**	0.010	0.004**	0.010	0.004***
ln x_L ln q_{COM}	−0.005	0.003	−0.005	0.003	−0.007	0.005	−0.007	0.005
ln x_C ln q_{WLU}	−0.015	0.006***	−0.015	0.006***	−0.011	0.005**	−0.011	0.005**
ln x_C ln q_{COM}	0.009	0.005*	0.009	0.005	0.006	0.005	0.006	0.005
ln x_{IC} ln q_{WLU}	0.008	0.003**	0.008	0.003**	0.001	0.004	0.001	0.004
ln x_{IC} ln q_{COM}	−0.003	0.003	−0.003	0.003	0.001	0.004	0.001	0.004
ln q_{WLU} ln q_{COM}	0.036	0.066	0.028	0.066	0.042	0.063	0.035	0.064
ln ratcarpax	−0.028	0.006***	–	–	−0.028	0.006***	–	–
ln ratcarwlu	–	–	−0.030	0.006***	–	–	−0.028	0.006***

Notes: *, **, and *** denote parameters significant at 10%, 5%, and 1%, respectively.

CHAPTER 5

AIRPORT–AIRLINE ARRANGEMENTS: AN INTERPRETIVE REVIEW OF INDUSTRY PRACTICES AND RECENT STUDIES

Xiaowen Fu and Hangjun Yang

ABSTRACT

With significant changes in the aviation industry, various airport–airline arrangements have been formed to achieve alternative objectives. However, no consensus has been reached on such arrangements' economic effects and the associated optimal public policy. This chapter aims to provide an interpretive review of the common types of airport–airline arrangements, the different modeling approaches used and key conclusions reached by recent studies. Our review suggests that airport–airline arrangements can take diverse forms and have been widely used in the industry. They may allow the airport and its airlines to internalize demand externality, increase traffic volume, reduce airport investment risks and costs, promote capacity investment, enhance service quality, or simply are a response to the competition from other airport–airline chains. On the other hand, such vertical arrangements, especially for those exclusively between airports and selected airlines, could lead to collusive outcomes at the expenses of non-participating organizations. The effects of such arrangements are also significantly influenced by the contract type, market structure and bargaining power between the airport and

The Economics of Airport Operations
Advances in Airline Economics, Volume 6, 97–122

ISSN: 2212-1609/doi:10.1108/S2212-160920170000006005

airline sectors. While case by case investigations are often needed for important economic decisions, we recommend policy-makers to promote competition in the airline and airport segments whenever possible, and demand more transparency or regulatory reporting of such arrangements. Policy debates and economic studies should be carried out first, before intrusive regulations are introduced.

Keywords: Airline–airport arrangements; vertical structures; airport; air transport

JEL Classifications: R48; L52; L93

INTRODUCTION

Significant changes have taken place in the aviation industry since the late 1970s, leading to the formation of various airport–airline arrangements that have significant implications for airlines, airports, passengers, and regulatory policies.

Most airports around the world were traditionally owned and operated directly by national or local governments, with a designated department/agency acting as both the regulator and operator of the airports. In the early 1970s, a number of countries began to create airport corporations under public ownership, in order to improve productive efficiency and tap into capital markets. With a global wave of privatization and commercialization started in the 1990s, dramatic changes have taken place in the airport industry. Many airports are now required to be financially independent and free from government subsidy, which implies that even public airports need to put a high priority on revenue and costs. Traditionally, airports were passive providers of aviation infrastructure that predominantly focused on providing reliable and safe operations. Today, many airports operate like commercial organizations that proactively promote aviation services and explore new revenue opportunities by working closely with airlines (Jarach, 2001; Tretheway & Kincaid, 2010). Meanwhile, with sustained growth in traffic volume, there is an increasing pressure for new airports to be built and major expansion projects to be carried out at existing airports. Such huge capital needs impose great challenges to the aviation industry at a time when an increasing number of governments no longer treat airports as public utilities that they must attend to. Many airports, thus turn to airlines for solutions. In markets with sufficient demand and limited airport competition, this may be achieved by simply increasing airport charges. In other cases, airports form various arrangements with airlines to jointly deal with the challenges (Xiao, Fu, & Zhang, 2016).

The airline sector has always been a major driver of changes in the airport sector. Deregulation in the airline industry started in the US domestic market in 1978, promoted the adoption of new airport policies and alternative ownership forms. Moreover, the substantial growth of low-cost carriers (LCCs) in the 1990s has played an important role in reshaping airport–airline relationships. Compared with full service airlines (FSAs) that rely heavily on hub-and-spoke operations, LCCs provide differentiated services that consume fewer airport resources (Barrett, 2004; Dresner, Lin, & Windle, 1996; Fu, Homsombat, & Oum, 2011; Gillen & Morrison, 2003). In Europe, there were about 200 under-utilized airports, most of which operated at a loss and relied on government subsidies (Caves & Gosling, 1999; Scheers, 2001). Because LCCs demand simple terminal and ground services, the marginal cost for these airports to serve additional LCC traffic tends to be very low thanks for the availability of spare capacity. This gives airports great incentives to proactively attract LCC services with negotiated charges and various airport–airline arrangements (Starkie, 2012). At large airports, a dominant airline can often achieve a substantially higher mark-up above cost than fringe competitors (Borenstein, 1989; Lijesen, Rietveld, & Nijkamp, 2001). Such a benefit of "hub premium" gives airlines a strong incentive to dominate an airport, often by cooperating with the airport (Fu et al., 2011).

In addition to airlines and airports, governments can become influential stakeholders which intervene in important decisions. In many cases, governments are directly involved because they are the owners of the airports and/or airlines involved. In a more general setting, governments are involved as an independent regulator to ensure fair business practices, service quality and safety, and to promote the well-being and social welfare of the whole society.

Despite the numerous examples of airport–airline cooperations, the two sectors often have fundamentally different views with respect to issues related to government policies and regulations governing airports and airport–airline relationships. The Airports Council International (Europe, 2013) argued that many legacy airport regulations should be removed because airports, especially those in Europe, operate under competitive environments. It argued that with deregulation and liberalization, airlines have choices of serving different airports and destinations. In comparison to airlines, airports cannot relocate. Because investments are capital intensive, airports have a large proportion of fixed costs and thus a strong incentive to compete for traffic. The Airports Council International (2013) argued that "there is a strong case for the regulator standing back and allowing the commercial parties to negotiate commercial outcomes", because the airport sector is increasingly competitive. It noted that 96% of all European airports, small or large, are actively marketing their airports to the airlines. With 81 more airports in Europe with commercial jet services in 2008 than in 1996, airports compete for airline traffic and thus the regulations should be replaced with commercial negotiations. However, such views are not supported by airlines. IATA (2013) argued that while liberalization and deregulation in the airline sector have driven cost efficiency and competition, too many airports are "shielded from these competitive pressures" and thus "economic regulation is required to force airports to operate efficiently". Indeed, even government agencies in the same country may have different views (Czerny, Guiomard, & Zhang, 2016). For example, in some cases, formal price regulation has been replaced by a "light-handed regulation" under which regulators can only monitor airport performance and encourage airport and airlines to negotiate solutions. In Australia, the Australian Productivity Commission was positive about the performance of light-handed regulation, while the Australian Competition and Consumer Commission (ACCC) had shown concerns of airports' pricing power and service quality (Arblaster, 2014, 2016; Australian Competition & Consumer Commission, 2010, 2014, Forsyth, 2003, 2008; Productivity Commission, 2011; Yang & Fu, 2015). In the United States, although many airports have been cooperating with their airlines in providing services and building infrastructures, the Federal Aviation Administration (FAA) (1999) cautioned against exclusive agreements between airports and particular airlines if such agreements involve a preferential use of key airport facilities.

To summarize, significant changes in the aviation industry have shaped the relationships between airports, airlines, passengers, government, and regulators. Many airports and airlines have chosen to form various vertical arrangements to achieve various objectives. Although, there are numerous examples where favorable outcomes have been achieved, key stakeholders may have very different views on the general outcomes and policy options on a wide range of issues. Although, quite a few studies have been devoted to airport–airline arrangements in recent years, this literature is not as well established as other topics such as airline competition, demand modeling, airport ownership, and productivity. This study aims to contribute to this literature by summarizing the various forms of airport–airline arrangements and to conduct an interpretative review of the key conclusions obtained in existing studies. We hope our work will identify the key findings of this burgeoning literature, and contribute to further investigations on this important issue. Although, our analysis is focused on the aviation industry, findings may be applicable to some other industries too. For example, the vertical integration and arrangement between shipping firms and ports have been widely used in the maritime sector. Maersk, e.g., operates approximate 50 container terminals (Alvarez-Sanjaime, Cantos-Sánchez, Moner-Colonques, & Sempere-Monerris, 2013). These kinds of vertical relationships have also raised similar competition and efficiency concerns in the maritime sector (Notteboom, 2006; Notteboom, Pallis, & Farrel, 2012; Yip, Liu, Fu, & Feng, 2014).

The rest of the chapter is organized as follows: the "Alternative Forms of Airport–Airline Arrangements" section reviews the types of airport–airline vertical arrangements used in the aviation industry. The "Analytical Approaches and Key Findings of Recent Studies" section reviews the modeling approaches used in the literature and the key findings. The last section summarizes and identifies the research gaps and opportunities.

ALTERNATIVE FORMS OF AIRPORT–AIRLINE ARRANGEMENTS

Although, various forms of airport–airline arrangements have been discussed by a few studies, notably in Fu et al. (2011) and D'Alfonso and Nastasi (2014), an overview is still provided here because the structure and form of such arrangements have significant implications. In the literature, the term of "vertical relationship" has also been frequently used. The meaning of such a relationship can be very broad. The relationship between airports and airlines can always be defined as upstream vs. downstream, supplier vs. consumer (of airport services), partners and/or stakeholders. In comparison, we would like to focus on the effects of particular arrangements between airport and airlines, many of which have been introduced due to the dynamic changes in the aviation industry. Therefore, we will use the term "arrangement" exclusively in this chapter. Basso and Zhang (2007, 2008) emphasized the need to consider the vertical structures of passengers–airlines–airports, because the market structure at the airline level plays an important role in determining the demands faced by airports. This is another example highlighting the importance to recognize that airports' demands are derived/dependent on airlines' decisions and their strategic interactions. Explicitly modeling such a vertical structure also allows other strategic effects commonly observed in the upstream–downstream setting, such as the double-marginalization effects and market foreclosure, to be fully identified. Such an approach has been routinely applied in recent studies on a wide range of issues (for a review, see Zhang & Czerny, 2012) especially airport pricing (see, e.g., Czerny, Cowan, & Zhang, 2017; Czerny & Zhang, 2015a, 2015b) and capacity choice (Xiao, Fu, Oum, & Yan, 2017; Xiao, Fu, & Zhang, 2013; Zhang & Zhang, 2003, 2006a, 2010). Whereas the study of airport–airline arrangements will naturally be considered in a vertical structure, our study goes beyond the standard upstream–downstream model by focusing on particular forms of arrangements in addition to treating airports as a simple input provider. Among others, such arrangements may include revenue sharing, joint venture, financial guarantor, airline consortium at particular airports, etc., which are summarized below. The classifications of these practices follow predominantly Fu et al. (2011) and D'Alfonso and Nastasi (2014), thus some details and examples are not reported again to avoid duplications.

Residual RATE-Setting Method and Signatory Airline Status

The determination of airport service charges can be quite complex and varies across different markets. It is also significantly affected by the types of regulations imposed on airports. In the United States where almost all airports are owned by local governments,[1] there are in principal three methods of determining airport charges: (a) compensatory, (b) residual, and (c) hybrid. Under a compensatory rate-setting model, airlines are required to cover the costs of providing the airport facilities and services. Under such a scheme, the airport–airline relationship is like a standard seller (service provider) – buyer structure. In comparison, under a residual agreement, some airlines sign the master use-and-lease agreements so that they will be held responsible for paying the cost shortfall if the airport's revenue does not fully cover its costs. These airlines signed master use-and-lease agreements are entitled as "signatory airlines". The airport aeronautical charges are determined after the revenues from non-signatory airlines and non-aeronautical revenues have been deducted from the airports' total costs. As a result, signatory airlines effectively become the guarantors of the airport, bearing the airport's financial risks. The service and finance guarantee by airlines reduces the airport's operation risks, allowing the airport to reduce capital costs when securing loans from banks and financial markets (Fu et al., 2011). In exchange for the risks borne, signatory airlines obtain varying degrees of control of airports' operations and investments. Airports cannot proceed with major capital investments unless approved by signatory airlines, a requirement referred as the "majority in interests" principal. Another benefit is that signatory airlines often end up paying lower charges than non-signatory airlines when there is sufficient travel demand. Similar airport–airline agreements have been observed in other markets such as in the Sydney and Melbourne airports (Barbot, 2009). A hybrid method uses a mix of the first two approaches to determine airport charges.

Airlines Control and/or Invest in Airport Facilities

Many airports provide dedicated space and facilities to major airlines; thus airlines have significant control over the operations, design, and investments in these facilities. Even at the design and construction stage of the new Denver International Airport, concourse B had already been reserved for United Airlines. The carrier also designed and built its own baggage system. Other examples include Lufthansa's investment in the Terminal 2 of the Munich airport (Kuchinke & Sickmann, 2005); JetBlue's US$80 million investment in the Terminal 5 of the New York JFK airport; Ryanair's US$10 million investment of a low-cost terminal at the Bremen Airport (Fu et al., 2011); and airline investments ($400 million, $33 million, $229 million, and $412 million from Southwest, American, Delta, and United, respectively) in the Los Angeles International Airport (Xiao et al., 2016).[2] In many countries, governments encourage private investments in airport facilities in general, often through either privatization or public private partnership (PPP). Private investors may enter a concession or build-own-transfer (BOT) contract with an airport or the government, under which the private entity finances, builds or upgrades, and then operates the facility until the ownership is transferred back to the airport or the government. The International Civil Aviation Organization (2016) noted that the Indian PPP model appeared to be effective in financing airport investments, and improved the efficiency and quality of services available.

Airlines' investments in airports per se have not received much regulatory concern, probably because airlines mostly invested in terminals and hangars for their own use. However, because of the vertical relationship, airlines' control of the airport may raise some concerns. The US General Accounting Office (1996) and the Asian Development Bank (2000) both noted that when considering airport privatization in Italy, national government-owned airlines divested their shares in the Rome and Milan airports, two of the major airline hubs in the country. The concerns are probably similar to those raised in the case of long-term usage contracts as discussed below.

Long-Term Usage Contract

Although aircraft can be easily redeployed, there are significant sunk costs invested when airlines develop their networks or serve new destinations. Therefore, it is natural for them to sign long-term contract to secure the use of key facilities. Many full service airlines (FSAs) had long-term use and/or lease over key facilities such as check-in gates and parking spaces at their hubs (FAA, 1999). In deregulated markets including Europe and Australia, airports have tried to proactively attract airlines, especially LCCs, to initiate new services by offering them favorable terms and incentive packages. To lock in such favorable terms, airlines often sign long-term agreements and contracts with airports (Fu et al., 2011; Starkie, 2012). It should, however, be cautioned that signing a longer agreement is not always a universal trend. In the United States, many airports had set the use-and-lease agreements in accordance with the term periods of airport bonds. As a result, 30-year agreements were commonplace (Messina & Smith, 2016). However, the US aviation markets have been very dynamic in the new millennium. In addition to demand shocks following unexpected events such as the 9/11 terrorist attack and the global financial crisis, airline bankruptcies and mergers also lead to dramatic market structure and traffic flow changes (e.g., hub consolidation and de-hubbing). As a result, there can be significant changes in an airport's demand and actual traffic volume (De Neufville & Barber, 1991; De Neufville & Odoni, 2003; Xiao et al., 2013). These market volatilities have led some airlines to prefer shorter agreements that allow for flexibility and reduce operational risks. The different practices in the aviation industry calls for an in-depth understanding of the implications of alternative airport–airline arrangements.

Although specific market conditions need to be considered in evaluating long-term usage contracts between airports and airlines, regulators such as

FAA (1999) have shown concerns that key airport facilities such as checking-in counters and boarding gates may be exclusively leased to dominant airlines, which may become entry barriers for other airlines to initiate new services to an airport. Indeed, Dresner, Windle, and Yao (2002) studied the airline entries into the top 500 US non-stop city-pair routes, which led them to conclude that airport slot control and gate access are important airline entry barriers.

Airports Issue Revenue Bonds Backed by Airlines

With sustained traffic growth, many airports now face substantial capacity constraints. Although governments had historically financed such capital needs, an increasing number of countries are considering relying on commercial arrangements and capital markets. Even in the US where airports have remained under government ownership and control, it is clear that the private sector will have to play an important role. The US General Accounting Office (1996) noted that since 1946, the federal government paid more than $23.5 billion in grants for airport investment. In 1970, the Airport and Airway Trust Fund was established and financed from taxes on airline travel, air cargo, and non-commercial aviation fuel. In 1982, the Airport Improvement Program (AIP) was set up to collect passenger facility charges (PFC) to fund airport grants. However, these federal grants are not sufficient, only covering about one-third of the US airports' capital needs during 2001–2004 (Transportation Research Board, 2007; Xiao et al., 2016; Zhang, 2012).

Many airports now choose to rely on the capital market by issuing various airport bonds, such as the General Obligation (GO) Bonds that are backed by general tax revenue of the local government (city, county or state) that owns the airport; General Airport Revenue Bonds (GARBs) backed by airports' general revenue; Passenger Facility Charge (PFC) Bonds that are to be paid by airports' future PFC revenue; bonds backed by Customer Facility Charges (CFCs); and Special Facility Revenue Bonds (SFRBs) (Transportation Research Board, 2007). SFRBs are issued to fund a facilities (e.g., terminals, hangar and maintenance facilities, cargo buildings, ground equipment support facilities, fuel storage and distribution facilities, and car facilities) that are to be used by a single or multiple airlines. In exchange, these airlines are entirely responsible for SFRBs in case of a default; thus all related investment and operational risks are transferred to airlines. Such arrangements have allowed airports to undertake major projects with the assistance of airlines. For example, Continental and Southwest backed US$323.5 million and US$519 million SFRBs for the Houston Airport and Dallas Love Field Airport, respectively, so that dedicated facilities could be built for their use.

Many airport bonds are tax-exempt and enjoy a high credit rating. FAA estimated that these features had allowed large hub airports in the US to reduce their interest rate by about 2% during 1985–1995 (GAO, 1996). This is one of the reasons that airport bonds have played an important role in financing facility investments. In 2010, a total of US$18.5 billion airport revenue and special facility bonds were issued in the United States (DIA, 2014). So far, no airport bond has defaulted.

Revenue and Risk Sharing between Airports and Airlines

Non-aeronautical charges have become a major revenue source for large airports worldwide. According to the ATRS airport benchmarking report (2014), the average shares of aeronautical revenue (in airport total revenue) are 50% in North America, 52.3% in Europe, 43.5% in Oceania, and 52.8% in Asia. Because demands for commercial services at an airport are greatly influenced by passenger volumes, there is a positive externality between the air travel demand and the demand for airport commercial services. Some airports (e.g., Tampa International Airport in the US) thus have shared their revenues with their airlines. In other cases, only specific income sources are included in revenue sharing (e.g., Ryanair demands sharing parking revenue from the airports it serves). If airlines and airports have jointly invested facilities such as passenger and cargo terminals, de facto revenue sharing may be achieved. Such a mechanism enables airports to share some of the benefits of commercial services with airlines, thus encourage airlines to bring additional traffic volumes.

Initiating new services at an airport may incur quite some sunk costs to airlines. In an effort to promote new services, airports may choose to share carriers' operational risks. Hihara (2012, 2014) described a "Load Factor Guarantee Mechanism" developed by the Noto airport in central-northern Japan. The airport pays (or receives) a contingent payment based on the difference between an airline's actual and target load factors for flights offered at the airport. If the airline's actual load factor is below (above) the target agreed in the contract, the airport will subsidize (share profit with) the airline. Therefore, such a mechanism protects airlines from downside risks and allows the airport to share airline revenue at upside.

Airport–Airline Consortium

Demkovich, Crosby, Muchow, Bender, and Copelan (2014) defined an airport–airline consortium as "a special-purpose business entity that is usually owned and operated by a group of airlines, and that may be assigned the responsibility of developing and/or managing certain facilities, equipment, systems, or services at an airport". First established in 1962, a total of 39 airport–airline consortiums had been established in the US by 2014. In essence, such consortiums may be regarded as cooperation programs between selective airlines at specific airports. Airlines have long formed strategic alliances (e.g., Star Alliance and Oneworld) to coordinate their strategies and operations at the company level (Oum & Zhang, 2001; Park, 1997; Zhang & Zhang, 2006b). However, in certain cases, airlines may want to cooperate with each other at a particular airport without forming long-term strategic partnerships. For example, the DEN Consortium allows its member airlines to jointly hold a common de-icing fluid supply contract at the Denver International Airport, whereas the LAX Shared Use Lounge Company, enables airlines not belonging to the same alliance to maintain and use common lounge at the Los Angeles airport. Airlines may be reluctant to enter into a long-term lease contract with the airport, or to sponsor and/or build its own lounge. Meanwhile, it can involve substantial administration costs for an airline to share or use the lounge managed by an airline in another (rival) alliance. An airport–airline consortium only involves the arrangements at a particular airport, and membership can be changed over time. As a result, the decisions are limited to a particular airport only, which greatly simplifies the decision process. In fact, airlines may not know exactly which airlines have confirmed to become a member until consortium documents are distributed for execution. As a result, it is possible that competing airlines may enter the same consortium.

A consortium may be formed to share the financing and operation of terminals (e.g., Terminal One Group Association for the JFK Terminal One project), sharing equipment, baggage systems, escalators (e.g., Detroit Airlines North Terminal Consortium), operating and maintaining the aviation fuel system (e.g., BOSFUEL Corporation in Boston, MEMFUEL in Memphis), or other functions such as representing airlines on designated issues (e.g., Airlines Committee of Hawaii for three airports).

Compared to the case when an airline directly controls or owns airport facilities as explained in the "Airlines Control and/or Invest in Airport Facilities" and "Long-Term Usage Contract" sections, airport–airline consortiums have some distinctive features: (a) a consortium is a legal business identity, which acts on behalf of its members. It can collect funds from member airlines, take out loans (from the airport, an airline, or a bank), or advance invoicing of member airlines; (b) membership can be changed, which allows flexibility and reduces airlines' risk of long-term commitments; (c) in a few cases, airports have direct, albeit limited, involvement in consortium governance (e.g., the Detroit Airlines North Terminal Consortium (DANTeC) and the San Antonio Airlines Consortium (SAAC)). That is why it can be called an "airport–airline consortium".

Common Ownership and Joint Decision of Airport and Airline

Although, many airports around the world are still directly owned or controlled by governments, governments increasingly act as independent regulators instead of airline owners or managers. Although the largest airlines in China are still majority owned by the central government, airports had been divested to provincial and city governments. Therefore, airports and airlines behave like independent businesses. Still, in some countries the common ownership of airlines and airports may lead to joint or coordinated decisions.

Lohmann, Albers, Koch, and Pavlovich (2009) noted that Singapore and Dubai used tightly combined airline, airport, and tourism strategies in developing their own cities to become major aviation hubs and tourism destinations. Singapore Airlines (SIA) contributed about one-third of the Changi airport's phase 1 investment costs of S$1.5 billion. With the support of the country's tourism authorities, the Singapore Stopover Holiday provided transit passengers of SIA and SilkAir (SIA's regional subsidiary) with complementary free services such as free shuttles, discounts at designated stores, and free admissions to some tourism destinations. In Dubai, civil aviation is controlled ultimately by the Maktoum family, which owns both airports and the hub carrier Emirates, and is in charge of aviation policy. Airport landing charges are extremely low and traffic control charges for Emirates were reported to be less than half of those paid by major European airlines (Lohmann et al., 2009). Qatar Airways and Etihad Airways are also owned by their, respectively, state governments, who also control and/or manage major airports in the country.[3]

Information Sharing and Joint Marketing

As airport charges may be based on both aircraft movements and passenger volumes, airports and airlines have long been sharing information, such as traffic statistics. To ensure service quality, airports have been reporting key performance indicators, either on a voluntary basis or per regulatory requirement. Service quality for Australian airports is reviewed by the ACCC regularly. The London Heathrow airport reports service quality monthly, which may be used to adjust service charges (as rebates). As commercial services become more important, some airports invested in software to monitor passenger spending by flight number using boarding pass information (Humphreys, Ison, & Francis, 2006). Airports have also used a broad range of data and analysis when negotiating with airlines, or to persuade airlines to initiate service. Gold coast gathered supporting data to persuade Qantas to restart its services in 2012, whereas the Brisbane airport monitors load factors of flights to avoid route suspension (Lohmann & Vianna, 2016). Many large airports are reported to have significant route development teams, and airport managers regard transparent information sharing as a key to sustained cooperation between airlines and airports (Lohmann & Vianna, 2016). In certain cases, airports and airlines also work together to jointly market aviation services. The Charleroi airport in Belgium provided direct financial support to Ryanair's advertisement and promotion (Barbot, 2006). The Dalian airport in China works closely with airlines flying to Dalian and alliance airports, and also facilitates cooperation among these airlines in providing flights to the airports (Cui, Wang, Tuck, Su, & Wang, 2014).

Incentive Programs and Other Agreements

Although the International Air Transport Association (IATA, 1997) and the EU Airport Charges Directive (European Commission, 2009) both forbid price discrimination by airports and demand that airlines pay the identical price for the same services, in practice airports may end up charging airlines different prices. As discussed earlier, signatory airlines in the US often end up paying lower charges in exchange for the risks they bear for the airport. In many other cases, airports may offer targeted incentives through rebates and discounts on aeronautical charges, bonus payments or marketing support, which are aimed for growth in either traffic volume or routes/destinations (Allroggen, Malina, & Lenz, 2013). In a study that included 200 airports in Europe, Malina, Albers, and Kroll (2012) found that only 50.5% had not adopted incentive programs. In particular, airports (or local authorities) may enter into bilateral agreement with airlines to provide the latter with financial support. Malina et al. (2012) found evidence for airport (authority)–airline agreements at 33 (26) airports, or one-third of the airports studied. Fichert and Klophaus (2011) noted that in Germany not only the low-cost airports, but also the nine largest airports had applied incentive programs, although the discount models and incentive magnitudes varied significantly. Ryerson (2016) studied air service incentive programs (ASIPs) in the top 70 airports in the US, of which 36 offered domestic ASIPs, 37 offered international ASIPs, and 29 offered both. These incentives are mostly designed to help airlines initiate new routes and services and/or increase flight frequencies, with incentives being reduced charges and marketing budgets. By March 2016, the US airports with ASIPs had provided incentives for 149 domestic and 97 international routes. Among these routes, about 60% of routes had sustained aviation services after the incentive programs expired, with large airports achieving more sustainable routes.

Both the European Commission (2005) and the Federal Aviation Administration (2010) have imposed various regulations on incentive programs. For example, FAA forbids airports from guaranteeing passenger revenue or ticket sales, and also forbids airports from providing airlines with direct payment, or interest-free loans, to pay for leased property. Still, airports and regional governments are getting "innovative" in providing airline incentives to grow business, sometimes from communities instead of from the airport directly. The Youngstown-Warren Regional Airport's (YNG) "Travel Bank – Air Service Initiative" collected more than 6 million pledges and support from more than 200 businesses and individuals to support regular services to the airport.[4] The Niagara Falls International Airport Stakeholders Group has been working with local businesses, including hotel and casino operators, to promote local aviation services with incentive programs.[5] Because many airports are still owned by local governments, it is not surprising that local authorities and communities are willing to support their own airports and provide incentives to airlines. More alternative programs may be developed to promote airport–airline cooperation and the initiation of additional aviation services.

ANALYTICAL APPROACHES AND KEY FINDINGS OF RECENT STUDIES

With various airport–airline arrangements being introduced to the aviation sector, different views have been proposed regarding the best policies toward such arrangements in particular, and airport regulation in general. One the one hand, researchers such as Starkie (2012) and Bush and Starkie (2014) argued that the deregulation in the airline industry, especially the growth of LCCs, had led to significant changes. Airlines can freely change their network configuration and route entry. With recent airline mergers, an increasing number of network carriers now operate multi-hub networks. With increased airport competition and (airline) buyer power, they argued that ex ante airport regulation is generally redundant and only common competition laws need to be maintained. As one piece of supporting evidence, these studies show that in Western Europe, there are a large number of airports that have overlapping catchment areas; thus, there is significant (potential) competition among these airports. As shown in Fig. 1, Starkie (2012) noted that for the 21 airports in England and Wales that had an annual passenger throughput of at least 400,000 in 2005/6, the average driving time to the nearest airport is only about 1 hour.

These observations and arguments have, at least partially, been recognized by regulators. The European Commission (2014) noted that there has been a shift in bargaining power toward airlines at certain, generally smaller, airports with the growth of LCCs. Whereas the Australian government admitted that some airports might have strong market power, it encouraged airlines and airports to negotiate on commercial arrangements including airport charges. The formal price-cap regulation has been replaced with the "light-handed" regulation (Arblaster, 2014, 2016; Forsyth, 2003, 2008; Yang & Fu, 2015; see also the recent literature by Czerny et al., 2016).

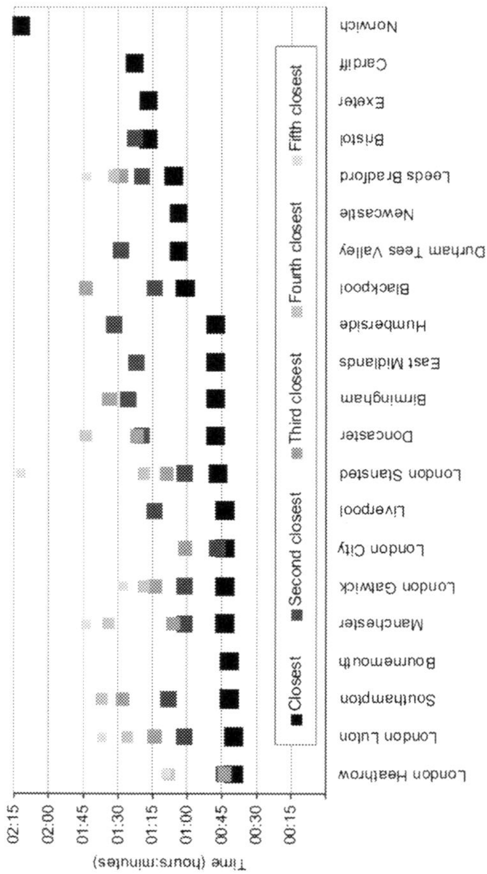

Fig. 1. Driving times between English/Welsh airports. *Source:* Starkie (2012).

On the other hand, many regulators and airlines have expressed considerable concerns over possible removal or reduction in regulation, or over problems emerging from light-handed regulation. In airlines' submission to the UK Civil Aviation Authority (Civil Aviation Authority, 2014) they argued that due to asymmetric information and market power between airlines and airports, "it is clear that commercial negotiations may not lead to the most efficient outcome", and may lead to inefficient pricing and allocation of risks. Airlines further argued that the existence of commercial contracts does not mean these contracts are reasonable or successful. The UK Competition Commission was concerned about the airport competition in the London area; thus it requested BAA to divest its airports in the city other than Heathrow. In New Zealand where light-handed regulation was introduced on airports, NZCC (2013) concluded that the "information disclosure regulation is not limiting excessive profits, as Wellington Airport is expected to recover at least $38 million from airport users over the current 5-year pricing period."

These policy debates have led to an increasing number of academic investigations on the implications of airport–airline arrangements. Since it is impossible to review all related studies, we will summarize these studies based on their analysis and modeling approaches, with a brief summary of the key conclusions.

Revenue Sharing

Airport–airline revenue sharing is among the first vertical arrangements that have been modeled. Notable studies include Fu and Zhang (2010, 2010) and Saraswati and Hanaoka (2014). All these studies considered a case when an airport shares a proportion of its commercial revenue with one or multiple airlines in exchange for a fixed payment. The main differences in these studies are due to differences in market structure at the airport and airline sectors. Fu and Zhang (2010) analyzed the case of a monopoly airport, Zhang et al. (2010) considered the case of duopoly airports which offer either complementary or substitutable services, whereas Saraswati and Hanaoka (2014) considered the setting of airport/airline networks. In general, these studies found that revenue sharing may bring both benefits and competition concerns. On the one hand, revenue sharing allows airlines and airports to internalize a positive demand externality between aeronautical services and commercial services. This will increase traffic volume and improve social welfare. On the other hand, airport(s) may prefer to cooperate with the dominant airline only, and thus may harm competition and social welfare. However, in the case of competing airports, airport–airline cooperation may be formed as a competitive response to other airport–airline chains. In general, whether there is inter-airport competition and whether airport–airline arrangement is exclusive are critical to the welfare effects of revenue sharing arrangements.

Bargaining Game

The airport revenue sharing studies discussed above mostly considered "take-it-or-leave-it" contract offers between airlines and airports. That is, it is implicitly assumed that the bargaining power is entirely with one side. Such an assumption is unlikely to change the main conclusions as a more balanced power distribution may simply change the fixed payment but not the market outcome. Still, such a simplification allows these studies to focus on the overall effects of such arrangements per se, but does not offer rich insights into the effects of market power distribution on the formation of airport–airline arrangements, and how airports and airlines' well-being are differently affected by such arrangements. As regulators, notably those in the UK, New Zealand, and Australia, are encouraging commercial negotiations to play more important roles in airport operations and management, it would be useful to model airport–airline negotiation explicitly. As far as we are aware, the only study following this approach is Yang, Zhang, and Fu (2015), which considered a Nash bargaining game between one airport and multiple competing airlines to determine the share of airport revenue to be shared with airlines. Their analytical results suggest that airport–airline arrangements are more likely to be reached when airlines have greater market power or higher costs, airport charges are higher, or the airport puts more priority on maximizing social welfare.

Collusion or Joint Venture

Another approach used by Barbot (2009) and Barbot, D'Alfonso, Malighetti, and Redondi (2013) is to consider collusion between airports and airlines. For example, Barbot (2009) considered the case of "successive duopolies" with two airlines and two airports. Collusion is modeled as a participating airport and airline maximizing their joint profit as in a full merger. Although merger between airports and airlines are not frequently observed in practice, the "integrated strategy" adopted by Singapore and Dubai governments, which are the owners of both flag carriers and domestic hub airports, may be considered/modeled as joint decision making. It should be cautioned that although the Singapore government did support Singapore Airlines' market expansion in the early years, the country has since adopted a very liberal aviation policy and direct supports to the airline have largely phased over the years.

Xiao et al. (2016) analyzed the effects of airport–airline arrangements on an airport's capacity choice. They considered the case in which each airline contributes a proportion of the capital needed for airport capacity investment, and in exchange shares the same proportion of the airport's revenue. In such a setting, the airport and airlines may be regarded as partners in a joint venture for capacity investment. However, in their study capacity choice is determined by the airport, thus the decision/modeling process is similar to a standard vertical structure as that in Basso and Zhang (2007, 2008).

Contract Design and Moral Hazard

Barbot and D'Alfonso (2014) considered a contract in which an airline commits to carry to an airport the quantity that maximizes the joint profits of the airport–airline pair, whereas the airport commits to advertise the airline. Their modeling results suggest that such agreement is not sustainable. However, with demand uncertainty, especially a large probability of high demand, the airport may prefer to commit to such contract. Hihara (2012, 2014) modeled the load factor guarantee mechanism between the Japanese Noto airport and its airlines as an incomplete contract under asymmetric information, and discussed how the contract could be designed to induce optimal efforts by the airport and airlines and allow them to share risks. These studies have led Minato and Morimoto (2017) to calibrate a similar model with observed data at the airport, which suggest airport–airline cooperation can be sustained in the long term.

Case Studies

Lohmann et al. (2009) studied the integrated (airline, airport, and government) strategy and development history of Singapore and Dubai. Without revealing the names of the airport, Francis, Fidato, and Humphreys (2003) reviewed the implications of LCC service growth to selected European airports and identified the important issues that airport managements were trying to address in forming new airport–airline relationships. Studies like Fu et al. (2011), Starkie (2012), and Bush and Starkie (2014) may also be included in this category, although they aim to provide general reviews instead of focusing on specific markets and airports. Because different researchers may interpret the same fact and observation differently, conclusions and policy recommendations provided in these studies can be subjective. However, these studies offer rich details and insights into actual industry practices and management philosophy, which motivate and justify analytical models developed in the literature.

Other Study Approaches

Some additional arrangements have been analyzed in the literature, which mostly models the decisions by airlines and airports within a vertical structure similar to that defined in Basso and Zhang (2007, 2008). For example, Barbot (2011) and D'Alfonso and Nastasi (2012) considered different types of arrangements between airlines and airports, including the scenario in which an airline controls some airport facility (e.g., terminal) and resells it to other airlines, and airport price discrimination (such as lower prices paid by signatory airlines).

A few other studies have tried to analyze the effects of airport–airline arrangements. Alcobendas (2014) modeled the effects of airport charge determination (through airport–airline agreement) on market equilibrium. The main conclusion is that different methods to compute airport charge will influence airlines' decisions, which lead to a different airport congestion level. An empirical investigation by Ha, Wan, Yoshida, and Zhang (2013) identified an inverse U-shaped relationship between airline market concentration and airport efficiency. That is, too much or too little downstream concentration is associated with airport inefficiency. Although their study is motivated by the effects of airport–airline vertical arrangements, the identified effects cannot be directly or fully attributed to such vertical arrangements because there can be many other factors influencing the concentration of an airline market.

Interpretation of Findings and Implications

It has been well recognized that competition concerns may arise from a vertical structure. For example, collusion between selected up- and down-stream firms may lead to "foreclosure", in which a firm controlling essential facilities may deny proper access to its good/service in order to extend monopoly power to downstream segment (Rey & Tirole, 2007). That is one major reason for the US FAA's concern over airlines' control over or exclusive use of key airport facilities, as this may deter potential entry (Dresner et al., 2002). Although airports rarely own or control airlines, there are many ways for airlines and airports to "compensate" each other via revenue bonds, long-term service commitments, revenue and risk sharing, etc. Therefore, Fu and Zhang (2010) and Fu et al. (2011) argued that both an airport and its dominant airline have incentives to exclusively cooperate with each other, which could harm competition. On the other hand, it has also been long recognized that vertical cooperation may eliminate the damages caused by double-marginalization, thus leading to improved consumer surplus (Comanor, 1967). Even at airports where aeronautical charges are regulated or cost based, vertical arrangements may allow airport and airlines to internalize the positive demand externality of aviation services (traffic volumes) on commercial services, and thus increases market output (traffic volume and commercial revenue) and social welfare. Because of such countervailing effects, Fu and Zhang (2010, 2010), Fu et al. (2011), and Barbot (2011) all concluded that the effects of airport–airline vertical arrangements are two-sided in that they may increase social welfare but can also harm competition.

Starkie (2008) and Bush and Starkie (2014) argued that in Europe, the airport market is competitive and airlines have high bargaining power. Although, such a conclusion is likely to hold in some markets, policy-makers and researchers should always bear in mind that the airport sector has extremely diversified market structures and is increasingly dynamic due to commercialization, privatization, and liberalization processes in the airport and airline industries. Even in the UK where the airport sector is believed to be more competitive than most other regions, the BAA had been requested to sell many of its airports as the Competition Commission is concerned about possible negative competition effects, including the (former) common airport ownership in London. The diversity of the airport industry can be appreciated by differences in airports' profitabilities. ACI (2014) and CAPA (2015) reported that as many as 69% of airports worldwide operated at a loss in 2013. On the other hand, large airports like the Hong Kong International Airport and Sydney Kingsford Airport achieved impressive financial returns. In terms of EBITDA margin, the two airports' figures in the first 6 months of the financial year 2015 reached 69.13% and 82.11%, respectively.

Although the results and conclusions of the studies are largely compatible with each other, significant differences can be observed which are mostly due to the different scenarios and arrangements considered. For example, Barbot and D'Alfonso (2014) found airport–airline contracts are likely to fail, whereas Minato and Morimoto (2017) reached the opposite conclusion. Both studies are motivated by real cases (e.g., the agreement failure between the Angouleme airport and Ryanair, and the sustained cooperation between the Noto airport and ANA). The different conclusions may be due to the different types of contract studied – a quantity commitment contract vs. a load factor guarantee mechanism. Although not analyzing airport–airline arrangements directly, the study by Ha et al. (2013) found a reverse U-shape relationship between airline market concentration and airport efficiency. The authors argued that when the airline concentration is very high, a dominant airline has strong bargaining power to get favorable airport treatment without passing the benefits to passengers, which leads to sub-optimal traffic volume. On the other hand, when there is no dominant airline, competition leads to excessive output volume and congestion, and deep airport–airline collaboration may be difficult to reach. As a result, either too much or too little airline concentration is associated with airport inefficiency.

Due to the issues discussed above, any attempts to give very general conclusions and recommendations on airport–airline arrangements should be cautious. Case by case analysis should be conducted for important policy decisions. That said, some common themes emerged during our review: First, increased competition, either in the airline sector or the airport sector, is likely to increase social welfare. For example, both Fu and Zhang (2010) and Zhang et al. (2010) studied airport–airline revenue sharing using similar models, albeit with different market structure in the airport sector. Fu and Zhang (2010) studied the case of a monopoly airport, in which cooperation between the airport and its dominant airline will harm competition. In comparison, Zhang et al. (2010) found that if inter-airport competition is present, airport–airline vertical cooperation might be formed as a competitive response to other airport–airline pairs, which could lead to increased competition and put airport–airline chains into a prisoners' dilemma. Introducing more competition seems to be a generally acceptable strategy when there are regulatory concerns. Indeed, Comanor (1967) argued that it is the lack of competition in the upstream market, not the vertical cooperation, that is harmful. He questioned the claim that leading firms in specific manufacturing industries extended their market power by acquiring scarce raw materials to erect entry barriers to competitors. He argued that it is the scarce resource, not the manufacturing production, that limits the degree of competition. Therefore, forbidding upstream and downstream merger will simply let the upstream firms retain the rents associated with scarce resources, and consumers may be harmed due to the double-marginalization effects.

Another recommendation that seems generally helpful is the importance of transparency of airport–airline arrangements. Currently, such commercial arrangements do not always have to be released to the public, although regulators such as the UK Competition Commission and the Australian Productivity Commission encourage airports and airlines to settle disagreements via commercial negotiation and consultation. Because increased transparency is likely to deter arrangements and collusion that may harm the third party, imposing such requirements is likely to maintain competition levels.

However, these two conditions are unlikely to be fully met. Airport investments tend to be lumpy and costly, particularly when there is significant demand uncertainty (Oum & Zhang, 1990; Xiao et al., 2013, 2017). As a result, it is often difficult or even infeasible to introduce airport competition. Moreover, imposing reporting requirements on airports is feasible, but can also be costly like other regulations. The interpretations of airport–airline arrangements can also be different, as evidenced by the diverse views expressed by the airport and airline industry in IATA (2013) and ACI Europe (2013). All these calls for more in-depth investigations on this important issue.

SUMMARY AND CONCLUSIONS

With the significant changes that have taken place in the aviation industry in the past decades, airports increasingly operate like commercial business and form various arrangements with downstream airlines to achieve alternative objectives. In some markets, like Australia, New Zealand, and the UK, regulators encourage airports and airlines to settle disagreements and address new challenges via negotiation or consultation, either as a substitute or complement to strict airport regulation. However, no consensus has been reached on the optimal public policy in the presence of significant market dynamics. Some airport–airline vertical arrangements, such as the one between the Charleroi airport and Ryanair, had led to complicated litigations and policy debates.

This chapter aims to provide an interpretive review of the common types of airport–airline arrangements, and the different modeling approaches used by recent studies on such an important issue. Our review suggests that airport–airline arrangements can take very diverse forms and have been widely used in the aviation industry. They may allow the airport and its airlines to internalize demand externalities, increase traffic volume, reduce airport investment risks and costs, promote capacity investment, enhance service quality, or simply are a response to the competition from other airport–airline chains. On the other hand, such vertical arrangements, especially for those exclusively between selected airports and airlines, could lead to collusive outcomes at the expense of non-participating organizations. The effects of such arrangements are also significantly influenced by the contract type, market structure and bargaining power distributions of the airport and airline sectors. Therefore, policy-makers should be cautious in making simple general conclusions.

While case by case investigations are often needed for important economic decisions, we recommend that policy-makers promote competition in the airline and airport levels whenever possible, as they are likely to reduce the negative "side-effects" of vertical arrangements, if any. In addition, requiring more transparency or regulatory reporting of such arrangements can be an effective method to deter anti-competition actions. Finally, more in-depth analyses should be carried out on this important issue. As far as we are aware, the only empirical investigation that directly examined the effects of airport–airline arrangements are Yang et al. (2015), which found positive effects on airport traffic volume and capacity investments overall. However, they have used simple t-tests without simultaneously controlling for possible moderating factors. We believe that airport–airline arrangements can be an important source of welfare and efficiency gains in the aviation sector. Policy-makers should be prudent in introducing additional regulations at the current stage. Instead, promoting policy debates and economic studies are probably the best solution before intrusive regulations are introduced.

NOTES

1. Other than the two airports in Washington DC that are directly controlled by the federal government, virtually all commercial airports in the US are owned by local governments, either directly under county/city/state governments (i.e. civil aviation department), or through airport/port authorities.
2. All the currencies mentioned in the chapter are in terms of USD, unless explicitly indicated otherwise.

3. The Hamad International Airport at Doha is under the control of Qatar Civil Aviation Authority, whereas the state-owned Abu Dhabi Airport owns and operates five airports in the state.
4. News available at http://yngairport.com/documents/pressreleases/travelbank_final.pdf.
5. See, various reports including http://news.wbfo.org/post/falls-airport-gets-business-boost.

ACKNOWLEDGMENT

Financial supports from the OECD-ITF and the University of Sydney Industry Partnership grant are gratefully acknowledged.

REFERENCES

Airports Council International. (2013). Airport competition. International Civil Aviation Organization Working Paper ATConf/6-WP/90.

Airports Council International (ACI 2014). (2014). ACI airport economics report. http://www.aci.aero/Publications/ACI-Airport-Economics-and-Statistics

Airports Council International Europe (ACI Europe). (2013). How airports compete. Report Retrieved from www.aci-europe.org

Air Transport Research Society (ATRS). (2014). Airport Benchmarking Report – Global standards for airport excellence, publications and data available for purchase at www.atrsworld.org.

Alcobendas, M. A. (2014). Airline–airport agreements in the San Francisco Bay Area: Effects on airline behavior and congestion at airports. *Economics of Transportation*, *3*(1), 58–79.

Allroggen, F., Malina, R., & Lenz, A. (2013). Which factors impact on the presence of incentives for route and traffic development? Econometric evidence from European airports. *Transportation Research Part E*, *60*, 49–61.

Alvarez-Sanjaime, O., Cantos-Sánchez, P., Moner-Colonques, R., & Sempere-Monerris, J. (2013). Vertical integration and exclusivities in maritime freight transport. *Transportation Research Part E: Logistics Transportation Review*, *51*, 50–61.

Arblaster, M. (2014). The design of light-handed regulation: Lessons from experience in Australia and New Zealand. *Journal of Air Transport Management*, *38*, 27–35.

Arblaster, M. (2016). Negotiate-arbitrate regulation of airport services: Twenty years of experience in Australia. *Journal of Air Transport Management*, *51*, 27–38.

Asian Development Bank. (2000). Developing best practices for promoting private sector investment in infrastructure – Airports and air traffic control. ISBN No. 971-561-282-5. Retrieved from http://www.adb.org

Australian Competition and Consumer Commission. (2010). *Airport monitoring report 2008–09: Price, financial performance and quality of service monitoring*. Canberra: ACCC.

Australian Competition and Consumer Commission. (2014). *Booming demand and price increases drive airport profits higher while quality of service remains flat*. ACCC media release at http://www.accc.gov.au/media-release/booming-demand-and-price-increases-drive-airport-profits-higher-while-quality-of-service-remains-flat.

Barbot, C. (2006). Low-cost airlines, secondary airports, and state aid: An economic assessment of the Ryanair – Charleroi Airport agreement. *Journal of Air Transport Management*, *12*(4), 197–203.

Barbot, C. (2009). Airport and airlines competition: Incentives for vertical collusion. *Transportation Research Part B*, *43*, 952–965.

Barbot, C. (2011). Vertical contracts between airports and airlines: Is there a Trade-off between Welfare and competitiveness? *Journal of Transport Economics and Policy*, *45*(2), 277–302.

Barbot, C., & D'Alfonso, T. (2014). Why do contracts between airlines and airports fail? *Research in Transportation Economics*, *45*, 34–41.

Barbot, C., D'Alfonso, T., Malighetti, C. P., & Redondi, R. (2013). Vertical collusion between airports and airlines: An empirical test for the European case. *Transportation Research Part E*, *57*, 3–15.

Barrett, S. D. (2004). How do the demands for airport services differ between full-service carriers and low-cost carriers? *Journal of Air Transport Management*, *10*, 33–39.

Basso, L., & Zhang, A. (2007). Congestible facility rivalry in vertical structures. *Journal of Urban Economics*, *61*, 218–237.

Basso, L., & Zhang, A. (2008). Sequential peak-load pricing: The case of airports and airlines. *Canadian Journal of Economics*, *41*, 1087–1119.

Borenstein, S. (1989). Hubs and high fares: Dominance and market power in the US airline industry. *RAND Journal of Economics*, *20*, 344–365.

Bush, H., & Starkie, D. (2014). Competitive drivers towards improved airport/airline relationships. *Journal of Air Transport Management*, *41*, 45–49.

Caves, R., & Gosling, G. (1999). *Strategic airport planning*. Oxford: Pergamon.

Center for Aviation (2015). *Airport financial results 1H2015 – Primary airports, hubs, alliances, retail, sustain profitability*. Retrieved from https://centreforaviation.com/analysis/. Accessed on February 2016.

Civil Aviation Authority. (2014). *Economic regulation of new runway capacity: Airline Response*, 19 Dec 2014. Retrieved from https://www.caa.co.uk/WorkArea/DownloadAsset.aspx?id=4294974418

Comanor, W. (1967). Vertical mergers, market powers and the antitrust laws. *American Economic Review*, *57*, 254–265.

Cui, M., Wang, J., Tuck, J., Su, J., & Wang, S. (2014). *Dalian airport's alliance management dilemma*. Ontario, Canada: Ivy Publishing, Case W13561.

Czerny, A. I., Cowan, S., & Zhang, A. (2017). How to mix per-flight and per-passenger based airport charges: The oligopoly case. *Transportation Research – Part B*, In Press.

Czerny, A. I., Guiomard, C., & Zhang, A. (2016). Single-till versus dual-till regulation of airports: Where do academics and regulators (dis)agree? *Journal of Transport Economics and Policy*, *50*(4), 350–368.

Czerny, A. I., & Zhang, A. (2015a). How to mix per-flight and per-passenger based airport charges. *Transportation Research Part A: Policy and Practice*, *71*, 77–95.

Czerny, A. I., & Zhang, A. (2015b). Third-degree price discrimination in the presence of congestion externality. *Canadian Journal of Economics*, *48*, 1430–1455.

D'Alfonso, T., & Nastasi, A. (2012). Vertical relations in the air transport industry: A facility-rivalry game. *Transportation Research Part E*, *48*, 993–1008.

D'Alfonso, T., & Nastasi, A. (2014). Airport-airline interaction: Some food for thought. *Transport Reviews*, *34*(6), 730–748.

Demkovich, B. P., Crosby, J. J., Muchow, L. D., Bender, G. G., & Copelan, A. J. (2014). *A Guidebook for Airport-Airline Consortiums*, ACRP Report 111, Research sponsored by the Federal Aviation Administration, The Transportation Research Board.

De Neufville, R., & Barber, J. (1991). Deregulation induced volatility of airport traffic. *Transportation Planning and Technology*, *16*(2), 117–128.

De Neufville, R., & Odoni, A. (2003). *Airport systems – Planning, design and management*. New York: McGraw-Hill.

DIA (Denver International Airport). (2014). Airport financing models – An overview. Presented by Patrick Heck, Chief Financial Officer of Denver International Airport on 8 April, 2014. Retrieved from http://www.aci-na.org/sites/default/files/cs1b-patrick_heck.pdf.

Dresner, M., Lin, J. S. C., & Windle, R. (1996). The impact of low-cost carriers on airport and route competition. *Journal of Transport Economics and Policy*, *30*(3), 309–328.

Dresner, M., Windle, R., & Yao, Y. (2002). Airport barriers to entry in the US. *Journal of Transport Economics and Policy*, *36*, 389–405.

European Commission. (2005). Community guidelines on financing of airports and start-up aid to airlines departing from regional airports. *Official Journal of the European Union C*, *312*(1), 1–14.

European Commission. (2009). Directive 2009/12/EC of the European Parliament and of the Council of 11 March 2009 on airport charges; OJ L 70, 14.3.2009.

European Commission (2014). Report from the commission to the European parliament and the council on the application of the airport charges directive. COM (2014)278 Final, Brussels 19.5.2014.

Federal Aviation Administration. (1999). *Airport business practices and their impact on airline competition*. Washington DC: FAA/OST Task force Study.

Federal Aviation Administration (2010). Air carrier incentive program guidebook: A reference for airport sponsors, TC10-0034. Washington, DC.

Fichert, F., & Klophaus, R. (2011). Incentive schemes on airport charges—Theoretical analysis and empirical evidence from German airports. *Research in Transportation Business and Management*, *1*(1), 71–79.

Forsyth, P. (2003). Regulation under stress: Developments in Australian airport policy. *Journal of Air Transport Management*, *9*(1), 25–35.

Forsyth, P. (2008). Airport policy in Australia and New Zealand: Privatization, light-handed regulation and performance. In C. Winston & G. de Rus (Eds.), *Aviation infrastructure performance: A study in comparative political economy*. Washington, DC: Brookings Institution Press.

Francis, G., Fidato, A., & Humphreys, I. (2003). Airport–airline interaction: The impact of low-cost carriers on two European airports. *Journal of Air Transport Management*, *9*, 267–273.

Fu, X., Homsombat, W., & Oum, T. H. (2011). Airport-airline vertical relationships, their effects and regulatory policy implications. *Journal of Air Transport Management*, *17*, 347–353.

Fu, X., & Zhang, A. (2010). Effects of airport concession revenue sharing on competition and social welfare. *Journal of Transport Economics and Policy*, *44*(2), 119–138.

Gillen, D., & Morrison, W. (2003). Bundling, integration and the delivered price of air travel: Are low cost carriers full service competitors? *Journal of Air Transport Management*, *9*(1), 15–23.

Ha, H. K., Wan, Y., Yoshida, Y., & Zhang, A. (2013). Airline market structure and airport efficiency: Evidence from major Northeast Asian airports. *Journal of Air Transport Management*, *33*, 32–42.

Hihara, K. (2012). An analysis of airport-airline relationship under a risk sharing contract. *Transportation Research Part E*, *48*, 978–992.

Hihara, K. (2014). An analysis of airport-airline relationships with risk sharing contracts under asymmetric information structure. *Transportation Research Part C*, *44*, 80–97.

Humphreys, I., Ison, S., & Francis, G. (2006). A review of the airport-low cost airline relationship. *Review of Network Economics*, *5*(4), 413–420.

IATA. (2013). Airport Competition, Economics Briefing No. 11. James Wiltshire. IATA, November 2013.

International Air Transport Association. (1997). *IATA policy on user charges aspects of the commercialization of airports and air traffic service entities*. Montreal: International Air Transport Association.

International Civil Aviation Organization. (2016). *Assessment of the airport PPP experience in India*. Working Paper/Information paper A39-WP/294.

Jarach, D. (2001). The evolution of airport management practices: Towards a multi-point, multi-service, marketing-driven firm. *Journal of Air Transport Management*, *7*(2), 119–125.

Kuchinke, B. A., & Sickmann, J. (2005). The joint venture terminal 2 at Munich Airport and the consequences: A competition economic analysis. 4th Conference on applied infrastructure research, Berlin (Vol. 8).

Lijesen, M., Rietveld, P., & Nijkamp, P. (2001). Hub premiums in European civil aviation. *Transport Policy*, *8*, 193–199.

Lohmann, G., Albers, S., Koch, B., & Pavlovich, K. (2009). From hub to tourist destination – An explorative study of Singapore and Dubai's aviation-based transformation. *Journal of Air Transport Management*, *15*, 205–211.

Lohmann, G., & Vianna, C. (2016). Air route suspension: The role of stakeholder engagement and aviation and non-aviation factors. *Journal of Air Transport Management*, *53*, 199–210.

Malina, R., Albers, S., & Kroll, N. (2012). Airport incentive programmes: A European perspective. *Transport Reviews*, *32*(4), 435–453.

Messina, J. F., & Smith, E. T. (2016). Emerging trends in airport-airline use and lease agreements in the USA. *Journal of Airport Management*, *10*(3), 273–282.

Minato, N., & Morimoto, R. (2017). Dynamically interdependent business model for airline–airport coexistence. *Journal of Air Transport Management*, In Press.

New Zealand Commerce Commission (NZCC). (2013). Report to the Minister of Commerce and Transport on how effectively information disclosure regulation is promoting the purpose of part 4 for Wellington Airport, Section 56G of the Commerce Act 1986, 8 February. http://www.comcom.govt.nz/regulated-industries/airports/section-56g-reports/

Notteboom, T. (2006). Concession agreements as port governance tools. *Research in Transport Economics*, *17*, 437–455.

Notteboom, T., Pallis, A. A., & Farrel, S. (2012). Terminal concessions in seaports revisited. *Maritime Policy & Management*, *39*(1), 1–5.

Oum, T. H., & Zhang, A. (2001). Key aspects of global strategic alliances and the impacts on the future of Canadian airline industry. *Journal of Air Transport Management*, *7*, 287–301.

Oum, T. H., & Zhang, Y. (1990). Airport pricing: Congestion tolls, lumpy investment, and cost recovery. *Journal of Public Economics*, *43*(3), 353–374.

Park, J. H. (1997). The effects of airline alliances on markets and economic welfare. *Transportation Research*, *E33*, 181–195.

Productivity Commission. (2011). *Economic regulation of airport services*. Productivity Commission Inquiry Report, No. 57, 14 December 2011.

Rey, P., & Tirole, J. (2007). A primer on foreclosure. In M. Armstrong & R. Porter (Eds.), *Handbook of industrial organization* (Vol. 3, pp. 2145–2220). New York, NY: Elsevier.

Ryerson, M. S. (2016). Incentivize it and they will come? How some of the busiest U.S. airports are building air service with incentive programs. *Journal of the American Planning Association*, *82*(4), 303–315.

Saraswati, B., & Hanaoka, S. (2014). Airport–airline cooperation under commercial revenue sharing agreements: A network approach. *Transportation Research Part E: Logistics and Transportation Review*, *70*, 17–33.

Scheers, J. (2001). Attracting investors to European regional airports. *What are the Prerequisites? International Airport Review*, *5*(4), 55–63.

Starkie, D. (2008). *The airport industry in a competitive environment: A United Kingdom perspective*. Joint Transport Research Centre, International Transport Forum, OECD.

Starkie, D. (2012). European airports and airlines: Evolving relationships and the regulatory implications. *Journal of Air Transport Management*, *21*, 40–49.

TRB (Transportation Research Board). (2007). *Innovative finance and alternative sources of revenue for airports*. Airport Cooperative Research Program Synthesis 1.

Tretheway, M., & Kincaid, I. (2010). Competition between airports: Occurrence and strategy. In P. Forsyth, D. Gillen, J. Müller, & H. M. Niemeier (Eds.), *Airport competition* (pp. 119–136). Farnham, Surrey: Ashgate.

US General Accounting Office. (1996). Airport privatization: Issues related to the sale or lease of U.S. Commercial airports. Chapter Report, 11/07/96, GAO/RCED-97-3.

Xiao, Y., Fu, X., Oum, T. H., & Yan, J. (2017). Airport capacity investments with real options. *Transportation Research – Part B*, *100*, 93–114.

Xiao, Y., Fu, X., & Zhang, A. (2013). Demand uncertainty and airport capacity choice. *Transportation Research – Part B*, *57*, 91–104.

Xiao, Y., Fu, X., & Zhang, A. (2016). Airport investment with vertical arrangements. *Transportation Research – Part A*, *92*, 298–309.

Yang, H., & Fu, X. (2015). A comparison of price-cap and light-handed airport regulation with demand uncertainty. *Transportation Research – Part B*, *73*, 122–132.

Yang, H., Zhang, A., & Fu, X. (2015). Determinants of airport-airline vertical arrangements: Analytical results and empirical evidence. *Journal of Transport Economics and Policy*, *49*(3), 438–453.

Yip, T. L., Liu, J., Fu, X., & Feng, J. (2014). Modeling the effects of competition on seaport terminal awarding. *Transport Policy*, *35*, 341–349.

Zhang, A. (2012). Airport improvement fees, benefit spillovers, and land value capture mechanisms. In G. K. Ingram & Y.-H. Hong (Eds.), *Value capture and land policies* (pp. 323–348). Cambridge, MA: Lincoln Institute of Land Policies.

Zhang, A., & Czerny, A. I. (2012). Airports and airlines economics and policy: An interpretive review of recent research. *Economics of Transportation*, *1*, 15–34.

Zhang, A., Fu, X., & Yang, H. (2010). Revenue sharing with multiple airlines and airports. *Transportation Research – Part B*, *44*(8-9), 944–959.

Zhang, A., & Zhang, Y. (2003). Airport charges and capacity expansion: Effects of concessions and privatization. *Journal of Urban Economics*, *53*(1), 54–75.

Zhang, A., & Zhang, Y. (2006a). Airport capacity and congestion when carriers have market power. *Journal of Urban Economics*, *60*(2), 229–247.

Zhang, A., & Zhang, Y. (2006b). Rivalry between strategic alliances. *International Journal of Industrial Organization*, *24*, 287–301.

Zhang, A., & Zhang, Y. (2010). Airport capacity and congestion pricing with both aeronautical and commercial operations. *Transportation Research Part B*, *44*(3), 404–413.

CHAPTER 6

AIRPORT AND AIRLINE RELATIONSHIP OF MULTIPLE FUNCTIONAL STRUCTURES

Katsuya Hihara

ABSTRACT

The relationship between airports and airlines is very interesting from an economics perspective, and analysis of this relationship is wide open for new research endeavors. For instance, airport and airline interactions can be viewed as a zero-sum game of deciding, say, airport landing charges, while at the same time both entities have an incentive making a joint effort to enhance their ability to generate passenger demand and to contribute to growing regional economies. Within this theoretical framework, their relationship consists of not only a binary choice of conflict or cooperation, but also suggests the possibility of complex mixtures of conflict and cooperation. While understanding the interdependence of airports and airlines is an important issue in transportation economics, research examining the complexity of airport and airline relationships is relatively new to the field. This chapter contributes to this research area, in part, by introducing one very interesting example of an airport and airline relationship that considers an element of conflict and cooperation. Specifically, this chapter examines the economic consequences of a risk sharing contract. Analysis of the risk sharing contract recognizes the relevance of microeconomic theories, such as contract theory and principal–agent theory and reveals how these concepts can be applied to traditional transport economics. Predictions of risk sharing between airlines and airports using these theories are derived using numerical examples.

The Economics of Airport Operations
Advances in Airline Economics, Volume 6, 123–152

ISSN: 2212-1609/doi:10.1108/S2212-160920170000006006

Findings reveal that the risk-sharing agreement based on the Noto Airport Load Factor Guarantee Mechanism (LFGM) contract enables the airport side and the airline side not only to share the monetary consequences of demand fluctuation, but also to secure air flights from a local airport to Tokyo, to jointly enhance their various demand-inducing efforts, and to increase their utilities in order to meet the common target they set in the contract. With the LFGM contract, both sides have consistently maintained the air transport network in a relatively low demand area for more than 10 years without significant outside financial assistance. The findings from this chapter also contribute to better understanding the complex relationships among aviation entities, to the recognition of importance and potential to design properly the airport and airline contract, and to the advancement of economic and public policy analysis of this sector.

Keywords: Airport–airline vertical relationship; risk sharing contract; Load Factor Guarantee Mechanism; contract theory; incomplete contract; principal–agent theory

JEL classifications: C70; D81; D86; L93

INTRODUCTION – AIRPORT AND AIRLINE VERTICAL RELATIONSHIP

Background – Complex and Risky Business

The relationship between airports and airlines is on one hand, conflicting, like a zero-sum game, in the issue for deciding landing charges or gate payment. On the other hand, their relationship is very much interdependent, and sometimes airlines and airports can be seen as forming joint venture type business relationship, in a sense that airport and airline are jointly providing air travel-related services to the passengers of the airline using the airport to whatever the destinations. So, the relationship consists of multi-functional strings of interactions, and thus it is very complex.

Adding to this complexity is the volatile nature of the aviation business itself, as historically major airlines merged to expand their network as an approach for contending with market uncertainty. And still many of these companies faced bankruptcy and in some cases, foreclosure.[1] The penalty associated with the inability to compete in a relatively volatile business environment was exacerbated with the policy move toward liberalization of airline services beginning in the late 1970s.[2] In this more globally competitive business environment, airlines tend to be more cautious about new investments especially regarding network expansions using airport services in low demand–low population density destinations.

Risk associated with the airline–airport relationship is also apparent for airports. For instance, the airport business is susceptible to cyclical variations in passenger demand and local airports have the incentive to secure gates to airline companies to reduce profit losses associated with cyclical downturns. Airports, though, make construction investments tailored to the specific aircraft size/type of specific airlines. The gate/passenger steps tailored for the biggest A380 is the typical example of such aircraft-specific ground investment.

Since many of such investments made by airports or airlines are unique to specific airports/airlines/routes, the facilities and the monetary cost associated with these investments are difficult to recover and reuse, once these investments are executed. Micro-economics define such investments as "relationship-specific." They are investments that are unique to their particular businesses and are meaningful only in such specific relationship. This chapter examines the economic consequences associated with airline–airport relationships within an incomplete contract theory framework in part because of this theory's heavy dependence on the concept of relationship-specific investment. Findings from using this theoretical approach on the airline–airport relationship provide new insights on the economics of aviation and airport relationship.

Risk Sharing Across Industries

It makes sense that in highly risky and interdependent businesses companies in a vertical relationship negotiate contractual arrangements to share risk among themselves. We can find many examples of risk sharing contracts across many industry sectors including aviation and transport sectors. Negotiating over fuel surcharges is a good example. Oil prices fluctuated widely in the last 10 years or so, starting from the US asset bubble period, followed by collapsing demand after the financial market crash in 2008, and continuing with the current new energy market era characterized by the shale oil revolution with relatively suppressed oil prices. So, in this uncertain business environment, airlines, maritime shipping companies, trucking companies, and even electric power companies make contractual arrangements to hedge some of fuel price fluctuation risk with passengers, shippers, cargo owners, and electricity-end users. The following presents a brief overview of the ubiquitous activity of risk sharing across industries.

In manufacturing, an example of risk sharing can be found in the production of aviation engines and commercial aircraft manufacturing. Companies in this business sector negotiate several risk sharing contracts between assembling/integrating companies and parts/components-supplying companies as risk sharing partiers. The risk of investing in the manufacturing new aircraft engines or new aircrafts is so large that companies jointly shoulder huge development costs associated with the occurrence of project failure. In retail, industries have introduced vendor buy-back contracts to transfer large merchandise left-over risk in case of low demand to vendors/suppliers. Also, real estate development industries invented co-sharing cost/profit with retail store owners to share the risk of uncertain consumer demand.

Risk sharing is not exclusive to the private sector as public–private partnership (PPP) in the development of infrastructure projects (and Private Finance Initiatives in the UK and other countries in road, ports, railways, and utility projects) designs proper risk sharing mechanisms in contractual arrangements in order to allocate the numerous project risks among suppliers, partners, stakeholders, and public sectors. Examples of project risks are, land-procurement risk, project cost over-run risk, project period-prolongation risk, environmental damage risk, litigation risk, project liquidity risk, interest risk, to mention just a few.

The risk-sharing arrangement, though, for public–private partnerships differs from the examples reported for manufacturing, and retail in that the former tend to design complicated, multi-parties relationships and the latter partnerships tend to form a vertical relationship (such as supplier and purchaser). Risk sharing arrangements among airline companies and airports also depict a vertical association. Traditionally, airports are greatly affected by the business decision of airline companies that can be viewed as transport service decisions by airport customers.[3] Airline companies' decision to use hub and spoke network formation rather than point-to-point, and decisions on flight frequencies along routes are examples of airline business choices that influence passenger use of airports. Hence, airport decision on the construction of gates has been influenced by uncertainty of airline demand for slots. Airports and airlines have been sharing demand fluctuation risk with each other with respect to gate expansion investment projects in such a way that airports, i.e., investors, receive some funding from airlines, and thus airline companies become risk sharing partners with airports. Also, airline companies, especially low cost carriers (LCCs), face uncertainty associated with airport-related costs. Passing on such costs to airlines from LCC serving airports can introduce a competitive disadvantage to LCCs. So, many local airports in EU countries negotiate contracts to attract LCCs to their airports by cutting landing charges and offering monetary incentives based on their performances during the first several years.

In sum, while the relationship between airports and airlines has been examined in past research there is a dearth of research examining risk sharing among these two entities. This chapter contributes to our understanding the vertical relationship of airlines and airports by using micro-economic analysis to examine risk-sharing among companies in these two industries. Making such an analysis is significant in part because incorporating the framework to examine risk sharing among airlines and airport can reveal how to design a contract that enhances effort to increase the demand for routes of an airport, and to reduce potential utility loss among airports and airlines by introducing proper risk sharing contractual agreements. In the following section, an actual risk sharing contract will be examined. This contract pertains to the Noto airport in Japan and its agreement with the airline company it serves. The contract is entitled the Load Factor Guarantee Mechanism (LFGM) contract. Following that section, this chapter numerically gauges the balance of risk sharing between the two parties and provides an analytical framework to assess risk sharing balance. In the "Incomplete Contract Framework Analysis" section, we introduce Contract Theory and Principal–Agent Theory to the analyses and show how the proper contractual design can enhance efforts to increase the demand of airports and restore utility losses of airport and airline companies. In the "Summary and Concluding Remarks" section, risk sharing contract's contribution to maintaining air transport network and public policy implications are discussed.

AIRPORT AND AIRLINE RISK SHARING CONTRACT

Risk Sharing Contract between Airport and Airline

Airports are an indispensable component of the infrastructure in the air transportation network system. Overall there reportedly exist more than 45,000 civil aviation airports worldwide. Of these 45,000 there are about 59 multiple airports system, like that of La Guardia, JFK, and Newark in New York metropolitan area. Previous research indicates that these airport systems are important sources of local economic growth.[4] However, as discussed in the "Introduction – Airport and Airline Vertical Relationship" section, the linkage between economic growth and profitability of aviation has seemingly weakened in the face of stepped-up competition. Under these more competitive circumstances, many airports are faced with revenue and profit level fluctuations. Some airports and airlines are forming vertical contractual relationships to share their revenue fluctuation risk of the routes to/from airports, and to stabilize their financial conditions so that air transport services by those routes could be maintained. Examples of these cases are reported in Barbot (2009), Fukuyama, Kagawa, and Ikeda (2009), and Zhang, Fu, and Yang (2010).

In Japan, about 100 civil aviation airports exist nationwide, including Noto airport. This airport is pertinent to our analysis because the Noto Airport LFGM contract provides an interesting example for the risk sharing contract between airport and airline and is discussed in detail in the "Noto Airport Load Factor Guarantee Mechanism (LFGM)" section (Fig. 1).

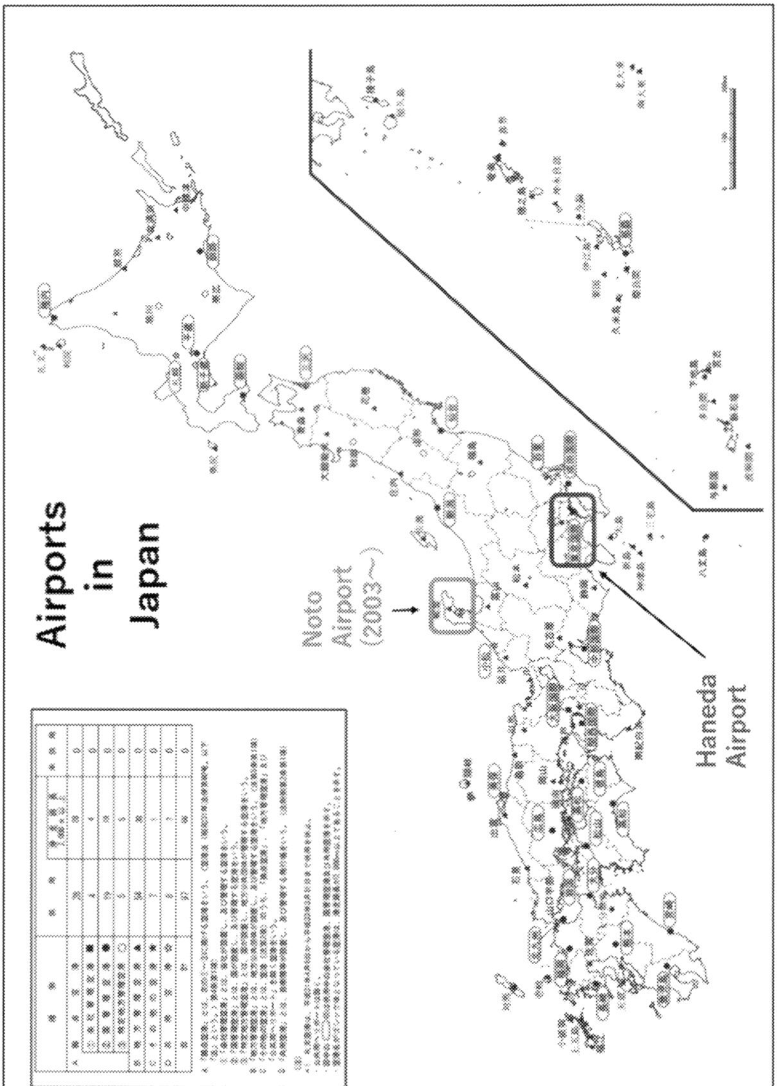

Fig. 1. Aviation airports in Japan (Noto and Tokyo (Haneda)).

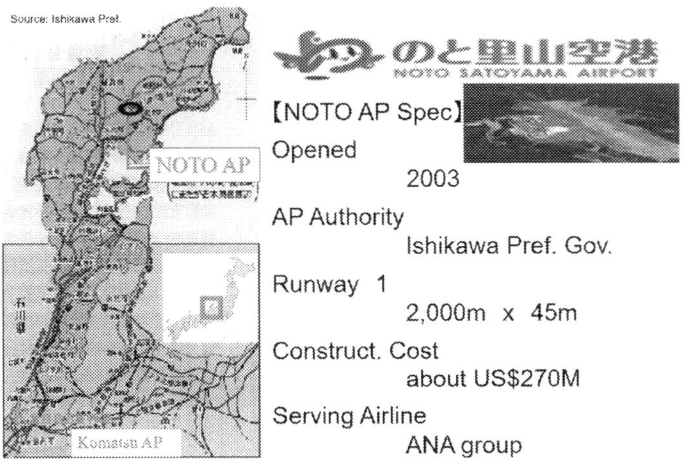

Fig. 2. Noto airport.

Information on the Noto Airport

Noto airport is located in the Noto peninsula of Ishikawa prefecture in the mid-northern part of the main land of Japan. The population of Ishikawa prefecture, where Noto airport is located as indicated in Fig. 2, with about 1.16 million inhabitants. The population of the surrounding municipalities is about 0.1 million, which is very small as compared with Tokyo metropolitan area of about 30 million inhabitants. The entire area of Noto peninsula is one of the most rural areas of Ishikawa Prefecture with residents engaging mainly in agriculture and fishery.

The passenger access to Noto had been historically provided by either railroad or road only. The travel time between Tokyo and Noto area was more than 7 hours, which meant it was almost inaccessible for most of the people except for local excursions or limited business/leisure trips. Given this traveler's surface transportation shortcomings, inhabitants in the surrounding area of Noto had long yearned for a local airport that would help alleviate their local transport challenges. As part of the process to secure a local airport, local leaders engaged in a long and enduring effort to tap into national funding for the purpose of constructing it. After a long struggle, finally in 2003, the new airport, Noto airport, was opened.

Noto airport is owned and controlled by the Ishikawa prefecture government, which is Noto area's local government. It has one runway of 2,000 m × 45 m. Its construction cost is about 270 m US$ at that time. The airport was funded roughly half by national government and half by the local government and is served by the All Nippon Airways (ANA) group with two flights a day between Noto and Tokyo (Haneda).[5]

Noto Airport Load Factor Guarantee Mechanism (LFGM)

The relationship between Noto airport and the ANA is heavily shaped by the Noto Airport LFGM, which is a contract between the local airport (Noto airport) and the airline using its services (ANA). This contract covers the revenue fluctuation risk for both airports and airlines for the period of 1 year (specifically from July 7th the current year to July 6th the next year) stipulated in each year's LFGM contract. In contract-closing negotiations each year, both parties set a target load factor before the start of a year in each year's LFGM contract. They also set aircraft type (mostly A320) for the year period of the contract and the payment unit per seat in the payment structure. Information on aircraft type and number of passengers is used to compute the actual load factor of the Noto and Haneda route. The difference between the target load factor outlined in the Noto-ANA LFGM contract and the actual load factor is calculated and, based on the difference, the payment is made according to the payment schedule specification stipulated in the LFGM contract.

The specification of the LFGM is illustrated in the diagram presented in Fig. 3. If the actual load factor (LF) is less than the target load factor as in the light colored range above the zero-payment line in Fig. 3, airport (AP) makes a payment according to a linear payment structure up to a ceiling to airline (AL). If, on the other hand, the actual load factor is more than the target load factor as in the dark colored range below the zero-payment line in Fig. 3, then airline (AL) makes a payment to airport (AP) in a linear payment structure up to limit (the floor in the diagram of Fig. 3). In the actual Noto airport case, the contractual structures evolved several times to a final stable structure. During the starting 3 years, both parties changed their contracts at every year's period end. Finally, they agreed to the fourth year's contract contents and have kept that agreement structure for the duration.

The LFGM contract of Noto airport was first signed in 2003 between Noto airport and the ANA group. The objective route of the contract is the route

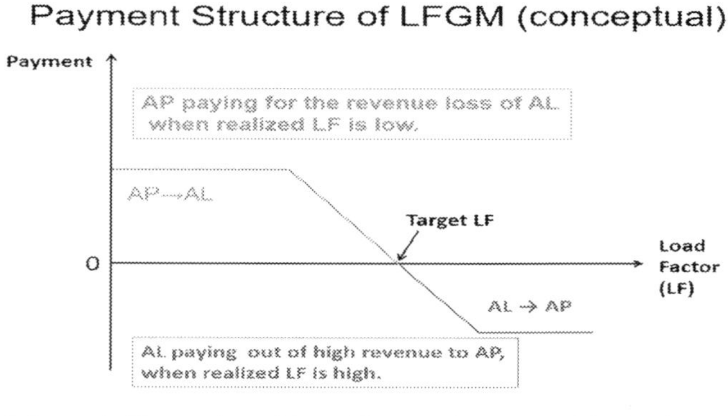

Fig. 3. Schematic illustration of Load Factor Guarantee Mechanism (LFGM).

between Noto airport and Haneda airport (the biggest domestic hub airport in Japan). The ANA group flies two flights a day between Noto and Haneda with the initial flight originating from Haneda airport every day. In the usual case for a local government to assist a start-up airline at a local airport, many contracts or programs cover usually for the revenue downside risk only for the airline. Upside opportunity is not shared and gains from the upside are kept by the airline. However, the ANA group is an established airline company, and for their airline–airport agreement the Noto airport LFGM stipulates that the airport and airline share both the downside risk and upside opportunity. In a sense, the LFGM contract is just like a joint venture between airport and airline, as often seen in the other project fields such as construction or property developments. So, the mechanism is not just a local government's aid to airline, but airport and airline truly share the revenue fluctuation risk, both upside and downside in a joint venture in air transport services flying to/from the airport.

In addition to sharing risk, the Noto LFGM contract has multiple functions for the negotiating parties. Also, the contract works as an incentive device for both parties. With the clear manifestation of load factor before the start of a year, airport and airline share a common goal, a target load factor set by the contract for the year. They make efforts trying to meet the target load factor, to receive the payment, and to avoid the situation of ending up in paying money to the other party. So, both parties jointly make efforts to meet the common target load factor. The contract also serves as a commitment manifestation by the airline to serve the airport for at least the year period the contract covers. This means a great deal to local airport authorities since they usually get threatened by airlines serving there to reduce the frequencies or to totally stop the entire service at any time. However, by signing a contract, the airline makes commitment based on the legal document to serve the airport during the period covered by the contract, hence giving some assurances of airline service activity to local airport authority. Such assurances may create an incentive for the local airport authority/government to make more aggressive efforts to entice more local people or tourists to use the airline serving the airport, by offering subsidizing some part of air tickets to local residents or providing extra gifts of the local agricultural or fishery products or distributing some campaign coupons for local hot spring loggings.

The LFGM contracts have several payment schedule variations as we mentioned above. In fact, the contracts evolved from the renegotiations between airport and airline before the start of the next contractual year for the first 4 years. In Fig. 4, all the variations of the payment schedules are shown. Also, in Table 1 we have the comparison of the target load factors, the actual load factors and the payment made based on the contracts for the starting 4 years. In the first year of Noto airport case, the airport assumed bigger risk than the airline since the airport agreed to the relatively high target load factor (70%) and accepted steeper payment schedule than that for the receiving schedule. The paying amount grew faster than receiving amount as load factor changes

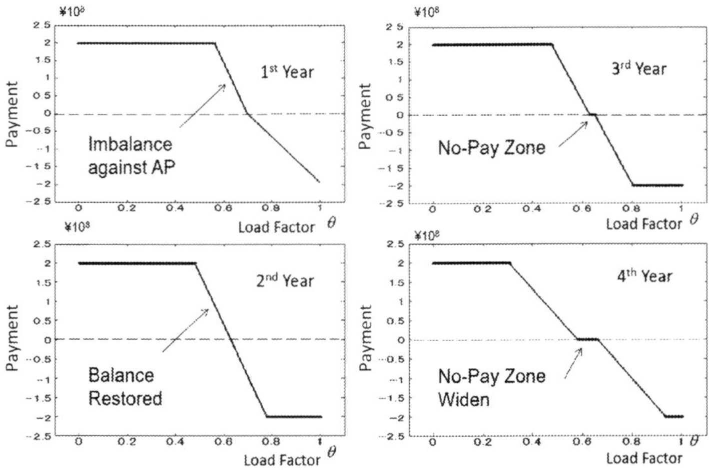

Fig. 4. Payment schedules of Noto Airport Load Factor Guarantee Mechanism (LFGM).

Table 1. Actual Results for Noto Airport Load Factor Guarantee Mechanism (LFGM).

Year	Target LF (%)	Estimated LF (%)	Realized LF (%)	Payment AL → AP (¥10^8)
1	70	65.0	79.5	0.97
2	63	63.7	64.6	0.15
3	64	63.5	66.5	0.20
4	62	65.1	65.1	0

for the airport. In the second year, payment and receiving schedules became aligned and both parties were sharing the same slope for payment as well as receipt. Receiving amount by airport had acquired the limit just like the limit of payment from airport. In the third year, they agreed to set up a no-payment zone around the target load factor so that the possibility of each year's actual payment would become relatively small. By the fourth year, the no-payment zone around the target load factor was widened and the common slope of payment/receiving schedule became more flat. By this renegotiation, the prospect that the actual payment would take place became highly unlikely. Even if the payment was made, the actual amount would become very modest.

The contents of Table 1, show the actual results of the Noto LFGM contract. These findings show the realizations of the actual load factors and the actual payment made by the parties in more detail. Target load factor ("Target LF") in the table is the target load factor indicated in each year's LFGM contract. "Realized LF" is the actual load factor for the Noto–Haneda route for each year. "Payment AL → AP" is the actual payment from the airline to the airport based on the payment schedule of the contract. "Estimated LF" is the predicted mean values of load factor random variable modeled and calculated by the estimation model. The estimation model will be explained in more detail in the "Balance of Airport and Airline Risk Sharing" section. (As we can see in the table, the first year's target load factor (70%) is remarkably higher than the same year's estimated load factor (65%) predicted by the model. This can be interpreted as the situation that the airport side took a significant risk in the opening year to gain the commitment of the airline side to serve the airport.) Nonetheless, findings in Table 1 show that actual load factors are exceeding target levels for each observation year.

These load factor results are very much surprising since prior to the opening of Noto airport, most observers thought that airport could not attract many passengers and the LFGM contract would be one-sidedly skewed against the airport only for the airport to pay a lot of money for the airline's loss. This expectation was based on the observation that the Noto airport was in such a remote place with very few inhabitants, that an economic growth prospect for the area was very low and hence air transport service demand would be a modest one around the area. So, many observers expected the airport had to take more risk. The first-year contract's contents of high target load factor and steep payment schedule from airport to airline were all in line with these general assessments.

In an effort to achieve a high target load factor outlined in the LFGM contract, the Noto airport/Ishikawa prefectural government made various promotion efforts. The publicly known examples, including those from the second year of the contract, are the follows:

- introducing monetary incentive to local residents who purchase the airline's flight ticket from the airport (30 US$ a ticket or so, depending on the conditions),
- cutting landing charges by 2/3,
- improving the secondary transport (bus and taxi) service to/from the airport by coordinating their frequencies and stoppings,
- making parking free of charges for Noto–Haneda flight passengers,
- registering the surrounding mountainous areas for a world agricultural heritage, which serves as an attraction point for air travel passengers,
- negotiating with an academic school to open a new flight engineering school at the airport,
- relocating a prefectural government's administrative branch office to the terminal building,
- running many series of magazine/press campaigns in the Tokyo area,
- setting up a famous comedian's demo-flight just before the opening.

The total budget of such efforts by the airport for the first year alone exceeded 1 million US$.

For their part, ANA group also instituted business practices to enhance airline performance as dictated by the LFGM, such as,

- setting up special discount price package to accommodate Noto airport passengers,
- improving connection flights at Haneda airport for many destinations from Noto through Haneda hub airport,
- introducing a wide area excursion discount travel package for combining Noto–Haneda flight route and local hot spring loggings.

With these aggressive efforts, both parties achieved staggering performance results. The first year's actual load factor was 79.5%, which was well above the target load factor of 70%. 70% was thought to be a substantial stretch since the average load factor for the previous year, 2002, was only 64.8% and the average load factor for the last 50 years' period is about 66.8%. In addition, this was calculated by including the trunk routes connecting the major airports, such as Haneda, Osaka (Itami), Fukuoka, and Sapporo (Chitose). *A priori*, given that the that the city of Noto area is a very remote locality with a very small population, 70% target load factor for the Noto–Haneda route in the opening year, 2003, predictions suggested that such a strong performance was almost impossible. It should also be noted that the actual load factor of 79.5% in the first year of the contract was a real surprise to all even when we take account of the possibility that the first year's performance could be exceptionally high. This strong performance made it possible for the Noto airport to receive about 970 million yen (roughly about a million dollars) in accordance with the Noto LFGM contract.

In the second year, both parties adjusted the contracts in reaction to the surprisingly strong demand. They agreed to introduce a larger aircraft (B737 → A320) and lower target load factor (70% → 63%). Even with this revision, Noto airport still received some money from the contract, but the amount reduced to a modest one of about 15 million yen (roughly about 0.15 million dollars). By the third year, both parties introduced no-payment zone around the new target load factor (±1% around 64%). Both made enough efforts to reach the target load factor of the contract. With the introduction of no-payment zone, the actual payment based on the contract remained small amount, about 20 million yen (roughly about 0.2 million dollars).

In the fourth year, Noto airport and the ANA enlarged the no-payment zone to ±2% around the target load factor, which was also adjusted to 62% from 64%. During the renegotiation process of the three revisions of the contract, both airport and airline closely monitored the actual load factor, payment schedule slope, no-payment zone, and both parties' effort known to them to attract more passengers to the flight route. With these monitoring and preparation works, they narrowed down the contents of Noto airport LFGM contract to the stable form of the fourth year with very low possibility of actual payment. This is the final form of the contract and its contents have not changed until now.

Noto airport and the ANA group have continued to keep the Noto airport LFGM in the contract every year from the beginning of 2003. The contents of Table 2 show the results of the last 12 years of the Noto airport LFGM contract from 2003 to 2015. The findings in this table show both parties consistently achieved the target load factor, except for the year 2011. That was the year of the great east Japan earthquake that devastated the eastern part of Japan with the famous Fukushima nuclear power plant meltdown accidents to the detriment of the Japanese economy. In 2011, they shared the view that the year was exceptional, and that the year's economic activity downturn had no direct connection with their own efforts. So, they agreed that the year's contract should be suspended due to force majeure and that no payment would be made. This kind of flexible interpretation would be thought as a sign of one of the interesting relationships between airport and airline. They formed a kind of a joint venture type project by agreeing to the contract. Both might share the view that the long-term mutual trust and commitment to continue the joint venture by the contract should be preserved over short-sighted behaviors of seeking the disaster-led windfall profit.

With the introduction of the no-payment zone, the fine-tuning of target load factors, and continuous promotional efforts to bring more passengers to the flight route, Noto airport and the ANA group have consistently achieved target load factors and no actual payment was made since the third-year result payment. The no-payment results might also contribute to the stability of the contractual relationship because consistent no-payment results made the monetary cost of maintaining the contractual relationship cheaper than otherwise while both enjoyed the increased demand of the flight route.

BALANCE OF AIRPORT AND AIRLINE RISK SHARING

Framework of Gauging Risk Sharing Balance

Evidence presented in this chapter thus far has revealed significant performance gains associated with the risk-sharing agreement between Noto airport and the ANA group. Despite these impressive gains, there is still the issue of which negotiating entity shoulder the burden of risk based on the terms of the negotiation agreements. Indeed, possible future economic downturns may create a situation such that performance falters. Knowing the balance of risk-sharing then becomes an important issue. In this section, a numerical model is introduced to estimate the balance between the airport and the airline in the LFGM contract.[6] Initially, we examine route level load factor time-series data in Japanese domestic airline market for more than 50 years and apply time series analysis to provide a predictive model of load factor trends. Below is the historical

Table 2. Noto Airport Long-term Results Summary.

Contract Period	1	2	3	4	5	6	7	8	9	10	11	12
Calendar Period	2003.7– 2004.7	2004.7– 2005.7	2005.7– 2006.7	2006.7– 2007.7	2007.7– 2008.7	2008.7– 2009.7	2009.7– 2010.7	2010.7– 2011.7	2011.7– 2012.7	2012.7– 2012.7	2013.7– 2014.7	2014.7– 2015.7
Target Load Factor (%)	70.0	63.0	64.0	62.0	62.0	62.0	62.0	62.0	62.0	62.0	62.0	62.0
Actual Load Factor (%)	79.5	64.6	66.5	65.1	65.4	62.3	62.3	55.8[a]	62.0	63.2	62.7	63.6
Payment AL → AP (¥10^8)	0.97	0.15	0.2	0	0	0	0	0[a]	0	0	0	0

[a]In March 2011, the great earthquake hit the eastern part of Japan. It had a huge negative impact on the travel demand of entire Japan. Both parties agreed that in 2011, the missing the target LF is because of force majeure and that no payment was made from AP to AL.

Fig. 5. Load factor data in Japan (1951–2014).

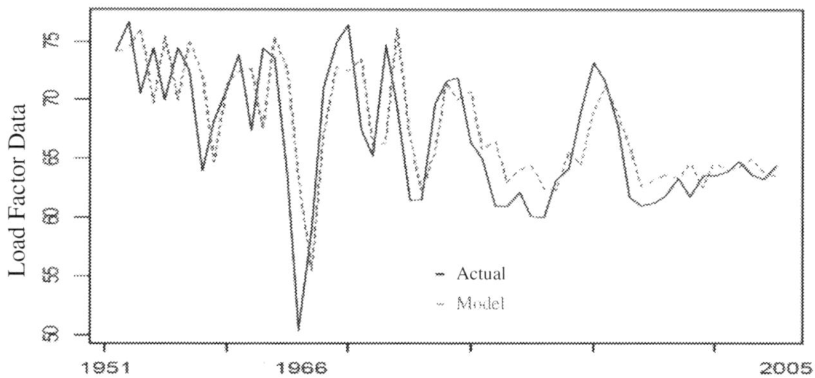

Fig. 6. Actual load factor data and model estimates in Japan (1951–2005).

average load factor data in Japanese domestic flight routes between 1951 and 2014. The trend shows noticeable load factor fluctuations in the mid-1960s to the early 1990 and relative stability thereafter (Fig. 5).

Model Formulation for Risk Sharing Balance

Load factor information in Fig. 6 is used to conduct time-series analysis of the historical average load factor data up until 2005, which was starting years' period of Noto Airport LFGM contract. From several standard tests, we identified the structure of Auto Regressive Integrated Moving Average (ARIMA) Model and specified ARIMA (1,1,4) structure in the historical data.

The red dotted line is the estimated value by the ARIMA (1,1,4) model and black line is the actual historical data in Fig. 6. The findings presented in Fig. 6

show a reasonably close approximation of the actual load factor for the Japanese domestic air transport market.

In order to construct a predictive model to gauge the risk sharing balance of the Noto LFGM contract, we introduce a numerical framework with probability settings, in which the load factor value can be thought of as a random variable. By the property of ARIMA modeling, the following year's value can be predicted with normal distribution. With the historical time-series analysis, we are already able to construct the following year's normal distribution of load factor. The mean values of the predicted normal distributions for the starting 4 years of Noto LFGM contract are calculated and presented in the "Estimated LF" column of Table 1. But in order to gauge the risk balance of the actual contract, we must combine the actual contractual payment schedules and the load factor normal distribution into a numerical framework. In the "Gauging the Balance" section, we explain how actual contractual payment schedules and the load factor normal distribution can be combined into a predictive numerical model to assess the risk balance of the actual risk sharing contract.

Gauging the Balance

As a property of the ARIMA model, the succeeding year's load factor value can be predicted with a normal distribution as we stated above. Based on this theoretical property, we construct the actual prediction values for the following year load factor with the normal distribution. Using the payoff schedules of the contracts and the normal distributions of the predicted load factor derived from estimating the ARIMA model, we calculate the payoff probability distributions for airports paying airlines, and the expected payoffs to the airport based on the agreed contract.

To illustrate how to make this calculation of the expected payoff of the piece-wise linear payoff schedule contracts with load factor related clauses indicated in Fig. 4. We use a similar piece-wise linear payment schedule of a hypothetical contract as shown in Fig. 7.

Here we can consider load factor as a random valuable. The random variable of load factor follows the normal distribution $N(\mu, \sigma^2)$ from the ARIMA model as we stated. We can calculate one party's expected payoff E_{payoff} from

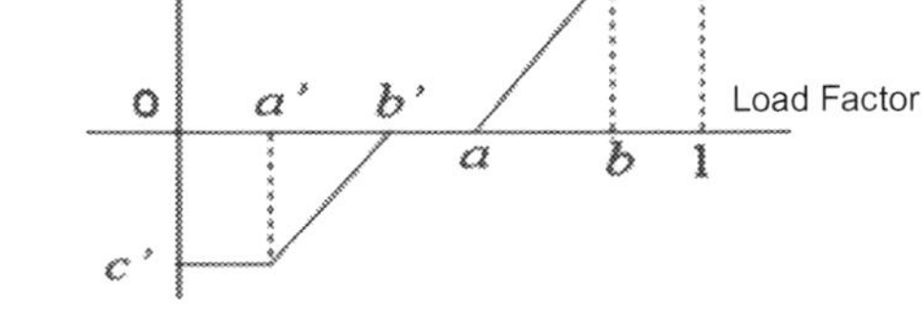

Fig. 7. Payoff schedule illustration of a model contract.

a specific contract set by *a*, *b*, *c*, *a*', *b*', and *c*', where the variables *a*, *b*, *a*', and *b*' are specific values stipulated by the model contract of load factors with normal distribution, $N(\mu, \sigma^2)$, and the values *c* and *c*', respectively, denote the upper and lower range of the payoff boundaries stipulated by the model contract when the load factor lies within [*b*, 1] and [0, *a*'].

Then the expected payoff E_{payoff} from the contract for a party can be calculated as follows.

$$E_{payoff} = G(a, b, 0, c, \mu, \sigma) + G(a', b', c', 0, \mu, \sigma) + H(c, b, 1, \mu, \sigma) + H(c', 0, a', \mu, \sigma) \tag{1}$$

In (1), $G(a, b, 0, c, \mu, \sigma)$ and $H(c, b, 1, \mu, \sigma)$ can be derived as follows.

$$G(a, b, 0, c, \mu, \sigma) = \left(\frac{c}{b-a}\mu - \frac{ac}{b-a}\right)[\Phi_{\mu,\sigma^2}(b) - \Phi_{\mu,\sigma^2}(a)] - \frac{c}{b-a}\sigma^2[\phi_{\mu,\sigma^2}(b) - \phi_{\mu,\sigma^2}(a)] \tag{2}$$

$$H(c, b, 1, \mu, \sigma) = c[\Phi_{\mu,\sigma^2}(1) - \Phi_{\mu,\sigma^2}(b)] \tag{3}$$

The terms $\phi(\mu, \sigma^2)$ and $\Phi(\mu, \sigma^2)$ denote the normal distribution function and the cumulative normal distribution function respectively with mean μ and standard deviation σ. The function $H(c, b, 1, \mu, \sigma)$ is an expected payoff of the contract illustrated by Fig. 7, if a load factor, which follows $\phi(\mu, \sigma^2)$, is within the range [*b*, 1]. Also, we can think of the function $G(a, b, 0, c, \mu, \sigma)$ as an expected payoff of the contract illustrated in Fig. 7, if the load factor lies within the range [*a*, *b*]. The details of this derivation can be provided upon request.

In addition, the payoff distribution $D_{\text{payoff }(y)}$ can be calculated using the piece-wise linear payoff contract schedule above as the function of the payoff amount *y* as follows. Again, we skip the detailed derivation, which can be provided upon request.

$$D_{payoff}(y) = \begin{cases} 0 & y < c' \\ \Phi(a') - \Phi(0) & y = c' \\ \phi\left(\dfrac{y - \beta_2}{\alpha_2}\right) & c' < y < 0 \\ \Phi(a) - \Phi(b') & y = 0 \\ \phi\left(\dfrac{y - \beta_1}{\alpha_1}\right) & 0 < y < c \\ \Phi(1) - \Phi(b) & y = c \\ 0 & y > c \end{cases} \tag{4}$$

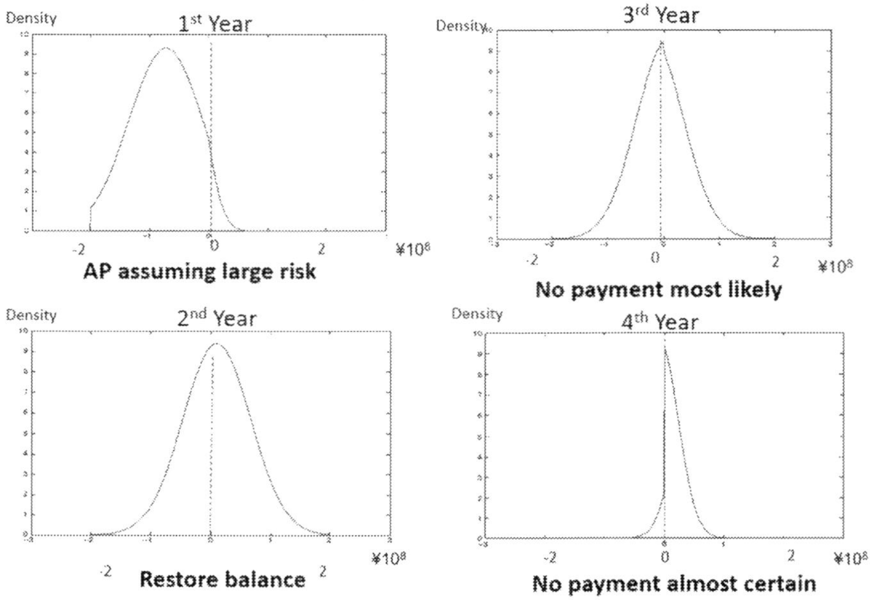

Fig. 8. Estimated airport's payoff probability distributions for the starting 4 years of Noto LFGM contracts. *Source:* Hihana (2008).

Based on Eq. (4), we can draw graphs of payoff distribution $D_{\text{payoff }(y)}$ for Noto airport side of Noto airport LFGM contract from year 1 to year 4. The four graphs of Fig. 8 are those payoff probability distributions for Noto airport by the Noto LFGM contract.

Findings presented in the first graph show the first year's payment probability distribution for Noto airport is skewed to the left. This means the most likely result of the first-year contract is for the airport to pay a little short of about a million US$. This is exactly the expectation of observers, and it suggests that Noto airport took significant risk to gain the commitment of ANA airline to serve the local small size airport. In contrast, both parties agreed to enlarge the capacity by substituting the previous aircraft (B737-500; 126 seats) for a bigger aircraft (A320; 166 seats) and lowered the target load factor from 70% to 63% in the second year. Because of this capacity increase, the payoff probability distribution gets more centered and the airport's risk taking became more balanced with the airline's risks. The introduction of the third year's no-payment zone resulted in the tighter distribution around the zero payment. The enlargement of no-payment zone made the distribution even tighter around zero in the fourth year. By the fourth year's contract, the probability distribution peaked at zero payment and depicts the tightest distribution around zero among the four distributions thus far. The actual contractual payoff of the fourth year was in fact zero. This is consistent with the prediction above.

As stated earlier, both parties have kept the fourth-year contract up until now. The target load factor (62%) of the fourth-year contract is reasonable when we consider the aircraft size and the basic demand for air transport services. The no-payment zone (±2%) around the target load factor is a quite effective provision for suppressing the actual payment possibility. So, one could say that the running cost of agreeing and keeping the Noto LFGM contract every year became drastically low by introducing and enlarging the no-payment zone around the target load factor.

During the starting 4-year contract period, both parties gathered information on the potential demand, tried several efforts to increase the passengers of the Noto–Tokyo (Haneda) route, and adjust their efforts to include more effective and enduring types of efforts. An example of such efforts is depicted by the organization of the local promotional league mainly of Noto area local cities with the help of Ishikawa prefectural government and 30 other local business entities. The league continues to pay promotional fee about 30$ a ticket for local residents who use the air flight between Noto and Tokyo (Haneda). In addition, this league and Ishikawa prefectural government engaged in new campaigns, such as setting up special events during every season of the year in the entire surrounding area, forming a sort of supporters' membership club of Tokyo area residents who have some form of connections with the Noto/Ishikawa area. They also negotiated with airlines, train companies, and travel companies to introduce special air-rail combination tickets for using Noto–Tokyo (Haneda) air route and newly opened Hokuriku Shinkansen (bullet train) between Ishikawa prefecture and Tokyo area. In Japan, Noto LFGM contract and local efforts to attract more demand are thought to be one of the most successful vertical relationships. In fact, the airport regulatory authority of Japan (MLIT) began to consider such vertical relationship, like Noto airport LFGM contract, in allocation of scarce slots at the congested Haneda airport in 2012.

INCOMPLETE CONTRACT FRAMEWORK ANALYSIS

Incomplete Contract Theory and its Application to Risk Sharing Contracts[7]

Contracts cannot account for all the possible contingencies in real world situations. Neither can be negotiated provisions cover all the possibilities in the covenants of each contract. In this sense, a contract is inevitably incomplete. Also, the investment by airports or airlines could be relationship-specific. What we identify as relationship-specific in this chapter means that investment of one party of a contract is highly specialized in that particular relationship.

The party virtually cannot stop the process of the investment or reuse the investment in the other relationship, once they make investment in the current relationship. It is considered that this possibility is very important in analyzing the incomplete contract. In the relation-specific investment case, each of the parties is bound with the other parties in the relationship. This type of investment relationship challenge is called a hold-up problem.

The following is an example of the hold-up problem in the context of the airline–airport relationship. If an airport would like to make some gate improvement or passenger/baggage system renovation in one location based on some contract about a particular aircraft or system with an airline, it would be difficult or even virtually impossible to dislocate the improved facility and to reuse it in other locations. So, the airport, which is in such specific relationship in the gate/system improvement contract, cannot freely change its investment. This can be seen as hold-up situation, since the airport is tied into with the specific airline/system, once they start the relation-specific investment of such contract.

In the case of Noto airport, the demand was estimated, by many experts, to be appreciably low level, namely about 31 million passengers.[8] So, airlines, which potentially considered serving Noto airport, were thought to exercise caution when committing to serving to Noto airport. In order to attract airlines, Noto airport, which Ishikawa prefectural government owns, decided to offer the LFGM contract to the airline for confirming the airline's commitment to serving the airport. This contract can be seen as incomplete contract and all the efforts based on the risk sharing contract can be seen as relationship-specific. This specificity can also be viewed as a strategic complementarity relationship. The condition for such a relationship is satisfied when increasing one party's marginal effort contributes to also increase the other party's marginal effort. The outcome from a complementarity relationship between an airline and an airport then is enhanced performance for both parties.

In sum, within this theoretical framework airports and airlines are in a sense forming a joint venture type project to serve the passengers using the airline's flights to and from the airport. Negotiating terms that promote risk sharing among these two parties have the ability to motive greater effort from airlines and airports to enhance their performance as well as the welfare of both parties. The 'Model' section illustrates how the incomplete contract affects effort and welfare level.

Model

This chapter uses the canonical Hart and Moore (1988) model of incomplete contract framework to illustrate the intricate relationship between airport and airline of the LFGM contract. In their model, both parties are risk neutral, and a simple one buyer – one seller specific relationship was analyzed. Here we modify their model by adding two more degrees of freedom to it. Technically, the airport is buying the airline's flight service from the airline in exchange for the risk sharing contractual payment arrangement, and the airport is also selling airport-related services for fees such as landing fee or gate payments to airline. The airline is also buying airport-related services from the airport and selling air flight service to the airport. In this sense, each party of the contract is buyer and seller at the same time. Thus, we need two more variables in addition to the simple one buyer – one seller model of Hart and Moore (1988).

Here, we just briefly describe the hold-up problem without contract case according to the Hart and Moore model. If no contract is agreed to beforehand, then the efforts are made only when such efforts are efficient. This is the case of no contract. So, naturally, no contractual payment is made. After the realization of θ, the uncertainty, i.e., load factor, both parties are assumed to play Nash Bargaining game, and they share the realized gain according to the Nash Bargaining solutions. Because some part of the gain made possible by the relationship is always bargained away from one to the other by the Nash Bargaining, both parties, who anticipate this, just decrease the level of effort that is less than the first best situation. This under-effort and inefficient situation is an example of the so-called hold-up problem. This no contract case process is depicted in Fig. 9.

If we introduce a risk sharing contract to the relationship, and both parties agree to the specific conditions of its contents, then payment according to the contract could be rewarding enough to overcome the hold-up problem and to attain the first best level of efforts. This contract case process is depicted in Fig. 10.

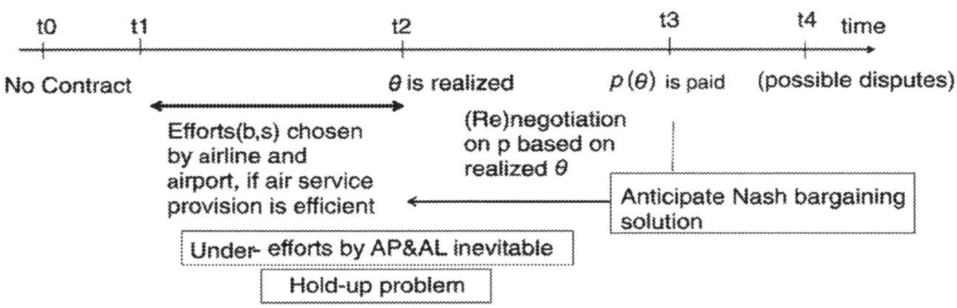

Fig. 9. Timeline for no contract case.

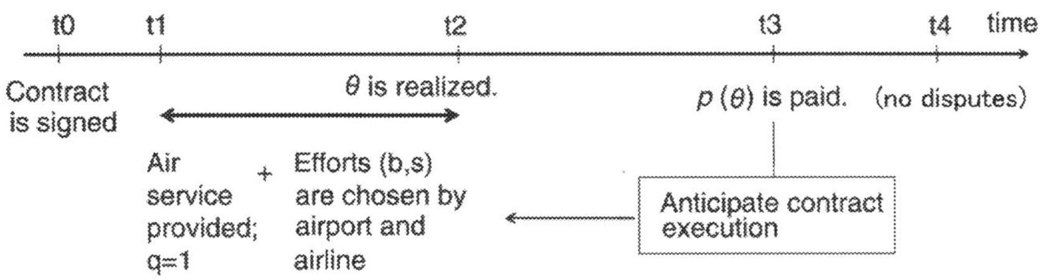

Fig. 10. Timeline for contract case.

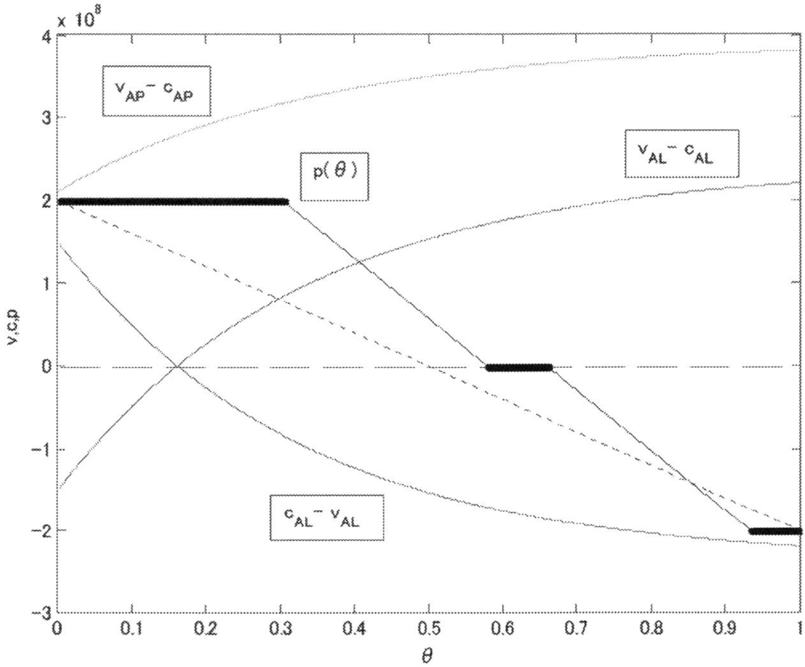

Fig. 11. Contract payment schedule satisfying Proposition 1.

What is the condition for such efficient risk sharing contract? The gist of the conditions and main argument are given in Proposition 1. Also, we provide such conditions graphically in Fig. 11. But here, we drop the detailed derivation and formal proof, which are provided in Hihara (2012).

Proposition 1 If the entire payment schedule $p(\theta)$ of the LFGM contract is within the range $\{p(\theta) : c_{AL} - v_{AL} \leq p(\theta) \leq v_{AP} - c_{AP}\}$, i.e., if $p(\theta)$ satisfies the following inequalities (5)

$$c_{AL} - v_{AL} \leq p(\theta) \leq v_{AP} - c_{AP} \tag{5}$$

which are constructed by airport's net position $v_{AP} - c_{AP}$ and the minus of the airline's net position $c_{AL} - v_{AL}$for all the possible values of $\theta(\theta \in [0, 1])$, then the LFGM contract achieves the first best effort level, where,

$P(\theta)$ denotes payment of the LFGM contract,

$c\{p, q\} = c\{p(\theta), 1\}$ denotes the LFGM contract,

v_{AP} denotes airport's buyer's valuation of the flight service from the airport,

c_{AP} denotes the airport's seller's the cost of effort,

v_{AL} denotes the airline's buyer's valuation of using the airport, and

c_{AL} denotes the airline's seller's the cost of effort.

The following graph in Fig. 11 shows how a piece-wise linear payment schedule of a contract satisfies the conditions of Proposition 1. The piece-wise linear function of the payment schedule $P(\theta)$ of the contract has to be within the range $(c_{AL} - v_{AL} \leq P(\theta) \leq v_{AP} - c_{AP})$ of the light colored curving airport's net position $(v_{AP} - c_{AP})$ and the minus of the airline's net position $(c_{AL} - v_{AL})$, which is the decreasing curve, during the entire range of θ, the load factor, in order for the contract to achieve the first best effort level.

If the actual LFGM contract satisfies the condition in Proposition 1, then the contract overcomes the hold-up problem arising from the airport–airline relation-specific commitment/investment, and it enhances each party's efforts level and attains the higher welfare level above.

Numerical Illustrations

To illustrate the effect of the contract which satisfies the conditions of Proposition 1, we introduce some numerical settings. Here we set a simple linear payment schedule with a payment ceiling 2×10^8 and payment floor-2×10^8. This is actually the dotted simple line of the payment schedule indicated in Fig. 11. In addition to the buyer and seller valuations presented in proposition 1 (v_{AP}, c_{AP}, v_{AL}, and c_{AL}), additional values are given as follows:

$$p(\theta) \equiv 2 \times 10^8 - 4 \times 10^8 \theta$$

$$\nu_{AP}(b,\theta) = B_1 - (B_1 - A_1)e^{\{-\lambda_1(\theta+b)\}}, \quad C_{AP}(b,\theta) = C_1 - (C_1 - D_1)e^{\{-\lambda_2(\theta+b)\}},$$

$$\nu_{AL}(s,\theta) = B_2 - (B_2 - A_2)e^{\{-\lambda_3(\theta+s)\}}, \quad C_{AL}(s,\theta) = C_2 - (C_2 - D_2)e^{\{-\lambda_4(\theta+s)\}},$$

$$P(\theta) = E - F\theta, \qquad \theta \tilde{} N(\mu,\sigma^2), \qquad \phi(b) = e^b, \qquad \psi(s) = e^s, \quad A_1 = 2.4 \times 10^8,$$

$$B_1 = 4 \times 10^8, \quad C_1 = 0.3 \times 10^8, \quad D_1 = 0.1 \times 10^8,$$

$$A_2 = 0.7 \times 10^8, \quad B_2 = 2.5 \times 10^8, \quad C_2 = 2.2 \times 10^8,$$

$$D_2 = 0.1 \times 10^8, \quad E = 2 \times 10^8, \qquad F = 4 \times 10^8$$

From the numerical setting, we can derive the expected utility level of airport $\overline{U}_{AP}$ and airline$\overline{U}_{AL}$.

$$\overline{U}_{AP} = E_\theta[U_{AP}(b,\theta)] = B_1 - D_1 - \{(B_1 - A_1) + (C_1 - D_1)\}e^{\{-\lambda\mu - \lambda b + \frac{\lambda^2\sigma^2}{2}\}} - (E - F\mu) - e^b$$

$$\overline{U}_{AL} = E_\theta[U_{AL}(s,\theta)] = B_2 - D_2 - \{(B_2 - A_2) + (C_2 - D_2)\}e^{\{-\lambda\mu - \lambda s + \frac{\lambda^2\sigma^2}{2}\}} + (E - F\mu) - e^s$$

For simplicity, we set the parameters as follows:

$$\mu = 0.7, \quad \sigma = 2.38, \quad \lambda = \lambda_1 = \lambda_2 = \lambda_3 = \lambda_4 = 3\,.$$

Also, we assume the Nash bargaining solution with no contract case for airport is $\alpha = 0.5001$ (So the solution for airline is $1 - \alpha = 0.4999$).

From the first order conditions of the first best situation in $\overline{U}_{AP} + \overline{U}_{AL}$ with respect to b, airport's effort and s, airline's effort, we get the first best level of efforts for both parties.

$$b^{FB} = \frac{1}{\lambda + 1}\ln(MN_1), \quad s^{FB} = \frac{1}{\lambda + 1}\ln(MN_2)$$

$$M = \lambda e^{\{-\lambda\mu + \frac{\lambda^2\sigma^2}{2}\}}, \quad N_1 = B_1 - A_1 + C_1 - D_1, \;\; N_2 = B_2 - A_2 + C_2 - D_2$$

If both parties cannot agree on a contract, then we have a situation of a no-contract case. Both parties have no rule of agreement to follow. So, we assume they just play a Nash bargaining game and share the result by α and $1 - \alpha$ according to standard assumptions. We can calculate the following second-best utility levels for airport and airline under effort (hold-up) situation.

$$\begin{aligned} \overline{U}^{SB}_{AP} &= \alpha[E_\theta[U_{AP}(b,\theta)] + E_\theta[U_{AL}(s,\theta)]] - e^b, \\ \overline{U}^{SB}_{AL} &- (1 - \alpha)[E_\theta[U_{AP}(b,\theta)] + E_\theta[U_{AL}(s,\theta)]] - e^s. \end{aligned}$$

$$b^{SB} = \frac{1}{\lambda + 1}\{\ln\alpha + \ln(MN_1)\}, \quad s^{SB} = \frac{1}{\lambda + 1}\{\ln(1 - \alpha) + \ln(MN_2)\}$$

By solving the FOC of the maximization problem of the two utility levels above, we get the following second-best level of effort (under effort level).

We can draw the graph for both the first best level of efforts and the second-best (hold-up situation) level of efforts as the function of the two moments μ and σ of the underling normal distribution $N(\mu, \sigma^2)$ of the random variable, load factor. Fig. 12 indicates those graphs. The left two graphs are for airport, the light colored sheet being the first best level, and the dark colored sheet being the second-best level of efforts. The right ones are for airline, the the light

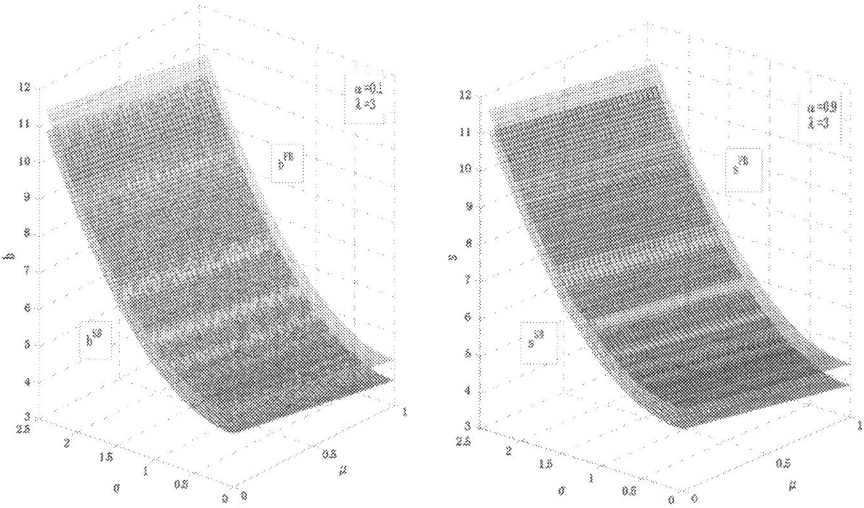

Fig. 12. Effort levels for the first best and the second best.

colored sheet being the first best, and the the dark colored one being the second-best efforts. A comparison of these figures reveals the vertical difference of the two sheets is the difference of efforts levels between the first best and the second best. We can think of the effort level differences as the recovery by making the proper risk sharing contract from the no contract case.

What is the effect of underlying load factor expected level change on effort levels of the airport? What is the impact of underlying load factor uncertainty level change on effort levels of the airport? These effects between the effort level and the underlying load factor distribution can be checked by deriving the analytical relationship between effort levels and underlying load factor normal distribution. With our numerical model, we can analytically obtain such relationships. By taking partial derivatives of second-best effort levels b^{SB} from the results we already have with respect to μ and σ, we can derive the following relationships for each moment of the normal distribution, μ and σ,

$$\frac{\partial b^{SB}}{\partial \mu} = \frac{-\lambda}{\lambda + 1} < 0, \quad \frac{\partial b^{SB}}{\partial \sigma} = \frac{\lambda^2}{\lambda + 1} > 0$$

The same relationships can be derived for the effort levels of the airline, s^{SB}. The concrete results are omitted here since the basic relationships are similar to the case of b^{SB}.

The interpretation of these inequalities suggests that as the expected load factor μ improves, either party needs less effort to reach the same level of utility even in the second-best case. If the expectation of load factor improves, then you do not have to do as much as before even in the second-best case. If the uncertainty, or volatility (standard deviation), of the load factor σ increases, the effort level also increases. If uncertainty increases, then you have to make more efforts even in the second-best situations. These results are common to both first best and second-best levels of efforts.

In addition to the effort levels, we would like to observe graphically the difference of utility levels of the first best cases and the second-best cases. Next, we show such utility level differences of the two parties. Once we get the first best and second-best effort levels above, we can put them into the expected utility levels of both parties, $\overline{U}_{AP} + \overline{U}_{AL}$ already derived above, and calculate the difference. ResU indicated below, is the difference of total utility levels between the first best case and the second-best case for both the airport and the airline,

$$\mathrm{Res}U \equiv \overline{U}_{AP}(b^{FB}) + \overline{U}_{AL}(s^{FB}) - \{\overline{U}_{AP}(b^{SB}) + \overline{U}_{AL}(s^{SB})\} \equiv E[\overline{U}^{FB} - \overline{U}^{SB}]$$

In the numerical example, we can analytically derive ResUas functions of μ and σ by putting back the first and the second-best effort levels in the equation above. ResU can be thought of as the degree of under-effort problem of no contract case, or at the same time, the restoration level of the total utilities by agreeing on the contract that satisfies the proper conditions stated in Proposition 1. Fig. 13 is the graphs of ResU. The effects of the perturbations of μ and σ on ResU are virtually the same as those on the effort levels already stated.

Next, we can check the perturbation effects of asymmetric levels of Nash Bargaining solutions for the no contract case on the restoration levels of the total utilities of both parties, $\mathrm{Res}U \equiv E[\overline{U}^{FB} - \overline{U}^{SB}]$. While fixing the risk sharing contract by holding the underlying load factor normal distribution unchanged, we can change the level of the asymmetricity of Nash bargaining solutions by shifting the values of α and observe the change of the restoration of total utility level, ResU. As we can see below, the changes of the asymmetric levels of Nash bargaining solution α in the case of no contract have big impacts on the restoration level, ResU.

In Fig. 13, we graphically provide the different levels of Re$sU$with respect to different values of α, which can be thought of as the indicators of asymmetricity level of Nash Bargaining solutions. Each sheet of a different color level indicates the level of utility restoration ResU for each value of α. As shown in the graphs, the more asymmetric the Nash bargaining solution becomes (α becomes extreme, or gets closer values away from 0.5 to either 0 or 1), the larger the restoration of the total utilities (different layers of ResU) the proper contract can provide. As we stated, different layers of sheets represent difference cases of α values. The highest (layer 1) sheet represents the case of $\alpha = 0.9$, which means that airport takes 90% of the gains. The 2nd highest (layer 2) represents the case of $\alpha = 0.1$, which means that airline takes 90% of the gains. The bottom

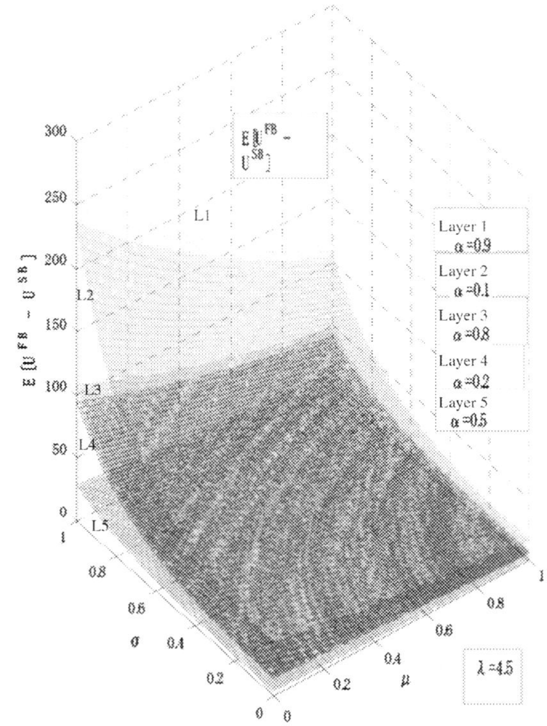

Fig. 13. The levels of utility recovery by the proper contracts.

(layer 5) represents the case of $\alpha = 0.5$, which means that airport and airline takes 50% each. Evenly shared case of the bottom (layer 5) ($\alpha = 0.5$) sheet is the limited level of total utility levels recovery (lower value of Re*sU*). Extreme share cases of the highest (layer 1) ($\alpha = 0.9$) sheet the 2nd highest (layer 2) ($\alpha = 0.1$) sheet are the greater levels of total utility recovery (lower value of Re*sU*) in Fig. 13. So, the restoration effects of agreeing on the proper risk sharing contract on utility levels is greater when the asymmetric level in no contract case is greater (the value of the Nash Bargaining solutions α is extreme).

SUMMARY AND CONCLUDING REMARKS

The relationships between airlines and airports are very complex, but also profoundly interesting. However, only relatively recently have the relationships attracted significant attention from researchers. In this chapter, we contribute to this research trend by examining the several functions of risk sharing relationships between airport and airline. To name just a few examples, airport and airline share revenue/profit fluctuation risk by the contract. The contract also serves as an incentive device to enhance their effort levels by setting a common goal, like a target load factor. Third, the contract promises a commitment by airlines to serving airports in exchange for downside revenue fluctuation risk sharing by airports.

As an interesting real example of risk sharing contract, we describe the Noto Airport LFGM contact in the "Airport and Airline Risk Sharing Contract" section. In addition, we proposed an analytical framework to numerically gauge the risk sharing balance by combining time series analyses and numerical illustrations in the "Balance of Airport and Airline Risk Sharing" section. In the "Incomplete Contract Framework Analysis" section, we showed the analysis of Noto LFGM from the stand points of contract theory (incomplete contract) and principal–agent theory with some numerical explanations about how the proper contractual designs can restore utility losses of no-contract case.

With these analyses, we could say that the risk sharing contract of proper designs can improve both efforts and utility levels of airlines and airports. This enhancement could help to maintain profitable operations on low-density air routes without major outside financial contributions. This performance would lead to maintaining the aviation networks at rural low demand areas or even in the low growth economy environment by sharing risks and making efforts to attract more passengers and to attain the common goal. This kind of effect is very important from the public policy standpoints. In fact, the Ministry of Land, Infrastructure, Transport and Tourism (MLIT) of Japan, which is in charge of allocating flight slots of congested airports, like Tokyo (Haneda), began considering whether airlines are making risk sharing contracts or other type of cooperation with airports or local governments in 2012. Those who are making risk sharing or similar types of cooperative agreements, like the Noto airport LFGM contract, can present their concrete contents of risk sharing cooperation, and compete with other airlines for additional slots under allocation.

While this chapter has described some of the attributes of risk-sharing contracts, there is potential for further research within the context of contract analysis on the airport–airline relationship. For instance, new work in this area includes examining contracts for a multi-year dynamic model, which captures the evolving nature of the enduring relationship. In addition, further work could examine more specific joint efforts by airlines and airports, to profitably offer price discounts or increase flight departure and arrival frequency. These modifications could contribute to the airline–airport relationship literature by allowing analysis of more interdependent and plausible relationships between airports and airlines. With these refinements, we have a better ability to more closely model the complex relationship and dynamic negotiations between airports and airlines in the real world. The results of such analyses could contribute further to better public policy analysis on this matter.

Nonetheless, the findings in this chapter reveal that the mechanisms of risk sharing LFGM contract agreements of multiple functions between airlines and airports enable the two sides not only to share the monetary consequences of demand fluctuation, but also to secure air route from a local airport to Tokyo, to enhance the various demand-inducing efforts, and to increase both parties' utilities, in order to meet the common target load factor they set in the contract. With LFGM contract, both sides have consistently maintained the air transport network in a relatively low demand area for more than 10 years without significant outside helps. Our findings also contribute to better understanding the complex relationships among aviation entities, to the recognition of importance and potential to design properly the airport and airline contract, and to the advancement of economic and public policy analysis of this sector.

NOTES

1. Examples of major carriers that filed for bankruptcy or ended in breakups are Pan Nam Airways, Eastern Airlines, Continental Airlines, Japan Airlines, and World Airways.
2. Among these policies are Airline Deregulation Act (ADA) of 1978 in the US, and a series of negotiations of open skies agreement (OSA) starting from KLM (The Netherlands)–US bilateral agreement in 1992 and continuing with the EU–US Open Sky Agreement in 1995.
3. This kind of approach is a traditional one, where airports and airlines are considered in vertical relationship. In recent years, researchers tend to pay more attention to airports' retail/merchandise business function as well as aeronautical business functions. This approach is called two-sided platform approach. See, e.g., Ivaldi, Sokullu, and Toru (2015, 2012). Some additional materials are provided in the Reference.
4. Many researches show that airport systems are an important source of global/local economic growth. See, e.g., Kasarda & Lindsay (2011). Some additional materials are provided in the Reference.
5. The ANA group is one of the two major airline groups in Japan.
6. This section is based on Hihara (2008).
7. This section is based on Hihara (2012).
8. Still in reality, the real demand for the opening year was just over 15 million passengers.

ACKNOWLEDGMENTS

Financial supports from the Airport Environment Improvement Foundations, Kansai International Airport Co., Ltd., Narita International Airport Co., Ltd. Japan Airport Terminal Co., Ltd. and JSPS KAKENHI Grant Number 16K03695 are gracefully acknowledged.

REFERENCES

Barbot, C. (June 2009). Vertical Relationship between airports and airlines: Is there a trade-off between welfare and competitiveness? ATRS 2009 Abu Dhabi working paper.

Fukuyama, T., Kagawa, T., & Ikeda, Y. (2009). Chihou-Kuukou Kokusai Teiki Rosenn "Yonago-Seoul Rosen" Ni Taisuru Chiiki Shien Ni Kansuru Bunseki (in Japanese). *Journal of International Transport Safety Society*, *34*, 90–98.

Fundenberg, D., & Tirole, J. (1991). *Game theory*. Cambridge, MA: MIT Press.

Hart, O., & Moore, J. (1988). Incomplete contracts and renegotiation. *Econometrica*, *56*, 755–785.

Hihara, K. (2008). Numerical analysis on payoff of load factor guarantee mechanism for Noto airport. *Transportation Research, 2007 FY Annual of Japan Society of Transportation Studies*, pp. 169–178 (in Japanese).

Hihara, K. (2012). Analysis of an airport-airline relationship under a risk sharing contract. *Transportation Research Part E*, *48*, 978–992.

Ivaldi, M., Sokullu, S., & Toru, T. (2012). Chapter 10 are airports two-sided platforms? A Methodological Approach. In J. Peoples (Ed.), Pricing behavior and non-price characteristics in the airline industry. *Advances in Airline Economics* (Vol. 3, pp. 213–232). Bingley: Emerald Group Publishing Limited.

Ivaldi, M., Sokullu, S., & Toru, T. (2015). Airport prices in a two-sided market setting: major US airports. *Working paper* http://www.cepr.org/sites/default/files/events/Ivaldi%20-%20Airport%20Prices%20IST%20180515.pdf (Accessed March 2017).

Kasarda, J., & Lindsay, G. (2011). *Aerotropolis*. London, UK.

Zhang, A., Fu, X., & Yang, H. (2010). Revenue sharing with multiple airlines and airports. *Transportation Research Part B*, *44*, 944–959.

CHAPTER 7

PRICING OF AIRPORT OPERATIONS

Gisle Solvoll and Terje A. Mathisen

ABSTRACT

It is demonstrated how an analysis of airports' cost structures and the calculation of long-run marginal costs (MCs) of serving passengers and airplanes can be used as a basis for setting airport charges according to the principles of welfare economics. Based on Norwegian data, the MC for an extra passenger (PAX) and extra air traffic movement (ATM) are used to set airport charges under the assumption that the charges should be equal for all airports in the country. When adjusting the estimates to meet revenue restrictions and comparing the estimates to current charges, we observe that PAX should be charged more and ATM less. This finding is in line with recommendations from the International Air Transport Association (IATA). When allowing charges to vary between airports, we demonstrate how a Ramsey pricing approach can be applied to set differentiated PAX and ATM charges, considering both the supply side (the competitive conditions between the airlines operating at the airports) and the demand side (the passengers' price elasticity of demand).

Keywords: Airports; air traffic movements; marginal cost pricing; aviation charges; Ramsey-style pricing

JEL classifications: D24; E64; L93

The Economics of Airport Operations
Advances in Airline Economics, Volume 6, 153–180

ISSN: 2212-1609/doi:10.1108/S2212-160920170000006007

INTRODUCTION

Airport infrastructure is, in most countries, financed by airport charges for the services offered at the airport together with revenues from commercial activities (Losada, Eraso, & Garcia, 2012). International air transport organizations that aim to standardize airport charges have a general policy stating that charges, among other things, should be based on costs and should be non-discriminatory (ICAO, 2009; Martin-Cejas, 1997). Most airports charge both passengers (PAX) and air traffic movement (ATM). However, there are variations with respect to the distribution of charges between PAX and ATM both between countries and based on type of airport ownership (e.g., Graham, 2013). The similarity in the charging structure has occurred because most countries have adopted the recommendations made by the International Civil Aviation Organisation (ICAO) and the International Air Transport Association (IATA) for the standardization of airport charges.

Because of the influence that airport charges have on airport financing and the economics of airlines, the charging policy draws the attention of many stakeholders. From the airlines' viewpoint, the design of airport charges is important since they directly affect their operating costs. According to Doganis (2010), airport and en-route charges represent approximately 7% of total operating costs for ICAO member airlines on average. For low-cost operators flying short-haul operations, this share can be as high as 25%. Although, the aeronautical charges constitute a small part of most airlines' total costs, a more competitive airline environment and falling yields have resulted in airlines giving their external costs, such as airport charges, greater attention (Graham, 2013).

From the airports' viewpoint, the income from airport charges must provide a secure basis for airport operations and future infrastructure investments. Hence, for many airports, it appears that the motivation in setting charges is financing concerns rather than economic efficiency concerns. Because the efficient allocation of airport resources necessitates that the charges reflect the costs that each flight imposes, the shortcomings of traditional pricing policies makes alternative pricing strategies, such as marginal cost pricing or Ramsey pricing, interesting. However, since marginal cost pricing does not cover total costs, the charges must be increased above the marginal costs when budget constraints exist. The Ramsey rule helps us to set charges in an economically optimal way (Button, 2010). A simple interpretation of this rule is that it is a form of price discrimination where charges are set based on the consumer's ability to pay.

Aviation charges based on a Ramsey pricing approach has been discussed both principally and empirically in the literature on airport pricing. Morrison (1983) developed a pricing model for uncongested airports by using the

Ramsey rule with profit constraints. Based on a hypothetical "representative" airport, Morrison (1983) found that the take-off charges increased too rapidly with the aircraft weight, and based on "Ramsey thinking," he recommended to increase the charges for small planes on long flights and decrease the charges for large planes on short flights. A numerical example with the use of the Ramsey rule in setting aviation charges is given by Martín-Cejas (1997). He analyzes the structure of landing charges at uncongested airports in Spain using the same model formulation as Morrison (1983). In Martín-Cejas (1997), the charges depend on the marginal costs of airport operations (differentiated by aircraft size and flight distance) and the price elasticity of demand (dependent on trip distance). The results from the analysis show the same trend as found in Morrison's work. The model was further extended by including CO_2 emission costs (Martín-Cejas, 2010). The analysis with emission costs imposes a penalty ranging from 70% to almost 100% for all planes and distances compared to the analysis without emission costs. Hakimov and Mueller (2014) present a list of landing charges for five uncongested German airports using Ramsey pricing. The calculated charges are compared to the actual weight-based charges at these airports. Unlike Morrison and Martin-Cejas, Hakimov and Mueller (2014) found that Ramsey prices increase with distance and aircraft weight faster than the real charges, especially in short-distance markets. However, they note that the difference between the theoretical optimum and practice needs to be better understood.

The aim of this chapter is to demonstrate how estimates of the marginal cost of serving passengers and airplanes can be used as a basis for setting airport charges according to the principles of welfare economics. Attention is also given to the effect of the pass-on rate, i.e., to what extent a change in charges is passed on to the passengers via the ticket price. The empirical evidence is based on a project initiated in 2010 by the Norwegian Ministry of Transport and Communications with the main objective of revising present airport charges based on principles of economic welfare under revenue restrictions. Some results from this project are discussed by Jørgensen, Mathisen, and Solvoll (2011) and Mathisen, Jørgensen, and Solvoll (2014).

The remaining of this chapter is organized as follows: the "Norwegian Airport Network, Airport Charges and Operating Costs" section provides a brief presentation of the Norwegian airport network, the structure of the airport charges and marginal cost estimates for airport operations in Norway. In the "Marginal Cost-Based Airport Charges" section, the marginal cost estimates are applied in new schemes for national airport charges, where the cost of raising public funds is also taken into consideration. In the "Ramsey Pricing Approach under Budget Constraints" section, an example of how Ramsey thinking can be used to differentiate charges between airports is considered. Finally, in the "Conclusions and Implications" section, we present conclusions and implications from this study.

NORWEGIAN AIRPORT NETWORK, AIRPORT CHARGES AND OPERATING COSTS

Most Norwegian airports are operated by the state-owned company Avinor (see e.g., Lian, 2010) according to commercial principles. In total, the airport network in Norway does not require state subsidies, but there is substantial cross-subsidization between the largest airports and those located in rural areas. The total operating costs vary considerably between the airports due to the different sizes and amount of traffic, as does their cost efficiency (GAP, 2012). In this section, we will elaborate on the airport network in Norway, the way in which the infrastructure is financed through charges imposed on airlines, and show the results from an analysis of the cost structure.

Norwegian Airport Structure

Norway has some of the highest air transport dependence in Europe (Williams, Fewings, & Fuglum, 2007). While Norway had a domestic air trip rate per capita of 2.27 in 2003, most European countries had less than one-third of this value. The airports in the network represent a heterogeneous group. One part is characterized by airports with high traffic volume near the largest cities. A second part includes airports characterized by low traffic and a location in what can be classified as peripheral areas (Kjærland & Mathisen, 2012). These airports contribute to Norway having the highest number of commercial airports with short runways (<1,000 m) in Europe (Williams et al., 2007).[1] Despite its low population level, several routes in Europe with the highest frequency and number of passengers are found domestically in Norway (http://ec.europa.eu/eurostat).

To maintain a satisfactory provision of the routes at the local airports, the Norwegian Ministry of Transport and Communications procures air transport services at many of these airports through a Public Service Obligation (PSO) system. Norway is, according to the European Commission (2009), a dominating "PSO country" in Europe, holding nearly 20% of all restricted PSO routes. In 2014, the government spent approximately NOK 677[2] million (€ 75 million) to subsidize PSO operations to and from these airports. The subsidized contracts are awarded as net contracts using competitive tendering every fourth year (in the southern part of Norway) and fifth year (in the northern part of Norway). The PSO regulations give the winning operator exclusive rights to operate the defined routes with a predetermined set of quality factors such as frequency, size of aircraft and maximum fare level. In 2017, the air transport company Widerøe, the largest regional airline company in Scandinavia, operates almost all Norwegian PSO routes.

The state-owned company Avinor owns and operates 45 airports and one helipad in Norway with a total annual traffic of approximately 51 million terminal passengers (PAX) in 2016. Avinor organizes the airports into three groups in which the main airport of Norway (OSL), located near the capital city Oslo, comprises the first "group." The three other large airports located near the cities of Bergen (BGO), Stavanger (SVG), and Trondheim (TRD) comprise the second group, and the remaining 41 airports comprise the third group, as illustrated in Fig. 1.

In 2016, OSL had 25.8 million terminal passengers, the airports in the second group had an average of 4.8 million terminal passengers, and the airports in the third group had an average of 0.26 million terminal passengers (Avinor, 2016). The main part of the third group consists of 28 local airports characterized by particularly low traffic (50,000 terminal passengers on average in 2016). At these airports, virtually all passenger traffic is subject to PSO. The remaining regional airports are in more densely populated areas, and air traffic is based on routes operated on a commercial basis. However, the road infrastructure has improved since most small airports were built approximately

Fig. 1. Norwegian airports owned by Avinor.

45 years ago (Mathisen & Solvoll, 2012), and there is an increasing leak of passengers to the larger airports in the network where commercial routes are operated by jet planes (Lian and Rønnevik, 2011). Consequently, there is an ongoing debate on the future structure of the local airport network in Norway.

Current Airport Charges

The general purpose of Avinors' charging policy is to provide revenues that allows the company to accomplish the tasks that their owner has instructed them to complete. Primarily, this means that the charges should be considered compensation for services related to air navigation, the operation of airports and security. However, in addition, the aviation policy shall fulfill a number of other goals. The policy shall ensure operating efficiency and at the same time consider social considerations, such as the effects on settlement and economic development in rural areas, as well as environmental considerations. The aviation policy shall also aim to ensure competition between airlines and must comply with international rules in this area (The Norwegian Ministry of Transport and Communication, 2012).

The airport charges imposed on air traffic in Norway are composed of five elements[3]: the take-off charge, passenger charge, security charge, Terminal Navigation Charge (TNC), and en-route charge.[4] The security charge, TNC, and en-route charge are set to cover Avinors' costs of providing these services. Avinor sets the two remaining categories, the take-off charge and passenger charge – which are the focus in this article – according to guidelines from the Norwegian Ministry of Transport and Communication. The take-off charge is weight-based and the passenger charge is levied per departing passenger. This is also the basic pricing structure for most airports from different countries (Graham, 2013; Martin-Cejas, 1997). Avinor also generates revenues from commercial activities, such as rent from shops, tax-free sales, and parking. The authorities do not regulate prices for commercial activities. The total revenue for all airports operated by Avinor is almost evenly distributed between air transport charges and income from commercial activities.

The basis for the present study is the airport charge system and the airport charges in 2009.[5] This forms a reference year for all comparisons between revised and present charges. The charges in NOK for 2009 and 2016 are shown in Table 1. In 2009, passenger charges were NOK 36 and NOK 59 for domestic and international flights, respectively. The take-off charge was NOK 96 per ton based on the aircrafts' maximum take-off weight (MTOW). For particularly large aircrafts, the charge was reduced to NOK 48 per ton exceeding 100 tons. Consequently, an aircraft with an MTOW of 70 tons was required to pay a take-off charge of approximately NOK 6,700. According to the accounting figures for Avinor airports, there was a total of 35.8 million PAX and 596,000

Table 1. Aviation Charges of Norwegian Airports Owned by Avinor in 2009 and 2016. Numbers are in NOK.

Charge Type		2009	2016
ATM charge (MTOW)	<75 tons	96	64
	75–100 tons		32
	100–150 tons	48	
	>151 tons		12.8
PAX charge	Domestic flights	36	54
	International flights	59	54
	Security charges	60	56
Terminal navigation charge (TNC)[a]		0	1,251
En-route charge[b]		547	381

[a]TNC per service unit. The number of service units is calculated based on the formula $(MTOW/50)^{0.7}$.
[b]The en-route charge is a per-unit rate. The charges are set by Eurocontrol and vary between states (charging zones); see www.eurocontrol.int/articles/establishing-route-charges.

ATM in 2009, generating revenues of NOK 833 million and NOK 1,280 million, respectively. This yields NOK 23 per PAX and NOK 2,150 per ATM on average (the figures can be doubled since a departure and arrival is charged only once). This implies that an average ATM in 2009 was approximately 45 tons. The entire ATM scheme was revised in 2011 when part of the take-off charge was collected as a Terminal Navigation Charge (TNC).

Costs at Norwegian Airports

An important basis for the analysis of airports' costs is to define which services are provided by an airport and how they can be measured. The most central output measures when studying airports are the number of passengers (PAX), the number of air traffic movements (ATM), and the amount of freight (FRT) handled (Graham, 2013). Since most airports handle both passengers and freight, an output measure that combines the two, such as work load units (WLUs), can be used. The WLU uses a weight criteria for combining these two types of traffic; one WLU equals one PAX or 100 kg of FRT. This output measure has, however, been shown to be imprecise and vague and therefore has rarely been used in recent studies (see e.g., Martín & Voltes-Dorta, 2011). Ideally, the WLU-formula should include an ATM element. An example of such an output measure is the air throughput unit (ATU) (LeighFisher, 2012). This output measure implies that 1 ton of freight counts the same as handling 10 passengers. Moreover, one additional ATM counts the same as handling 100 passengers. However, as freight handling at airports is very much an airline activity, it has little impact on an airport's economic performance, and the focus should be on PAX and ATM. Thus, we are left with the output measures PAX and ATM as the most relevant variables to use when analyzing the cost structure at airports. However, a potential problem for econometric analyzes is that these two explanatory variables are highly correlated; when PAX increases, the number of ATMs will also increase to meet the increased demand and vice versa. The use of ATM is also not ideal because it does not differentiate between aircrafts of different sizes.

An example of marginal cost estimation in Scandinavia was carried out by Carlsson (2003) using an exponential model with the number of passengers as the only independent variable, accounting for approximately 96% of the variation in costs between airports. Morgado and Macario (2012) estimated the marginal costs at Portuguese airports and used these to suggest new charges. Our demonstration of Ramsey-style pricing is based on a cost study by Mathisen et al. (2014) using both PAX and ATM in a model estimating the marginal costs of airport operations in Norway.

The panel data model applied by Mathisen et al. (2014) is presented in Eq. (1) and argued to have properties in accordance with reasonable a priori assumptions regarding the cost structure at Norwegian airports. It is clear from Eq. (1) that the marginal cost with respect to $PAX = X_1$ is $\partial C/\partial PAX = \beta_1$. To reduce multicollinearity, the independent variable X_2 is processed using a deviation from both a mean transformation and logarithmic transformation of ATM. Since it is reasonable to consider the mean value, $ln\overline{ATM}_t$, to be a relatively constant variable, the marginal cost for ATM is $\partial C/\partial ATM \approx \beta_2/ATM$.

$$C_{it} = \beta_0 + \beta_1 X_{1it} + \beta_2 X_{2it} + \beta_3 D_{1i} + \beta_4 D_{2i} + v_{it} \tag{1}$$

where $\beta_0,\ \beta_1,\ \beta_2, \beta_3, \beta_4 > 0$ and $X_{2it} = lnATM_{it} - ln\overline{ATM}_t$

The cost function in Eq. (1) estimates the total operating costs measured in Norwegian kroner (NOK) at the 2009 price level for airport i at time t, (C_{it}), where the subscript i denotes the cross-section dimension and t denotes the time-series dimension. The intercept term β_0 is fixed and thereby independent of both time and the airport. The independent variables, X_{1it} and X_{2it} are observable time-varying factors. Moreover, X_{2it} is represented by a deviation from the annual mean for ATM as defined in (1).

PAX is defined as the number of terminal passengers (sum of arrival and departure and transfer) at both route and charter flights and *ATM* is the sum of arrival and departure flights, including both route and charter categories. The dummy variable D_{1i} is defined as 0 if the airport is classified as category 1 or 2, else $D_{1i} = 1$.[6] This follows the BSL E 3-2 categorization which mainly separates airports with runways shorter than 1,199 meters ($D_{1i} = 0$) from larger airports and, broadly speaking, corresponds with the group of regional and local airports defined in the "Norwegian Airport Structure" section. This separation is important, since runways shorter than 1,199 meters are not suited for jet planes. Since D_{1i} is an imprecise and weak indication of capacity, the estimates can be interpreted as long-run.[7] The dummy variable D_{2i} is defined as 1 if the observation relates to the main national airport OSL (Oslo airport, Gardermoen), which is considerably larger than all other airports in the network; otherwise $D_{2i} = 0$. Both dummy variables are observable time-invariant factors.

A priori assumptions are that all β-parameters are positive, implying that all factors are positively correlated with costs. Furthermore, the disturbance term $v_{it} = u_i + \varepsilon_{it}$ is divided between the unobservable airport-specific effect, u_i, and the remainder of the disturbance, ε_{it}. u_i is time-invariant and accounts for the airports' unobserved characteristics, whereas the remainder of the disturbance, ε_{it}, varies with airports and time and can be thought of as the usual disturbance term in the regression (see e.g. Wooldridge, 2006).

The data set analyzed by Mathisen et al. (2014) consist of annual observations of production and accounting figures for all 45 airports owned by Avinor for the years 2007, 2008, and 2009. The cost variable includes depreciation and excludes security and rents paid by commercial activity at the airport. The traffic statistics are publicly available on the website of the airport owner Avinor (2016). All airports have reported the figures for all 3 years, and this is consequently a balanced data set without missing values. Consequently, the selection in the data set is a complete representation of the population since all Avinor airports are included, and the 3 years with 45 airports comprise a total of 135 observations. The mean values for the variables *PAX* and *ATM* are 860,410 and 13,625, respectively. The average airport in the data set has annual operating costs of NOK 72.7 million. If OSL is excluded, the average costs would decrease to approximately NOK 40 million.

The cost estimations derived by Mathisen et al. (2014) are presented in Table 2. The random effects model, using both within and between variations, is argued by Mathisen et al. (2014) as consistently providing the best unbiased estimates. The unobserved individual effects (rho) explain about half of the

Table 2. Estimation Results.

Variable		Random Effects (GLS)		
		Coefficient	Std. dev.	*t*-value
β_0	Constant	1.98×10^7	1,604,496	12.3
β_1	X_1 (*PAX*)	34	1.71	19.7
β_2	X_2 (ln*ATM*)	5,974,870	1,709,082	3.5
β_3	D_1 (Category)	1.54×10^7	2,493,248	6.2
β_4	D_2 (OSL)	8.01×10^8	2.75×10^7	29.1
Rho		0.52		
R^2 (Overall)		0.9988		

variation in operating costs, which can be properties such as quality and organizational structure.

The results in Table 2 indicate that the long-run marginal costs for handling an extra passenger (*PAX*) are rounded to NOK 34. According to the derivative presented in the "Norwegian Airport Network, Airport Charges and Operating Costs" section, the costs for an extra air traffic movement (*ATM*) amount to approximately NOK 439 and is an average value independent of the weight of the plane.[8] Fixed costs amount to approximately NOK 20 million per year, with an additional element of NOK 15.4 million if the airport is large (qualifies for category 3 or 4). Finally, for the main airport OSL, the total costs shift positively by approximately NOK 800 million.

MARGINAL COST-BASED AIRPORT CHARGES

The Norwegian Ministry of Transport and Communications have decided that airport charges at airports owned by Avinor should be based on three main objectives of the Directive 2009/12/EC of the European Parliament (2009). This implies:

- Improving the transparency of the costs and related charges: Avinor must presents the allocation of their costs to their users and thus justify the calculation of airport charges.
- Prohibiting discrimination between users: airlines receiving the same service at a given airport must pay the same charge. A differentiation of charges should be based on clear and transparent criteria.
- Establishing consultation mechanisms: Avinor must consult their users before setting charges.

In addition to the bullet points, the above charges should, as much as possible, be based on the principles of welfare economics. Changes in charges should generate approximately the same revenues as the current charges (revenue neutrality), and the charges should be equal for all airports throughout the country.

Price Equal to Long-run Marginal Cost

Estimates of long-run marginal costs (MCs) were discussed in relation to Eq. (1). MC-values are valid for both departure and arrival, implying that estimated values are multiplied by 2 if charged only once per trip. Hence, in 2009, the prices of the marginal cost-based airport charges imposed on air transport companies should amount to NOK 68 (34×2) for each passenger and by a fixed element of NOK 878 (439×2) for each air traffic movement.

Hence, the model specification implies that the ATM charge is the same for aircrafts of all sizes. However, the increased importance of the PAX element indirectly ensures a differentiation in charges according to plane size. For example, when using these figures and assuming a load factor of 80%, a "landing and take-off" procedure with a Boeing 737-800 (186 seats) and a Dash 8 100 (39 seats) will be charged NOK 10,996 and NOK 3,000, respectively.

It should be noted that this ATM charge is based on the average traffic volume for all airports in the network. Due to the ln specification in Eq. (1), the marginal cost-based ATM charge will depend on the number of ATMs independent of the size of the aircraft. The derivative with respect to ATM implies that airports with high traffic should have a lower ATM charge, with the opposite applying to smaller airports. While marginal cost-based pricing suggests lower ATM charge at larger airports, setting charges based on this rule is problematic in meeting the Norwegian Ministry of Transport and Communications' directive that charges should be equal for all airports. Moreover, it is difficult from a regional policy perspective because airports with low traffic are usually located in rural areas, where the airport is regarded as an important mainstay for continued settlement and further economic development. However, it is possible to differentiate the ATM charge with respect to the size of the aircraft by taking into account that an average ATM has an MTOW of 45 tons. If it is assumed that the marginal cost of an ATM increases linearly with tonnage, an ATM could be charged 20 NOK per ton (878/45), instead of a flat rate per movement. With this approach, a Boeing 737-800 (79 tons) and a Dash 8 100 (16 tons) would be charged NOK 1,580 and NOK 320, respectively.

A comparison between these marginal cost-based charges and charges in 2009 shows that, on average for domestic and international flights, the ATM charges are reduced from NOK 4,300 to NOK 878 for the average ATM, and PAX charges are increased from NOK 46 to NOK 68 (see average values in Table 3, which compares ATM and PAX charges under various charge schemes). This corresponds to an average charge reduction of 80% for ATM and an increase of 48% for PAX. Consequently, marginal cost pricing implies a significant shift in taxation from ATM to PAX. This indicates that even though

Table 3. Charge Schemes based on MC Pricing and Average Revenues (2009 Prices). Numbers are in NOK.

	PAX Charge	ATM Charge[a]
MC (no cost of raising public funds, λ=0.0)	68	878
MC (cost of raising public funds is 20%, λ=0.2)	82	1,054
MC (revenue adjusted)	97	1,249
Actual average charge in 2009	46	4,300

[a]Using an average ATM in Norway in 2009 of 45 MTOW.

both elements should still be taxed, the PAX charge should be increased and the ATM charge reduced.

However, if marginal cost pricing is implemented, there would be large reductions in total revenues. Appendix A provides an estimate of the reduction in revenues that would occur with marginal cost pricing under reasonable assumptions. For example, if we assume that 50% of the change in charges is transferred to the passengers[9] and an average price elasticity of demand of −1.0, setting PAX and ATM charges according to MC will reduce the annual revenues for Avinor by NOK 602 million. The corresponding reduction in ticket prices increases the number of passengers, which both raise commercial revenues and impose increased operating costs on Avinor. Bearing this in mind, the total profit change for Avinor is estimated to be NOK 571 million. See the details in Appendix A, which form the basis for the figures in Table 4.

Thus, a consequence of MC pricing is that the total revenues are reduced from the present level. This is because the existing ATM charge is far above MC. Recall, however, that the Norwegian Ministry of Transport and Communications' directive states that changes in charges should be revenue neutral. Several approaches can be chosen to meet the revenue neutrality restriction. The first is to assume that a constant mark-up can be applied to PAX and ATM to keep total revenues at current levels without affecting the number of passengers. A second, more realistic approach, is to consider the costs of raising public funds and changes in the number of passengers resulting from the change in prices. These approaches are highlighted in the following sections, along with estimates of the PAX and ATM charges that would ensue (Table 3), the consequences for the airport owner (Table 4), and the overall

Table 4. Consequences for the Airport Owner Avinor of Long-run Marginal Cost Pricing. Numbers are in Million NOK.

	2009 Actual	Setting Price Equal to MC Cost of Raising Public Funds	
		$\lambda = 0.0$	$\lambda = 0.2$
Number of passengers	35.8	36.4	35.9
Income from PAX and ATM charges	2,113	1,511	1,790
Income from commercial activities	3,016	3,069	3,044
Change in number of passengers	–	0.6	0.2
Change in charge income	–	−602	−323
Change in commercial income	–	53	28
Change in total income	–	−549	−295
Change in operating costs	–	22	15
Change in profit	–	−571	−310

Table 5. Welfare Effects of Changing the Airport Charges According to Long-run Marginal Costs. Numbers in Million NOK (2009 prices).

	MC Pricing with	
	$\lambda = 0.0$	$\lambda = 0.2$
Benefit to passengers (consumer surplus)	315	166
Change in profit for airport owner	−571	−310
Change in profit for airline companies	315	166
Economic effects before tax costs	60	22
Tax costs	–	62
Economic effects after tax costs	60	−40

welfare effects (Table 5). Details regarding estimated impacts of these approaches are discussed in the following sections and in Appendices A and B.

Charges Adjusted to Meet Revenue Restrictions (Revenue-Adjusted MC)

One way to secure that total revenues from the revised charging system will meet the target level of 2009 is to apply constant mark-ups to both PAX and ATM. Since total revenues remain unchanged, we assume that the number of PAX and ATMs does not change. However, it could be argued that a given percentage increase in the ATM charge will have a relatively larger impact on the number of ATMs than a corresponding change in the PAX charge will have on the number of passengers. This is because an increased ATM charge directly influence the airlines' costs by operating at an airport, and thereby leads to supply changes that could influence demand. Consequently, in practice it is likely that the number of PAX and ATMs would change somehow. However, we do not have any unambiguous information on the impact on demand. Therefore, the calculations forming the basis for the figures presented in Tables 4 and 5 assume unchanged demand and supply.

Following the tradition of setting airport charges (*AC*) equal for all airports, a reasonable approach is to raise all long-run marginal costs (*MC*) by the same factor (f) as indicated in Eq. (2) – i.e., adjusting the marginal costs to be sufficiently high to match the revenues generated by the current charge scheme.

$$AC = MC \times f \tag{2}$$

In Eq. (2), f is the relative mark-up on *MC* to meet the revenue restriction. Such an adjustment would raise the airport charges above *MC* by approximately 43% ($f = 1.43$) to NOK 97 for PAX and NOK 1,249 for an average ATM.[10]

Charges when Considering the Cost of Raising Public Funds

If the deficit arising from MC pricing must be financed by the state, the question of whether the raising of public funds to finance the revenue loss has any welfare economic consequences should be addressed. The costs for general taxation have been studied empirically, and the Norwegian Ministry of Finance (2014) recommends a mark-up factor of 20% as a rule of thumb. The welfare optimal airport charges (AC^*), given that all loss of revenue is financed by the state, can be derived by the maximization of social surplus under budget constraint as in Eq. (3). Welfare optimal charges are obtained at the point where the impact on social welfare from increasing the amount raised through the charge is the same as the impact from raising it through taxes; see Appendix B.

$$AC^* = MC \times f^* \text{where } f^* = \frac{1}{(1 + \frac{\alpha}{e})} \text{ and } \alpha = \frac{\lambda}{(1 + \lambda)} \leq 1 \text{ and } 0 \leq \alpha \leq 1 \qquad (3)$$

In Eq. (3), e is the price elasticity of demand. The adjustment factor considering the costs of raising public funds, f^*, includes the parameter λ, representing the reduction in social surplus when the requirement for profit is increased by NOK 1. Hence, λ can be interpreted as welfare loss by taxation. If $\lambda = 0$, then $\alpha = 0$ and the optimal charge will, according to Eq. (3), be equal to MC.

From Eq. (3), it can be derived that f^* increases with λ (higher taxation costs) and decreases when $|e|$ increases (more price elastic demand). For example, the value of f^* is 1.26, 1.20, and 1.16 for price elasticities of -0.8, -1.0, and -1.2, respectively, given a welfare loss by taxation of $\lambda = 0.2$. Hence, assuming a price elasticity of -1.0 and the Norwegian Ministry of Finance (2014) recommendations of the cost of raising public funds, the optimal charges based on MC are a PAX charge of NOK 82 and an ATM charge of NOK 1,054. As demonstrated in Table 4, these charges imply a revenue loss for Avinor of approximately NOK 295 million.

Consequences of Long-run Marginal Cost Pricing – A Numerical Example

Table 3 summarizes the results from the different marginal cost pricing strategies. It is clear from Table 3 that PAX should be charged more and ATM less. By comparing charges of equal revenue-adjusted MC with the PAX and ATM charges in 2009, we can calculate that the PAX charge increases by approximately 110% and the ATM charge decreases by approximately 71% (for an airplane weighing 45 tons). The benefits relate to improved accountability for passengers and lower risk for airline companies. More specifically, such a change will make a higher proportion of the operators' costs variable and thereby reduce the cabin factor required to establish new routes. Moreover, a higher emphasis on PAX charges ensures that large and heavy aircrafts are charged more than small and light aircrafts even though the ATM charge is independent of the aircraft size.

In the following discussion, we will study the consequences for different actors in the air transport market if MC pricing is implemented in greater detail.

Consequences for the Airport Owner (Avinor)

In Table 4, the consequences for the number of passengers, income and operating costs for all 45 airports owned by Avinor are summarized.

The reference year is 2009, and the calculations are based on an average price elasticity of demand of -1.0, an average ticket price one-way (in 2009) of NOK 1,000, and an average pass-on rate of 50% (the proportion of the change in charges passed on to passengers). This is, of course, a significant simplification since the airline companies are actively practicing revenue management. The calculations are carried out assuming that the cost of raising public funds (λ) is either 0% or 20%. The calculation is shown in Appendix A.

Under these assumptions, it is demonstrated in Table 4 that income from PAX and ATM charges are reduced, while income from commercial activities increases. However, for the airport owner, total revenues will decrease and profit will decrease more due to the growth in operating costs because of the increased number of passengers. The yearly profit decreases by NOK 571 million and NOK 310 million when the charges based on MC are implemented when $\lambda = 0.0$ and $\lambda = 0.2$.

Consequences for the State

The consequences for the State will be the fiscal effects of the change in profits for Avinor. Assuming that the income in the reference year is necessary for Avinor to operate the airports and meet investment obligations, the company will need capital injection if the charges equal MC. This capital can be obtained by reduced dividends to shareholders (the State), borrowing or increased general taxation. If the capital is raised through general taxation, and the welfare loss through taxation is 20%, a capital injection of NOK 310 million implies a tax cost of NOK 62 million; see Table 5. See Appendix A for details regarding the calculation.

A reduction in aviation charges also implies that the transport authorities may experience reduced subsidy requirements to PSO routes, at least in the short run (partially offsetting the need for raising capital through taxation). This is due to reduced costs for the airline companies operating these routes. However, in a situation where aviation charges are based on a Ramsey approach, the charges at airports with "inelastic" demand will increase substantially. The Norwegian Ministry of Transport and Communications must compensate the increased costs for operators of the PSO routes.

Consequences for the Airline Companies and Passengers

For the airline companies, any change in airport charges leads to a change in operating costs. The consequences for the airlines' profit depends on the structure of the charging system and the extent to which the airline companies will pass on changes in charges to the passengers' ticket prices. Since we assume a 50% pass-on rate, the charge change will be evenly distributed between a reduction in the airline companies' profits and an increased ticket price for passengers.

As suggested in Table 3, more of the aviation charge should be based on the number of passengers (PAX charge) and less on the number of air transport movements (ATM charge). This favors airline companies with the lowest load factors and the highest ticket prices. In Norway, this gives some advantage to Scandinavian Airlines (SAS) and the regional carrier Widerøe and some disadvantages for the low-cost carrier Norwegian. Furthermore, if the ATM charge does not consider the weight of the plane, the operators of small aircrafts are disadvantaged relative to companies operating large aircrafts. Thus, this change will be a significant disadvantage for Widerøe in Norway.

A central question is how much the airline companies will raise/lower ticket prices when aviation charges increase/decrease. With a decrease in charges, the answer to this question determines who enjoys the largest benefit – the airline companies or the passengers. The competitive situation, the airline companies' cost structure and the travelers' price elasticity of demand will affect the impact that changes in the charges have on the ticket prices. It is likely that increased charges equal the increase in price of the most expensive tickets, while the price of the cheapest tickets remains unchanged, at least in the short term. This is due to different price elasticities of demand for passengers buying from different ticket categories. Considering that the airline companies practice yield pricing, it is difficult to have a firm opinion about the degree of pass-on for a specific charge change.

Welfare Considerations

The welfare effects of a new fare system based on MC pricing will be the sum of the consequences for the passengers (change in consumer surplus), for Avinor (change in profit), for the airline companies (change in profit), and for the State through the tax effect. These effects are summarized in Table 5. The calculation details are given in Appendix B.

As can be seen from Table 5, passengers will be better off due to a reduction in ticket prices. The benefit for the passengers increases with price sensitivity and pass-on rate. Due to the assumption of an average pass-on rate of 0.5, the benefits for the passengers equal the change in profit for the airline companies. Using a pass-on rate of 0.7, the consumer surplus will increase to NOK 442 million and NOK 233 million, and the profit for the airline companies will decrease to NOK 190 million and NOK 100 million when λ

equals 0.0 and 0.2, respectively. The airport owner will also benefit from lower ticket prices due to increased traffic compared to a situation with a lower pass-on rate and thereby a higher fare level. However, the airline companies will be facing a lower increase in profit the more of the charge reduction they must "give away" to the passengers. Nevertheless, a higher pass-on rate has a positive effect on the net welfare effects of a reduction in aviation charges.

When we take into account the costs of raising public funds, Table 5 demonstrates that the total welfare effect of implementing marginal cost pricing is negative. It is, however, worth noting that a tax cost of 20% implies a welfare loss if the entire revenue loss is financed through general taxation. The latter is a strict condition because it is reasonable to assume that Avinor can compensate for reduced revenues through different efficiency measures related to the operation of the airports.

RAMSEY PRICING APPROACH UNDER BUDGET CONSTRAINTS

If the transport authorities allow airport charges to vary between airports, welfare optimal charges can be derived by the Ramsey approach. This rule provides guidelines on how to find the second-best charges – that is, how the charges of different airports should deviate from marginal costs when aiming to maximize the total surplus subject to a financial constraint. Assuming that the cross-elasticities of demand between different airports are negligible, Eq. (3) can be rephrased as follows:

$$AC_i^R = MC_i \times f_i \text{ where } f_i = \frac{1}{(1+\frac{\alpha}{e_i})} \text{ and } 0 \leq \alpha \leq 1 \tag{4}$$

In Eq. (4), AC_i^R is the Ramsey charges at airport i, MC_i is the long-run marginal costs at airport i, f_i is the mark-up factor, and e_i is the price elasticity of demand. The parameter α is dependent upon available subsidy funds and has a value of between 0 and 1; the less public funds are available the higher the value of α and, hence, the higher the value of f_i. When $\alpha = 0$, no binding financial constraints are present, and the value of $f_i = 1$ and charges can be set equal to MC_i (first-best charges). The Ramsey rule implies that the relative deviation between marginal costs and charges should be largest at airports where the price elasticities of demand are lowest, regardless of the available funds. It can also be deduced from Eq. (4) that the value of e_i influences f_i more the higher the value of α is. This means that the less available funds are, the more will demand conditions at different airports influence the second-best charges. For a thorough review of Ramsey pricing, we refer to Brown and Sibley (1986) and Hensher and Brewer (2001).

An increase or decrease in airport charges will totally or partially be passed on to the ticket price that the passengers must pay. According to Jørgensen and Santos (2014), the pass-on rate will vary depending on the competitive conditions at the airports and the shape of the airlines' demand functions at the various airports, together with the shape of the airlines' cost functions. This implies that the Ramsey rule should be adjusted when taking into account that the effect the changes in charges will have on the demand for flights from various airports can be different even if the price elasticity of demand at the airports are equal.

One way that Eq. (4) can be adapted to take into account different pass-on rates, defined by the variable φ, is shown in Eq. (5).

$$AC_i^P = MC_i \times f_i^P \text{where } f_i^P = \frac{1}{1 + \frac{\alpha}{e_i \times \varphi_i}} \text{ and } \alpha < |e_i \times \varphi_i| \tag{5}$$

In Eq. (5) AC_i^P is the pass-on rate-adjusted Ramsey charges at airport i where φ_i is the pass-on rate at airport i. According to Eq. (5), the value of f_i^P increases when $|e_i \times \varphi_i|$ decreases. This implies that the relative deviation between MC and AC should be largest at airports where the price elasticity of demand is the most price inelastic and the pass-on rate is lowest, regardless of available funds.

Applying a Ramsey Pricing Approach at Norwegian Airports: A Calculation Example

We will now apply the principle of Ramsey pricing in Eq. (5) using Norwegian airports as an illustrative case. The assumption regarding the pass-on rate (φ_i) is based on a relatively rough assessment of the actual competitive situation at the airport. Three types of competitive environments were identified by Jørgensen et al. (2011). First, at several airports, the two major commercial airlines, SAS and Norwegian, compete in a duopoly. Assuming linear demand functions, linear cost functions and price competition, this situation corresponds to a pass-on rate above 0.5. The pass-on rate at these airports is set to 0.7. Second, many smaller airports are operated by only one operator due to the limited commercial potential. The pass-on rate in these "monopoly" cases is set to 0.5. Third, airports without commercially attractive routes are served by PSO routes operated by one airline company only. These airlines operate at regulated maximum prices on the flexible tickets sold, and the state compensates the operator for any changes in airport charges. Although the charges change, the maximum prices remain unchanged. On other tickets sold, the pass-on rate is likely to be close to 100%. Hence, a rough estimate gives us an average pass-on rate of 0.4. For a thorough discussion of reasonable values on the pass-on rate, see Jørgensen and Santos (2014).

The assumptions regarding the price elasticities of demand (e_i) are based on differences in alternative transport options to air transport for the inhabitants in the airport catchment area; see, e.g., InterVISTAS (2007). The presence of alternatives is divided into four categories according to local knowledge and the best judgment of the authors. The larger cities are well connected by both coaches and railway (and fast-craft services in coastal areas) and have a well-developed road infrastructure for private vehicles. Hence, there are many alternatives, and the average price elasticity of demand is set to −1.2, which indicates high sensitivity to price. As a special case, alternatives are even more abundant at the main airport located near the capital of Norway, Oslo, and the price elasticity of demand is set to −1.4. Airports located far from the main airport, where travel alternatives are fewer, are assigned an elasticity of −1.0. Some local airports are rural, and people have few alternatives to air transport. The price elasticity of demand is relatively inelastic at these airports and is set to −0.8.

The above discussion of variations in the parameters produces eight airport categories. These are listed in Table 6. The assumptions regarding price elasticities and pass-on rates at different airports place most of the small PSO airports in category VIII, while the largest airport, OSL (Oslo airport, Gardermoen), ends up in category I.

Based on the parameters in Table 6, we are able to calculate the adjustment factor f_i^p to be used for deriving the Ramsey charges for PAX and ATM

Table 6. Airport Categories Classified By Market Structure, Pass-on rate, Transport Alternatives and Passengers' Price Elasticities of Demand.

Airport Category	Number of Airports	Market Structure	Pass-on Rate	Transport Alternatives	Price Elasticity of Demand
I	1	Duopoly	0.7	Many	−1.4
II	3	Duopoly	0.7	Middle	−1.0
III	5	Duopoly	0.7	Many	−1.2
IV	7	Duopoly	0.7	Few	−0.8
V	2	PSO	0.4	Many	−1.2
VI	3	Monopoly	0.5	Middle	−1.0
VII	2	PSO	0.4	Middle	−1.0
VIII	22	PSO	0.4	Few	−0.8

Table 7. Airport Charges with Revenue Restrictions According to a Ramsey Approach. All Prices are in NOK at the 2009 Price Level.

Airport Category	Adjustment Factors (f_i^p)	PAX Charge	ATM Charge
I	1.27	87	1,117
II	1.43	97	1,254
III	1.33	91	1,171
IV	1.60	109	1,405
V	1.78	121	1,561
VI	1.72	117	1,514
VII	2.11	143	1,848
VIII	2.91	198	2,554
MC ($\lambda = 0$)	1.00	68	878
MC ($\lambda = 0.2$)	1.20	82	1,054
MC adjusted to meet revenue restrictions	1.43	97	1,249

following the use of Eq. (5); see Table 7. Calculations show that revenue restriction is met if $= 0.21$.[11] For a comparison, the uniform charges derived in the "Ramsey Pricing Approach under Budget Constraints" section are included in Table 7. When adjusting the charges to meet the revenue constraints, we have adjusted both the PAX charge and the ATM charge by the same factor. We have assumed that *MC* is equal for all airports. It should also be noted that long-run marginal cost estimates are applied at all airports even though it can be argued that short-run estimates would be more appropriate at some smaller airports that are not operating on the capacity limit.

As can be seen from Table 7 the PAX charge varies from NOK 87 to NOK 198, while the variation in the ATM charge ranges from NOK 1,117 to NOK 2,554, depending on airport category. It is therefore clear that the charges depend on departure airport, which may imply different charges on the same route depending on the travel direction. If we assume an average ATM charge per ton based on MTOW, based on the discussion in Chapter 3.1, an aircraft of 16 tons (typically a Dash 8-100 with 39 seats) will have a take-off charge of NOK 397 [(1,117/45)×16] at a category I airport and NOK 908 [(2,554/45)×16] at a category VIII airport. If the cabin factor is 80% (31 passengers), the PAX charges will be NOK 2,697 (87×31) and NOK 6,138 (198×31) at category I and VIII airports, respectively. Thus, the total charges are NOK 3,952 higher (almost 128%) when the aircraft operates at a category VIII airport compared to a category I airport.

The diversity in airport locations, from rural areas to large cities, enables differentiation according to the presence of alternative transport options for passengers. The price elasticity will be less negative (less price sensitive) if there are few alternative transport options. Hence, according to Ramsey thinking, such airports should have a higher rise in marginal costs than airports located in regions with many transport alternatives. However, setting airport charges according to these criteria could be problematic from a regional policy perspective. Passengers with few travel alternatives (which would see the highest increase) are usually located in rural areas where the airport itself is regarded as an important means for further economic development (Halpern & Bråthen, 2011).

Another issue to consider is that small airports rarely meet the capacity limit. Since a marginal increase in traffic movements or passengers does not imply an extension of capacity, it is not appropriate to use long-run estimates as the basis for setting charges. Charges should rather be based on short-run marginal costs reflecting the increased use of the existing infrastructure only. See, for example, the discussion on the use of long- and short-run estimates by Viton (1981). The fact that short-run estimates are lower than long-run estimates implies that the differences addressed above are reduced.

CONCLUSIONS AND IMPLICATIONS

This chapter investigates how an analysis of airports' marginal costs (MCs) of serving passengers and airplanes can be used as the basis for setting airport charges according to the principles of economic welfare. The data are from 45 airports in Norway and are operated by the state-owned company Avinor. The analysis indicates that a revision of the Norwegian aviation charges towards MC pricing implies a shift towards relatively higher charges levied on passengers (PAX charge) compared to charges based on aircraft movements (ATM charge). This shift is in line with IATA (2010) recommendations that, wherever possible and practical, airports should transition to passenger-based charges. For 2009 prices, the marginal cost-based airport charges indicate charges of NOK 68 (7.6 €) for each passenger and NOK 878 (97.6 €) for an average air traffic movement.

However, charges based on MC do not cover the total costs of operating an airport, and the income from the PAX and ATM charges are reduced. If the loss of income is covered through general taxation and takes into consideration the costs of raising public funds, the charges should be set above MC. The higher the tax costs are, the higher the mark-up is from MC. With a revenue restriction stating that the new PAX and ATM charges should generate approximately the same revenues that the current ones do, our estimations show that MC-based charges must be set at approximately 43% above MC. The airport owner (the state) has decided that charges on all airports owned by Avinor should be equal. However, if charges are allowed to vary between airports, a Ramsey pricing approach indicates that the mark-up from MC should be highest at airports where the passenger price elasticity of demand is lowest (in absolute values) and where the pass-on rate (the proportion of a tax change passed on to passengers via the ticket price) is low.

By using our approach to Ramsey pricing on airports owned by Avinor, most local airports located in areas characterized by few transport alternatives to air transport will be given the maximum charge, while the main airport in Norway, where travel alternatives are numerous, will be assigned the minimum charges. Such distributional effects using our Ramsey pricing approach will be difficult to accept for policy makers, and it will conflict with Avinor's goal of promoting economic development in rural areas. Professionally speaking, it is legitimate to argue for lower charges at airports with significant spare capacity since optimal charges should then be set equal to short-run marginal costs. Then, however, the funding requirements increase considerably so that airports need additional funding from the state budget to cover operating costs and necessary investments.

Aviation charges based on MC pricing imply a reduction in the present charges and the income from these charges. From a welfare perspective, MC pricing is desirable when no financial bindings exist. However, as demonstrated in the calculation example, a change in MC pricing can imply a reduction in welfare for society if all losses of income for the airport owner are compensated by general taxation. In principle, the economic benefits of financing revenue loss with public funds increase with lower taxation costs and decrease the less price sensitive the market in question is.

Our estimations of MC and the use of the estimated results in setting airport charges have weaknesses. First, it is technically difficult to estimate the marginal cost of both passengers and air transport movements in the same model due to the strong correlation between these production measures. This makes the estimates uncertain. Second, the estimations are based on a panel data set of 3 years, which we have treated as a pooled data set. Such a pooling approach is not unproblematic. The estimation results are calculated from the reported costs at Norwegian airports that are operated by the state-owned company Avinor. Therefore, the estimated marginal costs indicate how efficiently Avinor runs these airports. If the airports are run inefficiently, the size of the marginal costs would reflect this. Thus, the actual parameter values cannot be directly transferred to airports in other countries, although it is corrected for factor price differences and differences in operating efficiency and other framework conditions that will influence costs. Nevertheless, the method used is transferable to countries that have organized their airports in the same way as in Norway and can thus be used to carry out similar analyses to the Norwegian case.

NOTES

1. Short Take-Off and Landing (STOL) planes, such as the Bombardier Dash 8 100 (DHC-8), operates in local airports with runways as short as 800 m. Local airports with sufficiently long runways are, in some cases, operated by jet planes.

2. For all conversions from the Norwegian kroner (NOK) to Euro (€), we have assumed that € 1 ≈ NOK 9.

3. All taxes are charged to the airlines once per trip. Charges passed on to passengers are paid as part of the ticket price. A trip (without transfer) includes two air traffic movements (ATMs) and visits at terminals at both departure and landing. It is, however, not typical for these services to be charged separately for the origin and destination airports.

4. The en-route charge is set to meet the cost generated by the air space surveillance services provided by the control centers of Avinor. The TNC was introduced in 2011 to cover the control tower operating costs and was designed as a concavely increasing function of airplane weight (MTOW). Before 2011, this charge was included in the take-off charge. The charges for security, tower services, and en-route costs are changed when the costs or traffic amount changes.

5. The reason for using this reference year is that the analysis of the cost structure at Norwegian airports is based on a research project initiated by the Norwegian Ministry of Transport and Communications, where cost data for 2007, 2008, and 2009 for all airports owned by Avinor formed the basis of the analysis.

6. This refers to the size of the airport according to the categories ranging from 1 (small) to 4 (large) following the regulations on the design of large airports (BSL E 3-2) defined by the Norwegian Ministry of Transport and Communication (2006). Generally, the infrastructure requirements increase substantially for higher categories, which again increase both the investments and operation costs. The difference between the categories is most easily seen by the runway length and safety zones.

7. Although the cost function assumes airports minimize long-run costs, there are some costs required by aviation authorities that are relatively independent of the number of passengers or the size of the airport.

8. If $\beta_2 = 5,974,870$ and average $ATM = 13,625$, then $\frac{\partial C}{\partial ATM} = \frac{\beta_2}{ATM} \approx 439$. The use of average ATM is a simplification implying that airports with more (less) traffic will have a lower (higher) value.

9. The extent to which a change in charges is passed on to passengers is discussed by Jørgensen and Santos (2014). They show that this pass-on rate is always 50% in the case of linear demand and supply curves under monopoly. In a situation with a duopoly, the pass-on rate will exceed 50 percent. However, for subsidized PSO routes, the situation would depend on whether the authorities change the maximum fares accordingly and compensate the operator. If reduced charges lead to an equal (or no) reduction in the regulated maximum fares, then all (or no) changes in charges will be passed on to the passengers. On other discounted tickets, where prices are set freely in the market, it can be assumed that the normal market mechanism applies.

10. In the remainder of the chapter, all references to charges per PAX and ATM assume that only one charge applies per trip (i.e., twice the charge that would apply per departure and arrival).

11. The value of $\alpha = 0.21$ gives unchanged revenues from PAX and ATM charges when the 45 airports included in the calculation are given price elasticities of demand and pass on rates as shown in Table 6.

12. When using the number of arriving and departing passengers (PAX) as an analysis unit, the calculations of the impact that MC pricing has on the change in the number of passengers and the income from these components must be halved since a passenger

contributes to two terminal visits, and the taxation is related to only one of these visits. The charges are set to 2 $\times MC$.

REFERENCES

Avinor. (2016). Traffic statistics. Retrieved from http://www.avinor.no/en/avinor/traffic.

Brown, S. J., & Sibley, D. S. (1986). *The theory of public utility pricing*. Cambridge, MA: Cambridge University Press.

Button, K. (2010). *Transport economics* (3rd ed.). Cheltenham, UK: Edward Elgar.

Carlsson, F. (2003). Airport marginal cost pricing: Discussion and an application to Swedish airports. *International Journal of Transport Economics*, *30*(3), 283–304.

Doganis, R. (2010). *Flying off course: The economics of international airlines* (4th ed.). London: Routledge.

European Commission. (2009). *Public service obligations – List of routes concerned*. Working document based on information from the Official Journal and on data delivered by Member States. Retrieved from 11th January 2010 http://ec.europa.eu/transport/air/internal_market/doc/2009_11_03_pso_inventory.pdf.

European Union. (2009). Directive 2009/12/EC of the European Parliament and of the Council of 11 March 2009 on airport charges *Official Journal of the European Union*, 52.

GAP. (2012). *Comparative study (benchmarking) on the efficiency of Avinor's airport operations*. Berlin.

Graham, A. (2013). *Managing airports: An international perspective* (4th ed.). London: Routledge.

Hakimov, R., & Mueller, J. (2014). Charges of uncongested German airports: Do they follow Ramsey pricing scheme? *Research in Transportation Economics*, *45*, 57–65.

Halpern, N., & Bråthen, S. (2011). Impact of airports on regional accessibility and social development. *Journal of Transport Geography*, *19*(6), 1145–1154.

Hensher, D. A., & Brewer, A. (2001). *Transport: An economics and management perspective*. Oxford: Oxford University Press.

IATA. (2010). Passenger based airport charges. Retrieved from http://www.iata.org/whatwedo/airport-ans/charges/Documents/Passenger-based-airport-charges.pdf.

ICAO. (2009). *ICAO's policies on charges for airports and air navigation services*. Doc 9082.

InterVISTAS. (2007). *Estimating air travel demand elasticities*. Final Report.

Jørgensen, F., Mathisen, T., & Solvoll, G. (2011). *Lufthavnavgifter i Norge – takstsystemets struktur og betydning for tilbud og etterspørsel* (Airport charges in Norway). SIB report 2/2011, Bodø Graduate School of Business, Norway (in Norwegian).

Jørgensen, F., & Santos, G. (2014). Charges on transport – To what extent are they passed on to users? *Transportation Research Part A: Policy and Practice*, *69*, 183–195.

Kjærland, F., & Mathisen, T. A. (2012). Assessing the peripheral status of local airports. *Journal of Air Transport Studies*, *3*(2), 1–22.

LeighFisher. (2012). *Airport performance indicators 2012*. London.

Lian, J. I. (2010). Network dependency and airline competition – Consequences for remote areas in Norway. *Journal of Air Transport Management*, *16*(3), 137–143.

Lian, J. I., & Rønnevik, J. (2011). Airport competition – Regional airports losing ground to main airports. *Journal of Transport Geography*, *19*(1), 85–92.

Losada, J. M. S., Eraso, J. C., & Garcia, P. D. (2012). Airport management: The survival of small airports. *International Journal of Transport Economics*, *39*(3), 349–367.

Martín, J. C., & Voltes-Dorta, A. (2011). The econometric estimation of airports' cost function. *Transportation Research Part B: Methodological*, *45*(1), 112–127.

Martín-Cejas, R. R. (1997). Airport pricing systems in Europe and an application of Ramsey pricing to Spanish airports. *Transportation Research Part E: Logistics and Transportation Review*, *33*(4), 321–327.

Martín-Cejas, R. R. (2010). Ramsey pricing including CO_2 emission cost: An application to Spanish airports. *Journal of Air Transport Management*, *16*(1), 45–47.

Mathisen, T. A., Jørgensen, F., & Solvoll, G. (2014). Marginal costs pricing of airport operations in Norway. *Research in Transportation Economics*, *45*, 49–56.

Mathisen, T. A., & Solvoll, G. (2012). Reconsidering the regional airport network in Norway. *European Transport Research Review*, *4*(1), 39–46.

Morgado, F., & Macário, R. (2012). Landing fees in portuguese airports. *Transportation Research Record*, *2300*, 119–128.

Morrison, S. A. (1983). Estimation of long-run prices and investment levels for airport runways. In T. E. Keeler (Ed.), *Research in transportation economics* (Vol. 1, pp. 103–113). Greenwich, Connecticut: JAI Press.

The Norwegian Ministry of Finance. (2014). *Veileder i samfunnsøkonomiske analyser*.

The Norwegian Ministry of Transport and Communication. (2006). FOR 2006-07-06 nr 968: Forskrift om utforming av store flyplasser (BSL E 3-2). Oslo (in Norwegian).

The Norwegian Ministry of Transport and Communication. (2012). Verksemda til Avinor AS. Meld. St. 38 (2012-2013).

Viton, P. A. (1981). A translog cost function for urban bus transit. *The Journal of Industrial Economics*, *29*(3), 287–304.

Williams, G., Fewings, R., & Fuglum, K. (2007). Airport provision and air transport dependence in European countries. *Journal of Airport Management*, *1*(4), 398–412.

Wooldridge, J. M. (2006). *Introductory econometrics: A modern approach* (3rd ed.). Mason, OH: Thomson South-Western.

APPENDIX A

Below, we show how the consequences of MC pricing for the airport owner (Avinor) and for the society (welfare effects) are calculated. The central assumptions for the calculation are that we assume an average ticket price (P) of NOK 1,000 (one way), an average price elasticity of demand (e) of -1.0 and an average pass-on rate (φ) of 0.5. The following symbols are used:

ATM_{2009} = Number of air transport movements in 2009.

PAX_{2009} = Number of arriving and departing passengers in 2009.

PAX_{new} = Number of arriving and departing passengers with charges equal to MC.

AC^{pax}_{2009} = Passenger charge in 2009.

$\overline{AC}^{atm}_{2009}$ = Average ATM charge per passenger in 2009.

AC^{pax}_{new} = MC-based passenger charge.

AC^{atm}_{new} = MC-based ATM charge.

I^{AC}_{new} = Income from MC-based PAX and ATM charges.

I^{com}_{new} = Income from commercial activities when PAX and ATM charges are set equal to MC.

C = Operating costs.

Consequences for the Airport Owner (Avinor)

The number of passengers when PAX and ATM charges are set equal to MC are calculated using Equation (A.1).[12]

$$PAX_{new} = PAX_{2009} + e \times 0.5 \times \left(\frac{\Delta AC}{P} \times PAX_{2009}\right), \qquad (A.1)$$

where $\Delta AC = \left(AC^{pax}_{2009} + \overline{AC}^{atm}_{2009}\right) - \left(AC^{pax}_{new} + \frac{AC^{atm}_{new}}{PAX_{2009}} \times ATM_{2009}\right)$

Income from MC-based PAX and ATM charges are calculated using Eq. (A.2).

$$I^{AC}_{new} = 0.5 \times \left(AC^{pax}_{new} + \frac{AC^{atm}_{new} \times ATM_{2009}}{PAX_{2009}}\right) \times PAX_{new} \qquad (A.2)$$

The income from commercial activities when PAX and ATM charges are set equal to MC are calculated as follows:

$$I^{com}_{new} = I^{com}_{2009} + 0.5 \times \left[\frac{I^{com}_{2009}}{PAX_{2009}} \times (PAX_{new} - PAX_{2009})\right] \quad (A.3)$$

The operating costs with an increased number of passengers due to MC pricing are calculated as follows:

$$\Delta C = MC^{pax}_{2009} \times \Delta PAX \quad (A.4)$$

Welfare Effects

The welfare effects of implementing MC pricing are calculated as follows:

Change in consumer surplus (*CS*):

$$\Delta CS = \left(0.5 \times PAX_{2009} \times \Delta AC^{P}\right) + \left(0.5 \times \Delta PAX \times \Delta AC^{P}\right) \times 0.5 \quad (A.5)$$

Change in profit (π) for the airport owner ($\Delta\pi^{AO}$):

$$\Delta\pi^{AO} = I^{AC}_{2009} - I^{AC}_{new} + I^{com}_{2009} - I^{com}_{new} + \Delta AC \quad (A.6)$$

Change in profit for airline companies ($\Delta\pi^{AC}$):

$$\Delta\pi^{AC} = \left(0.5 \times PAX_{2009} \times \Delta AC^{A}\right) + \left(0.5 \times \Delta PAX \times \Delta AC^{A}\right) \times 0.5 \quad (A.7)$$

APPENDIX B

To analyze the problem of setting charges according to the principles of economic welfare, we use the condition for maximizing economic surplus under budget constraints (Ramsey pricing):

$$MaxSO = \int_{P}^{\infty} X(P) + (P \times X(P)) - C(X(P)) \quad \text{given} \quad P \times X(P) - C(X(P)) \leq \pi^{*} \quad (B.1)$$

where *SO* is economic surplus, *P* is the charge, *C*(*X*) is the airport owner's cost function, *X*(*P*) is the demand function for airport services, and π^* is the surplus requirements ($\pi^* < 0$ implies deficit and $\pi^* > 0$ implies surplus). First order conditions for the maximization of *SO* (Lagrangian) imply:

$$L(P) = \int_{P}^{\infty} X(P) + P \times X(P) - C(X(P)) + \lambda[P \times X(P) - C(X(P)) - \pi^{*}]$$

$$\frac{\partial L}{\partial P} = -X(P) + P\frac{\partial X}{\partial P} + X(P) - \frac{\partial C}{\partial X}\times\frac{\partial X}{\partial P} + \lambda\times P\frac{\partial X}{\partial P} + \lambda\times X(P) - \lambda\times\frac{\partial C}{\partial X}\times\frac{\partial X}{\partial P} = 0 \Rightarrow$$

$$(1+\lambda)\times P\times\frac{\partial X}{\partial P} + \lambda\times X(P) = (1+\lambda)\times\frac{\partial C}{\partial X}\times\frac{\partial X}{\partial P}$$

If the expression above is divided by $(1+\lambda)\times\frac{\partial X}{\partial P}$ on both sides, we get:

$$P + \frac{\lambda\times X(P)}{(1+\lambda)\times\frac{\partial X}{\partial P}} = \frac{\partial C}{\partial X} \Rightarrow$$

$$P\left(1 + \frac{\lambda\times X(P)}{(1+\lambda)\times P\times\frac{\partial X}{\partial P}}\right) = \frac{\partial C}{\partial X} \Rightarrow$$

$$P\left(\frac{\frac{\partial C}{\partial X}}{1 + \frac{\lambda}{1+\lambda}\times\frac{X(P)}{P}\times\frac{\partial X}{\partial P}}\right) = \frac{\frac{\partial C}{\partial X}}{1 + \frac{\lambda}{1+\lambda}\times\frac{1}{e}} \Rightarrow$$

$$P^* = \frac{\frac{\partial C}{\partial X}}{1 + \frac{\alpha}{e}} \tag{B.2}$$

where

$$0 \le \alpha = \frac{\lambda}{1+\lambda} \le 1$$

where P^* is the optimal charge and e is the price elasticity of demand. Since e is negative, $|e| > \alpha$ if $P^* > 0$.

It can be shown that $\frac{\partial SO^*}{\partial \Pi^*} = -\lambda$, where SO^* is the maximum economic surplus when the surplus requirement is π^*. This implies that λ indicates the reduction in economic surplus from the airport operation when the surplus requirement increases by NOK 1. Hence, λ can then be interpreted as the welfare loss by taxation. When $\lambda = 0$, $\alpha = 0$, and the optimal charge will, according to (B.2), equal the marginal costs.

The above helps us calculate how much optimal airport charges (*AC*) should deviate from *MC* ($\partial C/\partial X$) when the deficit is to be financed by general taxation.

$$AC = P^* = MC\times f \text{ where } f = 1/(1+\alpha/e) \text{ and } 0 \le \alpha = \lambda/(1+\lambda) \le 1 \text{ and } |e| > \alpha. \tag{B.3}$$

In (B.3), f is the in-percentage mark-up (in decimals) to be levied on *MC* to reach the surplus requirements.

CHAPTER 8

THE COST STRUCTURE OF THE AIRPORT INDUSTRY: METHODOLOGICAL ISSUES AND EMPIRICAL EVIDENCE[☆]

Anna Bottasso and Maurizio Conti

ABSTRACT

This chapter examines the main methodological issues involved in the comprehension of the cost structure of the airport industry and suggests considerations for future airport cost analyses. Such understanding has become a crucial concern for policy makers, regional planners, and managers in order to deal with optimal market design (e.g., regulation and market configuration) and airport strategies (e.g., pricing, investments, and alliances). An in-depth analysis of the economics of cost functions is presented, together with a description of the relevant multi-output cost economies measures (average incremental costs, scale and scope economies, and cost complementarities). We also discuss the assumptions underlying estimates of total versus variable cost functions and the importance of estimating a sufficiently flexible functional form. Moreover, we provide a critical survey of the international empirical literature on the cost structure of the airport industry, which

[☆]The content of this chapter does not reflect in any case the opinion of the Joint Research Centre of the European Commission and the Joint Research Centre is not responsible for the use that third parties can make of the data contained in this chapter.

The Economics of Airport Operations
Advances in Airline Economics, Volume 6, 181–212

ISSN: 2212-1609/doi:10.1108/S2212-160920170000006008

highlights how econometric estimates strongly depend on the sample choice and the empirical model considered. Indeed, while econometric studies on international samples based on long-run cost function estimates show that long-run scale economies are never exhausted, single country studies mostly estimate variable cost functions and find lower values for scale economies at median sample points that tend to decrease with size. We discuss why we believe that studies based on the estimation of short-run variable cost functions offer more reliable results, given the reasonable assumption of airport overcapitalization in the short run. We conclude our work by noting that underlying policy issues related to planning and regulation, as well as to the optimal market structure of the airport sector, need to take into account the role played by vertical relationships between airports and airlines.

Keywords: Airport industry; cost function; scale economies; scope economies; regulation

JEL Classifications: D24; L51; L9

INTRODUCTION

Over the last decades, fast growth of air traffic has taken place all over the world, leading to significant changes in the airport sector. Airports, far from being regarded as public utilities that offer aviation services to airlines and passengers, are now multiproduct firms supplying the market with a bundled group of aviation and non-aviation services, with increasing shares of revenues coming from non-aeronautical business. In addition, institutional and governance reforms of the utility and transport industries in most OECD countries have had a major impact on the role of airports. Institutional and governance changes have often entailed the privatization of public enterprises and the introduction (or revision) of economic regulation. Within this framework, airports are increasingly considered critical assets for economic growth, suggesting that an understanding of the economics of the sector has become a crucial concern for policy makers (authorities), regional planners, and managers. In particular, a rigorous analysis of airport cost structure is important, including information concerning the nature and extent of scale and scope economies and an understanding of cost complementarities. Similarly, an understanding of efficiency and productivity aids in comprehend which factors determine performance differentials and favor its improvement. These issues are particularly relevant in order to deal with optimal market design and airport strategies. Because of the importance of understanding the nature of airport costs for policy, pricing, and airport investment decisions, this chapter examines our current understanding of airport costs, methodological issues in examining airport costs (including the choice of inputs and outputs), and important considerations for future airport cost analyses.

The study of the existence and breath of economies of scale and scope, together with possible sub-additivity of the airport cost function, are key elements in the debate on the natural monopoly nature of the airport infrastructure and the associated need for regulation. Moreover, cost analysis sheds light on the optimal size and number of airports in a particular region as well as on competition and (price) regulation issues. In addition, pricing decisions should be based on cost structure and productivity analysis so that price signals can provide the correct incentives for investment decisions and diversification strategies. Indeed, if economies of scale do not prevail over the entire output range, minimum efficient scale can be identified so that capacity expansion investments and opening of new airports decisions can be supported; moreover, when charges are regulated, understanding whether airports are operating in the region of decreasing or increasing average costs provides guidance for price regulation.

Also, the widespread tendency to develop commercial activities within the airport area deserves special attention: possible scope economies and cost complementarities between aeronautical services and commercial activities should be accounted for in the price regulation process and in diversification strategies. Similarly, the existence of economies of scope in the production of different aviation services, e.g., between international and domestic passengers or between passengers and cargo, might provide support for decisions on alliances with different kinds of airlines, like low-cost carriers, and for specific investments.

Despite the fact that airport cost structure analysis can advise policy makers and airport managers on several policy issues, the economic literature has devoted more attention to the analysis of efficiency determinants. Such studies represent complementary tools for policy analysis and strategy decisions, since they can help us understand which elements enable efficiency improvement. Often, factors that are beyond the managers' control might have an important role in determining airports performance; e.g., things like the regulatory framework and the governance structure. Most papers that examine such efficiency drivers analyze technical efficiency and its determinants by means of the Data Envelopment Analysis approach, which identifies the sample best practice frontier and compares decision-making units against it. In these DEA studies, the analysis of cost economies is not the main focus and, when present, cannot be considered as fully reliable given the modeling approach adopted, which often neglects the multi-output nature of the airport business. Moreover, as Lechmann and Niemeier (2013) note, DEA studies draw conclusions about economies of scale from the estimation of returns to scale, which may not be always correct. For these reasons, we do not discuss DEA results in this essay; instead, we focus on the applied literature that has analyzed airport cost structure by econometrically estimating cost or input distance functions and frontiers.[1]

Before illustrating the main results of the empirical literature on airports cost structure, we discuss issues involved in the choice of input and output variables. Indeed, the richer the specifications of the cost function, the more precise estimates of cost economies are; however, the definition and choice of such variables are not always immediate and might raise collinearity problems. In particular, the older studies adopted very parsimonious specifications of the cost function in terms of outputs, while more recent papers reflect the evolution of the airport business model and analyze multi-output models which take into account commercial services alongside with aeronautical outputs.

An in-depth description of the economics of cost functions is presented in the third section where we illustrate necessary and sufficient conditions for the existence of a natural monopoly and we review relevant multi-output scale and scope economies measures and the relationships that exist among them. Moreover, we present a discussion on the main methodological difficulties that one faces when studying the sub-additivity nature of a multi-output cost function, which requires the researcher to take into account not only global scale economies, but also the average incremental cost of each output as well as scope economies.

Turning to the choice of the cost function, we argue the importance of estimating a sufficiently flexible functional form, which allows recovering scale economies measures over different sample points. We also discuss the assumptions underlying estimates of total versus variable cost functions. This distinction is associated with input indivisibilities and is very important in the context of the airport sector where the infrastructures are built in order to meet future demand and are not freely adjustable in the short run. In such a framework, it is not realistic to assume that airports are operating over their long-run equilibrium path so that it might be more reasonable to estimate variable cost functions.

The last section of the essay reports a critical survey of the international empirical literature on the cost structure of the airport industry.

A detailed analysis of the empirical evidence suggests that results on scale economies measures are mixed. Econometric studies based on international samples show that long-run scale economies are never exhausted, even for airports with about 80 million passengers (e.g., Martin & Voltes Dorta, 2011a). Such results are based on long-run cost function estimates that assume airports are operating at the optimal size of installed capacity. However, evidence in favor of a certain degree of overcapitalization reported by several studies (e.g., Bottasso & Conti, 2012) casts some doubts on the appropriateness of such an approach and of the associated results. Moreover, it is important to remember that the use of international samples would perhaps require a more rigorous treatment of the heterogeneity related to the presence of airports located in countries with different institutional and regulatory settings.

Single country studies mostly estimate variable cost functions and find low values for scale economies at median sample points that tend to decrease with size; moreover, some authors suggest the presence of diseconomies of scale for larger airports. (e.g., Voltes Dorta & Pagliari, 2012 on Spanish data, McCarthy, 2016 for the US, and Bottasso & Conti, 2012 on UK data).

OUTPUT AND INPUT MEASUREMENT IN THE AIRPORT INDUSTRY

Outputs

If one reads the empirical literature dealing with airport' technology, productivity, and efficiency, she will easily find out that the definition of output is a hotly debated issue. Indeed, as the discussion in the "Scale and Scope Economies in the Airport Industry: A Critical Survey of the Recent Literature" section of this study and Table 1 in the Appendix will hopefully make clear, the empirical literature is not unanimous on the definition of the set of goods produced by an airport.

Earlier studies usually considered airports as single product firms, by focusing either on total passengers or on work load units (*wlu*), the latter being defined as one passenger or 100 kg of freight.[2] More recently, the assumption that airports produce one single output has been seriously called into question, as it would neglect important features of the modern airport industry for a variety of reasons. First, airports can be considered as the interface between aircraft, on one side, and passengers and freight transported by air (Doganis, 1992) on the other: the actual number of aircraft movements need therefore to be taken into account in order to understand the cost structure of the airport industry. Second, different types of flights (e.g., domestic versus international) might impose a different burden on airport costs. Third, the business model and related costs of modern airports cannot be fully understood if one does not recognize that terminals are used to provide a number of non-aviation related services, such as shopping centers and restaurants, so that airports have been recently defined as big shopping malls with "wide parking." Finally, some of the activities generally carried out by airports share various subsets of their infrastructures (runways, terminal spaces, check-in desks, and aprons), possibly generating non-negligible cost complementarities and economies of scope.

Although, in most airports the various components of the output vector are highly correlated, assuming away the multiproduct nature of the airport industry in econometric work might lead to important biases in parameters that represent the underlying production technology. By way of example, Martin, Roman, and Voltes Dorta (2011) show that the magnitude of scale economies is upward biased if a single output structure is imposed on the data. Similarly, the empirical results in McCarthy (2016, 2014), which share the same sample, inputs, and econometric methodology (and mainly differ in terms of how rich the output vector specification is), suggest that the single output model yields much higher values for economies of scale.

The consideration of working load units as an output variable was the first attempt at taking into account the multiproduct nature of the airport industry by jointly considering passengers and cargo. However, the use of *wlu* has an important drawback, because it assumes equivalence between one passenger and 100 kg of freight that is unlikely to be valid in practice. As a matter of fact, passengers and freight require different airport facilities (e.g., check-in desks are used only by passengers) and are therefore unlikely to have a similar impact on airports costs.[3] Moreover, there might be economies of scope between freight and passengers as they share some production facilities like the conveyor belts. For these reasons, it is surely advisable to include freight and passengers as separate outputs in the cost function,[4] even if some authors have justified the use of *wlu* on statistical grounds, given the large correlation between passengers and freight and the possible associated multicollinearity problems.

Even if the separate inclusion of freight and passengers in the cost function is an improvement with respect to single output studies, it is still far from satisfactory. Indeed, as correctly noted by Martin and Voltes Dorta (2011a), airports are infrastructure providers and the use of some of these infrastructures, such as runways, are unrelated to the number of passengers or the tons of freight moved in the airports. It is for this reason that many recent studies have considered air transport movements (*atm*), defined as the number of landings and take-offs of aircrafts engaged in the transportation of passengers, cargo or mail, as an (additional) output, alongside passengers and freight (Bottasso & Conti, 2012; Oum et al., 2008; Martin & Voltes Dorta, 2011a; McCarthy, 2016, among the others).

However, Martin and Voltes Dorta (2011a) note that different aircrafts can have a differential impact on airport costs because heavier airplanes require longer, wider and stronger runways, and more space on the aprons. In principle, one might want to distinguish between *atm* of different types of aircraft, although this strategy might generate a proliferation of parameters in the cost function and create serious econometric estimation problems.

A very simple way of dealing with this issue is to control (in the cost function) for the shares of international passengers or low-cost flights in the airport (Bottasso & Conti, 2012). Indeed, bigger airplanes are disproportionally used on long-haul (international) routes, while low-cost carriers usually focus on short-haul routes and employ relatively smaller aircrafts. Alternatively, one could follow Martin and Voltes Dorta (2011a) and employ a hedonic-adjusted number of *atm*. Following the pioneering work of Spady and Friedlaender (1978), the authors propose to build the following hedonic function of air transport movements: $atm_{mtow} = atm{*}mtow^{v}$. The variable *mtow* represents an airport's maximum take-off weight that has been shown to act as a proxy for the damage costs imposed on airports by aircrafts (Hogan & Starkie, 2003), while v is a parameter that has to be jointly estimated alongside the conventional cost function parameters. The obvious drawback of this strategy is that the econometric model is no longer linear and such non-linearity can complicate the estimation of the cost function parameters.[5]

On a different issue, Martin and Voltes Dorta (2011a) argue that international and domestic passengers might be modeled as separate outputs. Indeed, the joint provision by an airport of domestic and international passengers is a likely source of economies of scope because they share facilities, such as terminal areas and check-in desks. However, to some extent, they may impose different costs on airports, because of the different aircrafts used in long-haul versus short-haul routes (see above) and because of the dedicated spaces to international passengers in the terminal areas.[6] Also in this case, controlling for the passenger mix might help to alleviate biases but, if sufficient variation in the data is available, a separate inclusion into the cost function of international and domestic passengers might be preferred.

A somewhat different direction is however taken by Pels, Nijkamp, and Rietveld (2003) who argue that air transport movements should be better considered as an intermediate output that is "consumed" by the airport in the production of passenger movements. They, therefore, propose to consider passengers (and perhaps cargo, as in Chow & Fung, 2009) as the primary output of an airport, provided that air transport movements are considered as an additional input in the production technology. However, the idea of considering *atm* as an additional input has not got much traction in the empirical literature that has sought to estimate the cost structure and technology of the airport industry.[7]

Another important issue in the definition of airport output is related to the increasing importance of non-aviation revenues. Indeed, Oum and Fu (2008) argue that non-aviation output accounts for 40–80% of an airport total revenues and such a trend is confirmed by Bottasso and Conti (2012). The authors report that, in 2005, the non-aviation turnover of the BAA airports in the UK accounted for 70% of total revenues, and that profits generated by aviation services were negative in the case of Gatwick and Manchester. For this reason, some authors have included deflated non-aviation revenues into the cost function as an additional output.[8]

Finally, a few recent studies have acknowledged that airports, as a by-product of their activities, generate negative externalities and bad outputs (Martini, Manello, & Scotti, 2013; Scotti, Dresner, Martini, & Yu, 2014; Voltes Dorta & Martin, 2016, among the others). However, to the best of our knowledge, the impact that the inclusion of a bad output can have on the cost structure of the airport industry in terms of scope and scale economies has yet to be explored in the literature. Similarly, no study has so far attempted to incorporate delays as an additional bad output, probably for the lack of available data. In addition to this, it is important to note that the cost function framework might not be ideal to address these issues: indeed, as we will discuss at length in the "Technology of Multiproduct Firms" section, the cost function exists only insofar as firms minimize costs. While this is more or less reasonable in the case of private costs, it is methodologically questionable to assume that airports minimize social costs as well (e.g., the costs associated with noise and pollution imposed onto society), unless specifically instructed to do so in the case of government-owned operators or when forced to internalize external costs by particular policy interventions. This, of course, does not mean that a better understanding of the wider social costs associated with the performance of airports is not important, but that future research should probably focus more on the estimation of input distance functions, as the latter do not impose a particular behavioral assumption on producers and allows inclusion of bad outputs in the empirical model.[9]

Inputs

The definition and measurement of inputs in the airport literature do not seem to raise substantial disagreement among economists. This does not mean that the treatment of some inputs in the empirical literature is completely satisfactory.

By way of example, if one looks at the studies surveyed in Table 1, capital inputs are generally proxied by technical variables. Most studies use the number of runways,[10] or the number of runways together with the airport surface area and the apron areas, or the number of check-in desks. The advantage of using technical variables is that they are easily available and relatively comparable across airports,[11] the latter advantage being particularly attractive in the case of cross-country data. However, the use of technical variables presents some drawbacks too. First, because in general only one or two technical variables are considered, a non-negligible share of an airport's capital inputs is not taken into account; second, the quality and the different vintages of the infrastructures are not considered. Finally, as noted by Yan and Oum (2014), physical capital stocks cannot take into account gold plating phenomena, typically associated with rate of return regulation, in lounges and other airport facilities. From this point of view, the computation with the perpetual inventory method of a monetary measure of the capital stock, as in Bottasso and Conti (2012), might be an interesting avenue for future research.[12]

The measurement of capital stock can also have important spillovers on the definition of capital costs in the case where authors opt for the estimation of a total cost function. Indeed, while the correct procedure would be to multiply the price of capital by the monetary value of the capital stock, the absence of the latter has forced virtually all studies to use the sum of depreciation and interest reported in the airport's balance sheet, normalized by some scale variable (see below). This solution is, however, problematic for two reasons. First, accounting depreciation is based on balance sheet data for the value of fixed assets, while a value of the capital stock reconstructed from the flow of investment is likely to be a better approximation to the "true" economic value of the capital stock. Second, not only does the price of capital include the depreciation rate and the average interest rate on debt (as it is implicitly assumed in most studies), but also the opportunity cost of equity capital. In other words, the price of capital should be more properly measured as the weighted average cost of capital plus the depreciation rate. Again, more efforts on a better definition of capital costs would be welcomed in the field of airport cost function estimation.

Finally, a few words might be spent on the definition of other input prices. In general, the price of labor is estimated as the ratio of labor costs to employees. This approach may generate two problems: first, the labor price might be endogenous;[13] second, various business solutions as far as outsourcing is concerned might lead to differences in labor prices across airports that are simply associated with differences in the type (and quality) of workers that are on the airports' payrolls. For this reason, Bottasso and Conti (2012) proxied the price of labor with the average wage paid in UK localities where the airports were located and, reassuringly, they did not find major differences with respect to the more traditional proxy.

As far as the other inputs (maintenance, utilities, energy, materials, etc.) are concerned, the common practice in most airport studies is to bundle these costs together and divide them by a measure of size, namely *atm* or *runways*.[14] Of course this practice, although standard, might be subject to criticisms as far as the scale variable is concerned.

An interesting alternative is that proposed by McCarthy (2016) who uses national level price indices (e.g., for fuel) adjusted by regional price differences, thus introducing some variation across both airports and years. Finally, Voltes Dorta and Lei (2013) propose to normalize other input expenditures for a scale measure built as the weighted average of various infrastructure variables that can be considered as expenditures drivers, where the weights are the infrastructures relative marginal productivities.[15] The latter are in turn obtained from a multi-output ray production frontier estimated in Martin and Voltes Dorta (2011a).[16]

TECHNOLOGY OF MULTIPRODUCT FIRMS

In this section, we first discuss necessary and sufficient conditions for the existence of a natural monopoly. Then we provide a detailed analysis of the instruments that allow researchers to fully characterize the technology of multiproduct firms.

An intuitive definition for natural monopoly refers to the higher efficiency of organizing industry production within an individual firm rather than splitting output into two or more producers. In the past, the occurrence of natural monopoly was associated with the existence of increasing returns to scale. However, we know, at least since the work of Baumol, Panzar, and Willig (1982) that, in the realistic case of a multiproduct industry, the existence of returns to scale is neither a sufficient nor a necessary condition for the industry to be a natural monopoly.

More formally, Baumol et al. (1982) associate the occurrence of a natural monopoly with the concept of sub-additivity of the cost function. In particular, given an output vector $q = (q_1, \ldots, q_n)$, a cost function $C(q,w)$, where w is a vector of input prices, is said to be strictly subadditive if $\sum_{i=1}^{n} C(q^k, w) > C(q, w)$ for every k such that $\sum_{k=1}^{K} q^k = q$. In other words, if the cost function is subadditive, then the cost of producing q in a single firm is lower in comparison to any possible subdivision of the same vector of output among $k > 1$ firms.

According to Panzar (1989), "an industry is said to be a natural monopoly if the cost function is subadditive over the relevant range of output." It is important to note that sub-additivity is inherently a local concept: indeed, sub-additivity can be verified for an output vector q and not verified for another output vector q'. In the case of the airport industry this means that, in a given region, a unique airport might be the efficient way of organizing production while, in another area, perhaps because of differences in the overall level of demand or in the output mix (international versus domestic passengers, cargo versus passengers), the industry could be better described as a natural duopoly.

At this point, a distinction between the (somewhat abstract) case of a single product and a multiproduct industry is warranted. Indeed, it is well known that, in the single product case, increasing returns to scale imply sub-additivity, although the converse is not true: in other words, increasing returns to scale are a sufficient but not a necessary condition for the sub-additivity of the cost function. In the more interesting multiproduct case, as we noted above, increasing returns to scale are neither a necessary nor a sufficient condition for sub-additivity. To better understand why, some further definitions are necessary.

Following Baumol et al. (1982), we can define as Global or Multiproduct Scale economies as follows:

$$GSE = \frac{C(w,q)}{\sum_{i=1}^{n} (\partial C/\partial q_i) q_i} = \frac{1}{\sum_{i=1}^{n} \varepsilon_{Cq_i}} \tag{1}$$

GSE is the inverse of the elasticity of total costs with respect to an equal proportional change in the level of outputs, leaving the proportion of outputs fixed. For particular industry configurations, it is possible to show that values of $GSE > 1$ (indicating increasing global scale economies) do not imply sub-additivity. This fact can be explained by noting that, in a multiproduct context, a firm can increase its size either by increasing the volume of all products proportionally[17] or, as it is perhaps more likely, by changing its output mix.

Other dimensions of scale behavior need therefore to be introduced. In particular, Baumol et al. (1982) define product-specific scale economies, which show how costs change as one output (or a group of outputs) changes, while keeping other outputs unchanged:

$$SE_i = \frac{IC_i}{\sum_{i=1}^{n}(\partial C/\partial q_i)q_i} = \frac{AIC_i}{\sum_{i=1}^{n}(\partial C/\partial q_i)} = \frac{IC_i}{\sum_{i=1}^{n}\varepsilon_{Cq_i}c(q)} \tag{2}$$

where $IC_i = C(q) - C(q_{-i})$ represents the incremental cost of producing i, $C(q_{-i})$ is the cost of producing all outputs other than i, and $AIC_i = IC_i/q_i$ is the average incremental cost.

In order to better understand the technology of a multiproduct firm, it is also necessary to define the concept of scope economies; i.e., the cost saving that can be achieved by producing a given output set in a single firm rather than in specialized ones. Given a subsect of products T, scope economies can be measured as:

$$SCOPE_T = \frac{C(q_T) + C(q_{-T}) - C(q)}{C(q)} \tag{3}$$

Eq. (3) measures the percentage increase in costs that would arise by breaking up production into two product lines. Scope economies are generally justified on the grounds of the existence of (quasi) public inputs; i.e., of inputs that, once they are bought by a firm in order to produce one good, are available at zero cost for the production of other outputs (e.g., managerial expertise). Indeed, the managerial expertise that is required to efficiently manage the movement of international passengers in an airport is unlikely to be much different from that required to move domestic ones; it can, therefore, be safely considered at least as a quasi-public input.

Another source of economies of scope might instead arise from the indivisibility of some capital assets that can easily be shared by the joint production of different outputs. Prominent examples in the case of the airport industry are aprons and runways that can be shared by the production processes of passengers and cargo, the terminal buildings in the case of passengers and non-aviation commercial services, or check-in desks that in turn might be shared by both domestic and international passengers.

Panzar (1989) highlights an important relationship between economies of scope, global, and product-specific scale economies:

$$GSE = \frac{\sum_{i=1}^{n}\gamma_i SE_i}{1 - SCOPE_T} \tag{4}$$

where $\gamma_i = \frac{\varepsilon_{Cq_i}}{\sum_{i=1}^{n}\varepsilon_{Cq_i}}$. The above equation shows that, in the absence of scope economies, global scale economies are just the weighted average of product-specific scale economies; in turn, if SCOPE > 0, "the presence of scope economies magnifies the extent of overall economies of scale beyond that would result from a simple weighted sum of product specific levels" (Panzar, 1989). Therefore, Eq. (4) makes it clear that the presence of sufficiently strong scope economies might yield global scale economies even when some products are characterized by constant or decreasing product-specific scale economies.

A sufficient (but not necessary) condition for scope economies, which has been often exploited in the empirical literature, is based on the notion of cost complementarity (Panzar, 1989).

A twice-differentiable cost function is characterized by weak cost complementarity over the product set N and up to product level q if $\partial^2 C(\frac{\hat{q}}{\partial q_i \partial q_j}) \equiv C_{ij} < 0, i \neq j$, for all $0 < \hat{q} < q$.

A cost function that is characterized by weak cost complementarity[18] over the product set N up to the output level q, is also characterized by economies of scope.

Baumol et al. (1982) showed that the joint existence of global economies of scale and scope might not imply sub-additivity of the cost function, and that therefore the existence of scope and global scale economies is not per se a sufficient condition for an industry to be a natural monopoly. However, the authors show that if an industry is characterized by decreasing average incremental costs through q for each product $i \in N$ and scope economies at q, then the cost function is subadditive at q.[19]

The implication of this condition is that if a cost function is characterized by decreasing average incremental costs for output i, then the production of this output should be monopolized into a single firm if industry costs are to be minimized. Moreover, if the cost function is characterized by decreasing average incremental costs for all N outputs and there are economies of scope among them all, then production of the N outputs should be consolidated within a unique firm.

The empirical implementation of the test for sub-additivity described above is by no means trivial. An example with just two outputs and two possible firms, first proposed and implemented by Evans and Heckman (1983), can clarify the point. After estimating a suitable cost function, one should compute the following:

$$SUB = \{C(q_1, q_2) - [C(\phi q_1, \varpi q_2) + C((1-\phi)q_1, (1-\varpi)q_2)]\}/C(q_1, q_2) \quad (5)$$

where φ and ϖ are the weights which say how the industry output vector is split between the two firms. If SUB < 0 for whatever possible combination of weights, then the cost function is subadditive and the industry is a natural monopoly.

This test might be criticized on the grounds that some weights might require that the parameters of the cost function are valid beyond the range of outputs actually experienced in the industry. This was clearly a problem for the industry the test was first proposed for, namely the US telecom industry in 1984. Indeed, in 1984 the US monopolist produced both local and toll services, and therefore assuming that a firm would not have produced one of the two outputs clearly required extrapolation. This argument led Evans and Heckman (1984) to restrict the weights in order to prevent problems of extrapolation, although the test they proposed is simply a local test for sub-additivity.

Shin and Ying (1992) in turn proposed an alternative test that is somewhat "less local" as it does not impose minimum output bounds and splits the output vectors produced by hypothetical firms into sequential 10% increments (without allowing firms to produce zero outputs). This procedure, which has also been employed by Bitzan (2003) on a sample of US railroads, allows deriving, for each observation of the sample, a set of hypothetical output vectors that can be compared to the monopoly case.

Turning to the airport industry, a similar approach could be implemented by considering an appropriate group of airports. By way of example, let us suppose that we were to consider the catchment area of Berlin and we wanted to study whether aggregation into a single large airport would make economic sense.[20] In this case, we could estimate a cost function using a sample of small-medium-large non-specialized international airports (as in Martin & Voltes Dorta, 2011b), probably attenuating the extrapolation bias.[21] Of course, if the research question was different, we would need a different sample: for instance, should we aim to assess whether or not it is optimal to turn a diversified airport into an international passengers only airport, we would need a sample with both specialized and diversified operators in order to avoid extrapolation bias.

Another possible drawback of this test is that it implicitly assumes that a firm which produces positive quantities of each output shares the same technology with firms that specialize in a subset of products. Indeed, this assumption is likely to be false, and wrongly imposing it in the econometric estimation might bias parameter estimates as well as the measurement of economies of scale and scope. Bottasso, Conti, Piacenza, and Vannoni (2011) and Triebs, Saal, Arocena, and Kumbhakar (2016) have tackled this issue for the case of the UK water and sewerage industry and for a sample of US electric utilities, respectively.

The former study estimates the General specification of a Composite Cost function that nests various commonly employed functional forms, such as the Generalized Translog, the Translog, the Composite, and the Separable Quadratic (see below). The main advantage of the Composite family of technologies is that it is not characterized by the zero output problem that plagues the translog form. Moreover, Bottasso et al. (2011) allow all parameters to take on different values between the two types of firms (diversified and undiversified) and reject (by means of a LR test) the hypothesis that the parameters are invariant to the type of producers (water only and water and sewerage).

The approach taken by Triebs et al. (2016) is somewhat different. In practice, they posit a translog functional form and interact each regressor with dummy variables for each category of firms (upstream only, downstream only, integrated). In this way, they are both able to deal with the zero-output issue and are not forced to restrict the technology to be the same for diversified and undiversified producers. The advantage of this approach is that it does not need the non-linear terms associated with the Box-Cox transformations that are involved in the General specification of the Composite. Nevertheless, we believe that in sufficiently large samples, the latter might be preferred because it is a more flexible functional form and it allows to test whether the technology is indeed better represented by a translog.[22]

This reminds us of another important point that some decades of empirical research on the cost structure of various public utility industries have made clear; i.e., the sensitivity of economies of scale and scope estimates to the choice of the functional form for the cost function.[23]

The common simple Cobb-Douglas functional form is not a suitable representation of the industry technology, as it imposes a unitary elasticity of substitution among inputs and it does not allow scale economies to take on different values at different output levels. For these reasons, empirical researchers have turned to estimate more flexible functional forms that do not impose strong a priori restrictions on certain key parameters representing the underlying industry technology. The most popular are the Translog, the Generalized MacFadden, the Generalized Quadratic and, especially, the General Specification of the Composite. While the Translog is by far the most popular in applied work (also in the case of airports), the other functions are particularly attractive when scope economies need to be computed or when some firms in the sample produce only a subset of the industry output vector, so that the use of the Translog is not feasible.

Finally, a point that is worth making before discussing the recent empirical literature on the cost structure of the airport industry, concerns the importance of careful consideration of the appropriate cost function to estimate: i.e., a variable versus a total cost function. In principle, if the assumption that firms minimize costs is warranted,[24] the estimation of a total cost function enables a researcher to retrieve all the information that is needed to describe the industry technology (Baumol et al., 1982). However, total cost minimization rests on the assumption, often implicit in the airport literature, that airports can instantaneously adjust their capital stock in the absence of important fixities in capital inputs.

Indeed, the capacity of an airport, in terms of apron areas, terminal spaces, runways, and other infrastructures, is unlikely to be easily modifiable in the short run. As a matter of fact, the existence of strict environmental and planning restrictions severely limits the possibility for airports to rapidly adjust capacity in response to even large fluctuations in demand. It is true that most airports routinely invest and that capital costs depend on the level of output;

however, this does not mean that, in a given year, airports are able to fully adjust their capital stock in order to minimize total production costs, as if they could "re-build" the airport from scratch. Moreover, the lumpy nature of most capital investments in the airport industry implies that some infrastructures are built in order to meet future and not current demand: as a result, it seems unlikely that airports can be thought of as total cost minimizer firms.

Martin and Voltes Dorta (2011a) is perhaps the only study that offers a justification for the estimation of a total cost function in the airport industry. In particular, the authors note that cross-sectional estimates of total cost functions based on samples composed by airports with sufficient variability in size might be used to recover the long-run effect of output on costs, thereby "legitimizing" the estimation of a total cost function.[25] By way of contrast, a time series sample would be more likely to identify short-run impacts of output changes on costs. Along with this line of reasoning, one could say that panel data characterized by important size differentials and estimators that do not identify parameters on the basis of the within variation only, could be used to estimate a total cost function because they would identify the long-run effects of output on costs.

Although, there might be some merit in this distinction between the short and the long-run effects identified by different types of data (time series versus cross-section), it is important to recall that this distinction reflects an empirical problem (Hsiao, 2003) and, more importantly, it is conditional on the use of the same dependent variable. However, in the total versus variable cost function debate, the issue is mainly a theoretical one; namely, whether the assumption that airports minimize total costs is defendable or not. If it is not, then the total cost function does not even exist.[26]

A possible way out of the variable versus total cost function debate is the performance of a formal statistical test that allows a researcher to discriminate between deviations from the optimal expansion path due to random factors (in which case the estimation of a total cost function would be warranted) from those arising from systematic failures to minimize total costs. Schankerman and Nadiri (1986) have proposed such test: only if the hypothesis that airports minimize total costs cannot be rejected is the estimation of a total cost function warranted.[27]

The estimation of a variable cost function enables researchers to test for returns to scale, cost complementarity or any other key technological parameter, distinguishing between the short and the long run.

For instance, a measure of short-run global scale economies, which some authors prefer to define as economies of capacity utilization, can be recovered as:

$$SESR = 1/\sum_{i=1}^{N} \varepsilon_{Cq_i} \tag{6}$$

In turn, long-run global economies of scale can be computed by using the following formula:

$$GSE = SESR*(1 - \varepsilon_{Ck}) \quad (7)$$

where ε_{Ck} is the elasticity of costs with respect to the capital stock.

However, as shown in Schankerman and Nadiri (1986) and, for the case of the airport industry, in Bottasso and Conti (2012), the evaluation of (7) at the actual level of the capital stock is correct provided that the airport's capital stock is at its optimal long-run level[28] or when the technology is homothetic. Unfortunately, some studies simply evaluate GSE at the actual level of the capital stock, even when the technology is not homothetic and without checking whether or not the capital stock is at its long-run equilibrium level. Bottasso and Conti (2012) implemented the test proposed by Schankerman and Nadiri (1986) and showed, for the UK airport industry case, that airports were not minimizing total costs and that, in particular, smaller airports were slightly undercapitalized, while larger ones displayed clear evidence of overcapitalization.[29] Also, Voltes Dorta and Lei (2013) and McCarthy (2016) find evidence of a positive elasticity of variable costs with respect to capital stock, a clear indication of short-run disequilibrium and a failure of total cost minimization.[30]

Before turning to a review of the studies that have considered the cost structure of the airport industry, it is worth noting that the theoretical literature on scale and scope economies in multiproduct industries briefly surveyed above, has made it clear that the estimation of global scale economies, although important, cannot say the last word on important policy questions.

Indeed, in addressing important policy issues the multiproduct nature of the airport industry requires researchers to pay much more attention to aspects related to scope economies and, if possible, to explicitly test for the sub-additivity of the cost function. For example, local authorities might need to decide whether it is more convenient to expand an existing airport or to build a new one in the surrounding area, or whether it is convenient to close small airports in the catchment areas of larger ones and expand the latter. Alternatively, it might be important to understand whether it is cost-efficient to separate freight from passengers, or whether the construction of specialized airports (e.g., on international flights) should be encouraged.[31]

SCALE AND SCOPE ECONOMIES IN THE AIRPORT INDUSTRY: A CRITICAL SURVEY OF THE RECENT LITERATURE

1. For expositional purposes, we have decided to organize the recent literature on scale and scope economies in the airport industry according to the type

of sample analyzed. In particular, we have grouped papers into four groups: "The United States" section will deal with studies that have analyzed the US airport industry; the "Other Single Country Studies" section will consider other single country studies (Italy, Spain, UK, and China), while the "Cross-Country Studies" section will be based on the analysis of multi-country studies; finally, the "A Critical Assessment" section will provide an overall assessment.

The United States

The cost structure of the US airports has been analyzed in a series of papers by McCarthy (2011, 2014, 2016) on a sample of 50 airports (27 large hubs and 23 medium hubs) observed over the period 1996–2008. The three papers share the econometric approach (a translog variable cost function with cost shares and airport fixed effects[32] estimated by SURE) as well as variable and quasi-fixed inputs (see Table 1). The difference between the three studies is associated with the output set and the various control variables included in the cost function. While McCarthy (2014) considers airports as a single output industry, using *atm* as a proxy, McCarthy (2011) takes into account both a one output specification, using passengers, and a more extended model that also incorporates freight. In turn, McCarthy (2016) estimates a three output model by adding *atm* to passengers and freight. Parameter estimates allow the author to recover economies of capacity utilization, equivalent to short-run scale economies in Eq. (6) above; moreover, the formula in Eq. (7) is used to retrieve long-run scale economies, evaluated at the sample mean of the variables, including the capital stock. Interestingly, empirical results show that single output studies tend to produce higher economies of scale. For instance, McCarthy (2014) finds economies of capacity utilization of 3.5 at the sample mean,[33] and long-run economies of scale of 4.1, while the two output model in McCarthy (2011) reports long-run economies of scale of about 1.6, using the output and capital variable cost elasticities reported in the paper. Finally, the three output model in McCarthy (2016) finds essentially constant scale economies in the short run and diseconomies of scale in the long run. Unfortunately, scale economies are not computed at different cuts of the sample, although the fact that the mean airport serves about 11 million *wlu* shows that economy of scale might be exhausted even for medium-sized airports.

Moreover, McCarthy (2016) employs the cost complementarity test discussed above and finds some evidence of anti-cost complementarities between non-aeronautical revenue, *wlu* and *atm*, while the positive cost complementarity between *wlu* and *atm* is not statistically significant.

An interesting methodological innovation introduced in the airport cost function literature by McCarthy (2016) is that the paper corrects for first-order serial correlation in both the cost function and the share equations. Since the author does not report scale economies estimates from a model without such controls, it might be interesting to analyze the impact of serial correlation on scale and scope economies estimates in future research.

A study that was not focused on scale economies estimation but that is worth citing, as it finds somewhat conflicting results with McCarthy (2016), is that by Yan and Oum (2014). The authors estimate a three output stochastic variable cost frontier model on a sample of 55 US airports observed over the period 2001–2009 and find evidence of short-run economies of scale (1.7) at the sample mean. Moreover, on the basis of the first-order cost function coefficients and Eq. (6), empirical results suggest the existence of lower long-run scale economies (about 1.3).

Other Single Country Studies

Two recent studies have estimated cost functions for the UK airport industry providing information on economies of scale. Leaving aside the pioneering work of Tolofari et al. (1990), who reported scale economies up to 20 million passengers, using *wlu* as output, we can mention Bottasso and Conti (2012) and Voltes Dorta and Lei (2013). The former study estimates by SURE a variable cost function with the monetary value of the capital stock as a quasi-fixed input, for the 24 largest UK airports observed over the period 1994–2005, using both a three and a four output specifications. By applying the test suggested by Schankerman and Nadiri (1986) the authors find evidence of short-run disequilibrium (and, in particular, of overcapitalization for the largest operators) and long-run scale economies that are exhausted at approximately 5 million passengers, with diseconomies of scale that start to prevail for airports with more than 14 million passengers.

In turn, Voltes Dorta and Lei (2013) estimate both a two output variable and total translog stochastic cost frontier with Bayesian techniques for 27 UK airports observed over the period 1994–2009. In the case of the variable cost frontier, they used a weighted average of the number of runways and terminal surface (see the "Output and Input Measurement in the Airport Industry" section) as quasi-fixed inputs. In the case of the total cost function, the authors report significant economies of scale (2), at the translog approximation point (2 million passengers), slightly larger but broadly consistent with the values reported in Bottasso and Conti (2012) for airports serving approximately 2 million passengers. Their results also show that scale economies are almost exhausted for the largest airports in the sample. In the case of the variable cost function, the authors report only economies of capital utilization at the mean (1.69). Moreover, the positive and significant capital stock elasticity denotes that airports are not in long-run equilibrium and that therefore the estimation of a variable cost function should be preferred. Using the estimated capital elasticity and Eq. (7), long-run scale economies of about 1.5 would arise for the mean airport, although, as explained in the "Technology of Multiproduct Firms" section, this procedure is not correct when airports are not in long-run equilibrium.[34]

Abrate and Erbetta (2010) estimate a three output input distance function together with input share equations for a sample of 26 Italian airports observed over the 2000–2005 period. By exploiting the duality relationship between the input distance function and the shadow cost function, they report evidence of mild short run increasing returns to scale at the sample mean (3.8 million passengers), although they do not discuss returns to scale at different sample points. Abrate and Erbetta (2010) is perhaps the only paper that features handling revenue as an output: Interestingly, they use a complementarity test and find, at the sample mean, evidence of significant diseconomies between passengers and handling revenues. They also find some heterogeneity since, focusing on airports serving more than 1 million passengers, the diseconomies between handling and passengers seem to arise only in the case of airports that already outsource a significant fraction of handling. In turn, airports with very low outsourcing seem to benefit from joint provision of handling and passengers.

Another study that reports empirical evidence on returns to scale without using the cost function framework is that of Chow and Fung (2009) which is based on a sample of 46 Chinese airports in 2000, that includes both international and regional hubs as well as regional airports. Their paper, based on the methodology of Pels et al. (2003), estimates a series of production frontiers for passenger and cargo movements as well as an input distance function that features passenger and cargo as outputs, and *atm* as well as various technical variables as inputs. Their main results suggest that, at the approximation point, there are constant returns to scale, and scope economies between cargo and passengers.[35]

Finally, Martin et al. (2011) estimate multiproduct total and variable cost functions for a sample of 36 Spanish airports observed over the period 1991–1997. In the case of the total cost function, there is evidence of mild scale economies for the average airport (1.18), with larger airports operating at approximately constant returns.[36] In turn, the variable cost function suggests the existence of short-run scale economies (1.70) for the average airport, while long-run scale economies are not reported. Nevertheless, the positive coefficient for the capital stock suggests the existence of important overcapitalization for the average Spanish airport, so that a variable cost function should be relied on to retrieve estimates of the long-run scale economies.

Cross-Country Studies

One of the first studies exploring the extent of scale economies in the airport industry using cross-country data was Doganis et al. (1995). Authors used data for 25 European airports observed in 1993 assuming *wlu* as output and found scale economies up to five million passengers for airports located in the UK and southern Europe and essentially constant returns for northern European ones.

More recently, there has been a surge in the use of international data, perhaps because this allows a comparison of the costs of several very large airports with medium-sized ones, while the use of country-level data usually prevent such analysis since there are very few large airports in each sample. Of course, the use of cross-country data has its own limitations; important differences in accounting conventions, institutions, rules on planning and noise emissions (among others) might introduce biases in parameter estimates if not properly controlled for.

Pels et al. (2003) estimate a series of translog production frontiers for the production of air transport movements and passenger movements, respectively, for a sample of 33 European airports observed over the period 1995–1997. The authors find essentially constant returns for the production of a*tm* and increasing returns (1.2) in the production of passengers for the average airport which, in their sample, produces 150,000 atm and 12.5 million wlu.[37] Martin and Voltes Dorta (2008) estimate a translog total cost function for a sample of 41 international airports observed over the period 1991–1995 using *atm* and *wlu* as outputs. They find mild scale economies that range from 1.3 to 1, with an average of 1.13 at the translog approximation point (about 8 million passengers).

In two companion papers, Martin and Voltes Dorta (2011a, 2011b) estimate a five output stochastic total cost frontier featuring both technical and allocative inefficiency with Bayesian techniques for a sample of 191 international airports observed over the period 1991–2008. The main innovation of these studies is the five output specification that includes domestic and international passengers, cargo, non-aeronautical revenue and a hedonic function of air transport movements.[38] The authors find large scale economies ranging from 2, at the sample mean of 12 million passengers, to about 1.4 for airports serving more than 40 million passengers. One possible drawback of the study is the failure to include airport fixed effects or at least regional dummies to capture the unobserved heterogeneity that surely characterizes the airports considered in the sample.[39] Moreover, Martin and Voltes Dorta (2011b) include an interesting exercise aimed at assessing whether it might be better to serve the future expected increase in demand either by expanding an existing airport (e.g., constructing new runways, terminals, etc.) or by building an entirely new airport in the same catchment area. The authors test the hypothesis that the aggregate costs of some Multi Airport Systems (MAS), such as those of Milan, London, and Berlin, are higher than the costs of an individual airport producing the whole output of the airports included in the MAS. The authors, after estimating a stochastic cost frontier on the sample of airports, use estimated parameters and aggregate data at the MAS level to derive the efficient cost of a hypothetical airport corresponding to the aggregate size of each MAS. This measure is obtained by dividing the predicted expenditure by the observed total costs and is used to approximate the inefficiency of each MAS. The inefficiency of each individual airport belonging to an MAS is proxied with the traffic weighted average of the inefficiency estimated for airports with a similar size included in the sample. In this way, the authors can subtract from the overall inefficiency of the MAS the inefficiency of the individual airports, thereby deriving a residual inefficiency that the authors interpret as the potential savings "related to the consolidation of air traffic into a single location."

Using this procedure, Martin and Voltes Dorta (2011b) report costs in excess of about 20–44% associated with the fragmentation of production into a multi-airport system. It goes without saying that this result, as recognized by the authors, is largely driven by their finding that scale economies are not exhausted at any output level. While this is a badly needed paper, because it is the first serious work that attempts to provide an answer to a very important policy question, it is however also important to recall that what is really necessary to tackle such issue is the sub-additivity kind of analysis described in the "Technology of Multiproduct Firms" section.

Finally, Voltes Dorta and Pagliari (2012) use a sample of 194 world airports observed over the period 2007–2009 in order to estimate a five output variable stochastic cost frontier, estimated with Bayesian techniques and report, at the approximation point of the translog, short-run economies of scale of 2.13. The positive square terms are consistent with short-run scale economies decreasing with size. While the authors do not compute scale economies at different sample points, they note that, in the case of Heathrow, short-run scale economies are about constant. The positive elasticity of both the quasi-fixed factors is yet again a sign of short-run disequilibrium, which in turn would call for the computation of long-run scale economies.[40]

A Critical Assessment

Our overall reading of the empirical literature is that a consensus on the existence of scale economies in the airport industry does not seem to exist yet. Indeed, a series of papers, especially from Voltes Dorta and coauthors report unexhausted scale economies even in the case of large international airports that serve more than 100 million passengers per year. In turn, other recent single country studies, like McCarthy (2016) in the case of the US and Bottasso and Conti (2012) for the UK, have found diseconomies of scale, at least for the largest operators.[41]

Such contrasting results could be explained by differences in model specification related to control variables and inputs definition, but not on the choice of output variables, as both series of papers consider quite rich output vectors, ranging from 3 to 5. Furthermore, differences in the methodological approach adopted (cost function versus stochastic cost frontiers) are likely to be associated with discrepancies in results. All these possible explanations would call for future studies to provide more sensitivity checks in order to probe the robustness of their main results to changes in the sets of control variables, estimation methodology, and functional form assumptions.

However, in our opinion there can be two other, perhaps more important, reasons for this lack of a consensus. First, country level studies usually feature only one or two very large operators: if these airports, for idiosyncratic reasons, tend to have relatively higher costs, returns to scale might appear lower than they actually are. From this point of view, larger international samples (as those used, say, in Martin & Voltes Dorta, 2011a) should be less prone to what is essentially a small sample problem. It goes without saying that this type of sample opens up new difficulties that, in our opinion, have not yet been satisfactorily addressed in the empirical literature, such as differences in accounting conventions, institutions,[42] and regulations that might impose barriers to airport expansions that vary across countries and that, if not controlled for, might bias parameter estimates. Along with this line, we believe that, controlling for airport unobserved heterogeneity (as done in McCarty, 2016; Kutlu & McCarty, 2016) by including of a full set of airport fixed effects into the cost function, might make both single country and especially cross-country studies more convincing.[43]

However, we also believe that the widespread finding of overcapitalization in the airport industry calls seriously into question the hypothesis of total cost minimization. The latter is the theoretical underpinning of the link between the total cost function and the production technology, that in turn allows researchers to interpret the (inverse of) the scale elasticity as a returns to scale measure. From this point of view, when firms are in disequilibrium, a variable cost function should be estimated and long-run scale elasticities recovered using the long-run optimal capital stock, as shown in Schankerman and Nadiri (1986). In other words, we would suggest that future research would make more use of variable cost functions and input distance functions.[44]

Moreover, our reading of the literature reveals that, notwithstanding the multiproduct nature of the airport industry, the empirical evidence about the existence of scope economies is surprisingly almost non-existent. Indeed, Chow and Fung (2009) use a complementarity test and report evidence of scope economies between passengers and cargo at the sample mean, while McCarthy (2016) finds some evidence of anti-cost complementarities between *atm* and non-aeronautical revenue and between *wlu* and non-aeronautical revenue.[45] However, we should recall that a failure of finding a cost complementarity between any two outputs is not necessarily evidence of absence of scope economies, as the cost complementarity test is a sufficient but not necessary condition for scope economies to exist. Similarly, we have not been able to find any study that has quantified the magnitude of product-specific returns to scale, although McCarthy (2016) has provided a test for their existence. Furthermore, to the best of our knowledge, neither the existence of scope economies in the airport industry has been analyzed, nor a sub-additivity test has been implemented.

We believe that in order to try to address issues such as airport expansion versus construction of new airports, or airport diversification versus specialization, it becomes crucial to reach a more thorough knowledge about scope economies. In particular, it becomes crucial to understand how scope economies interact with global and product-specific scale economies and how the magnitude of these interactions changes at different scales of production and product mixes.

Related to this, researchers should recognize that the translog, being undefined at zero-output levels, should be abandoned in favor of the estimation of more flexible functional forms because the computation of scope and product-specific returns to scale requires the comparison of costs of diversified and specialized airports.

Finally, we believe that an issue that might deserve some further work is that concerning the econometric estimation of the cost function and, in particular, the exogeneity assumption about outputs. Indeed, such an assumption is likely to be a reasonable approximation in the case of those public utility sectors where an output is largely demand-driven, as firms are required to satisfy demand at the prices set by regulators (distribution of gas, water, and electricity being perhaps the clearest examples). By way of contrast, in the case of airports, output is the result of the complex interactions between passengers, airlines, and airports, with aeronautical charges that depend on airports costs, being the transmission channel. In other words, if an unobserved (by the econometrician) shock to airport costs leads to changes in aeronautical charges, which in turn are transferred to airline customers, the output level becomes endogenous. The importance of this effect depends on various factors, such as whether the airport is regulated or not, whether regulation is of the single or dual till type. Again, tackling the endogeneity of output seriously might be another important step to address in future studies.

CONCLUSIONS AND POLICY IMPLICATIONS

The analysis of the empirical literature on the airport industry cost structure provides mixed results as far as the existence and breadth of scale economies. We believe that studies based on the estimation of short-run variable cost functions offer more reliable results, given the reasonable assumption of airport overcapitalization in the short run. Most studies that adopt this approach analyze single country data and suggest that economies of scale do exist but tend to be exhausted for larger airports. Indeed, as long as the scale of operation grows, costs might significantly increase because of inefficiency of the management in running very large airports, more stringent environmental constraints, and land scarcity. Moreover, as Gillen (2011) suggests "doubling throughput more than doubles the space needed so there may well be diseconomies of scale with terminals." Furthermore, it is important to remember that most studies do not include in their analysis external costs linked to expanding airports, like noise and emissions, congestion in the nearby areas, and longer times for passengers operations. Although, as discussed above, a cost function might not be the correct theoretical framework to deal with such issues, it should be tackled in future analysis, possibly within the framework of an approach that takes into account the multi-output nature of the airport business. Indeed, as we stressed in this essay, a deep knowledge of airport technology helps to address several policy questions. However, it is important to remember that some policy issues related to planning and regulation as well as on the optimal market structure require an analysis of the relationship between airports and airlines. In fact, some authors suggest that airlines countervailing power might guarantee a certain degree of competition among airports and would prevent the exploitation of possible market power (Bottasso, Bruno, Conti, & Piga, 2017).

NOTES

1. We refer to Liebert and Niemeier (2013) for a survey on the applied literature on efficiency and productivity of airports. Within this strand of literature, various studies have sought to assess the impact of ownership and regulation on airport efficiency: see Assaf & Gillen, 2013; Craig, Airola, & Tipu, 2012; Oum, Yan, & Yu, 2008)) for recent works on this issue.

2. See Tolofari, Ashford, and Caves (1990), Doganis, Lobbenberg, and Graham (1995), Martin Cejas (2002), and Low and Tang (2006).

3. See Martin and Voltes Dorta (2011a) and in particular their Figure 1.

4. However, Bottasso and Conti (2012), for a sample of UK airports, report an elasticity of variable costs with respect to *wlu* very similar to the sum of the elasticities of passengers and freight.

5. Martin and Voltes Dorta (2011a) estimate a stochastic cost frontier using Bayesian techniques.

6. Voltes Dorta and Lei (2013) model passengers as a hedonic function of the share of passengers flying with low-cost carriers and with charters.

7. Indeed, it is not clear how to implement the approach suggested by Pels et al. (2003) in a cost function framework. On the empirical side, one would need to assume that the airport is buying *atm* from itself and then impute a price into the cost function. More seriously, most airports impute a charge to airlines for each air transport movement, and therefore most researchers might have considered odd not to consider *atm* as a conventional output. However, a few papers employing Data Envelopment Analysis have followed the approach of Pels et al. (2003).

8. See Voltes Dorta (2011a), Bottasso and Conti (2012), and McCarthy (2016).

9. The case of delays is similar. However, if delays would determine a "penalty" for airport operators, the estimation of a cost function could be theoretically justified. For a discussion of delays, pricing, and airport capacity, see Morrison and Winston (1989).

10. McCarthy (2016) uses a refined version, namely the number of effective runways, which takes into account also the width and the length of each airport's runways.
11. However, see Liebert and Niemeier (2013) on the comparability of runways across airports.
12. The use of a monetary value for the capital stock is, however, not without problems, particularly in the case of studies that pool data of airports located in several countries, for the existence of different accounting conventions.
13. The number of employees is under the control of the airport: as a result, an unobserved shock (by the econometrician) to costs might introduce a correlation with the price of labor, thus inducing a bias in the results.
14. This is the common procedure for the price of capital, too.
15. By way of example, in the case of material costs, Voltes Dorta and Lei (2013) consider as infrastructure variables the number of check-in desks and boarding gates.
16. See Martin and Voltes Dorta (2011a) for a detailed explanation of the estimation of the multi-output ray production frontier and its use in the computation of input prices.
17. In a network industry, a firm might also increase size by extending its network. See on this the discussion in Panzar (1989).
18. The cost complementarity test simply checks whether the marginal costs of good i does not grow as the production of good j increases.
19. Another sufficient condition is based on the notion of trans-ray supportability of the cost function. See Panzar (1989).
20. Of course assuming away any "disciplining effects" on airport costs (and prices) brought about by competition between airports, as discussed in Bottasso et al. (2017).
21. Extrapolation bias might also be a concern for estimates of scope economies computed as in Eq. (3).
22. Bottasso et al. (2011) and Fraquelli, Piacenza, and Vannoni (2005), among the others, reject the null hypothesis that the underlying technology is translog.
23. See Salvanes and Tjotta (1998) for a discussion.
24. It might be argued that, in the case of government-owned firms that are poorly exposed to competitive pressures, the cost minimization assumption could be questioned, because airports managers might be instructed to pursue various social goals other than strict cost minimization. For this reason, some authors have preferred the estimation of input distance functions, which do not impose any behavioral assumption on producers. For the airport industry case, see Chow and Fung (2009) and Abrate and Erbetta (2010).
25. The idea is that the disequilibrium positions of some airports (some with a too large and others with a too small capital stock) would wash out, on average.
26. In other words, it is not possible to use parameter estimates to recover the underlying production technology.
27. See Kulatilaka (1985) for a test based on the difference between the actual and the shadow price of capital.
28. In this case, a total cost function can be estimated, because short run total cost minimization (which takes the capital stock as fixed) and long run total cost minimization coincide when the capital stock is optimally chosen.
29. As in the case of scale economies, it is important to recall that, as shown in Casarin (2007), also testing for the presence of scope economies using the cost complementarity test requires ultimately the computation of the long run optimal capital stock level.
30. The finding of a positive coefficient of the capital stock at the sample mean of the data is per se an indication that the mean airport is not in long-run equilibrium with respect to the capital stock. This is because standard microeconomic theory posits that a larger capital stock should reduce variable costs so that we should expect a negative elasticity. Moreover, if an airport is operating at long-run equilibrium scale, the marginal

effect of the capital stock on variable costs is equal (in absolute value) to the market price of capital. When this does not happen and one finds a positive elasticity of variable costs with respect to the capital stock, it is because the latter is so large, compared to production, that further increases would raise variable costs, i.e. the shadow value of the capital stock is negative (see Bottasso & Conti, 2012). A positive elasticity of the capital stock, a result that is not uncommon in the empirical literature related to various public utility industries, might be associated to the existence of infrastructures built in order to meet future demand that is yet to materialize; however, in the meantime, that infrastructure needs to be operated, thereby requiring extra operating expenditure (e.g., for heating an underutilized terminal building over the winter). Alternatively, the positive elasticity of capital might simply be the result of multicollinearity problems associated to a positive correlation between the capital stock and the output variables, or the results of failing to control for capacity utilization (Oum & Zang, 1991). See also Bottasso and Conti (2009) for a discussion of this issue.

31. Of course, we are not discussing very important issues that should take a central role in the policy issues above, such as the preferences of consumers, their time spent traveling, and the disciplining effects of competition on airports productivity and charges.

32. To the best of our knowledge, McCarthy's are the only papers that include a full set of airport specific fixed effects in the papers included in this survey.

33. See Kutlu and McCarthy (2016) who estimate a one output translog stochastic frontier with the true fixed effects approach and find large short run returns to scale.

34. Assaf (2010) uses bootstrapped DEA techniques for 27 UK airports in 2007 and finds that most large airports are operating either at constant or decreasing returns to scale, confirming the results in Bottasso and Conti (2012) with a radically different methodology.

35. This result is again based on the computation of a complementarity test, as in Abrate and Erbetta (2010). The drawback of the study is the failure to consider important inputs such as labor, material, and services.

36. For example, the three largest airports, Madrid, Palma de Mallorca, and Barcelona, have returns to scale equal to 1.06, 1.08, and 1.08, respectively.

37. One possible drawback of this paper is its failure to control for labor and other operating expenditure.

38. The hedonic function of *atm* has the purpose to take into account the differential impact on airport costs imposed by the take-offs and landings of different types of aircrafts.

39. Indeed, the airports are located in various EU countries plus USA, Mexico, Panama, Canada, Japan, South Korea, New Zealand, Thailand, South Africa, China, and Australia.

40. Although not focusing on scale economies, Oum et al. (2008) estimate a three outputs variable cost frontier, for a sample of 109 world airports observed over the period 2001–2004, and report cost elasticities of outputs which give raise to short-run returns to scale of about 1.35 at the sample mean (about 19 million passengers). Similarly, Zhao, Choo, and Oum (2014) consider a panel of 54 major Canadian and US airports observed over the period 2002–2008 and estimate a variable restricted translog stochastic cost frontier and find quite large short run returns to scale at the translog approximation point (about 1.4) and positive elasticities for the quasi-fixed capital inputs.

41. Yan and Oum (2014) have found significant short run scale economies for the US case at the sample average, while Martin et al. (2011) report, in the case of Spain, unexhausted scale economies, even if the three largest airports seem to operate under essentially constant returns to scale. In turn, Chow and Fung (2009) find constant returns to scale for a sample that include large, medium, and small Chinese airports.

Overall, the evidence on single country studies seems therefore to be more geared toward constant scale economies or diseconomies of scale.

42. For example, employment protection legislation might differ, as well as regulation governing the scope of outsourcing and they can both have implications on input usage and optimal size of an airport.

43. A potential pitfall of including airport fixed effects is that only the within airport variation is used to identify output cost elasticities. If this variation is low, compared to the variation across airports, estimates might be imprecise, especially in multi-output models.

44. Hajargasht, Coelli, and Prasada Rao (2008) and Nemoto and Furumatsu (2014) are two recent papers that measure global, product-specific returns to scale and economies of scope using an input distance function framework.

45. Moreover, the existence of diseconomies of scope between non-aeronautical services and aeronautical outputs would call, strictly speaking, for airports to divest their commercial activities: this might seem odd, as it would go against the trend characterizing most commercial airports (both private and public) around the world. However, diseconomies of scope between commercial activities and aeronautical outputs might be just an indication that in some airports too much space has been devoted to shops, maybe at the expense of check-ins and gates, thereby creating congestion and increasing costs. In other words, future research should spend more effort in finding better proxies for non-aviation activities than simple deflated revenues, in particular by paying attention to the issue of space allocation, within the terminal buildings, to non-aviation related services.

REFERENCES

Abrate, G., & Erbetta, F. (2010). Efficiency and patterns of service mix in airport companies: An input distance function approach. *Transportation Research Part E, 46*(5), 693–708.

Assaf, A. (2010). Bootstrapped scale efficiency measures of UK airports. *Journal of Air Transport Management, 16*(1), 42–44.

Assaf, A., & Gillen, F. (2013). Measuring joint the impact of governance form and economic regulation on airport efficiency. *European Journal of Operations Research, 220*(1), 187–198.

Baumol, W. J., Panzar, J. C., & Willig, R. D. (1982). *Contestable markets and the theory of industry structure*. Harcourt Brace Jovanovic.

Bitzan, J. (2003). Railroad costs and competition: The implication of introducing competition to railroad networks. *Journal of Transport Economics and Policy, 37*(2), 201–225.

Bottasso, A., & Conti, M. (2009). Scale economies, technology and technical change in the water industry: Evidence from the English water only sector. *Regional Science and Urban Economics, 39*(2), 138–147.

Bottasso, A., & Conti, M. (2012). The cost structure of the UK airport industry. *Journal of Transport Economics and Policy, 46*(3), 313–332.

Bottasso, A., Conti, M., Piacenza, M., & Vannoni, D. (2011). The poolability assumption for multiproduct technologies: Evidence from the English water and sewerage utilities. *International Journal of Production Economics, 130*(1), 112–117.

Bottasso, A., Bruno, M., Conti, M., & Piga, C. (2017). Competition, vertical relationship and countervailing power in the UK airport industry. *Journal of Regulatory Economics*, forthcoming.

Casarin, A. (2007). Efficient industry configurations in downstream gas markets. An empirical assessment. *Energy Economics, 29*, 312–328.

Chow, C. K. W., & Fung, M. K. Y. (2009). Efficiency and scope economies of Chinese airports in moving passengers and cargo. *Journal of Air Transport Management, 15*, 324–329.

Craig, S. G., Airola, J., & Tipu, M. (2012). General purpose of special district governance? Technical efficiency versus rent dissipation in airport finances. *Public Finance Review*, *40*(6), 712–735.

Doganis, R. (1992). *The airport business*. London: Routledge.

Doganis, R., Lobbenberg, A., & Graham, A. (1995). *The economic performance of European airports*, Research Report 3, Department of Air Transport, College of Aeronautics, University of Westminster, London.

Evans, D. S., & Heckman, J. J. (1983). Multiproduct cost function estimates and natural monopoly tests for the bell system. In D. S. Evans (Ed.), *Breaking up bell: Essays on industry organization and regulation*. New York: North-Holland.

Evans, D. S., & Heckman, J. J. (1984). A test for subadditivity of the cost function with an application to the bell system. *American Economic Review*, *74*, 615–627.

Fraquelli, G., Piacenza, M., & Vannoni, D. (2005). Cost savings from generation and distribution with an application to Italian electric utilities. *Journal of Regulatory Economics*, *28*(3), 289–308.

Fraquelli, G., Piacenza, M., & Vannoni, D. (2007). Scale and scope economies in multi-utilities: Evidence from gas, water and electricity combinations. *Applied Economics*, *36*, 2045–2057.

Gillen, D. (2011). The evolution of airport ownership and governance. *Journal of Air Transport Management*, *17*, 3–13.

Hajargasht, G., Coelli, T., & Prasada Rao, D. S. (2008). A dual measure of economies of scope. *Economic Letters*, *100*(2), 185–188.

Hogan, O., & Starkie, D. (2003). Calculating the runway damage component in the marginal cost pricing of airport services: An application to Dublin airport. In D. Gillen et al. (Eds.), *The economic regulation of airports – Recent developments in Australasia, North America and Europe*. Aldershot: Ashgate.

Hsiao, C. (2003). *Analysis of panel data* (2nd ed.), Econometric Society Monograph. Cambridge University Press.

Kulatilaka, N. (1985). Testing on the validity of static equilibrium models. *Journal of Econometrics*, *28*, 253–268.

Kutlu, L., & McCarthy, P. (2016). US airport ownership, efficiency and heterogeneity. *Transportation Research Part E*, *89*, 117–132.

Lechmann, M., & Niemeier, H. M. (2013). Economies of scale and scope of airports – A critical survey. *Journal of Air Transport Studies*, *4*, 1–25.

Liebert, V., & Niemeier, H. M. (2013). A survey of empirical research on the productivity and efficiency measurement of airports. *Journal of Transport Economics and Policy*, *47*(2), 157–189.

Low, J., & Tang, L. C. (2006). Factor substitution and complementarity in the Asia airport industry. *Journal of Air Transport Management*, *12*, 261–266.

Martin Cejas, R. (2002). An approximation to the productive efficiency of the Spanish airports network through a deterministic cost frontier. *Journal of Air Transport Management*, *8*, 233–238.

Martin, J. C., Roman, C., & Voltes Dorta, A. (2011). Scale economies and marginal costs in Spanish Airports. *Transportation Research Part E*, 238–248.

Martin, J. C., & Voltes Dorta, A. (2008). International airports: Economies of scale and marginal costs. *Journal of Transportations Research Forum*, *47*, 1.

Martin, J. C., & Voltes Dorta, A. (2011a). The econometric estimation of airports' cost function. *Transportation Research Part B*, 112–127.

Martin, J. C., & Voltes Dorta, A. (2011b). The dilemma between capacity expansion and multi-airport systems: Empirical evidence from the industry's cost function. *Transportation Research Part E*, 382–389.

Martini, G., Manello, A., & Scotti, D. (2013). The influence of LLC, fleet mix and ownership on airports' technical and environmental efficiency. *Transportation Research Part E*, *50*, 37–52.

McCarthy, P. (2011). Airport costs and production technology: A translog cost function analysis with implications for economic developments. *Georgia Department of Transportation*.

McCarthy, P. (2014). Airport costs and production technology: A translog cost function analysis. *Journal of Transport Economics and Policy*, *48*, 3.
McCarthy, P. (2016). Multi-product cost analysis of US airports. In J. D. Bitzan, J. H. Peoples, & W. W. Wilson (Eds.), *Airline efficiency* (Vol. 5, pp. 243–281). Advances in Airline Economics. Emerald Group Publishing Limited.
Morrison, S. A., & Winston, C. (1989). Enhancing the performance of the deregulated air transportation system. *Brookings Papers on Economic Activity: Microeconomics*, 61–123.
Nemoto, J., & Furumatsu, N. (2014). Scale and scope economies of Japanese private universities revisted with an input distance function approach. *Journal of Productivity Analysis*, *41*(2), 213–226.
Oum, T. H., Yan, J., & Yu, C. (2008). Ownership forms matter for airport efficiency: A stochastic frontier investigation of worldwide airports. *Journal of Urban Economics*, *64*, 422–435.
Oum, T. H., & Zang, Y. (1991). Utilization of quasi-fixed inputs and estimation of cost functions. *Journal of Transport Economics and Policy*, *25*(2), 121–134.
Panzar, J. C. (1989). Technology determinants of firm and industry structure. In R. Schmalensee & R. D. Willig (Eds.), *Handbook of industrial organization* (Vol. I). Elsevier.
Pels, E., Nijkamp, P., & Rietveld, P. (2003). Inefficiencies and scale economies of European airport operations. *Transportation Research Part E*, *39*, 341–361.
Pulley, L. B., & Braunstein, Y. M. (1992). A composite cost function for multiproduct firms with an application to economies of scope in banking. *Review of Economics and Statistics*, *74*, 221–230.
Salvanes, K. G., & Tjotta, S. (1998). A test for natural monopoly with application to Norwegian electricity distribution. *Review of Industrial Organization*, *13*, 669–685.
Schankerman, M., & Nadiri, M. (1986). A test of static equilibrium models and rate of return to quasi-fixed factors. *Journal of Econometrics*, *33*, 97–118.
Scotti, D., Dresner, M., Martini, G., & Yu, C. (2014). Incorporating negative externalities into productivity assessments of US airports. *Transportation Research Part A*, *62*, 39–53.
Shin, R., & Ying, J. (1992). Unnatural monopolies in local telephonies. *The Rand Journal of Economics*, *23*(2), 171–183.
Spady, R., & Friedlaender, A. (1978). Hedonic cost functions for the regulated trucking industry. *Bell Journal of Economics*, *9*(1), 155–179.
Tolofari, S., Ashford, N., & Caves, R. (1990). The cost of air service, department of transport technology. Loughborough: University of Loughborough.
Triebs, T. P., Saal, D., Arocena, P., & Kumbhakar, S. (2016). Estimating economies of scale and scope with flexible technology. *Journal of Productivity Analysis*, *45*(2), 173–186.
Voltes Dorta, A., & Lei, Z. (2013). The impact of airline differentiation on marginal cost pricing of UK airports. *Transportation Research Part A*, *55*, 72–88.
Voltes Dorta, A., & Martin, A. (2016). Benchmarking the noise-oriented efficiency of major European airports: A directional input distance function approach. *Transportation Research Part E*, *91*, 259–273.
Voltes Dorta, A., & Pagliari, R. (2012). The impact of recession on airports' cost efficiency. *Transport Policy*, *24*, 211–222.
Yan, J., & Oum, T. H. (2014). The effects of government corruption on the efficiency of US commercial airports. *Journal of Urban Economics*, *80*, 119–132.
Zhao, Q., Choo, Y. Y., & Oum, T. H. (2014). The effects of governance forms on North American airport efficiency: A comparative analysis of airport authority vs. government branch. *Journal of the Transportation Research Forum*, *53*(2), 93–110.

APPENDIX

Paper	Sample	Inputs	Outputs	Econometric Methodology, Functional Form	Main Results
Tolofari et al. (1990)	7 BAA airports (1975–1987)	Labor, capital stock, material, residual input + control variables	wlu	OLS, Translog total cost function	Scale economies up to 20.3 mln wlu
Doganis et al. (1995)	25 European airports (1993)	Labor and capital	Wlu and value added		Scale economies up to 5 mln wlu
Pels et al. (2003)	33 European airports (1995–1997)	Atm production function: surface area, no. of aircraft parking positions, no. of runways. APM production function: predicted atm, no. of check-in desks, no. of baggage claims units	Atm and atm	Stochastic translog production frontiers	Constant returns to scale in production of atm and increasing returns in the production of atm (12.5 mln pax)
Martin and Voltes Dorta (2008)	41 international airports (1991–1995)	Labor, materials, capital	Atm and wlu	SURE, translog total cost function	Mild scale economies (1.13) at the geometric sample mean (8.5 mln pax, 114,000 atm), but scale economies unexhausted for larger airports with about 80 mln pax.
Chow and Fung (2009)	46 Chinese airports in 2000	Atm, terminal area, cargo facilities area, no. of airport parking position, airport surface area, length of runways	Pax movements cargo movements	ML, Stochastic translog input distance frontier	Constant returns to scale at the sample mean. Complementarity between cargo and pax
Abrate and Erbetta (2010)	26 Italian airports (2000–2005)	Labor costs, other opex costs as variable inputs; apron area, total airport surface area as fixed inputs	Pax, handling revenue, commercial revenue	SURE, stochastic input distance function with cost shares	Short run increasing returns at the sample mean (3.8 mln pax)

McCarthy (2011)	50 US airports (1996–2008)	Labor, outsourced services, repairs and maintenance, plus effective no. of runways as a quasi-fixed input	One output: pax; two outputs: pax, cargo	SURE, variable cost function	Two outputs model: short- (1.34) and long-run scale economies (1.57) at the sample mean. No clear evidence of scope economies between cargo and pax
Martin and Voltes Dorta (2011a)	161 international airports (1991–2008)	Capital, labor, materials	International pax, domestic pax, cargo, non-aviation revenue, hedonic function atm	Bayesian inference. Stochastic total cost frontier	Large scale economies at the sample mean (2 at 12 mln pax), and for airports serving more than 40 mln pax (1.4)
Martin and Voltes Dorta (2011b)	161 international airports (1991–2008)	Capital, labor, materials	International pax, domestic pax, cargo, non-aviation revenue, hedonic function atm	Bayesian inference. Stochastic total cost frontier	Large scale economies at the sample mean (2 at 12 mln pax), and for airports serving more than 40 mln pax (1.4)
Martin et al. (2011)	36 Spanish airports (1991–1997)	Capital, labor, materials in the total cost function. Labor, materials plus no. of runways as a quasi-fixed factor in the variable cost function	Atm, wlu, commercial revenue	SURE. Stochastic variable and total cost function	Total cost function: mean scale economies 1.2 (average airport has 2.5 mln pax). Variable cost function: short-run scale economies (1.69) at the sample mean
Bottasso and Conti (2012)	24 UK airports (1994–2005)	Labor, other opex plus capital stock as a quasi-fixed input	Atm, pax, cargo and non-aviation revenue	SURE, variable cost function	4 output model: Long-run scale economies at the sample median (2 mln pax), constant returns after the 75th percentile (6 mlm), diseconomies of scale after 14 mln pax
Voltes Dorta and Pagliari (2012)	194 worldwide airports (2007–2009)	Labor, materials plus terminal surface and runways length as quasi-fixed inputs	Domestic pax, international pax, cargo, commercial revenues, hedonic function of atm	Bayesian inference, variable cost frontier	Large short-run scale economies (2.13) at the mean (13 mln pax), decreasing with size. Positive elasticity of capital stock variables evidence of excess capacity

(Continued)

Paper	Sample	Inputs	Outputs	Econometric Methodology, Functional Form	Main Results
Voltes Dorta and Lei (2013)	27 UK airports (1994–2009)	Capital, labor and other opex in the total cost function, labor and other opex plus combination of runways and terminal surface	Hedonic function of pax, commercial revenue	Bayesian inference, variable cost frontier	Total cost function: Long-run scale economies (2 at mln. Pax); Variable cost function: short-run scale economies (1.7 at 2 mln pax). Positive elasticity of capital stock variables evidence of excess capacity
McCarthy (2014)	50 US airports (1996–2008)	Labor, outsourced services, repairs and maintenance, plus effective no. of runways as a quasi-fixed input	Atm	SURE, variable cost function	Short-run scale economies (3.5 for 130,000 atm), long-run scale economies at the sample mean (4.1)
McCarthy (2016)	50 US airports (1996–2008)	Labor, outsourced services, repairs and maintenance, plus effective no. of runways as a quasi-fixed input	Atm, wlu, nonaeronautical level	SURE, variable cost function	Constant short-run scale economies for the average airport, long-run scale diseconomies (0.75) at the sample mean. Positive elasticity of capital stock variables evidence of excess capacity. Some evidence of increasing product-specific scale economies in non-aeronautical revenue. Some evidence of scope diseconomies

CHAPTER 9

AIRPORT CHARGES – INTERACTIONS BETWEEN AIRLINES AND AIRPORTS

Terje A. Mathisen, Finn Jørgensen, Pål A. Pedersen and Georgina Santos

ABSTRACT

A substantial part of airports' revenues relates to charges covering the costs of services supplied by the airport. Charges are imposed on carriers, which in turn pass them or a percentage of them, on to passengers. In the present chapter, special attention is given to regional airports characterized by low traffic volumes, enabling only one or a few carriers to serve each destination. A classic economic model is presented to analyze how the pass-on rate depends on supply and demand characteristics and market structure. Some illustrative examples assuming combinations of common specifications for market characteristics are also presented, showing pass-on rates ranging from 50% to more than 100%. Consequently, market structure and characteristics of carriers and passengers are decisive for how passengers experience changes in airport charges. The differences between the optimal charge from the perspectives of the airport and the welfare of society are specifically addressed. It is demonstrated that knowledge of the pass-on rate in the monopoly cases may be sufficient to infer how the mark-up will be affected by a change in marginal costs. Consequently, the understanding of the

The Economics of Airport Operations
Advances in Airline Economics, Volume 6, 213–234

ISSN: 2212-1609/doi:10.1108/S2212-160920170000006009

pass-on rate is relevant for airport owners and for decision-makers when considering the welfare of passengers and other politically stated goals.

Keywords: Airport charge; pass-on rate; carrier; passenger; regional airport; competition; airlines

JEL Classifications: L93; L12; D21

INTRODUCTION

Whether airports are public or private bodies, they have revenues as part of their objective (e.g., Zhang & Czerny, 2012). In large part, revenues can be generated by either aeronautical revenues, commercial revenues or subventions (Losada, Eraso, & Garcia, 2012). Airports often act to maximize profit from commercial activities. As a part of the general public infrastructure, airport charges are often regulated by central governmental authorities, both for publicly and privately owned airports.

Traditionally, airport charges relate to air traffic movements (ATM) with landing fees based on the weight of aircraft (MTOW) and passenger (PAX) fee per departing passenger.[1] Airports throughout the world tend to have both per-passenger charges and per-flight charges, and indeed they collect as much revenue from one as from the other (Czerny & Zhang, 2015). Silva and Verhoef (2013) show that airports require both per-passenger charges and per-flight charges to maximize welfare, which they define as the sum of consumer surplus, airlines' profits, and airport's profit.

The International Air Transport Association (IATA) aims for standardization of airport charges (Martin-Cejas, 1997), which are fair and cost-efficient[2] and the International Civil Aviation Organization (ICAO, 2012, point 13.II) emphasizes that public policy objectives should include ensuring "non-discrimination and transparency in the application of charges." However, some attempts on charges based on the ability to pay have been addressed in the literature. Studying private airports, Hakimov and Mueller (2014a) introduced the use of Ramsey pricing at uncongested airports with Germany as a case study. Mathisen, Jørgensen, and Solvoll (2014) discussed distribution problems of strictly following the Ramsey rule by raising charges most aggressively at rural airports characterized by generally less elastic demand due to few alternative modes of transport.

The design of passenger fees varies between countries (e.g., Gordijn, 2010). In Germany, the *Air Travel Tax* was introduced in 2011 to promote environmental friendly travel behavior. In the United Kingdom, the *Air Passenger Duty* is a fiscal charge without environmental arguments but rather based on its distributional effects, charging higher rates for more expensive ticket categories. In The Netherlands, the *Air Passenger Tax* was introduced in 2008 with the argument of making polluters pay. The introduction of this charge coincided with the financial crisis which, in combination with leakage to Belgium and Germany (Gordijn & Kolkman, 2011), resulted in a decline in passenger volume and discontinuation of the charge. In 2011, the (former) British Midland International (BMI)[3] complained to the UK Civil Aviation Authority, about London Heathrow discriminating against short-haul airlines by charging them the same fees it charged long-haul ones (Zuidberg, 2014). In July 2016, a fiscal fee was introduced in Norway and it is unclear whether environmental impacts were part of the argument (Haanshuus & Jodalen, 2016). Also, in this case, the introduction coincided with a period of developing economic problems. It got much attention when Ryanair used the introduction of this fee to justify their leaving a private airport, which in turn resulted in a decision by the owners to close down the airport.

A change in the level of airport charges naturally has direct impacts on carriers' costs. However, carriers do not necessarily pass on all charges to passengers. Jørgensen and Santos (2014) discuss theoretically how transport firms pass on output taxes to passengers under different types of competition and goals, using a model of differentiated services dating back to Singh and Vives (1984). In their review of airport charging, Zhang and Czerny (2012) discuss the welfare optimizing airport charge, considering external costs, such as congestion not internalized by passengers.

The aim of this chapter is to provide a discussion on how characteristics of cost and demand and type of competition influence the extent to which airport charges are passed on from carriers to passengers. Moreover, attention is given to how optimal charges from the airport perspective, deviate from what could be preferable from a welfare point of view. Even though taxation in different types of markets has been widely studied in the literature, this study stands out for two reasons. First, in contrast to many earlier studies using general relationships, we introduce specific functional forms. Evidently, the choice of function influences both the optimal charge and the pass-on rate. By operationalizing the functions, we are able to capture common relationships relevant for air transport. Second, we focus on low traffic airports where few or only one transport firm operate(s). Knowledge on how carriers and passengers respond to changes in the charge scheme is important for both public authorities and airport owners when deciding upon charge policies and the actual charge. They should be aware of market structure when designing charges to meet their objectives.

The chapter is structured as follows. In the "Models for Airlines and Airports Behavior" section, the model is presented, with attention to the interaction between airlines and airports. In the "Pass-On Rates Under Different Market Characteristics" section, the conditions for transfer of fares are derived from common cost and demand specifications, and the model is then set to the duopoly case with price competition. In the "Discussion and Numerical Example" section, the results are discussed and summed up. Finally, in the "Concluding Remarks" section, some conclusions and implications are presented.

MODELS FOR AIRLINES AND AIRPORTS BEHAVIOR

Both the US and EU airline markets have been subject to deregulation (Janic, 1999) and markets are increasingly being considered as oligopolies with imperfect competition (Zhang & Czerny, 2012). This is the case for studies of airports at the network level. However, when studying airports at route level, travel demand may be sufficient for only one carrier serving the different destinations. This is particularly prominent at small airports where Public Service Obligation (PSO)[4] subsidies are more frequently used (see, e.g., Williams & Pagliari, 2004).

Let us assume an airline market including a value chain consisting of four bodies as illustrated in Fig. 1. The State (represented by the national government, including parliament or equivalent), decide on public policy regarding airports, including charges. Airports then instruct airlines to collect the charges from the passengers.

In the simple principal–agent model illustrated in Fig. 1, the state authority cares about the overall welfare and subsidy needs when designing public policy for the part of air transport infrastructure costs financed through airport charges. Moreover, within the limits of this national policy, an airport maximizes a goal function depending on profit, revenues, and welfare (see the "Airport Charging Under Different Objectives" section) when deciding upon the actual airport charge.[5] For the airlines, the airport charge is a given variable when they choose the profit maximizing ticket price. Finally, passengers choose their optimal demand for flights by minimizing generalized travel cost, which, needless to say, includes all monetary and time costs. In our model, we particularly focus on the relationship between the bodies in the three boxes to the right ("Airport," "Airline," and "Passengers"). Hence, we do not explicitly look into the details of designing and implementing an optimal policy from the perspective of the state.

Airlines Response to Airport Charges – A General Model

Suppose an airline faces the following demand function for passenger transport to and from an airport

$$X = X(P) \text{ where } dX/dP < 0, (d^2X)/(dP^2) \geq 0 \quad (1)$$

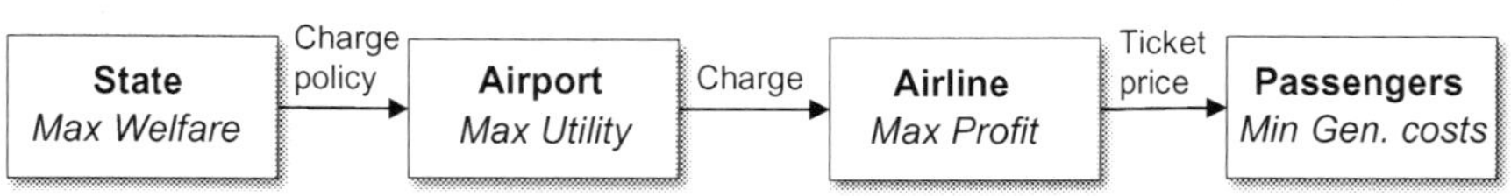

Fig. 1. The value chain in the airline market.

where X is the number of passengers transported and P is ticket price (fare). Moreover, let the airline's total costs be given by the following function

$$C(X,t) = C_o(X) + t \cdot X$$
$$\text{where } \partial C(X,t)/dX > 0, d^2C(X,t)/(dX^2) \geq 0, \partial C(X,t)/dt = X > 0 \qquad (2)$$

In Eq. (2), parameter t is a per unit tax imposed by the airport on each passenger traveling to and from it. C_0 represents all costs excluding airport fees and depends on the number of passengers (PAX). PAX is widely used as output indicator for transport activity and related to airline cost either alone, through Work Load Units (WLUs) or in combination with other indicators, such as Air Traffic Movements (ATMs) (Martín & Voltes-Dorta, 2011). Empirical studies show that PAX relates closely to other production measures. According to Carlsson (2003), PAX accounted for 96% of the variation in costs at Swedish airports when used as a single independent variable. In the case of no airport charges ($t = 0$), then $C = C_o(X)$. The airline profit (π) is given by

$$\pi = P \cdot X(P) - C(X,t) \qquad (3)$$

When the airline maximizes profits, optimal price (P) is implicitly given by the following first order condition (e.g., Pindyck & Rubinfeld, 2013)

$$P \cdot \frac{dX(P)}{dP} + X(P) = \left(\frac{dC_o(X)}{dX} + t\right) \cdot dX/dP \qquad (4)$$

Equation (4) can be rephrased to $P = \frac{\frac{dC_o(X)}{dX}+t}{(1+\frac{1}{EL_PX(P)})}$ where $EL_PX(P) = \frac{dX}{dP} \cdot \frac{P}{X}$ represents price elasticity of demand and where $EL_PX < -1$. The value of EL_PX decreases (becomes more negative) when passengers have more substitutes, such as better access to other airports or better surface transport alternatives.[6] Equation (4) implicitly defines the optimal price, P^*, as a function of t, i.e., $P^* = P^*(t)$.

Using Eqs. (1) and (3) in combination yields the airline's optimal number of passengers transported (X) as a function of the tax (t) in Eq. (5).

$$X(t) = X(P^*(t)) = X\left(\frac{\frac{dC_o}{dX} + t}{(1 + \frac{1}{EL_PX(P)})}\right) \qquad (5)$$

The per unit tax pass-on rate from the airline to its passengers $\left(\frac{dP}{dt}\right)$ can be defined as the ratio between the change in price and the change in tax. In other words, it measures the impact that an infinitesimal change of a per unit tax, t, imposed on each passenger, has on the equilibrium price, P^*. The lower (higher) the value of $\frac{\partial P^*}{\partial t}$, the less (more) of the tax increase is paid by travelers to and from the airport and the more (less) is paid by the airline operating at the airport. When $\frac{dP^*}{dt} \geq (<) 1$ the final price (tax inclusive) to passengers goes up by more than, the same as or less than the amount of the tax. Consequently, the magnitude of the increase in the travelers' fare, after introducing the airport charge (t), is $(\frac{dP^*}{dt} \cdot t)$.

Differentiating the first order conditions for profit maximization in Eq. (4) with respect to tax (t) we get, after some mathematical manipulation (see Bulow & Pfleiderer, 1983; Kate & Niels, 2005)[7]:

$$\frac{dP^*}{dt} = \frac{X_P(P)}{2X_P(P) + X_{PP}(P)(P^* - C_X(X) - t) - C_{XX}(X)X_P^2(P)} > 0 \tag{6}$$

It should be noted that the second order condition for maximization of the airline's profits (π) implies that the denominator in Eq. (6) is negative. Hence, $\frac{dP^*}{dt} > 0$, meaning that increasing the charge will always lead to higher fares for passengers. Moreover, by parameterizing the general expressions we can discuss in more detail how functional forms of demand and cost influence the relationship between tax and optimal price. Such operationalization of the functions is given in the "Pass-On Rates Under Different Market Characteristics" section.

Using Eq. (1) in combination with Eq. (6) gives the effect of a tax increase on the optimal number of passengers (X^*)

$$\frac{dX^*}{dt} = X_P \cdot \frac{dP^*}{dt} < 0 \tag{7}$$

Airport Charging Under Different Objectives

Let the airport cost function of serving the airline be $K(X)$ and revenues be given by the number of passengers to and from the airport multiplied by the airport fee (t). We here isolate revenues from airport charges and do not consider commercial revenues. Then profit for the airport (ρ) can be written as

$$\rho = t \cdot X^*(t) - K(X^*(t)), \text{ where } dK/dX > 0 \text{ and } (d^2K)/dX^2 \geq 0 \tag{8}$$

Profit Maximizing Airports

When airports want to maximize profit, they will set the level of charge (t^*) according to the first order conditions for profit maximization, as follows

$$\frac{d\rho}{dt} = X^*(t) + \left(t - \frac{dK(X^*(t))}{dX^*}\right)\frac{dX^*(t)}{dt} = 0 \tag{9}$$

Equation (9) can be reformulated to $t^* = \frac{\frac{dK(X^*(t))}{dX^*}}{(1+\frac{1}{EL_tX^*(t)})}$ where $EL_tX^*(t) = \frac{dX^*}{dt}\cdot\frac{t}{X^*}$ is the elasticity of X^* with respect to t. It follows from Eq. (9) that $t > \frac{dK(X^*(t))}{dX}$, meaning that the charge (t^*) is greater than the marginal cost of serving the passengers. Whether such pricing procedure is welfare optimal or not depends on the level of social costs imposed by each passenger that the airport authorities ignore (Δ). Examples of this include carbon emissions and noise caused by aircraft (European Commission, 2014; Martín-Cejas, 2010). If $\Delta \geq (<)(t^* - \frac{dK(X^*(t))}{dX})$, the airport sets too low, correct and too high a charge, respectively. Consequently, if all social costs are internalized in the airport's calculations ($\Delta = 0$), passengers are charged above the welfare optimal level.

Welfare Maximizing Airports

When the airport is owned or regulated by the state, it is likely, at least to some extent, that it will pursue other goals rather than pure profit maximization. One common goal within the transport sector is the maximization of social welfare when the loss of revenues is financed by the state (e.g., Button, 2010). In line with the literature dating back to Ramsey (1927) we formulate this problem as maximizing social welfare subject to a subsidy restriction (budget). When solving the Lagrangian function, the optimal charge can be written as

$$t^{**} = \frac{\frac{dK(X^*(t))}{dX^*}}{(1 + \frac{\tau}{EL_tX^*(t)})} \tag{10}$$

where $0 \leq \tau = \frac{\gamma}{1+\gamma}$ and γ is the social cost of raising public funds by 1 Euro (see e.g., Mathisen et al., 2014). By comparing Eqs. (9) and (10) it can be verified that $t^* > t^{**}$ but t^{**} will increase and tend to t^* when γ increases (t^{**} increases with τ). If the social cost of raising public funds is 0 ($\gamma = 0$) then $\tau = 0$ and the optimal charge will be equal to the airport's marginal costs ($\frac{dK(X^*(t))}{dX^*}$).

Utility Maximizing Airports

It could also be argued that airports' managers have particular interests in running a big airport and that they have some power to pursue other goals (see, e.g., Button (2010) and Jørgensen and Mathisen (2014) and the literature dating back to Baumol (1962) and Williamson (1966) for discussions of this issue). If the goal were to maximize utility, the goal function (U) could be described as a weighted sum of profits and revenues, as follows

$$U = \rho + \beta \cdot R \text{ where } 0 \leq \beta < 1 \text{ and } R = t \cdot X^*(t) \text{ are the airport's revenues.} \tag{11}$$

The restriction imposed on β implies that airports may put some weight on size, but they always put a higher weight on profits. After some mathematical manipulation, the optimal charge, t^{***}, when U is maximized, can be written as

$$t^{***} = \frac{1}{1+\beta}\frac{\frac{dK(X^*(t)}{dX^*}}{(1+\frac{1}{EL_t X^*(t)})} \tag{12}$$

It can be seen from Eq. (12) that the higher the weight the airport places on revenues (given by β) the lower the charge, t^{***}, will be.

PASS-ON RATES UNDER DIFFERENT MARKET CHARACTERISTICS

We will now discuss in more detail how different specifications of market characteristics (i.e., the demand- and costs functions) influence the pass-on rate $\left(\frac{dP^*}{dt}\right)$. Furthermore, we will pay attention to the difference between the level of airport charge and the airport's marginal cost of serving airlines and their passengers $(t - \frac{dK(X^*(t)}{dX})$. In the present discussion, we focus purely on the profit maximizing airports of the "Profit Maximizing Airports" section. When all social costs are internalized in the airports' costs, this mark-up indicates how the profit maximizing airport charge (t^*) deviates from the welfare optimal situation, most easily described by the marginal cost pricing rule. In all cases, we assume linear cost functions for both the airline (13) and the airport (14), as follows

$$C = (c+t)X + F \quad \text{where} \quad c, t, F > 0 \tag{13}$$

$$K = qX + H \quad \text{where} \quad q, H > 0 \tag{14}$$

In Eq. (13), the airline's total costs and fixed costs of operating at the airport are given by C and F, respectively. The element $(c + t)$ represents the extra cost of carrying one more passenger to/from the airport. The marginal costs $\left(\frac{dC}{dX}\right)$ are, thus, constant and equal to $(c + t)$. In Eq. (14), the airport's total costs, fixed costs, and marginal costs of serving the airline are given by K, H, and q, respectively. Even though linear specifications are less flexible than more advanced cost functions, they are often used in the literature as an approximation to the cost structures for both transport modes and transport infrastructure (see e.g., Pels & Rietveld, 2008). Moreover, such functions give often mathematically tractable solutions that are easy to interpret (Blauwens, De Baere, & van de Voorde, 2008).

The demand functions considered are standard in transport economic textbooks and in econometric analyzes – namely linear functions, power functions and exponential functions (see, e.g., Hensher & Brewer, 2001; McCarthy, 2001). Additionally, we introduce a two firm case (duopoly) competing on price assuming linear functions only. Our approach is similar to that in Bulow and Pfleiderer (1983), using constant marginal costs in combination with Power and Exponential demand functions when analyzing the effect of cost changes on prices in a monopoly market. However, in our four cases, described below, we extend on the reasoning by Bulow and Pfleiderer (1983) in three ways. First, we address additional cases by including the linear demand function often found in the transport industry and duopoly price competition. Second, we study the interactions in vertical integration between airports and airlines when designing charges. Finally, we briefly comment on the monopoly case when airlines' cost functions are convexly increasing.

The variation in number of suppliers and the proposed demand functions in combination with the linear cost function produces the following four cases:

I. Linear demand – monopoly
II. Power demand – monopoly
III. Exponential demand – monopoly
IV. Linear demand – duopoly

For the sake of simplicity, when presenting the model results we use the same symbols for optimal values and parameters in the different cases. Alternatively, indexing of all parameters to match the case in question could have been used, but it would have made the algebra heavy-handed. Therefore, in the sections that follow it should be borne in mind that, e.g., even if a and b represent aspects of demand conditions by market size and price sensitivity, respectively, in all cases, the strict interpretation of the parameters depends on each specification (I, II, III, and IV).

Case I – Linear Demand

The relationship between the number of passengers (X) traveling to and from an airport and average ticket price (P) is given by

$$X = a - bP \text{ where } a, b > 0 \text{ and } EL_P X = \frac{-bP}{a - bP} \tag{15}$$

The value of a indicates the size of the market, while b represents the price sensitivity of demand; the value of b increases when passengers get better access to other transport alternatives. The demand curve in Eq. (15) implies that price elasticity of demand, $EL_P X$, decreases concavely with price.

Inserting (13) and (15) into (3) and deriving the first order conditions for maximization of the airline's profits lead to the following equilibrium

$$P^* = \frac{a + b(c + t)}{2b} \text{ and } X^* = \frac{a - b(c + t)}{2} \tag{16}$$

Equation (16) enables us to derive the influence of the charge imposed on the airline, as shown by Eq. (17).

$$\frac{dP^*}{dt} = \frac{1}{2} \text{ and } \frac{dX^*}{dt} = -\frac{b}{2} \tag{17}$$

The results in Eq. (17) show that an increase in airport charges (t) by 1 Euro will always increase the ticket price by 0.5 Euro, at the (optimal) equilibrium. In other words, the airline passes on to passengers' ticket price half of the change in the airport's charge. Hence, the change in ticket prices due to an increase in airport tax is independent of the demand conditions the airline faces, its productivity and the initial level of the tax. This implies equal pass-on rates across all airports. Consequently, the relative changes in ticket price will be greater for passengers at airports where prices are lowest.

Moreover, it follows from Eq. (17) that the impact of a change in the airport charge on demand is greater if price sensitivity is higher (greater b). This means that reduction in travel demand will be greatest at airports where passengers have many alternative means of transport (presence of substitutes). It is also worth noting that the change in demand resulting from a change in the airport charge is independent of the airline's productivity (c-value).

When the airport maximizes profits (ρ) we can derive optimal airport charges (t^*) using Eqs. (9), (14) and (16), as follows

$$t^* = \frac{a - bc + bq}{2b} = \frac{a - b(c - q)}{2b} \tag{18}$$

Keeping in mind Eq. (17), the part of the tax (t^*) passed on to each passenger is just half ($\frac{1}{2} \cdot t^*$). From Eq. (18) it follows that a higher market potential (greater a) and higher marginal costs at the airport (greater q) will always increase t^*, while increasing marginal costs for the airlines (greater c) and more price sensitive demand (greater b) lead to lower t^*.[8]

The difference (Δ) between the airport charge maximizing the airport's profits and the airport's costs of serving an extra passenger (q) is given in Eq. (19).

$$\Delta = t^* - q = \frac{a - b(c + q)}{2b} > 0 \tag{19}$$

It follows from Eq. (19) that $\Delta > 0$. The value of Δ is reduced when the market potential declines, when passengers become more price sensitive and when the marginal costs of the airline and the airport increase.

Case II – Power Demand Function

Let us now address the situation where the demand curve for transport to and from the airport decreases convexly with price as in Eq. (20) and where the airline and airport cost functions are the same as those specified in Eqs. (13) and (14), respectively.

$$X = aP^{-b} \text{ where } a, b > 0 \textit{ and } EL_P X = -b < -1 \qquad (20)$$

The demand curve in Eq. (20) implies that $EL_P X$, is constant and equal to the exponent $(-b)$. Also, in this specification the parameter a indicates market size.

By inserting (13) and (20) into (3), the first order conditions for maximization of the airline's profits can be derived. This yields the following market solution

$$P^* = \frac{b(c+t)}{b-1} \text{ and } X^* = a\left(\frac{b(c+t)}{b-1}\right)^{-b} \text{ where } b > 1 \qquad (21)$$

Equation (21) implies the following changes in equilibrium solutions when the per unit tax increases:

$$\frac{dP^*}{dt} = \frac{b}{b-1} \text{ and } \frac{dX^*}{dt} = -\left[\frac{b(c+t)}{b-1}\right]^{-b-1} \frac{ab^2}{b-1} \qquad (22)$$

It follows from Eq. (22) that $\frac{dP^*}{dt} > 1$ when $b > 1$. This implies that a monopolist facing constant marginal costs and a demand curve with constant price elasticity will always pass on to passengers more than the change in the charge. Evidently, $\frac{dP^*}{dt}$ will decrease when b increases. Hence, the pass-on rate from airlines to passengers is lower when airlines operate at airports with more elastic demand. For example, if the value of b is 1.5 and 2.0, passengers will experience an increase in ticket price of 3 Euros and 2 Euros, respectively, if the airport charge is increased by 1 Euro. In contrast to the case of a linear demand function, the pass-on rate now depends on the price sensitivity of the passengers, while airline marginal costs still do not influence the pass-on rate. Moreover, Eq. (22) shows that the magnitude of the impact of the charge on the number of passengers depends both on market- and cost conditions. Specifically, the reduction in the number of passengers is smaller if the charge (t) is higher to start with and if marginal costs (c) are high. The impact of price elasticity (b) on travel demand is not clear-cut.

Let us now pay attention to the airport owner tax setting again. From Eqs. (10), (14) and (22), we can derive the optimal airport charge for profit maximizing airports as follows

$$t^* = \frac{bq + c}{b - 1} \tag{23}$$

It is clear from Eq. (23) that $t^* > 0$ when $b > 1$. Moreover, the charge that maximizes profit for the airport increases with marginal costs for the airport (q) and when demand is less price elastic (lower b). In contrast to the case of linear demand, we find that the optimal charge for the airport owner increases when marginal costs for the carrier (c) increase. Also, it should be noted that t^* is independent of the value of a, meaning that the size of the market does not influence the optimal charge. Equation (22) in combination with (23) implies that the tax effect on ticket price is $(\frac{b}{b-1} \cdot \frac{bq+c}{b-1})$, implying a greater effect when the demand becomes less price sensitive.

The difference (Δ) between the airport charge maximizing profit for the airport (t^*) and its marginal costs of serving the passengers (q) is given in Eq. (24).

$$\Delta = t^* - q = \frac{c + q}{b - 1} > 0 \tag{24}$$

In contrast with Case I, it is clear from Eq. (24) that the difference between the airport's charge and its marginal costs is unaffected by the market potential of the airport (value of a). Moreover, it increases in c and q and decreases in b.

Case III – Exponential demand function

Let demand be given by the general exponential function in (25).

$$X = ae^{-bP} \text{ where } a, b > 0 \text{ and } EL_P X = -bP \tag{25}$$

Similar to (20) the demand decreases convexly with ticket price, but the absolute value of price elasticity increases proportionally with P. Consequently, ($100{\cdot}b$) can be interpreted as the percentage change in X when P changes by 1 Euro. Inserting Eqs. (13) and (25) into (3) gives the following optimal values of price and the number of passengers transported to and from the airport

$$P^* = \frac{1 + b(c + t)}{b} \quad \text{and} \quad X^* = ae^{-(1+b)(c+t)} \tag{26}$$

Equation (26) implies the following equilibrium effects of a marginal change of the airport charge

$$\frac{dP^*}{dt} = 1 \text{ and } \frac{dX^*}{dt} = -a(1+b)be^{-(1+b(c+t))} \tag{27}$$

The fact that $\frac{dP^*}{dt} = 1$ implies that a profit maximizing airline acting as a monopolist with constant marginal costs and facing an exponential demand curve, will always pass on the entire change in the airport charge to the passengers. Hence, an increase in the charge of 1 Euro increases the ticket price for passengers by exactly 1 Euro. Under these conditions, passengers are, thus, treated similarly at all airports, but the relative value of a change in charge is highest at airports dominated by low fare tickets.

From Eq. (27) we can see that reduction in travel demand due to an increase in the charge is greater when the market is large (greater a), marginal cost low (lower c) and when the charge is lower to start with (lower t). Hence, there is a negative convex relationship between travel demand and the airport charge. A more price sensitive demand (greater b) will increase this effect if $(b+1)(c+t) > 1+2b$.

When still assuming a profit maximizing airport with cost structure according to Eq. (14), we can derive its optimal airport charge as follows

$$t^* = \frac{bq+1}{b} \tag{28}$$

Because airlines pass along the entire tax to passengers (see Eq. (27)), the increase in fares due to the tax will be exactly (t^*). It follows from Eq. (28) that the optimal charge increases when airport marginal costs (q) increase and when demand becomes less price elastic (lower b). In this case, the optimal charge for the airport owner is unaffected by the airline marginal costs (c) and the size of the market (a).

The difference (Δ) between the airport charge that maximizes airport profit (t^*) and the airport marginal costs (q) is

$$\Delta = t^* - q = \frac{1}{b} > 0 \tag{29}$$

It follows from Eq. (29) that Δ decreases in b. In contrast to Cases I and II, Δ is independent of both the marginal costs of the airline (c) and the airport (q).

Case IV – Linear Demand – Duopoly

Even at small airports, some routes are served by more than one company. Hence, it is relevant to study the interaction between airlines and airports under duopoly competition. Let two airlines (1 and 2) offer symmetrically differentiated services (X_1 and X_2) at an airport and compete simultaneously in prices (Bertrand competition).[9] Moreover, we apply market conditions equal to Case I where both airlines face linear demand functions and identical linear cost functions. Their demand functions are

$$X_1 = a - bP_1 + sP_2 \text{ and } X_2 = a - bP_2 + sP_1 \text{ where } a, b > 0, 0 < s < b \tag{30}$$

In Eq. (30), parameter a indicates the market potential of the airport while parameter s measures the degree of substitutability between the services from the two airlines; the higher the value of s, the more intensely they compete. Their cost functions are

$$C_1 = (c + t)X_1 + F \text{ and } C_2 = (c + t)X_2 + F \tag{31}$$

where C_1 and C_2 are total costs of airlines 1 and 2, respectively.

Using Eqs. (30) and (31), profits for each airline ($\pi_i, i = 1, 2$) are then given by

$$\pi_1 = (P_1 - (c + t))(a - bP_1 + sP_2) - F \text{ and } \pi_2 = (P_2 - (c + t))(a - bP_2 + sP_1) - F \tag{32}$$

When the airlines maximize their profits by choice of the fare variable we get the following common equilibrium prices (P^*) and quantity (X^*)

$$P^* = \frac{a + b(c + t)}{2b - s} \text{ and } X^* = \frac{ab + b(c + t)(s - b)}{2b - s} \tag{33}$$

Based on Eq. (33), the influence on equilibrium values following changes in the per unit tax can be derived as follows

$$\frac{dP^*}{dt} = \frac{b}{2b - s} \text{ and } \frac{dX^*}{dt} = -\frac{b(b - s)}{2b - s} \tag{34}$$

Under the restriction placed on the b and s parameters it is easy to verify from Eq. (34) that $\frac{dP^*}{dt} > \frac{1}{2}$ and that it decreases with b and increases with s; the less competition the airlines experience from other modes of transport and the more fiercely they compete the more of the tax is passed on to the passengers. The impact of the tax on the total number of passengers to and from the airport ($2 \cdot \frac{dX^*}{dt}$) will be higher when b increases and s decreases.

Let us now address the optimal charge from the airport perspective. By combining Eqs. (8), (14) and (33) it is clear that the optimal charge (t^*) for a profit maximizing airport is

$$t^* = \frac{(b - s)(q - c) + a}{2(b - s)} \tag{35}$$

By comparing Eqs. (18) and (35) it can be verified that the airport charges a higher tax when it serves two airlines rather than one. Moreover, it follows from Eq. (35) that t^* increases when the market potential for the airlines increases (greater a), the airport marginal costs (q) increase and the airlines' marginal costs (c) decrease. Finally, better alternatives from other transport modes (greater b) and less fierce competition between the two airlines (lower s) will lower the tax charged by the airport. From Eqs. (34) and (35) it follows that the effect on ticket price due to the tax is $(\frac{b}{2b-s} \cdot \frac{(b-s)(q-c)+a}{2(b-s)})$. As it can be seen, this effect is decreasing in b and increasing in s.

Equation (36) implies that the difference, Δ, between the charge set by the airport and the airport marginal cost (q) is

$$\Delta = t^* - q = \frac{(s-b)(q+c)+a}{2(b-s)} \tag{36}$$

Equation (36) demonstrates that Δ increases when both the airlines and the airport marginal costs decrease and when the market potential for the airlines increases. Increasing competition between the airlines also leads to a greater value of Δ.

DISCUSSION AND NUMERICAL EXAMPLE

Main Model Results

The model presented in the "Pass-On Rates Under Different Market Characteristics" section, addresses an airport system where routes are served by a single airline or two airlines in duopoly competition. This is particularly relevant for smaller airports or low demand destinations. One of the main findings is that demand characteristics have a substantial influence on how changes in airport charges are passed on to passengers. Consequently, information on demand characteristics should be obtained and used as part of the decision-making process when revising airport charges. This is particularly relevant for airport authorities pursuing political goals and taking into account distributional impacts between types of airports and groups of passengers. Table 1 summarizes the results for each of the four cases addressed in the "Pass-On Rates Under Different Market Characteristics" section.

When the demand function facing the airline is linear or exponential the airline will pass on half $\left(\frac{dP^*}{dt} = \frac{1}{2}\right)$ or all of the tax $\left(\frac{dP^*}{dt} = 1\right)$ to passengers, respectively, regardless of how sensitive demand is (b value) and the levels of marginal costs for the airline (c) and for the airport (q). When fares are lower, the relative changes in ticket price will be higher. If fares are assumed to increase with distance traveled (e.g., Mathisen, 2015), passengers using airports

Table 1. Summary of Impacts on Pass on Rates, Demand, Charges, and Mark-up in the Four Cases.

Case	Demand Function	$\frac{dP^*}{dt}$	Marginal Impact on Ticket Price	Marginal Impact on Demand, $\frac{dX^*}{dt}$	Impact on Airport Mark-up, Δ
I	Linear (Monopoly) $X = a - bP$	$= 0.5$	Half of the charge is passed on to passengers. Independent of demand conditions and thereby equal pass-on rate for all airports. Relative change in ticket price is greatest where prices are lowest.	Reduction increases with b. Independent of a and c.	Δ increases with a and decreases with b, c, and q
II	Power (Monopoly) $X = aP^{-b}$	>1	Always pass on more than change in charge. Increase in price due to charge is reduced with elasticity value (b).	Reduction is smaller if charge is large to start with. Decreases with c. Uncertain influence of b.	Δ increases with c and q and decreases with b. Independent of a
III	Exponential (Monopoly) $X = ae^{-bP}$	$=1$	Entire change in charge is passed on to passengers. Other consequences are similar to Case I.	Reduction increases with a. Other consequences are similar to Case II.	Δ decreases with b, independent of a, c and q
IV	Linear (Duopoly) $X_i = a - bP_i + sP_j$, $i = 1, 2, i \neq j$	>0.5	Pass-on rate decreases with b and increases with s.	Reduction increases with b. Decreases with s.	Δ decreases with c and q and increases with a, b and s.

that serve short distances will, thus, be more affected by increasing charges, relatively speaking.

When the airline serving an airport faces a power demand function, the pass-on rate decreases when demand becomes more price sensitive. This suggests that passengers at airports with few transport alternatives (few substitutes) will be hardest hit by the tax. The impact is, however, still independent of the size of the market and the airline's and airport's marginal costs (values of c).

In Case IV (duopoly) the charge is influenced by the degree of product differentiation (parameter s in Table 1) in addition to the parameters discussed in the first three cases. The pass-on rate is always larger than 0.5 and increases when airlines experience less competition from alternative modes of transport and when airlines compete more fiercely in the market.

A profit maximizing airport serving an airline facing a linear demand function will increase the tax when the demand becomes less price elastic, when the marginal costs for the airport increase and when the marginal cost for the airline decrease. The same conclusions apply for a power demand function except that increasing marginal cost for the airline also increases the tax. Lastly, for the case of an exponential demand function, less price elastic demand and higher marginal cost of the airport of serving the passengers will increase the tax, but the airline's marginal cost does not affect the level of charge. It should be remarked that changes in the a, b, and c parameters affect t^* (optimal tax) and Δ (airport mark-up) in the same directions. Increasing q on the other hand, will always increase t^* but only increase Δ when assuming a power demand function.

The close relationship between pass-on rate and the impact on mark-up is demonstrated in the right column of Table 1. More specifically, knowledge of the pass-on rate in the monopoly cases may be sufficient to infer how mark-up will be affected by a change in marginal cost. For instance, when the pass-on rate is below 1, then an increase in airline or airport marginal cost will decrease the mark-up, while a pass-on rate equal to 1, implies that the mark-up is independent of these marginal costs.

It is well documented that firms could have other incentives than the owners and there is no reason to assume that airports differ from this reasoning (see the "Welfare Maximizing Airports" and "Utility Maximizing Airports" sections). For example, managers at the airport could put some weight on revenues. Then the airport will set a lower charge the more weight it places on revenues. In a situation where the airport tax is designed by the government, it could be more relevant to assume social welfare maximization under budget restrictions. The optimal charge will then increase with stricter budget restrictions and the cost of raising public funds.

Admittedly, the model relies on restrictive assumptions regarding demand and costs. Despite producing a good approximation to practice and intuitive results that can be easily interpreted, the use of linear costs is not always suitable. Therefore, using Eq. (6) we now briefly focus on the special monopoly case of a convex specification where costs increase with traffic, raising to the power of two (quadratic). When assuming such a quadratic cost function ($\frac{d^2C}{dX^2} \geq 0$ with linearly increasing marginal cost), then the pass-on rate is less than a half ($\frac{dP^*}{dt} < 0.5$) and less than one ($\frac{dP^*}{dt} < 1$) when the demand function is linear and exponential, respectively. Also in the case of a power demand function the pass-on rate will be lower when employing a quadratic cost function compared to a linear one, but it is not straightforward to establish intervals for the values of $\frac{dP^*}{dt}$. Consequently, increasing marginal cost will for all three specifications of the demand function lead to lower pass-on rates compared to a situation with constant marginal costs. Future applications of such a standard model can be extended to include other specifications found of particular relevance to the air transport industry.

Numerical Example

Let us now apply the model to a simple numerical example based on some empirical evidence from the regulated part of the Norwegian air transport industry. As mentioned in the "Models for Airlines and Airports Behavior" section, operations at these routes are licensed to one supplier by the PSO regime (e.g., Mathisen & Solvoll, 2012). Focusing on the Power function (Case II and discussed by Bulow and Pfleiderer (1983)), we need information on elasticity (b) and marginal costs for airports (q) and airlines (c). The study by InterVISTAS (2007) suggests an elasticity value for short trips at the route level in Europe of about -1.5, which if plugged into Eq. (22) yields a pass on rate equal to 3.

Mathisen et al. (2014, p. 54) estimate the long-run marginal costs of handling an extra passenger at small and mid-sized Norwegian airports at 34 NOK, which is about 3.5 Euros at 2016 exchange rates. This is the value we assume for the example below. While there are a number of studies that estimate airport marginal costs (e.g., Hakimov & Mueller, 2014b; Link, Götze, & Himanen, 2009; Martín, Román, & Voltes-Dorta, 2011; Martín & Voltes-Dorta, 2011; Voltes-Dorta & Lei, 2013) studies on airline marginal costs are very rare, probably because costs are highly sensitive information for airlines. We do not know of any estimates on airline marginal costs for the routes in question. Given this uncertainty, we can only make arbitrary assumptions on c, which we allow to take two values, 5€ and 10€, in our numerical calculations.

Plugging these values in Eq. (23) renders $t^* = \frac{1.5\times3.5+5}{1.5-1} = \frac{10.25}{0.5} = 20.50$ when $c = 5$ and $t^* = \frac{15.25}{0.5} = 30.50$ when $c = 10$. Using Eq. (21) and the same parameter values it is evident that $P^* = 77$ when $c = 5$ and $P^* = 122$ when $c = 10$. These estimates are within the fare interval estimated by Mathisen (2015) for the highly regulated air transport in Norway.

Currently, the airport owner Avinor charges passengers approximately 5€ (Mathisen et al., 2014). This suggests that the Norwegian airport authorities put some weight on goals other than profits. Additionally, a fiscal passenger seat fee amounting to about 9€ was introduced by the Norwegian government in 2016 producing a total fee of about 14€. When using the same parameter values in Eq. (21) it is evident that the 9€ environmental tax increased P^* from 30€ to 57€ when $c = 5$ and from 45€ to 72€ when $c = 10$. Summing up, the estimations above demonstrate clearly that the airport authorities' objectives can be of great importance for passenger fares.

CONCLUDING REMARKS

Many interesting questions remain to be modeled, discussed and empirically tested when analyzing airport charges. In our approach, we have restricted ourselves to analyzing airport charges and pass-on rates to passengers in a single airport and single flight route model. In a model describing a network of airports and several flight routes, possibly with differences in number of operating airlines and where costs and demand conditions might vary, the problem of designing airport charges and consequences for pass-on rates might be more complex.

Another issue that should be given more attention to when designing airport charges, is that the central government, in reality, has several political goals to consider. This is illustrated by the state owned Norwegian airports setting airport charges below profit maximizing level leading to lower ticket price. Securing overall welfare often means choosing a policy for airport charges where internal and external efficiency in the airport and airline markets should be seen in relation to possible private and public budget constraints, negative externalities from aviation and possible positive wider economic benefits on regional development and industries depending on the supply from airports and airlines. This means that in a more comprehensive analysis, the principal–agent relationship between the governments (labeled State in the first box from the left in Fig. 1) should be discussed in more depth. It is also worth mentioning that whether airports charges are optimal from a welfare perspective does not only depend on their goal function, but also on the degree to which they consider all social costs caused by airlines' activity. Finally, it is demonstrated that knowledge of the pass-on rate in the monopoly case may be sufficient to infer changes in the mark-up for the airport following a change in marginal cost.

As mentioned in the introduction, the Norwegian government and parliament introduced a new fiscal air charge as of 1 June 2016. The extra fee is about nine Euros per passenger. The new charge provoked an intense political and economic debate concerning possible negative effects on passengers and industries, especially in regions where few other transport alternatives exist. However, preliminary data shows that traffic volume has increased, although it may be too early to say what the long-term effect will be. This increase in traffic volume may be the result of other favorable changes having nothing to do with (low or no) pass-on rates for passengers. This is indeed likely to be a suitable explanation, especially bearing in mind that often air tickets are purchased well in advance, and in this case, probably before the new air charge become effective. Future studies could use this case to uncover the pass on rate in the Norwegian air transport market.

Nevertheless, the relatively simple model provides two important lessons. First, we have clear conclusions on how market characteristics influence the pass-on rate when using the chosen specifications. Second, and more importantly, we have demonstrated the interrelations between carriers' fare setting, pass-on rates and airports' tax level on the one hand and demand and costs conditions for carriers and airports on the other hand. It is evident that market characteristics have a considerable impact on pass-on rates and should be part of the decision-making process when designing airport charges.

NOTES

1. While charges put on PAX and ATM are collected by the carriers on behalf of the airport, the other charges either cover expenses, such as security, or are out of airports' control, such as en-route fees imposed by Eurocontrol.

2. http://www.iata.org/policy/infrastructure/Pages/index.aspx

3. BMI was acquired from Lufthansa by International Airlines Group and integrated into British Airways in 2012.

4. In order to keep appropriate scheduled air services, PSOs are imposed by Member States on routes which, although not commercially viable, are 'vital for the economic development of the region they serve'. When no air carrier is interested in operating such route(s), the Member State in question may restrict the access to the route to a single air carrier and compensate its operational losses with a PSO subsidy. The selection of the carrier is made by public tender at Community level (https://ec.europa.eu/transport/modes/air/internal-market/public-service-obligations-psos_en).

5. From the theory of industrial organization it is well-known that vertical integration of two monopolies in a value chain, as the airline and airport in our model, produces the problem of double marginalization (see, e.g., Lipczynski, Wilson, & Goddard, 2009; Pepall, Richards, & Norman, 2014). This could considerably increase producers' profits, and possibly also, consumers' welfare. However, our model assumes an airport deciding upon the optimal charge, being aware of the market situation in the airline market, which eliminates the problem of double marginalization.

6. For a discussion of different operational measures of the level of competition of individual airports, we refer to Merkert and Mangia (2014).

7. In Eq. (6) we denote $X_P = \frac{dX}{dP}$, $X_{PP} = \frac{d^2X}{dP^2}$, etc.

8. Note that $t^* > 0$ when X^* in Eq. (18) is positive and $\frac{dt^*}{db} = \frac{-2a}{(2b)^2} < 0$.

9. Another possibility is that airlines move sequentially when choosing prices or compete in quantities simultaneously (Cournot) or sequentially (Stackelberg). For discussion on such model approaches in the transport literature, see e.g., Pedersen, 1999.

REFERENCES

Baumol, W. J. (1962). On the theory of expansion of the firm. *The American Economic Review*, *52*(5), 1078–1087.

Blauwens, G., De Baere, P., & van de Voorde, E. (2008). *Transport economics* (3rd ed.). Antwerpen: De Boeck Hoger.

Bulow, J. I., & Pfleiderer, P. (1983). A note on the effect of cost changes on prices. *Journal of Political Economy*, *91*(1), 182–185.

Button, K. (2010). *Transport economics* (3rd ed.). Cheltenham, UK: Edward Elgar.

Carlsson, F. (2003). Airport marginal cost pricing: Discussion and an application to Swedish airports. *International Journal of Transport Economics*, *30*(3), 283–304.

Czerny, A. I., & Zhang, A. (2015). How to mix per-flight and per-passenger based airport charges. *Transportation Research Part A: Policy and Practice*, *71*, 77–95.

European Commission. (2014). Update of the Handbook on External Costs of Transport.

Gordijn, H. (2010). *The Dutch Aviation Tax; Lessons for Germany?* Paper presented at Infraday-2010, Berlin 8-9 October.

Gordijn, H., & Kolkman, J. (2011). *Effecten van de vliegbelasting: Gedragsreacties van reizigers, luchtvaartmaatschappijen en luchthavens*. Den Haag, The Netherlands: Kennisinstituut voor Mobiliteitsbeleid.

Haanshuus, S. H., & Jodalen, T. M. (2016). *Flypassasjeravgiften – troverdige motargumenter?* Bodø, Norway: Nord University.

Hakimov, R., & Mueller, J. (2014a). Charges of uncongested German airports: Do they follow Ramsey pricing scheme? *Research in Transportation Economics*, *45*, 57–65.

Hakimov, R., & Mueller, J. (2014b). Marginal costs estimation and market power of German airports. *Research in Transportation Economics*, *45*, 42–48.

Hensher, D. A., & Brewer, A. (2001). *Transport: An economics and management perspective*. Oxford: Oxford University Press.

ICAO. (2012). *ICAO's policies on charges for airports and air navigation services*. Ninth edition. Doc 9082.

InterVISTAS. (2007). *Estimating air travel demand elasticities*. Final Report.

Janic, M. (1999). Behaviour of Western European scheduled airlines during the market liberalisation process. In M. Beauthe & P. Nijkamp (Eds.), *New contributions to transportation analysis in Europe*. Aldershot: Ashgate.

Jørgensen, F., & Mathisen, T. A. (2014). Market equilibriums for transport operators with several goals. *European Transport Research Review*, *6*(3), 241–251.

Jørgensen, F., & Santos, G. (2014). Charges on transport – To what extent are they passed on to users? *Transportation Research Part A: Policy and Practice*, *69*, 183–195.

Kate, A. T., & Niels, G. (2005). To what extent are cost savings passed on to consumers? An oligopoly approach. *European Journal of Law and Economics*, *20*(3), 323–337.

Link, H., Götze, W., & Himanen, V. (2009). Estimating the marginal costs of airport operation using multivariate time series models with correlated error terms. *Journal of Air Transport Management*, *15*(1), 41–46.

Lipczynski, J., Wilson, J., & Goddard, J. (2009). *Industrial organization: Competition, strategy, policy* (3rd ed.). Harlow: Prentice Hall/Financial Times.

Losada, J. M. S., Eraso, J. C., & Garcia, P. D. (2012). Airport management: The survival of small airports. *International Journal of Transport Economics*, *39*(3), 349–367.

Martín, J. C., & Voltes-Dorta, A. (2011). The econometric estimation of airports' cost function. *Transportation Research Part B: Methodological*, *45*(1), 112–127.

Martín, J. C., Román, C., & Voltes-Dorta, A. (2011). Scale economies and marginal costs in Spanish airports. *Transportation Research Part E: Logistics and Transportation Review*, *47*(2), 238–248.

Martin-Cejas, R. R. (1997). Airport pricing systems in Europe and an application of Ramsey pricing to Spanish airports. *Transportation Research Part E: Logistics and Transportation Review*, *33*(4), 321–327.

Martín-Cejas, R. R. (2010). Ramsey pricing including CO_2 emission cost: An application to Spanish airports. *Journal of Air Transport Management*, *16*(1), 45–47.

Mathisen, T. A. (2015). Empirical evidence on the relationship between fare and travel distance. *International Journal of Transport Economics*, *42*(1), 111–126.

Mathisen, T. A., & Solvoll, G. (2012). Reconsidering the regional airport network in Norway. *European Transport Research Review*, *4*(1), 39–46.

Mathisen, T. A., Jørgensen, F., & Solvoll, G. (2014). Marginal costs pricing of airport operations in Norway. *Research in Transportation Economics*, *45*, 49–56.

McCarthy, P. S. (2001). *Transportation economics: Theory and practice – A case study approach*. Blackwell, Oxford.

Merkert, R., & Mangia, L. (2014). Efficiency of Italian and Norwegian airports: A matter of management or of the level of competition in remote regions? *Transportation Research Part A: Policy and Practice*, *62*, 30–38.

Pedersen, P. A. (1999). Strategical interactions within transport markets. In H. Meersman, E. van de Vorde, & W. Winkelmans (Eds.), World Transport Research: Selected Proceedings of the 8th World Conference on Transport Research (Vol. 4, pp. 611–622). Transport Policy, Amsterdam: Pergamon.

Pels, E., & Rietveld, P. (2008). Cost functions in transport. In K. Button & D. A. Hensher (Eds.), *Handbook of transport modelling* (2nd ed.), (Vol. 1, pp. 381–394). Amsterdam: Pergamon.

Pepall, L., Richards, D., & Norman, G. (2014). *Industrial organization: Contemporary theory and empirical applications* (5th ed.). Hoboken, NJ: Wiley.

Pindyck, R. S., & Rubinfeld, D. L. (2013). *Microeconomics* (8th ed.). Upper Saddle River, NJ: Pearson.

Ramsey, F. P. (1927). A contribution to the theory of taxation. *The Economic Journal*, *37*(145), 47–61.

Silva, H. E., & Verhoef, E. T. (2013). Optimal pricing of flights and passengers at congested airports and the efficiency of atomistic charges. *Journal of Public Economics*, *106*, 1–13.

Singh, N., & Vives, X. (1984). Price and quantity competition in a differentiated duopoly. *The RAND Journal of Economics*, *15*(4), 546–554.

Voltes-Dorta, A., & Lei, Z. (2013). The impact of airline differentiation on marginal cost pricing at UK airports. *Transportation Research Part A: Policy and Practice*, *55*, 72–88.

Williams, G., & Pagliari, R. (2004). A comparative analysis of the application and use of public service obligations in air transport within the EU. *Transport Policy*, *11*(1), 55–66.

Williamson, J. (1966). Profit, growth and sales maximization. *Economica*, *33*(129), 1–16.

Zhang, A., & Czerny, A. I. (2012). Airports and airlines economics and policy: An interpretive review of recent research. *Economics of Transportation*, *1*(1-2), 15–34.

Zuidberg, J. (2014). Key drivers for differentiated airport passenger service charges. *Journal of Transport Economics and Policy*, *48*(PART 2), 279–295.

CHAPTER 10

SPATIAL EVOLUTION OF AIRPORTS: A NEW GEOGRAPHICAL ECONOMICS PERSPECTIVE

Tay T. R. Koo and Andreas Papatheodorou

ABSTRACT

Airports and urban developments in their vicinity constitute a highly specialized type of agglomeration based on air connectivity that epitomizes the importance of mobility in the modern service economy. However, in a frictionless world of backyard capitalism and perfect competition, such agglomeration of civil aviation services would not have been necessary. Thus, concepts such as imperfect markets, path dependence, and cumulative causation may be alternatively used to explain the spatial aspects of airport developments. Focusing on "second-nature" concentration, the "new geographical economics" (NGE) literature offers a potential theoretical framework that organizes these concepts into a coherent economic framework. This chapter aims to highlight the unique relevance of the NGE approach in developing an economics-based understanding of the spatial distribution of airports. Drawing from the existing NGE knowledge-base, this conceptual chapter explains that the NGE approach can be adopted as a microfoundation to show how the spatial aspects of airport development, including core-periphery dynamics of regional disparity and parity, can emerge from economic mechanisms. The chapter concludes with

The Economics of Airport Operations
Advances in Airline Economics, Volume 6, 235–259

ISSN: 2212-1609/doi:10.1108/S2212-160920170000006010

potential implications for airport economics and regional policy, along with the discussion of some of the main critiques of the theory.

Keywords: Airport location choice; new economic geography; new geographical economics; regional economic development; agglomeration

JEL classifications: R12; R58; O18

INTRODUCTION

It is widely acknowledged that firms within an industry can cluster together forming a self-reinforcing agglomeration (Dicken & Lloyd, 1990). This agglomeration can be a potent force for industrial specialization of regions. As trade barriers break down, favorable conditions may develop for this specialization to take place where at some point it may become economically more viable to serve the market from a single location than from many dispersed locations (Krugman & Venables, 1996). The study of how these circular processes may shape the concentration and dispersion of economic activities across space under different structural economic conditions is undertaken by a subfield of economics, known as "new economic geography."[1] Krugman and Venables (1996, p. 960), e.g., ask the following questions in the context of European integration in developing models of new economic geography: where will the industrial specialization ("districts") emerge? Will the formation of such districts be beneficial? How will the spatial adjustment process play out? As explained below, this type of question is highly relevant for air transport economics too.

Aviation has an obvious spatial dimension. Airports are unevenly distributed across space, as areas with high concentration of airports coexist with areas where such infrastructure is completely absent. Most places are dependent on few large hubs to meet their air mobility needs. Airports can be viewed as agglomerations of air services with considerable external economies, which are not entirely pre-determined by factor endowments. Regional and national specialization in air services clearly exists as evidenced by international air transport hub cities such as Dubai, Abu Dhabi, and Singapore, but also at a domestic level such as Atlanta in the United States. In fact, airports can in some instances account for about 10–30% of the employment in a region (Flores-Fillol, Garcia-Lopez, & Nicolini, 2016). Airports are thus significant specialized industrial clusters where air services are produced and exchanged, and economic value created. The air transport industry has mobile factors of production such as aircraft and airlines, but as noted by Burghouwt (2007), its spatial development is also subject to significant path dependence. It is also a regulated sector that has come under significant liberalization at some levels, thus representing a quasi-natural experiment environment in which the spatial effect of trade barrier removal can be assessed. Thus, new geographical economics (NGE) may have an interesting perspective on the spatial evolution of airport development.

In fact, the spatial effects of policy regulation and deregulation on the characteristics of air transport access, network, supply, and demand have been subjects of considerable research (Bowen, 2010; Burghouwt, 2007; Burghouwt, Hakfoort, & Eck, 2003; Chou, 1993; Derudder & Witlox, 2009; Dobruszkes, 2006; Goetz & Sutton, 1997; Graham, 1997; Hooper, 1998; Koo, Halpern, Papatheodorou, Graham, & Arvanitis, 2016; O'Connor, 2003; Papatheodorou & Arvanitis, 2009; Reynolds-Feighan, 1998, 2010; Shaw, Feng, Chen, & Zhou, 2009; Small, 1993, etc.). However, the relevance of the NGE research has not been a subject of discussion in many of these studies. One exception is Papatheodorou and Arvanitis (2009), who examine the implications of air transport liberalization for the development of peripheral destinations in Greece. They note that despite the prominence of Greece as a tourism destination, the low-cost carrier services between Western Europe and Greece have been spatially very concentrated. Here, the NGE theory is invoked to highlight the potential risks for the periphery if access costs improve. However, it is argued that tourism in the periphery is largely a spatially fixed activity where, unlike most imports, the consumers travel to the destination for consumption. Thus, rather than risking the loss of terms of trade, through lower access costs (e.g., by attracting low cost carriers), the peripheral destinations may be able to trigger tourism-led regional economic development.

While NGE has not been a primary focus of many post-liberalization studies, as done in Papatheodorou and Arvanitis (2009), aspects of NGE have been invoked in the context of a territorial rivalry between airports in attracting airline services in a liberalized environment. The evolution of low-cost carriers (LCCs) in a post-liberalization environment in Europe has brought the territorial rivalry to new levels; many remote areas that had limited air access in the past have been given the opportunity to tap into the aviation network. The self-reinforcing agglomeration mechanism (an important element of NGE) has been alluded to in observing that LCC may help destinations to partially overcome the "agglomeration shadow" cast by large metropolitan areas on the peripheries as the airlines actively look for opportunities to serve secondary and regional airports. This, in turn, may help regenerate the periphery through economic activities such as tourism while contributing to the gradual decongestion of the "core." Thus, just as the core may gain at the expense of the periphery, it is possible for the reverse to happen.

As implied by the discussion above, NGE may be able to provide guidance on the underlying economic conditions (e.g., level of trade barriers) that may lead to regional parity/disparity in access to air services. Against this background, this chapter examines whether NGE can provide a suitable microfoundation framework to better understand the spatial evolution of airports.

The chapter is organized as follows. First, the main ingredients of the NGE framework are explained and their relevance for air transport discussed. Second, a qualitative description of the vertical linkages model of NGE (based on Krugman & Venables, 1995) is provided and the main outcomes most relevant for airport development are highlighted. This is followed by a section on the theory's implications for issues of significance in the interface of airport economics and regional policy. The chapter then explains some of the main critiques of the NGE theory before concluding.

CONCEPTUAL FRAMEWORK OF NEW GEOGRAPHICAL ECONOMICS

Studies mentioned previously have found overwhelming evidence that the pattern of air transport development is uneven at all spatial scales. This uneven distribution has important consequences; for instance, it has direct implications for how mass tourism – a significant contributor to the global economy – develops especially in decentralized, free-market economies (Papatheodorou, 2003). The core-periphery dualism is observed at various levels; for instance, referring to mass sunlust tourism developments for British travelers, Papatheodorou (2004) notes that asymmetries are apparent at different levels of spatial hierarchy globally (e.g., Mediterranean and the Caribbean regions vis-à-vis the rest of the world), nationally (e.g., Spain is at the core of Mediterranean tourism while Algeria is clearly a periphery), regionally (e.g., the popularity of the South Aegean island region in Greece compared to many destinations on the mainland), and locally (e.g., within the South Aegean region there are highly popular islands such as Rhodes and Kos and relatively off-track such as Karpathos). These patterns of geographic concentrations are at clear odds with the prediction of the perfectly competitive markets where an even distribution because of "backyard capitalism" would be expected instead (Krugman, 1991). In fact, airports are important because our economy is based on spatial friction and interaction. In a world of backyard capitalism, such concentrations would not be necessary because all our needs could be fulfilled locally through divisibility. This follows from Starrett (1978)'s *spatial impossibility theorem*, the result from which states: "if space is homogeneous, transport is costly, and preferences are locally non-satiated, there is no competitive equilibrium involving transportation" (Fujita & Thisse, 2002, p. 35). However, indivisibilities generate the need for transport, because not all activities can be performed in autarky (Fujita & Thisse, 2002). Clearly, the demand for mobility (permanent or temporary, e.g., migration or tourism, respectively), which is related to the indivisibilities of factor endowments, results in the need for air services. The latter are subject to indivisibilities themselves often requiring large fixed (and in many cases sunk) costs. A priori, however, the location of the airport can be ambiguous, i.e., there is some degree of flexibility as to where the agglomeration (of air services) occurs.

Because of their spatially fixed nature, a theoretical framework to trace the evolution of airports requires an economic mechanism enhanced with territorial connotations. To infuse a spatial dimension in trade theory is to adopt what is commonly known as (and what will be alternatively called geographical economics in this chapter) the "new economic geography" (NEG) models. In fact, as noted by Krugman (1991) himself, the NEG model has emerged from the need to explicitly model geography in what has traditionally been "aspatial" mainstream economics. The ideas contained in the economic geography models may have implications for policy and management of economic spaces. For instance, the economic geography-based models have been important in debates surrounding the trade liberalization policies in the European Union in the 1990s (Brakman et al., 2009). Krugman and Venables (1996), for instance, presented a vertical linkage model to examine the questions on where and how industrial specialization may emerge as European integration takes place under a geographically immobile work force. The reduction of barriers to trade essentially reduces transport costs of moving goods/services from one point to another; this can help certain regions/industries/firms to capitalize on increasing returns, thus resulting in greater concentration of economic activities. An important consequence of this process is the growing regional disparities because the development of the Core may occur at the expense of the Periphery. Understandably, this raises important distributional policy issues.

A long tradition exists in the study of geographical concentration in sub-fields within economics. The ideas and work from the various sub-fields such as urban and regional economics, international trade and growth theories, have all contributed to the "core model of economic geography" developed by Krugman (1991) and Krugman and Venables (1995) (Fujita et al., 1999). We adopt the work by Head and Mayer (2004, p. 2) in summarizing the following five essentials of economic geography: (a) internal increasing returns to scale; (b) imperfect competition; (c) transportation costs; (d) endogenous firm location decisions; and (e) the endogenous location of demand. Below we focus on the basic insights of each component, and then describe how these features are integrated to form a model that accounts for "circular cumulative causation" (Myrdal, 1957). As shown by Head and Mayer (2004), in the margin, it is the fifth aspect (endogenous location of demand) that differentiates economic geography from the preceding international trade theory. These ingredients are combined in a general equilibrium framework, where it is possible to trace how two regions with initially identical factor endowments may, although not necessarily, proceed on a path to a core-periphery equilibrium.

Increasing Returns

This refers to the increasing returns that exist within a firm and should be distinguished from external economies of scale, which include technological and pecuniary externalities. Internal economies of scale are an important source of industrial concentration because as production expands, the unit cost of production decreases; thus, it makes economic sense to continue production within the same firm.

There are several sources of internal increasing returns in the airline industry (e.g., Caves, Christensen, & Tretheway, 1984; Oum & Zhang, 1997; Quinet & Vickerman, 2004). Economies of scope in an airline context can be viewed as those closely related to network economies where cost savings arise from the ease of adding a new node to an existing network. The new linkage then enjoys the benefits of the entire network. Density economies clearly exist as the cost of operating a flight per seat decreases as aircraft size (and thus the number of seats within an aircraft) increases. Economies also exist in relation to fleet size where unit cost savings may be available in crewing, maintenance and pilot costs, etc. Having the above in mind, Holloway (2008)'s argument that economies of scale exist "to the extent that it is rarely twice as expensive to operate two flights as it is to operate one" (p. 341) is adopted in this chapter to consider increasing returns as a broad concept encompassing all of the above types of economies at an airline level. Finally, the NGE models also account for external economies to a limited extent. Of the Marshallian external economies (knowledge spill-over, access to specialized labor pool, and backward–forward linkages), NGE models incorporate the third (i.e., backward–forward linkages) because it is more readily explicated in the model (Fujita & Krugman, 2004).

Imperfect Competition

Perfect competition is an inadequate analytical framework for analysis in the presence of increasing returns, as the latter imply that marginal costs are lower than average costs. Clearly, this is not financially sustainable as firms would then be operating below the break-even point. Dixit-Stiglitz (1977)'s monopolistically competitive market structure is most often used to model imperfect competition. This well-known framework involves the assumption that the producer of the good/service in question specializes in the production of one differentiated variety. The way economies of scale work in the Dixit-Stiglitz formulation (which is important for NGE) is that each firm focuses on a single type of the differentiated product's variety to capitalize on the internal economies of scale it enjoys with respect to its production. In the airline context (and while trying to avoid being too literal in the interpretation of an abstract model), the firm's differentiated product could be an exclusive shuttle service on a given route (e.g., such as that common in Ryanair's network or charter services), or a unique combination of the routes (a given carrier's network, which rarely overlaps completely with the network of another carrier). Consumers, in turn, are assumed to exhibit preferences for variety (i.e., the "love-for-variety" effect) and purchase a bit of every variety on offer. The consumer utility is enhanced as a larger number of destinations become accessible from a particular airport. The issue here is that although this is a "strategic simplification" that is necessary in modeling (Fujita & Krugman, 2004), it is also important to balance the benefits of modeling simplification against the appropriateness of the assumptions in the given aviation market. Dynamic oligopolistic market structure is appropriate in many route-level competition cases (Fu & Oum, 2014), and to reduce the complex interplay of airlines' airport location decisions to a collection of independent route entry decisions by each airline may be challenging to accept. Nonetheless, as it is the case with many economic models, the trade-off between modeling ease and realism is a much broader issue concerning the inter-disciplinary area of economic geography. In this context, these issues are revisited in the section "Main Critique of the New Geographical Economics Approach" of this chapter.

Transportation/Trade Costs

In NGE, geography exists by allowing transport costs in the economy. Note that "transport costs" do not pertain only to the airfares but represents a much broader notion of freedom of movement and trade. Transport costs can be abstracted to represent trade barriers due to physical geography and/or cultural barriers. The transport dimension in geographical economics can be viewed from two perspectives: as an individual sector of an economy or as a cost that is attached to the traded good/service. The former is not considered in the core models of NGE (see, Takahashi, 2011 for an NGE model that does), rather the core models treat transport as an exogenous cost and model it using the Samuelson's "iceberg" function where transport cost is specified as the number of units that must be "shipped" from the origin for one unit to arrive at the destination.

In the NGE model, economic agents across regions are assumed to be free but the product incurs transport costs when imported/exported across region. A heavily regulated environment is a situation where this transport cost is high enough to warrant that every economic agent (i.e., an airline in the present context) will locate in the respective home region as a rational choice even under free mobility. In an extreme case, this means that every region has an airport serving all the air access needs of its own population. Specifically, transportation cost is the access cost to an airport that provides an air service to the desired destination. If every region serves the air mobility needs of all its residents, as in the theoretical case described above, then there will not be any access cost because the consumers do not have to travel to an airport in another region (say, to another city or country) to access the destination. In a case where access to another region is required, in NGE parlance, the flight is "imported", where the transportation cost of importing this service is the access cost. Thus, the transportation cost is the cost to access the airport that has the direct access to the final destination, e.g., transit costs.

Moreover, in air transport parlance, transportation cost could represent the degree of air liberalization between states. Domestic and international liberalization policies have effectively reduced trade barriers. For areas without capacity constraints, the policies have allowed greater freedom for airlines to "locate" where the market is and greater opportunities for airports to seek profits by enticing airline entry. Europe prior to air deregulation in the 1990s, and prior to the collapse of the Soviet Union, can be viewed as a situation where there was a high cost attached to accessing another country's air services.

Endogenous Firm Locations

According to NGE models, firms are mobile across space and choose a region that maximizes profits. The force that keeps each firm in one location is the indivisibility expressed as increasing returns. Firms must provide the services to many consumers in other regions incurring transportation costs, which increases the break-even price for the firm's services – this is a dispersion force. The assumption that firms can change location freely in response to profits is important to the NGE model. Although airlines are not always mobile to such a degree, there is also some supporting evidence for mobility: the existence of demonstrated and potential demand for air services (and by implication, revenue and profits) is clearly the most important factor in the airport entry decisions of LCC (e.g., Ito & Lee, 2003). More importantly, in a liberalized aviation environment where airlines have greater freedom to follow the market and where airports are increasingly under competitive pressure to generate profits, the entry and exit decision is more flexible and market-based.

Given free mobility, firms will respond to their profit function. While demand is higher in the core, the labor cost is comparatively high. In an event of declining profits due to higher cost of production in the hub (especially if an airline needs to secure new, expensive slots in order to keep its network at competitive levels), relative attractiveness of secondary or regional airports increases. For example, an airline may choose to provide air access to Seoul, Korea from Gold Coast or Sydney in Australia. If costs in Sydney become too high as a result of agglomeration pressures, the airline may have an economic incentive to locate in Gold Coast where the cost of production is lower and rely on a domestic connection (possibly in the context of a code-sharing agreement with another carrier) to transport passengers to their end destination. Similarly, as trade barriers were removed and the completion of the European single aviation market was realized, airlines reaped the benefits of developing and consolidating into larger hubs (as an agglomeration force) by choosing to locate in the hubs even if it meant crossing country borders. However, concentration has also resulted in rising costs and congestion, which in the NGE model induces a firm to move to the periphery. In air transport parlance, this is analogous to the emergence of the low-cost model, which was a dispersion force as it provided incentives for airlines to seek alternative airports in the inner periphery as well as the outer regions.

Endogenous Location of Demand

As outlined by Head and Mayer (2004) this is what advances the geographical economics theory from the ("new") international trade theory. Broadly, there are two mechanisms through that the location of demand is endogenized in the general equilibrium model of geographical economics.[2] First is the core model by Krugman (1991). The demand is endogenously determined because firm's location decision determines the number of workers. Ceteris paribus, a larger production (in terms of number of varieties as well as overall quantity levels) is associated with a lower unit cost, which reduces the aggregate price index thus effectively raising real wages and favoring labor migration. The workers, who are also consumers, demand final goods, which in turn set off a cumulatively causative process of the increased demand attracting further number of firms. Therefore, if for some reason one region has more firms located than other regions, then this will trigger a cumulative causation process (as the greater the number of firms, the greater is the number of workers and subsequently the demand for the goods produced by the firm: this will attract even more firms). But this mechanism is not always readily applicable. In fact, it may prove challenging to observe it many contexts because labor is often not mobile.

The original core-periphery model based on the mechanism described above (the core model by Krugman, 1991) aimed to encapsulate the general agglomeration process such as the emergence of cities. However, there are many cities specializing in a narrower range of industries, which is particularly important for regional and international specialization and trade (Fujita & Krugman, 2004; Krugman & Venables, 1996). This second mechanism is concerned with the location of demand determined by access to intermediate goods, and requires relatively minor modification of Krugman (1991)'s core-periphery model (Krugman & Venables, 1995). Here demand increases not due to increased workers/consumers, but as the number of firms using each other's outputs increases. This means the airlines will be attracted to a place where the access to inputs such as catering, security, cleaning, maintenance, freight forwarders and fueling firms and ancillary services such as hotels for layover crews and pilots, are the greatest. The presence of these airline services also increases the incentives for a web of intermediate good providers to locate in the region. A different way to look at this is airlines as intermediate goods providers for other goods and services in the wider tourism supply chain. Tourism services such as accommodation are used as inputs by airlines, and in turn, the accommodation sector uses air services as inputs in producing the tourism product. The demand for tourism attracts greater number of airlines whose outputs are used as inputs by other airlines (connecting passengers), which seems to explain the presence of large hubs, and importantly, the presence and emergence of cities and states specializing in the air services and transit tourism industry. Thus, agglomeration is important in the aviation industry. The place of such agglomeration is the airport and the surrounding areas.

In the above model industrial/sectoral mobility of labor is completely free but only within a given region, i.e., there is spatial immobility. The model introduces a new centripetal force: that when the price index decreases because the number of varieties increases (due to the presence of a larger number of firms), the fixed and marginal costs of the spatially mobile sector of the economy (e.g., manufacturing) decrease. Combes et al. (2008) state that this is equivalent to introducing a Marshallian externality through intermediate inputs – which departs from the pure internal economies of scale of the core-periphery model. This is similar to the economies of scale experienced by all firms as a result of an increase in through-traffic at the airport hub.

MODEL OUTCOMES

The Vertical Linkages Model

It may be possible to view aviation as a sector where its relative size in the core or the periphery is endogenously determined by the NGE dynamics. This section of the chapter focuses on core-periphery models with intermediate goods as encapsulated by Krugman and Venables (1995). The chapter approaches the general equilibrium model from a qualitative perspective: for a much more detailed (and technical) exposition of a family of NGE models, see Baldwin et al. (2003), Combes et al. (2008), and Brakman et al. (2009). The intermediate inputs in this model are the main channel of agglomeration: vertical linkages in the production process exist where one's final product is used as an input by another. The products demanded by consumers are also used by firms as inputs, and all varieties are demanded by consumers and all varieties are used by firms as inputs. This is an intuitively appealing framework to study the mechanisms of airport development. For instance, the products of airlines (disembarking passengers) are used as feeder traffic for other airlines, which in turn also produce traffic to/from the hub airport. It is reasonable to assume that consumers (travelers) will exhibit preference for access to more than fewer diverse destinations.

In this general equilibrium model, the basic setup entails the following (summarized in Fig. 1):

- Two identical regions.
- Two sectors: agriculture (the immobile sector with perfectly competitive market under constant returns to scale) and manufacturing (the mobile sector with imperfect markets under increasing returns).
- Workers are homogenous but spatially immobile: labor is immobile across regions but mobile across sectors.
- Agricultural goods have zero transport cost, while manufacturing goods have positive transport costs.

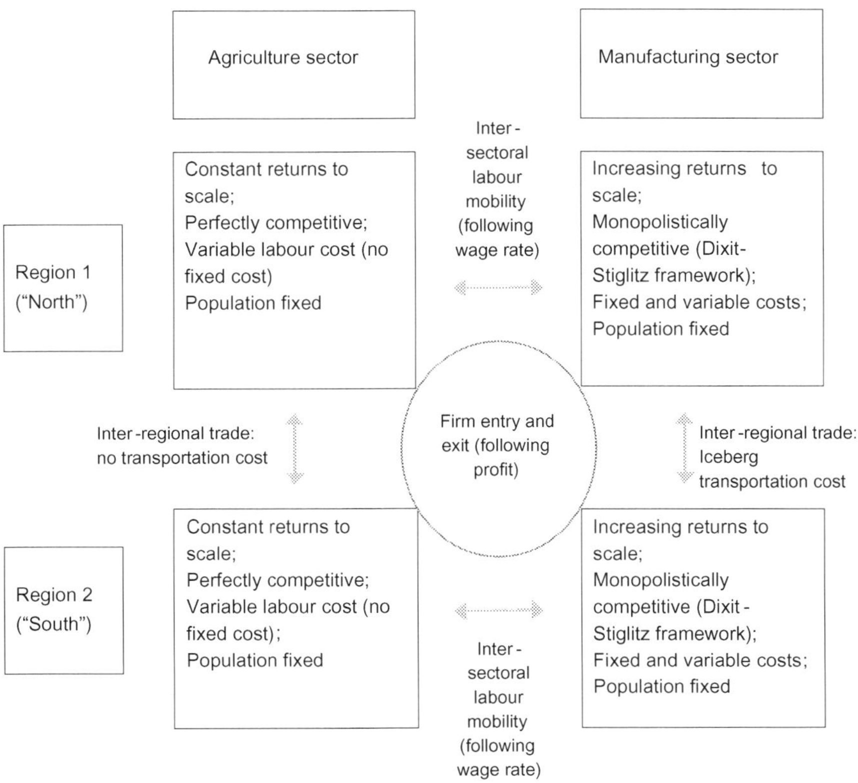

Fig. 1. The Core-Periphery Vertical Linkage Model. Modified on the schematic diagram by Baldwin et al. (2003, p. 194).

- The manufactured goods are horizontally differentiated, and have identical transport costs.
- Each firm in the manufacturing sector has monopoly power, represented by the Dixit-Stiglitz framework. Thus, each firm produces one variety and all are of equal size. The increase in the size of the sector is represented by increase in the variety (i.e., number of firms).
- Consumer utility is of Cobb-Douglas form with expenditure shared across agriculture and manufacturing. The manufacturing share of the Cobb-Douglas function is represented by constant-elasticity of substitution (CES).
- Each firm produces one variety of fixed quantity using both labor and a composite of intermediate goods.
- Labor market equilibrium in and across the two sectors is determined by wage.
- The manufacturing firms locate where profit is the greatest.
- The share of the number of mobile firms in each region is the main indicator of the level of agglomeration/dispersion.

The movements of mobile factors and goods are summarized in Fig. 1.

The models are usually not analytically solvable (although there are linear versions – see Baldwin et al., 2003 for a summary of several varieties) and thus simulation is a norm in NGE to identify the long-run equilibrium points. First, short-run equilibrium is determined by fixing the labor share in each sector within the region. Long-run equilibrium is ascertained by relaxing this and allowing free mobility between sectors within the region (Brakman et al., 2009). Following Combes et al. (2008), four possible outcomes are possible:

1. Both sectors exist in each region.
2. One region specializes in the sector with increasing returns while the other region has both sectors.
3. One region specializes in the constant returns sector while the other region has both sectors.
4. One region specializes in the constant returns sector while the other region specializes in the increasing returns sector.

One of the most interesting findings from the NGE models is the effect of the exogenous changes of transportation costs on the spatial distribution of mobile firms. This can be shown by the famous Tomahawk diagram due to Krugman (1991) and discussed numerous times in the NGE literature.

The bold lines represent the stable long-run equilibria. The break point represents the lowest transportation cost that allows symmetry to be the long-run stable equilibrium. If transportation cost drops beyond this point symmetry becomes unstable and the agglomeration will become the stable equilibrium.[3] The sustain points represent the highest transport cost where the agglomeration equilibrium is stable. Any higher transportation cost will render the agglomeration unstable and move the equilibrium into that of symmetry. Interestingly, there are overlapping areas of transport cost between the sustain points and the break point where both the agglomeration and symmetric equilibria are stable long-run outcomes. This point will be revisited in the context of path dependence.

By specializing in airport services Middle East hubs such as Dubai and Abu Dhabi, as well as Singapore have become industrial clusters of air and tourism services. The transit flows in these cities and the corresponding cluster of air services, is an expression of export-oriented localization. In other words, these cities can be viewed as net exporters of air mobility services where intermediate inputs include the various inputs within the tourism supply chain. These points have leveraged on their natural geographical advantages to build an agglomeration of air services by attracting mobile airlines to locate their services to/from those points. In other words, places such as Dubai and Singapore capitalized on intermediacy (i.e., being strategically located along the Kangaroo route) and fifth freedom air traffic rights in the 1990s to acquire centrality features and sustain autonomous development thereafter (Fleming & Hayuth, 1994).

In cases of market liberalization, there is a first-class opportunity to examine what happens when trade costs decrease rapidly and economic agents are mobile. Aviation satisfies these two conditions quite well: liberalization has occurred and airlines, especially low-cost carriers, have considerable mobility. The degree of this mobility varies, and the risk sharing arrangements exist (Fu, Homsombat, & Oum, 2011); however, in extreme cases low-cost carriers have in the past played destinations against each other to secure added concessions (Papatheodorou & Arvanitis, 2009). Consequently, airline behavior (such as its entry and exit decisions), from an NGE perspective, is an endogenous component that in turn shapes potential market demand, contributing to the core-periphery development of airports. Note, however, that there is a degree of inertia in regards to the long-run equilibrium. Along some levels of transportation costs, agglomeration patterns do not change. Consequently, despite the assumption of mobile firms, incremental changes in the parameters do not always result in incremental changes in the final outcome. As often pointed out, the NGE models are non-linear, and this is related to the point below.

The concept of path dependence has been invoked in the air transport literature to explain airline and airport development, although the NGE approach has not been directly applied as a potential candidate to explain the economic mechanics. Burghouwt (2007) identifies air transport regime, network economies, nodal drivers, and path dependence as four main groups of factors driving the airline network configurations in Europe. Specifically, he observed that the location of European hubs is not usually the result of a rational choice by economic agents (airlines) but more by "seemingly trivial historical events" that resulted in the accumulation of traffic rights. The regulatory barrier could lock the hub carriers to an airport for a long time.

Fig. 2 explains how this may happen. When transport cost is very high the long-run stable equilibrium is to have the mobile sector located in every region.

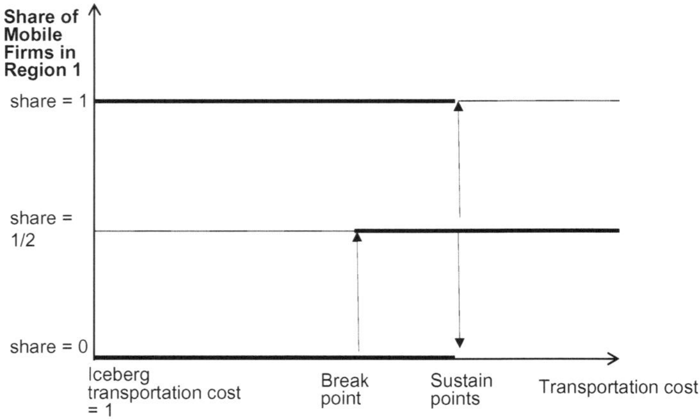

Fig. 2. Tomahawk Diagram (drawn based on the illustration in Baldwin et al., 2003; Brakman et al., 2009). *Note*: Samuelson's Iceberg transportation cost refers to the number of units that must be "shipped" from the origin for one unit to arrive at the destination. An increase in transportation cost is synonymous to an increase in the number of units that must be "shipped" for one unit to arrive.

When the transport cost falls sufficiently, the equilibrium becomes unstable and may shift away if there is a shock. Although, rather dramatic, according to the core-model the exogenous shock can trigger an agglomeration process which will stop only when complete agglomeration takes place. In fact, in the case of the vertical linkages model, when the final consumption's (rather than the intermediate sector's consumption) share of manufacturing (the mobile sector) is high, it is possible to have stable long-run equilibria with partial agglomeration where the Core specializes only in the mobile industry while the Periphery has some share of the mobile industry and a large immobile industry (Combes et al., 2008). Thus, this is a case representing, e.g., a situation where one region has a large hub and the other a smaller secondary airport. Returning to Fig. 2, as it happens, if the trade barrier is imposed again through re-regulation, which raises transport costs to the same level as before, the economy does not return to the original equilibrium where all activities disperse across the regions. What this suggests is that there exists a range of transport costs where spatial equilibrium can be either dispersion or agglomeration. The stable equilibrium is in fact determined by how the transport cost was reached. With an alternative "history," the same level of transport cost may have produced an entirely different long-run equilibrium. This suggests that it may not be possible to "undo" the effect of previous deregulation by re-regulating – an important point in the case of domestic aviation markets such as India (Hooper, 1998) and Brazil (Bettini & Oliveira, 2008) where such re-regulation had occurred in the past.

This type of path dependence clearly influences the spatial configuration of airports. In the United States, the Civil Aeronautics Board (CAB), which was created during the vast expansion of government in the Great Depression, profoundly affected the geography of the United States airline industry in ways that are still evident, long after it ceased to exist (Solberg, 1979) (Bowen, 2010, p. 18). In fact, Delta airlines' hub at Atlanta was an outcome of an agreement between the carrier and CAB in 1940. The agreement was that Delta would be given rights to operate longer routes from Atlanta in exchange for establishing services to declining rural communities in the South. This was an initial advantage Atlanta enjoyed over other cities with respect to air access. Throughout the regulated era, Atlanta built on this advantage to grow its role as a hub for Delta, and today, it is, among several other airports in the US, somewhat a "specialist" in providing connecting air services for domestic passengers. As discussed by Bowen (2010), following deregulation Delta was able to intensify its hubbing so as to increase the number of non-stop cities linked to Atlanta and the share of the total flights emanating from the hub (24% in 2008). One may view this as a path dependent process where the initial advantage of Atlanta was locked-in to create a major hub airport.

NGE: IMPLICATIONS FOR AIRPORT ECONOMICS AND POLICY

NGE as an Approach to Transport Project Appraisal

The spatial distribution of economic activities affects welfare by influencing the net wealth an area can produce as well as the geographic distribution of this wealth (Ottaviano, 2003). Ottaviano argues that this means any policy that influences the location of economic activities will have "regional side-effects" that are unlikely to be captured by policy analyses which tend to be focused and narrow in coverage. Furthermore, the NGE models enable the mapping of the implications of transport cost reduction for spatial inequality without relying on comparative advantage-based explanations, which was the case in trade theory prior to NGE (Puga, 2002). This is important for airport economics and policy because as discussed earlier the location of an airport and a region's specialization in the air services sector are not always determined by underlying endowments. Thus, even between seemingly similar regions, core-periphery disparity can arise due to lock-ins and threshold effects.

Although, the nature of the NGE model can result in model outcomes that are extreme (such as hyper-sensitivity to small changes, while in others, insensitivities), the focus on the interrelations between transport costs, agglomeration and regional inequalities in a common analytical framework makes NGE models particularly suitable to study the impact of transport infrastructure improvements (Puga, 2002).[4] For instance, in regards to the relations between transport cost and welfare, in a simple case of two regions, the Krugman and Venables (1995) model suggests three phases of spatial evolution of regional disparity/parity (as summarized in Combes et al., 2008):

> Phase 1. When transport costs are high, the regions are initially characterized by autarky and backyard capitalism. As transport costs decrease, both regions benefit from a decrease in the price index and a rise in welfare.
>
> Phase 2. If for some reason one region gains an advantage over the other, the divergence process begins, resulting in the core-periphery outcome. The periphery imports an increased variety of services and therefore the price index increases, thus welfare drops. The real welfare gap becomes greater because on balance the welfare increase arising from a greater number of varieties may not offset the increase in the import costs experienced in the periphery.
>
> Phase 3. This is a phase where convergence may occur because the increasing level of concentration in the core results in high labor costs, which becomes a disincentive for firms to locate there. As transportation costs drop further, firms' incentives to relocate to the periphery are enhanced. As the periphery enjoys an increasing share of self-produced (and non-imported) varieties, the price index decreases and real wage (therefore welfare) improves. Meanwhile, the core experiences the opposite effect as real wage declines (as a result of the increased share of the imported varieties).

In a theoretical case where complete disappearance of transport cost occurs, the labor market will equalize and so would the price index in both regions. Interestingly, the welfare in both regions would be equal but at a higher level compared to the autarky case. The phases above in face-value have some interesting similarities with the phases in the way regulation and deregulation of aviation plays-out. For example, in Graham (1997), the regulation era is characterized by point-to-point type of services with limited competition and high costs; this is followed by the initial stages of deregulation where hub-and-spoke develops and low-cost operators make entry. Costs fall and competition increases. In the mature stages of deregulation, multiple hubs and alliances develop; the latter may also involve niche operators, such as regional carriers but also low cost carriers; thus, the market consolidates and new entry becomes more restricted. The general spatial trajectory of these phases is from high-cost point-to-point operations towards an agglomerated, yet closely integrated, economy.

Implications for the Approach and Analysis of a Specific Airport Location Problem

Although there are interesting parallels to draw, it has also been argued that NGE approaches are too abstract to be taken literally. Therefore, their use for policy is somewhat limited and premature (Neary, 2001). However, as Puga (2002) argued, NGE when applied in a specific context is useful because it shows how the overall spatial outcome of a project depends not only on the project attributes but also the characteristics of the economic environment, including the characteristics with respect to factor mobility and interregional wage differentials. In fact, although its simplistic nature is problematic, the model (due to its epistemological strength) also offers the capability to analyze counterfactual, "what if", scenarios, which are useful for policy analysis (Martin & Sunley, 2011).

Due to the spatial economic nature of airports, it is not surprising that NGE encapsulates key economic relationships and trade-offs used to frame debates around specific airport policies. In particular, for a given region, or country, the NGE theories are useful for airport economic issues such as whether or not it is better to serve a region/country's air mobility needs from a single location (a large hub) or several airports, and in which region the hub should be located, and how beneficial the airport location (and agglomeration) will be for the economy. These questions involve the economics of airport operations as well as the wider economic impact. In the United Kingdom, for instance, there has been a continuing debate over where and how the additional airlift capacity in Greater London should be located. There are several options, one involving the large-scale expansion of an already congested hub West of London (Heathrow), additional capacities in other airports serving Greater London such as Gatwick, Stansted and Luton, or an entirely new location East of London in the Thames Estuary (Economics of Aviation Capacity, 2015).

Some of the main prevailing views and "hypotheses" about the relative merits of different airport development options are readily encapsulated by the internally consistent economic logic of NGE theories. This is evident in the fact that debates often involve the following assertions:[5] the tendency for airlines to favor hubs, and passengers to favor direct connections; the fact that airlines tend to be quite mobile to an extent there is a degree of freedom over which airport to serve/base in both interregional (e.g., London or Frankfurt) and intraregional (e.g., Heathrow or Gatwick) contexts; the need for substantial public funding for the airport (therefore, the location of taxation and subsidy matters); the importance of couching airport development in terms of the wider regional growth strategies aimed at poorer areas; the significance of the airport access time and costs given the large employment base (estimated to be around 100,000) the airport supports, including the closely inter-related sectors supporting leisure tourism and business travel; and the importance of understanding the impact on those who gains (urban renewal as a result of the new airport) as well as those left behind (as a result of downscaling or relocation).

In NGE, economic principles are invoked in a common framework to derive agglomeration/dispersion outcomes that address the above issues relevant for a variety of stakeholders. This is one of the key differences from other approaches used in transport infrastructure appraisal such as cost-benefit analysis, which traditionally does not assess the transport impact on regional economic development (Puga, 2002). The endogenization of agglomeration in a general equilibrium framework produces outcomes that are insightful and not immediately obvious. For instance, despite factor mobility, the model predicts a degree of agglomeration inertia where incremental policy will be ineffective. Moreover, the marginal effect of a change in policy will depend on the initial condition; as an example, the single European aviation market resulted in some airlines changing hub location but this does not necessarily mean the reversal of this policy will result in the airlines switching back.

In airport economics research, the concepts of Krugman's (1991) core-periphery model have been invoked in the interpretation of the spatial computable general equilibrium analysis commissioned by the UK Airports Commission (2015). Similarly, the qualitative implications of the NGE were discussed in Shen and Cao (2016) in the context of "aerotropolis" policy development in China. There is a family of NGE models that may be more appropriate in differential circumstances, however. Beyond the foundational core-periphery model, for instance, a model particularly suited for assessing the economic implications of airport location may be the localization spill-over model by Martin (1999). In this model, economic growth is affected by agglomeration. Agglomeration benefits are related to the increasing returns in the "manufacturing" sector as well as spill-overs. The latter occur locally when there is a learning curve such that producing capital from one region becomes cheaper faster than producing the same unit elsewhere. As discussed in Baldwin et al. (2003), the ultimate implication of the model is the trade-off between spatial equity and growth, i.e., a policy to trigger agglomeration in the poorer region may not necessarily bring the highest total growth. However, they also note that one can mitigate the seemingly inevitable trade-off by correctly identifying the market failure (in this case the spill-overs) and targeting it with policy such as by enhancing transportation links to facilitate the spill-overs to be dispersed across regions. In the airport location problem context, these results suggest the need to consider facilitating efficient flows of people between airports – another important airport infrastructure policy dimension. Thus, in this case, the NGE model provides insights into the need to consider multimodal transportation issues in the airport location problem. In general, these approaches highlight how transport projects will have to simultaneously influence several key parameters to provide an environment conductive for growth across regions while also reducing regional inequality.

Finally, there are many challenging issues for empirical research, some of which are related to more generic econometric issues such as endogeneity, and some more nuanced such as establishing quantitatively specific ranges of benchmark threshold levels. In airport catchment area analysis, a field of airport economics and marketing research increasing in industry interest as airports actively pursue opportunities through route development, the key objective is to estimate the real market potential of the airport. One may approach the airline's airport location problem as a discrete choice problem involving the real market potential as one of the key deterministic attributes of airports. As mentioned by Combes, et al. (2008), such a multinomial logit (or variant) application to the firm location choice is a common approach. On this issue, NGE suggests there is an endogeneity of firm location and demand arising from the simultaneity of firm location choice and real market potential, i.e., the real market potential of the airport depends on the number of airlines serving it. Clearly, in the presence of these effects, bias in the estimates will likely occur. The feedback effect means the selection of a given option by others increases the market potential (if airline entry increases the hubbing potential of the airport) or decreases the market potential (if airline entry induces increases in costs such as congestion). An example of a recent extension of the multinomial logit that addresses these types of problems is by de Grange et al. (2015), who introduces a logit model with network externalities.

MAIN CRITIQUE OF THE NEW GEOGRAPHICAL ECONOMICS APPROACH

NGE is an area of academic study concerned with economic mechanisms determining the spatial distribution of economic activities. Although related closely to regional science, urban economics, international trade, and growth theories, the key contribution of the economic geography theory in the body of economics is the endogenization of the location choice of economic agents and demand (e.g., Combes, et al., 2008). This allows the model to determine the spatial distribution of economic activities based on the "second-nature" concentration. The latter is defined by Krugman as the forces of concentration and dispersion that are independent of factor endowments, which its distribution can be regarded as "first nature," often represented by physical geography. Thus, economic geography attempts to focus on economic mechanisms that can result in a concentration of economic activities over a homogenous space.

A brief note on the nomenclature is warranted. The following is not as trivial as it may first seem as it can be a source of confusion and controversy. Economic geography was subject to four major theoretical waves since the 1960s: location theory and neoclassical approach; behavioral approach; Marxist political economy; and the new economic geography (Coe, Kelly, & Yeung, 2010). The new economic geography based on the seminal work by Krugman is directly linked to the earlier location theory and neoclassical approach (the first wave), and it is not the same theoretical wave as the new economic geography mentioned by Coe et al. (2010) in the four-wave list. Thus, in this context, it is a "new" and more sophisticated form of the earlier neoclassical approach "reborn" with an upgrade. However, as hinted earlier, there are considerable disagreements over the appropriateness of the term new economic geography in the field of economic geography, which is rich and diverse in disciplinary perspectives. Furthermore, new economic geography can be confused with other meanings as it is not the first time a theoretical upheaval in economic geography has been called as such – for instance the new economic geography in the mid-1990s sees the economic processes as social, cultural and institutional factors from an eclectic standpoint ranging from post-structuralism and post-modernism to institutionalism and feminism (Coe et al., 2010, p. 13). Furthermore, the models in this class should be in no way seen as superseding the "old" economic geography, as they address a limited set of questions, often in limited ways (Anderson, 2012, p. 137). As a result, this chapter used the term new geographical economics following Brakman et al. (2009)'s rationale that the use of geographical economics more clearly states the fact that the theory is firmly grounded in international economics and it is an attempt to introduce more geography into economics. This then avoids the confusion that new economic geography is a theory developed by economic geographers, a suggestion that the geographers may reject.

As alluded to earlier, economic geography is a field of very diverse perspectives. This chapter roughly painted a picture of one narrow area specializing in neoclassical economics of geography. NGE is also what is "arguably the most sustained and systematic recognition of the importance of location and geography by mainstream economics to date" (Garretsen & Martin, 2010, p. 129). Other than the use of the term "new", NGE has been a subject of various critiques. Some of the main critiques are briefly presented below to situate the preceding sections in broader context of the importance of space and time, and what this means for the economics of air transport.

Following Garretsen and Martin (2010), the focus of NGE is on two important issues: the way in which geography (space) and history (time) are incorporated into the models. In the two-region case, transport cost represents geography in NGE modeling framework, whereas history matters in a sense that different equilibrium outcomes (dispersion or agglomeration) are possible depending on which path is followed. Once this happens the nature of the equilibrium is pre-determined; nonetheless, the initial condition will determine which path, and therefore equilibrium, is eventually followed. The main critique by Garretsen and Martin (2010) is that despite subsequent extensions to the core model of NGE, the role of geography and history remains (limited) as above. In this context, the key concern regarding geography is that it is far from certain whether the two-region setting and the resultant symmetric transport cost can adequately capture what is important in a multi-region setting.[6] Similarly, there is concern with the way history has been reduced to the separable role of a "shock" and the role of guiding hand to equilibrium. The equilibrium approach to history and path dependence is problematic at least because this implies that once stability (equilibrium) is reached, it is as if history comes to an end (Martin, 2010). These concerns are compounded by the fact that there is a strong downside to empirical and policy application of the NGE models; partly because, as noted by Garretsen and Martin (2010) there are many competing theories that are similar. Moreover, historical determinism as suggested by path dependence assumes that economic agents and spaces are too weak to change their fate when faced with historical accidents and the self-reinforcing mechanism of cumulative causation. This seems to deny the very existence of "path-breaking" and "path creation" (Ma & Hassink, 2014) which lies at the heart of strategic spatial management as previously discussed in the cases of Dubai and Singapore.[7]

In any case, there is also a compelling counter-argument. In regards to the simplification of geography and history in the models, one may see NGE as an important initial attempt to improve it. As Krugman (2010) puts it, "the economist's way of thinking may have blind spots, but it also has a great deal of power and depth; there should be a way to persuade economists to learn from geography without sacrificing the good in the field" (p. 2). In Krugman's terms, the "intention of the NGE model was to answer the "what if" questions … an important result in this regard has been the finding that the geographical structure of an economy depended on a few key parameters: transportation costs, economies of scale, and factor mobility" (p. 6). However, Krugman does concede that the original core-periphery model was also modeled based on 1900s industry conceptualizations with a "steampunk" feel. Although this is still very much relevant to newly industrializing nations, nowadays, the external economies in advanced industrial economies are more subtly expressed through channels such as knowledge spill-overs. This point is consistent with that of Garretsen and Martin (2010) who argued that better models are needed that account for these, and perhaps more "invisible," effects. With all the above in mind, the chapter is ready to conclude on its main points.

CONCLUSION

In a backyard capitalism setting where everything is divisible, concentrations in civil aviation services (and perhaps even the aviation sector itself) may not exist, because there will be no need for transportation costs and trade. In order to address the issue of how "second-nature" concentration may take place, NGE models have incorporated increasing returns and imperfect markets to endogenize firm location *and* demand where the location choices of economic agents influence, and are influenced by, market potential. These models provide a possible economic mechanism through which path dependence and multiple equilibria may arise. This chapter's intention was to introduce and discuss what aspects of the NGE approach may be relevant to the study of the spatial evolution of airports as well as how. Although the discussion was conceptual in nature, the applicability could readily be seen due to the presence of imperfect markets, path dependence, trade barriers (transportation costs) and various forms of increasing returns, as well as the prevailing importance of both "first"- and "second"-nature concentrations in aviation.

However, adopting the essential elements of the NGE in an air transport context is not without significant challenges. A simple substitution of the NGE modeling nomenclature with aviation terms is not sufficient. The appropriateness of the strategic modeling simplifications adopted in NGE needs to be examined; for instance, there are issues as to how to reconcile the assumption about factor mobility. While it is true that some low cost carriers have demonstrated considerable mobility in route entry/exit decisions, many airlines also do not have the same degree of flexibility not least due to airport slot constraints. Furthermore, as previously mentioned, the dynamic oligopolistic market structure may be a more suitable characterization of aviation markets, which are often assessed at the route-level. This diverges from the way in which increasing returns operate in NGE through the Dixit-Stiglitz framework. Thus, the interplay of increasing returns, endogenous location and demand mechanisms will be context-specific and will need to be justified on a case-by-case basis. In this regard, different variants within the family of NGE models may be suitable for particular situations.

One way to move forward is to leverage the unique opportunities the study of air transport sector offers for the empirical work around NGE. For instance, due to its regulatory history, aviation is a quasi-natural experiment in which the effect of trade barrier removal can be assessed. Furthermore, the economic mechanics of airport specialization, such as a transit tourism city and an aerotropolis may suitably be explored using NGE models. Another area of potential contribution is in offering policy guidance on airports and regional economic development. While not suggesting that all regions aim to be the Core, there are cases where regions invest considerably in airport infrastructure to develop tourism and growth. The NGE approach is a particularly suitable framework for the analysis of publicly funded transport projects with significant regional economic development content. The NGE approach may provide an economic framework to think about the effectiveness of these investments from the perspective of the risks of peripherality, dependency and "regional side-effects." These, in turn, may feed back into improving NGE modeling to address some of the main concerns about the approach raised by economic geographers, namely, a more nuanced representation of the complexity of spatial effects.

NOTES

1. This term 'new economic geography' can be controversial and as will be seen this chapter adopts the term 'new geographical economics (NGE)' following Brakman, Garretsen, and van Marrewijk (2009).

2. For more information on variants please see, for example, Baldwin, Forslid, Martin, Ottaviano, & Robert-Nicoud, 2003; Combes, Mayer, & Thisse, 2008; Brakman et al., 2009.

3. In the NGE research literature, sometimes this is referred to as a "catastrophic" change from a symmetric equilibrium to an asymmetric one.

4. Puga (2002) discusses how NGE approaches can contribute to high-speed rail and road transport policies involving European Union's structural funds.

5. Based on the issues discussed in "Economics of aviation capacity (2015), *The Economist*, viewed 1st January 2017, http://www.economist.com/blogs/gulliver/2015/12/economics-aviation-capacity"

6. There are multi-region extensions of the two-region model (e.g., see Fujita, Krugman, & Venables, 1999 for "racetrack economy"), however, the broader critiques about geography and history mentioned still applies (Garretsen & Martin, 2010).

7. Aspects of the role of self-fulfilling prophecies and expectations have been examined within the NGE framework (Baldwin et al., 2003).

REFERENCES

Anderson, W. (2012). *Economic geography*. Routledge.

Baldwin, R., Forslid, R., Martin, P., Ottaviano, G., & Robert-Nicoud, F. (2003). *Economic geography & public policy*. Princeton University Press.

Bettini, H. F. A. J., & Oliveira, A. V. M. (2008). Airline capacity setting after re-regulation: The Brazilian case in the early 2000s. *Journal of Air Transport Management*, *14*, 289–292.

Bowen, J. (2010). *Economic geography of air transportation*. Routledge.

Brakman, S., Garretsen, H., & van Marrewijk, C. (2009). *The new introduction to geographical economics*. Cambridge University Press.

Burghouwt, G. (2007). *Airline network development in Europe and its implications for airport planning*. Ashgate.

Burghouwt, G., Hakfoort, J., & Eck, J. (2003). The spatial configuration of airline networks in Europe. *Journal of Air Transport Management*, *9*, 309–323.

Caves, D., Christensen, L., & Tretheway, M. (1984). Economies of density versus economies of scale: Why trunk and local service airline costs differ. *Rand Journal of Economics*, *15*(4), 471–489.

Chou, Y. (1993). Airline deregulation and nodal accessibility. *Journal of Transport Geography*, *1*(1), 36–46.

Coe, N., Kelly, P., & Yeung, H. W. C. (2010). *Economic geography*. Blackwell Publishing.

Combes, P., Mayer, T., & Thisse, J.-F. (2008). *Economic geography*. Princeton: Princeton University Press.

de Grange, L. et al. (2015). A logit model with endogenous explanatory variables and network externalities. *Networks and Spatial Economics*, *15*(1), 89–116.

Derudder, B., & Witlox, F. (2009). The impact of progressive liberalization on the spatiality of airline networks: A measurement framework based on the assessment of hierarchical differentiation. *Journal of Transport Geography*, *16*(5), 305–312.

Dicken, P., & Lloyd, P. E. (1990). *Location in space* (3rd ed.). New York: Harper & Row.

Dixit, A. K., & Stiglitz, J. E. (1977). Monopolistic competition and optimum product diversity. *American Economic Review*, *67*, 297–308.

Dobruszkes, F. (2006). An analysis of European low-cost airlines and their networks. *Journal of Transport Geography*, *14*(4), 249–264.

Economics of aviation capacity. (2015). The Economist. Retrived form http://www.economist.com/blogs/gulliver/2015/12/economics-aviation-capacity. Accessed January 1, 2017.

Fleming, D. K., & Hayuth, Y. (1994). Spatial characteristics of transportation hubs: Centrality and intermediacy. *Journal of Transport Geography*, *2*(1), 3–18.

Flores-Fillol, R., Garcia-Lopez, M.-A., & Nicolini, R. (2016). Organization of land surrounding airports: The case of the aerotropolis. *Land Economics*, *92*(1), 57–81.

Fu, X., Homsombat, W., & Oum, T. H. (2011). Airport-airline vertical relationships, their effects and regulatory policy implications. *Journal of Air Transport Management*, *17*, 347–353.

Fu, X., & Oum, T. H. (2014). Air Transport Liberalization and its Effects on Airline Competition and Traffic Growth – An Overview. In *Advances in airline economics* (Vol. 4, pp. 11–44). Bingley: Emerald Publishing.

Fujita, M., Krugman, P., & Venables, A. J. (1999). *The spatial economy. Cities, regions and international trade*. Cambridge, MA: MIT Press.

Fujita & Krugman. (2002). Should not be in the paper. It should be Fujita and Krugman (2004) instead.

Fujita, M., & Krugman, P. R. (2004). The new economic geography: Past, present and the future. *Papers in Regional Science*, *83*, 139–164.

Fujita, M., & Thisse, J.-F. (2002). *Economics of agglomeration*. Cambridge: Cambridge University Press.

Garretsen, H., & Martin, R. (2010). Rethinking (new) economic geography models: Taking geography and history more seriously. *Spatial Economic Analysis*, *5*(2).

Goetz, A., & Sutton, C. (1997). The geography of deregulation in the U.S. airline industry. *Annals of the Association of American Geographers*, *87*(2), 238–263.

Graham, B. (1997). The geography of air transport in Australasia: A global perspective. *Australian Geographical Studies*, *37*(2).

Head, T., & Mayer, T. (2004). The empirics of agglomeration and trade. Retrieved from http://www.cepii.fr/PDF_PUB/wp/2003/wp2003-15.pdf. Accessed on August 4.

Holloway, S. (2008). *Straight and level: Practical airline economics*. Burlington, VT: Ashgate.

Hooper, P. (1998). Airline competition and deregulation in developed and developing country contexts – Australia and India. *Journal of Transport Geography*, *6*, 105–116.

Ito, H., & Lee, D. (2003). *Low cost carrier growth in the U.S. airline industry: Past, present, and future*. Working Paper, Cambridge.

Koo, T., Halpern, N., Papatheodorou, A., Graham, A., & Arvanitis, P. (2016). Air transport liberalisation and airport dependency: Developing a composite index. *Journal of Transport Geography*. doi:10.1016/j.jtrangeo.2015.04.006

Krugman, P. (2010). *The New Economic Geography, Now Middle-Aged*. In Prepared for presentation to the Association of American Geographers, April 16, 2010.

Krugman, P. R. (1991). *Geography and trade*. Cambridge, MA: MIT Press.

Krugman, P. R., & Venables, A. J. (1995). Globalization and inequality of nations *Quarterly Journal of Economics*, *110*(4), 857–880.

Krugman, P. R., & Venables, A. J. (1996). Integration, specialization, and adjustment. *Eurpean Economic Review*, *40*(3-5), 959–967.

Ma, M., & Hassink, R. (2014). Path dependence and tourism area development: The case of Guilin, China. *Tourism Geographies*, *16*(4), 580–597.

Martin, P. (1999). Public policies, regional inequalities and growth. *Journal of Public Economics*, *73*(1), 85–105.

Martin, R., & Sunley, P. (2011). The new economic geography and policy relevance. *Journal of Economic Geography*, *11*, 357–369.

Martin, R. (2010). Roepke lecture in economic geography – Rethinking regional path dependence: Beyond lock-in to evolution. *Economic Geography*, *86*(1), 1–27.

Myrdal, G. (1957). *Economic theory and underdeveloped regions*. London: University Paperbacks, Methuen.

Neary, P. (2001). Of hype and hyperbolas: Introducing the new economic geography. *Journal of Economic Literature*, *39*, 536–561.

O'Connor, K. (2003). Global air travel: Toward concentration or dispersal? *Journal of Transport Geography*, *11*, 83–92.

Ottaviano, G. (2003). Regional policy in the global economy: Insights from new economic geography. *Regional Studies*, *37*(6-7), 665–673.

Oum, T. H., & Zhang, Y. (1997). A note on scale economies in transport. *Journal of Transport Economics and Policy*, *31*, 309–315.

Papatheodorou, A. (2003). Modelling tourism development – A synthetic approach. *Tourism Economics*, *9*(4), 407–430.

Papatheodorou, A. (2004). Exploring the evolution of tourism resorts. *Annals of Tourism Research*, *31*(1), 219–237.

Papatheodorou, A., & Arvanitis, P. (2009). Spatial evolution of airport traffic and air transport liberalisation: The case of Greece. *Journal of Transport Geography*, *17*, 402–412.

Puga, D. (2002). European regional policies in light of recent location theories. *Journal of Economic Geography*, *2*, 373–406.

Quinet, E., & Vickerman, R. (2004). *Principles of transport economics*. Cheltenham: Edward Elgar.

Reynolds-Feighan, A. (1998). The impact of U.S. airline deregulation on airport traffic patterns. *Geographical Analysis*, *30*(3), 234–253.

Reynolds-Feighan, A. (2010). Characterisation of airline networks: A North American and European comparison. *Journal of Air Transport Management*, *16*, 109–120.

Shaw, S., Feng, L., Chen, J., & Zhou, C. (2009). China's airline consolidation and its effects on domestic airline networks and competition. *Journal of Transport Geography*, *17*, 293–305.

Shen, D., & Cao, Y. (2016). Aerotropolis fromation and evolution: Insights from new economic geography. *International Journal of Sustainable Development*, *19*(3).

Small, N. (1993). A victim of geography, not policy? Canada's airline industry since deregulation. *Journal of Transport Geography*, *1*(3), 182–194.

Solberg, C. (1979). *Conquest of the Skies: A history of commercial aviation in America*. Boston, MA: Little, Brown & Company.

Starrett, D. (1978). Market allocations of location choice in a model with free mobility. *Journal of Economic Theory*, *17*, 21–37.

Takahashi, T. (2011). Directional imbalance in transport prices and economic geography. *Journal of Urban Economics*, *69*(1), 92–102.

UK Airports Commission. (2015). Economy: Wider impacts assessment. Retrieved from https://www.gov.uk/government/uploads/system/uploads/attachment_data/file/371810/2-economy–wider-impacts-assessment.pdf. Accessed on January 1, 2017.

CHAPTER 11

THE HETEROGENEOUS IMPACT OF AIRPORTS ON POPULATION AND EMPLOYMENT GROWTH IN CITIES☆

Marquise J. McGraw

ABSTRACT

This chapter examines the effects that airports have had on economic development in cities from 1950 to 2010. It uses a novel dataset consisting of previously unexploited data on the origins and history of the aviation system in the United States. Applying the method of synthetic controls to a set of medium and small airports, I examine both the overall impacts and the heterogeneity within the outcomes of various airports. Then, I use regression analysis to determine key factors differentiating successful airports from less successful ones, as it pertains particularly to population and employment growth. I find that, first, on average, cities have benefited from airports over this period. Airports, overall, provided a causal contribution of 0.2– 0.6% per year on population and employment growth over the time period. Second, I show that city-level factors contributing to airport success include: (1) closer proximity to a major research university, (2) a capital city location,

☆This chapter is the result of the author's independent research while at Middlebury College and the University of California, Berkeley, and does not necessarily represent the views of the Consumer Financial Protection Bureau or the United States. All errors are my own.

The Economics of Airport Operations
Advances in Airline Economics, Volume 6, 261–312

ISSN: 2212-1609/doi:10.1108/S2212-160920170000006011

and (3) climate factors, particularly higher January mean temperatures and/or hours of sunshine. City size is a consideration as well; cities in larger metropolitan areas, with larger shares of employment in nontradables in the 1950s, were also better positioned to reap the benefits that airports provided on city growth. Significant differences were not found across regions, airport governance structures, or other factors.

Keywords: Airports; cities; economic development; local labor markets; agglomeration

JEL classifications: L93; R11; R4

INTRODUCTION

To the casual observer, airports and aviation in general appear to be beneficial for cities. In fact, many cities consider their airports a vital part of their local economies. Consistent with this belief, the Federal government subsidizes air travel through the provision of funds to necessary infrastructure, such as the air traffic control system. It also subsidizes service to very small airports through programs, such as the Essential Air Service. These expenditures are not trivial; as of October 2012, 120 communities in the contiguous United States received a total of nearly $225 million dollars yearly in such subsidies (Wittman et al., 2013). Local municipalities themselves also subsidize aviation by offering incentives to air carriers for service to their cities with the goal of increasing economic activity within their borders. For example, in 2010, Huntsville International Airport, a 12-gate airport in Madison County, Alabama, spent $1.5 million in local taxpayer money to attract service from AirTran Airways. In 2013, it set aside $5 million in hopes of luring more service.[1] Local leaders fear that the loss of service would hurt Huntsville's ability to attract new jobs and to compete for new conventions and tourists.

The same is true for larger airports as well. In September 2016, the Commonwealth of Virginia secured a long-term lease agreement with United Airlines, its largest tenant, to continue operations at Washington-Dulles International Airport through 2024. "Today's agreement is critical to the economic prosperity of Northern Virginia and air service throughout the Commonwealth," said Governor Terry McAuliffe. "The extension of the United lease solidifies Dulles as Virginia's gateway to the country and the world and a critical piece of our efforts to build a new Virginia economy." This deal was accompanied by a package of $50 million in funding to "reduce airline costs and further strengthen the competitive position of Dulles International."[2]

As these two examples show, the conventional wisdom is that airports are always beneficial for cities. While this, however, may be true on average, there is little research examining whether this benefit exists across all commercial airports. Would Huntsville, the area around Washington-Dulles, and cities of all shapes and sizes in between, be different had it not been for their airports? If so, how might those differences come about? And if not, why not? How is it that airports might play such an important role, and through what mechanism? Answers to these questions are unclear from the current literature. In an era where many airlines are pulling out of smaller airports, this is a critical question. In fact, Wittman et al. (2013) note that between 2007 and 2012, 24 airports lost all their commercial service at some point. Understanding how aviation might affect cities, particularly smaller cities, is critical to understanding whether there is a proper policy response. This is also important for understanding how transportation infrastructure, more generally, might affect cities, and how those effects may have developed over time.

The aims of this chapter are twofold. First, I examine the question of how airports have, on average, affected their local economies over the post-World War II period, 1950–2010. Second, and most critically, this chapter examines the heterogeneity in airport success and failure cases across individual airports. The hope is to provide new evidence of the role of airports in these cities, particularly in medium-sized and smaller communities.

In identifying the causal effect of airports on population and employment, econometrically, the major concern is endogeneity. Airports, similar to other pieces of infrastructure, such as roads, are not randomly assigned to cities, which could lead to statistically biased estimates of their impacts. In the case of airports, this is even more of a concern, given the law in the United States specifically stipulates that the construction and operation of airports is a local responsibility. This gives rise to questions which may complicate estimation of these effects. Were airports strategically constructed in cities that expected to thrive anyway, so that effects casually attributed to the airport could potentially result from other unexplained factors? Or, alternatively, were airports built in places with relatively dim prospects in the hope of stimulating growth in those local economies, with the true effect of aviation actually larger than initially thought?

A key innovation of this study is a research design that examines the entire recent history of aviation in the United States during the period 1900–2010, while employing previously unexploited historical aviation and economic data to address endogeneity concerns. I employ synthetic controls (Abadie et al., 2003; Abadie, Diamond, & Hainmueller, 2010) as the estimator of choice. This estimator, which at its core extends the widely used difference-in-difference framework to individual case studies and aggregate outcomes, uses that historical data to generate a "counterfactual" estimate. Specifically, it generates an estimate of what would have happened in the absence of the airports being constructed and operated in the city. Differencing these estimates from the actual outcomes, one can obtain a measure of the average treatment effect.

It is certainly the case that on average, the set of mostly small- and medium-sized airports in this study have caused growth in employment and population over the 60-year period. Given the size of the compounded effects over the 60-year time horizon, they are best conceptualized in terms of annual growth rates. That is, an airport contributes, on average, 0.2–0.4% of population/employment growth per year. However, there is widespread heterogeneity in terms of those outcomes. The top airport in the sample is estimated to contribute 4% of growth per year to its economy, while over 70% of the airports in the sample have statistically insignificant, or in some cases, negative causal effects.[3] This chapter argues that city fundamentals, particularly as it relates to the quality of human capital in cities, play a key role in differentiating between airports that are successful and those that are not.

LITERATURE REVIEW

The literature on the specific topic of airports and regional economic development, while growing, is relatively small. In addition, the questions posed in this chapter are also related to the broader literature on the effects of public infrastructure, as well as the literature on roads and economic development. For instance, Aschauer (1989). was one of the first to provide evidence that public capital, specifically "core" infrastructure, plays a significant role in economic growth.[4] Munnell (1990) showed that, states that have invested more in infrastructure tend to have greater output, more private investment, and more economic growth. She notes, but cannot conclusively prove, that causation seems to run from investment to increased productivity.

Closely related to the topic of airports and urban development is the literature on roads. In his seminal paper, Baum-Snow (2007) estimated the effect of highways on suburbanization using the 1947 national highway plan as an instrument for the highway system which was eventually constructed. Specifically, he examined the number of planned highway "rays" passing through a city to instrument for the number of rays ultimately constructed.[5] His primary finding is that one new highway passing through a central city reduced the city's population by roughly 18%. He found if the interstate highway system had not been built, aggregate central city population in each metropolitan statistical area (MSA) would have increased by 8% between 1950 and 1990.

Michaels (2008) found that the opening of the interstate highway system increased trade-related activities in rural counties. In so doing, the highways raised the demand for skilled workers in skill-abundant counties and reduced it elsewhere. Duranton, Morrow, and Turner (2013), using the 1947 national highway plan as an instrument, showed that highways play an important role in determining the specialization of urban sectors in terms of production and trade in heavy goods. Duranton et al. (2012) examine causality between road transportation and city growth, finding significant effects of road miles on employment and population growth. For the period between 1983 and 2003, they find that a 10% increase in a city's initial stock of highways leads to a 1.5% increase in employment over the 20-year period.

In aviation, Brueckner (1982) was the first study to explicitly consider the question of whether and how the quality of airline service received by a city impacts its business climate. Focusing on smaller cities, he was unable to obtain conclusive evidence of a relationship. He did note, however, that traffic was higher when a military base was nearby and was also increasing in the share of professional ("white-collar") jobs. Brueckner (2003) found that a 10% increase in passenger enplanements in a metro area leads approximately to an 1% increase in employment in service-related industries, with no effect on manufacturing or other types of employment, based on 1979 data. Green (2007) uses time-series data and finds that a 10% increase in boardings per capita leads to a 3.9% increase in population growth and a 2.8% higher employment growth for the 10-year period of 1990 to 2000. Taken together, these papers indicate a likely relationship between air service and local economic outcomes.

Cohen et al. (2003) apply spatial econometrics techniques to a cost function approach. They find that increasing investment in own-state airport infrastructure tends to generate cost-savings for the manufacturing industry, primarily due to non-production-related labor and materials savings. They also find that such expansion is accompanied by spillover benefits to other airports, especially when investment is concentrated in a connected hub. Small airports were the focus of Button, Doh, and Yuan (2010). They use a sample of 66 small airports in Virginia to estimate their effects on economic development, and find that a doubling of passenger numbers produces up to a 4% increase in per capita income in the areas studied. Percoco (2010) considers the impact of airports on Italian provinces. Building on Brueckner (2003) and accounting for spatial spillover effects, he finds that the elasticity of service-sector employment to airport passengers is 0.045, and that of spillover effects is almost 0.017. Blonigen et al. (2015) exploit the market changes induced by the 1978 Airline Deregulation Act to examine the relationship between air traffic and local economic growth. Using time-series variation in local growth rates over a 20-year period centered around deregulation (1969–1991), they find that air service has a positive and significant effect on regional growth, with the size of these effects differing by the size of the MSA and its industrial mix. LeFors (2014) constructs a measure of air accessibility, and uses it to examine how it contributes to growth. He finds increasing air accessibility increases the growth rate of employment in tradable services; however, he finds weak effects on productivity and total employment growth.

Sheard (2014) uses the Civil Aeronautics Administration's 1944 National Airport Plan as an instrument for the current distribution of airports (by size, as measured by air traffic) in the U.S. His dependent variable of interest is employment shares. He estimates that airport size has a positive effect on local employment in tradable services, with an elasticity of approximately 0.1, and a negative effect on manufacturing. He finds no measurable effect on nontradable services. Note that his instrument is relevant to his question (of employment shares), but endogenous if one is interested in understanding aggregate population or employment outcomes, since, by 1944, planners were basing their assessments on outcomes observed well after the aviation system had become established, and were thus assigning airports to places that planners believed would need them in the future. Sheard (2015), using a different identification approach similar to the Bartik instrument, finds that the elasticity between airport size and employment is 0.02, and that between airport size and GDP to be 0.035.

This study is conceptually most similar to Baum-Snow (2007), adapted for the aviation context. Here, instead of focusing on traditional (and possibly endogenous) metrics of air traffic, whether measured by enplanements or flights, I adapt a treatment effect approach. The definition of "treated" here is a binary indicator for having an airport in a CBSA. Since airports receive traffic from multiple points in space, conceptualizing the treatment in this way makes sense. Additionally, I diverge from Baum-Snow in that I adopt a research design more akin to a difference-in-differences approach than Baum-Snow's instrumental variables approach. Availability of data, as well as specific factors in aviation history that will be further discussed in the "Estimating the Effect of Airports on Cities" section, make a compelling case for this approach. I build on this difference-in-difference design to understand the heterogeneity of airport effects as well. This is accomplished by using a synthetic control approach, which is more akin to a reweighting/matching estimator applied to difference-in-differences. This method has the advantage of uncovering not only the overall impacts of airports, but the heterogeneity in these effects as well. The synthetic control method is further discussed in the "Synthetic Control Analysis" section.

This study thus contributes to the literature in four ways. First, unlike other papers that consider the effects of aviation only over limited periods, I consider the entire period of aviation in the United States (1900–2010), allowing for a better understanding of how the role of airports may have shifted over time. Second, by explicitly focusing on (mostly) mid-sized and smaller airports, and using new data from the formative period of aviation to better identify counterfactual cities, I am able to examine these effects in a context that more closely resembles a natural experiment, improving the likelihood of identifying the effects of interest.[6] Third, by focusing on airports in CBSAs as the unit of observation, rather than air traffic, I reduce the likelihood that the estimated effects of aviation are unfairly weighted toward the largest cities, which allows for a better understanding of how airports impact smaller metropolitan areas.

Finally, the use of the synthetic control estimator is novel and sheds new light on the heterogeneity in the productivity of airports.

LOCAL LABOR MARKETS AND AIRPORTS

Why, theoretically, might we expect airports, or any type of public infrastructure, to affect economic activity in a city? This may happen through one of at least four mechanisms: (1) by acting as an unpaid factor of production in a firm's production function, (2) by working to making other inputs more productive, (3) by helping to attract other inputs from elsewhere, and/or (4) by stimulating demand for more infrastructure (e.g., roads) and related services (Eberts et al., 1999). In this chapter, I focus on the first channel, but note the other three channels could potentially be of importance as well.

The effect of the airport shock on a representative local labor market is shown in the highly stylized model given in Fig. 1. In this city, labor demand is assumed to be downward sloping, while labor supply slopes upward. In the short run (panel a), the opening of the airport acts as a shock to labor demand, which, being a productive amenity increases as the airport makes (some)

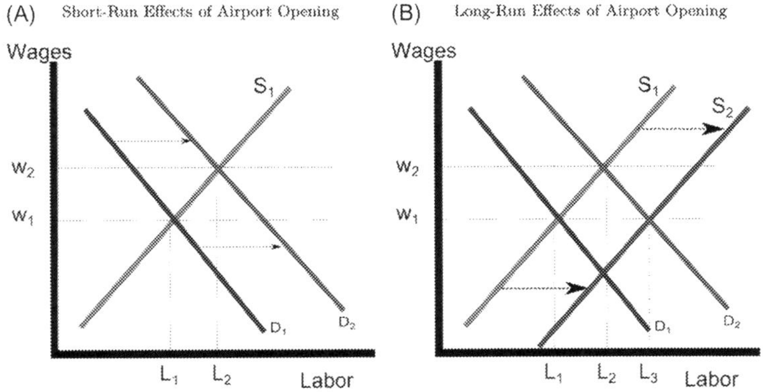

Fig. 1. Stylized Model of Airports and Local Labor Markets. *Notes*: In this highly stylized model, labor demand is assumed to be downward sloping, while labor supply slopes upward. In the short run (panel A), the opening of the airport acts as a shock to labor demand, which increases as the airport makes (some) existing firms more productive and also attracts new firms to the city. Hence, demand shifts from D_1 to D_2. Wages increase as well, from w_1 to w_2. In the long run (panel B), workers in non-airport cities see the higher wages in the airport city and move there, increasing the supply of labor and shifting labor supply from S1 to S2. This shift depresses the short-run wage gains. However, long-run employment rests at L_3, which represents a larger gain ($L_3 - L_1$) relative to the original employment boost ($L_2 - L_1$). As a result, the airport is expected to increase employment, but not necessarily wages, in long-run equilibrium.

existing firms more productive and also attracts new firms to the city. Hence, demand shifts from D_1 to D_2. Wages increase as well, from w_1 to w_2. In the long run (panel b), workers in non-airport cities see the higher wages in the airport city and move there, increasing the supply of labor and shifting labor supply from S_1 to S_2. This shift depresses the short-run wage gains. However, long-run employment rests at L_3, which represents a larger gain $(L_3 - L_1)$ relative to the original employment boost $(L_2 - L_1)$. As a result, the airport is expected to increase employment, but not necessarily wages, in long-run equilibrium.

The magnitude of the employment effect $(L_3 - L_1)$ could potentially vary by industry. This would be true if an airport affected certain industries more than others. Assume that firms in all cities produce goods of two types – tradable and nontradable. Tradable goods – goods that are destined for consumption outside the city where they were produced – are found in the agriculture, mining, manufacturing, and wholesale trade sectors. Nontradable goods consist of output in the construction, retail trade, finance, insurance and real estate, public administration, and services sector.[7] Let X represents the set of goods produced in the economy. This is then composed of two subsets, tradable x_t and nontradable x_m firms. There are J tradable industries producing goods x_{t1} through x_{tj}, and K nontradable industries producing goods x_{m1} through z_{mk}.

Suppose the airport serves as a shock primarily to the tradable industry x_1 in city c. The direct effect of this is an increase in employment for industry x_1. The indirect effect is composed of changes in employment in both sectors. With the positive shock to x_1, aggregate income increases because there are more jobs and, if the labor supply curve slopes upward, local wages are higher, at least in the short run. This, in turn, stimulates local demand for nontradable goods. The size of this effect will depend on consumer preferences, the types of jobs in the tradable sector (skilled versus unskilled), and the elasticities of land and labor. The shock to x_1 may also stimulate additional demand for tradable goods in other tradable industries. However, this need not be a positive effect: the citywide increase in production costs reduces the competitiveness of the other tradable firms. As the price of tradables is fixed on the national market, if the local metropolitan area's cost of production becomes too high, it may become beneficial for some of these firms to shift production to other, less costly areas.

If airports are shown to affect employment in the tradable sector, then potentially gains in the nontradable sector could be observed as well. However, the reverse would not be true if any employment growth is entirely due to increasing levels of nontradable employment. I posit that if air travel has an effect on employment, it is likely due to the fact that it promotes information flows (Bel et al., 2008; Giroud, 2013; Hovhannisyan et al., 2011), enhancing local-level productivity. This could occur in either tradable industries, nontradable industries, or both. It could also be the case that, just as the role of cities has changed over time from hubs of agricultural trade to information-based knowledge economies (see, e.g., Boustan, Bunten, & Hearey, 2013), the role of airports may have shifted over time as well.

DATA

Now we turn to the estimation of these effects. A novel dataset consisting of a balanced panel of Census Based Statistical Area (CBSA) level outcomes for 1900–2010, inclusive, was constructed to estimate the effects of interest. It includes data on population, land areas, employment levels by sector, geography and climate characteristics, and previously unexploited, newly digitized historical information related to the development and creation of the aviation system. Most of the data was obtained at the county level, and then aggregated into 2010 CBSAs.[8]

Population and Employment. Employment data were obtained for the following sectors, in addition to total employment: Agriculture and Mining, Construction, Manufacturing; Transportation, Communications, and Utilities; Wholesale Trade; Retail Trade; and Services. Data from these sub-areas were used to come up with the "Tradable Sector" and "Nontradable Sector" employment estimates. In general, data from 1900 to 1940 were obtained from the IPUMS database (Ruggles, Alexander, Genadek, & Schroeder, 2010) by aggregating the microdata to the county level; 1950–1970 data were obtained from aggregate county-level data found in the City and County Data Book; and the remainder was downloaded from National Historical Geographic Information System (NHGIS) at the county level. Population data (by county) were obtained from the NHGIS U.S. Census database as well. More details on the construction of the population and employment data can be found in Appendix A.

Geography, Climate, and Complementary Transportation Networks. Data were collected on a variety of geographic, transportation, and climate characteristics as controls. Region controls include dummy variables for each of the nine Census divisions and CBSA land area. Other controls for 1887 straight-line rail mileage, planned 1947 highway mileage, having a port, having a political capital city, mean January temperature and sunshine levels, having a coastal location, and a dummy variable for close proximity to a river. Data on whether a CBSA was home to a land grant college, the distance to the nearest military base, as given by the Bureau of Transportation Statistics, and the distance to the nearest top 200 research university, as given by the 2010 NRC rankings,[9] were included as well. See Appendix A for more details on the source and construction of each of these variables.

Airport Location. The placement of airports was not "random," but rather, was influenced by a number of local-level historical factors. The Air Commerce

Act of 1926 stipulated that the construction of airports is a local-level responsibility. Hence, while certain Federal actors, namely the Post Office Department and the Army Air Service were interested in the construction of airports to foster commerce and national defense, they could not directly establish airports. Thus, they had to influence local actors to do so. Some of these factors, controlled for in the relevant parts of this study, are as follows: (1) the locations of collection points on the Air Mail system, as it developed from the early 1920s until 1938; (2) the primary cities located on a 1922 plan of airways for national defense, (3) the locations of a network of Federally constructed emergency airfields from the early years of aviation, and (4) the locations of airfields designated by the Army Air Service as suitable landing fields in 1926.[10]

As early as 1918, the U.S. Post Office Department was interested in developing a network of air routes to speed mail delivery and increase its revenues for its growing Air Mail service.[11] The Postmaster General originally drew routes with specific objectives (e.g., San Francisco to New York), with the placement of intermediate stops along these trunk lines in large part due to the constraints of early aircraft. Local municipalities, through lobbying efforts, were encouraged to build airports with the promise of profits that would later flow. The Post Office contracted out the actual work of carrying the mail to enterprising airlines, which would later add passenger service as well. In fact, by the mid-1930s, four of the major airlines that would go on to dominate domestic commercial travel for most of the twentieth century began operations as contractors for the Post Office: United, American, Eastern, and Transcontinental and Western Air (TWA). The result is that by 1938, a substantial number of airports had been established and their locations would generally remain fixed. Hence, Air Mail played a pivotal role in the establishment of the national aviation network as we currently know it. See Fig. 2 for a map. Data on Air Mail were hand-entered from the First Edition of the *American Air Mail Catalogue*, published in 1940. The Catalogue provides an index of all Air Mail routes and cities, including their start dates.

At around the same time, the Post Office was growing its Air Mail service, the Army Air Service was seeking to establish itself as a player in National Security. In 1923, the Army Air Service published the first comprehensive plan of airways and air routes deemed necessary for military navigation in *Airways and Landing Facilities*, a circular providing a template for cities to build their own airports. According to the original document, those airways would "promote commercial aviation, be an important transportation factor in the progress of civilization, and be available for national defense." The Plan stipulated that airways would have main stations 200 miles apart, substations 100 miles apart with landing fields and some level of basic services, and intermediate airfields 25 miles apart for emergency use. Hence, the location of places chosen as main stations on this plan was stipulated by the requirements above. These airfields were envisioned as places where Army pilots, the National Guard and Reserve units could train. The network was also envisioned to

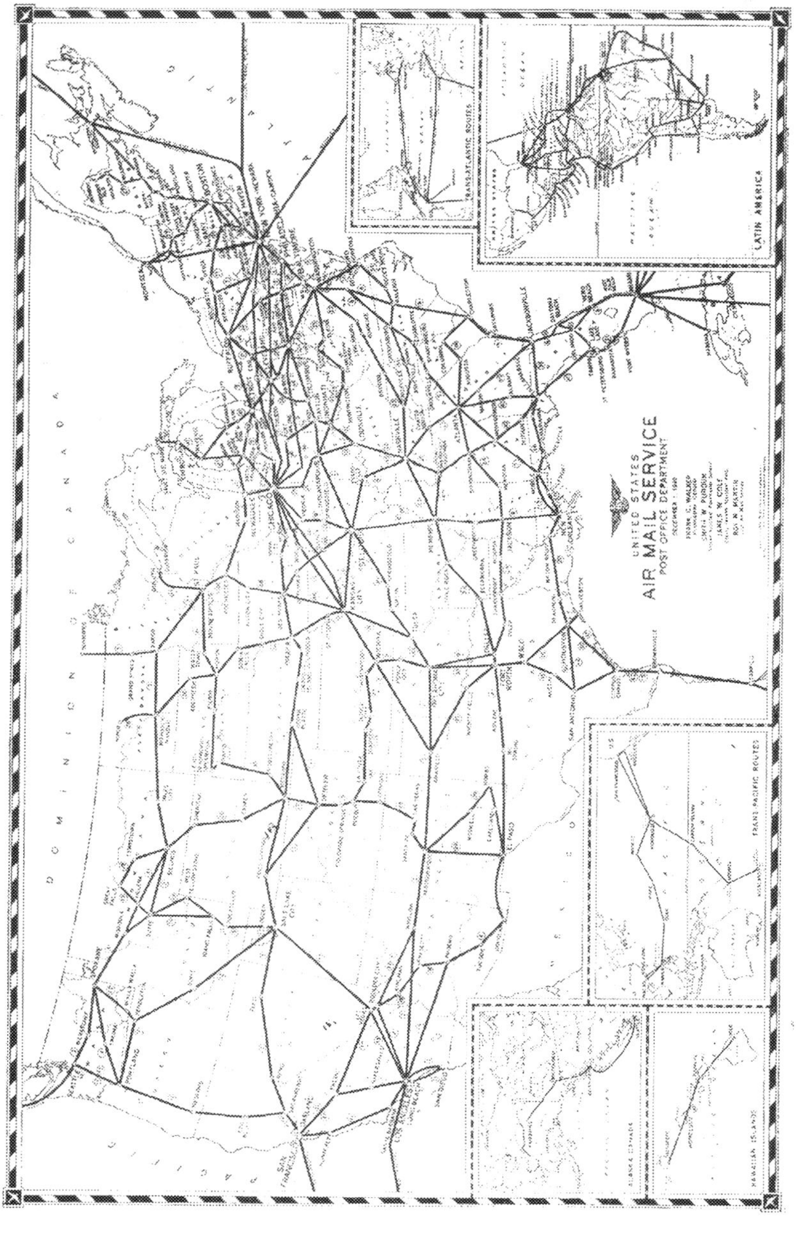

Fig. 2. Air Mail Network, 1938. *Source:* American Air Mail Society (1939).

connect parts of the Air Service located in disparate places. For example, one of the first lines was a route between New York City, Washington DC, and Rantoul, Illinois via Dayton, Ohio, where the Air Service's engineering division was located. This plan is relevant as places located along this network likely were lobbied to construct airfields, as the Army Air Service did not have the budget to carry this out on their own. In some cases, there may have been overlapping with the efforts of the Post Office as well. Main cities on the Army Air Service Plan were hand-entered directly from the map. Fig. 3 shows a reproduction of this map.

As private and commercial aviation established itself throughout the 1920s and 1930s, the Army Air Service (AAS), and later, the Civil Aeronautics Administration, began to create resources and policies to ensure the safe use of the airspace. In 1926, AAS published the first census of emergency air field locations. This data, hand-entered from the Army Air Service's *Landing Fields in the United States*, can serve as a proxy for a set of places that could support an airport, based on land availability, engineering considerations, and the presence of local-level knowledge required to construct an airport. In many (though certainly not all cases), it would have been rather easy to upgrade these facilities during the pre-period to full airport status if desired. Thus, I use this source to help identify a set of "control" CBSAs in the study.

ESTIMATING THE EFFECT OF AIRPORTS ON CITIES

Research Design

In the absence of any endogeneity concerns, and under the strong assumption of identical cities with identical populations and sectoral employment structures, if airports were randomly assigned to cities, estimating the treatment effect of airports would be trivially given by the difference in outcomes between airport and non-airport cities. However, even after controlling for differences in city size and employment, there are numerous reasons to believe that airports were not randomly assigned to cities. As stated previously, the Air Commerce Act of 1926 stipulates that the construction of airports is a local responsibility. The demand for airports at a local level can be expected to be heterogeneous – e.g., places with larger populations or that expect to grow faster could be more likely to establish airports. The opposite might be true as well – places that foresaw a loss in population or in key industries may have turned to airports as a way to rescue their troubled cities. Furthermore, places where policymakers believed in the "winged gospel" of aviation may have been more likely to put substantial local resources behind airport construction and maintenance (Bednarek, 2001).

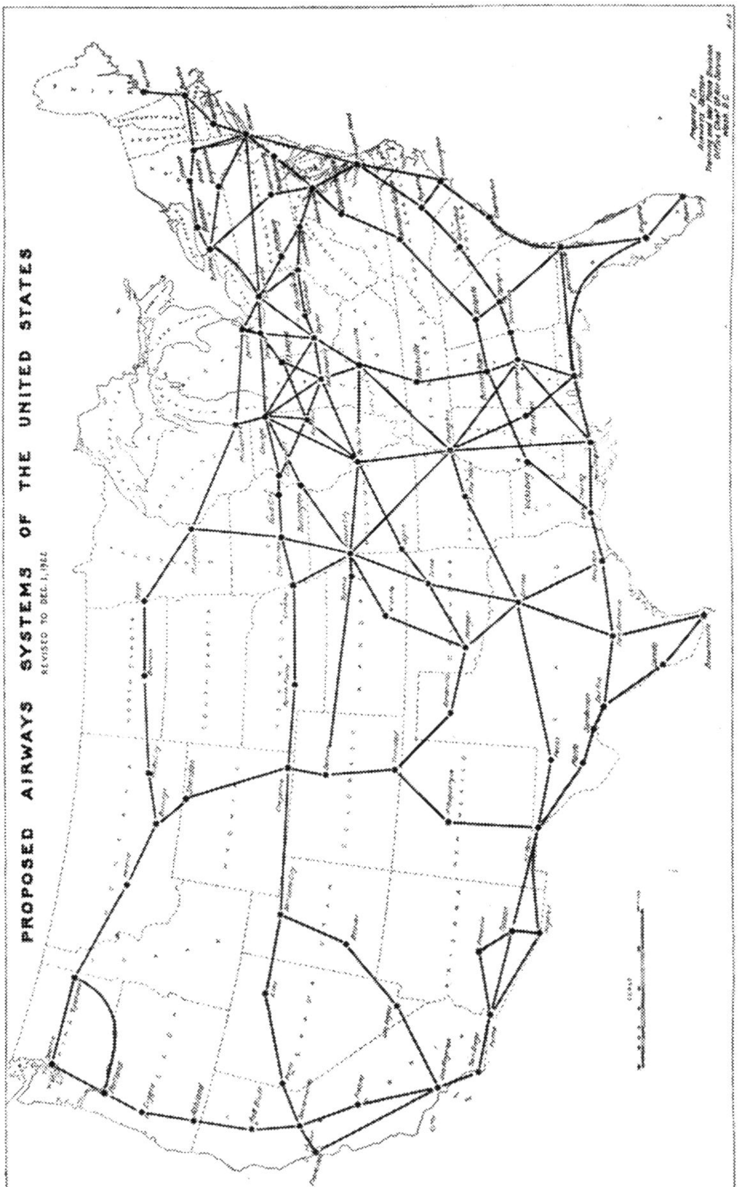

Fig. 3. Army Air Service 1922 Proposed Airways Systems of the United States. *Source:* U.S. Army Air Service (1923).

The timing of airport openings is also a concern. Although comprehensive data on opening dates are unavailable, information is available on service activation dates.[12] In order for commercial aviation to affect the economy, not only did airports have to be built, but other pieces of infrastructure, such as airways, beacons, and crucially, aircraft, had to be in place and capable of carrying significant numbers of passengers. Such technology did not exist until the post-World War II period. Smaller, expensive-to-operate DC-3 propeller aircraft were used by most major airlines in the late 1940s and 1950s. With the advent and proliferation of jet aircraft through the 1960s, air travel quickly became the de facto mode of choice for long distance travel. Consistent with these factors, I follow Bednarek (2001) and consider the beginning of the postwar period as the key structural break. Since my data is decadal in nature, I consider 1950 as the base year for estimating treatment effects.[13] Hence, the treatment effect of interest in this study is the effect of a CBSA having an airport activated anytime before 1950, under the assumption that 1950 is the year during which the effects of aviation may first be measured. I also examine the effects by decade. The synthetic control method, the details of which will be presented in the next section, aims to provide causal effects in the presence of this endogeneity.

In this study, cities of interest are those containing one (and only one) airport that is fully capable of handling commercial flight activity. To identify this set of airports and corresponding cities, airports are included in the study based upon certain criteria. First, the airport's FAA activation date must be 1950 or prior.[14] Second, an airport, by 1950, must be publicly owned and fully available for public use. As a proxy for capability of handling commercial operations, the airport must have an air traffic control tower. Moreover, because the process of receiving an airport in larger cities is determined by factors not common to other cities, an airport must not have been classified by the Federal Aviation Administration (FAA) as a "large hub" airport in 1964.[15] Data from FAA Form 5010 (Airport Master Record), as well as the *FAA Statistical Handbook*, was used to derive the initial sample.[16] Since I am interested in metropolitan area level outcomes, I use Core Based Statistical Areas (CBSAs) as the unit of observation. Next, in order to reduce confounding, any CBSAs with multiple airports are dropped from the sample, along with CBSAs whose airports are less than 40 miles away from the nearest airport are dropped.[17] CBSAs that contained a large-hub airport were removed as well. Airports that moved were also removed from the sample, giving the main sample of 131 airports. Fig. 4 shows their locations.

To identify a suitable set of control CBSAs, I restrict the sample to the set of control CBSAs that (1) had, at a minimum, limited experience with aviation in the 1920s or (2) were slated to receive a first commercial-level airport under the Civil Aeronautics Administration's National Airport Plan of

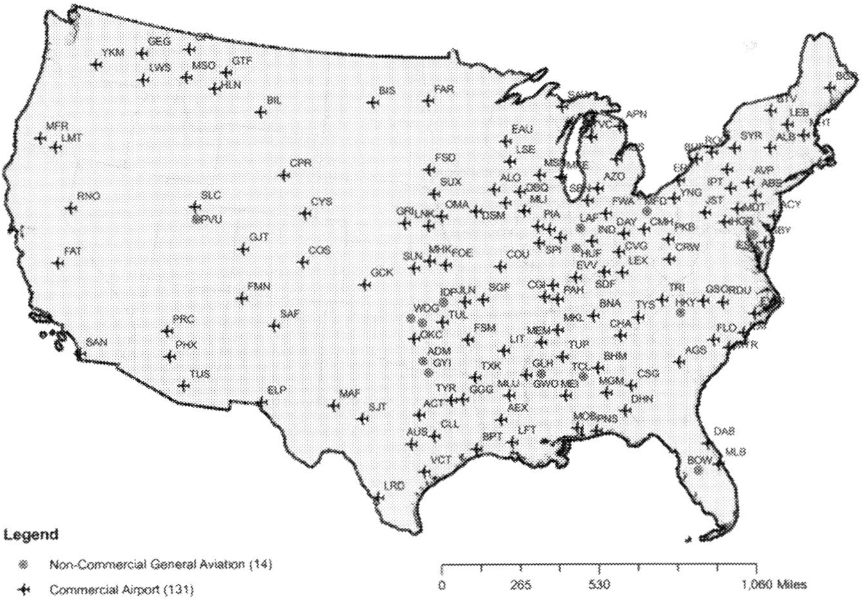

Fig. 4. Map of Sample Airports.

1944.[18] For the former, I used the 1926 locations of emergency airfields, hand-entered from the Army Air Service's *Landing Fields in the United States*, as a proxy for a set of places that could support an airport, based on land availability, engineering considerations, and local-level knowledge required to construct an airport. In many (though certainly not all cases), it would have been rather easy to upgrade these facilities during the pre-period to full airport status if desired. Any CBSA with a large-hub airport, or multiple airports, is dropped. After accounting for CBSAs dropped due to inconsistent geography, 379 CBSAs serve as controls. Of these, 110 CBSAs share a boundary with treated CBSAs. Fig. 5 shows the treated, control, adjacent, and GA airport CBSAs. Table 1 gives information on characteristics pertaining to the airports themselves. Because there is the possibility of spillover effects onto adjacent CBSAs in some cases, an ideal research design would use only non-adjacent CBSAs as controls. However, data limitations make this impossible; hence, there is the possibility of slight downward bias in the final estimates.

Table 2 gives characteristics of CBSAs with and without airports. Airport CBSAs are more likely to contain political capital cities and to have a land grant college. They are also more likely to have larger amounts of other transportation infrastructure, such as roads, ports, or river access, and to be larger

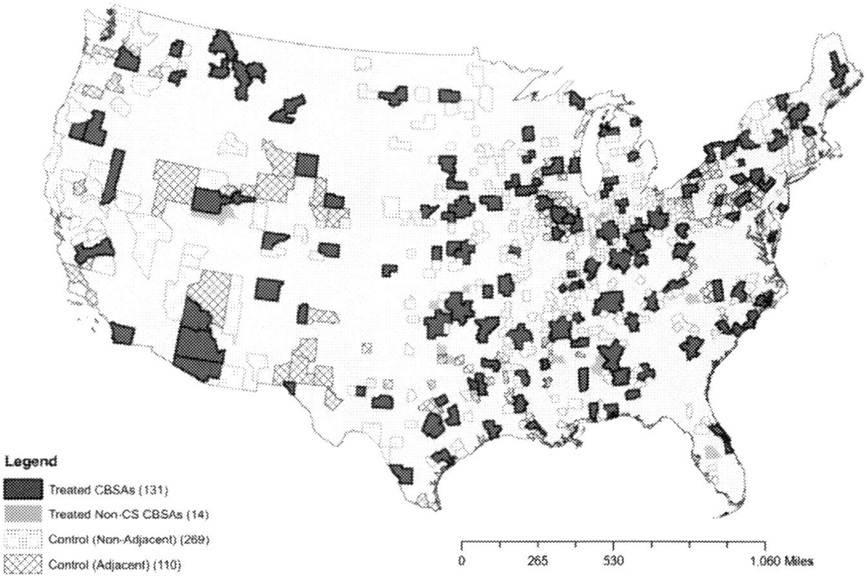

Fig. 5. Map of Sample CBSAs.

Table 1. Sample Means – Airport Characteristics.

Variable	All Airports (n = 131)	
	Mean	SD
Activation Year	1940.66	2.91
Distance to nearest CBD (miles)	4.79	2.53
Land Area of Airport (acres)	2185.52	1667.94
Current length of longest runway (feet)	8894.42	1730.72
Distance to nearest comm. airport (miles)	87.6	39.46
Boardings/Enplanements [thousands] (1960)	103.22	165.25
Boardings/Enplanements [thousands] (1980)	369.78	570.63
Boardings/Enplanements [thousands] (2010)	869.2	2091.69
Flights/Operations [thousands] (1960)	6.04	7.39
Flights/Operations [thousands] (1990)	35.13	56.23
Flights/Operations [thousands] (2010)	35.98	61.77
Per Capita Boardings (1960)	0.29	0.39
Per Capita Boardings (1980)	0.95	0.94
Per Capita Boardings (2010)	1.13	1.19

Notes: Standard Deviations (SDs) in parentheses. Boardings/enplanements and flights include air carrier, air taxi (on-demand) and commuter flights.

Table 2. Covariates by Airport Status.

Variable	Controls (n = 379)		Airport CBSAs (n = 131)	
	Mean	SD	Mean	SD
Airport Predictors				
On 1938 Air Mail Network	0.087	0.282	0.679	0.469
On 1922 Army Air Service Defense Plan	0.026	0.16	0.313	0.465
CBSA County on 1944 National Airport Plan	0.135	0.342	0.092	0.29
Had CAA Intermediate Airfield	0.314	0.465	0.412	0.494
Transport				
Planned Highway Mileage as of 1947	18.261	24.417	60.267	58.424
Located near river	0.348	0.477	0.534	0.501
Has Port	0.032	0.175	0.099	0.3
1887 Straight-Line Rail Mileage	79.749	63.59	170.672	151.773
Geography/Climate				
Has Political Capital City	0.018	0.135	0.168	0.375
NOAA Coastal County	0.251	0.434	0.244	0.431
Has Land Grant College	0.042	0.201	0.153	0.361
Mean January Temperature	32.11	11.119	32.838	11.865
CBSA and Region				
CBSA Land Area (std. to 2010)	1440.966	2168.268	2571.252	2080.955
Region 1: Northeast	0.127	0.333	0.122	0.329
Region 2: Midwest	0.38	0.486	0.321	0.469
Region 3: South	0.314	0.465	0.382	0.488
Region 4: West	0.179	0.384	0.176	0.382

in overall land area as well. However, climate does not vary substantially between CBSAs with airports and those without. Additionally, the distribution of airports and non-airport CBSAs across regions are similar. Airport CBSAs were more likely to have been located on the 1938 Air Mail network, and to have been home to a city listed in the 1922 Army Air Service Proposed System of Air Routes. Moreover, airport CBSAs are more likely to have been home to CAA intermediate airfields, political capital cities, and to have a land grant college. They are more likely to have larger amounts of other transportation infrastructure, such as roads, ports, or river access, and to be larger in land area as well. In general, climate does not vary substantially between CBSAs with airports and those without. Finally, the distribution of airports and non-airport CBSAs across regions, access to a coast, and right-to-work state status are roughly similar. In what follows, controls for many of these characteristics will be included.

Estimation Strategies

Baseline OLS Estimates of Aggregate Airport Effects

Let Y represents an outcome of interest, e.g., population, in metropolitan area m. Let $\Delta Y^i_m = ln(Y^i_{m,2010}) - ln(Y^i_{m,1950})$, which gives the 60-year change in the dependent variable of interest.[19]

First, I run the following regression to get the OLS baseline estimate:

$$\Delta Y^i_m = \alpha^i_2 + \beta^i_1 A_m + \beta_2 Z_m + \varepsilon^i_{2,m} \tag{1}$$

where $i\varepsilon I$ is a set of sectors in the economy, A is a dummy variable for having an airport in CBSA m, $\mathbf{Z}$ is a vector of exogenous controls for pre-period outcomes in the sector of interest (with both level and growth effects included[20]), geography, climate, and information on other transportation networks; α^i is an intercept, and β^i is the parameter of interest. We may interpret β^i as the contribution of having an airport to a CBSA's local economic outcome at time $t>0$, after controlling for pre-period characteristics, relative to time $t = 0$, where 1950 is normalized to $t = 0$. ε_m represents the error term.

A key disadvantage of OLS in non-randomized studies, such as this, is that estimation can be sensitive to parametric assumptions (e.g., normality). This is particularly possible when the baseline covariates are highly imbalanced, which is likely the case given the differences in size and population levels in airport cities relative to non-airport cities. While there is overlap between airport and non-airport counties in the sample, it is a relatively limited amount. In a case like this, regression will tend to extrapolate outside of the region of common support, potentially biasing the results. Because this estimate is potentially biased, I now turn to a second method of causal inference.

Difference-in-Differences Estimation of Aggregate Airport Effects and Standard Errors

Given the treated and control units estimated for each airport for each of the four outcomes of interest, it is possible to pool the units to estimate treatment and control units. First, a dataset is created that includes all estimated treated and control units. Then, a differences-in-differences estimator is run. Following Reber (2005) and Mora et al. (2012), I implement an "event-time" version of the differences-in-differences (DD) estimator. It differs from the standard DD approach in that instead of a simple "post-treatment" indicator, I create a series of dummy variables indicating time (in decades) relative to implementation

($k = 0$ is normalized to 1950) in order to estimate the dynamic effects of the airports on their local economic outcomes. The specification is:

$$y_{it} = \alpha + \theta_i + \gamma_t + \sum_{k=-5}^{6} \lambda_k \delta_{k,it} + \varepsilon_{it} \tag{2}$$

where α is a constant, θ_i is a CBSA fixed effect, and γ_t is a year fixed effect. $\delta_{k,it}$ is an indicator variable equal to 1 if the CBSA is in year k of having its airport, and 0 otherwise. In the regressions, $k = 0$ is left out as the reference year. The pattern of λ_ks describes the change in trend in the outcome of interest, y_{it}, associated with having an airport. For example, $\lambda_1 - \lambda_0$ gives the change in the dependent variable associated with moving from $k = 0$ (1950) to $k = 1$ (1960). Hence, λ_6 identifies our coefficient of interest, the cumulative causal growth in the dependent variable (population or employment) attributable to airports over the 60-year period of our study.

The DD estimator relies heavily on the assumption of parallel trends; that is, population and employment trends in airport cities, prior to 1950, should be roughly parallel to those after. The specification estimated above allows for a partial test of the identifying assumption that absent receiving an airport, the growth trends of treated and control CBSAs would have trended similarly. Unfortunately, in most cases, this assumption does not hold (λ_k for $k<0$ are not statistically insignificant). In practice, many places receiving airports were smaller than average in the pre-period, relative to their eventual position in 1950, and yet were growing faster than the average.

In order to ameliorate these endogeneity concerns, I next turn to the synthetic control estimator. It extends the difference-in-difference framework essentially by allowing an application of a more flexible weighting scheme of the pre-treatment outcomes, providing, in principle, treated and control unit estimates that satisfy the parallel trend criteria. Additionally, because the synthetic control estimator is applied to each individual airport city in the sample, it is possible to uncover the heterogeneity in airport city outcomes.

Synthetic Control Analysis

The use of synthetic controls was first proposed by Abadie et al. (2003, 2010). It allows for the extension of the traditional differences-in-differences framework by allowing treatment effects to vary over time. In my case, the synthetic control is constructed as the weighted average of CBSAs in the "donor pool" – that is, the set of control counties selected by the criteria described in the "Research Design" section. Under the identifying assumption that conditional on controls, a treated unit would have otherwise evolved as an estimated control unit does, the difference between the actual "treated" outcome and the synthetically constructed "control" outcome gives us the causal treatment effect of airports on local employment and population.

Suppose there is a sample of $C+1$ CBSAs, indexed by c, among which unit $c=1$ is the treated CBSA and $c=2$ to $c=C+1$ are potential controls. We also assume a balanced panel with a positive number of pre-intervention periods, T_0, as well as a positive number of post-intervention periods, T_1, with $T_0+T_1=T$. Let Y_{ct} represent the outcome of unit c at time t. For a given t (with $t \geq T_0$), the synthetic control estimator of airport's effect is given by the difference between the treatment and synthetic control at that period:

$$Y_{1t} - \sum_{c=2}^{C+1} w_c^* Y_{ct}$$

where $\mathbf{W} = (w_2, ..., w_{C+1})^T$ is a $(C \times 1)$ vector of positive weights that sum to 1; $\mathbf{X}_1$ is a $(k \times 1)$ vector containing a set of pre-intervention characteristic values; and $\mathbf{X}$ is a $(k \times C)$ matrix collecting the values of the same variables for the CBSAs in the set of airport potential CBSAs.

The synthetic control algorithm chooses optimal weights $\mathbf{W}^*$ that minimizes the mean square prediction error (MSPE) given by

$$\text{MSPE} = \|X_1 - X_0 W\|_V = \sqrt{(X_1 - X_0 W)^T V (X_1 - X_0 W)},$$

where an optimal choice of variable weights $\mathbf{V}$ assigns weights to linear combinations of the variables in X_0 and X_1. In practice, I implement this estimation strategy using Abadie, Diamond, and Hainmueller (2011)'s R package Synth.

For concreteness, Fig. 6 shows the hypothetical counterfactual for the Springfield, MO, CBSA as well as the actual CBSA outcome. Differencing these give the treatment effect at each point in time. Further differencing, namely, subtracting the 1950 estimated treatment effect from the 2010 estimated treatment effect, gives the 60-year difference of interest that is the primary quantity of interest in this study.

This estimation method, which has quickly gained prominence in empirical microeconomics and political science, certainly advances a practitioner's ability to estimate causal effects in a wider variety of settings. The method, however, is not without some important drawbacks and caveats. For example, as noted by Doudchenko et al. (2016), difference-in-differences allows for a non-zero intercept corresponding to permanent differences; the synthetic control method applied here does not. Also, the constraint that the set of weights $\mathbf{W}$ must sum to one is also not trivial; a more flexible estimation method could yield somewhat different results. Athey et al. (2016) note that in cases where a unit may be on the extreme end of a distribution of units, allowing for a different set of weights could be more ideal. In practice, I use the difference-in-differences method in the "Difference-in-Differences Estimation of Aggregate Airport Effects and Standard Errors" section to deal with intercept issues. A similar approach is adopted by Kreif et al. (2016). The synthetic control method will

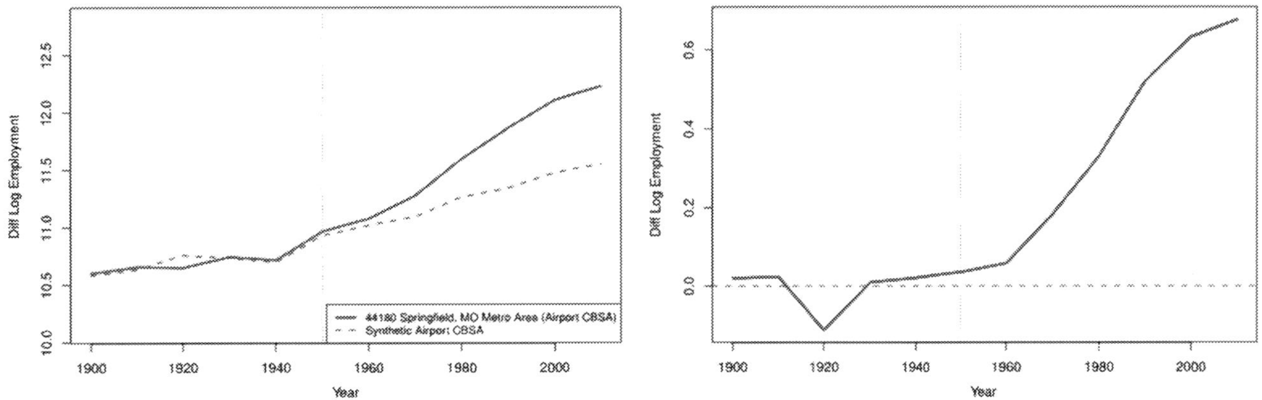

Fig. 6. Synthetic Control Case Outcomes: counterfactual Unit and Gaps (treatment effect) Plot. *Notes*: Figures show the synthetic control estimate of total employment in the Springfield, Missouri metropolitan area. The figure on the left shows the CBSA outcome (solid line) and the estimated synthetic unit (dotted line). The gaps plot on the right shows the difference between these two figures, which is the estimated treatment effect.

fail to consistently estimate control units on the extreme upper end of the distribution (such as large cities with large airports), hence the focus here on medium and smaller sized airports.

Importantly, one must bear in mind the synthetic control matches units based solely on pre-treatment outcomes. In practice, the fact that the population and employment distributions between airport and non-airport cities differ substantially in this study means that the synthetic control method cannot always account for the effect of regional macroeconomic shocks that would have not been predictable from the vantage point of the 1950s. For example, given how the estimator works, the best match for Elmira, New York, e.g., may be a western city less exposed to regional shocks. Although, such a match might be counterintuitive, it is a valid match if it minimizes MSPE. Yet, the estimator has no way of "penalizing" the estimator for the fact that it is matching to a region outside of its own. In fact, as will be shown in the "Conclusion and Policy Implications" section, the treatment effect estimate on Elmira's airport is negative. Yet, it seems implausible how an airport itself can cause a decline in an area's outcomes directly. Thus, in some analyses to come later, I will constrain the minimum contribution of any airport at zero as a way of mitigating this concern.

An additional downside of the synthetic control estimator is that, unlike other matching strategies, there is no way to estimate standard errors analytically. Unlike regression-based or other matching estimators, the goal is to find a single counterfactual outcome for a single treated unit, meaning the necessary variation within treated units does not exist. Abadie et al. (2003) propose the use of a permutation test to visually estimate statistical significance. In such a test, each member of the donor pool is considered to be a "treated" unit, and differenced. Then, these estimated outcomes (treated unit minus control unit) are plotted on a graph with the estimated outcome, which allows the viewer to visually assess the statistical significance of the outcome. A representative plot of this is shown below for Springfield Airport.

Given the aims of the present study, however, such a measure would not suffice. First, in the permutation test framework, it is unclear at what point an outcome should be deemed statistically significant. Different researchers analyzing the same permutation test plot may come to different conclusions. Second, there are yet other variables that are up to the researcher's control. For example, in the permutation test, poorly fit hypothetical outcomes are often removed; again, however, the choice of at what threshold to set for this process is also up to the researcher. This complicates the difficulty in using solely these plots to assess statistical significance.

In order to address these difficulties, I propose the use of bootstrapping to generate standard errors on both the level and overall growth effects produced by the synthetic control estimator. This is done by repeatedly generating counterfactual control units generated from resampling members of the donor pool.[21] This allows for the estimation of standard errors, clustered by CBSA.

The method is similar in spirit, but not identical to, the "leave-one-out" method as in Kreif et al. (2016), where responses are estimated and plotted in response to iterative removal of units from the donor pool. Fig. 7 shows the result of this process for Springfield Airport. Note that it is similar to the outcome that was suggested by the permutation test.

CASE STUDIES

This section presents two case studies illustrating the links between a region's airport and its economy: Springfield, Missouri (Springfield-Branson National Airport) and Elmira, New York (Elmira Corning Regional Airport). The Springfield case study illustrates how an airport, coupled with a vibrant local economy, can benefit a metropolitan area, while the Elmira case illustrates how an airport could fail to substantially impact a city's fortunes over the long term. Each case considers population and employment outcomes. I also present, for comparative purposes, the results of a one-to-one matching routine which finds the most similar place to an airport CBSA for comparative purposes.

Springfield-Branson National Airport (SGF) opened in 1945 and the Springfield metropolitan area has since boomed. A recent economic impact study finds that SGF generated 4,454 jobs, $154 million in payroll, and $402 million in total output as of 2012, accounting for 2.48% of total metropolitan area output.[22] A glance at Fig. 8 reveals Springfield has experienced large levels of population and employment increase since 1950, with only the tradable sector seeing employment declines limited to more recent years. In comparison, Pittsfield, Massachusetts, a city with similar pre-1950 population and employment levels but no airport, experienced peak population during the 1960s with subsequent decline, and a relatively flat employment profile overall. It appears that Springfield's ability to attract and subsequently retain tradable sector jobs, coupled with its ability to capitalize on tourism and boost its non-tradable sector employment, was due in no small part to the presence of SGF.

In contrast to Springfield, Elmira, New York, always a heavily manufacturing based economy, has experienced continued population and employment decline since the 1960s, a trend that Elmira's airport was unable to help reverse. Elmira's county-owned airport, Elmira-Corning Regional (ELM), opened in 1945. A 2011 economic impact study estimates that ELM supported 1,669 direct jobs and 1,708 indirect jobs.[23] The airport also accounts for $208 million in payroll and $1.5 billion in output.[24] Danville, Ohio was similarly positioned to Elmira before 1950, sharing many similarities with Elmira. However, Danville never received an airport. In the past, both Danville and Elmira were major thoroughfares for rail freight. A look at Fig. 9 reveals that in both places, total employment has been essentially flat since 1950. Additionally, tradable sector employment, driven by manufacturing increased, then declined

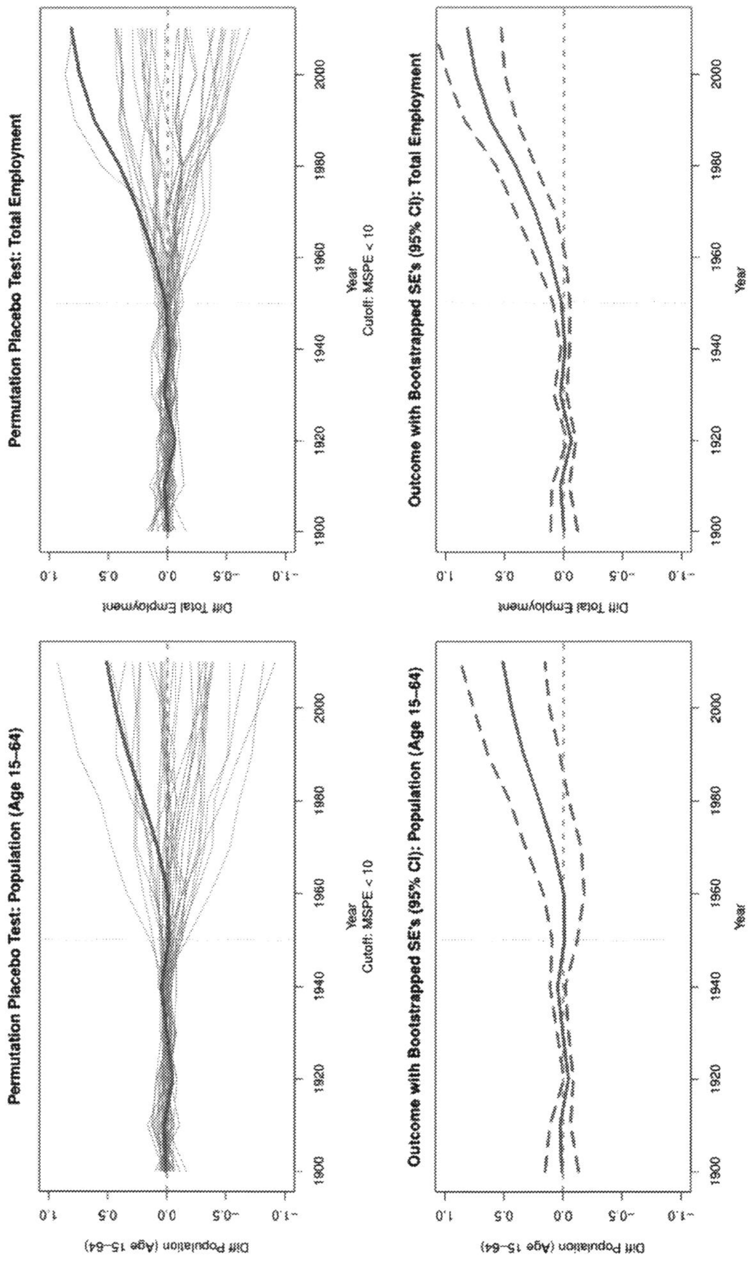

Fig. 7. Assessing Significance of Synthetic Control Cases.

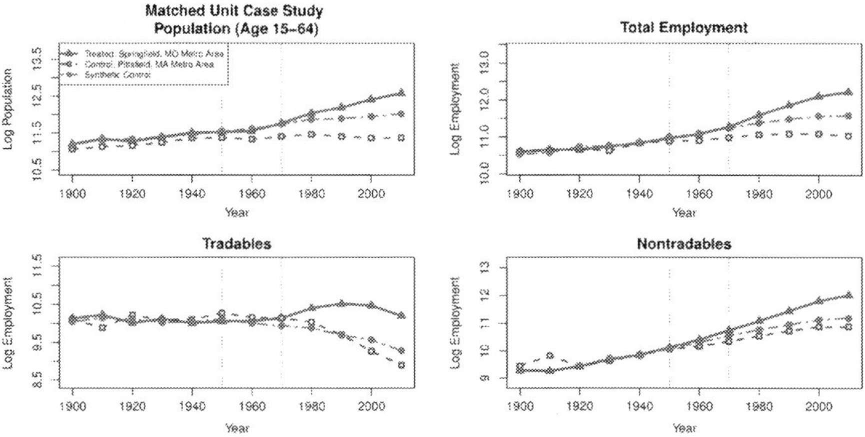

Fig. 8. Springfield Airport Case Study. *Notes:* Graphs show sectoral employment and population outcomes for the treated airport CBSA, a control unit identified by using a one-to-one matching strategy, and a synthetic control unit. See "Estimation Strategies" section for more details.

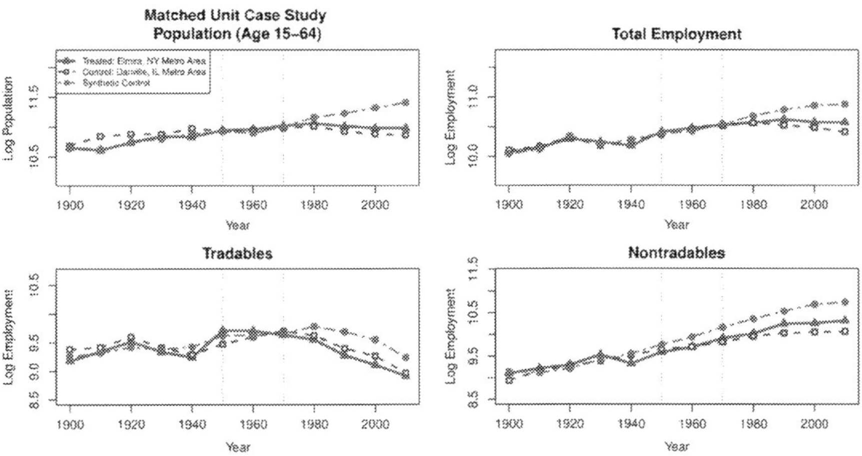

Fig. 9. Elmira Airport Case Study. *Notes:* Graphs show sectoral employment and population outcomes for the treated airport CBSA, a control unit identified by using a one-to-one matching strategy, and a synthetic control unit. See "Estimation Strategies" section for more details.

starting in the 1950s, never to recover. Both places were positioned similarly before Elmira's airport opened, and have followed similar trajectories since, indicating that ELM did not have a substantial effect on its local economy. In fact, a look at the synthetic control unit, shown in Fig. 10 shows that Elmira

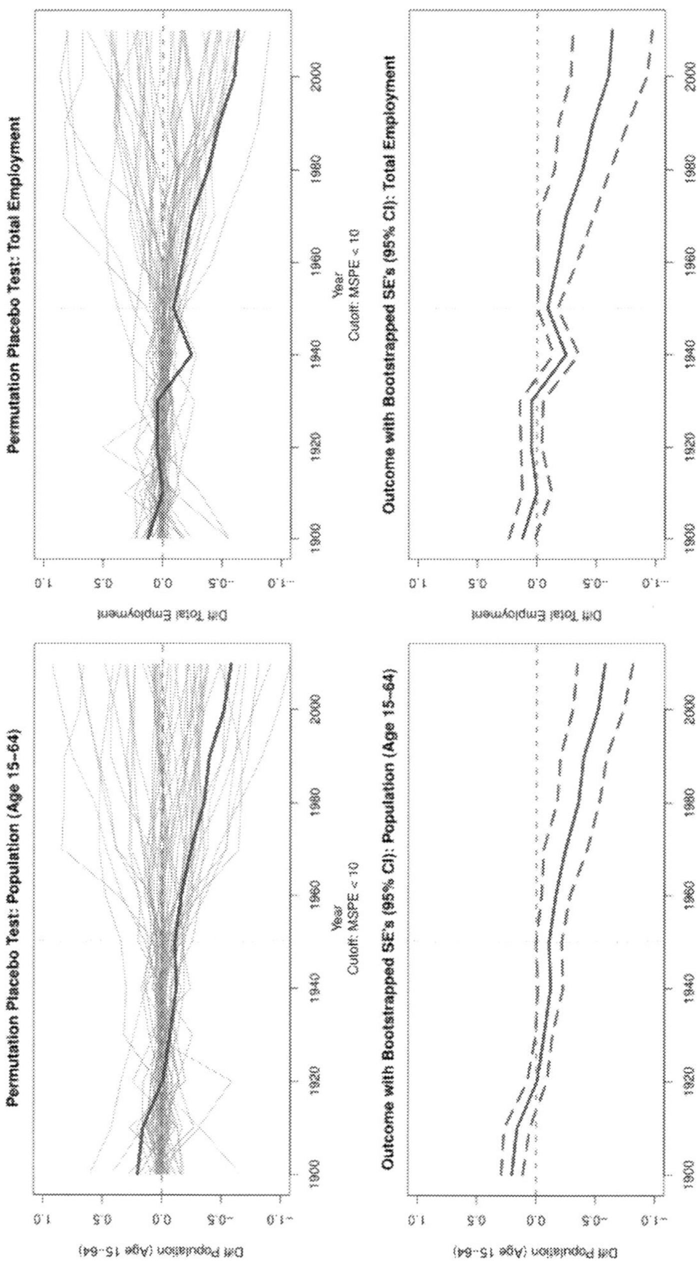

Fig. 10. Elmira Airport Case: Outcome and Statistical Significance.

performed worse than what would be expected even in the absence of an airport. Unlike the case of Springfield, Elmira's airport was not able to stem the region's gradual decline, resulting from unanticipated regional shocks.[25]

The case study also allows us to visually assess the performance of the permutation test versus the bootstrap method, upon which the remainder of this paper is based. Considering again the case of Springfield Airport, we see that for both employment and population, the synthetic control outcome is more conservative than the matching routine. Fig. 6 shows the results for the permutation test and bootstrap methods for illustrative purposes. We see that both give identical conclusions, though note how for Elmira, the synthetic control estimator estimates a negative overall outcome that appears to be statistically significant. The bulk of the remainder of this chapter aims to understand the difference between those airports which had positive and significant outcomes versus others. As a result, in the analysis that follows, airports with "negative and significant" effects will be assumed to be equivalent to airports that did not have a positive effect on their local area.

RESULTS

Consistency of Synthetic Control Estimator

To demonstrate that the synthetic control method produces estimates in the aggregate similar to those given by traditional estimators, such as ordinary least squares regression (OLS), which serves as a baseline, and difference-in-differences regression (DD), which aims to estimate causal effects. Results of this exercise are presented in Table 3. In the OLS regression, the dependent variable is either total population, total employment, or employment in the tradable or nontradable sector. The independent variable of interest is a dummy variable indicating CBSA airport status. A full set of controls is included, which account for regional and geographic characteristics, airport location factors, human capital controls, and past values of population and employment as relevant.[26] While the choice of treated and control CBSAs should mitigate some potential endogeneity bias, these should not be interpreted as "causal" estimates. Nevertheless, these estimates indicate airports have contributed to roughly 20% population and 24% total employment growth over the 60-year period. OLS estimates also indicate that effects on the tradable and nontradable sectors have been mostly equal, at roughly 16%.

The second column presents the difference-in-differences (DD) estimate. These estimates include year fixed effects, as well as controls for pre-existing trends. In contrast to the OLS estimates, the DD estimates can be interpreted as causal. The population DD estimate is very close to the OLS estimate (0.191 for OLS, 0.197 for DD) but there is some divergence in the total employment

Table 3. Summary of Estimates: Long Difference in Sectoral Employment Outcomes, All Methods, 1950–2010. Dependent Variable: CBSA has Commercial Airport (Binary 0/1 Outcome). 60-Year Estimates and Standard Errors Below; Percent Growth Rates in Brackets [..].

Sector/Outcome by Analysis	OLS	DD	Synth	Synth (Constrained)
Population	0.191*** [0.32]	0.197*** [0.33]	0.136** [0.23]	0.219*** [0.37]
	(0.053)	(0.036)	(0.067)	(0.039)
Total Employment	0.231*** [0.39]	0.332*** [0.55]	0.160** [0.27]	0.247*** [0.41]
	(0.058)	(0.037)	(0.073)	(0.051)
Tradable Sector	0.155*** [0.26]	−0.469*** [−0.78]	0.255*** [0.43]	0.523*** [0.87]
	(0.069)	(0.039)	(0.086)	(0.083)
Nontradable Sector	0.158*** [0.26]	0.913*** [1.52]	0.027 [0.0]	0.218*** [0.36]
	(0.05)	(0.035)	(0.067)	(0.042)

Notes: See "Estimation Strategies" section for details regarding each estimation strategy. OLS and Synthetic Control estimates include all covariates as specified below. Annual growth rates, in PERCENT, follow in brackets [], simply the 60-year coefficient divided by 60. Pre-period controls include employment controls specific to the sector being analyzed, in log levels, for 1900–1950 in 10-year increments. (Log population is substituted for log employment where applicable.) Population controls, included for the employment estimates, are comprised of controls for pre-period 15–64 population, in log levels, for 1900–1950 in 10-year increments. Region controls include dummy variables for each of the nine Census divisions and CBSA land area. Geography/transport includes controls for 1887 straight-line rail mileage, planned 1947 highway mileage, having a port, being a political capital city, mean January temperature, having a coastal location, and for close proximity to a river. Tradable sector employment is the sum of agricultural, mining, manufacturing, and wholesale trade sector employment. Nontradable sector employment is the sum of retail trade, finance/insurance/real estate, business professional and other services, construction, and public administration sector employment. The difference-in-difference estimates include year and CBSA fixed effects, as well as additional controls for pre-1950 trends. Synthetic control estimates in the third column allow individual airport estimates to be negative, while in the fourth column any negative estimates are constrained to a zero lower bound. All standard errors are clustered at the CBSA level.
* $p < 0.1$, ** $p < 0.05$, *** $p < 0.01$.

estimates (0.231 for OLS, 0.332 for DD), though the gap does not appear to be statistically significant. Tradable and nontradable estimates are markedly different from the OLS estimates, which is concerning. One plausible explanation is that the estimates for the tradable sector exhibit classical measurement error that worsens in the presence of multicollinearity (see, e.g., Carroll, Ruppert, Stefanski, & Crainiceanu, 2006). For this reason, while Appendix A provides a few results based on tradable and nontradable service-sector outcomes, caution should be used in interpreting any of these estimates.

The third column of Table 3 presents the average synthetic control estimates based upon treatment effects estimated for each individual airport in the sample. Note that population and total employment estimates, of 0.136 and 0.160 are smaller than their OLS and DD counterparts; nevertheless, these estimates do not appear to significantly differ from the OLS and DD estimates, which is reassuring. This does not hold true for the tradable and nontradable sector estimates, however, which again is of concern. A key drawback of the synthetic control method, as explained in the "Synthetic Control Analysis" section, is that it cannot effectively control for regional-scale macroeconomic phenomena (such as the decline of manufacturing in parts of the northeast and midwest). Thus, I impute zero for any negative synthetic control estimate and then obtain the average treatment effect in the final column. Here, we see the estimates on employment and population are very close to their OLS and DD counterparts, which is reassuring. Again, however, there is divergence in the sectoral employment estimates to such an extent that further analysis on these, using the methods in this study, would likely be problematic.

Finally, I consider the implications of the study's focus on medium and small airports as it pertains to the generalizability of the results that follow. Table 4 compares the OLS and DD estimates presented in Table 3 to their counterparts when larger airport[27] and multiple airport communities are included.[28] Importantly, note that inclusion of large airports, or even large airport and multiple airport communities, results in little change to the estimates. Hence, although the synthetic control method, due to sample overlap issues, is unable to estimate the individual effects of the largest airports, it does appear that the results presented here are robust, on average, to their removal from the main sample. Because of this, although what follows will consist mainly of estimates from smaller and medium-sized airports, the conclusions should reasonably generalize to the set of U.S. airports as a whole.

Identification of Airports with "Significant Impact"

Individual airports are deemed to have had a significant impact if, according to the 60-year synthetic control estimator, they had a statistically significant, and positive, impact on either employment *or* population cumulative growth outcomes at the usual 95% level of confidence.[29] From the initial sample of 131 airports, 28 airports met this criterion. Of these, seven served as airline hubs for some part of the 60-year period. The airports are geographically distributed around the country, as shown in the map below. Cities such as Lexington, Kentucky, and Memphis, Tennessee, likely benefited from their status as UPS and FedEx hubs, respectively. Cities such as Reno, Nevada, and Daytona Beach, Florida benefit from the increased tourism opportunities brought by their airports. Burlington, Vermont, Madison, Wisconsin, and College Station, Texas, are able to exploit the synergies between the access their airports provide and their large state research universities. Table 5 shows the full list of 28

Table 4. Comparison of Samples. Dependent Variable: CBSA has Commercial Airport (Binary 0/1 Outcome).

Sector/Outcome by Analysis Sample Group	60-Year Estimates and Standard Errors Below; Percent Growth Rates in Brackets [..]					SP + LA + MA
	SP	OLS SP + LA	SP + LA + MA	SP	DD SP + LA	
Population	0.191*** [0.32]	0.190*** [0.32]	0.188*** [0.31]	0.197*** [0.33]	0.199*** [0.33]	0.197*** [0.33]
	(0.053)	(0.053)	(0.052)	(0.036)	(0.036)	(0.036)
Total Employment	0.231*** [0.39]	0.229*** [0.38]	0.226*** [0.38]	0.332*** [0.55]	0.335*** [0.56]	0.334*** [0.56]
	(0.058)	(0.057)	(0.057)	(0.037)	(0.037)	(0.037)
Tradable Sector	0.155*** [0.26]	0.153** [0.26]	0.149** [0.25]	−0.469*** [−0.78]	−0.471*** [−0.79]	−0.475*** [−0.79]
	(0.069)	(0.069)	(0.069)	(0.039)	(0.039)	(0.038)
Nontradable Sector	0.158*** [0.26]	0.156*** [0.26]	0.144*** [0.24]	0.913*** [1.52]	0.917*** [1.53]	0.916*** [1.53]
	(0.050)	(0.050)	(0.050)	(0.035)	(0.035)	(0.035)

Notes: See "Estimation Strategies" section for details regarding each estimation strategy. OLS and Synthetic Control estimates include all covariates as specified below. Annual growth rates, in PERCENT, follow in brackets [], simply the 60-year coefficient divided by 60. Pre-period controls include employment controls specific to the sector being analyzed, in log levels, for 1900–1950 in 10-year increments. (Log population is substituted for log employment where applicable.) Population controls, included for the employment estimates, are comprised of controls for pre-period 15–64 population, in log levels, for 1900–1950 in 10-year increments s. Region controls include dummy variables for each of the nine Census divisions and CBSA land area. Geography/transport includes controls for 1887 straight-line rail mileage, planned 1947 highway mileage, having a port, being a political capital city, mean January temperature, having a coastal location, and for close proximity to a river. Tradable sector employment is the sum of agricultural, mining, manufacturing, and wholesale trade sector employment. Nontradable sector employment is the sum of retail trade, finance/insurance/real estate, business, professional and other services, construction, and public administration sector employment. The difference-in-difference estimates include year and CBSA fixed effects, as well as additional controls for pre-1950 trends. SP = Sample Airports only, referring to the set of airports used in the synthetic control analysis that follows. LA = Large Airport communities. MA = Multiple Airport communities. All standard errors are clustered at the CBSA level.
* $p < 0.1$, ** $p < 0.05$, *** $p < 0.01$.

Table 5. Airports with Statistically Significant Impact on Local Economies Since 1950: Population/Employment Index.

Airport ID	Airport Name	City	State	Growth Index (%)	Ever Hub?
PHX	Phoenix Sky Harbor Intl	Phoenix	AZ	4.2	Yes
AUS	Austin-Bergstrom Intl	Austin	TX	4	No
COS	City Of Colorado Springs Muni	Colorado Springs	CO	2.5	Yes
SAN	San Diego Intl	San Diego	CA	2.5	Yes
SLC	Salt Lake City Intl	Salt Lake City	UT	2.5	Yes
MHT	Manchester	Manchester	NH	2.3	No
CLL	Easterwood Field	College Station	TX	2.2	No
MYR	Myrtle Beach Intl	Myrtle Beach	SC	2.2	No
RDU	Raleigh-Durham Intl	Raleigh/Durham	NC	2.2	Yes
ILM	Wilmington Intl	Wilmington	NC	1.8	No
TUS	Tucson Intl	Tucson	AZ	1.8	No
SGF	Springfield-Branson National	Springfield	MO	1.7	No
BNA	Nashville Intl	Nashville	TN	1.6	Yes
LIT	Bill And Hillary Clinton National/ Adams Fi	Little Rock	AR	1.6	No
BTV	Burlington Intl	Burlington	VT	1.5	No
COU	Columbia Rgnl	Columbia	MO	1.5	No
LEX	Blue Grass	Lexington	KY	1.5	No
MSN	Dane County Rgnl-Truax Field	Madison	WI	1.5	No
BMI	Central Il Rgnl Arpt At Bloomington-Normal	Bloomington/ Normal	IL	1.4	No
RNO	Reno/Tahoe Intl	Reno	NV	1.4	Yes
CMH	Port Columbus Intl	Columbus	OH	1.3	Yes
LNK	Lincoln	Lincoln	NE	1.3	No
MEM	Memphis Intl	Memphis	TN	1.3	Yes
MGM	Montgomery Rgnl (Dannelly Field)	Montgomery	AL	1.3	No
DAB	Daytona Beach Intl	Daytona Beach	FL	1.2	No
DSM	Des Moines Intl	Des Moines	IA	1.1	No
OKC	Will Rogers World	Oklahoma City	OK	1.1	No
IND	Indianapolis Intl	Indianapolis	IN	1	No
JLN	Joplin Rgnl	Joplin	MO	1	No
LAF	Purdue University	Lafayette	IN	1	No
OMA	Eppley Airfield	Omaha	NE	1	No
CID	The Eastern Iowa	Cedar Rapids	IA	0.5	No

Notes: Growth index refers to the annual average percentage by which the average of working-age population and total employment grew, due to the presence of the airport as estimated by the synthetic control estimator for each airport. "Ever Hub" indicates whether an airport was ever designated as a "hub" by a major carrier at some point after 1978.

airports. In the table, I create an average annual growth rate measure by averaging the 60-year population and employment outcomes for each airport, dividing by 60, and then multiplying by 100 in order to convert the growth rates to percentages. We see from the table that these airports have, on average, contributed 1.6% per year of growth to these cities since 1950. Note, however, that these are the highest performing airports in the sample; recall from the previous section that the average annual growth rate across the entire sample of airports is 0.4%. This fact alone demonstrates the amount of heterogeneity present when it comes to how various airports were able to contribute to urban growth. Fig. 11 shows the geographic distribution of the airports.[30]

A glance at Fig. 12 shows a substantial distribution in outcomes across airports. The majority of the outcomes are not statistically significant. Those that are significant, and above zero are considered "significant." It is also clear from the plot that the overall average effect is being pulled up mostly by a small group of airports which have had outsized impacts on their cities, as represented toward the right-hand side of the figure.

I now turn to the question of what factors make these 33 airports so successful. A glance at Table 5 gives some insight into possible characteristics driving this behavior. Overall, it appears that cities that were positioned to take advantage of the transition from a manufacturing-based to a service- based economy in the postwar period benefited the most from their airports. For example, in 1950, these cities were larger, employed more people, and had a higher share of employment in nontradable services as opposed to tradables. Also, significant airports were much more likely to have a land grant college in its CBSA and to have a top research university nearby. (In fact, while the table indicates the mean distance from an airport to a top research university is roughly 32 miles, the median distance is actually about 9 miles, with the mean and median distance for other airports being roughly 66 miles.) Further evidence that the growth came through human capital comes from the fact that airports in political capital cities are more likely to have significant impacts on their cities. Other characteristics appear to play a role, such as designation as an airline hub, or the number of non-stop destinations served, on average, from 1980 to 2012, by that particular airport. The question of whether the city's airport was successful because of its hub/traffic patterns, or whether the airport attracted a hub/lots of non-stop flights, because of its positioning for success, is left for future research.

Other potential factors that could lead to the success of an airport are its proximity to tourist destinations and military bases. While measures of tourism are difficult to obtain, the USDA ERS Amenity Scale, and climate measures can somewhat proxy for this. Hours of January sunshine, and location in a metropolitan area, are both important factors, for example. The amenity scale is a measure of an area's desirability constructed from measures of climate, topographic variation, and water area. These are permanent features that are unlikely to be affected by local economic activities or human settlement. Hence,

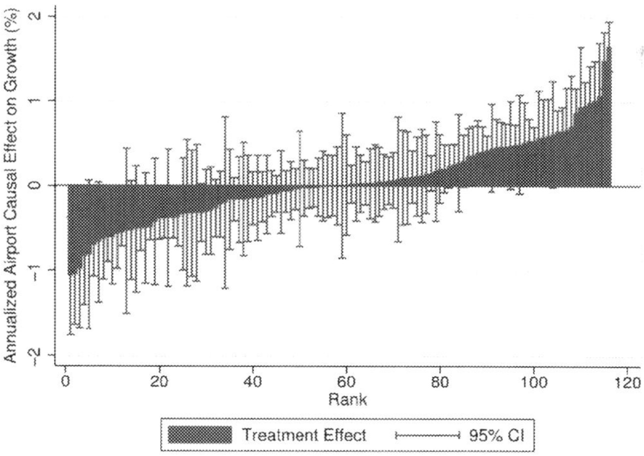

Fig. 11. Heterogeneity in Estimated Annual Growth Outcomes. *Note:* This figure shows all 117 outcomes that were estimated by the synthetic control method, ranked by the size of the treatment effect on an annualized percentage basis. The soild shaded bars are the individual outcomes and the bars represent 95 percent confidence intervals.

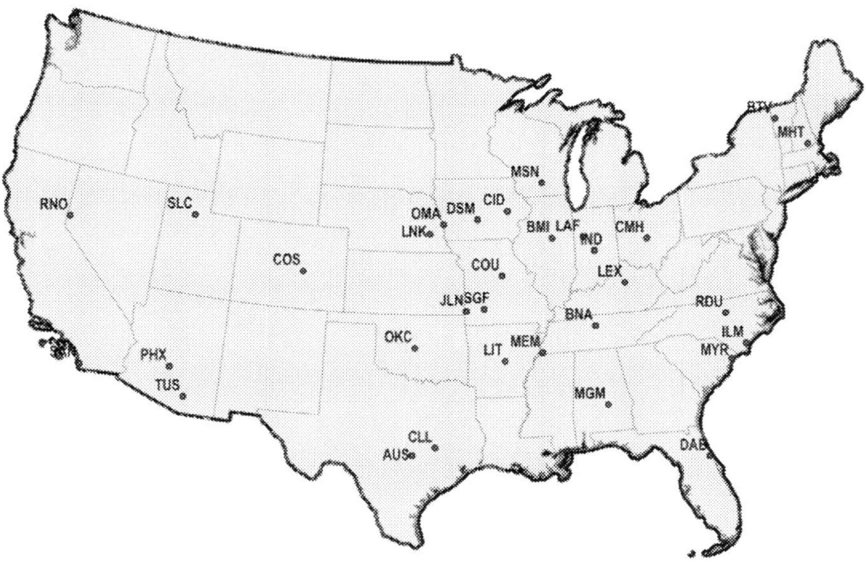

Fig. 12. Geographic Distribution of Significant Airports.

the fact that successful airports have significantly higher amenity scale values than less successful ones indicate support for the role that natural advantage plays in an airport's success as well. Capitalizing on these advantages via the development of tourism options can lead to city growth as well, in places such as Reno, Nevada (RNO) and Daytona Beach, Florida (DAB). Airports such as Colorado Springs (COS) and Austin-Bergstrom (AUS) might additionally benefit from the presence of a military base nearby as well.

Most of these findings hold when only employment in tradable industries is considered, with the exception of the amenity scale, which does not seem to remain a predictor of airport success. This can be seen from an examination of Appendix Table B3. When nontradable employment is considered separately, as in Appendix Table B4, it appears that the most important predictors (based on statistical significance) are still the share of nontradable employment, having a land grant college, mean hours of sunshine in January, and status as having been an airline hub (or having a high number of non-stop destinations as would be expected of an airline hub). Region is not a significant predictor of airport success or failure. (Table 6).

Given that many of the factors considered above are likely working together, it is important to consider the correlations between them. Thus, I turn to various forms of linear regression as a final exercise. In order to assess the robustness of the result to a variety of specifications of the regression model, I consider five versions of these models. The main version is presented in Table 7. Appendix Tables B5 and B6 provide model estimates for the tradable and nontradable sector data. Model 1 is a Logit model with a binary dependent variable (Significant/Not Significant). Model 2 is a linear probability model for comparison to Model 1. Results from these first two models come closest to mirroring the exercise performed previously in Table 5–B3.

Models 3 through 5 aim to tell us more about what correlates with the actual estimated value of the airport's contribution to the local economy. As mentioned previously, some of the estimated treatment effects were negative, due to the relatively small number of "airport-like" CBSAs in the donor pool. In Model 3, the estimated treatment effect (regardless of sign) is regressed on the variables in the left-hand column. In Model 4, any treatment effect estimated to be negative is replaced with a zero and then the regression is repeated. This imputation makes sense, because, in practice "negative" treatment effects in this framework are really cities that declined relative to their expectation in the 1950s, often due to outside, unanticipated macroeconomic shocks, that could not be foreseen at the time of treatment, and were thus erroneously attributed to the causal impact of the airport. In Model 5, I introduce a Tobit model. The Tobit adjusts for this "truncation" at zero and provides consistent estimates in the presence of that truncation. While all the models aim to estimate the same outcome, I take Model 5 as my preferred specification.

A glance across the regressions indicate that having an airport in a capital city is a major contributor to growth, as well as having an airport in a

Table 6. Characteristics of "Successful" Airports (Population/Employment Index).

Outcome	Significant ($n = 33$)		Non-Significant ($n = 87$)		*P*-value
	Mean	SE	Mean	SE	
Log 1950 Population	11.688	0.14	11.403	0.094	0.109
Log 1950 Employment	11.141	0.14	10.82	0.098	0.078
Log 1950 Payroll Per Worker	3.166	0.031	3.195	0.034	0.622
1950 Share of Nontradable Employment	56.652	1.905	47.724	0.932	0
Planned (1947) Highway Miles Per Sq Mi	0.028	0.003	0.024	0.002	0.279
Straight-Line Rail Mileage Per Sq Mi (1887)	0.087	0.01	0.105	0.008	0.213
Distance to Nearest NRC Research University (miles)	32.219	6.624	65.99	5.379	0.001
CBSA Has Land Grant College	0.424	0.087	0.092	0.031	0
Distance to Nearest U.S. Military Base (miles)	27.01	4.96	44.97	4.73	0.032
CBSA Composite Amenity Scale (USDA ERS)	0.443	0.528	−0.318	0.194	0.095
Mean January Temperature (F)	34.98	2.04	32.212	1.23	0.243
Mean Hours of Sunlight in January	163.108	6.235	140.729	2.91	0
In Metropolitan Area (Census)	1	0	0.862	0.037	0.022
In Coastal Location (NOAA)	0.152	0.063	0.276	0.048	0.16
Political Capital City	0.394	0.086	0.08	0.029	0
Port City	0.121	0.058	0.092	0.031	0.636
Ever Airline Hub	0.273	0.079	0.046	0.023	0.001
Number of Non-Stop Destinations (Average 1980–2010)	36.92	5.735	21.02	2.87	0.007
Northeast Region	0.061	0.042	0.149	0.038	0.443
Midwest Region	0.364	0.085	0.345	0.051	0.443
South Region	0.394	0.086	0.402	0.053	0.443
West Region	0.182	0.068	0.103	0.033	0.443

Note: p-values are from a standard two-sided t-test on individual outcomes EXCEPT in the case of region, where *p*-values are based on a chi-square test of independence.

metropolitan area. In contrast to the tables, mean January temperature appears to surface as an important predictor. This is consistent with one of Edward Glaeser's main findings – which January temperature is a strong predictor of urban growth (see, e.g., Glaeser, 2011). Additionally, the number of non-stop destinations is included as a predictor in some of the specifications as well.[31] The most consistent, and compelling, result across the five specifications is distance to a Top 200 Research University is a strong predictor of an airport's success. Specifically, an 1% increase in the distance from the university reduces

Table 7. Regression Results: Predictors of "Significant" Airport Status: Main Index.

Variables	(1)	(2)	(3)	(4)	(5)
	Significant Impact		Est. Treatment Effect		
	(Logit)	(OLS)	(OLS, No Truncation)	(OLS, With Truncation)	(Tobit, With Truncation)
Coastal Location	−0.262	−0.0628	0.0502	−0.00607	−0.00763
	(0.976)	(0.089)	(0.083)	(0.051)	(0.094)
Airport in Capital City	1.561	0.183	0.17	0.191**	0.246**
	(1.106)	(0.133)	(0.133)	(0.096)	(0.110)
Port City	−0.973	−0.0679	−0.197	0.032	−0.0329
	(1.468)	(0.167)	(0.135)	(0.082)	(0.130)
In Metropolitan Area (Census)	–	0.167*	0.442**	0.0906	0.374**
	–	(0.097)	(0.171)	(0.058)	(0.159)
CBSA Has Land Grant College	1.133	0.250*	0.137	0.129	0.0824
	(0.861)	(0.133)	(0.105)	(0.081)	(0.107)
Log Hours of January	4.047	0.117	0.382	0.262	0.674**
Sunshine	(3.618)	(0.253)	(0.299)	(0.172)	(0.267)
Log January Temperature	2.753*	0.329*	0.295*	0.236**	0.301**
	(1.501)	(0.169)	(0.161)	(0.109)	(0.142)
ERS Amenity Scale (USDA)	0.202	0.0471	0.0329	0.0257	0.0111
	(0.325)	(0.038)	(0.035)	(0.024)	(0.033)
Log Distance to Nearest Research Univ	−0.569**	−0.0594*	−0.0975***	−0.0459**	−0.0904***
	(0.268)	(0.035)	(0.031)	(0.020)	(0.030)
Log Number of Non-Stop	0.529*	0.0627*	0.0412	0.0273	0.0667*
Destinations	(0.312)	(0.035)	(0.038)	(0.023)	(0.037)
Log Distance to Nearest	−0.32	−0.032	−0.0181	−0.0164	−0.0324
Military Base	(0.260)	(0.026)	(0.035)	(0.020)	(0.026)
Log CBSA Land Area	0.0913	0.00842	0.108	0.024	0.0368
	(0.590)	(0.079)	(0.091)	(0.058)	(0.091)
Constant	−27.35	−1.144	−3.291**	−1.620*	−4.147***
	(20.750)	(1.292)	(1.578)	(0.964)	(1.330)
Observations	82	103	99	99	99
R-squared	–	0.453	0.557	0.604	–

Robust standard errors in parentheses, clustered at the CBSA level. Census division fixed effects also included in all specifications but not shown. *** $p < 0.01$, ** $p < 0.05$, * $p < 0.1$.

Notes: "Significant Impact" refers to a binary outcome as to whether the synthetic case estimator found a positive and significant impact caused by the airport to the city. "Estimated Treatment Effect" refers to the actual 60-year cumulative treatment effect outcome that was estimated by the synthetic control case estimator for each CBSA in the study. "Truncation" in Specifications (4) and (5) involve replacing the estimated (negative) treatment effects with zeros, since, technically, the effect of an airport should be nonnegative. See "Estimation Strategies" section for more information.

the 60-year treatment effect by between 0.05% and 0.1%. Taking Model 5 as my preferred specification, it appears the most important determinants of an airport's success are: being located in a capital city, in a metropolitan area, with significantly more hours of January sunshine and higher January mean temperatures, and, a research university in close proximity. Airports containing these ingredients were, on average, poised to exhibit the most success in transforming the cities that they serve. As a glance at Appendix Tables B4 and B5 show, proximity to a research university remains a key predictor of how transformational an airport can be on its local economy when examining outcomes for tradable and nontradable employment.

CONCLUSION AND POLICY IMPLICATIONS

The goal of this chapter was to better understand how airports might contribute to urban growth, both on average and in a distributional sense. To do so, a novel panel dataset and the method of synthetic controls were employed, which provided insight into both questions. First, I argued that on average, airports have contributed to growth in population and employment in cities, at a rate of on average 0.4% per year over the period 1950–2010. Second, I showed that the heterogeneity in the responses of cities to their airports can be explained by factors related to cities' initial positioning as of 1950. I showed that the strongest predictors of airport success were: shorter distance to a research university, a capital city location, and a location with higher January mean temperatures or greater hours of January sunshine. Size is a consideration as well; cities in larger metropolitan areas, with larger shares of employment in nontradables in the 1950s, were better positioned to take advantage of their airports for city growth. Significant differences were not found across region, airport governance, or other similar factors.

The broader lesson of this study is that infrastructure, coupled with other human capital investments, allowed cities to grow the most quickly. This is evident in the rise of cities such as, among others, Austin, Texas and Colorado Springs, Colorado. This also suggests that many of these benefits (though by no means all) are accrued from factors, such as knowledge spillovers, as opposed simply from the jobs generated in airports and at cargo companies. It is interesting to note the market access variable (number of non-stop destinations) was not significant in a robust manner in the final analysis, suggesting that while service levels are important to an airport's success, it is more simply having access to an airport that drives most of these outcomes. That is, it appears that traffic levels will be more a function of supply and demand factors, themselves correlated with city size and some of the other factors considered here.

The key policy takeaway here is that not all infrastructure investments are created equally. I have shown that, on balance, infrastructure investment stimulates growth in the economy. I have also shown, however, that the ability of a city to take advantage of their airport for success was also dependent upon a number of other factors. The lesson here is certainly not that cities should rush to open new airports. Rather, it is that developing robust amounts of human capital, at universities and in other ways, will ensure that infrastructure investments are able to have the greatest impact on their cities. That being said, it appears worthwhile to continue to invest in airports, both as physical assets, and also the air traffic network that guides aviation activity, to ensure that firms and individuals who can benefit from the aviation system can do so, at least until the next innovation in long-distance transportation infrastructure comes along.

NOTES

1. Carey, Susan. "Why Small Airports are in Big Trouble". Wall Street Journal. http://online.wsj.com/news/articles/SB10001424052702304688104579465711898215996

2. Office of Governor Terry McAuliffe. Governor McAuliffe Announces Airports Authority and United Airlines Signing of Long-Term Lease at Dulles International. https://governor.virginia.gov/newsroom/newsarticle?articleId=17931

3. These negative causal effects are likely due to a key limitation of the research design; namely, that it is impossible to fully control for macroeconomic regional shocks occurring in local economies post-1950. This will be elaborated upon later in the chapter.

4. Aschauer includes streets, highways, airports, electrical and gas facilities, mass transit, water systems, and sewers in this group.

5. In his study, a highway ray is defined as a segment of road that connects the central business district (CBD) of the central city with the region outside the central city. If the highway passes through the city, it counts as two rays; if it terminates in the city it counts as one ray.

6. The effect of larger effects are more difficult to ascertain in the framework used in this study, and could bias estimates. Additionally, understanding the effects of airports on the New York City or San Francisco-Oakland Metropolitan Area is a daunting challenge, given their history with other types of transportation, settlement patterns, and the like. It is relatively straightforward, by comparison, to assess how an airport has affected a smaller, more isolated regional economy, hence, the focus of this study on medium and small cities.

7. The transportation, communications, and utilities sector are considered separately, but is included in all estimates of total employment.

8. Census Based Statistical Areas (CBSAs) consist of the county or counties or equivalent entities associated with at least one core (urbanized area or urban cluster) of at least 10,000 population, plus adjacent counties having a high degree of social and economic integration with the core as measured through commuting ties with the counties associated with the core. "CBSAs" refers collectively to metropolitan statistical areas and micropolitan statistical areas. CBSAs were selected as the unit of observation for the analysis since the service areas of airports are generally diffuse, and would thus most closely capture the effect of an airport on a given city. The Data Appendix gives more

information on how the data were aggregated and adjusted, where necessary, to ensure consistent geography throughout.

9. The National Academies, 2010 Rankings. http://sites.nationalacademies.org/PGA/Resdoc/

10. A fifth factor, though one that will not be considered in the research, is Charles Lindbergh's efforts to popularize aviation through his 1926 Guggenheim Tour. http://www.charleslindbergh.com/history/gugtour.asp

11. See VanDerLinden (2002) for a comprehensive survey of the history of this program.

12. Activation dates indicate when the Federal government added the airport to the National Airport System. Given that these records were not maintained until 1926, airports opening earlier than 1926 are shown as being activated in 1926.

13. One might argue that I could normalize each airport to its opening date, and look at its evolution after that. However, this would only complicate the analysis, and could even confound it. This is due to a variety of reasons: (a) actual "opening dates" are really difficult to track down and are unavailable in many cases (though I have access to an "activation date", but this need not be the opening date; (b) since air service essentially started in earnest in the 1945-1950 period in many places, without the technology and conditions for the rest of the aviation network in place, such an analysis would fail to pick up the desired effect of the post-WW II effects of aviation on the economy; and (c) the effects of government efforts in fighting the second World War would be picked up in such a normalization (airport closures to civilian traffic, repurposing of some airfields as temporary military bases, etc.).

14. 17 commercial airports were opened after 1950; these were excluded from the sample.

15. Given all the economic processes at work in these larger cities, including such airports could lead to bias in the estimated effects. For example, one might be concerned about confounding arising from multiple issues in this initial sample. Cities such as, say, New York and San Francisco, were destined to get airports with high-frequency service, and to continue to grow independent of any single piece of infrastructure. Moreover, in these extremely large locales, air traffic is often constrained by capacity. Given these complications, and the lack of credible counterfactual CBSAs for such places, identifying the effect of one single piece of infrastructure on population or employment growth could be a task fraught with peril, particularly within the constraints of this project's research design. Therefore, I drop any airport that was classified as a "large hub city" airport in 1964. 1964 was the first year in which a Federal agency classified airports by their size and relevance to the national aviation system.

16. FAA Form 5010 Data: http://www.faa.gov/airports/airport_safety/airportdata_5010/

17. ArcGIS software was used for these calculations.

18. More precisely, locations proposed to receive airports of Class 3 or greater in the National Airport Plan.

19. While in this chapter I will consider this the main outcome of interest, for ease of interpretation, coefficients can be divided by 6 to obtain decadal growth rates or 60 for annual growth rates.

20. In an attempt to ensure that the OLS model fit the data as well as possible, decadal outcomes (such as population for each of the years 1910 through 1950), as well as interactions of adjacent terms, was included.

21. The bootstrap is repeated for 100 iterations.

22. MO Statewide Airports Economic Impact Study: http://www.modot.org/other-transportation/aviation/documents/Missouri-2012-Economic-Impact.pdf

23. https://www.dot.ny.gov/divisions/operating/opdm/aviation/repository/NYS%20Economic%20Study%202010%20Technical%20Report_0.pdf

24. Since the ELM economic impact figure included the now-defunct Sikorsky Aircraft Corporation's output in its totals, the case of nearby, slightly smaller Greater Binghamton Regional may provide a better idea of ELM's true economic impact. There, total payroll generated by the airport was estimated at $23 million, and total output was estimated at $52 million, with 483 jobs supported by the airport.

25. In the absence of data constraints, within-region matches, where the members of the donor pool were restricted to the same geographic region as the airport, should eliminate the issue of negative estimated treatment effects. However, due to considerations of covariate overlap, it is impossible to do so.

26. See notes in Table 3 for full details on the vector of controls.

27. Defined as a "large hub" airport by the FAA in 1964.

28. These airports are: DTW, MSP, STL, PIT, PHL, and HOU. If airports in multiple hub communities are added, then LAX, SFO, ORD, BOS, JFK, CLE, and SEA are added. (BFL, SBA, SJC, RDD, BDL, TPA, LAN, DLH, CLT, and EUG comprise the set of smaller airports excluded from the main sample because they are in multiple airport communities. OLS estimates when multiple airport communities are included are similar to those reported above with those communities excluded.).

29. Any airports, such as Elmira's, that were estimated to have a negative and statistically significant outcome, would be classified as "not significant" for purposes of what follows below.

30. A similar exercise was performed separately for the tradable and nontradable sectors; see Appendix Table 7 and B1.

31. Omitting this variable from the model does not change the findings in any meaningful way.

32. http://www.icpsr.umich.edu/icpsrweb/ICPSR/studies/20660

33. Atlas of Historical Counties Project: http://publications.newberry.org/ahcbp/

34. http://www.higher-ed.org/resources/land_grant_colleges.htm

35. ICPSR County Characteristics, 2000-2007; ICPSR Study 20660.

36. http://www.ngs.noaa.gov/RSD/coastal/projects/coastal/ports_list.html

37. I thank Nate Baum-Snow for sharing this data.

38. I thank Jeremy Atack for sharing this data.

39. http://www.faa.gov/about/office_org/headquarters_offices/apl/aviation_forecasts/taf/

REFERENCES

Abadie, A., Diamond, A., & Hainmueller, J. (June 2010). Synthetic control methods for comparative case studies: Estimating the effect of California's tobacco control program. *Journal of the American Statistical Association*, *105*(490), 493–505.

Abadie, A., Diamond, A., & Hainmueller, J. (June 2011). Synth: An R package for synthetic control methods in comparative case studies. *Journal of Statistical Software*, *42*(13), 1–17.

Abadie, A., & Gardeazabal, J. (March 2003). The economic costs of conflict: A case study of the Basque country. *American Economic Review*, *93*(1), 113–132.

American Air Mail Society. (1940). *American Air Mail Catalogue. The Airpost Journal*. (1st ed., pp. 232–240). Albion, PA: American Air Mail Society.

Aschauer, D. A. (March 1989). Is public expenditure productive? *Journal of Monetary Economics*, *23*(2), 177–200.

Athey, S., & Imbens, G. (July 2016). The state of applied econometrics – Causality and policy evaluation.

Baum-Snow, N. (2007). Did highways cause suburbanization? *The Quarterly Journal of Economics*, *122*(2), 775–805.

Bednarek, J. R. D. (September 2001). *America's airports: Airfield development, 1918-1947* (1st ed.). College Station, TX: Texas A&M University Press.
Bel, G., & Fageda, X. (July 2008). Getting there fast: Globalization, intercontinental flights and location of headquarters. *Journal of Economic Geography*, *8*(4), 471–495.
Blonigen, B. A., & Cristea, A. D. (March 2015). Air service and urban growth: Evidence from a quasi-natural policy experiment. *Journal of Urban Economics*, *86*, 128–146.
Boustan, L. P., Bunten, D., & Hearey, O. (May 2013). *Urbanization in the United States, 1800-2000*. Working Paper 19041, National Bureau of Economic Research.
Brueckner, J. K. (1982). *Metropolitan airline traffic: Determinants and effects on local employment growth*. BEBR No. 894, College of Commerce and Business Administration, Bureau of Economic and Business Research, University of Illinois at Urbana-Champaign.
Brueckner, J. K. (July 2003). Airline traffic and urban economic development. *Urban Studies*, *40*(8), 1455–1469.
Button, K., Doh, S., & Yuan, J. (January 2010). The role of small airports in economic development. *Journal of Airport Management*, *4*(2), 125–136.
Carroll, R., Ruppert, D., Stefanski, L., & Crainiceanu, C. (2006). *Measurement error in nonlinear models* (2nd ed.). Boca Raton, FL: Chapman and Hall.
Cohen, J. P., Paul, M., & Catherine, J. (2003). Airport Infrastructure Spillovers in a Network System, SSRN Scholarly Paper ID 2819582, Social Science Research Network, Rochester, NY.
Doudchenko, N., & Imbens, G. W. (2016). *Balancing, regression, difference-in-differences and synthetic control methods: A synthesis*. Working Paper 22791, National Bureau of Economic Research October. DOI: 10.3386/w22791.
Duranton, G., & Turner, M. A. (October 2012). Urban growth and transportation. *The Review of Economic Studies*, *79*(4), 1407–1440.
Duranton, G., Morrow, P. M., & Turner, M. A. (November 2013). Roads and trade: Evidence from the USA. *The Review of Economic Studies*, *81*(2), 681–792.
Eberts, R. W., & McMillen, D. P. (1999). Chapter 38 Agglomeration economies and urban public infrastructure. In P. Cheshire & E. S. Mills (Eds.), *Handbook of regional and urban economics* (Vol. 3, pp. 1455–1495). Amsterdam, The Netherlands: Elsevier.
Giroud, X. (May 2013). Proximity and investment: Evidence from plant-level data. *The Quarterly Journal of Economics*, *128*(2), 861–915.
Glaeser, E. (2011). *Triumph of the city: How our greatest invention makes us richer, smarter, greener, healthier, and happier*. New York, NY: Penguin Books.
Green, R. K. (March 2007). Airports and economic development. *Real Estate Economics*, *35*(1), 91–112.
Hovhannisyan, N., & Keller, W. (May 2011). *International business travel: An engine of innovation?* Working Paper 17100, National Bureau of Economic Research.
Kreif, N., Grieve, R., Hangartner, D., Turner, A. J., Nikolova, S., & Sutton, M. (2016). Examination of the synthetic control method for evaluating health policies with multiple treated units. *Health Economics*, *25*(12), 1514–1528. HEC-14-0564.R1.
LeFors, M. (2014). The role of air accessibility in urban development. Unpublished manuscript. University of California, Irvine. Retrieved from http://www.economics.uci.edu/grad/Job%20Market%20Paper%20-%20Michael%20LeFors.pdf
Michaels, G. (2008). The effect of trade on the demand for skill: Evidence from the interstate highway system. *Review of Economics and Statistics*, *90*(4), 683–701.
Mora, R., & Reggio, I. (December 2012). *Treatment effect identification using alternative parallel assumptions*. UC3M Working Papers, Economics.
Munnell, A. (June 1990). How Does Public Infrastructure Affect Regional Economic Performance? In Is There a Shortfall in Public Capital Investment? Federal Reserve Bank of Boston, Conference Proceedings, No. 34.
Percoco, M. (October 2010). Airport activity and local development: Evidence from Italy. *Urban Studies*, *47*(11), 2427–2443.

Reber, S. J. (2005). Court ordered desegregation: Successes and failures integrating American schools since brown versus board of education. *Journal of Human Resources*, *40*(3), 559–590.

Ruggles, S., Alexander, J. T., Genadek, K., & Schroeder, M. (2010). Integrated Public Use Microdata Series: Version 5.0 [Machine-readable database].

Sheard, N. (March 2014). Airports and urban sectoral employment. *Journal of Urban Economics*, *80*, 133–152.

Sheard, N. (2015). *Airport improvements and urban growth*. AIX-Marseille Working Paper, February.

U.S. Army Air Service. (March 1923). Airways and landing facilities. *Air Service Information Circular*, *5*(404), 1–13.

VanDerLinden, R. (2002). *Airlines and air mail: The post office and the birth of the commercial aviation industry*. Lexington: University Press of Kentucky.

Wittman, M., & Swelbar, W. (May 2013). *Trends and market forces shaping small community air service in the United States*. White Paper ICAT-2013-02.

APPENDIX A: DATA APPENDIX

CENSUS POPULATION AND EMPLOYMENT DATA

Population data were obtained from the National Historical Geographic Information System (NHGIS) for 1900–2010. These include total population, nonwhite population and urban population. The key limitation of the County Business Patterns data is that it begins in 1946 (and my series begins in 1951), right around the time at which I claim airports are opening and aviation is coming into its own. Moreover, there appears to be some concern that the CBP datasets are not as comparable over time as one would like, likely due to changes in the way firms were selected for inclusion in this, especially early on. As a result, the primary employment data used in this analysis is derived from the Industry data of the U.S. Census, allowing for consistent series of census-derived industrial data from 1900 to 2010. Sources for each employment data point:

- Agriculture and Mining: 1900–1940 from IPUMS 1% Sample, 1950–1960 from CCDB (note: mining imputed from 1950 to 1970 values since missing), 1970–2010 from NHGIS Construction: 1900–1940 from IPUMS 1% Sample, 1950–1960 from CCDB, 1970–2010 from NHGIS.
- Manufacturing: 1900, 1920, 1930, 1940 from NHGIS; 1910 from IPUMS (derived from 1% microdata); 1950 from City and County Data Book (CCDB) using 1949 manufacturing employee count; 1960 from CCDB using 1958 manufacturing employee count; 1970–2010 from NHGIS.
- Transportation, Communication and Utilities: 1900–1930 from IPUMS 1% microdata, 1940–1960 from CCDB entries, 1970–2010 from NHGIS.
- Wholesale Trade: 1900–1940 from IPUMS 1% microdata, 1950 from CCDB 1948 wholesale employment count; 1960 from CCDB 1958 wholesale employment count; 1970–2010 from NHGIS.
- Retail Trade: 1900–1930 from IPUMS 1% microdata; 1940 from CCDB 1939 retail employment count; 1950 from CCDB 1948 retail employment count; 1960 from CCDB 1958 retail employment count; 1970–2010 from NHGIS.
- Finance, Insurance, and Real Estate (FIRE): 1900–1940 from IPUMS 1% microdata; 1950 and 1960 from CCDB 1950/1960 FIRE employment count; 1970–2010 from NHGIS.
- Services: 1900–1940 from IPUMS 1%, 1950–1960 linearly imputed from 1940 to 1970 values, 1970–2010 from NHGIS.
- Public Administration: 1900–1940 from IPUMS 1%, 1950–1960 from CCDB, 1970–2010 from NHGIS.
- All employment: 1900–1940 from IPUMS 1%, 1950–1960 from CCDB; 1970–2010 from IPUMS From these, employment shares were defined as the share of employment in the industry of interest divided by total employment

(by year). Missing data were imputed by taking the geometric mean of neighboring data points (this affected 121 out of roughly 250,000 cells). Finally, cells that still were missing were imputed with values from the next 10 years (this affected 10 out of roughly 250,000 cells). Finally, cells missing 1900 population or employment data were flagged, as in many cases, these counties were not officially part of the United States until 1912 or after.

- Tradable Employment = Wholesale + Manufacturing + Agriculture + Mining.
- Nontradable employment = Retail + Finance + Services + Construction + Public Administration.

Other variables derived from the U.S. Census: Data on land and building prices from 1900 to 1950 were obtained from the NHGIS (missing post-1950). Data on median family income from 1950 to 2010 were obtained from NHGIS (missing prior to 1950). Data on median housing values were taken from CCDB for 1930 and 1940, and NHGIS from 1980 to 2010. Other years missing. Data on median rents were taken from CCDB for 1940 and 1950, and NHGIS from 1980 to 2010. Other years missing. Data obtained from the Bureau of Economic Analysis (BEA) include earnings, earnings per worker, personal income, and per capita personal income for 1970–2010.

OTHER DATA SOURCES

- County Characteristics 2005 – data on Census division, region, latitude, longitude, January temperature and other climate characteristics, topography measure, from ICPSR study 20660.[32]
- Planned highway mileage – courtesy of Nate Baum-Snow, aggregated to the county level using GIS software.
- Railway straight-line mileage in 1887 – courtesy of Jeremy Atack, aggregated to the county level using GIS software.
- Coastal Counties – U.S. Census Bureau and National Oceanic and Atmospheric Administration: https://www.census.gov/geo/landview/lv6help/coastal_cty.pdf
- Port Cities – NOAA http://www.ngs.noaa.gov/RSD/coastal/projects/coastal/ports_list.html Land grant colleges – http://espnational.org/about-us/land-grant-universities.html
- County/CBSA Size: County land areas over time were derived for each 10-year interval by obtaining data on county boundaries from the Atlas of Historical Counties Project.[33] CBSAs with changes in land areas greater than 3% were dropped from the analysis.
- Geography/Human Capital: These include a dummy variable for whether a county contains a political capital city or a land grant college.[34]

- Climate and Geography: From the ICPSR's county characteristics study, I use a measure of mean January temperature.[35] Dummy variables were derived for whether a county contains a port, is located on a coast, or on a river.[36] I also control for planned highway mileage in as of 1947,[37] as well as total straight-line rail mileage in 1887.[38]
- Air Traffic Data: I use air traffic data (enplanements and operations) from the FAA's Terminal Area Forecast for 1976–2012 traffic.[39] Between 1964 and 1976, where available, I hand-collected data from annual versions of the *FAA Statistical Handbook* to obtain traffic data.

The next step is to aggregate this data to the level of the Core Based Statistical Area (CBSA). 2010 CBSA data were obtained from the National Historical Geographic Information System. The overriding goal of what follows is to create a consistent data series from 1900 to 2010 in which data are compiled for a consistent geography. This means that both the composition of counties in each CBSA and the size of each CBSA, in terms of land area, must be the same for each data point in the time series. This will allow for a consistent estimation of the effects of the airport over time. As counties form the building blocks of CBSAs, much of what follows involves operations on county level data. The steps involved are: (1) standardize county sizes, and flag counties in which counties change " too much"; (2) aggregate county-level census, employment, airport, aviation history, and county characteristics data; and (3) remove CBSAs where geography cannot be made consistent due to political changes.

County size. Counties were standardized to their 2010 land areas. County land areas over time were derived for each 10-year interval by obtaining data on county boundaries from the Atlas of Historical Counties Project. Next, for each county, a flag was created indicating if the county's area had changed more than 3% since 1930. CBSAs flagged in this way are dropped. To standardize county areas, a ratio of the then-year county area to the 2010 county area was derived. Dividing employment and population data through by this ratio yields the adjusted county level information used in the analysis. Aggregation subsequently yielded the CBSA information used in this study.

APPENDIX B

Table B1. Airports with Statistically Significant Impact on Local Economies Since 1950: Tradable Employment.

Airport ID	Airport Name	City	State	Growth Index	Ever Hub?
AUS	Austin-Bergstrom Intl	Austin	TX	0.037	No
RNO	Reno/Tahoe Intl	Reno	NV	0.033	Yes
TUS	Tucson Intl	Tucson	AZ	0.028	No
LFT	Lafayette Rgnl	Lafayette	LA	0.027	No
SAN	San Diego Intl	San Diego	CA	0.027	Yes
COS	City Of Colorado Springs Muni	Colorado Springs	CO	0.024	Yes
DAB	Daytona Beach Intl	Daytona Beach	FL	0.024	No
LIT	Bill And Hillary Clinton National/ Adams Fi	Little Rock	AR	0.02	No
PHX	Phoenix Sky Harbor Intl	Phoenix	AZ	0.019	Yes
SLC	Salt Lake City Intl	Salt Lake City	UT	0.019	Yes
ACT	Waco Rgnl	Waco	TX	0.018	No
RDU	Raleigh-Durham Intl	Raleigh/ Durham	NC	0.018	Yes
CLL	Easterwood Field	College Station	TX	0.017	No
LNK	Lincoln	Lincoln	NE	0.017	No
TUP	Tupelo Rgnl	Tupelo	MS	0.016	No
BTV	Burlington Intl	Burlington	VT	0.015	No
LAF	Purdue University	Lafayette	IN	0.015	No
MSN	Dane County Rgnl-Truax Field	Madison	WI	0.015	No
SDF	Louisville Intl-Standiford Field	Louisville	KY	0.015	No
BNA	Nashville Intl	Nashville	TN	0.014	Yes
LEX	Blue Grass	Lexington	KY	0.014	No
MHT	Manchester	Manchester	NH	0.014	No
FSM	Fort Smith Rgnl	Fort Smith	AR	0.013	No
MEM	Memphis Intl	Memphis	TN	0.013	Yes
CMH	Port Columbus Intl	Columbus	OH	0.011	Yes
IND	Indianapolis Intl	Indianapolis	IN	0.011	No
MDT	Harrisburg Intl	Harrisburg	PA	0.011	No
FWA	Fort Wayne Intl	Fort Wayne	IN	0.01	No
MGM	Montgomery Rgnl (Dannelly Field)	Montgomery	AL	0.01	No
FAR	Hector Intl	Fargo	ND	0.009	No
FSD	Joe Foss Field	Sioux Falls	SD	0.009	No

Table B1. *(Continued)*

Airport ID	Airport Name	City	State	Growth Index	Ever Hub?
OKC	Will Rogers World	Oklahoma City	OK	0.008	No
OMA	Eppley Airfield	Omaha	NE	0.008	No
AZO	Kalamazoo/Battle Creek Intl	Kalamazoo	MI	0.007	No
CVG	Cincinnati/Northern Kentucky Intl	Covington	KY	0.007	Yes
FAT	Fresno Yosemite Intl	Fresno	CA	0.007	No
JLN	Joplin Rgnl	Joplin	MO	0.007	No
TYR	Tyler Pounds Rgnl	Tyler	TX	0.007	No
TXK	Texarkana Rgnl-Webb Field	Texarkana	AR	0.006	No
SUX	Sioux Gateway/Col. Bud Day Field	Sioux City	IA	0.005	No
MKE	General Mitchell Intl	Milwaukee	WI	0.004	Yes
ABE	Lehigh Valley Intl	Allentown	PA	0.003	No

Notes: Growth index refers to the annual average percentage by which the average of working-age population and total employment grew, due to the presence of the airport as estimated by the synthetic control estimator for each airport. "Ever Hub" indicates whether an airport was ever designated as a "hub" by a major carrier at some point after 1978.

Table B2. Airports with Statistically Significant Impact on Local Economies: Non-Tradable Employment.

Airport ID	Airport Name	City	State	Growth Index	Ever Hub?
PHX	Phoenix Sky Harbor Intl	Phoenix	AZ	0.022	Yes
AUS	Austin-Bergstrom Intl	Austin	TX	0.02	No
ILM	Wilmington Intl	Wilmington	NC	0.019	No
COS	City Of Colorado Springs Muni	Colorado Springs	CO	0.017	Yes
RDU	Raleigh-Durham Intl	Raleigh/Durham	NC	0.015	Yes
HGR	Hagerstown Rgnl-Richard A Henson Fld	Hagerstown	MD	0.013	No
SGF	Springfield-Branson National	Springfield	MO	0.013	No
MHT	Manchester	Manchester	NH	0.012	No
SAN	San Diego Intl	San Diego	CA	0.011	Yes
TUS	Tucson Intl	Tucson	AZ	0.01	No
BMI	Central Il Rgnl Arpt At Bloomington-Normal	Bloomington/Normal	IL	0.009	No
BNA	Nashville Intl	Nashville	TN	0.009	Yes
BTV	Burlington Intl	Burlington	VT	0.009	No
PVU	Provo Muni	Provo	UT	0.009	No
LAF	Purdue University	Lafayette	IN	0.008	No

Table B2. *(Continued)*

Airport ID	Airport Name	City	State	Growth Index	Ever Hub?
CLL	Easterwood Field	College Station	TX	0.007	No
PNS	Pensacola Gulf Coast Rgnl	Pensacola	FL	0.007	No
TVC	Cherry Capital	Traverse City	MI	0.007	No
CMH	Port Columbus Intl	Columbus	OH	0.006	Yes
CID	The Eastern Iowa	Cedar Rapids	IA	0.005	No
LSE	La Crosse Muni	La Crosse	WI	0.004	No
IND	Indianapolis Intl	Indianapolis	IN	0.003	No

Notes: Growth index refers to the annual average percentage by which the average of working-age population and total employment grew, due to the presence of the airport as estimated by the synthetic control estimator for each airport. "Ever Hub" indicates whether an airport was ever designated as a "hub" by a major carrier at some point after 1978.

Table B3. Characteristics of "Successful" Airports (Tradable Employment).

Outcome	Significant ($n = 42$)		Non-Significant ($n = 75$)		*P*-value
	Mean	SE	Mean	SE	
Log 1950 Population	11.824	0.132	11.288	0.097	0.013
Log 1950 Employment	11.265	0.135	10.707	0.099	0.001
Log 1950 Payroll Per Worker	3.194	0.027	3.184	0.039	0.855
1950 Share of Nontradable Employment	54.32	1.616	47.95	1.091	0.001
Planned (1947) Highway Miles Per Sq Mi	0.031	0.002	0.022	0.002	0.015
Straight-Line Rail Mileage Per Sq Mi (1887)	0.097	0.01	0.1	0.008	0.805
Distance to Nearest NRC Research University (miles)	36.04	7.42	68.4	5.44	0.001
CBSA Has Land Grant College	0.333	0.073	0.107	0.036	0.003
Distance to Nearest U.S. Military Base (miles)	30.42	5.51	45.67	5.03	0.056
CBSA Composite Amenity Scale (USDA ERS)	0.314	0.456	−0.302	0.197	0.154
Mean January Temperature (F)	34.57	1.93	32.18	1.3	0.292
Mean Hours of Sunlight in January	157.5	5.35	140.7	3.25	0.005
In Metropolitan Area (Census)	0.976	0.024	0.853	0.041	0.039
In Coastal Location (NOAA)	0.167	0.058	0.293	0.053	0.132
Political Capital City	0.31	0.072	0.08	0.031	0.002
Port City	0.119	0.05	0.093	0.034	0.662
Ever Airline Hub	0.262	0.068	0.027	0.019	0
Number of Non-Stop Destinations (Average 1980–2010)	37.88	5.13	19.6	2.94	0.001
Northeast Region	0.095	0.045	0.147	0.041	0.728

Table B3. (*Continued*)

Outcome	Significant ($n = 42$)		Non-Significant ($n = 75$)		*P*-value
	Mean	SE	Mean	SE	
Midwest Region	0.333	0.073	0.333	0.055	0.728
South Region	0.405	0.076	0.413	0.057	0.728
West Region	0.167	0.058	0.107	0.036	0.728

Note: *p*-values are from a standard two-sided *t*-test on individual outcomes EXCEPT in the case of region, where *p*-values are based on a chi-square test of independence.

Table B4. Characteristics of "Successful" Airports (Nontradable Employment).

Outcome	Significant ($n = 22$)		Non-Significant ($n = 97$)		*P*-value
	Mean	SE	Mean	SE	
Log 1950 Population	11.56	0.176	11.46	0.089	0.634
Log 1950 Employment	10.98	0.179	10.9	0.092	0.665
Log 1950 Payroll Per Worker	3.204	0.035	3.181	0.031	0.743
1950 Share of Nontradable Employment	55.6	2.35	49	0.975	0.005
Planned (1947) Highway Miles Per Sq Mi	0.026	0.004	0.025	0.002	0.967
Straight-Line Rail Mileage Per Sq Mi (1887)	0.088	0.013	0.102	0.007	0.431
Distance to Nearest NRC Research University (miles)	40.7	10.5	60.4	4.99	0.093
CBSA Has Land Grant College	0.364	0.103	0.144	0.036	0.019
Distance to Nearest U.S. Military Base (miles)	26.8	4.99	43.4	4.44	0.089
CBSA Composite Amenity Scale (USDA ERS)	0.668	0.683	−0.258	0.194	0.077
Mean January Temperature (F)	34.4	2.75	32.8	1.15	0.546
Mean Hours of Sunlight in January	160.9	9.002	143.8	2.81	0.02
In Metropolitan Area (Census)	0.955	0.045	0.887	0.032	0.343
In Coastal Location (NOAA)	0.227	0.09	0.247	0.044	0.843
Political Capital City	0.273	0.095	0.144	0.036	0.15
Port City	0.136	0.073	0.093	0.03	0.543
Ever Airline Hub	0.273	0.095	0.072	0.026	0.008
Number of Non-Stop Destinations (Average 1980–2010)	37.8	8.63	22.9	2.65	0.033
Northeast Region	0.091	0.062	0.134	0.035	0.401
Midwest Region	0.364	0.103	0.34	0.048	0.401
South Region	0.318	0.1	0.423	0.05	0.401
West Region	0.227	0.09	0.103	0.031	0.401

Note: *p*-values are from a standard two-sided t-test on individual outcomes EXCEPT in the case of region, where *p*-values are based on a chi-square test of independence.

Table B5. Regression Results: Predictors of "Significant" Airport Status: Tradable Employment.

Variables	(1) Significant Impact	(2)	(3) Est. Treatment Effect	(4)	(5)
	(Logit)	(OLS)	(OLS, No Truncation)	(OLS, With Truncation)	(Tobit, With Truncation)
Coastal Location	−0.915	−0.0839	0.173	0.0379	0.0862
	(1.127)	(0.093)	(0.145)	(0.100)	(0.129)
Airport in Capital City	1.046	0.135	−0.103	0.0359	−0.0117
	(1.021)	(0.145)	(0.154)	(0.117)	(0.137)
Port City	0.0999	−0.032	−0.300*	−0.0786	−0.186
	(1.015)	(0.132)	(0.166)	(0.125)	(0.156)
In Metropolitan Area (Census)	–	0.113	0.527**	0.153	0.272*
	–	(0.115)	(0.216)	(0.092)	(0.137)
CBSA Has Land Grant College	−0.806	−0.0128	0.137	0.0843	0.084
	(1.157)	(0.142)	(0.143)	(0.120)	(0.120)
Log Hours of January Sunshine	7.121**	0.434*	0.249	0.319	0.418
	(3.205)	(0.245)	(0.325)	(0.228)	(0.284)
Log January Temperature	0.961	0.0747	0.0534	0.0426	0.039
	(1.295)	(0.165)	(0.179)	(0.132)	(0.160)
ERS Amenity Scale (USDA)	0.162	0.0251	0.0642	0.0706*	0.0797*
	(0.379)	(0.037)	(0.056)	(0.041)	(0.041)
Log Distance to Nearest Research Univ	−1.395***	−0.161***	−0.129**	−0.131***	−0.156***
	(0.298)	(0.036)	(0.052)	(0.039)	(0.040)
Log Number of Non-Stop Destinations	0.476	0.0549	0.0147	0.0347	0.042
	(0.367)	(0.043)	(0.040)	(0.033)	(0.037)
Log Distance to Nearest Military Base	−0.132	−0.0212	−0.0742*	−0.0366	−0.0492
	(0.288)	(0.031)	(0.039)	(0.029)	(0.030)
Log CBSA Land Area	0.213	0.048	0.218*	0.0114	0.0811
	(0.691)	(0.086)	(0.118)	(0.073)	(0.086)
Constant	−33.97*	−1.728	−2.463	−0.942	−1.994
	(17.710)	(1.310)	(1.705)	(1.243)	(1.480)

Table B5. (*Continued*)

Variables	(1) Significant Impact	(2)	(3)	(4) Est. Treatment Effect	(5)
	(Logit)	(OLS)	(OLS, No Truncation)	(OLS, With Truncation)	(Tobit, With Truncation)
Observations	91	100	100	100	100
R-squared	–	0.492	0.593	0.607	–

Robust standard errors in parentheses, clustered at the CBSA level. Census division fixed effects also included in all specifications but not shown. *** $p < 0.01$, ** $p < 0.05$, * $p < 0.1$.

Notes: "Significant Impact" refers to a binary outcome as to whether the synthetic case estimator found a positive and significant impact caused by the airport to the city. "Estimated Treatment Effect" refers to the actual 60-year cumulative treatment effect outcome that was estimated by the synthetic control case estimator for each CBSA in the study. "Truncation" in Specifications (4) and (5) involve replacing the estimated (negative) treatment effects with zeros, since, technically, the effect of an airport should be nonnegative. See "Estimation Strategies" section for more information.

Table B6. Regression Results: Predictors of "Significant" Airport Status: Nontradable Employment.

Variables	(1) Significant Impact	(2)	(3)	(4) Est. Treatment Effect	(5)
	(Logit)	(OLS)	(OLS, No Truncation)	(OLS, With Truncation)	(Tobit, With Truncation)
Coastal Location	0.39	0.0273	0.156	0.0748	0.172
	(0.791)	(0.101)	(0.105)	(0.068)	(0.111)
Airport in Capital City	0.472	0.0474	−0.00768	0.0385	0.0195
	(0.797)	(0.124)	(0.122)	(0.087)	(0.123)
Port City	0.328	0.0588	−0.138	0.02	−0.0271
	(1.063)	(0.151)	(0.163)	(0.110)	(0.156)
In Metropolitan Area (Census)	0.326	0.0373	0.310*	0.0454	0.126
	(1.217)	(0.138)	(0.186)	(0.077)	(0.151)
CBSA Has Land Grant College	1.032	0.187	0.0972	0.0677	0.0447
	(0.822)	(0.148)	(0.105)	(0.083)	(0.105)
Log Hours of January Sunshine	1.051	0.11	0.587*	0.359*	0.756**
	(2.328)	(0.266)	(0.302)	(0.185)	(0.288)
Log January Temperature	1.281	0.195	0.228	0.152	0.135
	(1.343)	(0.172)	(0.180)	(0.122)	(0.153)

Table B6. *(Continued)*

Variables	(1)	(2)	(3)	(4)	(5)
	Significant Impact		Est. Treatment Effect		
	(Logit)	(OLS)	(OLS, No Truncation)	(OLS, With Truncation)	(Tobit, With Truncation)
ERS Amenity Scale (USDA)	0.148	0.0219	0.0149	0.00734	0.0084
	(0.330)	(0.050)	(0.042)	(0.028)	(0.039)
Log Distance to Nearest Research Univ	−0.14	−0.0169	−0.0754**	−0.0293	−0.0702**
	(0.291)	(0.037)	(0.034)	(0.022)	(0.031)
Log Number of Non-Stop Destinations	0.0804	0.00908	0.014	0.0166	0.027
	(0.250)	(0.033)	(0.034)	(0.022)	(0.036)
Log Distance to Nearest Military Base	−0.315	−0.0415	−0.00862	−0.00656	0.00138
	(0.196)	(0.031)	(0.034)	(0.021)	(0.032)
Log CBSA Land Area	0.116	0.0137	0.076	−0.00805	0.058
	(0.711)	(0.088)	(0.089)	(0.058)	(0.095)
Constant	−9.064	−0.558	−3.913**	−1.765	−4.240***
	(11.530)	(1.505)	(1.628)	(1.064)	(1.534)
Observations	90	102	102	102	102
R-squared		0.244	0.414	0.369	

Robust standard errors in parentheses, clustered at the CBSA level. Census division fixed effects also included in all specifications but not shown. *** $p < 0.01$, ** $p < 0.05$, * $p < 0.1$.

Notes: "Significant Impact" refers to a binary outcome as to whether the synthetic case estimator found a positive and significant impact caused by the airport to the city. "Estimated Treatment Effect" refers to the actual 60-year cumulative treatment effect outcome that was estimated by the synthetic control case estimator for each CBSA in the study. "Truncation" in Specifications (4) and (5) involve replacing the estimated (negative) treatment effects with zeros, since, technically, the effect of an airport should be nonnegative. See "Estimation Strategies" section for more information.

CHAPTER 12

THE EFFECT OF INTERNATIONAL AIRPORTS ON COMMERCIAL PROPERTY VALUES: CASE STUDIES OF TORONTO, ONTARIO, CANADA AND VANCOUVER, BC, CANADA

Jeffrey P. Cohen and Mike Brown

ABSTRACT

Airports are the portals where international air transport networks, which are increasingly important in a globalized, services-oriented economy, intersect with regional and metropolitan ground transportation networks. Our hypothesis is that, at this nexus, the degree of international connectivity at an airport and distance from the airport manifests itself in the value of commercial properties. As such airports are shaping the urban form around them and highlight the importance of integrated metropolitan and airport planning. Looking at Canada's two largest international airports at Toronto, Ontario and Vancouver, BC, and controlling for other factors, we see evidence that commercial properties decrease in value as distance to the airport increases and increase in value as the range of international frequencies and destinations available at the airport increase. We introduce a new concept of land-use at and around airports of "aviation-dependent" which would include hotels and corporate head offices, in addition to the traditional "aviation-related" and "aviation-compatible" uses. We see the effects of distance and

The Economics of Airport Operations
Advances in Airline Economics, Volume 6, 313–333

ISSN: 2212-1609/doi:10.1108/S2212-160920170000006012

connectivity are particularly pronounced on commercial properties occupied by aviation-dependent uses.

Keywords: Airports; commercial property values

JEL classifications: R3; R4

BACKGROUND

Most airport authorities study and report on airport economic impacts in terms of direct, indirect, and induced employment associated with on-going operations at the airport or with a particular capital investment program. Others go further and also analyze the wider economic or catalytic benefits – i.e., jobs facilitated by trade, tourism and FDI flows – stimulated and enabled by the connectivity available at the airport. These efforts are undertaken mainly to ensure that political decision makers and the community appreciate the economic importance of the airport and therefore the value of policies and investments aimed at supporting its growth. Other uses of economic impact assessments are to ensure sufficient ground access and parking capacity for employees is planned and available, as well as other employee services.

This chapter takes a further step and looks at how an airport's economic impact manifests itself in terms of commercial property values in the surrounding area which, in turn, speaks to the concept of airport cities or the Aerotropolis.

Ease of access to international markets for business travel or the distribution of their products is one way in which firms can benefit from access to an airport. This is particularly significant in Canada where 31% of GDP is accounted for by international exports compared to 13% in the United States. If these beneficial effects are strong enough, this can lead to a higher demand for real estate near the airport, which in turn can lead to higher value for the land near the airport. These effects can vary across industries due to the differences in intensity with which firms in each industry utilizes air transportation services.

If airports are affecting land values around them, then they are, in effect, shaping the form of metropolitan areas and no longer are they neutral transportation installations. This is highly significant for region wide land-use and transportation planning and we look at these effects around the two busiest airports in Canada: Toronto Pearson International Airport and Vancouver International Airport.

PAST RESEARCH: THE ECONOMIC EFFECT OF AIRPORT OPERATIONS

There is an extensive literature on the wider economic benefits of airports deliver to their communities. Many of these are studies of the impacts on employment from enhanced airport operations. Others focus on how better "connectivity" leads to improvements in economic development. Some of the studies focus on how particular industries flourish with airport improvements. We review some of the more prominent studies below. The majority of studies of employment impacts include coverage for airports in the United States and Europe, with a smaller number in Canada and elsewhere. Our analysis below of two of the largest Canadian airports – Vancouver (YVR) and Toronto (YYZ) – will fill the gap in this literature.

Among the US studies, Irwin and Kasarda (1991) examined the relationship between the structure of airline networks and employment growth at 104 metropolitan areas in the United States. Using data for a 30-year period, their statistical analysis, using least squares regressions, found that expansion of the airline network serving a region had a significant positive impact on employment in that region, particularly in service sector employment.[1]

Another US study on the employment impacts, by Button and Taylor (2000), examined the link between international air service and economic development. Using data for 41 metropolitan areas in the United States, the authors statistically analyzed the links between "high-tech" employment and the number of direct routes to Europe offered by airports in the region. The analysis found that there was a strong and significant relationship between employment and air services to Europe, such that increasing the number of European routes served from three to four generated approximately 2,900 "high-tech" jobs. While the results focussed on North Atlantic services, we believe these results are generalizable to all international linkages.

In a similar study, Brueckner (2003), also looked at the impact of air service on employment in the United States. The analysis found that a 10% increase in passenger enplanements in a metropolitan area leads to an approximately 1% increase in employment in service-related industries. Frequent service to a variety of destinations, reflected in the high levels of passenger enplanements, was found to both attract new firms to the metro area and stimulate employment at established enterprises. However, the analysis found that there was no impact on manufacturing and other goods-related employment suggesting that air travel is less important to these industries than it is to service-related industries.[2]

Among the studies covering airports outside of the United States, Cooper and Smith (2005) examined the contribution of air transportation to tourism, trade, location/investment decisions, and productivity in Europe. The study estimated that the net contribution of air transportation to trade (i.e., export minus imports) was €55.7 billion (roughly c$75 billion) in 2003 across the 25 current EU members, or approximately 0.6% of GDP.

There have been several other studies focusing on international settings. One of these other international studies was done by the consulting firm Inter*VISTAS* (2006), which used a global dataset on economic performance and national air service connectivity. That study found a 10% increase in a nation's air connectivity increased national GDP by 0.07%. While this may seem a small figure, when applied to the total economy and compounded over the years, it results in GDP that is 0.73% after 10 years. Bel and Fageda (2008) analyzed the relationship between international air service and the location of large firm's headquarters across major European urban areas. The authors found that supply of non-stop intercontinental flights was a significant factor in determining headquarters locations (along with other economic, business, labor, and tax factors). Empirical research indicated that a 10% increase in supply of intercontinental air service was associated with a 4% increase in the number large firm headquarters located in the corresponding urban area. These international studies generally used regression techniques to estimate these elasticities.

Another international study commissioned by IATA surveyed 625 businesses in five countries. These survey results indicated that 63% of firms considered, air transport to be vital or very important to investment decisions, while a further 24% said it was somewhat important. On average, 18% of firms reported that a lack of good air transport links had affected their past investment decisions.[3] This study was different from most of the others in that it is survey-based, rather than focused on statistical analysis of existing data.

Another interesting aspect of airport connectivity is the intersection of connectivity and Foreign Direct Investment (FDI). The strong relationship between FDI and aviation connectivity is also well-documented in academic literature, with some estimates suggesting that FDI increases by 50% after a first direct connection to a foreign region.[4] A recent study by the University of Brescia sought to establish impact of new routes on the creation of European inward FDI in Italy. The study concluded that inward FDI increased overall by 33.7% in the 2 years after the opening of new routes while, in the same period, FDIs in the control group decreased by 16.6% (*ibid.*).

In addition to the relationship between connectivity and FDI, connectivity is also an important factor influencing companies' decisions on where to locate. For example, according to a European Cities Monitor survey, 52% of companies consider international transport links to be an essential factor when locating businesses in Europe.[5] Similarly, other surveys have found that the investment decisions of firms in a wide range of countries have been significantly affected by the absence of good air transport links. These surveys are reflected in numerous academic studies examining the determinants of the location of large firms' headquarters across a range of countries and concluding that good airport facilities are very important to firms' relocation decisions (*ibid.*).

The European section of the Airports Council concludes that international global accessibility is "absolutely essential" to businesses making location decisions.[6] Direct examples of air connectivity via a well-connected global hub causing the relocation of global HQs include the decision by KPMG to move its European Headquarters to offices adjacent to Frankfurt Airport, and Philips' earlier 1997 decision to relocate from Eindhoven, where the company had historically been based, to Amsterdam.

There are numerous other international examples of catalytic development occurring along a development corridor from the airport fence to a central city location featuring HQs. Sectors that are considered most likely to relocate (or establish) within development corridors associated with a new airport are:

- The banking and finance sector, which is highly aviation dependent – two-thirds of the sector's total travel spend relates to air travel.
- The scientific/technical and R&D sector – which spends 34% of its overall travel spend on aviation.[7]

Another important aspect of airport impacts is the relationship between airports and property values. It is expected that ceteris paribus, better airports should enhance the desirability of living near the airports, which should become capitalized into house prices. But there are other potential "externalities" that could detract from property values, such as air and/or noise pollution. Among the many studies that have examined the impacts of transportation infrastructure on property values, most of these compare the tradeoffs between enhanced residential property values and greater noise associated with airport (and/or other transportation infrastructure) improvements. For instance, Tomkins, Topham, Twomey, and Ward (1998) find the benefits of residential location near airports exceed the costs. Since noise is less of a concern for commercial property, the focus for commercial property studies is more properly placed on the benefits from proximity to the airport.

While many of the real estate impacts have focused on residential property values, a smaller number of others have focused on commercial property impacts. One recent study of the commercial property improvement impacts of airports is Cohen and Paul (2007). They assess the impacts on manufacturing property values of airport infrastructure stocks aggregated to the US state-level. They find airport infrastructure improvements in a particular state enhance the commercial property values for the manufacturing sector in that state.

An earlier study that focuses on both residential and commercial property impacts of airport proximity is Crowley (1973), who studies the Toronto area. They find significant increases in residential sales prices near the airport in years in which there are significant airport improvements. They also find that there

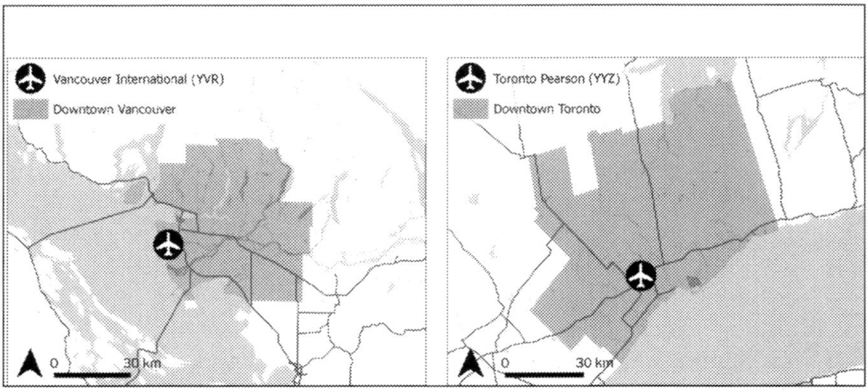

Fig. 1. Location of Toronto Pearson and Vancouver International Airports.

are significant increases in the number of lots converted from residential to commercial land-use zoning in these years of significant airport improvements in the Toronto suburb of Etobicoke. These zoning changes are evidence that commercial establishments place greater value upon land near the airport when the airport is improved.

Given the relatively small number of recent studies that focused on Canadian airports, an analysis of two of the largest airports in Canada – Vancouver (YVR) and Toronto (YYZ) – is worthy of our attention below (Fig. 1).

VANCOUVER INTERNATIONAL AIRPORT

Vancouver International Airport (YVR) is situated in the City of Richmond, BC, one of the constituent municipalities of Metro Vancouver. In 2014, Vancouver International Airport served 19.3 million enplaned-deplaned and 257,000 tons of cargo.[8] By way of comparison, Seattle–Tacoma International Airport served 37.5 million passengers in 2014 and processed 327,240 tons of air cargo.[9] Overall, 49% of global GDP is accessible by daily, non-stop scheduled air service from YVR.[10] The airport also has the most scheduled flights to China of any airport in North America and considerably more on a per capita basis which reflects Vancouver's and YVR's role as a North American gateway to Asia.

Proximity to YVR may be particularly valuable for businesses shipping products and documents by air express. Vancouver is geographically the most distant major North American metro area from global air freight hubs such as Louisville, KY (UPS) and Memphis, TN (Fed Ex) and Vancouver is also two time zones behind them. The upshot is that cargo aircraft have to leave YVR by 1800 hours in order to arrive in time for the "Big Sort" at these two hubs and, furthermore, Vancouver packages must also clear US Customs. Package pick up from commercial premises in parts of Metro Vancouver distant from the airport must, therefore, occur in the early to mid-afternoon thereby reducing the time available for production and putting a premium on locations closer to the airport. These issues underscore the importance of our analysis on the property value impacts of proximity to YVR.

We used the City of Richmond's business license database which provides an address and the major 2012 North American Industry Classification System (NAICS) two-digit industries (obtained from Statistics Canada) that operated in Richmond, BC. Table 1 describes these industries, which included the following: construction (23); manufacturing (31–33); wholesale (41); retail (44–45); transportation and warehousing (48–49); finance and insurance (52); professional, scientific, and technical services (54); corporate head offices (55); healthcare (62); and accommodation and food (72). While we also examined several other industries, the two-digit industries mentioned above were generally statistically significant and worthy of further analysis and discussion.

Table 1. Value of Proximity to Vancouver Airport (YVR) By Industry Least Squares Regression Results. Dependent Variable: Log (Assessed Land Value, C$ 2012).

Distance to YVR Times Dummy Variables for Properties in Each Industry:	NAICS Code	Examples	Regression Coefficient
Accommodation	721		−0.65
Corporate Head Offices	55		−0.64
Manufacturing	31–33	Food manufactures including seafood	−0.43
Construction	23	Builders and maintenance contractors	−0.38
Wholesale	41		−0.31
Professional, Scientific and Technical Services	54	Lawyers, immigration consultants	−0.29
Health Care	62		−0.21
Finance and Insurance	52	Banks, mortgage brokers, investment houses, brokerages	−0.19
Transportation and Warehousing	48–49		−0.11
Food	722		0.24
Retail	44–45		0.35

There were 5,776 commercial businesses in Richmond in 2013, and nearly 2,200 of these businesses in the sectors described above matched with data on Gross Land Area in the BC Assessment database. Our analysis focuses on these 2,200 businesses. "Retail" comprised the largest sector among the industries in our sample, consisting of over 30% of the commercial properties in Richmond. "Transportation and warehousing," "wholesale," and "accommodation and food" each comprise approximately 10% of the properties in our sample in Richmond. The remaining two-digit industries each occupy less than 10% of the commercial properties in Richmond. The two-digit industries listed in Table 1a comprised 91.4% of all two-digit industries that occupied commercial property in Richmond in 2013. We also have data on (81), "Other Services (except public administration)", but due to the requirement of the statistical model that we omit one sector from the estimation, this is the sector that we omit because of this sector's tangential relationship to air travel.

Data on assessed values, Gross Land Area (GLA), effective year built, and property class were obtained from BC Assessment. We also obtained the business license database from the City of Richmond. We merged the two databases and geo-coded the resulting dataset to obtain distance from each property to YVR. The average commercial property in Richmond had a land value assessed at approximately $25.3 million, with a minimum of $300 and the highest property had an assessed land value of $106 million. Approximately 25% of the commercial properties were Class 05, while the remaining commercial properties were Class 06.[11] The average property had an effective year built of 1991, and a Gross Land Area (GLA) of 42,500 ft. The average commercial property in Richmond was located 5.17 miles from YVR, with the furthest distance of 17.7 miles and the shortest distance of 1.17 miles.

We used regression analysis to examine the relationships between assessed value of land and distance from YVR of commercial properties in the various two-digit sectors in Richmond. Regression analysis is particularly useful because it enables a researcher to isolate the effect of one variable on the assessed value of land. In our analysis, we consider the two-digit NAICS industries described above, one-by-one, while holding constant the other industries and other variables that were expected to affect land values (such as GLA, property class, and effective age). We constructed "indicator" or "dummy" variables for each of the industries. For each of the 2,197 observations, each of these dummy variables equals a value of 1 if the observation is for a business in industry i, and 0 otherwise. We then multiply the distance from YVR vector by each of these dummy variables, so that we can estimate the average impact of distance for firms in industry i on assessed land values in industry *i*, where *i* consists of each of the 2-digit industries described above. In addition to obtaining an estimate of the magnitude and sign of each industry's coefficient, we also test whether each coefficient is statistically significantly different from zero.

As shown in Table 1, Accommodation, Wholesale, Construction, Manufacturing, and Corporate Head Offices valued proximity to YVR the most among the industries we included in our analysis. Specifically, assessed land values for Corporate Head Offices increased by approximately 0.64% for every 1% decrease in distance to YVR, and this relationship was statistically significant. A similar interpretation can be applied to the other industry estimates that were negative and statistically significant. Fig. 2 shows the sectors that moderately value access to YVR. The transportation and warehousing coefficient is approximately −0.11, but this is not a statistically significantly different from zero relationship. This result implies the transportation and warehousing valuation of proximity to YVR is only marginally meaningful. There were several other sectors that had a statistically insignificant relationship to assessed land values in Richmond. These sectors included "information and cultural industries," "real estate and rental and leasing," "administrative and support, waste management and remediation services," "educational services," and "arts, entertainment, and recreation".

In our regression analysis, we separated sector 72 into two parts – accommodation (721) and food (722). We found the coefficient on 721 is approximately −0.65 and statistically significant, while the coefficient on 722 is +0.24 and statistically significant. This implies for every 1% decrease in the distance to YVR for accommodation establishments, the assessed land value rose by approximately 0.65%. Food establishments had the opposite effect. This underscores the importance of the accommodation industry to the air travel industry while food establishments are more oriented to

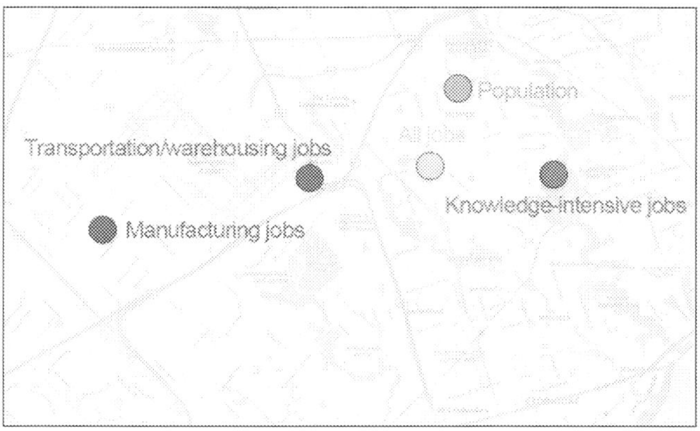

Fig. 2. Centroids of Population and Employment in the Toronto Metropolitan Area. *Note*: Toronto Pearson Airport is in the upper left quadrant of Fig. 2.

serving the local market. Likewise for retail establishments which are primarily locally focused although the airport can be an appropriate site for specialty retail with a regional, provincial, national, and even international catchment area such as the designer outlet mall scheduled to open at YVR in July 2015.

We also looked at a sub-set of the transportation and warehousing NAICS codes to focus on businesses engaged in the customer brokerage and freight forwarding (NAICS Codes 4885). There are a number of such businesses located at the YVR but the Airport Authority is aware that a number of these businesses had moved off the airport: the number of freight forwarders and customs brokers in Richmond increased by 15% from 2004 to 2013 but the number at the airport declined by 28%. There are various reasons including more competitive rents, electronic customs clearance and the multi-modal nature of the business. The results support this with coefficient was −0.12 but it was not statistically significant. Freight forwarders and customs brokers in Richmond and it confirms that these businesses have only a weak attraction to the airport and, in fact, there is a cluster in East Richmond adjacent to provincial highway #91, a Class A railroad and seaport. It does appear, as the prior literature would suggest, that effects are concentrated in the service-related sectors. Cargo and freight (characterized by "transportation and warehousing") play less of a role than might otherwise be expected.

TORONTO PEARSON INTERNATIONAL AIRPORT

The underlying policy and business motivations for the research, which has been funded by the airport authorities, at Toronto Pearson were somewhat different to Vancouver so we did not undertake an analysis of industry location relative to the airport by NAICS code. Nonetheless, many of the findings from the Vancouver work were replicated in Toronto.

Toronto Pearson International Airport (YYZ) is Canada's largest airport it served 41.3 million enplaned-deplaned passengers in 2015 and is the second largest international airport in North America after John F. Kennedy Airport in New York City. Toronto Pearson is connected to 67% of the global economy by daily, non-stop scheduled service.[12] Canada's two major air carriers, Air Canada and WestJet, have major hubs at Toronto Pearson.

Toronto Pearson is Canada's busiest cargo airport with 435,000 tons of cargo enplaned and deplaned in 2015 of which an estimated 73% was international cargo.[13] Exports account for 34% of Ontario's economy, higher than the national average, and Pearson is also the port of exit for $31.5 billion of Ontario's exports or 15% of the total and a key link in the supply chain of Ontario's businesses.[14] One the biggest exports through Toronto Pearson are pharmaceutical products and Mississauga, Ontario is home to a significant cluster of pharmaceutical companies aka "Pill Hill" and $2.3 billion worth of pharma products were exported from Toronto–Pearson in 2014 which accounts for 36% of Ontario's total pharma exports.[15]

In broad terms, Toronto Pearson processes twice the volume of passengers and cargo as Vancouver International.

Airport Employment Zone

Toronto Pearson Airport anchors an employment zone which, in 2011, 288,000 people worked within a 5-mile radius and 45,000 worked within a 2-mile radius.

The Airport Employment Zone (AEZ) is the second largest concentration of employment in Canada after the central business district of Toronto[16] and also of note are the centroids[17] of employment in key sectors in the Toronto metropolitan area[18] which are all adjacent to Toronto Pearson International Airport. This may be due to "random acts of geography" with respect to the historical location of the airport but it may also signify the role of the airport as an attractor of employment.

Toronto Pearson's Impact on Commercial Property Values: Time Series Analysis

We looked at a wide range of factors that could explain the value of a commercial property including its type, size, age, interest rates, the cost index for constructing commercial buildings in Toronto, the neighborhood and some "airport-related" measures such as driving distance to the airport, the number of international flights per day as a proxy for global connectivity. Table 2 shows statistics for the Toronto Pearson International Airport AEZ.

Table 2. Toronto Pearson Airport Employment Zone Labor Force Statistics.

Distance From Toronto Pearson Airport	Total Employed Labor Force Total	Total Employed Labor Force Working At Home	Total Employed Labor Force With Usual Place of Work
0–2 miles	44,805	0	44,805
2–5 miles	243,670	6,795	236,875
Total	288,475	6,795	281,680

Source: Statistics Canada.

Our dataset include 470 commercial properties around Toronto Pearson that sold between the years 2000 and 2015. This is a cross section of properties that sold during this time period; it is not a panel in the sense that these properties sold once during this time period. Commercial property is defined to include small and large office buildings and hotels. It does not include warehouses or industrial properties (although these will be studied later). Sales prices and property characteristics were obtained from Geowarehouse, a Toronto-based company that sells these data and to which the GTAA subscribes. Driving distance is defined as the shortest driving distance between the property and the airport on Google Maps. It is understood that the road network is essentially unchanged over the study period, that is, there have been no major changes to the driving distance, if not the time. SeeTable 3 for results.

Lot size is the most powerful factor explaining sales price. We also tested and controlled for neighborhood effects, that is, unique local conditions that

Table 3. Impact of Toronto Pearson Commercial Property Values: Dependent Variable: Log Real Sale Price Ordinary Least Squares Regression Results.

Included observations:	$n = 470$
R-squared:	0.547663
Adjusted R-squared:	0.539813
Variable	Coefficient
	Probability
CONSTANT	6.751599
	0
LOG(LOTSIZE)	0.659003
	0
LOG(DRIVING)	−0.157981
	0.009
LOG(INTLFLIGHTS)	0.691426
	0.0011
L5B_DUMMY	0.425638
	0.0423
L5S_DUMMY	−1.620679
	0.0076
L6T_DUMMY	−0.95933
	0.0002
L6Z_DUMMY	−0.95933
	0.0002
L7E_DUMMY	−2.710099
	0

p-values are in bold.

may affect property prices by using the Forward Sortation Area (FSA) of the post code. The only neighborhoods where intrinsic local effects were significant and positive were the Mississauga City Centre (L5B) and Hurontario and Bovaird (L6Z) which is major intersection in west central Brampton. In other words there are inherent characteristics in the areas that boost the value of commercial property, possibly benefits of co-locating with similar businesses.

Neighborhoods where there were significant and negative, intrinsic effects on commercial property sales prices were immediately north of the airport: between Derry road and the Mississauga/Brampton city boundary (L5S), the area bounded by the Mississauga/Brampton city boundary, Highway 410, Highway 7 and the Vaughan/Brampton line (L6T) and in Caledon (L7E).

In a separate analysis (available from the authors upon request), we also created dummy variables to control for other factors that we are not able to observe or measure that could affect property sales prices over time. For example, the number of international flights at Pearson grew by over 100% between 2000 and 2015 and we want to be sure that we are capturing the impact of those flights as distinct from other factors that may have been at work over those years, e.g., increasing construction costs. Neither the year nor construction cost index (an index for the cost of constructing properties) was significant so we can be confident that we are capturing the impact Pearson's international connectivity and not some other variable that has changed over time.

International flights have had a bigger impact on hotels' value and explain more of the variation in their sales prices compared to office buildings. It makes sense in that hotels' response to airport growth is more "elastic" in that they cater to passengers and aircrew more directly than offices do.

In summary lot size, the number international flights, driving distance from the property to the airport and certain neighborhood effects explain 55% of the variation in commercial property sales prices around Toronto Pearson Airport from 2000 to 2015.

One of the sources of contention over commercial development at an airport that is not explicitly aviation related is that it comes at the expense of established commercial centers in the surrounding municipalities. This is particularly the case if the airport is under a separate land-use authority. In the case of Toronto Pearson, and other Canadian airports, by virtue of being on federal land means that airports are not subject to municipal zoning. The evidence is that this is not a zero-sum game, e.g., commercial property values in Mississauga City Centre, the nearest commercial center to Toronto Pearson, have increased as a result of Toronto Pearson's international connectivity. In practical terms, the company occupying an office building at an airport will need lawyers, accountants, marketing and government relations consultants who may choose to locate in an adjacent city center. A 10% increase in international flights translates into a 28% increase in commercial property values in Mississauga City Centre and explains 14% of the change in those property values over the last 15 years. See Table 4.

Table 4. Impact of Toronto Pearson's International Connectivity on Commercial Property Values in Mississauga City Centre: Least Squares Regression Results: Dependent Variable: Log Real Sale Price.

Included observations:	$n = 27$
R-squared:	0.143273
Adjusted R-squared:	0.109004
Variable	Coefficient
	Probability
CONSTANT	3.458593
	0.5512
LOG(INTLFLIGHTS)	2.814978
	0.0515

p-values are in bold.

Toronto Pearson's Impact on Commercial Property Values: Cross-Sectional Analysis

Hotels

The assessed value of a hotel around Toronto Pearson Airport is a function of its size, rating and distance from the airport. A hotel is worth 2.3% less every 10% further away it is from the airport.

The demand for hotel rooms around Toronto Pearson is primarily driven by passengers and aircrew. Airport hotels are also used by those doing business with companies and organizations operating at the airport and other companies seeking a convenient location for internal meetings or training courses. Proximity to the airport, therefore, has value to hotel owners through shorter travel times for guests and lower shuttle bus operating costs.

Our dataset include 53 hotels around Toronto Pearson. We obtained the assessed value of the hotel for 2016 property tax purposes from Geowarehouse, a Toronto-based company that sells these data and to which the GTAA subscribes. The rating of the hotel, that is, the number of stars was obtained from Trip Advisor. Driving distance is defined as the shortest driving distance between the property and the airport on Google Maps. See Table 5 for results.

The strongest predictor of a hotel's assessed value is the land it occupies as a surrogate for its size. A 10% increase in land area translates into a 6.4% increase in value which is to be expected as value does not increase proportionately with size.

The next strongest predictor is the hotel's rating with a 10% increase translating into an 18.3% increase in value. So, going from three stars to four stars is a 33% increase and a 60% increase in assessed value.

Driving distance to the airport is the next strongest predictor with a 10% increase in distance by road resulting in a 2.3% decline in assessed value. This

Table 5. Impact of Toronto Pearson Airport on Hotel Values. Least Squares Regression Results: Dependent Variable: Assessed Hotel Values 2016.

Included observations:	$n = 43$
R-squared:	0.661502
Adjusted R-squared:	0.635464
Variable	Coefficient
	Probability
CONSTANT	8.119401
	0
LOG(AREA)	0.641082
	0
LOG(DISTANCE)	−0.229857
	0.0022
LOG(RATING)	1.838964
	0.0001

p-values are in bold.

result is consistent with the one from an earlier analysis of Pearson's impact on hotel values over time.

We also tested and controlled for neighborhood effects, that is, unique local conditions that may affect property prices by using the Forward Sortation Area (FSA) of the post code but none were significant.

In summary, lot size, hotel rating and driving distance to the airport explains 66% of the variation in hotel values around Toronto Pearson Airport in 2016.

Warehouses

The multi-modal nature of the freight forwarding, logistics, and warehouse business, the need for land to support truck operations and for easy highway access means that a warehouse increases in value the further away it is from Toronto Pearson airport.

This illustrates how Toronto Pearson's growth is affecting the Airport Employment Zone. As land values increase, it is pushing warehouse operations further away.

Our dataset include 80 businesses around Toronto Pearson that report themselves as being freight forwarders or warehouses.[19] We obtained the assessed value of the properties these companies occupied for 2016 property tax purposes from Geowarehouse, a Toronto-based company that sells these data and to which the GTAA subscribes. Driving distance is defined as the shortest driving distance between the property and the airport on Google Maps. See Table 6 for results.

Table 6. Impact of Toronto Pearson Airport on Warehouse Values. Least Squares Regression Results: Dependent Variable: Assessed Warehouse Values 2016.

Included observations:	$n = 62$
R-squared:	0.819287
Adjusted R-squared:	0.813161
Variable	Coefficient
	Probability
CONSTANT	6.960381
	0
LOG(AREA)	0.829324
	0
LOG(DRIVING)	0.30242
	0.0005

p-values are in bold.

Our basic assumption is that the assessed value of the property is a proxy for what the occupant is paying in rent or, if owner-occupied, the opportunity cost of capital. The strongest predictor of a warehouse value is the amount of land it occupies. A 10% increase in land area translates into an 8.3% increase in value which is to be expected as value does not increase proportionately with area.

Driving distance to the airport is the next strongest predictor with a 10% increase in distance by road resulting in a 3.0% increase in assessed value. Why would this be the case: generally we expect to see commercial property values decline with distance from the airport? It's probably due to the truck orientation of the freight forwarding and logistics business. Large amounts of land are needed to accommodate the loading, unloading, and storage of trucks and easy access to highways is important as well.

Unlike hotels which are constantly shuttling people to and from the airport, only a small percentage of cargo handled by forwarders is probably transported to and from the airport every day. Since land values and highway congestion increase with proximity to Toronto Pearson airport, a location close-by is not a necessity.

These results are consistent with analysis undertaken at Vancouver International Airport which showed that freight forwarders exhibited little appetite for a location close to the airport.

The sample size has been adjusted downwards to exclude freight forwarders occupying office buildings and an outlier in unit assessed value.

Offices

Our dataset include 98 office buildings greater than 7,500 square feet around Toronto Pearson Airport. We obtained the assessed value of the properties these companies occupied for 2016 property tax purposes from Geowarehouse, a Toronto-based company that sells these data and to which the GTAA subscribes. Driving distance is defined as the shortest driving distance between the property and the airport on Google Maps.

The assessed value of offices around Toronto Pearson is affected by driving distance to the airport but only beyond a 7.0 km (4.4 miles) driving distance. Within 7.0 km, neighborhood effects are dominant.

Assuming an average urban driving speed of 30 km/h, a 7.0 km journey to the airport would take just under 15 minutes. There is no evidence that gradations within 7.0 km driving distance show up in property values presumably because the number of people moving between an office building and the airport are fewer on a daily basis than to and from hotel it's not really material whether the journey takes 10 minutes or 15 minutes. The risk of significant variance around the trip length is minimized because of proximity and availability of alternative routes and modes.

Beyond a 7.0 km of the airport, driving distance does become significant with a coefficient of −0.36. We think this is because the variability of the time it takes to drive to the airport increases with distance and the routing and mode options decrease putting a higher premium on proximity (see Table 7).

There are two main concentrations of office buildings within 7.0 km driving distance of the airport denoted by their post code: L4V and L4W. The fixed neighborhood effects of the former are negative as it's an older area, collocated with warehouses, poor public transit, and highway access and few amenities such as sidewalks and parks. It's also directly under the flight path of one of Toronto Pearson's main runways: 05–23. In contrast, the L4W post code is known as the Airport Corporate Centre and is a planned office campus with

Table 7. Impact of Toronto Pearson Airport on Office Values.[a] Least Squares Regression Results: Dependent Variable: Log Assessed Unit Office Building Values 2016.

Included observations:	$n = 57$
R-squared:	0.089593
Adjusted R-squared:	0.07304
Variable	Coefficient
	Probability
CONSTANT	6.233015
	0
LOG(DISTANCE)	−0.361208
	0.0237

[a]Office buildings greater than 7 km and less than 30 km driving distance from the airport. *p*-values are in bold.

Table 8. Impact of Toronto Pearson Airport on Office Values in Postal Code L4W.[a] Least Squares Regression Results: Dependent Variable: Log Assessed Unit Office Building Values 2016.

Included observations:	$n = 39$
R-squared:	0.640389
Adjusted R-squared:	0.630669
Variable	Coefficient
	Probability
CONSTANT	4.922028
	0
DUMMY_L4W	0.488284
	0

[a]Office buildings greater than 7 km driving distance from the airport.
p-values are in bold.

Table 9. Impact of Toronto Pearson Airport on Office Values in Postal Code L4V.[a] Least Squares Regression Results: Dependent Variable: Log Assessed Unit Office Building Values 2016.

Included observations:	n = 39
R-squared:	0.110608
Adjusted R-squared:	0.062282
Variable	Coefficient
	Probability
CONSTANT	5.185988
	0
DUMMY_L4V	−0.249204
	0.0386

[a]Office buildings greater than 7 km driving distance from the airport.
p-values are in bold.

good amenities, public transit and highway access and not directly under the flight path of a runway (see Tables 8 and 9).

CONCLUSIONS

Our analyzes show that proximity to and international connectivity at Canada's two largest airports, Toronto Pearson International and Vancouver International manifest themselves in the value and use of commercial property around them. Airports are therefore shaping the form of the metropolitan areas they serve which has implications for regional land-use and transportation planning. In the case of Toronto Pearson, it anchors an employment zone that's the second largest in Canada after the Toronto CBD and the airport is close to the centroid of population and certain types of employment in the broader metropolitan area.

In the case of Toronto Pearson, international connectivity and proximity are significant in explaining commercial property values on both a time series and cross-sectional basis. Hotels show the largest elasticity with respect to both because of the costs associated with transporting passengers between the hotel and the airport and the more immediate relationship between international flight activity and the demand for rooms from aircrew and passengers.

Our results show the importance of proximity to Vancouver International Airport for several industries. The "value" that the airport creates for those industries is reflected through increases in assessed land values, after we control for a variety of other factors that also affect land values. Hotels also show up as having a high elasticity with respect to distance to the airport while other sectors (such as locally oriented food services and retail) face higher land values as distance to Vancouver Airport increases.

A common finding between Vancouver and Toronto was a weak affinity amongst freight forwarders and customs brokers for proximity to the airport. In Vancouver, we deduced this through an analysis of NAICS codes while in Toronto, we can infer it from the fact that the value of warehouses increases with distance from the airport. We can advance several probable reasons for this. One reason is the freight forwarding business is increasingly multi-modal and the volume if not, the value of goods traveling by air is small relative to truck. Another reason is the electronic clearance of international goods weakens the link between airport and warehouse, and warehouses it on large lots of land. The fact that land values close to the airport are increasing and proximity to freeways is probably most important because of the truck focus of the business.

There are also implications for airport planning. Traditionally airports have been home to aviation-related businesses and clearly any business that requires direct access to the runways and taxiways will locate an airport, e.g., aircraft maintenance, general and corporate aviation facilities, air cargo. Land with direct access to a runway or taxiway is generally referred to as airside land. Airport land that does not have direct access to a runway or taxiway, generally referred to as groundside land, has traditionally been occupied by businesses that are still "aviation-related," e.g., facilities supporting rental car operations at the airport, flight kitchens and aviation fuel tanks.

In many jurisdictions airport land-uses are restricted to "aviation-related" ones through official plans and zoning ordinances. However, airports are operating in a competitive environment with air carriers demanding lower land fees and are motivated to generate new, incremental and diverse sources of non-aeronautical revenue. Where airports are under federal jurisdiction as they are in Canada and Australia, they are not bound by the regulations of state, provincial or municipal governments. While airports and surrounding jurisdictions generally endeavor to co-ordinate their respective plans, because airports ultimately control the zoning and development of their land, there have been conflicts with local or regional government over what constitutes appropriate land-uses at an airport.

The analysis presented here suggests that the traditional distinction between "aviation-related" and "non-aviation related" may longer be helpful and that we can contemplate new category which we refer to as "aviation dependent." These are businesses that are large consumers of air passenger and freight transportation services and place a premium on proximity to an airport accordingly. In terms of regional economic competitiveness, it's important to accommodate and enable these businesses. An optimal regional approach would be ensure that the lands at or close to an airport, that are not required for aviation related uses are occupied by those industries with the greatest need for proximity to air transportation services. Ordinarily, one would expect the market to do this, but if there are regulatory prohibitions that prevent "aviation dependent" businesses from locating at an airport because they are not deemed to be "aviation-related" in the traditional sense, then there is an inefficient land allocation.

In summary, airports influence urban form and highlight the importance of integrated airport and metropolitan planning.

NOTES

1. The analysis was conducted using 'non-recursive' models which confirmed that increases in the air service network were a cause rather than a consequence of this employment growth.
2. Similar results have been found by later work, e.g., Blonigen and Cristea (2015) and McGraw (2015).
3. IATA (2006).
4. Bannò and Redondi (2014); cited in Airports Commission Discussion Paper 02: Aviation connectivity and the economy Heathrow Airport Limited, 19th April 2013.
5. Cited by the UK Airports Commission (2013) Discussion Paper 02: Aviation Connectivity and the Economy.
6. ACI (2004).
7. Oxford Economics/Ramboll (2012).
8. Source: Vancouver Airport Authority.
9. Source: Port of Seattle.
10. Source: Vancouver Airport Authority and defined as daily, non-stop, scheduled flights. GDP for the US and Canada is calculated on a state/province level and other countries at a national level.
11. BC Assessment defines class 05 as "light industry" while class 05 is other commercial. See: https://www.bcassessment.ca/Services-products/property-classes-and-exemptions/understanding-property-classes-and-exemptions
12. Source: Greater Toronto Airports Authority. Defined as daily, non-stop, scheduled service with GDP calculated at the state/province level for the US and Canada and national level overseas.
13. Source: Greater Toronto Airports Authority.
14. Source: Statistics Canada.

15. Source: Statistics Canada.

16. Source: "Planning For Prosperity: Globalization, Competitiveness and the Growth Plan for the Greater Golden Horseshoe", Neptis Foundation, 2015.

17. These centroids were determined by randomly distributed points across each traffic analysis zone one point per job in each category and then QGIS "mean coordinates" function to determine the centroid of each point's dataset.

18. Referred to as the Greater Golden Horseshoe or GGH and essentially a contiguous urban area from east of Toronto around Lake Ontario to Niagara and including Hamilton, Ontario.

19. NAICS codes 48551 and 49311.

REFERENCES

Airports Council International (ACI). (2004). *The social and economic impact of airports in Europe*. Gennaio.

Bannò, M., & Redondi, R. (2014). Air connectivity and foreign direct investments: Economic effects of the introduction of new routes. *European Transport Research Review*, *6*(4), 355–363.

Bel, G., & Fageda, X. (2008). Getting there fast: Globalization, intercontinental flights and location of headquarters. *Journal of Economic Geography*, *8*(4), 471–495.

Blonigen, B. A., & Cristea, A. D. (2015). Air service and urban growth: Evidence from a quasi-natural policy experiment. *Journal of Urban Economics*, *86*, 128–146.

Brueckner, J. K. (2003). Airline traffic and urban economic development. *Urban Studies*, *40*(8), 1455–1469.

Button, K., & Taylor, S. (2000). International air transportation and economic development. *Journal of Air Transport Management*, *6*(4), October 2000.

Cohen, J. P., & Paul, C. M. (2007). The impacts of transportation infrastructure on property values: A higher-order spatial econometrics approach. *Journal of Regional Science*, *47*(3), 457–478.

Cooper, A., & Smith, P. (2005). *The Economic Catalytic Effects of Air Transport in Europe*, EUROCONTROL.

Crowley, R. W. (1973). A case study of the effects of an airport on land values. *Journal of Transport Economics and Policy*, *1*(May), 144–152.

International Air Transport Association (IATA). (2006). Airline Network Benefits – Measuring the Additional Benefits Generated by Airline Networks for Economic Development.

InterVISTAS Consulting Inc., Measuring the Economic Rate of Return on Investment in Aviation, December 2006.

Irwin, M., & Kasarda, J. (1991). Air passenger linkages and employment growth in U.S. Metropolitan areas. *American Sociological Review*, *56*(4), 524–537.

McGraw, M. J. (2015). Perhaps the Sky's the Limit? Airports and Employment in Local Economies.

Neptis Foundation. (2015). Planning for prosperity: Globalization, competitiveness and the growth plan for the greater golden horseshoe.

Oxford Economics/Ramboll. (2012). Impact of new hub options on business locations, FDI and alignment with strategies.

Tomkins, J., Topham, N., Twomey, J., & Ward, R. (1998). Noise versus access: The impact of an airport in an urban property market. *Urban Studies*, *35*(2), 243–258.

UK Airports Commission. (2013). Discussion Paper 02: Aviation connectivity and the economy Heathrow Airport Limited, 19th April.

CHAPTER 13

AIRPORT CONGESTION AND AIRLINE NETWORK STRUCTURE

Xavier Fageda and Ricardo Flores-Fillol

ABSTRACT

We investigate the relationship between airline network structure and airport congestion. More specifically, we study the ways in which airlines adjust capacity to delays depending on the network type they operate. We find some evidence suggesting that airlines operating hub-and-spoke structures react less to delays than airlines operating fully connected configurations. In particular, network airlines have incentives to keep frequency high even if this is at the expense of a greater congestion at their hub airports. We also show that airlines in slot-constrained airports seem to react to higher levels of congestion by using bigger aircraft at lower frequencies; thus, we conclude that conditioning the number of available slots on the levels of delays at the airport seems an effective measure that creates the right incentives for airlines to reduce the congestion they generate.

Keywords: Airline networks; airport congestion; delays

JEL classifications: L13; L93; R41

INTRODUCTION

The deregulation of air transportation allowed carriers to make strategic choices about fares and networks. Network airlines increasingly concentrate their services at a small number of hub airports at which they channel a high

The Economics of Airport Operations
Advances in Airline Economics, Volume 6, 335–359

ISSN: 2212-1609/doi:10.1108/S2212-160920170000006013

proportion of their total flights. At these hubs, dominant network carriers exploit transfer traffic through coordinated banks of arrivals and departures. The operation of such hub-and-spoke (HS) configurations enables airlines to reduce their costs since they can exploit economies of traffic density and offer high flight frequencies, the latter being greatly valued by business and connecting passengers.[1] As Flores-Fillol (2010) points out, network carriers have strong incentives to add new routes to their HS networks because by doing so they gain simultaneous access to one new local market and many connecting markets. By offering a wide diversified range of destinations, hub airports contribute substantially to the competitiveness of firms located in the urban areas under their influence.[2] While low-cost carriers (LCC) may also concentrate their traffic in just a few airports, they basically operate fully connected (FC) networks in which most air services are point-to-point.

However, the concentration of traffic favored by HS networks has contributed to an increase in airport congestion causing delays, cancellations, and missed connections, all of which ends up having a detrimental impact on passengers and airlines alike. Congestion is a severe problem and it is especially worrisome in HS networks.[3]

HS networks, therefore, are associated with both positive and negative effects. Our main aim is to examine the negative effects associated with congestion. In particular, this chapter aims at understanding the extent to which airlines react to airport congestion. More specifically, we seek to test the impact of airline network type on carriers' reactions to congestion: that is, do airlines operating HS and FC networks behave differently?

The theoretical analysis in Fageda and Flores-Fillol (2015) shows that airline profits are higher under HS networks without congestion and that this result is typically reinforced in the presence of congestion. Therefore, this analysis suggests that network airlines have few incentives to deviate flights out of their hub airports. The empirical analysis performed in this chapter extends the work in Fageda and Flores-Fillol (2016) and confirms that the effect of airline network structure on airport congestion is fundamental and provides some evidence about the different reaction to congestion of carriers operating HS networks as compared with carriers operating FC networks. Using data for the period 2005–2015 from all US airports located in urban areas having more than two million inhabitants in 2015, we find that airlines operating under HS networks react less to delays than the other airlines in their decisions about capacities. Thus, airlines operating HS networks seem to ignore the social costs (i.e., airport congestion) resulting from their network choice. Therefore, network airlines have incentives to keep capacity high even if this is at the expense of greater congestion at their hub airports. The rationale behind this result would seem to lie in the higher yield associated with flight banks; the cost savings from an intense exploitation of economies of traffic density; and the strategic behavior of airlines that may adopt a preemptive strategy so as to avoid losing market power, which involves releasing slots that might be taken over by other competing airlines. In addition, our analysis also shows that airlines in slot-constrained airports seem to react to higher levels of congestion by using bigger aircraft at lower frequencies. Thus, the criteria governing the allocation of slots (in particular the "use-it-or-lose it" rule) may create incentives for airlines to operate higher frequencies with smaller aircraft. Therefore, conditioning the number of available slots on the levels of delays at the airport seems an effective measure that creates the right incentives for airlines to reduce the congestion they generate.

The rest of this paper is organized as follows. In the next section, we present a literature review. The theoretical framework is presented in the "Model and Equilibrium Analysis" section. The "Data" section explains the data used in the empirical analysis. In "The Empirical Model" section, we specify the empirical model and state our expectations for the explanatory variables. The "Estimation and Results" section reports the regression results. The last section contains our concluding remarks along with some policy implications.

LITERATURE REVIEW

In this section, we review the different literature strands that are related to our analysis.

Network choice. Brueckner (2004) studies a monopoly network choice between HS and FC networks and shows that airlines exhibit an inefficient bias toward HS networks. Fageda and Flores-Fillol (2015) extend the analysis to a duopoly market structure and obtain a similar result as in Brueckner (2004). Flores-Fillol (2009) adopts a game-theoretic approach to study network choice in partially served markets. He shows that carriers adopt hubbing strategies when costs are sufficiently low and that flight frequency can become excessive under HS network configurations.

Internalization of congestion. Most studies of airport congestion analyze the relationship between delays and airport concentration, focusing on the internalization debate. The internalization hypothesis states that airlines at heavily concentrated airports are likely to internalize the effects of self-imposed congestion. Daniel (1995) is the first that recognizes the potential for internalization. However, he supports the idea that carriers behave atomistically due to the competitive pressure exerted by fringe carriers (a result that is confirmed in Daniel & Harback, 2008). Differently, Brueckner (2002) proposes a model that relates internalization of congestion with market power. Mayer and Sinai (2003) demonstrate that, even though delays at hub airports can be longer than those at non-hub gateways, increasing airport concentration does reduce these delays. Rupp (2009), however, reverses Mayer and Sinai's findings, using a different measure of delays. Brueckner and Van Dender (2008) seek a consensus in the internalization debate by showing that some competitive scenarios do lead to self-internalization, while others do not.

Negative effects of congestion. The potentially negative effects associated with congestion may be substantial both for passengers and airlines, as reported in several empirical studies. For example, Forbes (2008) uses data from New York–La Guardia airport (one of the four slot-constrained airports in the United States) to study price responses to flight delays. She finds an average price reduction per additional minute of delay of \$1.42 for direct passengers; this price decrease amounts to \$0.77 for connecting passengers. Britto, Dresner, and Voltes (2012) examine the impact of delays on consumer and producer welfare for a sample of the US routes. They find that delays raise prices and reduce demand. From their results, a 10% decrease in delays implies a benefit of \$1.50–\$2.50 per passenger, while the gains for airlines of reducing delays are about three times higher. Peterson, Neels, Barczi, and Graham (2013) use a recursive-dynamic model to examine the costs of flight delays both for airlines and passengers, finding that a 10% reduction in delayed flights increases net US welfare by \$17.6 billion.

Impact of delays on airline frequencies. While several works analyze the determinants of delays, less attention has been devoted to the impact of delays on airline frequencies.[4] The exceptions are the studies by Pai (2010) and Zou and Hansen (2014), which yield contradictory results that are reconciled in Fageda and Flores-Fillol (2016). Using data for a sample of the US routes, Pai (2010) finds a negative relationship between frequencies and delays. More precisely, he concludes that every extra minute of delay at the airports of origin or destination could result in 2–3 fewer flights per month. By contrast, Zou and Hansen (2014), also using a sample of the US routes, find a positive relationship between frequencies and delays.[5] Finally, Fageda and Flores-Fillol (2016) use data on 50 large US continental airports, including all hubs and the country's most congested airports during the period 2005–2013 and show that airlines operating FC configurations reduce frequencies in response to more frequent delays, whereas airlines operating HS structures increase frequencies.

Airline network structure and airport congestion. There are few previous studies relating airline network structure and airport congestion. Brueckner (2002) shows that delays are higher in hub airports after controlling for airport size and other airport attributes. Baumgarten, Malina, and Lange (2014) suggest that HS operations may aggravate congestion problems at peak times because more flights are operated for a given capacity during banks. Furthermore, the larger number of connecting passengers results in an increasing complexity of airport and airline operations. Finally, Daniel and Harback (2008) show that dominant airlines at many major US hub airports concentrate their flights at peak times, thereby forcing non-hubbing airlines to cluster their traffic in uncongested periods. They do not observe this effect in non-hub airports.

Slot-distribution regimes. Brueckner (2009) finds that a slot-distribution regime, where slots are distributed to the carriers and then traded through a clearing house, is equivalent to an efficient regime of differentiated congestion tolls. He recommends policy measures to endow carriers with clear property rights over slots to foster more active slot trading. Vaze and Barnhart (2012) show that a small reduction in the allocated slots at a congested airport results in a large reduction in average passenger delays.

The main contribution of our analysis takes place in the latter two literature strands, since (i) we study the different behavior of network and point-to-point airlines with respect to airport congestion and (ii) we also assess the effectiveness of slot-constraint regimes.

MODEL AND EQUILIBRIUM ANALYSIS

In the material that follows, we present a reduced version of the model in Fageda and Flores-Fillol (2015) that contains the main insights motivating our empirical exercise.

We assume the simplest possible network with three cities (*A*, *B*, and *H*), two airlines (1 and 2), and three city-pair markets (*AH*, *BH*, and *AB*). *AB* can be served either nonstop (FC network) or via hub *H* (HS network), as shown in Fig. 1.

Passenger population size in each market is normalized to unity and we limit market power by assuming fully served markets. The two symmetric networks are compared, so that we are implicitly assuming a coordination game with two symmetric equilibria and our purpose is to develop a focal criterion to select the Pareto-superior equilibrium.

FC Network

Utility for a passenger traveling with carrier 1 is

$$u_1 = \underbrace{y - p_1}_{\textit{Consumption}} - \underbrace{\frac{\gamma}{f_1}}_{\textit{Expected schedule delay}} - \underbrace{\lambda(4f_1 + 4f_2)}_{\textit{Congestion damage}} + \underbrace{b + a}_{\textit{Travel benefit}} \tag{1}$$

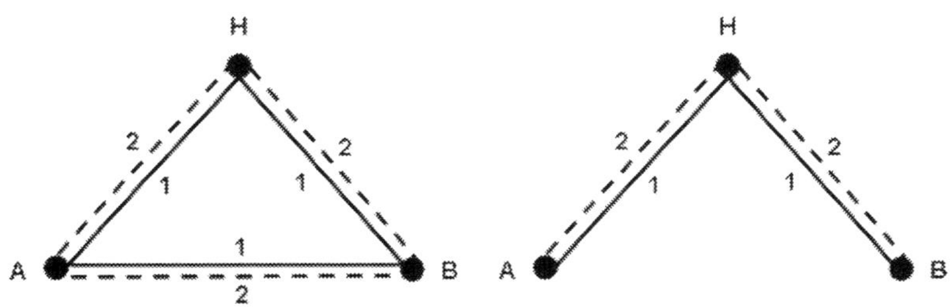

Fig. 1. The FC and HS Networks.

Consumption equals $y - p_1$, where p_1 is airline 1's fare and y denotes income. The *expected schedule delay* is decreasing with frequency, where $\gamma > 0$ captures the disutility of schedule delay (as Brueckner, 2004). The *congestion damage* depends on the aircraft movements at the origin and destination airports ($2f_1 + 2f_2$ at each airport), where $\lambda \geq 0$ captures the disutility of congestion (as Flores-Fillol, 2010). Finally, *travel benefit* includes the gain from travel (b) and the airline brand-loyalty (a), which is uniformly distributed over $[-\alpha/2, \alpha/2]$ and denotes the utility gain from using airline 1 (as Brueckner & Flores-Fillol, 2007). Interestingly, α measures product differentiation. The analysis is presented for carrier 1 (expressions for carrier 2 are derived analogously).

A passenger loyal to 1 (with $a > 0$) will fly with her preferred carrier when $y - p_1 - \gamma/f_1 + b + a > y - p_2 - \gamma/f_2 + b$, i.e., when $a > p_1 - p_2 + \gamma/f_1 - \gamma/f_2 \equiv \hat{a}$. Then, carrier 1's traffic is

$$q_1 = \int_{\hat{a}}^{\alpha/2} \frac{1}{\alpha} da = \frac{1}{2} - \frac{1}{\alpha}(p_1 - p_2 + \gamma/f_1 - \gamma/f_2) \tag{2}$$

Carrier 1's total costs on a route are

$$c_1 = f_1 \left[\underbrace{\theta}_{\text{Fixed cost}} + \underbrace{\tau s_1}_{\text{Seat cost}} + \underbrace{\eta(4f_1 + 4f_2)}_{\text{Congestion cost}} \right] \tag{3}$$

where τ is the marginal cost per seat, s_1 is carrier 1's aircraft size, and $\eta \geq 0$ denotes airlines' congestion damage. As in Brueckner (2004), the cost per seat falls with aircraft size, capturing the presence of economies of traffic density. Frequency, aircraft size, and traffic are related by $s_1 = q_1/f_1$.[6] Therefore (3) can be rewritten as

$$c_1 = \theta f_1 + \tau q_1 + f_1 \eta(4f_1 + 4f_2) \tag{4}$$

Airline 1's profit is $\pi_1 = 3(p_1 q_1 - c_1)$ and, using (4), it becomes

$$\pi_1 = 3\left\{ \underbrace{(p_1 - \tau)q_1}_{\text{Margin}} - \underbrace{f_1[\theta + 4\eta(f_1 + f_2)]}_{\text{Congestion and fixed cost}} \right\} \tag{5}$$

Airlines maximize profits by choosing fares and frequencies. Plugging (2) into (5), $\partial\pi_1/\partial p_1$ and $\partial\pi_1/\partial f_1$ can be computed.[7] From $\partial\pi_1/\partial p_1$, after applying symmetry, we obtain $p = \tau + \alpha/2$ and $\partial\pi_1/\partial f_1$ yields

$$\underbrace{12\eta f^3}_{A(f)} = \underbrace{\frac{\gamma}{2} - \theta f^2}_{B(f)} \tag{6}$$

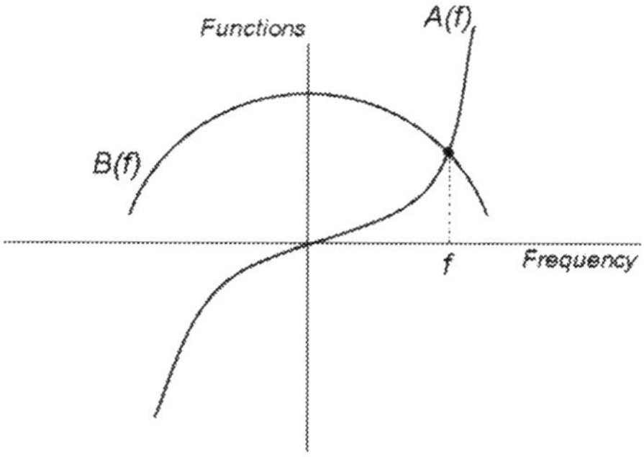

Fig. 2. The f Solution.

The equilibrium frequency is found graphically in Fig. 2, at the intersection between a cubic and a quadratic expression.

HS Network

Under HS networks, the route AB is eliminated and AB passengers change planes at the hub. Thus, airline 1 maximizes

$$\pi_1^h = \underbrace{2\left(p_1^h - \tau\right)q_1^h}_{\textit{Local margin}} + \underbrace{\left(P_1^h - 2\tau\right)Q_1^h}_{\textit{Connecting margin}} - \underbrace{2f_1^h\left[\theta + 3\eta\left(f_1^h + f_2^h\right)\right]}_{\textit{Congestion and fixed cost}} \tag{7}$$

where superscript h denotes HS and P_1^h and Q_1^h are fares and traffic in market AB. Airline's congestion cost on a route is given by $\eta\left(3f_1^h + 3f_2^h\right)$ because congestion on a route is caused by aircraft movements both at the hub $\left(2f_1^h + 2f_2^h\right)$ and at the spoke airport $\left(f_1^h + f_2^h\right)$. Profit maximization yields $p^h = \tau + \alpha/2$ and $P^h = 2\tau + \alpha/2$ and the condition for frequency is

$$\underbrace{6\eta\left(f^h\right)^3}_{A^h(f)} = \underbrace{\frac{\gamma}{2} - \frac{2\theta}{3}\left(f^h\right)^2}_{B^h(f)} \tag{8}$$

The equilibrium is generated by a diagram analogous to Fig. 2.

Comparison of Frequencies and Profits

Equilibrium frequencies are compared in Fig. 3, using Eqs. (6) and (8).

The f^2-coefficient and the height of the cubic curve in the positive quadrant are greater in the FC case.

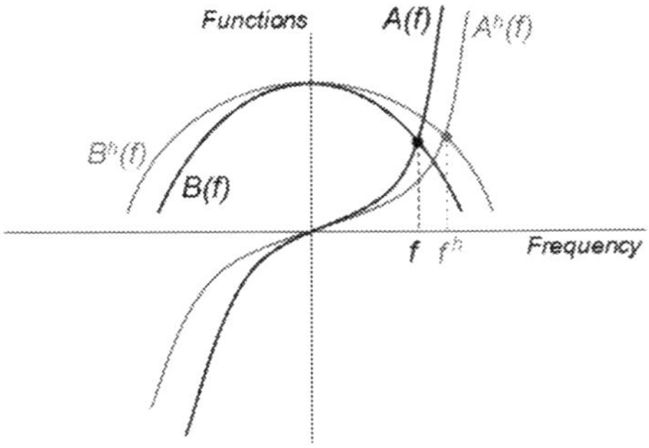

Fig. 3. Comparing f and f^h.

Proposition 1. Frequency is higher in HS networks: $f^h > f$.

Frequency is higher under HS networks because there is more traffic on each of the two active routes. The total number of flights operated by an airline under FC networks is $3f$ since three routes are active, whereas an airline under HS networks operates $2f^h$ flights.

Assumption 1. HS operations reduce the number of flights: $2f^h < 3f$.

This seems a natural expectation since HS networks are meant to cut airline costs by operating fewer routes. $s < s^h$ is a realistic implication observed under Assumption 1. HS configurations provide the passengers with higher frequency and allow airlines to make cost savings due to the presence of economies of traffic density as the aircraft size can be larger.

Comparing equilibrium profits is not trivial because the closed-form solution for frequency is complex. However, this comparison can be completed by recasting the optimization as a two-stage problem, where fares are first chosen conditional on frequency, and frequency is then chosen.

Substituting the equilibrium p into Eq. (5) and applying symmetry, we obtain

$$\pi_1(f) = \frac{3\alpha}{4} - 3\theta f - 24\eta f^2 \tag{9}$$

where the first factor 3 denotes the number of markets served; the second factor 3 indicates the number of routes operated; and the factor 24 shows that each of the routes is affected by eight aircraft movements.

Substituting the equilibrium p^h and P^h into (7) and applying symmetry, we obtain

$$\pi_1^h(f^h) = \frac{3\alpha}{4} - 2\theta f^h - 12\eta (f^h)^2 \tag{10}$$

where factors 3 and 2 denote that the airline serves three markets but only two routes; and the factor 12 shows that each of the routes is affected by six aircraft movements.

Using (9) and (10), the HS–FC profit differential yields

$$\Delta = \pi_1^h(f^h) - \pi_1(f) = \underbrace{\theta(3f - 2f^h)}_{>0\ (HS\ advantage)} + \underbrace{12\eta\left[2f^2 - (f^h)^2\right]}_{\substack{>0\ for\ f^h < 1.4f\ (HS\ advantage) \\ <0\ for\ f^h > 1.4f\ (HS\ disadvantage)}} \tag{11}$$

The first term is positive and captures the aircraft's fixed cost advantage of HS networks from operating only two routes. The second term can be positive or negative and captures the congestion cost advantage that can favor either network structure.

> **Proposition 2.** Without congestion ($\lambda = \eta = 0$), airline profits are higher under HS networks. In the presence of congestion, airline profits are higher under HS networks when $f^h \leq 1.4f$.

The sign of Δ is unclear for $f^h > 1.4f$. Corollary 1 analyzes the effect of congestion on Δ.

> **Corollary 1.** Congestion increases the profitability of HS networks ($\partial\Delta/\partial\eta > 0$) for $f^h < 1.4f$ and decreases the profitability of HS networks ($\partial\Delta/\partial\eta < 0$) for $1.4f < f^h < 3f/2$.

Congestion creates incentives for airlines to adopt HS networks, except for $1.4f < f^h < 3f/2$. When f^h is very high and falls within this interval, the sign of Δ is ambiguous and congestion acts as a brake on hubbing strategies.

DATA

We have data for all US airports located in urban areas having more than two million inhabitants in 2015. The analysis is made for the period 2005–2015. These urban areas are the following (airport codes in parentheses): Atlanta (ATL), Boston (BOS), Baltimore (BWI), Chicago (ORD and MDW), Dallas (DFW and DAL), Denver (DEN), Detroit (DTW), Houston (IAH and HOU), Miami (MIA), Minneapolis (MSP), New York (JFK, LGA, and EWR), Las Vegas (LAS), Los Angeles (LAX), Philadelphia (PHL), Phoenix (PHX), Portland (PDX), Sacramento (SMF), Saint Louis (STL), San Antonio (SAT), San Diego (SAN), Seattle (SEA), Washington (DCA and IAD), and Tampa (TPA). The data focus on domestic traffic (i.e., international flights are excluded).

We use the information provided by major carriers in the United States. In particular, our data considers flights offered by legacy carriers (Alaska, American, Continental, Delta, Northwest, United, and US Airways) and low-cost airlines (America West, AirTran, Frontier, Jet Blue, Midwest, Southwest, Spirit, Sun Country, and Virgin America).

The unit of observation of our regressions is the pair airline–airport and our final sample comprises 3,311 observations. The dependent variables in the empirical analysis are frequencies and mean aircraft size offered by airlines at the airport level. These data have been obtained from RDC Aviation (Capstats Statistics). As an explanatory variable, we include a measure of congestion at the airport level which is measured as the percentage of originating flights delayed by more than 15 minutes at a given airport. Data regarding delays have been obtained from the US Department of Transportation. We also consider other variables that may affect demand of flights at the airports of our sample: population and GDP per capita. These data are obtained from the US Census, which refer to the Metropolitan Statistical Area (MSA) where the airport is located. Furthermore, we also include the concentration index (in terms of departures) at the airport level, which is built using data from RDC Aviation.

Table 1 shows some descriptive statistics of the urban areas and airports included in the empirical analysis. In particular, this table provides information on the mean values of population (urban area), seats, and airport delays during the considered period. The sample of airports includes, on the one hand, the biggest US airports like ATL, ORD or DFW and, on the other hand, relatively small airports like SMF, SAT, PDX or the secondary airports in Dallas and Houston (DAL and HOU). The record of delays is high for all airports: even the airport with the lowest proportion of delayed flights, PDX, has around 15% of delayed flights. On the other extreme, we find that most congested airports in our sample, EWR and ORD, have a proportion of delayed flights of about 30%.

Fig. 4 shows the relationship between the levels of congestion and the size of the airports in our sample. The figure provides evidence of a positive relationship between both measures as it could be expected. However, the slope of the curve that depicts this figure does not seem to be too steep. In fact, we can find similar-size airports recording very different levels of congestion. For example, although HOU and SMF are very similar in terms of total seats, HOU is much more congested. In the same vein, EWR is much more congested than BWI; and PHL is much more congested than SEA for almost identical sizes (at least in terms of seats offered by major carriers for domestic flights). Hence, the size of the airport is not the only factor explaining the congestion level at an airport. Aside of the pressure that the demand imposes to a fixed capacity (in the short term), other relevant factors may include severe weather or congestion in the air space (particularly relevant for major urban areas). However, the focus of our study is on how airlines react to airport congestion as they choose

Table 1. Descriptive Statistics of the Airports Included in the Sample.

City	Airport	Population (millions)	Seats (millions)	Delays (percentage of total flights with delays exceeding 15 minutes)
Atlanta	ATL	4.6	51	24.65
Boston	BOS	4.1	16	23.50
Baltimore	BWI	2.2	15	22.47
Dallas	DAL	5.2	6	21.89
Washington	DCA	4.6	13	21.20
Denver	DEN	2.4	30	23.32
Dallas	DFW	5.2	33	25.18
Detroit	DTW	3.7	19	24.01
New York	EWR	18.3	15	30.58
Houston	HOU	5.1	8	24.33
Washington	IAD	4.6	11	24.67
Houston	IAH	5.1	19	22.13
New York	JFK	18.3	15	27.51
Las Vegas	LAS	2.0	26	21.82
Los Angeles	LAX	12.1	30	19.52
New York	LGA	18.3	17	26.48
Chicago	MDW	8.6	14	24.75
Miami	MIA	5.5	11	25.30
Minneapolis	MSP	2.7	19	22.17
Chicago	ORD	8.6	37	29.53
Portland	PDX	1.9	9	15.17
Philadelphia	PHL	5.4	19	26.13
Phoenix	PHX	3.7	27	19.30
San Diego	SAN	3.0	12	18.05
San Antonio	SAT	1.8	5	17.51
Seattle	SEA	3.1	19	18.84
San Francisco	SFO	3.2	20	24.53
Sacramento	SMF	1.8	7	17.63
Saint Louis	STL	2.1	10	20.98
Tampa	TPA	2.5	11	17.56

their capacity (measured either by frequency or aircraft size). In particular, we want to identify the effect of the type of network that the airline operates and whether the airport is subject to slot constraints.

We make the distinction between airlines that operate HS networks and airlines that operate FC networks (or point-to-point networks). Taking into

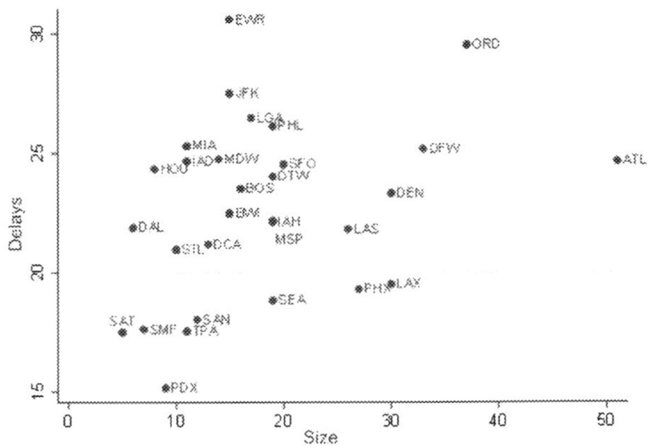

Fig. 4. Delays and Size of Airports in the Sample.

account that the unit of observation in our sample is the pair airline–airport, we consider airlines operating under HS network to be those airlines with a high share (more than 30%) at a certain airport. Our analysis assumes that the dominant airlines operate in an HS manner at their dominated airports, while the rest of airlines provide point-to-point connections.

Furthermore, we make the distinction between airports subject to slot constraints and the rest of airports. To address congestion, the Federal Aviation Administration (FAA) limits the number of flights that airlines make per hour in three airports in New York (EWR, JFK, and LGA) and one airport in Washington (DCA).[8] Indeed, airlines must obtain operating authorizations called slots from FAA to offer flights from/to these four airports. Slots may be leased and traded at any of the slot-controlled airports, taking into account that temporary restrictions to purchase or sell are often imposed at the airports of New York. The rules also contain a provision designed to encourage airlines to actively use their airport capacity. In particular, airlines are required to attain a minimum utilization rate of 80% of their assigned slots ("use-it-or-lose-it rule").

Table 2 shows the evolution of competition at the airport level using two measures: the share of the main airline at the airport and the Herfindahl–Hirschman concentration index (HHI). The HHI index is calculated as the sum of the squares of airlines' market shares in terms of flight frequencies. Both variables are expressed in terms of the total flights offered at the airport. We report the values for the first and the last year of the considered period. The share of the dominant airline is usually well above 50%. The only airports that are not clearly dominated by a particular airline are BOS, DCA, JFK, and LAX. In the cases of ORD and PHX, two airlines have a very high share of total flights. Consistently with these facts, most of airports are also characterized by a very high HHI index. In general, the intensity of competition

Table 2. Evolution of Competition at the Airport Level.

City	Airport	Share Main Airline (2005)	Share Main Airline (2015)	Concentration Index (2005)	Concentration Index (2015)
Atlanta	ATL	Delta (0.77)	Delta (0.78)	0.62	0.63
Boston	BOS	Delta (0.23)	Jet Blue (0.28)	0.15	0.15
Baltimore	BWI	Southwest (0.60)	Southwest (0.73)	0.38	0.54
Dallas	DAL	Southwest (0.96)	Southwest (0.90)	0.92	0.82
Washington	DCA	US Airways (0.42)	US Airways (0.29)	0.23	0.17
Denver	DEN	United (0.57)	United (0.42)	0.36	0.29
Dallas	DFW	American Airlines (0.81)	American Airlines (0.84)	0.67	0.67
Detroit	DTW	Northwest (0.75)	Delta (0.73)	0.58	0.55
New York	EWR	Continental (0.66)	United (0.72)	0.45	0.53
Houston	HOU	Southwest (0.91)	Southwest (0.93)	0.82	0.86
Washington	IAD	United (0.50)	United (0.70)	0.26	0.50
Houston	IAH	Continental (0.83)	United (0.78)	0.70	0.61
New York	JFK	Jet Blue (0.42)	Delta & Jet Blue (0.34)	0.29	0.26
Las Vegas	LAS	Southwest (0.40)	Southwest (0.46)	0.22	0.24
Los Angeles	LAX	United (0.26)	American Airlines (0.21)	0.17	0.16
New York	LGA	Delta & US Airways (0.24)	Delta (0.42)	0.17	0.24
Chicago	MDW	Southwest (0.67)	Southwest (0.96)	0.46	0.92
Miami	MIA	American Airlines (0.70)	American Airlines (0.76)	0.50	0.61
Minneapolis	MSP	Northwest (0.75)	Delta (0.70)	0.56	0.51
Chicago	ORD	United (0.51)	United (0.44)	0.41	0.35
Portland	PDX	Alaska Airlines (0.38)	Alaska Airlines (0.45)	0.22	0.26
Philadelphia	PHL	US Airways (0.63)	US Airways (0.58)	0.42	0.38
Phoenix	PHX	Southwest (0.37)	US Airways (0.36)	0.31	0.27
San Diego	SAN	Southwest (0.41)	Southwest (0.41)	0.22	0.22
San Antonio	SAT	Southwest (0.43)	Southwest (0.43)	0.25	0.28
Seattle	SEA	Alaska Airlines (0.51)	Alaska Airlines (0.54)	0.30	0.35
San Francisco	SFO	United (0.53)	United (0.46)	0.32	0.26
Sacramento	SMF	Southwest (0.57)	Southwest (0.57)	0.36	0.36
Saint Louis	STL	American Airlines (0.45)	Southwest (0.55)	0.32	0.35
Tampa	TPA	Southwest (0.30)	Southwest (0.40)	0.15	0.23

at the airport level remains constant during the considered period, although a sharp increase both in the share of the main airline and the HHI index is observed in BWI, IAD, and MDW. Note that Southwest, which is not a legacy carrier, is the airline with the highest number of dominated airports in our sample. Finally, it is also worth mentioning that slot constraints could impose an entry barrier to new carriers (GAO, 2012; Vaze & Barnhart, 2012) but data in Table 2 suggest that competition at slot-constrained airports is not weaker (and it is not getting worse) as compared to other airports.

Fig. 5 shows the evolution of the delayed flights at the airports included in our sample, differentiating by the type of airline that dominates the airport (legacy vs. low-cost). While the levels of congestion were clearly higher in airports dominated by legacy carriers at the beginning of the period, the performance of the airports dominated by low-cost airlines has worsened from 2013 onwards. In fact, the proportion of delayed flights in 2014 and 2015 has been higher in airports dominated by low-cost airlines. This may provide some indirect evidence on the convergence of network configurations of legacy and low-cost airlines, i.e., low-cost airlines are also adopting HS networks around their dominated airports.

Fig. 6 shows the evolution of the delayed flights at the airports in our sample, differentiating by the absence or presence of slot constraints. We focus on urban areas with more than 4 million in inhabitants because slot-constrained airports are located in populated cities (New York and Washington). Hence, this focus on big cities allows us to have a more comparable benchmark.

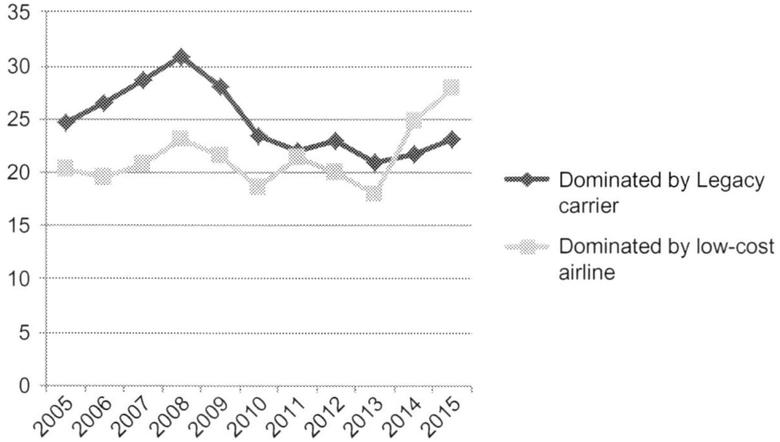

Fig. 5. Evolution of Airport Delays by Type of Airline. *Note*: Airports dominated by legacy carriers are ATL, DFW, DTW, EWR, IAD, IAH, MIA, ORD, PHL, SEA, and SFO; Airports dominated by low-cost airlines are BWI, DAI, HOU, MDW, SAN, SMF, and STL.

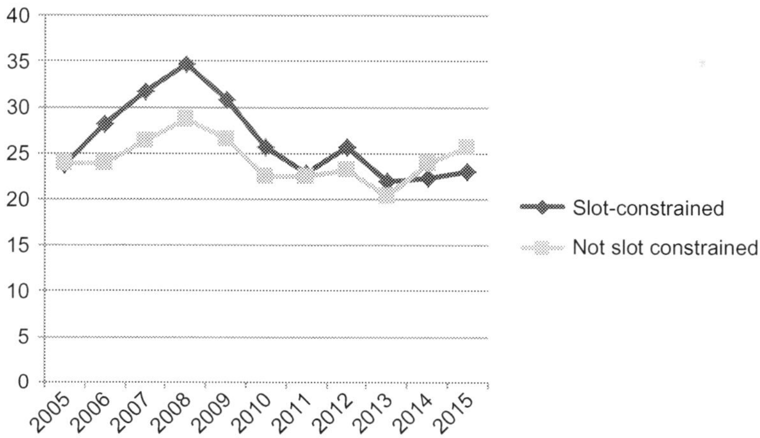

Fig. 6. Evolution of Delays by Type of Airport (urban areas > 4 mill. inhabitants). *Note*: Slot-constrained airports are EWR, JFK, DCA, and LGA; Airports that are not slot constrained include ATL, DFW, IAD, IAH, MIA, ORD, PHL, DAI, HOU, MDW, BOS, and LAX.

The performance of the slot-constrained airports has improved substantially since 2008. In fact, the proportion of delayed flights in the last 2 years of the considered period is lower in those airports. Taking into account this evidence, slot constraints could be seen as effective measures containing the levels of congestion and, therefore, their application to other congested airports could be a reasonable recommendation.

THE EMPIRICAL MODEL

We estimate the following equation for airline i at airport a from urban area u

$$\begin{aligned} Y_{i,a,t} = {} & \beta_0 + \beta_1 Pop_{u,t-1} + \beta_2 GDPpc_{u,t-1} + \beta_3 HHI_{a,t-1} + \beta_4 D_{i,a}^{mergers} + \beta_5 D_a^{slot} \\ & + \beta_6 Delays_{a,t-1} + \beta_7 D_{i,a}^{HS\_legacy} + \beta_8 D_{i,a}^{no\_legacy} + \beta_9 D_{i,a}^{dominant\_no\_legacy} \\ & + \beta_{10} D_{i,a}^{HS\_legacy} xDelays_{a,t-1} + \beta_{11} D_{i,a}^{no\_legacy} xDelays_{a,t-1} \\ & + \beta_{12} D_{i,a}^{dominant\_no\_legacy} xDelays_{a,t-1} + \beta_{13} D_a^{slot} Delays_{a,t-1} + \mu_t + \varepsilon \qquad (12) \end{aligned}$$

The dependent variables are the total number of annual flights and the mean annual aircraft size that each airline offers at the corresponding airport. The explanatory variables refer to year $t-1$ because airline capacity choices at the airport level in period t are influenced by airport and airline features in the previous period.

Among the explanatory factors, we include variables related to local demand: population ($Pop_{u,t-1}$) and GDP per capita ($GDPpc_{u,t-1}$). We can expect a positive sign for the coefficients associated with the population and income variables. Airlines may have incentives to increase the capacity on routes departing from airports located in areas with a higher local demand. Thus, the demand for airline services should be higher in airports located in more populated and richer urban areas. The HHI concentration index at the airport level is also considered ($HHI_{a,t-1}$). Airlines operating at more concentrated airports typically offer a higher capacity because they have higher yields and also due to a better exploitation of density economies. However, capacities could also be lower as a result of weaker competition (i.e., market-power effect), especially in terms of frequencies.

Furthermore, we include a variable that is aimed at controlling the mergers that have taken place during the considered period ($D_{i,a}^{mergers}$). This variable takes the value one for observations whose values may be distorted by a merger. This includes data for America West in 2007, Northwest in 2009, Continental in 2012, and AirTran in 2014. These airlines ended a merger/takeover process with other airlines during these years. Furthermore, this variable takes the value one for Delta in the hubs of Northwest since 2010 and for United in the hubs of Continental since 2012. The merger between American Airlines and US Airways finished in 2015 and, therefore, does not affect our analysis.

We also include a dummy variable that takes the value one for slot-constrained airports, as slot constraints may affect airlines' capacity choices (D_a^{slot}). Indeed, the criteria governing the slot allocation process are based on historical precedents and "use-it-or-lose-it" rules. Hence, airlines may have incentives to over-schedule flights in order to avoid losing the slots or underutilize the slots they do operate at slot-controlled airports by using smaller aircraft. In fact, GAO (2012) shows that airlines at slot-constrained airports use smaller aircraft than at other airports of similar size.

Along with these control variables, we consider a measure of airport congestion which is constructed as the percentage of total flights at the airport suffering a delay exceeding 15 minutes ($Delays_{a,t-1}$). Airlines could reduce capacities when delays increase due to higher operation costs but, alternatively, they could also increase capacities to obtain higher yields and to avoid losing market power (preemptive strategy).

Furthermore, we consider a set of dummy variables for airlines operating different network structures. First, we consider a dummy variable for legacy carriers at their hub airports ($D_{i,a}^{HS\_legacy}$).[9] We assume that these airlines operate HS networks. We also include a dummy variable that takes the value one for airlines that are not legacy carriers ($D_{i,a}^{no\_legacy}$). Additionally, we consider a dummy variable for airlines that are not legacy carriers and operate at airports they dominate ($D_{i,a}^{dominant\_no\_legacy}$).[10] This latter variable is only included in some specifications. In these specifications, the variable $D_{i,a}^{no\_legacy}$ does not include non-legacy carriers in their dominated airports. In all the cases, legacy carriers not operating at their hub airports are the reference case. We assume that, in such reference case, airlines operate FC networks.

Controlling for local demand, capacities of legacy carriers at their hub airports should be higher than the capacities of other airlines. The reason for this is the exploitation of connecting traffic, which is independent from local demand. Furthermore, we should not expect relevant differences between non-legacy carriers and legacy carriers that do not operate at their hubs in terms of capacities because both types of airlines operate FC networks. Having said this, frequencies may be higher and aircraft smaller for legacy carriers if they are using regional services from airports that are not their hubs.[11] Also note that Southwest can provide connecting services at its dominated airports, taking into account the high amount of flights that it offers. Hence, differences in capacity choices between Southwest at their dominated hubs and legacy carriers at their hubs could be modest.

Finally, we include interaction variables that are formed by the aforementioned set of dummy variables and the measure of congestion ($D_{i,a}^{HS\_legacy} xDelays_{a,t-1}$, $D_{i,a}^{no\_legacy} xDelays_{a,t-1}$, and $D_{i,a}^{dominant\_no\_legacy} xDelays_{a,t-1}$) and the dummy variable for slot-constrained airports and the measure of congestion ($D_{a}^{slot} xDelays_{a,t-1}$).

The relationship between capacities and delays for the legacy carriers operating at their hubs is determined by coefficients β_6 and β_{10}, while the same relationship for non-legacy carriers is determined by either β_6 and β_{11} or β_6 and β_{12}. If airlines operating HS networks (legacy carriers at their hubs and possibly non-legacy carriers at their dominated airports) react less to delays than airlines operating FC networks, we should expect $\beta_{10}>0$, $\beta_{12}>0$, $\beta_{10}>\beta_{11}$, and $\beta_{12}>\beta_{11}$. Furthermore, the relationship between capacities and delays for slot-constrained airports is determined by coefficients β_6 and β_{13}. If airlines operating at slot-constrained airports react less to delays than airlines operating in other airports, then we should expect $\beta_{13}>0$.

Finally, (12) also includes time fixed effects (μ_t) that capture shocks common to all airports and airlines occurred in the considered period.

ESTIMATION AND RESULTS

Table 3 shows the results of the estimation when the dependent variable is airline frequency at the airport level, while Table 4 shows the results when the dependent variable is the mean aircraft size offered by airlines at the airport

Table 3. Results of Estimates (Airline Frequencies at the Airport Level).

Explanatory Variables	(1)	(2)	(3)	(4)
$Pop_{u,t-1}$	0.50 (0.12)***	0.72 (0.13)***	0.66 (0.13)***	0.67 (0.12)***
$GDPpc_{u,t-1}$	−0.09 (0.03)***	−0.12 (0.03)***	−0.09 (0.03)***	−0.007 (0.02)
$HHI_{a,t-1}$	3010.68 (2319.2)	2356.79 (2307.14)	3616.09 (2318.72)	−1474.07 (1974.04)
$D_{i,a}^{mergers}$	−6643.39 (2435.38)***	−6469.60 (1822.41)***	−5179.60 (2020.36)***	−3507.98 (2016.09)***
$Delays_{a,t-1}$	179.18 (105.72)*	325.22 (110.52)***	23.86 (84.95)	116.19 (75.12)
D_{a}^{slot}	−1418.83 (1587.35)	25578.95 (5031.95)***	20991.1 (5100.05)***	20991.1 (5100.05)***
$D_{i,a}^{HSlegacy}$	129335.6 (5326.13)***	129329.4 (5293.52)***	45117.62 (19957.43)**	45072.11 (20017.12)**
$D_{i,a}^{nolegacy}$	683.87 (588.01)	611.03 (588.45)	−395.77 (2270.79)	−5180.50 (1632.90)***
$D_{i,a}^{dominant_{n}olegacy}$	–	–	–	10214.49 (8516.99)
$D_{i,a}^{HSlegacy} xDelays_{a,t-1}$	–	–	3518.62 (809.42)***	3517.61 (810.83)***
$D_{i,a}^{nolegacy} xDelays_{a,t-1}$	–	–	40.85 (100.96)	61.76 (73.42)
$D_{i,a}^{dominant_{n}olegacy} xDelays_{a,t-1}$	–	–	–	1764.61 (392.30)***
$D_{a}^{slot} xDelays_{a,t-1}$	–	−1121.14 (198.57)***	−915.71 (204.71)***	−1062.65 (191.58)***
Intercept	6632.06 (2435.38)***	4385.59 (2467.51)*	8858.71 (2111.06)	3945.94 (1908.24)**
Time fixed effects	YES	YES	YES	YES
R^2 Test F (joint sign.) Number observations	0.64 50.35*** 3311	0.66 44.48*** 3311	0.66 45.11** 3311	0.72 70.88*** 3311

Notes: Standard errors in parentheses (robust to heteroscedasticity); Statistical significance at 1% (***), 5% (**), and 10% (*).

Table 4. Results of Estimates (Mean Aircraft Size of Airlines at the Airport Level).

Explanatory Variables	(1)	(2)	(3)	(4)
$Pop_{u,t-1}$	0.0003 (0.0001)***	0.0002 (0.001)	0.0002 (0.0001)	0.0002 (0.0001)
$GDPpc_{u,t-1}$	0.00012 (0.00005)**	0.00014 (0.00004)***	0.00014 (0.00005)***	0.00014 (0.00004)***
$HHI_{a,t-1}$	−41.07 (2.78)***	−40.67 (2.79)***	−40.66 (2.80)***	−40.93 (2.83)***
$D_{i,a}^{mergers}$	−4.01 (2.70)	−4.11 (2.70)	−4.77 (2.66)*	−4.71 (2.66)*
$Delays_{a,t-1}$	−0.12 (0.12)	−0.21 (0.12)*	−0.68 (0.17)***	−0.67 (0.16)***
D_{a}^{slot}	−13.74 (1.86)***	−30.02 (5.91)***	−32.28 (5.87)***	−32.05 (5.89)***
$D_{i,a}^{HSlegacy}$	−17.04 (1.71)***	−17.03 (1.71)***	−31.55 (6.75)***	−31.47 (6.76)***
$D_{i,a}^{nolegacy}$	18.77 (0.89)***	18.81 (0.89)***	−4.13 (3.74)	−3.38 (3.83)
$D_{i,a}^{dominant_nolegacy}$	–	–	–	−10.09 (4.25)**
$D_{i,a}^{HSlegacy} xDelays_{a,t-1}$	–	–	0.63 (0.27)**	0.63 (0.28)**
$D_{i,a}^{nolegacy} xDelays_{a,t-1}$	–	–	1.02 (0.16)***	0.98 (0.16)***
$D_{i,a}^{dominant_nolegacy} xDelays_{a,t-1}$	–	–	–	0.53 (0.20)***
$D_{a}^{slot} xDelays_{a,t-1}$	–	0.67 (0.23)***	0.77 (0.23)***	0.76 (0.23)***
Intercept	125.62 (3.63)***	126.98 (3.66)***	137.34 (4.47)***	137.34 (4.47)***
Time fixed effects	YES	YES	YES	YES
R^2 Test F (joint sign.) Number observations	0.24 81.69*** 3311	0.24 77.37*** 3311	0.25 71.36*** 3311	0.25 71.36*** 3311

Notes: Standard errors in parentheses (robust to heteroscedasticity); Statistical significance at 1% (***), 5% (**), and 10% (*).

level. We report the results of different specifications. In the first specification, we do not include the interaction variables. In the second specification, we just include the interaction variable for the slot-constrained airports. In the third specification, we also include the interaction variables for the different types of airlines (legacy carriers at their hubs, non-legacy carriers). In the last specification, we differentiate between two types of non-legacy carriers: those operating at airports that they dominate and the rest.

In the estimation where $Y_{i,a,t}$ is the total number of annual flights, the coefficient of $Pop_{u,t-1}$ is positive and statistically significant in all specifications, as expected. Contrary to our expectations, the coefficient of $GDPpc_{u,t-1}$ is negative and statistically significant (except in the specification that differentiates between two types of non-legacy carriers, where it is negative but non-significant). Furthermore, the coefficient associated to $HHI_{a,t-1}$ is positive but not statistically significant (except in the specification that differentiates between two types of non-legacy carriers, where it is negative and non-significant). It may be the case that the variability of the income and concentration variables is too low in our sample, as most of airports are located in rich urban areas and have a high HHI. The interpretation of results for the coefficient of $D_{i,a}^{mergers}$ is unclear – it is basically included in the analysis to account for the distortion associated with merger operations.

In the estimation where $Y_{i,a,t}$ is the mean aircraft size, the coefficients of $Pop_{u,t-1}$ and $GDPpc_{u,t-1}$ are both positive as expected but only the variable of income per capita is clearly significant. By contrast, the coefficient of $HHI_{a,t-1}$ is negative and statistically significant. Given that frequencies are not higher and mean aircraft size is lower in more concentrated airports, we can conclude that airlines' capacity is lower in more concentrated airports. Since airlines compete both in airfares and capacities, weaker competition may lead airlines to reduce capacity by offering fewer seats.

We also find that frequencies are higher and the mean size of planes is lower at slot-constrained airports (see the coefficient of D_{a}^{slot}).[12] It may be the case that demand is higher in slot-constrained airports than predicted by the explanatory variables – this could explain the higher frequencies at slot-constrained airports. However, it could be also the case that the criteria governing the allocation of slots spur airlines to use the slots, even by operating smaller aircraft. Therefore, the use of higher frequencies with smaller aircraft may be a strategy of incumbent airlines to hold slots as a way to impose entry barriers to new entrants. However, the data provided above show that the intensity of competition is not lower in slot-constrained airports as compared to other airports. Consequently, other marked-based explanations like the existence of a larger demand or a higher number of short-haul destinations could explain this result.

As expected, legacy carriers that operate at their hub airports offer more frequencies and operate smaller aircraft than other airlines (see the coefficient of $D_{i,a}^{HS\_legacy}$). This result is in line with that obtained by Fageda and

Flores-Fillol (2012). Furthermore, non-legacy carriers at their dominated airports also offer higher frequencies and operate with smaller aircraft (see the coefficient of $D_{i,a}^{dominant\_no\_legacy}$), although the result for frequencies is not statistically significant.

The coefficient of $Delays_{a,t-1}$ is positive (and statistically significant in some of the specifications) in the frequency equation, while it is negative in the aircraft size equation (and statistically significant in some of the specifications as well). We must be cautious in the interpretation of this result because a simultaneous determination of frequencies and delays could occur, which would impose a bias in the estimation of the coefficient of $Delays_{a,t-1}$. Even if we use lagged values of the delays variable, the correlation over time may be high. Consequently, the positive sign of the coefficient of $Delays_{a,t-1}$ in the frequency equation might just reflect the fact that, historically, high frequencies contribute to higher delays. In any case, the relationship between frequencies and delays is jointly determined by the coefficients associated with the delays and the interaction variables. In fact, our main interest lies on the interaction variables since we aim at identifying the different behavior of airlines depending on the network structure they operate and the absence/presence of slot constraints.

When we include the interaction variables as regressors, the coefficient of $Delays_{a,t-1}$ can be interpreted in terms of the reaction to congestion of legacy carriers at airports they do not dominate (these are fully connected carriers, i.e., the reference case). The parameter estimate of the delays variable is positive in the airline frequency model, suggesting that legacy carriers operating away from their hubs increase frequency in response to delays. However, the delays variable is not statistically significant when we include the interaction variables. Looking at the interaction variables, we find evidence that airlines operating under HS networks react less to delays than the other airlines in their decisions about frequencies. Indeed, the coefficients of the interaction variables $D_{i,a}^{HS\_legacy} xDelays_{a,t-1}$ and $D_{i,a}^{dominant\_no\_legacy} xDelays_{a,t-1}$ are both positive and statistically significant in the frequency equation. By contrast, the coefficient of the interaction variable $D_{i,a}^{no\_legacy} xDelays_{a,t-1}$ is positive but non-significant.[13] The interpretation of the results in the aircraft size model is less clear: the coefficients of $D_{i,a}^{HS\_legacy} xDelays_{a,t-1}$ and $D_{i,a}^{dominant\_no\_legacy} xDelays_{a,t-1}$ are both positive and statistically significant but the coefficient of $Delays_{a,t-1}$ is negative and statistically significant (when we include the interaction variables). The coefficient of $D_{i,a}^{no\_legacy} xDelays_{a,t-1}$ is also positive and statistically significant.[14] In general, the estimation results of the two models suggest the concentration of traffic by major airlines (both legacy and low-cost carriers) in few airports located in big urban areas contributes to increase congestion (in particular, when we consider airlines' frequency choices). This result confirms empirically our theoretical predictions.

By contrast, we find some evidence that imposing constraints in the use of slots may help in mitigating the problem of congestion. More precisely, we find that the interaction variable $D_{a}^{slot}xDelays_{a,t-1}$ is negative and statistically significant in the frequency equation whereas it is positive and statistically significant in the aircraft size equation. Hence, airlines in slot-constrained airports seem to react to higher levels of congestion by using bigger aircraft at lower frequencies. Thus, the criteria governing the allocation of slots (in particular the "use-it-or-lose it" rule) may create incentives for airlines to operate higher frequencies with smaller aircraft. Therefore, conditioning the number of available slots on the levels of delays at the airport seems an effective measure that creates the right incentives for airlines to reduce the congestion they generate.

CONCLUDING REMARKS AND POLICY IMPLICATIONS

The importance of connecting traffic at hub airports (compared to that of local traffic) is dependent on the extensive number of potential destinations, which is of obvious benefit to HS networks and, consequently, to the urban areas around hubs. However, the concentration of traffic favored by HS networks has contributed to an increase in airport congestion resulting in delays, cancellations, and missed connections. Our analysis suggests that airlines operating under HS networks react less to delays than the other airlines in their decisions about frequencies. Thus, airlines operating HS networks seem to ignore the social costs (i.e., airport congestion) resulting from their network choice. This explains the fact that network carriers are reluctant to give up slots at their hub airports.

Airport congestion has yet to be adequately tackled from a public policy perspective. This is attributable to various factors including the difficulties encountered in implementing congestion pricing and the high investment costs associated with airport expansions. Another mechanism to deal with airport congestion is to impose slots constraints (extensively used in large European airports but only in three US airports). Our results show that airlines in slot-constrained airports seem to react to higher levels of congestion by using bigger aircraft at lower frequencies. Therefore, conditioning the number of available slots on the levels of delays at the airport seems an effective measure that creates the right incentives for airlines to reduce the congestion they generate.

Since network airlines do not react to congestion, our model predicts a further reinforcement of the existing hub airports over time unless new policies are adopted. We suggest that extending slot constraints to other US airports could be an effective measure. Other policy measures promoting direct connections at non-hub airports may have social benefits should problems of congestion become too severe. Policy makers and airport operators might also adopt such tools as congestion tolls, capacity investment, and a better marketing of cities in which the non-hub airports are located.

NOTES

1. It is generally accepted that the route operations of airlines are subject to density economies (Brueckner & Spiller, 1994), and that airlines can attract more connecting passengers in a HS structure by increasing service frequency than by increasing aircraft size (Wei & Hansen, 2006).

2. For instance, McDonald and McMillen (2000) discuss the centripetal force of Chicago O'Hare airport for industrial and commercial activities.

3. On the one hand, the magnitude of the problem can be noticed by looking at data over the period 2005–2013 for the top 50 US airports (data from RDC Aviation, Capstats Statistics), which reveals that the percentage of flights suffering a delay longer than 15 minutes was about 22%. On the other hand, the relationship between HS networks and congestion is empirically shown in Brueckner (2002), which shows that delays are higher in hub airports after controlling for airport size and other airport attributes.

4. Several empirical studies have examined the determinants of airline frequencies at the route level. These studies have generally focused on the effects of either route or airport competition (see, for example, Bilotkach, Fageda, & Flores-Fillol, 2010, 2013; Fageda, 2014).

5. Although, the authors acknowledge that airlines could reduce frequencies when delays increase due to higher operation costs, they justify the positive relationship between frequencies and delays by noting that congested flight segments may be associated with higher yields.

6. As such, we assume that all seats are filled. In Fageda and Flores-Fillol (2012), the 100% load factor assumption is relaxed. This distinction is not needed for the purposes of this analysis and, in any case, high load factors are a prerequisite for profitability.

7. $\partial^2\pi_1/\partial p_1^2$ and $\partial^2\pi_1/\partial f_1^2$ are satisfied by inspection. The positivity condition on the Hessian determinant, which is assumed to hold, requires $p_1 - \tau > \frac{\gamma}{4f_1} - \frac{4\alpha\eta f_1^3}{\gamma}$, i.e., margins have to be sufficiently large.

8. Slot control rules were implemented in the three airports of New York, DCA, and ORD in 1969. Rules at the airports of New York have been relaxed or suspended at certain times as a result of some statutory changes and FAA actions (GAO, 2012), while rules at ORD were removed in 2002.

9. Legacy carriers are considered to be *at their hub airports* when they operate more than 30% of the airport's overall traffic.

10. As in the case of legacy carriers, non-legacy airlines are assumed to *dominate an airport* when they operate more than 30% of the airport's overall traffic.

11. Legacy carriers usually feed their hubs with regional flights (these flights are provided by regional carriers may be subsidiaries or have a contract with the legacy carrier), using small aircraft (regional jets and turboprops). Our data does not distinguish between the flights provided by the legacy carrier and the regional carriers, as they are all coded as being provided by the legacy carrier. Hence, we may expect legacy carriers providing services with higher frequencies and smaller aircraft, as compared to low-cost airlines.

12. Note that this result does not hold in the specification that excludes the interaction variables.

13. Although, the positive and statistically significant parameter estimates on $D_{i,a}^{HS\_legacy} xDelays_{a,t-1}$ and $D_{i,a}^{dominant\_no\_legacy} xDelays_{a,t-1}$ suggest that airlines operating

under HS networks react less to delays than other airlines, it should be noted that the predicted reaction of non-HS airlines reducing frequencies in reaction to delays is also not observed.

14. The general model predicts that airlines operating FC networks will reduce capacity in reaction to delays, while those operating HS networks will increase capacity. In the aircraft size model, the findings of a negative and statistically significant parameter estimate for $Delays_{a,t-1}$ and the positive and statistically significant parameter estimates for $D_{i,a}^{HS\_legacy} xDelays_{a,t-1}$ and $D_{i,a}^{dominant\_no\_legacy} xDelays_{a,t-1}$ supports these predictions. However, the finding of a positive and statistically significant parameter estimate on $D_{i,a}^{no\_legacy} xDelays_{a,t-1}$ does not support them.

ACKNOWLEDGMENTS

We acknowledge financial support from the Spanish Ministry of Economy and Competitiveness (ECO2016-75410-P, ECO2013-42884-P, and ECO2015-69193-R) and Generalitat de Catalunya (2014SGR631).

REFERENCES

Baumgarten, P., Malina, R., & Lange, A. (2014). The impact of hubbing concentration on flight delays within airline networks: An empirical analysis of the US domestic market. *Transportation Research Part E*, *66*, 103–114.

Bilotkach, V., Fageda, X., & Flores-Fillol, R. (2010). Scheduled service versus personal transportation: The role of distance. *Regional Science and Urban Economics*, *40*(1), 60–72.

Bilotkach, V., Fageda, X., & Flores-Fillol, R. (2013). Airline consolidation and the distribution of traffic between primary and secondary hubs. *Regional Science and Urban Economics*, *43*(6), 951–963.

Britto, R., Dresner, M., & Voltes, A. (2012). The impact of flight delays on passenger demand and societal welfare. *Transportation Research Part E*, *48*, 460–469.

Brueckner, J. K. (2002). Airport congestion when carriers have market power. *American Economic Review*, *92*(5), 1357–1375.

Brueckner, J. K. (2004). Network structure and airline scheduling. *Journal of Industrial Economics*, *52*(2), 291–312.

Brueckner, J. K. (2009). Price vs. quantity-based approaches to airport congestion management. *Journal of Public Economics*, *93*(5-6), 681–690.

Brueckner, J. K., & Flores-Fillol, R. (2007). Airline schedule competition. *Review of Industrial Organization*, *30*(3), 161–177.

Brueckner, J. K., & Spiller, P. T. (1994). Economies of traffic density in the deregulated airline industry. *Journal of Law and Economics*, *37*(2), 379–415.

Brueckner, J. K., & Van Dender, K. (2008). Atomistic congestion tolls at concentrated airports? Seeking a unified view in the internalization debate. *Journal of Urban Economics*, *64*(2), 288–295.

Daniel, J. I. (1995). Congestion pricing and capacity of large hub airports: A bottleneck model with stochastic queues. *Econometrica*, *63*(2), 327–370.

Daniel, J. I., & Harback, K. T. (2008). When Do hub airlines internalize their self-imposed congestion delays? *Journal of Urban Economics*, *63*(2), 583–612.

Fageda, X. (2014). What hurts the dominant airlines at hub airports? *Transportation Research Part E*, *70*, 177–189.

Fageda, X., & Flores-Fillol, R. (2012). On the optimal distribution of traffic of network airlines. *European Economic Review*, *56*(6), 1164–1179.

Fageda, X., & Flores-Fillol, R. (2015). A note on optimal airline networks under airport congestion. *Economics Letters*, *128*, 90–94.

Fageda, X., & Flores-Fillol, R. (2016). How do airlines react to airport congestion? The role of networks. *Regional Science and Urban Economics*, *56*, 73–81.

Flores-Fillol, R. (2009). Airline competition and network structure. *Transportation Research Part B*, *43*(10), 966–983.

Flores-Fillol, R. (2010). Congested hubs. *Transportation Research Part B*, *44*(3), 358–370.

Forbes, S. J. (2008). The effect of air traffic delays on airline prices. *International Journal of Industrial Organization*, *26*(5), 1218–1232.

Government Accountability Office (GAO). (September 2012). (GAO-12-902). Slot-controlled airports: FAA's rules could be improved to enhance competition and use of available capacity. Report to the Committee on Commerce, Science, and Transportation, US Senate.

Mayer, C., & Sinai, T. (2003). Network effects, congestion externalities, and air traffic delays: Or why all delays are not evil. *American Economic Review*, *93*(4), 1194–1215.

McDonald, J. F., & McMillen, D. P. (2000). Employment subcenters and subsequent real estate development in suburban Chicago. *Journal of Urban Economics*, *48*(1), 135–157.

Pai, V. (2010). On the factors that affect airline flight frequency and aircraft size. *Journal of Air Transport Management*, *16*(4), 169–177.

Peterson, E. B., Neels, K., Barczi, N., & Graham, T. (2013). The economic cost of airline flight delay. *Journal of Transport Economics and Policy*, *47*(1), 107–121.

Rupp, N. (2009). Do carriers internalize congestion costs? Empirical evidence on the internalization question. *Journal of Urban Economics*, *65*(1), 24–37.

Vaze, V., & Barnhart, C. (2012). Modeling airline frequency competition for airport congestion mitigation. *Transportation Science*, *46*(4), 512–535.

Wei, W., & Hansen, M. (2006). An aggregate demand model for air passenger traffic in the hub-and-spoke network. *Transportation Research Part A*, *40*(10), 841–851.

Zou, B., & Hansen, M. (2014). Flight delay impact on airfare and flight frequency: A comprehensive assessment. *Transportation Research Part E*, *69*, 54–74.

CHAPTER 14

LOW-COST CARRIERS AND AIRPORTS: A COMPLEX RELATIONSHIP

Paolo Beria, Antonio Laurino and Maria Nadia Postorino

ABSTRACT

In the last decades, low-cost carriers (LCCs) have generated several changes in the air market for both passengers and airports. Mainly for regional airports, LCCs have represented an important opportunity to improve their connectivity levels and passenger traffic. Furthermore, many regional airports have become key factors to regenerate the local economy by improving accessibility and stimulating several markets, such as tourism. However, the relationship between LCCs and airports is rather complex and the outcomes not always predictable. In order to analyze and understand better such relationship and its outcomes, this chapter discusses the main underlying factors identified in: relation with the regional air market (secondary/primary airports), balance of power (dominated/non-dominated airports), and industrial organization (bases/non-bases). Starting from the proposed Relative Closeness Index, which combines yearly airport passengers and distance between airport pairs, a large sample of European airports is analyzed. Then, a smaller sub-sample – which includes selected, significant case studies referring to mid-sized airports – is discussed in detail. Among the main findings, airports sharing their catchment area with others are in a very risky position, due to the potential mobility of LCCs, while geographically isolated

The Economics of Airport Operations
Advances in Airline Economics, Volume 6, 361–386

ISSN: 2212-1609/doi:10.1108/S2212-160920170000006014

airports in good catchment areas can better counterbalance the power of carriers.

Keywords: Low-cost carriers; regional airports; airport–airline relationship; Relative Closeness Index

JEL classifications: C43; L93; R4

INTRODUCTION

Low-cost carriers (LCCs) have brought a crucial change to the air transport sector. In about 10 years, they have been able to transform the concept of flying for both passengers and airports. Many secondary airports that were previously, at best, spokes in the hub-and-spoke systems of traditional airline companies or seasonal destinations, nowadays represent a dynamic part of the European airport industry. The success of the relationship between airlines and airports entails greater connectivity and mobility for an area, and generally affects local economies around airports.

The positive results of some European airports in the last decade promoted the idea that *any* airport could improve the accessibility and connectivity level of an area and regenerate the regional economy (by stimulating tourism, creating new jobs and providing connections with larger cities, among others) provided it is capable of attracting LCCs. Therefore, airport operators have implemented different schemes to encourage the presence of these carriers, and especially to have their aircraft based there.

Generally, the relative dependency between airlines and airports is ruled by certain factors, among which are the market potential of an area for the carrier (population, GDP, and tourist attractions), airport technical aspects (turn-around time, level of congestion, availability of slots, and handling), possible incentives provided by the airport operators (airport charges and handling fees), and subsidies or financial guarantees from the airport/local authority. The combination of these elements, shapes the level of dependency between the two parts and affects the stability of the relationship, including the actual market power of the airline and its capability to bargain for favorable agreements from the airport manager.

After a literature review on the LCC phenomenon, this chapter provides a taxonomy of the relationship between LCCs and airports by identifying three main themes: the relation with the regional air market (secondary/primary airports), the balance of power (dominated/non-dominated airports), and the industrial organization (bases/non-bases). A large sample of airports is preliminarily analyzed with respect to the relation to the regional air market. Then, a selection of case studies is discussed thoroughly according to all the themes above to better understand the relationship between airport and airline. The concluding section summarizes the findings by discussing different forms of current relationships.

THE LOW-COST CARRIER PHENOMENON IN EUROPE: A SHORT OVERVIEW

One of the major results of the liberalization of intra-European air services has been the development of low-cost "no-frills" airlines (Doganis, 2010) that have increasingly gained market shares across Europe, impacting traditional carriers on short-haul routes thanks to their extensive pan-European networks. Despite having introduced some changes to better meet the needs of passengers[1] by hybridizing the original model in the second wave of development, (Fageda, Suau-Sanchez, & Mason, 2015; Klophaus, Conrady, & Fichert, 2012), the peculiar elements of the LCC scheme can still be identified according to three aspects (Table 1): organizational, commercial, and technical (de Wit & Zuidberg, 2012; Dobruszkes, 2006; Doganis, 2010; Hunter, 2006; Lawton, 2002).

Beyond the cost minimization and efficiency maximization approach of the low-cost/low-fare model (Doganis, 2010), several other factors may explain the dramatic rise of low-cost services:

- The difficult situation of some full-service carriers already in critical condition and further affected by the global financial crisis, which forced them to

Table 1. Main Features of the Low-Cost Model.

Organizational	Commercial	Technical
Point-to-point connections on short/medium haul routes rather than hub & spoke schemes	High commercial ability to bargain with the airports for favorable conditions (airport charges, handling, etc.)	Use of a single or restricted number of models of new aircraft
Non-integration into alliances and absence of frequent flyer program	In-flight catering services (i.e., meals, drinks, etc.) available for a fee	Short turnaround time with high utilization of aircraft and crew
Use of secondary non-congested airports with slots available at a relatively low price	High rate of advertising to promote the brand and increase the number of passengers	Single class cabin with a high-density configuration
Direct online selling, mainly ticketless	Heavy reliance on yield management to reach high load factors	Aircraft cleaning is done by the cabin crew to reduce cost and turnaround times
More intensive use of labor and higher productivity	Strict policy on baggage and, in general, payment of surcharges outside basic services	

downsize or cease services from some airports/routes, leaving space for LCCs (Dennis, 2005).

- The progressive enlargement of EU to new member states, which provided new markets (Dobruszkes, 2013).
- The presence of many secondary underused airports, often relatively close to big cities or located in districts with good catchment areas, whose potentialities have not been considered by full-service carriers.
- The incentives provided by airports and/or regional or local authorities (Allroggen, Malina & Lenz, 2013; Laurino & Beria, 2014; Malina, Albers & Kroll, 2011) that allowed LCCs to also provide services to low-density routes that, in many cases, have been dropped once the incentive ended (Wiltshire, 2013).

Between 2006 and 2014, the main European LCCs, such as *Wizz Air*, *Norwegian Air*, *Air Berlin*, *EasyJet*, and *Ryanair*, more than doubled the number of carried passengers (Table 2) from nearly 100 million in 2006 to more than 223 million in 2014. Dobruszkes (2013) shows how, also due to the higher impact of the financial crisis on full-service carriers, LCCs accounted for 70% of the 1995–2012 increase in the number of intra-European flights or seats and 64% of the number of seat-km. According to CAPA (2016), on average, LCCs currently provide 37% of intra-Europe seats, ranging from 60% of Hungary to 11% of Finland. In some cases, like in Italy, UK or Spain, they also play a major role in domestic routes.

RELATIONSHIP BETWEEN LCCS AND AIRPORTS

In the last decade, many studies have remarked on the positive relationship between LCCs and regional or secondary airports (see for example Lin,

Table 2. Passengers in Millions Carried by a Sample of Low-Cost Carriers.

Carrier	2006	2007	2008	2009	2010	2011	2012	2013	2014	CAGR[a] 06/14 (%)
Wizz Air	3	4.2	5.9	7.8	9.6	11	11.6	13.5	15.8	23
Norwegian air shuttle	5.1	6.8	9.1	10.8	13.0	15.7	17.7	20.7	24.0	21
Air Berlin	25.6	28.2	28.6	32.4	34.9	35.3	33.3	31.5	31.7	3
Easyjet	33.7	38.2	44.6	46.1	49.7	55.5	59.2	61.3	65.3	9
Ryanair	40.5	49.0	57.7	65.3	72.7	76.4	79.6	81.4	86.4	10

Source: Data from ELFAA – The European Low Fares Airline Association website.
[a]CAGR – Compound Annual Growth Rate represents the mean annual growth rate of traffic over a specified period of time.

Mak, & Wong, 2013; Jankiewicz & Huderek-Glapska, 2016). Before discussing the nature of such a relationship, the definition of "secondary" airport needs some further clarification. There is no unique definition of "secondary" airports, although they are generally identified as under-utilized airports that complement a network of "primary" or major airports – which, in turn, are defined as commercial service airports enplaning at least 10,000 passengers per year or airports where at least 10 network carriers are operating (Mason & Morrison, 2008). Secondary airports can be located close to some primary airports (such as in the London airport system, where Heathrow is the primary airport) or far from the main city they serve (such as Malmø in Sweden). Some common features are spare capacity, closeness to attractive cities, location in remote regions and low turnaround times. Strickland (2015) discusses and describes the role and the challenges secondary airports will be facing in the next years by analyzing many EU secondary airports.

In the EU, airports are classified depending on passengers (EC, 2005), namely *community* (more than 10 million passengers), *national* (5–10 million passengers), and *regional* (less than 5 million passengers). Recent data show that EU "secondary" airports handle about 260 million passengers per year, thus making a great contribution to European mobility. In the following, secondary airports will be identified as regional airports according to the EU classification, unless a more specific definition is given depending on the context.

The relationship between LCCs and airports is often reciprocal, because both try to take advantage of alternative demand markets and regions. In the deregulated environment that characterizes both airlines and airports, financial gain is due to the ability to capture as much demand as possible in a given catchment area by reducing operating costs at the same time (Graham, 2013). Then, on one side, airports try to adapt to LCC operating models by providing the basic facilities and services they require. On the other side, LCCs try to satisfy latent and unsatisfied travel demand by operating in areas characterized by poor alternative transport supply (mainly surface transport modes) and tourist attractiveness (Rey, Myro, & Galera, 2011). Although addressing common goals, LCCs and airports may have balanced or imbalanced relationships depending on the compromises they are able to realize and the strength of their attachment (Lin et al., 2013). Furthermore, the strength of this relationship is also measured by the choice of the airport as a base for the LCC. Such a choice represents a better integration between LCC, the airport – the main consequences are technical requests and maintenance for aircraft – and the host country – for example, crew overnight accommodations in the nearest city (Fuhr & Beckers, 2006), although it depends on the LCC's decision to maintain steady air services in the foreign country (Klein et al., 2015).

In this framework, the relationship between LCCs and airports is described based on three main themes:

- the role of the airport for the catchment area (secondary/primary airports);
- the industrial organization of the airline in the airport (bases/non-bases); and
- the balance of power between airport and airline (dominated/non-dominated airports).

Role of the Airport in the Catchment Area

The role of the airport in the catchment area is extremely relevant in defining the behavior of the carriers, since it determines the number and the characteristics of the options available to the airline to serve that particular demand. Three main cases of secondary airports are identified: airports in remote regions, airports competing with major airports for the same catchment area and exclusive airports serving secondary catchment areas.

Airports serving remote regions such as small islands can count on small catchment areas, but travelers have no real alternatives; neither inter-modal nor intra-modal. In this case, the limitedness of the market may leave space for only a few and monopolistic routes, typically toward the hub or the main base of the operating carrier. This situation may differ during holiday periods, when additional supplies provide services to tourists (by either charter or seasonal LCCs).

Secondary airports, totally or partially competing with major airports, lay on the other side of the range of the market structure spectrum. They may have a marginal role unless some conditions appear, such as congestion problems at the main airport (Bendinelli, Bettini, & Oliveira, 2016) or if they allow airlines to serve the captive market without bearing the higher costs of primary airports (as Rome Ciampino/Fiumicino, Girona/Barcelona El Prat, London Luton or Stansted/Heathrow). Many air markets have expanded toward secondary airports to search for extra capacity, given congestion and delay problems that affect major airports all over the world, particularly in Europe, where increasing traffic and lack of both airport development/expansion and strong regulatory policies have worsened the problem (Madas & Zografos, 2008). Even more frequently, LCCs have used secondary airports to serve the otherwise impenetrable markets of former flag carriers, which resulted in enlarged, overlapping and more heterogeneous catchment areas (Pantazis & Liefner, 2006). However, in the medium-long term, regional airports experiencing the highest traffic increase at the beginning are those that register the largest reductions during volatile periods (Halpern, Graham, & Dennis, 2016).

Without congestion at main airports or in the absence of relevant and unserved catchment areas, secondary airports do not develop or develop much less than the primary ones, typically specializing in niche markets (general aviation, charter, cargo). The main cause for such congestion is that air travelers prefer accessing larger airports to take advantage of lower fares and several airline services (Lian & Rønnevik, 2011), rather than having limited and expensive direct flights from the local airport. This phenomenon is also referred to as *traffic leakage* (Fuellhart, 2007; Fu & Kim, 2016). In these uncongested single-airport areas, there is often a one-to-one relationship between the catchment area and the airport. In this case, the relation of power in favor of one or the other depends mainly on the dimension of both the market (if large, more than one airline may exist) and the airline.

Airline Organization

The way airlines are organized is another factor making a difference in the relationship between airlines and airports. A primary difference is between hub-and-spokes (H&S) carriers and point-to-point ones, which refers to the organization of their networks (Zanin & Lillo, 2013). LCCs almost everywhere adopt a point-to-point-scheme, although the adjustments of the full carrier business models to maintain their market share have forced many LCCs to change their strategies and adopt hybrid network configurations (Klophaus et al., 2012). The impact of point-to-point LCC services on the airport organization depends on the airport's role in its catchment area and the number and type of air carriers operating there. For airports where H&S services are established, LCCs may fill the slots between hub waves[2] and spread air demand over uncongested (or less congested) time spans. Alternatively, LCCs settle in airports without H&S carriers, where they can assume a dominant role. However, incumbent airlines controlling most slots at their hub airports represent an important entry barrier for LCCs at full-carrier-established hub airports (Kappes & Merkert, 2013), while the rise of the LCC phenomenon has made the dimension of their supply far from marginal in many airports (Carballo-Cruz & Costa, 2014; Pyrialakou, Karlaftis, & Michaelides, 2012). In addition, where market conditions were favorable, LCCs have left their original secondary airports in favor of primary ones (de Wit & Zuidberg, 2012), where they compete for capacity with other traditional airlines.

The LCC organizational model may interfere with that of traditional airlines. Firstly, LCCs tend to be very demanding in terms of reliability, turnaround time and delays (Choo & Oum, 2013). Traditional H&S carriers plan very rigid timetables to coordinate the numerous flights arriving and departing from the hub (waves), but foresee broad buffers and leave spare capacity at the airport (Dennis, 2001). LCCs use the airport's capacity longer and more constantly, but timetables are tighter and allow no delays. Secondly, LCCs are organized in bases, where aircrafts and crews end the working day and where they usually come back after every return flight. Having aircrafts based there is a crucial element for an airport since, as suggested by Malighetti, Paleari, and Redondi (2016), it reduces the probability of suffering from downsizing due to the presence of switching costs.

Power Relations

Airline organization and catchment areas are among the factors influencing the power relations between airports and airlines. Airports have developed several forms of relationships with airlines, depending on mutual interests and revenue features. In some cases, they prefer to establish long-term relationships, which results in the development of H&S services and, generally, a dominant power of airlines in regards to airports (Fu, Homsombat, & Oum, 2011). Under these conditions, almost all supply is provided by one airline and the airport is completely dependent on the airline's strategy and conditions (price and operational conditions).

According to Lin et al. (2013), the relationship between airlines and airports could lead to several scenarios of power imbalance and mutual dependence. According to that study, the relationship between an LCC and an airport tends to be well-established as the airport capacity reaches saturation. In contrast, a negotiation approach is used more frequently when the airport capacity is under-utilized.

Another aspect of power balance relates to the presence of more airports in a shared catchment area; this is the case with multi-airport systems. Here, airlines, and then airports, compete according to their services and features; for example, when LCCs operating at secondary airports compete with full-service airlines operating at the primary airport (Pels, Njegovan, & Behrens, 2009), or similar airports compete to attract demand for the same catchment area based on their management and air service features (Postorino & Praticò, 2012). Furthermore, negotiations of suitable contracts addressed to attract LCCs, which generally reduce aeronautical revenues, could have several impacts on the airport's financial management, thus suggesting a careful analysis when negotiating preferential contracts (Francis, Fidato, & Humphreys, 2003).

The existence of small and dominated airports is also very unpredictable: small markets are more prone to be left by a dominating airline as soon as market conditions change, for example, in favor of another nearby airport offering better conditions. Single point-to-point routes can, in fact, be easily moved away, and this can make the difference in success or failure for a small airport. This dependence of the airport on the airline occurs also in the most common cases of partially dominated airports, like for LCC bases. Here, an airline which has a large share of traffic, peculiar conditions and local production factors (typically workforce) can enjoy large bargaining power under the threat of switching to another nearby airport to serve the same demand.

Even if the most obvious cases of airport abandonment are those of de-hubbing legacy carriers (for example, Milan Malpensa in 2008 as in Beria et al., 2012; Budapest in 2012 as in Bohl, 2013; or more in general in Redondi, Malighetti, & Paleari 2012), this airline activity has also occurred in many smaller airports dominated by LCCs[3] as clearly discussed in Malighetti et al. (2016). For example, Ryanair often threatens to relocate and/or withdraw routes in response to national normative changes[4] or to influence charges and conditions in the airport, as it did in Strasbourg, Altenburg, Frankfurt Hahn or Belfast (Olischer & Dörrenbächer, 2013).

DEGREE OF AIRPORT/AIRLINE DEPENDENCY

The three aspects discussed in the previous section contribute to the degree of airport/airline dependency and power relations. In general, it is possible to identify circumstances that can affect the role and potential power of the airport. In particular, whenever traffic is scarce, alternative airports exist in the area or the largest market share belongs to one carrier only, the secondary airport may have a weak role. In contrast, the presence of stable and well-functioning airline hubs and/or bases, the presence of a large captive traffic (especially business) attractive to airlines, the absence of a dominant airline, and the lack of alternative airports as good substitutes[5] could favor an airport increasing its market power.

However, airline market power is not the only determinant of the relationship between airlines and airports, since incentives can also play a role in tightening or weakening this relationship. Typically, the efficacy of incentives and subsidies in developing a market depend on how they are designed; in particular, they should promote a stable and constructive airport/airline relationship fostering sustainable and financially viable business plans, rather than stimulating short-term predatory practices by airlines that can only translate to a waste of public resources.

The liberalization of airline transport services and the rise of LCCs coupled with the presence of many formerly military airports in different areas of Europe (with a sufficiently attractive catchment area or not), resulted in the design and implementation of many programs by airports operators and/or local/regional governments to foster traffic supply. Different supporting typologies have been implemented in the last two decades, ranging from simple discounts on airport fees to more complex agreements defining many aspects of the relationship between airports and airlines. Four categories can summarize the most used schemes (Allroggen et al., 2013; Castillo-Manzano, López-Valpuesta, & González-Laxe, 2011; Copenhagen Economics, 2012; Fichert & Klophaus, 2011; Graham, 2013; Laurino & Beria, 2014; Malina et al., 2011):

1. Discount on airport charges: rebates or reductions over a relatively short period of time.
2. Direct subsidies from the airport or the local authority for starting new routes by fixing the minimum number of flights to be provided.
3. Revenues guarantees: under a threshold agreed with the airline, the airport directly covers the missing revenue of the airline.
4. Co-marketing agreement: the airline agrees to promote the area where the airport is located through marketing and advertising activities in exchange for money.

By analyzing a sample of 200 airports in the EU in 2010, Malina et al. (2011) found that two-thirds of incentives were granted on the basis of officially disclosed incentive programs; the remainder were bilateral agreements between airlines and airports (foreseeing discounts on certain fees, bonus payments or joint marketing initiatives for a limited period to airlines). While large airports rely mainly on published incentive programs, small and medium-sized airports use both mechanisms. Bilateral agreements are used in particular where airports aim at becoming a base for an airline. However, this is a two-sided decision. On the one hand, the airport could increase its traffic volume, but on the other, should it have no alternative airlines, it could turn the based airline into the dominant customer with a lot of bargaining power.

The new Guidelines on State aid to airports and airlines (EC, 2014a) try to take into account the new scenario resulting from the liberalization process as well as the numerous cases of potential discriminatory behavior of some airports in providing subsidies to airlines, suggesting a growth-oriented approach in the evaluation of state aid.

In particular, on one side the Guidelines acknowledge the potential role of regional airports for local development and for the accessibility of certain regions. On the other side, these guidelines highlight how, in the last decades, public funding to airport infrastructure often resulted in a proliferation of unprofitable airports, in many cases in the same catchment area, ghost airports or overcapacities while leaving congestion problems in the main airports (EC, 2014a). The new rules require that, in case an airport is located in the same catchment of another one with spare capacity, its business plan must identify the impact in terms of traffic variation on the existing one.

In terms of aid provided to the airlines, the new approach of the European Commission acknowledges that airlines are not willing, without adequate incentives, to start new routes from unknown and untested small airports (EC, 2014a) so, under specific conditions, airlines can receive start-up aid. In order to evaluate if aid (subsidies, co-marketing, tax rebates, etc.) could be provided to an airport, the Market Economy Operator (MEO) test[6] should be applied. In this case, using the MEO test provides the Commission guidelines to assess whether the conditions offered to an airline at the airport would have been offered by a profit-driven airport operator (EC, 2014a). This requires demonstrating *ex ante* that the deal between the airline and the airport contributes to the profitability of the airport, and that it should be able to cover all costs deriving from the arrangement plus a reasonable profit margin. To take into account that smaller airports may need more time to adjust their strategies (for example, in terms of airport charges to airline, increasing the non-aviation revenues, attracting new airlines, etc.) the Guidelines foresee a 10-year transitional period.

ANALYSIS

Methodology

As discussed in the "Relationship between LCCs and Airports" section, we study the relationship between airports and LCCs, looking at three aspects: (1) the relative power among airports, (2) the organization of the airline, and (3) the relative power between airport and airline, sometimes ruled by incentives, some others only by market forces. Limiting this to LCCs, the second element considers only if the airport is a base or not. Figure 1 schematizes the relationships.

According to this scheme, we start from a broad sample of 157 airports belonging to four European countries, and quantitatively analyze the relationship among airports (1) by means of a couple of indicators:

$$f\left(YCP_i, RCI_i\left(YCP_j\right)\right)$$

YCP_i indicates the dimension of the airport i in terms of yearly carried passengers while RCI_i, called Relative Closeness Index, represents the weight of the airports surrounding airport i calculated as follows:

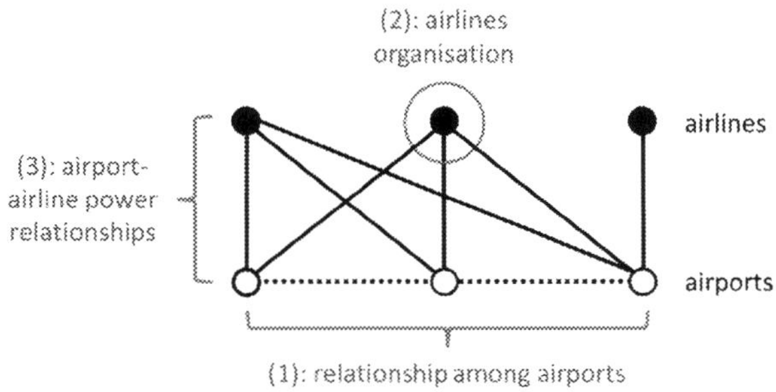

Fig. 1. Scheme of aspects determining airlines–airports relationships.

$$RCI_i = \sum_{j \neq i} \frac{YCP_j}{d_{ij}^2}$$

It divides the yearly carried passengers (YCP_j) at all j airports around airport i with the squared distance (d_{ij}) between i and j. The distance allows reducing the effect of far airports, in particular making negligible those farther than 100–150 km. In practice, a low index means that the airport is isolated or is surrounded by very small airports. A high value suggests that one or more large airports are located near to i.

To discuss the role of LCCs, it is important to also look at the dynamics of the two indicators over a 10-year period. Figure 2 provides an overview of the possible outcomes deriving from the variation over time of RCI and YCP values. By excluding the opening of new airports, four main patterns can be identified:

I. the airport grows together with the surrounding ones, but it loses some relevance;
II. the airport grows and also gains relevance with respect to the close ones;
III. the airport decreases its traffic together with the surroundings ones, but gains some relevance; and
IV. the airport decreases its traffic while the others grow and it loses some relevance in the area.

The analysis of the sample according to these two metrics, in the "Sample and Case Selection" section, will allow for selecting a more limited number of

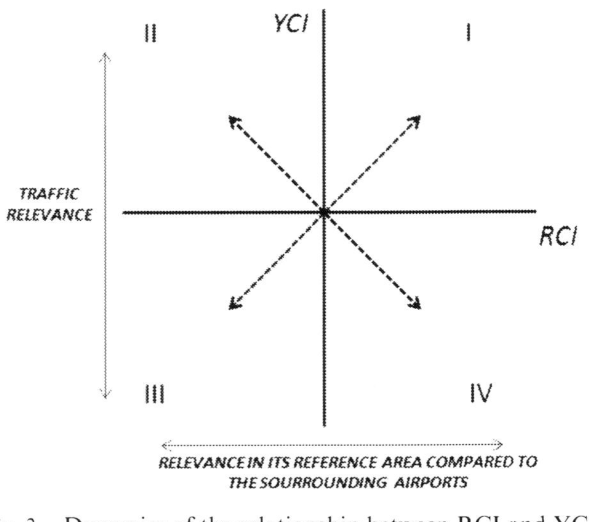

Fig. 2. Dynamics of the relationship between RCI and YCI.

case studies, for which all three elements of the relationship will be discussed in the "Discussion of the Case Studies" section.

Sample and Case Selection

This first analysis has been applied to four European countries (Italy, Germany, France, and Spain) and their airports, in order to identify, also quantitatively, if there are common determinants underlying the relationship between LCCs and airports. Table 3 reports the main characteristics of the examined countries useful to understanding and analyzing such a relationship.

Figure 3 depicts the 157 airports of the examined sample (reference year 2014) in a RCI-YCP diagram that allows for identifying some clusters. As a general comment, airports on the right side of the chart (whatever their dimension) have high RCI values, which is due to the presence of other airports in the same reference area (the closer they are, the higher the index). On the contrary, more isolated airports, such as those on small islands or in remote regions with poor surface transport supply, lie on the left part of the chart. As for the y-coordinate, airports characterized by good traffic volumes are on the top of the diagram, while airports with small traffic on a yearly basis are on the bottom. For a given airport *i*, its RCI value is a weighted combination of traffic volumes at surrounding airports and their distances from *i*. Then, the airport coordinates in the RCI-YCP diagram take into account both the

Table 3. Main Features of the Examined European Countries.

Country	France	Germany	Italy	Spain
Total land area [km^2]	547,571	348,520	294,152	498,535
Population (2016)	64,668,129	80,682,351	59,801,004	46,064,604
Density (inh/km^2)	118	232	203	92
Urban Pop. %	80.5	77.2	70.7	82
No. apts with scheduled services considered	47	27	40	43
No. apts with more than 1 M pax in 2014	12	17	23	20
Passengers volume 2014	164,682,473	209,844,141	150,243,055	195,863,599
% passenger traffic in top 5 apts	73.39	74.61	55.28	64.62
% passenger traffic in top 10 apts	89.89	91.29	74.82	83.06
CAGR 04-14 [%]	2.79	2.8	3.45	1.66

Source: www.worldometers.info for data on population and land area; airport data from ENAC (Italy), AENA (Spain), Direction Généralede l'Aviation civile (France), ADV, and Destatis websites of the airports (Germany).

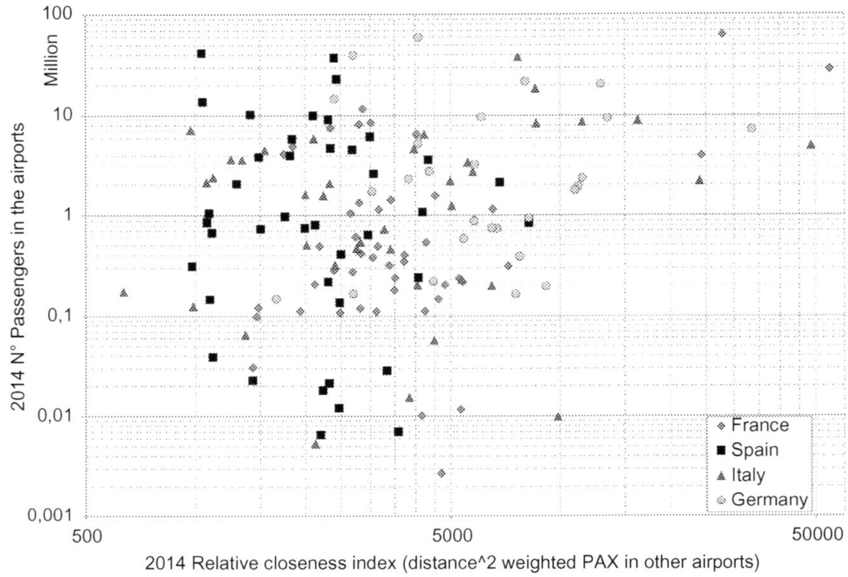

Fig. 3. RCI-YCP diagram for the airport sample in 2014 by using logarithmic scales. *Source:* Our elaborations on traffic statistics from AENA-Spain, ENAC-Italy, ADV-Germany, and Direction du Transport aérien-France.

size of the traffic volume at the airport itself and the presence of close airports, whose competing role depends on the amount of carried passengers. Small airports could be surrounded by large competitors and are consequently in the weakest position both in terms of demand (passengers are likely to opt for large airports due to the higher frequencies and destinations) and for the supply (carriers may concentrate on the main airports). Also among the mid-sized airports, the situation varies depending on the presence of large competitors nearby.

In this context, LCCs can modify the airport coordinates in the RCI-YCP diagram both directly and indirectly. The direct variation is due, for example, to the extra traffic due to the entry of an LCC, which moves up the position of the airport *i*. Instead, if LCCs bring extra traffic to neighboring airports *j*, the point indirectly moves right, toward a relatively weaker position.

Starting from these premises, four groups of airports have been identified. Group 1 encloses airports with YCP greater than 10 million, which also includes hubs; group 2 airports with YCP ranging between 1 and 10 million; group 3 airports with YCP ranging between 0.1 and 1 million, and group 4, the remaining airports. Mid-sized airports, belonging to groups 2 and 3, are historically more affected by LCCs than the other ones. In fact, airports belonging to group 1 have an established position and LCCs could add benefits (if operating at the airport itself) or satisfy latent demand (if operating at neighboring airports), but not modify their position. On the other hand, airports from group 4 are generally small airports in remote or isolated areas, often benefitting from Public Service Obligation[7] (PSO) or seasonal LCC services.

Furthermore, the consistency among airports in the groups has been determined by considering the population density in the region where the airport is located, the presence of LCCs and their role for the airport development as well as their impact on the surrounding airports, the compound growth rate of passenger traffic in the time span considered, the value of RCI and the airport specificity, if that is the case.

Based on these considerations, two significant cases within groups 2 and 3 for each country (16 cases on the whole) have been considered (Table 4) for further discussion. Airports in group 2 have been chosen by considering two different values of RCI, which correspond to low and high levels. Airports in group 3 have been selected based mainly on their location and the weight of LCCs.

The next section discusses these airports and their histories, looking both at their relative power and at the dynamics of the positioning due to LCC entrances, exits, and actions.

Discussion of the Case Studies

As discussed above, RCI and YCP provide an indication of the role played by airports with respect to the potential competitors serving the same catchment area. Figure 4 provides a comparison among airports in group 2, namely those with YCP ranging between 1 and 10 million,[8] while Table 5 shows the evolution of the compound annual growth rate between 2004 and 2014 for the RCI and YCP indexes.

The airport of Naples (NAP) in Italy evolved in the chart toward the right side. According to RCI, since in the same period there is no variation in d_{ij} – i.e., no new airports in the neighborhood – NAP evolution identifies an increase in YCP of neighboring airports. However, there was a general increase in the carried passengers also at NAP, where, during the same period, the percentage of LCC services increased significantly with the opening of an easyJet base in 2014. This aspect, together with the position in the territory and the absence of strong competing airports (FCO being about 200 km away), contributed to strengthening the locally dominant position of NAP. The other Italian airport in group 3, Verona (VRN), registered an increase in its RCI due to the presence, in a 150 km radius, of several competing airports that experienced relevant traffic growth in the time span analyzed (in terms of CAGR Bologna had 8.58%; Venezia 3.72%; Treviso 9.67%, Bergamo 10.13% and Linate 0.4%[9]). At the same time, there was also an evolution of the LCC services, with a good presence in 2011–2012 (about 34%) due to the increasing

Table 4. The Examined Airports of Groups 2 and 3.

Country	Airport	Group	RCI	Main Features of Airports
IT	Napoli (NAP)	2	Low	Important role in the area, good presence of LCCs
IT	Verona (VRN)	2	High	High population density, presence of alternative airports, tourism attractions
FR	Lione (LYS)	2	High	Good population density and important role in the area
FR	Nantes (NTE)	2	Low	Important role in the coastal area, good presence of LCCs
ES	Sevilla (SVQ)	2	Low	Role in the area and high presence of LCCs
ES	Girona (GRO)	2	High	Close to a large airport (BCN), tourism location and strong dependency on LCCs
DE	Hannover (HAJ)	2	High	Good population density and important role in the area
DE	Weeze (NRN)	2	Low	High presence of LCCs, strong population density
IT	Reggio Calabria (REG)	3	Low	Isolated airport and marginal role of LCCs
IT	Parma (PMF)	3	High	Presence of other airports in the same catchment area and strong dependency on LCCs
FR	Grenoble (GNB)	3	High	Close to a large regional airport (LYS) and good population density in the surrounding areas
FR	Pau-Pyrénées (PUF)	3	Low	Low population density, closeness to a similar airport (Lourdes) relative presence of LCCs
ES	Santander (SDR)	3	Low	Relatively isolated airport, but important role for the surrounding areas, high dependence on LCCs
ES	Valladolid (VLL)	3	Low	Central, not coastal, location; low population density and high dependence on LCCs
DE	Lubeck (LBC)	3	High	Relatively isolated airport, but important role for the surrounding areas and strong LCC role
DE	Karlsruhe (FKB)	3	High	High population density and strong LCC role

role of Ryanair which, in summer 2012, accounted for 13% of flights and almost 19% of seat capacity, just behind Meridiana.[10] In 2013, the presence of LCCs declined (from 34% to about 17%) due to the failure of WindJet and the withdrawal of Ryanair following the decision of VRN to cease the agreement,

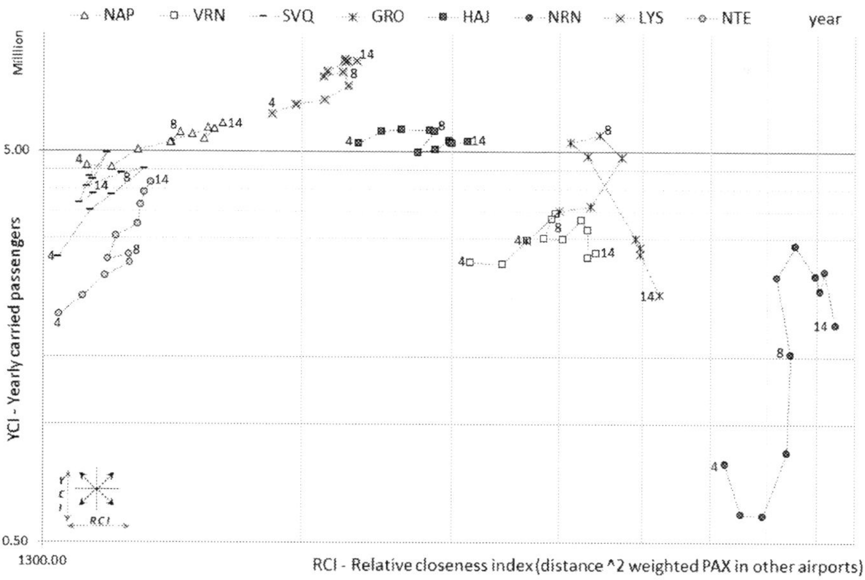

Fig. 4. Evolution of RCI between 2004 and 2014 for the airports in group 2. *Source:* Our elaboration on official statistics for the airports. *Note:* The numbers refer to years, thus 4 stands for 2004, 8 for 2008 and 14 for 2014.

Table 5. Evolution of the Compound Annual Growth Rate (CAGR) between 2004 and 2014 for the Relative Closeness Index (RCI) and Yearly Carried Passengers (YCP).

Group 2	IATA	CAGR – YCI 04/14 (%)	CAGR – RCI 04/14 (%)
Napoli	NAP	2.53	3.72
Verona	VRN	0.53	3.44
Siviglia	SVQ	4.00	0.93
Girona	GRO	−1.96	3.63
Hannover	HAJ	0.08	2.96
Weeze	NRN	8.53	3.00
Lione	LYS	3.12	2.31
Nantes	NTE	7.93	2.49

which foresaw financially unsustainable incentives paid to the carrier. Despite this critical situation, the airport is trying to slowly recover its traffic values thanks to carriers that were substituted for Ryanair, thus demonstrating the presence of a significant local demand and the role played by tourism attractions (VRN ranks second in terms of charter services nationwide).

Lyon Airport (LYS) is France's fourth busiest airport and is located in Rhône-Alpes, one of the most economically dynamic European regions. During the 10 years analyzed, traffic has steadily increased mainly on international routes that, also due to the increasing presence of LCC passing from 2.6% to 26.4% market shares, grew at a higher rate (52%) than domestic ones (23%). Despite this growth, the airport has lost some points in terms of RCI because of the presence of both Genève, located 150 km north-east, which registered a 6% CAGR, and Marseille airports, in the south, which had a 4% CAGR. The other French airport in the group, Nantes (NTE), has a low RCI and locally important results. In fact, it is isolated on France's Atlantic coast and its closest competing airports (Rennes, La Rochelle, Tours, and Poitiers) have a marginal role carrying, on average, less than 0.3 M passengers a year. The number of carried passengers at NTE has a positive trend in the examined period, with the percentage of LCC shares constantly increasing (from 0.2% in 2005 to 38.6% in 2014) despite the relevant presence of Air France and of its regional partner HOP!.

Looking at the Spanish airports, Sevilla has constantly increased the percentage of LCCs from less than 8% in 2004 to 85% in 2014, and traffic volumes registered a CAGR of 4% in the same period. Interestingly, the airport does not have a dominant carrier; two-thirds of the passengers are shared between Ryanair and Vueling, and the rest are carried by other airlines. In terms of RCI, despite the relative closeness of Malaga (4th in terms of traffic in Spain), the value has not significantly changed in the considered time span by evidencing a specific role for SVQ in the area that is confirmed by the data on population density, which is concentrated around Sevilla. Differently, the Girona airport, fully dominated by Ryanair, has experienced higher instability with two evident phases. In the first one, the traffic increased in an apparently successful way, thanks to the Ryanair base, but its neighbors also increased, resulting in a growing RCI. Between 2010 and 2014, Girona started losing traffic in favor of the near airport of Barcelona El Prat, where the dramatic expansion of Vueling, Ryanair and EasyJet determined traffic increase, together with the recovering of lost volumes due to the failure of Spainair in 2012 (CAPA, 2015). In these years the YCP of Girona has fallen while its RCI has grown, putting it into a difficult position.[11]

In Germany, the airport of Weeze (NRN) has increased its YCP, slowing down only in the last 4 years in part due to the financial crisis and in part to the introduction of an aviation tax, which resulted in Ryanair reducing its network. At the same time, the RCI has constantly grown due to the presence of many airports in the area both bigger, like Dusseldorf (75 km south) or Cologne (130 km south), and similar in traffic terms, such as Dortmund (130 km east) and Eindhoven (80 km west). The other German airport in group 2, Hannover, despite not being dominated by LCCs, has played an important role in its catchment area. Pantazis and Liefner (2006), demonstrate the impact of LCCs on traffic increase as well as on expansion of the Hannover catchment area, following the entrance of the LCC Hapag Lloyd Express, which exploited the free capacity resulting from the expansion of the airport before the start of the EXPO2000. The increase in RCI results from the traffic growth registered in the two closest airports of Bremen (CAGR 6%) and Hamburg (CAGR 4%), while in contrast, traffic figures for Hannover have only slightly changed in the 10 years analyzed.

Figure 5 provides a comparison among the airports in group 3, i.e., ranging from 0.1 to 1 million passengers, while Table 6 shows the evolution of the compound annual growth rate between 2004 and 2014 for the RCI and YCP indexes.

In Italy, Reggio Calabria (REG) and Parma (PMF) have similar vertical evolutions and a general increase of their YCP at the end of the examined period. However, in both cases traffic volumes declined during the last years – more significantly for PMF than REG. By looking at the LCC presence, its role has been very marginal and inconsistent for REG (only for 3 years in the time span considered). On the contrary, the LCC presence at PMF has been constantly increasing, reaching the considerable value of 94% in 2014 (91.3% during the 10-year period). However, this relevant presence has not led to

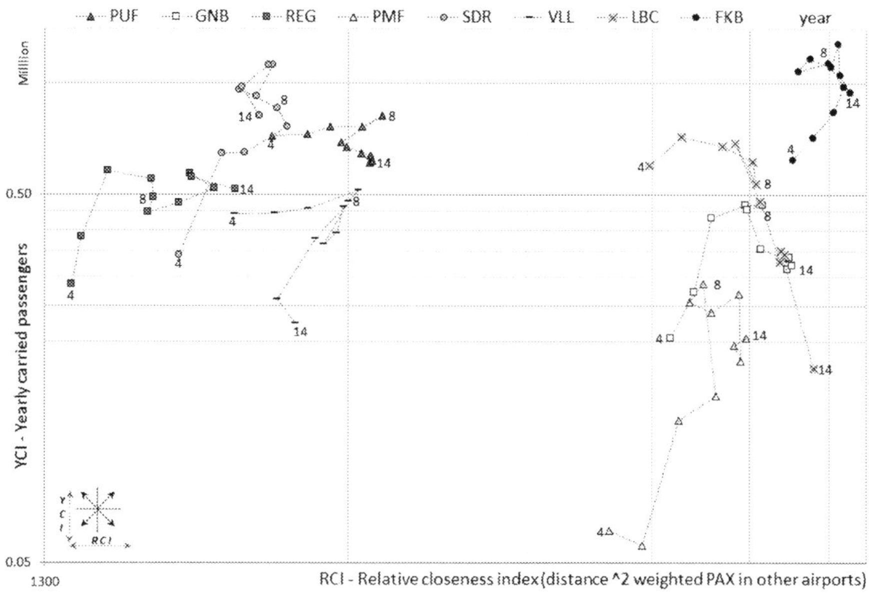

Fig. 5. Evolution of RCI between 2004 and 2014 for the airports in group 3 *Source:* Our elaboration on official statistics for the airports. *Note:* The numbers refer to years, thus 4 stands for 2004, 8 for 2008 and 14 for 2014.

Table 6. Evolution of the Compound Annual Growth Rate (CAGR) between 2004 and 2014 for the Relative Closeness Index (RCI) and the Yearly Carried Passengers (YCP).

Group 3	IATA	CAGR – YCI 04/14 (%)	CAGR – RCI 04/14 (%)
Reggio Calabria	REG	6.17	3.82
Parma	PMF	12.75	3.19
Santander	SDR	9.63	1.86
Valladolid	VLL	−6.86	1.41
Lubecca	LBC	−11.90	3.81
Karlsruhe	FKB	4.28	1.32
Grenoble	GNB	4.62	2.82
Pau-Pyrénées	PUF	−1.48	2.31

a constant traffic growth. These results should be combined with the RCI values for both airports. REG has small values, while the opposite happens for PMF. In the latter case, there is a significant presence of competing airports in the neighborhood, in particular the Bologna and Milan airport systems, which reduce the potential role of PMF. In contrast, REG has just one real competitor (Lamezia Terme, SUF, about 130 km away) and the presence of LCCs during 3 years did not produce significant positive or negative changes.

As for the French cases, GNB, located near to the Western Alps region, has experienced variable traffic trends, with ski tourists from abroad representing its main customers (98%). Despite the relevant role of seasonal charter services, regular flights have also increased thanks to the presence of LCCs, which on average have 43% of GNB's market share. However, the extremely seasonal character of passenger flows together with the closeness of similar alternative airports (Chambéry–Savoie) or bigger ones (Lyon and Geneva) translated to a constant increase in the RCI index by reducing the role of GNB in the area. Similarly, to GNB, the airport of Pau – Pyrénées (PUF) is located in a mountainous area and is less than 50 km away from the airport of Tarbes Lourdes Pyrénées (LDE), whose traffic is related to religious tourism and pilgrimages to Lourdes (Bernier, 2010). Traffic has been mainly domestic due to the strong presence of Air France on routes to both Paris airports.[12] Passengers in PUF grew until 2008, when LCCs reached their peak (20%); nonetheless, in 2009 PUF lost 15% of passengers while LDE grew by 53% without any LCCs. The presence of LDE together with the relative closeness of Toulouse (7th airport in France) and the withdrawal of Ryanair service in 2011[13] determined declining YCI and constantly increasing RCI values, which indicates a minor role for the airport (Table 6).

In Spain, the airport of Santander shows an increase in YCP, which follows the LCC's growing presence, while its RCI is substantially stable in the time period analyzed. As pointed out by Martinez and Marin (2015), the relatively small population of the city is offset by its isolation and the poor transport alternatives to the functional areas in Spain, which give Santander a role as a sub-regional center that is also attractive to the potential low-cost customers from the near agglomeration of Bilbao. In contrast, the Valladolid airport has changed its RCI in both directions. In the first years of the analysis, RCI has slightly grown, as has the LCC percentage. However, in the last 4 years, RCI decreased together with its YCI, probably due to traffic reduction in the biggest and closest airport of Madrid. There, the economic crisis, Iberia's restructuring process, the impact of high-speed train services on domestic routes and an increase in airport charges, which caused the cut of Ryanair's capacity and the closure of the EasyJet base, produced a drop in traffic figures.

As for the German cases, the Lubeck airport shows a particular trend, since its traffic grew until 2009 mainly due to LCCs. However, since 2010, the values have started to decrease, partly due to the financial crisis, while the nearby Hamburg airport (5th in traffic terms) kept growing, thanks to EasyJet, Germanwings and Condor establishing their bases at the airport. This translated to a constant RCI increase, which highlights a marginal role for Lubeck in favor of Hamburg, located only 60 km away, whose higher number of frequencies and destinations proved more attractive for passengers. The airport of Karlsruhe (FKB) has experienced a growing trend since 2003, when Ryanair started initial operations to London Stansted. In the same year, the carrier relocated its Strasbourg routes (25 km south of Karlsruhe) to FKB following a court judgment that imposed the repayment of subsidies received at the Strasbourg airport by the carrier (Olischer & Dörrenbächer, 2013). During the years, RCI moved toward the right side mainly due to the growth of the two bigger airports of Stuttgart (110 km east) and Frankfurt (160 km north). Moreover, in the last 2 years the airport has flat-lined, despite Ryanair launching its base in 2012.

CONCLUSIONS AND MAIN FINDINGS

Following the liberalization process, the presence of LCCs proved to be fundamental for the success of many airports in Europe. Nonetheless, quite often this presence represents only a necessary condition that needs other elements (such as the catchment area or the incoming market for tourist reasons) to guarantee long-term growth and sustainability. As a result, totally different outcomes may result from the interaction between airports and LCCs, which in turn influence the role of the airport in the catchment area.

This chapter provides an analysis of the two main aspects shaping the airport-LCC relationship: the role of the airport in the area and the balance of power between the LCC and the airport. These aspects have been analyzed starting from a sample of 157 airports in Europe, with a focus on a sub-sample of 16 representative airports in a 10-year time span. These airports have also been discussed narratively, commenting on the presence, the role and the organization of LCCs.

The analysis allows us to draw some common patterns:

- If several LCCs operate in an airport, the airport is less likely to be dominated by one carrier, in particular if there are no good substitutes in the region. This is the case of Sevilla or Nantes, where good population density and the relatively far distance of alternative airports results in a low RCI.
- In a context with a good catchment area and two airports, LCCs may opt for the secondary one instead of the primary airport due to its lower charges and entry barriers. As soon as the carrier decides to also serve the primary airport where it could also get business passengers, RCI increases. This is, for example, the case when Girona downsized in favor of Barcelona El Prat.
- Similarly, where there are many primary airports in the same catchment area, the airport hosting one LCC has a relatively low impact and is dominated by the carrier. This happened in Parma, Lubeck or Karlsruhe, all suffering from Ryanair's decisions. Only in the presence of a peculiar catchment area and where the airport manager favors a mix between low-cost and full-service carriers can the airport regain a role, as with the case of Verona.
- Tourism may be important for the success of an airport such as Verona, Girona or Sevilla, however where seasonality plays a part and similar airports compete to attract tourists, as in the case of Grenoble (with Chambery) or Pau–Pyrénées (with Lourdes Pyrénées), the outcomes can differ.
- Where the airport is rather isolated, due to poor surface transport services and relatively distant neighboring airports, the type of airline does not significantly modify its YCP, as the airport only serves its captive demand in the primary catchment area. This is the case of Reggio Calabria.
- Finally, good catchment areas and a good mix of traffic (business, leisure, and charter) allow more stable relationships between airports and airlines, preventing the dominance of one over the other (Naples and Lyon).

In conclusion, the relationship between LCCs and airports is not simply dual, but also heavily dependent on the role of the airport in its catchment area. It is not the sole presence of an LCC, even when growing for many years, which guarantees growth or even lasting traffic figures for any airport. Airports sharing the catchment area with others are in a very risky position, due to the mobility of the LCCs, even if the area they serve is very dynamic and guarantees a large demand. This aspect pushes airports to be extremely efficient and able to adapt to the changes in LCCs' business models, in order to continue to play a role in the catchment area. Differently, geographically isolated airports in good catchment areas can better counterbalance the power of carriers.

NOTES

1. In terms of product and service upgrades, such as the use of primary airports in addition to regional/secondary ones, the opening to the global distribution systems (GDSs) for ticket distribution, the introduction of customer-oriented features (longer seat pitch, apps for mobile phones, more flexible ticketing, and fast-track) and services (for business travelers, groups, and families).

2. It represents "a complex of incoming and outgoing flights, structured such that each incoming flight creates a bookable connection with every outgoing flight" (Danesi, 2006). This structure aims at maximizing the number of connections of an airline (historically a full carrier) available from the airport.

3. Olischer (2016) identifies 30 cases of threats of relocations/withdrawals within EU done by Ryanair (27), and EasyJet (2), Germanwings (1) together with the reasons: taxes (33%), subsidies (23%), airport fees (20%), no. of passengers (17%), and infrastructure (7%). Among them, 18 relocations/withdrawals have been completely executed, 10 partially and only 2 have been not executed.

4. This is the case in Italy, where the carrier has publically threatened to close two bases (Pescara and Alghero) as a result of a 40% increase in passenger departure taxes in 2016. Similarly, in Norway, the carrier announced the closure of its Oslo Rygge base following the introduction of an environmental tax for flights originating in Norway.

5. This is more likely in the case of short-haul traffic. Long-haul routes tend to concentrate more on hubs, and potentially important catchment areas may not be served by any resident airline (Milan, Barcelona, and Manchester).

6. There are two possible situations that can exclude the possibility of a state aid: "if (1) the price charged for the airport services corresponds to the market price and (2) the price charged for the airport services is shown, through an ex ante analysis, to lead to a reasonable return on capital for the airport manager" (EC, 2014a).

7. PSO refers to subsidies provided by governments (paid to airports, airlines or both) in order to guarantee a minimum level of air services to small or rural communities that, for example, may lack transport alternatives to reach main economic centers.

8. With the exception of Lyon, in the time span considered, the airports in this group had, on average, 5 Million passengers a year; thus they can be classified as regional airports according to the EU definition provided in paragraph 3.

9. In terms of Compound Annual Growth Rate. In the case of Linate, the growth path has been limited by law, reducing the number of hourly movements allowed following the opening of Malpensa in 1998.

10. http://www.anna.aero

11. In 2010 Ryanair launched its base in El Prat and it is now progressively downsizing its presence in Girona.

12. http://www.anna.aero

13. The European Commission found that airport service agreements and marketing arrangements concluded between the Chambre de Commerce et d'Industrie de Pau-Béarn and Ryanair/AMS between 2003 and 2011, as well as a contract signed with Transavia in 2006, gave these companies an undue economic advantage over their competitors (EC, 2014b).

REFERENCES

Allroggen, F., Malina, R., & Lenz, A. K. (2013). Which factors impact on the presence of incentives for route and traffic development? Econometric evidence from European airports. *Transportation Research Part E: Logistics and Transportation Review*, *60*, 49–61.

Bendinelli, W. E., Bettini, H. F. A. J., & Oliveira, A. V. M. (2016). Airline delays, congestion internalization and non-price spillover effects of low-cost carrier entry. *Transportation Research Part A: Policy and Practice*, *85*, 39–52.

Bernier, X. (2010). Regional airports and the accessibility of mountain areas: Networks, importance and contribution to development. *International Journal of Sustainable Development and Planning*, *5*(2), 130–140.

CAPA. (2015). Barcelona El Prat: Europe's leading airport for LCCs a battleground in fight for business travellers. Retrieved form http://centreforaviation.com. Accessed on June 2016.

CAPA. (2016). Airlines in Transition How FSCs can regain short haul share from LCCs Part 1 at the coal face. Retrieved from http://centreforaviation.com. Accessed on May 2016.

Carballo-Cruz, F., & Costa, V. (2014). Success factors of regional airports: The case of Oporto airport. *Tourism & Management Studies*, *10*(1), 37–45.

Castillo-Manzano, J. I., López-Valpuesta, L., & González-Laxe, F. (2011). The effects of the LCC boom on the urban tourism fabric: The view point of tourism managers. *Tourism Management*, *32*(5), 1085–1095.

Choo, Y. Y., & Oum, T.-H. (2013). Impacts of low-cost carrier services on efficiency of the major U.S. airports. *Journal of Air Transport Management*, *33*, 60–67.

Copenhagen Economics. (2012). *Airport Competition in Europe*. Report prepared on the request of ACI EUROPE.

Danesi, A. (2006). Measuring airline hub timetable co-ordination and connectivity: Definition of a new index and application to a sample of European hubs. *European Transport \ Trasporti Europei*, 34, 54–74.

de Wit, J. G., & Zuidberg, J. (2012). The growth limits of the low-cost carrier model. *Journal of Air Transport Management*, *21*, 17–23.

Dennis, N. (2001). Developments of hubbing at European airports. *Air & Space Europe*, *3*(1), 51–55.

Dennis, N. (2005). Industry consolidation and future airline network structures in Europe. *Journal of Air Transport Management*, *11*(3), 175–183.

Dobruszkes, F. (2006). An analysis of European low-cost airlines and their networks. *Journal of Transport Geography*, *14*(4), 249–264.

Dobruszkes, F. (2013). The geography of European low-cost airline networks: A contemporary analysis. *Journal of Transport Geography*, *28*, 75–88.

Doganis, R. (2010). *Flying off course: Airline economics and marketing* (4th edn.). New York: Routledge.

EC. (2005). Community Guidelines on financing of airports and start-up aid to airlines from regional airports, 2005. Brussels, 2005. Retrieved from http://eur-lex.europa.eu/. Accessed on November 2016.

EC. (2014a). Guidelines on State aid to airports and airlines, 2014. Brussels, 2014. Retrieved from http://eur-lex.europa.eu/. Accessed on November 2016.

EC. (2014b). State Aid: Further details on Commission decisions regarding public financing of airports and airlines in Germany, France and Austria. Brussels, 23 July 2014. Retrieved from http://europa.eu/. Accessed on June 2016.

Fageda, X., Suau-Sanchez, P., & Mason, K. J. (2015). The evolving low-cost business model: Network implications of fare bundling and connecting flights in Europe. *Journal of Air Transport Management*, *42*, 289–296.

Fichert, F., & Klophaus, R. (2011). Incentive schemes on airport charges—Theoretical analysis and empirical evidence from German airports. *Research in Transportation Business & Management*, *1*, 71–79.

Francis, G., Fidato, A., & Humphreys, I. (2003). Airport-airline interaction: The impact of low-cost carriers on two European airports. *Journal of Air Transport Management*, *9*(4), 267–273.

Fu, Q., & Kim, A. M. (2016). Supply-and-demand models for exploring relationships between smaller airports and neighboring hub airports in the US. *Journal of Air Transport Management*, *52*, 67–79.

Fu, X., Homsombat, W., & Oum, T. H. (2011). Airport-airline vertical relationships, their effects and regulatory policy implications. *Journal of Air Transport Management*, *17*, 347–353.

Fuellhart, K. (2007). Airport catchment and leakage in a multi-airport region: The case of Harrisburg International. *Journal of Transport Geography*, *15*, 231–244.

Fuhr, J., & Beckers, T. (2006). Vertical governance between airlines and airports – A transaction cost analysis. *Review of Network Economics*, *5*(4), 384–412.

Graham, A. (2013). Understanding the low-cost carrier and airport relationship: A critical analysis of the salient issues. *Tourism Management*, *36*, 66–76.

Halpern, N., Graham, A., & Dennis, N. (2016). Low-cost carriers and the changing fortunes of airports in the UK. Research in Transportation Business & Management, http://dx.doi.org/10.1016/j.rtbm.2016.05.002

Hunter, L. (2006). Low-cost airlines: Business model and employment relations. *European Management Journal*, *24*(5), 315–321.

Jankiewicz, J., & Huderek-Glapska, S. (2016). The air transport market in Central and Eastern Europe after a decade of liberalisation – Different paths of growth. *Journal of Transport Geography*, (50), 45–56.

Kappes, J. W., & Merkert, R. (2013). Barriers to entry into European aviation markets revisited: A review and analysis of managerial perceptions. *Transportation Research Part E: Logistics and Transportation Review*, *57*, 58–69.

Klophaus, R., Conrady, R., & Fichert, F. (2012). Low-cost carriers going hybrid: Evidence from Europe. *Journal of Air Transport Management*, *23*, 54–58.

Laurino, A., & Beria, P. (2014). Low-cost carriers and secondary airports: Three experiences from Italy. *Journal of Destination Marketing & Management*, *3*(3), 180–191.

Lawton, T. (2002). *Cleared for take-off: Structure and strategy in the low-fare airline business*. Aldershot: Ashgate.

Lian, J. I., & Rønnevik, J. (2011). Airport competition – Regional airports losing ground to main airports. *Journal of Transport Geography*, *19*(1), 85–92.

Lin, E., Mak, B., & Wong, K. (2013). *The business relationships between LCCs and airports in Southeast Asia: Influences of power imbalance and mutual dependence*. Transportation Research Part A: Policy and Practice, *50*, 33–46.

Madas, M. A., & Zografos, K. G. (2008). *Airport capacity vs. demand: Mismatch or mismanagement?* Transportation Research Part A: Policy and Practice, *42*, 203–226.

Malighetti, P., Paleari, S., & Redondi, R. (2016). Base abandonments by low-cost carriers. *Journal of Air Transport Management*, *55*, 234–244.

Malina, R., Albers, S., & Kroll, N. (2011). *Airport incentive programs: A European perspective*. Working Paper 107 of the Department of Business Policy and Logistics. University of Cologne No. 107.

Mason, K. J., & Morrison, W. J. (2008). Towards a means of consistently comparing airline business models with an application to the 'low-cost' airline sector. *Research in Transportation Economics*, *24*(1), *The Economics of Low-Cost Airlines*, 75–84.

Olischer, F. T. (2016). Concession Bargaining in the Aviation Industry Airlines vs Airports. Presentation at the workshop "New competition and the comparative locational advantage of airlines and airports", HTW Berlin, June 3rd–4th 2016. Retrieved from https://prezi.com. Accessed on June 2016.

Olischer, F. T., & Dörrenbächer, C. (2013). *Concession bargaining in the airline industry: Ryanair's policy of route relocation and withdrawal* (No. 73). Working Papers of the Institute of Management Berlin at the Berlin School of Economics and Law (HWR Berlin).

Pantazis, N., & Liefner, I. (2006). The impact of low-cost carriers on catchment areas of established international airports: The case of Hanover Airport, Germany. *Journal of Transport Geography*, *14*, 265–272.

Pels, E., Njegovan, N., & Behrens, C. (2009). Low-cost airlines and airport competition. *Transportation Research Part E: Logistics and Transportation Review*, *45*, 335–344.

Postorino, M. N., & Praticò, F. G. (2012). An application of the Multi-Criteria Decision-Making analysis to a regional multi-airport system. *Research in Transportation Business & Management*, *4*, 44–52.

Pyrialakou, V. D., Karlaftis, M. G., & Michaelides, P. G. (2012). Assessing operational efficiency of airports with high levels of low-cost carrier traffic. *Journal of Air Transport Management*, *25*, 33–36.

Redondi, R., Malighetti, P., & Paleari, S. (2012). De-hubbing of airports and their recovery patterns. *Journal of Air Transport Management*, *18*(1), 1–4.

Rey, B., Myro, R. L., & Galera, A. (2011). Effect of low-cost airlines on tourism in Spain. A dynamic panel data model. *Journal of Air Transport Management*, *17*, 163–167.

Strickland, J. (2015). Current challenges and future prospects for EU secondary airports. *Policy Department B: Structural and cohesion policies*. Brussels: European Parliament.

Wiltshire, J. (2013). IATA Economic Briefing No. 11: Airport Competition, IATA, November 2013.

Zanin, M., & Lillo, F. (2013). Modelling the air transport with complex networks: A short review. *European Physical Journal Special Topics*, *215*, 5–21.

CHAPTER 15

BENCHMARKING WORLDWIDE AIRPORT CONNECTIVITY WITH DEMAND DATA: GLOBAL HUB COMPETITION, NEW PLAYERS, AND THE HIDDEN POTENTIAL OF SELF-CONNECTIVITY

Pere Suau-Sanchez, Augusto Voltes-Dorta and Héctor Rodríguez-Déniz

ABSTRACT

The connectivity provided by full-service network carriers under the umbrella of airline alliances is increasingly challenged by the services of Middle Eastern airlines via their own hubs, and the rise of new passenger strategies like self-connectivity. While these two developments can potentially benefit consumers with more services and lower fares, the rise of Middle East carriers has been met with opposition by EU and US airlines that call for increased protectionism. In addition, only a few airports in the world actively support self-connections. In this context, this study aims to investigate (1) the markets in which Middle East carriers exert a stronger dominance in terms of the number of passenger connections, (2) whether EU, US, or Asian hubs provide a competitive quality of connectivity in terms of travel time, and (3) whether a significant potential for self-connections is hidden at

The Economics of Airport Operations
Advances in Airline Economics, Volume 6, 387–423

ISSN: 2212-1609/doi:10.1108/S2212-160920170000006015

major airports worldwide. To that end, several datasets of passenger bookings (MIDT), airline schedules, and minimum connecting times between 2012 and 2015 are combined in a connections-building methodology that delivers six market-specific airport connectivity indicators for our benchmarking exercise. Our findings show that although European and some Asian hubs have lost traffic in global markets, they remain competitive from a quality perspective. US hubs have maintained their market share and competitive position. Finally, we identify the airports and airlines with the highest potential to provide self-connecting travel options, which can become an attractive new source of revenue for the parties involved.

Keywords: Connectivity; hub competition; Gulf carriers; aviation policy

JEL classifications: L93; O18; R41

INTRODUCTION

Full-service airline networks are commonly organized in a hub-and-spoke fashion, with a limited number of large "hub" airports that consolidate originating and transfer traffic flows. This allows airlines to achieve higher load factors and benefits from economies of traffic density (Button, 2002; Doganis, 2010; Rodríguez-Déniz, Suau-Sanchez, & Voltes-Dorta, 2013). From an airport perspective, large hub airports have the opportunity to grow beyond their local market potential and enter into a competition for the global flows of transfer passengers (Suau-Sanchez, Voltes-Dorta, & Rodríguez-Déniz, 2016a). The number of global airports hosting a dominant hub is not increasing. In fact, the stronger airline competition has forced some airlines into bankruptcy (Ciliberto & Schenotne, 2012) and mergers, which have actually decreased the number of large hubs (Redondi, Malighetti, & Paleari, 2012).

During the last few years, two new dynamics have emerged that could challenge the status quo and current distribution of global passenger flows. The first is the rise of Middle Eastern carriers and their hubs (O'Connell, 2011a,2011b), which have benefited from the eastward displacement of the world's economic center of gravity (Airbus, 2012; Grether & Mathys, 2010; Quah, 2011). These Gulf-based carriers (e.g., Emirates, Etihad, and Qatar Airways), also known as "super connectors," have provided consumers with more services, travel options, and lower fares. By taking advantage of the increasing efficiency of wide-body twinjets (Bowen, 2010; O'Connor & Fuellhart, 2013), Gulf carriers use hub-bypassing strategies (Bel & Fageda, 2010; Maertens, 2010; Tembleque-Vilalta & Suau-Sanchez, 2016) and directly serve secondary airports in other continents from their main bases. In this way, Gulf carriers have been able to develop massive global hubs connecting worldwide destinations using sixth-freedom rights.[1]

Despite the potential benefit to consumers in terms of more services and lower fares, the rise of Middle East carriers has been met with opposition by EU and US airlines, which may be experiencing some demand leakage and are calling for increasing protectionism. For example, major carriers like American Airlines, Delta, United, and other industry bodies in the United States created the Partnership for Open and Fair Skies with the objective to "restore a level playing field under the Open Skies agreements with Qatar and the UAE" (Partnership for Open and Fair Skies, 2015). One of the arguments brought forward by this Partnership is that connections between North America and South East Asia via the Middle East result in longer travel distances than alternative routings provided by US airlines and their partners via Asian hubs (Partnership for Open and Fair Skies, 2015, pp. 47–48). This statement can be interpreted as a challenge to the quality of connectivity offered by Middle Eastern airlines and airports. In this context, our study aims to shed some light on these potential claims by identifying the air transport markets in which Middle East carriers exert a stronger dominance in terms of number of passenger connections and to quantify how much demand may have leaked from US and EU airlines and airports in recent years. We also investigate whether EU, US, or Asian hubs provide a similar quality of connectivity to Middle Eastern hubs in terms of travel time.

The second factor challenging the status quo is the popularization of a new way to connect flights among price-sensitive air travelers: self-connectivity (OAG, 2016). In a context where low-cost carriers (LCCs) have rapidly become the dominant players in short-haul markets (Dobruszkes, 2006, 2013), the substantial amount of flight frequencies at low-cost airport bases have created opportunities to transfer between those flights, even though flight connection services are not typically offered by the LCCs themselves[2] (Malighetti, Paleari, & Redondi, 2008; Maertens, Pabst, & Grimme, 2016). Only a few airports in the world actively support self-connections. Examples include London Gatwick and Milano Malpensa airports, which have introduced the GatwickConnects and ViaMilano platforms, respectively. These allow passengers to book their own flight transfer services between two flights not explicitly connected by the airline/s involved. In exchange for a fee (Gatwick) or for free (Milano), self-connecting passengers are offered a baggage transfer service and insurance against the risk of missing their onward flights. The limited implementation of this new business opportunity leads us to investigate whether a significant potential for self-connections is hidden at major airports worldwide, and to identify the airports where this potential is stronger given their current airline mixes.

In order to achieve our research objectives, we contribute to the literature on air transport geography with the first global connectivity analysis using demand data. To that end, several datasets of passenger bookings (MIDT), airline schedules, and minimum connecting times between 2013 and 2015 are combined in a connections-building methodology that delivers six market-specific airport connectivity indicators for our benchmarking exercise. These include factors that account for absolute amounts of connectivity, like traffic generation, number of destinations, or connecting passengers; but also factors that measure quality of connectivity offered by the different hubs, such as geographic detours and travel time increases. Finally, we find a large potential for self-connectivity in the world's busiest airports, which can become an attractive new source of revenue for the parties involved.

The remainder of this study is structured as follows. "Literature Review" section reviews the existing literature on the rise of Middle Eastern carriers and on self-connectivity, and discusses our contributions to the literature. "Data and Methodology" section describes the datasets employed and the connections-building methodology, and defines the connectivity benchmarks. "Results and Discussion" section presents the results and discusses the main policy and managerial implications. Finally, "Summary and Conclusions" section summarizes our main findings.

LITERATURE REVIEW

Measures of Connectivity

Traditionally, measuring airport connectivity has been a way of quantifying how accessible a region is in terms of air transport links. High levels of connectivity are linked to economic and social benefits to both cities and regions (Bel & Fageda, 2008; Brueckner, 2003; Florida, Mellander & Holgersson, 2015; Goetz, 1992; Van de Vijver, Derudder, & Witlox, 2014). Many previous studies have proposed different methods to measure airport connectivity (see, e.g., Burghouwt, 2007; Burghouwt & De Wit, 2005). A common approach is to refer to the topological properties of an air transport network (built upon published airline schedules) and the role that each airport plays, as a distinct node in said network, in facilitating connections between the other nodes. This framework allows researchers to employ many well-known topological indicators such as degree or betweenness centrality[3] as a proxy for airport connectivity (Guimerà, Mossa, Turtschi, & Amaral, 2005). The higher the level of airport centrality is, the closer the potential of an airport to serve as an intermediate gateway (hub) between other cities. To the extent that different airports may overlap in this gateway role for a given origin and destination market, varying degrees of hub competition can be inferred from the same measurements.

A second approach employs data on airline schedules to determine the number of potential flight connections available from/within a given airport that meet a set of criteria (typically both maximum and minimum connecting times). For example, the Netscan method employs a connection-building algorithm to search for valid flight combinations and performs a quality-weighted aggregation to calculate the airport's total number of connection units. The quality of a flight connection is linked to the detour imposed with respect to non-stop travel, which is measured in time units and has two components: (1) additional flying time associated to geographic detour (also known as circuity time) and (2) connecting time, with a maximum detour threshold always imposed to discard uncompetitive connections. In order to account for the fact that long-distance travelers will be less sensitive to travel detours, variable thresholds can be defined depending on travel distance (see, e.g., Global Connectivity Index by Allroggen, Wittmann, and Malina (2015)). In this context, airports that are able to organize flight arrivals and departures in coordinated waves (Burghouwt & De Wit, 2005) typically offer a higher amount of potential hub connections and also a higher quality of hub connectivity, translated into shorter connection times.

The methods described above can be classified as "supply-based" approaches (Suau-Sanchez, Voltes-Dorta, & Rodríguez-Déniz, 2015) since they are based on the analysis of published airline schedules (i.e., the supply side of air transport markets). Therefore, their results can be interpreted in terms of potential "flight connectivity" rather than actual "passenger connectivity." An important limitation of this approach is that not all flight connectivity has the same value. Potential flight connections serving large city-pair routes will be more valuable to the respective hubs than in city-pair routes where no passenger traffic is recorded. Schedules data does not provide information about the actual points of origin and destination of the passengers. Addressing this limitation requires the use of data on passenger bookings that have an explicit indication on the actual airport-pair market that is being connected (e.g., MIDT and PaxIS are two of the most well-known databases). Since this data cover the demand side of the market (i.e., the passenger), this approach can be referred to as "demand-based." For example, authors like Grosche and Klophaus (2015) and Rodríguez-Déniz et al. (2013) employ demand data to measure the share of connecting passengers served by a given hub within a given city pair. Comparing these "market shares" across different hubs allows for assessing the strength of hub competition in the same city-pair market.

A pure demand-based approach, however, does not provide any measures of quality of hub connectivity, which are still dependent on schedules data to calculate travel detours. Hence, in order to capture both hub competition and quality of hub connectivity, a combined approach with both supply and demand data is recommended. This can be implemented by means of demand-weighted connectivity indicators: using the supply data to build valid flight connections, but, at the time of aggregating them, a weighting associated to the actual passengers that travel on these routes can be implemented. This combined approach also allows us to disaggregate our results according to geographical market, which means that airports can have different rankings depending on the characteristics of their global destination networks. This is the novel approach employed in this study in order to serve our research objectives.

Deregulation, Airport Competition and the Rise of New Players

There is a general agreement in the literature that the deregulation and liberalization of air transport markets have overall benefited the passenger with more travel options from more airports (see, e.g., Bowen, 2002; O'Connor (2003)). This is true for intra-continental markets thanks to the rise of LCCs in the US and the EU (see, e.g., Dobruszkes, 2006, 2013). It is also true for intercontinental markets thanks to the reappearance of multihub strategies (Burghouwt, 2014) and the increasing use of hub-bypassing as a result of new aircraft technology and the growing economic importance of regions (Bel & Fageda, 2010; Bowen, 2010; Dijkstra, Garcilazo, & McCann, 2013; Suau-Sanchez et al., 2015). The Gulf carriers are indeed one of the main users of the hub-bypassing strategy that have benefited a number of European airports (O'Connell, 2011a).

However, there is a growing dissatisfaction among European and American carriers of the growing role of Gulf carriers in their home markets. They have complained to different regulators of an unlevel playing field and have called for a regulatory agenda that protects them from the Gulf carriers. A recent paper by De Wit (2014) analyzes in detail the reasons behind a possible unlevel playing field between Gulf carriers and European and US carriers. De Wit (De Wit, 2014) considers location as the main cause, since it allows Gulf carriers to develop long-haul hourglass hubs and to benefit from density, scope and scale economies. Conversely, European carriers have to operate from hinterland hubs and are challenged by costly short-haul feeder operations. In other words, Gulf carriers could have a comparative advantage from the perspective of the physical resource endowment (i.e., location). The location of a hub in relation to the global passenger flows can then be considered an exogenous comparative advantage. Different locations may promote dissimilar hub specializations (i.e., hub-and-spoke, hourglass hubs, etc.), which involve different network economics. In the case of a long-haul hourglass hubs, both the distance advantage and the technological economies of scale of the aircraft act to depress the unit costs (Doganis, 2002). Other possible reasons behind the unlevel playing field, but with a lower weight, highlighted by De Wit (*ibid.*) are related to the economic and institutional conditions in the Gulf States (e.g., fuel price, airport charges, fleet expansion and capacity dumping, state aid in financing, and fiscal regimes). These have been a matter of heated discussion in both academic and industry forums.

Recently, there has been an increase in the number of contributions analyzing the connectivity provided by Middle East carriers and its implications in terms of hub competition. There seems to be a general agreement that the

Middle East has earned a new central place in the worldwide travel flows and that the Gulf carriers are major providers of connectivity (Hooper, Walker, Moor, & Al Zubaidi, 2011; O'Connell, 2011a). Having said that, the available quantitative analyses on the competitive position of hubs may indicate that incumbent hubs remain competitive. For example, Grosche and Klophaus (2015) measure competition between the five largest European hubs (i.e., Amsterdam, Paris-Charles de Gaulle, Frankfurt, London-Heathrow, and Madrid) and the three Middle East hubs (i.e., Dubai, Doha, and Abu Dhabi) for the months of November 2009 and November 2012. They measure competition among hubs by ranking them according to the number of overlapping transfer city pairs. Results show that the main competitors to each of the five largest European hubs for extra-EU transfer traffic are Munich and Istanbul. None of the Gulf hubs were among the five main competitors to the largest European hubs. Similarly, Grimme (2011) looked into the passenger itineraries between Germany and Asia in 2008. They concluded that new services by Emirates stimulated passenger demand, while incumbent hubs did not lose transfer passengers. Their analysis showed that, on all relevant transfer itineraries, Emirates had a disadvantage when it comes to travel time due to the longer geographical detours imposed and long transfer times when connecting at Dubai. The importance of the hub's geographical position was also identified by Redondo, Malighetti, and Paleari (2011) for worldwide markets. Their results show that European airports seem to dominate the worldwide rankings and the Middle East hubs are not ranked among the most competitive.

In view of the above, there seems to be a contradiction between the scarce quantitative literature on hub competition (where incumbents still dominate) and the concerns expressed by the same incumbent airlines about the dominance of Middle East airlines and airports. This motivates us to provide a new analysis with more recent data than previous studies in order to re-evaluate the competitive position of Middle East hubs between 2013 and 2015.

Self-Connectivity: A New Niche Market Under Development

Traditionally, passengers that wish to connect between LCC flights must self-transfer. They travel on a combination of multiple tickets, enduring the inconvenience of an additional check-in process at the LCC airport base, taking care of their own baggage, and facing the added risk of a missed connection. In spite of this, an increasing number of price-sensitive passengers self-transfer (OAG, 2016). By designing their own flight itineraries outside the boundaries of traditional airline connectivity, these passengers are able to save some money.

During the last few years, LCCs have been through a process of "hybridization" (Klophaus, Conrady, & Fichert, 2012) and have distanced themselves from the "archetypical" LCC business model (Fageda, Suau-Sanchez, & Mason, 2015).

Price bundling, codesharing, and connecting flights have been the main additions to their services catalog. While, in the United States, Southwest has been offering connecting flights for quite a long time, in Europe there is a more limited number of LCCs offering this service. Vueling and Air Berlin were among the first LCCs to start offering flight transfers in their bases at Barcelona and Palma de Mallorca, respectively. More recently, Norwegian provides flight transfers between its flights and charges a connecting fee to cover the associated costs. Around the world, Air Arabia, Air Asia and Citilink are also known for offering flight connections at their main bases (ICAO, 2014). The provision of these services shows that LCCs are interested in generating new sources of revenue by catering to the needs of self-connecting passengers.

Airports may also see the benefits of exploiting this niche market as it can help increasing non-aeronautical revenues (Malighetti, Paleari, & Redondi, 2008). Recently, London-Gatwick and Milan-Malpensa airports implemented new platforms to facilitate self-connections and improve travel experience. Self-connecting passengers at Gatwick and Malpensa are offered a baggage transfer service as well as insurance against the risk of missing their onward flight in the event of delays. This service is free at Malpensa and available to any passenger, while at Gatwick a small fee needs to be paid and the transfer is only possible with a limited number of airlines. In this regard, the diversity of airlines participating in those self-connectivity platforms may indicate that this strategy can benefit route development strategies not only in short-haul markets, but also in medium- and long-haul markets.

As a very recent phenomenon, literature on self-connectivity is very limited. It was first defined by Burghouwt (2007) as "self-help hubbing." Later, it was analyzed in more detail by Malighetti et al. (2008) and hinted by Jimenez, Claro, and Pinho de Sousa (2013). More recently, Fichert and Klophaus (2016) and Maertens et al. (2016) scoped the self-connectivity market out. Using data on airline schedules, Malighetti et al. (2008) developed a method to find the quickest-travel-time itineraries within the European air transport network. Their main conclusion is that the majority (two-thirds) of the fastest indirect itineraries were provided outside the scope of the airline alliances. In regards to the airports with the highest potential, their results reveal that airports that are relatively "central" to the European network, in both a geographical and a topological sense, are found to be the ones with the highest potential for self-connections (e.g., Munich, Paris-CDG, Stockholm, and Helsinki). Fichert and Klophaus (2016) explore the self-connecting, hubbing and codesharing options of seven European airlines and suggest that airports support of self-connections is a soft approach for connection building. Using the same type of supply data as Malighetti et al. (2008), Maertens et al. (2016) also assess the potential of transfers between European LCC services. They identify Barcelona, London Gatwick and Stansted as the airports with the largest LCC transfer potential.

Overall, the studies above support the hypothesis that there is indeed an opportunity for widespread development of self-connecting travel services.

Our methodology can expand on the existing self-connectivity studies by broadening the definition of self-connectivity to include any connection between non-partner airlines alongside the intra- and inter-LCC connectivity. With this approach, we are able to account for potential connections between LCCs and full-service airlines or between airlines in different alliances. This is another dimension of self-connectivity that the existing studies have not explored so far. Similar to our other research objective, combining supply, and demand data allows us to measure the real market potential of those self-connections.

DATA AND METHODOLOGY

Definitions

Most publications on airport connectivity employ supply data (airline schedules and seat capacity) in order to measure an airport's potential to support air transport activity by (1) originating/receiving a large amount of airline seats and (2) coordinating flight schedules so as to enable good hub connectivity between arriving and departing seats in terms of shorter connecting times and a larger number of viable flight connections (see, e.g., Burghouwt & Redondi, 2013).

This study looks at the same concepts from the perspective of the actual passengers making these connections. This analysis, however, must be executed with caution: real-world flight itineraries may not properly characterize an airport's connectivity potential as passengers can decide to purchase plane tickets with longer-than-optimal connections in exchange for lower fares. This report addresses this issue by mixing data on passenger demand (MIDT) with published airline schedules in order to use only "best weekly connection" itineraries. Hence, while the focus of this paper remains on "potential" airport connectivity, the use of demand data brings two new dimensions to the analysis: (1) the possibility of assigning a "value" to the available flight connections according to the size of the relevant markets and (2) the possibility of disaggregating the results across different markets for a more detailed analysis. The importance of both aspects is discussed below.

Throughout this chapter, air transport markets will be defined by a place of origin (i.e., airport, city, country, region, etc.) and a place of destination for the air travelers. For example, in Fig. 1 above the market from B to D includes all seven passengers commencing their journeys in airport B and terminating in airport D, three of which travel indirectly through C. If the market is defined to cover the entire region (from all origins to all destinations), all ten passengers

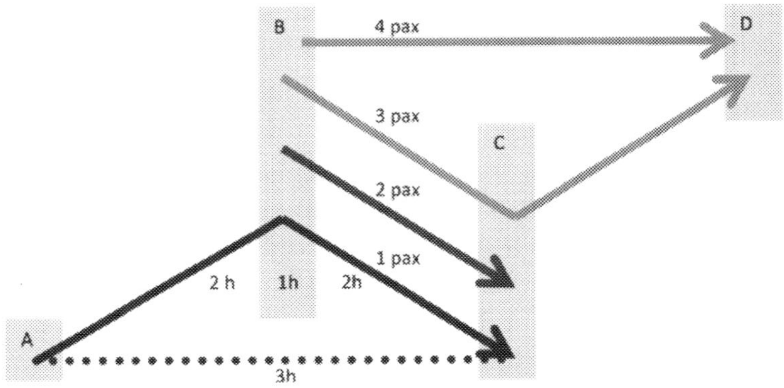

Fig. 1. Simplified Regional Air Transport Network.

will be considered, with six of them traveling non-stop and four traveling indirectly. From the perspective of passenger itineraries, airports can serve any given market as points of origin, final destinations, intermediate hubs, or not serve the market at all (e.g., airport A does not serve the B to D market in any way).

Looking at Fig. 1 from the perspective of each individual airport (e.g., airport B), it is possible to break down passenger departures in three main categories:

(1) Direct: Passengers starting their journey in airport B and flying non-stop to their destination (two passengers from B to C and four from B to D).
(2) Indirect: Passengers starting their journey in airport B and flying with at least one onward connection to their final destination (three passengers from B to D via C).
(3) Transfer: Passengers starting their journey in another airport and flying with at least one hub connection through airport B to their destination (one passenger from A to C via B).

Both direct and indirect passengers can be used to determine the role of airport B as "traffic generator," while transfer passengers can be used to assess the role of airport B as a "hub" or intermediate gateway to other markets. It is the combination of both roles that characterizes an airport's overall "connectivity" profile (Suau-Sanchez et al., 2016a). Note that the difference between indirect and transfer passengers is related to the perspective considered. For indirect passengers the perspective of the originating airport is taken. For transfer passengers the perspective of the hub airport is considered.

Based on these simple definitions, it is clear that any measure of airport connectivity depends on the market/s considered. London Heathrow, e.g., serves its largest number of passenger transfers in the markets between North America and Continental Europe where it does not generate any traffic (Tables 1 and 2). On the contrary, in the markets between the United Kingdom and the rest of the world, Heathrow appears to be mainly a traffic generator.

Table 1. Breakdown of Direct and Indirect Passenger Departures (in thousands) per Origin/Destination Market at Heathrow (June 2014).

From/to	UK	MAF	SAF	NAM	CAM	SAM	MEA	CEA	SOA	SEA	FEA	EEU	NEU	OCE
Direct	111	12	67	317	6	14	137	4	60	53	80	745	65	11
Indirect	3	3	33	92	9	17	21	2	38	39	29	64	21	33

Table 2. Breakdown of Transfer Passenger Departures (in thousands) per Origin/Destination Market at Heathrow (June 2014).

From/to	UK	MAF	SAF	NAM	CAM	SAM	MEA	CEA	SOA	SEA	FEA	EEU	NEU	OCE
UK	1		4	28		1	6		4	2	5	24	3	1
MAF	–	–	–	–	–	–	–	–	–	–	–	–	–	–
SAF	4	–	–	15	–	–	–	–	–	–	–	12	–	–
NAM	22	–	16	–	–	–	23	–	32	2	1	146	8	–
CAM	1	–	–	–	–	–	1	–	–	–	–	7	1	–
SAM	1	–	–	–	–	–	1	–	–	–	1	8	1	–
MEA	6	–	–	23	–	1	–	–	–	–	–	8	–	–
CEA	–	–	–	–	–	–	–	–	–	–	–	–	–	–
SOA	4	–	–	38	–	–	–	–	–	–	–	5	–	–
SEA	2	–	–	2	–	–	–	–	–	–	–	6	–	–
FEA	6	–	–	–	–	1	–	–	–	–	–	17	–	–
EEU	26	–	11	151	4	1	7	–	5	5	19	51	2	3
NEU	3	–	–	7	–	1	–	–	–	–	–	2	–	–
OCE	1	–	–	–	–	–	–	–	–	–	–	5	–	–

Source: Own Elaboration.
Note: Maghreb (MAF); Sub-Saharan Africa (SAF); N. America (NAM); Central Am. & Caribbean (CAM); S. America (SAM); Middle East (MEA); Central Asia (CEA); South Asia (SOA); South East Asia (SEA), Far East (FEA); European Econ. Area (EEU); non-EEA Europe (NEU); Oceania (OCE).

An additional layer of complexity is competition. For example, only by comparing Heathrow's traffic data above with other airports in the same market it is possible to determine if its degree of connectivity is relatively high, medium, or low. This highlights the importance of market disaggregation for the analysis of airport connectivity. A consequence is that airports can have as many different connectivity rankings as markets they serve, which, in extreme cases, can be up to tens of thousands of origin/destination pairs. For the sake of presentation, however, this paper will select only a few relevant geographic markets to present our results.

Connectivity Indicators

Six indicators are used to rank airport connectivity in each market. These can be classified between Quantity Connectivity Indicators, Quality Connectivity Indicators, and a Self-Connectivity Potential Indicator.

Quantity Connectivity Indicators:

(1) Destinations served (DEST): Total number of ultimate destinations that were reached by all passengers originating at the airport, separated between direct (i.e., non-stop) and indirect (i.e., requiring an onward connection). This aims to measure the airport's global or regional "reach." In Fig. 1, passengers traveling from airport B reach two destinations.
(2) Traffic Generation (OD): Ratio of direct plus indirect passengers generated by the airport to total passengers in the market. In simple words, it represents the airport's market share in terms of originating passengers. In Fig. 1, the OD ratio of airport B in the regional market is $9/10 = 0.9$.
(3) Connectivity (C): Ratio of transfer passengers served by the airport to total transfer passengers in the market. In simple words, it represents the airport's market share in terms of transfer passengers and it serves as an absolute measure of the airport's role as a hub in the selected market. In Fig. 1, the C ratio of airport B in the regional market is $1/4 = 0.25$.

Quality Connectivity Indicators:

The next indicators refer exclusively to transfer passengers and aim to measure the quality of the flight connections offered by the hub airport in similar fashion to previous studies, i.e., focusing on travel detours (Veldhuis, 1997). An indirect flight will lead to a travel time increase (TTI) for the passenger with respect to an actual or hypothetical non-stop alternative. TTI is simply calculated as the ratio between actual travel time and minimum non-stop travel time, minus one. In practical terms, the minimum travel time is obtained from the quickest direct flight available between the origin and destination pairs of the relevant market. In the absence of such direct flights, a minimum travel time is estimated taking into account great circle distance and average cruise speeds of comparable itineraries.

$$TTI = \frac{\text{total travel time}}{\text{minimum travel time}} - 1$$

In Fig. 1, the passenger traveling from A to C via B experiences a TTI of 66.67%. This value, however, can be disaggregated into two components: geographic detour (representing circuitry time) and connecting time, as follows: $TTI = (1 + DTI) \times (1 + CTI) - 1$

(4) Detour Time Increase (DTI): Ratio between total flying time (excluding connecting time) and minimum travel time, minus one. The calculation is made for each passenger itinerary within the relevant airport and market and then a traffic-weighted average is obtained.

$$DTI = \frac{\text{total flying time}}{\text{minimum travel time}} - 1$$

In Fig. 1, the passenger traveling from A to C via B experiences a DTI of 33.33%, meaning that the indirect flight takes 33% extra flying time with respect the non-stop alternative. The closer the DTE is to 0, the more time "efficient" the flight routing offered by a particular hub is (Fig. 2).
The DTI is linked to the hub airport's geographic location as it determines the actual flight distances, which in turn, determine flying times. The relationship between time and distance, however, is not directly proportional. A journey split in segments tends to be relatively slower than its non-stop equivalent, even if the total distance covered is the same, due to factors, such as the extra landing and take-off cycle or the use of different aircraft types. This makes DTI slightly different from a circuitry factor (flight distance/great circle distance), as shown in Table 3.

(5) Connecting Time Increase (CTI): Ratio between connecting time and total flying time. The calculation is made for each passenger itinerary within the relevant airport and market and then a traffic-weighted average is obtained.

$$CTI = \frac{\text{connecting time}}{\text{total flying time}}$$

In Fig. 1, the passenger traveling from A to C via B experiences a CTI of 25% meaning that the flight connection adds 25% of travel time on top of the geographic detour. The closer this indicator is to 0, the smaller the time cost for the passenger associated to the flight connection.
It is important to separate CTI from DTI, because they depend on different factors. DTI is completely determined by the geographical location of an airport in relation to the markets it serves. CTI is a function of factors, such as terminal size and geometry, destination mix (i.e., domestic vs.

Fig. 2. Top-50 Passenger Itineraries in the United Kingdom–South Africa Market. *Source*: OAG.

Table 3. Detour Time Increase in the London–Johannesburg Market.

London–Johannesburg	Distance (km)	Av. Flying Time (min)	Circuitry	DTI
Non-stop	9,069	665	1.00	1.00
via Amsterdam	9,378	730	1.03	1.10
via Dubai	11,901	905	1.32	1.37

Source: OAG.

international, short-haul vs. long-haul), border control regulations, time distribution of arriving and departing flights, or the physical distribution of alliance and codeshare partners in the terminal complex. The complexity of these interactions, especially at the largest airports, results in unique patterns for arriving and departing passenger transfers that determine the average duration of flight connections at an airport.

Using our dataset, we found that average "best weekly connecting times" for international transfers are 182, 133, and 114 minutes in Dubai, Heathrow, and Amsterdam, respectively. While there may be controllable factors that explain these differences, one must not forget the average market length of transfer passengers at Dubai is 12% longer than in Heathrow and 35% longer than in Amsterdam (Fig. 3). In simple words, this means that Dubai airport connects airport pairs that are, on average, further apart than the connections served by other hubs. This has implications on the amount of frequencies arriving and departing at the hub in a given day, as well as on the tolerance of long-distance passengers to travel detours. Moreover, it means that connecting time is a smaller proportion of total flying time at Dubai than it would be if it were connecting airports that were closer together. Having both DTI and CTI as relative measures over flying and travel times mitigates the distortion associated to different market lengths with the goal to improve comparability across airports.

Self-Connectivity Potential Indicator:

(6) Self-connectivity potential (SC): In addition to benchmarking the amount and quality of the actual connectivity provided by each airport, we are also interested in investigating each airport's "hidden potential" for self-connectivity. This is achieved by constructing a normalized indicator in which each self-connecting flight combination found by our algorithms in the schedules dataset is weighted by the average number of passengers per valid

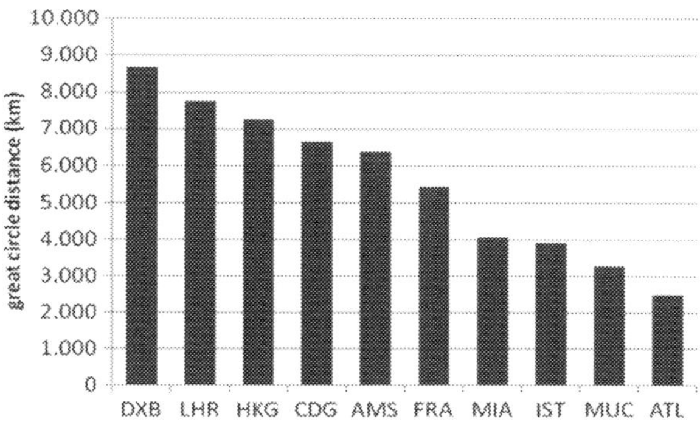

Fig. 3. Average Market Length of Transfer Passengers at Selected Airports (June 2014). *Source*: OAG.

frequency in the market it serves. In simple words, and in relation to Fig. 1, if there are three valid frequencies from B to D (one direct, one indirect-traditional via C, and one indirect self-connecting via C), the airport C will receive a SC score of 2.33 (7 passengers in the BD airport-pair multiplied by 1 self-connecting frequency and divided by 3 valid frequencies). While airport C could also potentially host valid flight combinations between A and D, these are not valuable to the airport because the market is empty of passengers (there are no passengers flying from A to D). This highlights the importance of using passenger data to complement the supply-based analysis of building connections with airline schedules. After aggregating all markets served by each airport, the SC score is normalized between 0 and 1 for ranking purposes, being 1 the airport with the highest SC value. While this is indeed a simplified approach to weight this type of connections, the results are expected to serve as a high-level indicator of the aforementioned "hidden potential" by combining supply and demand factors that affect the value of the available self-connections to the respective airports.

Datasets and Methodology

The first three indicators (*DEST, OD*, and *C*) will be calculated using monthly MIDT data between 2013 and 2015 in order to illustrate the evolution of connectivity profiles of selected airports in the relevant markets. The analysis of DTI, CTI, and SC will be provided for June 2015, which is the most recent period for which all required datasets are available. An algorithm to determine "best weekly connections" is developed, which combines supply (schedules and seats) and demand data (MIDT passenger itineraries).

The supply side is covered by a dataset of worldwide flight schedules during the first week of June 2015, for which the primary source is the OAG Schedules dataset. After simple data processing, the supply dataset comprises 667,534 unique records of scheduled passenger flight departures for 750 airlines that offered 90.3 million seats across a network of 3,018 commercial airports. Each record indicates the operating airline, alliance membership (if applicable), flight number, origin and destination airport codes, aircraft type, number of seats, flight distance, and Universal Time Coordinated (UTC) departure and arrival times.

The demand side is covered by a global MIDT dataset for an average week of June 2015. Each record contains information on the ticketing airline, as well as the points of origin and destination, the connecting airports (up to two intermediate stops), and the number of passengers. In total, the MIDT dataset contains 1.17 million different itineraries in 465,432 origin–destination markets, involving slightly over 57.6 million passengers, 19.7% of which (11.4 million) travel indirectly to their destinations. These passengers are heavily concentrated in North America, Asia-Pacific and the European Economic Area (EEA). These three intra-regional markets account for 45% of global connections. In regards to intercontinental markets, the busiest ones connect the three aforementioned regions as well as North America with Latin America and Caribbean.

The original sources of information for the MIDT dataset are Global Distributions Systems (GDSs), such as Galileo, Sabre, or Amadeus, among others. According to ARG (2013), 44% of all bookings of major airlines were done through GDSs in 2012. The proportion increases to 55% for network airlines, while LCCs, that prefer direct sales, only get 16% of their bookings via GDSs. This imbalance is an important limitation of the original dataset, as LCCs may be underrepresented. In order to correct that, the provider of our data (OAG Traffic Analyser) adjusted the market figures using mathematical algorithms based on frequencies and supplied seats in each flight sector. The reliability of these adjustments, in terms of LCC representation, can be judged by calculating the airline traffic shares in the intra-EEA market that result from our data. The combined market shares of LCCs are approximately 46%, which is virtually the same estimate provided by the European Commission for the EU Common Market in 2013 (EC, 2014). Additional explanations on the reliability of these adjustments have been covered in past studies that also employed these types of datasets for connectivity purposes (e.g., Suau-Sanchez et al., 2015, 2016a).

Besides MIDT and schedules, two additional datasets are required: (1) a full list of alliance, codeshare, and interline partners for each published airline in the MIDT file. This information was obtained both from OAG and the airlines' websites; and (2) Airport-specific minimum connecting times, including around 69,000 airline-specific exceptions valid on June 2015. This was obtained from the OAG Connections Analyser.

The CTI, DTI, and SC indicators are based on the determination of the best flight connections for each of the observed passenger itineraries in the relevant markets. To that end, there is need to match supply (airline schedules) and demand (MIDT) datasets across a sample week. For each MIDT record, a search is made for all available flights between the relevant airports, including intermediate stops. The resulting frequencies are then filtered by the codes of the published airline plus its alliance, codeshare and interline partners. Valid flight connections are built on the following restrictions (adapted from Seredyński, Rothlauf, & Grosche, 2014): (a) the published minimum connecting times must be met, (b) the maximum connecting time is arbitrarily set at 1 hour above the shortest weekly connection time,[4] (c) passengers on each first-leg flight prefer the alternative with the shortest travel time, and (d) passengers on each final-leg flight also prefer the shortest travel times. Once the valid flight combinations are selected, the number of passengers in the MIDT record is distributed among them according to seat capacity, which is determined by the minimum number of seats across all sectors. The proportion of passengers allocated to each travel option is equal to the proportion of its seat capacity to total capacity.

After a first round of processing, the resulting travel records are aggregated by flight number and departure date in order to check whether the number of passengers in all origin/destination markets assigned to each individual flight does not exceed the seat capacity of the aircraft. Passengers overcapacity are taken out of the travel records and brought into new rounds of processing with updated seat capacities in the schedules dataset. For this paper, three sequential rounds were enough to ensure that 95% of all passenger itineraries in the MIDT dataset were allocated. The final travel records can be then used to compute DTI and CTI values for any airport and market combination.

The process to calculate flight combinations for the SC indicator differs from the one above in that the search of travel itineraries fixes only the origin and destination airports in the MIDT records, with the objective to uncover all possibilities of connection (including "hidden" self-connections). In this case, there are no interline restrictions and self-connections are labeled as such if they involve two LCCs, or two airlines from different alliances, and there is no interline agreement between them. The same minimum connecting time restrictions are applied and maximum connecting times are based on the longest traditional connections in each market identified in the previous stage. This ensures that the self-connections are competitive in terms of travel time increase in comparison with the traditional ones.

All calculations were performed with SAS 9.4.

RESULTS AND DISCUSSION

The Evolution of Global Hub Connectivity

Table 4 reports the top-10 airports ranked by number of destinations, traffic generated and connectivity in worldwide international markets. The numbers reveal that European airports dominate when it comes to their global reach thanks to a high number of direct and indirect international destinations. Yet, the picture is quite different for traffic generation and connectivity. Regarding the former, London Heathrow sits at the top, but Asian airports located in large urban regions (Singapore, Seoul, and Hong Kong) seem to dominate the top 10. It is also important to highlight that, while the airlines based at London Heathrow might offer a relatively low number of direct destinations, the onward coverage by airline alliances helps in leveraging those into a larger number of indirect destinations compared to Dubai or Frankfurt.[5] In Europe, not only do the airports with strong local markets make it to the top in terms of traffic generation, but also others that are important tourist destinations (e.g., Amsterdam). Dubai on the other hand, appears in the fifth position as it

Table 4. Basic KPIs for Top-10 Airports, Worldwide International Markets, June 2015.

Destinations (direct + indirect)				Traffic Generation (OD)			Connectivity (C)		
Airport		All	Direct		Airport	%		Airport	%
1	London Heathrow (LHR)	1,527	185	1	London Heathrow (LHR)	3.8	1	Dubai International (DXB)	4.7
2	Frankfurt (FRA)	1,477	278	2	Singapore (SIN)	3.2	2	Frankfurt (FRA)	4.6
3	Paris CDG	1,454	245	3	Paris (CDG)	3.0	3	Istanbul Ataturk (IST)	3.7
4	Amsterdam (AMS)	1,330	264	4	Seoul Incheon (ICN)	2.8	4	London Heathrow (LHR)	3.1
5	New York (JFK)	1,237	125	5	Dubai International (DXB)	2.7	5	Paris (CDG)	2.7
6	Dubai (DXB)	1,216	214	6	Hong Kong (HKG)	2.7	6	Amsterdam (AMS)	2.7
7	Rome (FCO)	1,208	175	7	London Gatwick (LGW)	2.6	7	Doha (DOH)	2.6
8	Munich (MUC)	1,171	194	8	Taipei Taiwan (TPI)	2.5	8	Hong Kong (HKG)	2.4
9	Madrid (MAD)	1,170	164	9	Bangkok (BKK)	2.5	9	Munich (MUC)	2.2
10	Toronto (YYZ)	1,152	161	10	Amsterdam (AMS)	2.5	10	Atlanta (ATL)	2.1

Source: Authors from OAG Schedules and Traffic Analyser.

is a major business destination. In regards to connectivity, Dubai and Frankfurt are clearly ahead of the rest; they process more than 9% of the worldwide international connecting passengers. Generally, it can be said that European, Asian and Middle East airports dominate the international connecting markets. Atlanta, a well-known US hub is the only North American airport that makes it to the top 10. Overall, North American airports have little worldwide dominance, because of their less central geographical position with respect to the global flows, and therefore their more domestic focus (Rodríguez-Déniz et al., 2013).

While traffic generation is generally dependent on external factors, such as the size of the local market and business and tourism regional policies, the real competition takes place in the connecting traffic. This is the only traffic that allows airports to grow beyond their local market, but, due to its footloose nature, it can be subject to sudden changes. This strong degree of hub competition is illustrated in Fig. 4, which shows the evolution of connecting market shares in worldwide international markets between January 2013 and March 2015. Dubai (DXB) has clearly reinforced its role as main worldwide connecting airport, especially after the runway upgrade that took place between May and July 2014, which is shown in the graph as a big depression in connectivity. Istanbul (IST), Doha (DOH), and Abu Dhabi (AUH) have also progressively improved their position and gained market share over the recent years. On the other hand, Frankfurt (FRA), which shows quite a strong seasonality has been in a steady decline. Also, the other European airports, Heathrow (LHR), Paris

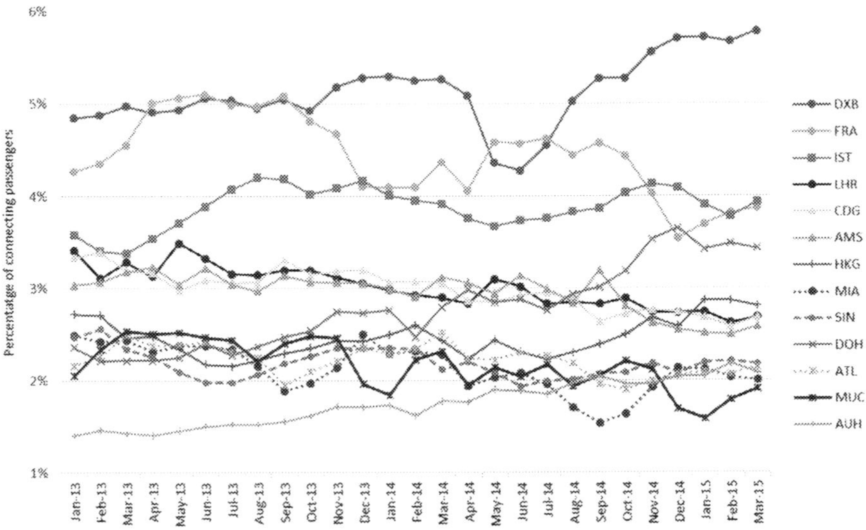

Fig. 4. Top 13 Worldwide Hubs in Terms of Percentage of Connecting Passengers (c) in International Markets: January 2013–March 2015. *Source*: MIDT.

(CDG), Amsterdam (AMS), and Munich (MUC) have gradually become smaller players. The situation for the top Asian and North American hubs is not that polarized. While Atlanta (ATL) and Hong Kong (HKG) remain relatively stable, Miami (MIA) and Singapore (SIN) present a slight decrease of connectivity. Overall, the picture is that the main winners are the Middle East hubs and Istanbul, and that the main losers (in terms of connecting market share) are the European hubs.

The rise of the Middle Eastern airports (and also Middle Eastern carriers) shown in Fig. 4 has been central to the complaints of the US carriers. In particular, they have denounced that, by using sixth-freedom rights, Gulf carriers are flooding the market with over capacity, especially between United States and Asia. In this regard, Figs. 5 and 6 look into the connectivity shares of a selection of hubs in the market between North America and Asia-Pacific. The results show that the Middle East hubs have slightly increased their market share at the expense of European and Japanese hubs, which host flight connections provided by US carriers and their alliance partners.

The fall of European hubs in terms of passenger connections can be illustrated further by exploring the Europe–Asia Pacific (Fig. 7) and the Europe–Africa markets (Fig. 8). In the former, Dubai (DXB), Istanbul (IST), and especially Doha (DOH) have been gaining some ground. While London Heathrow (LHR) and Paris (CDG) have been able to maintain a stable market share –probably because of the partnership of British Airways with Qatar

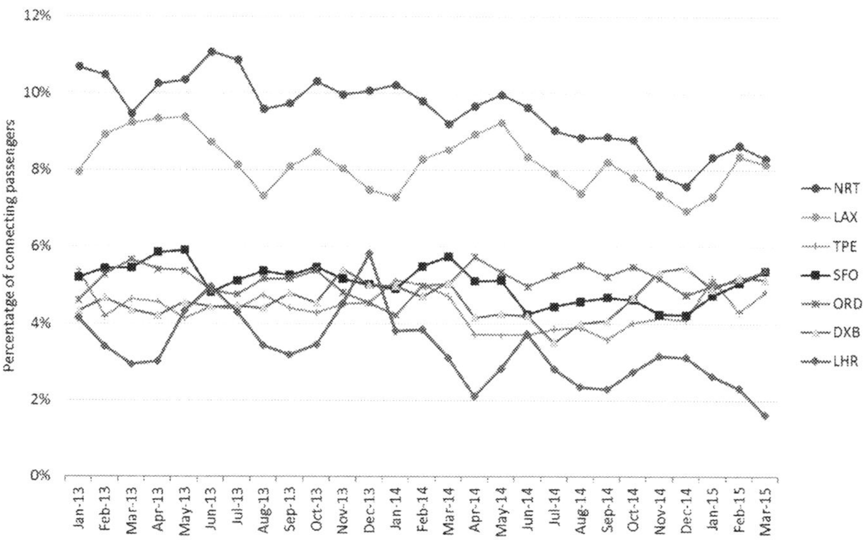

Fig. 5. Evolution of Connecting Shares for a Selection of Hubs in the North America–Asia Pacific market: January 2013 to March 2015. *Source*: MIDT.

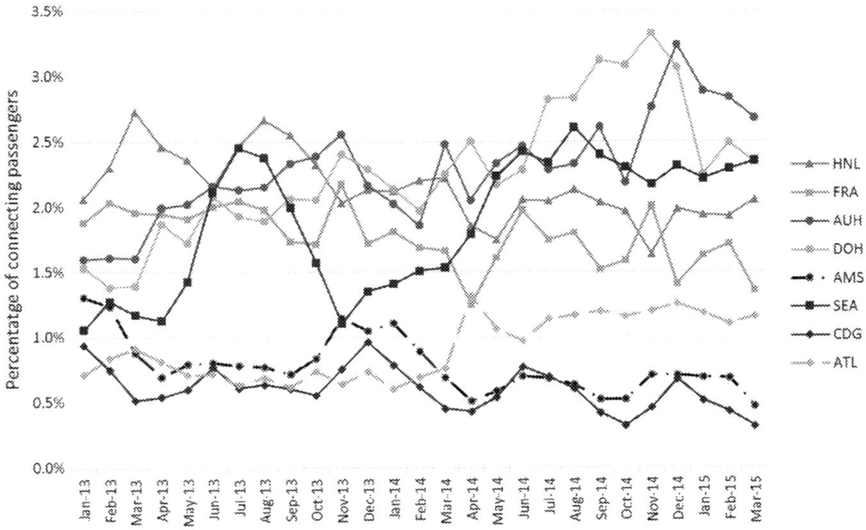

Fig. 6. Evolution of Connecting Shares for a Selection of Hubs in the North America–Asia Pacific Market: January 2013 to March 2015. *Source*: MIDT.

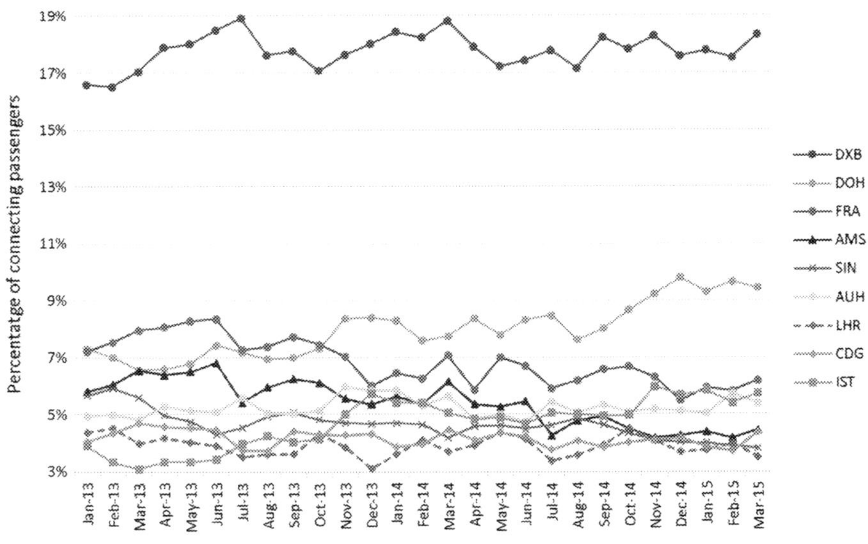

Fig. 7. Selection of Hubs in Terms of Percentage of Connecting Passengers in the European Economic Area–Asia Pacific Market. *Source*: MIDT.

Airways and the relationships between Air France and a significant number of Chinese airlines via the SkyTeam alliance–, the other European hubs have been losing terrain, especially Frankfurt (FRA) and Amsterdam (AMS). Singapore (SIN) has also lost significant market share, as a result of the continued decline followed the loss of the kangaroo route[6]. Concerning the European–Africa market (Figs. 8 and 9), the long-term leadership of Paris (CDG) is now contested by Dubai (DXB). In this regard, passengers seem willing to endure longer flying times in exchange for cheaper fares (Suau-Sanchez et al., 2016a). Also, Johannesburg (JNB) has substantially improved its position following a substantial development in the short-haul network of South African Airways, and the traffic from Turkish Airlines and Ethiopian to onward destinations that stop at Johannesburg to pick up and drop passengers.

Hence, we can conclude that Dubai, Doha, Istanbul and, to a lesser extent, Abu Dhabi are increasing their connecting share in global markets. As the greatest direct competitors, most of the European and some Asian hubs seem to be progressively lagging behind. While the Asian hubs only lose market share in particular markets and in relation to changes in airline strategies (e.g., the change in the kangaroo route), the European hub airports seem to be generally losing their position in most of the long-haul markets. A possible reason behind this could be airport capacity and noise-related operational restrictions because of environmental standards. Indeed, according to Burghouwt (2014) capacity shortages at primary European hubs have been one of the main

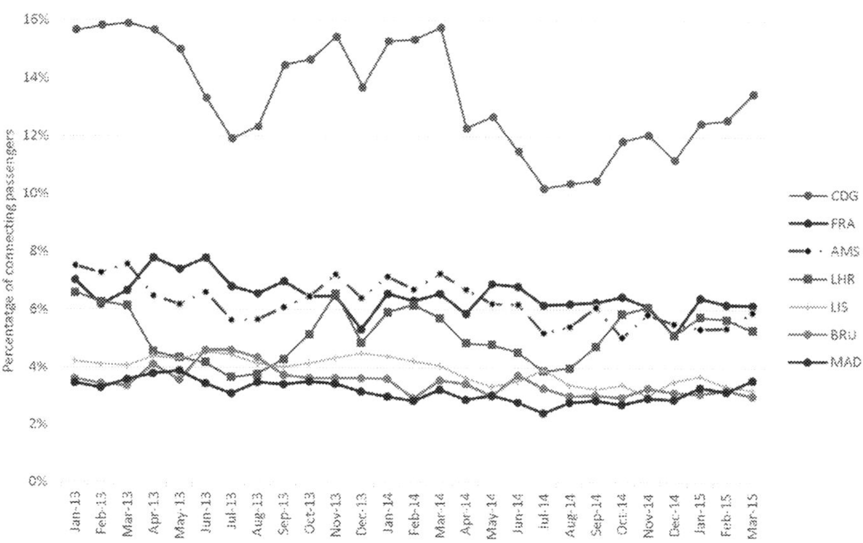

Fig. 8. Selection of European Hubs in Terms of Percentage of Connecting Passengers in the European Economic Area–Africa Market. *Source*: MIDT.

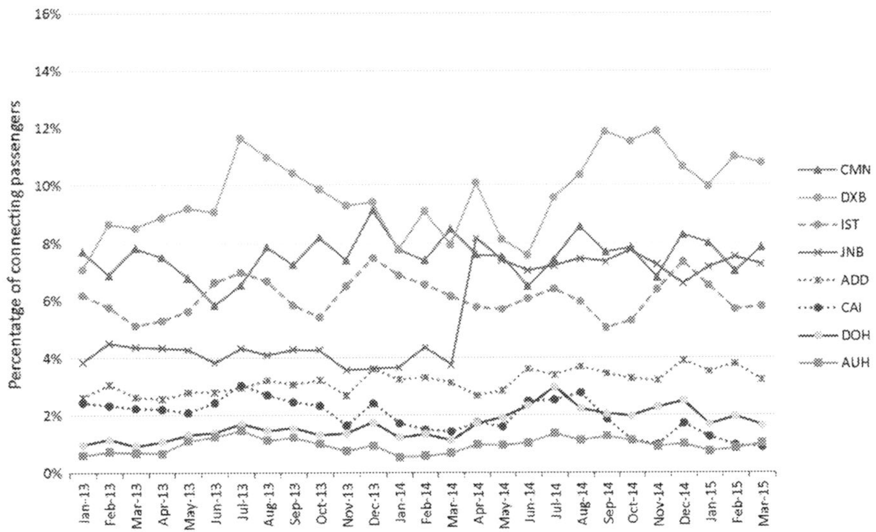

Fig. 9. Selection of African and Middle East Hubs in Terms of Percentage of Connecting Passengers in the European Economic Area–Africa Market. *Source*: MIDT.

motivations for airlines to open a secondary hub in order to accommodate market growth. A good example is the secondary hub of Lufthansa at Munich. This is usually translated into a weaker position in connecting markets, since one large hub attracts significantly more transfer passengers than two hubs of half the size (Goedeking, 2010). Our results do not show a deterioration of the North American hub airports regarding their capacity to capture market share in connecting markets. However, it is true that, due to their less central position in relation to the global flows, the North American hubs are mainly focused on being gateways for their domestic market and only lead in certain specific worldwide markets.

Quality of Airport Connectivity

Now we turn the attention to the quality of the airport connectivity, which is one of the decisive factors for the choice of the itinerary by the passenger (Hess & Polak, 2005). Table 5 presents the top-10 airports in terms of the quality of their connectivity (travel time increase and its components). Table 6 ranks the airports by average connecting time[7], and Table 7 presents the average travel distances and travel times of connecting passengers for the top-10 airports. All tables refer to worldwide international markets. While the previous section showed that Middle East hubs have been able to increase significantly the quantity of connecting passengers traveling through them and lead in several markets, from the perspective of quality our results show a general dominance of European hubs.

Table 6 shows that the North American, European, and Asian hubs generally provide the fastest connection times between flights. The Middle East hubs perform quite poorly, especially Dubai and Abu Dhabi, which have an average connecting time of 2 h 46 min, very far from the time of Atlanta and Miami (1 h 40 min), Frankfurt (1 h 46 min) or London Heathrow (1 h 59 min). Figs 10–12 provide a more detailed analysis and compare the distribution of connecting times of Heathrow, Frankfurt, and Atlanta to Dubai. In the first three cases, most of the connections take place within 2 hours after the passenger's arrival, whereas Dubai has a long tail of passengers with longer connecting times[8]. A more detailed breakdown is provided in Fig. 13, which shows the hourly distribution of connecting passengers at Heathrow, Dubai, and Frankfurt. Traditional wave-system analysis assumes that the existence of a clearly defined system of incoming and outgoing waves of flights that is a good proxy for hub efficiency, as most passengers connect within some predefined transfer windows. Figure 13 provides a new view on an airport's wave system by giving additional information on the time that the connecting passengers stay at the terminal until they are processed and depart with the onward flight. For example, Heathrow, that lacks of a wave system and British Airways

Table 5. KPIs for the Top-10 Airports in Terms of Airport Connectivity Quality, Selection of Airports Based on a 50% Similarity to LHR Connectivity, Worldwide International Markets, June 2014 and 2015.

2015								
Detour Time Increase (DTI)			Connecting Time Increase (CTI)			Total Time Increase (TTI)		
Airport		%		Airport	%		Airport	%
1	London Heathrow (LHR)	16.0	1	Singapore Changi (SIN)	16.6	1	Singapore Changi (SIN)	35.6
2	Singapore Changi (SIN)	16.3	2	Hong Kong (HKG)	16.6	2	London Heathrow (LHR)	36.2
3	Frankfurt (FRA)	16.6	3	London (LHR)	17.5	3	Hong Kong International (HKG)	38.6
4	Amsterdam (AMS)	16.6	4	Atlanta (ATL)	19.2	4	Amsterdam (AMS)	39.8
5	Dubai (DXB)	17.0	5	Amsterdam (AMS)	19.9	5	Frankfurt (FRA)	40.4
6	Paris (CDG)	17.2	6	Frankfurt (FRA)	20.5	6	Paris (CDG)	41.8
7	Abu Dhabi (AUH)	18.5	7	Abu Dhabi (AUH)	20.5	7	Dubai (DXB)	42.2
8	Doha (DOH)	18.5	8	Paris (CDG)	21.0	8	Abu Dhabi (AUH)	42.9
9	Madrid Barajas (MAD)	18.6	9	Doha (DOH)	21.1	9	Doha (DOH)	43.5
10	Hong Kong (HKG)	18.9	10	Dubai (DXB)	21.5	10	Madrid Barajas (MAD)	44.1
2014								
Detour Time Increase (DTI)			Connecting Time Increase (CTI)			Total Time Increase (TTI)		
1	London Heathrow (LHR)	16.5	1	Singapore Changi (SIN)	15.9	1	Singapore Changi (SIN)	36.0
2	Dubai (DXB)	17.1	2	Chicago O'Hare (ORD)	16.3	2	London Heathrow (LHR)	36.7
3	Singapore Changi (SIN)	17.4	3	Hong Kong (HKG)	16.5	3	Chicago O'Hare (ORD)	36.8
4	Chicago O'Hare (ORD)	17.6	4	London Heathrow (LHR)	17.3	4	Hong Kong (HKG)	39.1
5	Amsterdam (AMS)	17.7	5	Atlanta (ATL)	18.8	5	Amsterdam (AMS)	40.0
6	Abu Dhabi (AUH)	18.2	6	Amsterdam (AMS)	18.9	6	Abu Dhabi (AUH)	42.7
7	Paris (CDG)	18.7	7	Houston George Bush (IAH)	19.2	7	Madrid Barajas (MAD)	43.7
8	Madrid Barajas (MAD)	19.2	8	Madrid Barajas (MAD)	20.6	8	Dubai (DXB)	45.3
9	Bangkok (BKK)	19.2	9	Abu Dhabi (AUH)	20.7	9	Bangkok (BKK)	45.5
10	Hong Kong (HKG)	19.4	10	Bangkok (BKK)	22.1	10	Paris (CDG)	45.6

Source: Authors from OAG Schedules and Traffic Analyser.

Table 6. Average Connecting Times, Selection of Airports Based on a 50% Similarity to LHR Connectivity Value, Worldwide International Markets, June 2015.

Average Connecting Times		
	Airport	
1	Atlanta Hartsfield-Jackson Intl (ATL)	1 h 40 min
2	Miami International (MIA)	1 h 40 min
3	Frankfurt International (FRA)	1 h 46 min
4	Amsterdam (AMS)	1 h 54 min
5	Hong Kong International (HKG)	1 h 56 min
6	Singapore Changi (SIN)	1 h 56 min
7	London Heathrow (LHR)	1 h 59 min
8	Madrid Barajas (MAD)	2 h 05 min
9	Paris Charles de Gaulle (CDG)	2 h 15 min
10	Istanbul Ataturk (IST)	2 h 19 min
...		
	Doha	2 h 24 min
	Dubai (DBX)	2 h 46 min
	Abu Dhabi (AUH)	2 h 46 min

Source: Authors from OAG Schedules and Traffic Analyser.

operates a sort of rolling hub at the airport which seems to be relatively efficient in processing passenger connections (i.e., bands that separate between connecting passengers according to arrival time are more vertical, indicating a shorter stay at the airport). Dubai, on the other hand, presents more horizontal bands associated to Emirates' wave system. While one may argue that Dubai's hub is less efficient, it is important to note that airports with longer connecting times may serve longer city pairs. As indicated in Table 7, the average travel distance of a connecting passenger flying via Dubai is 9,743 km. This value is significantly larger than in the case of Atlanta (5,959 km) and Frankfurt (5,638 km) as most of their connections are between a short-haul and a long-haul flight.

Hence, comparing connecting times of hubs that serve markets with different city pairs lengths can be misleading due to the inverse relationship between flight length and daily frequency. The Connecting Time Increase (CTI) indicator (Table 5) improves comparability as it allows us to weight the connecting time inversely with the city-pair length. For example, London Heathrow, which serves very long city pairs (8,317 km), achieves an acceptable average connecting time (1 h 59 min), therefore increasing the travel time in only 17.5%. CTI

Table 7. Average Travel Distances and Times of Connecting Passengers for the top-10 Airports in teRms of Connectivity, Worldwide International Markets, June 2015.

Connectivity Rank	1	2	3	4	5	6	7	8	9	10
Airport	Dubai (DXB)	Frankfurt (FRA)	Istanbul (IST)	London (LHR)	Paris (CDG)	Amsterdam (AMS)	Doha (DOH)	Hong Kong (HKG)	Munich (MUC)	Atlanta (ATL)
Travel Distances										
Avg. direct great circle distance (km)	8,686	5,638	4,631	7,651	7,140	6,335	7,493	7,611	3,791	5,380
Avg. traveled great circle distance (km) (via hub)	9,743	6,159	5,158	8,317	7,864	6,942	8,379	8,384	4,185	5,959
Avg. geographic detour (%)	12.2%	9.2%	11.4%	8.7%	10.1%	9.6%	11.8%	10.2%	10.4%	10.8%
Travel Times										
Avg. minimum flying time	11 h 4'	7 h 25'	6 h 16'	9 h 47'	9 h 11'	8 h 14'	9 h 39'	9 h 51'	5 h 14'	7 h 9'
Avg. total flying time	12 h 57'	8 h 38'	7 h 54'	11 h 21'	10 h 45'	9 h 36'	11 h 27'	11 h 43'	6 h 18'	8 h 43'
Avg. total travel time	15 h 44'	10 h 25'	10 h 13'	13 h 20'	13 h 1'	11 h 30'	13 h 51'	13 h 39'	7 h 48'	10 h 23'

Source: Authors from OAG Schedules and Traffic Analyser.

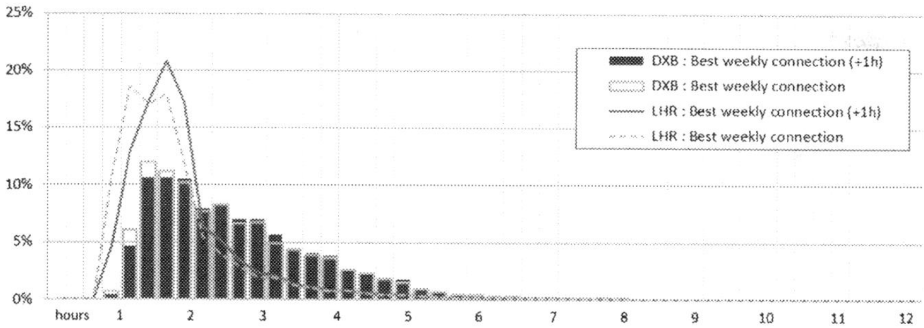

Fig. 10. Distribution of Connecting Times in Worldwide International Markets, Dubai and Heathrow, 2015. *Source*: MIDT.

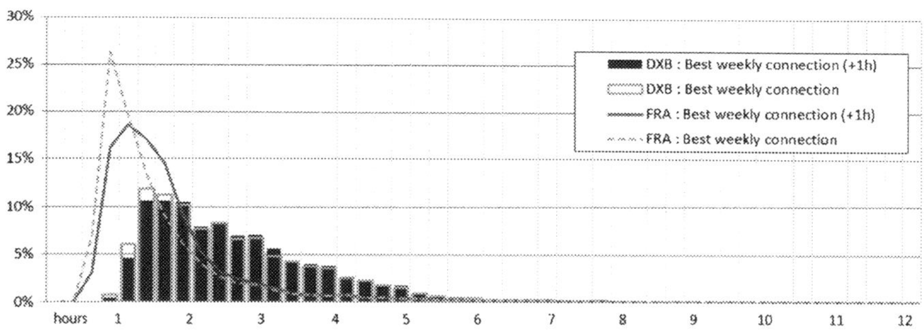

Fig. 11. Distribution of Connecting Times in Worldwide International Markets, Dubai and Frankfurt, 2015. *Source*: MIDT.

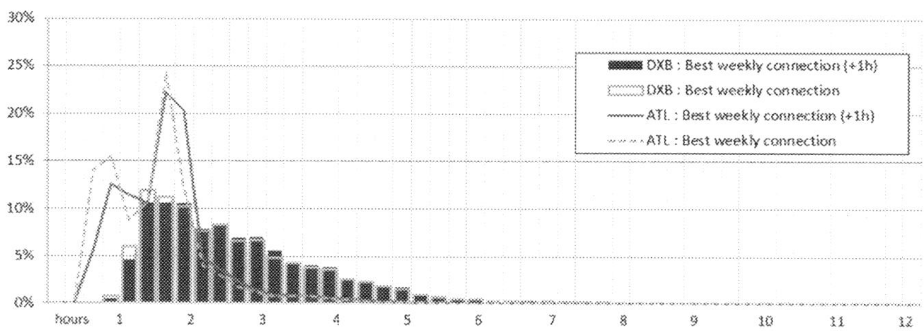

Fig. 12. Distribution of Connecting Times in Worldwide International Markets, Dubai and Atlanta, 2015. *Source*: MIDT.

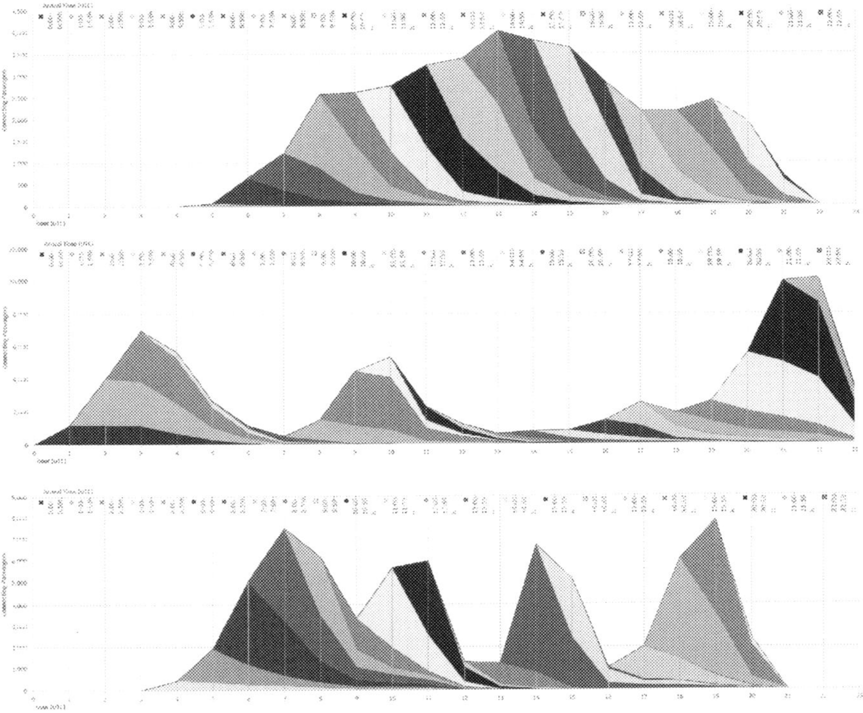

Fig. 13. Hourly Distribution of Connecting Passengers at London Heathrow (Top), Dubai (Middle) and Frankfurt (Bottom) in Worldwide International Markets, Breakdown by Arrival Time (Monday), 2015. *Source*: MIDT.

shows that, overall, the most efficient airports connecting passengers are the Asian (i.e., Singapore and Hong Kong), followed by the European (i.e., London Heathrow) and North American (i.e., Atlanta). Although, the Middle East hubs are in the top 10, they present CTI values very far from the top-3. Doha, for instance, serves city pairs of 8,379 km on average, the same length as Heathrow and Hong Kong, but its CTI is significantly higher (21.1%). Regarding the North American hubs, it is worth highlighting that from 2014 to 2015 Chicago and Houston dropped from the top 10, which is probably related to changes in network structure after the American Airlines and US Airlines merger.

Geography is one of the key factors for a successful hub (Redondo et al., 2011). Certainly, Qatar and the United Arab Emirates promote their location as the crossroads of Europe, Asia, and Africa, and highlight their central location with a motto reminding that they have access to a massive market: "80 percent of the world population within distance of an eight-hour flight." However, the geographical efficiency of a hub cannot be measured by the market size delivered by a central location, but should be measured in relation to the markets it actually serves. For example, some passengers might be willing to withstand big detours even when a quicker travel option is available. This is the case, for example, for Dubai in the European–African market (Suau-Sanchez et al., 2016a). This conforms to the findings of previous studies that identify a trade-off between airfares and travel time in air passengers' choice of itineraries (see, e.g., Hess, 2007). We use Detour Time Increase (DTI) to capture the geographical efficiency of the markets served by the airport. The results for 2015 show that Dubai, Abu Dhabi, and Doha have become slightly less geographically efficient than major European airports like Heathrow, Amsterdam, and Frankfurt. In other words, the combination of their central location and low fares provides opportunities to offer connections between regions along the great circle distance (e.g., Europe to South East Asia via the Middle East), but also between regions in which connecting in the Middle East means a relatively large detour (e.g., Europe to Africa via the Middle East), thus harming the overall DTI value.

Overall we can conclude this section saying that although Middle East hubs are, in quantitative terms, becoming leaders in connectivity, in qualitative terms, they lag behind in terms of average connecting times and geographical efficiency in worldwide international markets.

The Hidden Potential of Self-connectivity

Table 8 reports the results for the self-connectivity analysis by geographical region for June 2015, which comprises both domestic and international markets. The findings indicate that the airports showing major self-connectivity potential are those that have higher values of "traditional" connectivity and hence, this is not a phenomenon that is exclusive of low-cost airport bases as self-connections can be observed between non-allied full-service carriers and also between a full-service and an LCC. Atlanta is the airport with the most self-connectivity potential and it is used to normalize the values for all other airports. In fact, North American hub airports perform very well in terms of self-connectivity potential, clearly due to their high number and variety of domestic frequencies available. Asian and European hub airports also obtain fairly high SC values. Interestingly, in the European case, we find high self-connectivity potential in the top-10 airports, that are large low-cost bases serving big OD markets (i.e., London Gatwick, which has already launched the GatwickConnects service to facilitate connections between different airline services), and in smaller and medium hubs (i.e., Rome, Copenhagen, Vienna) in which the combination of the originating (mainly low-cost) and connecting traffic can result in a significant self-connectivity potential. For example, the

Table 8. Top-10 Airports by Region in Terms of Self-Connectivity (SC) Potential, June 2015.

	Europe - EEA	SC		Europe – Non-EEA and Middle East	SC		North America	SC
1	Frankfurt International (FRA)	0.380	1	Dubai (DXB)	0.392	1	Atlanta (ATL)	1.000
2	London Heathrow (LHR)	0.367	2	Istanbul Ataturk (IST)	0.263	2	Chicago O'Hare (ORD)	0.711
3	Rome Fiumicino (FCO)	0.342	3	Abu Dhabi (AUH)	0.181	3	Los Angeles (LAX)	0.664
4	Paris Charles de Gaulle (CDG)	0.320	4	Doha (DOH)	0.135	4	Phoenix Sky Harbor (PHX)	0.627
5	Amsterdam (AMS)	0.292	5	Moscow Domodedovo (DME)	0.128	5	Denver (DEN)	0.576
6	Munich International (MUC)	0.215	6	Jaddah (JED)	0.086	6	Las Vegas McCarran (LAS)	0.476
7	London Gatwick (LGW)	0.181	7	Riyadh (RUH)	0.069	7	New York (JFK)	0.367
8	Madrid Barajas (MAD)	0.178	8	Moscow Vnukovo (VKO)	0.047	8	San Francisco (SFO)	0.313
9	Copenhagen (CPH)	0.167	9	Istanbul Sabiha Gokcen	0.047	9	Dallas/Fort Worth (DFW)	0.282
10	Vienna (VIE)	0.128	10	Sharjah (SHJ)	0.036	10	Fort Lauderdale (FLL)	0.249
	Latin America	**SC**		**Africa**	**SC**		**Asia-Pacific**	**SC**
1	Sao Paulo Guarulhos (GRU)	0.329	1	Johannesburg (JNB)	0.083	1	Hong Kong (HKG)	0.506
2	Mexico City Juarez (MEX)	0.131	2	Nairobi (NBO)	0.028	2	Kuala Lumpur (KUL)	0.402
3	Sao Paulo Viracopos (VCP)	0.067	3	Lagos (LOS)	0.021	3	Delhi (DEL)	0.267
4	Brasilia (BSB)	0.072	4	Casablanca (CMN)	0.017	4	Mumbai (BOM)	0.263
5	Sao Paulo Congonhas (CGH)	0.075	5	Tunis (TUN)	0.012	5	Singapore (SIN)	0.343
6	San Juan (SJU)	0.043	6	Dar Es Salaam (DAR)	0.007	6	Bangkok (BKK)	0.192
7	Lima (LIM)	0.041	7	Douala (DLA)	0.005	7	Beijing Capital (PEK)	0.180
8	Rio de Janeiro (GIG)	0.048	8	Abuja (ABV)	0.009	8	Tokyo Haneda (HND)	0.196
9	Belo Horizonte (CNF)	0.044	9	Algiers (ALG)	0.011	9	Tokyo Narita (NRT)	0.155
10	Cancun (CUN)	0.048	10	Accra (ACC)	0.008	10	Sydney (SYD)	0.164

Source: Authors from OAG Schedules and Traffic Analyser.

combination of Vueling, an LCC, and Alitalia, (a full-service network carrier) explains the high potential at Rome Fiumicino. For the non-EEA Europe, the Middle East and Latin American, the results are quite polarized and only the main gateways show a significant self-connectivity potential. In Africa, the potential is very limited, as airline networks are still underdeveloped. Overall, the results show that the hubs in each region (e.g., Frankfurt, Atlanta) and the gateways between continents (e.g., Dubai) obtain the highest potential. According to Suau-Sanchez, Voltes-Dorta, and Rodríguez-Déniz (2016b), the reason behind that could be that, aside from the number of available flight connections, those type of airports have the highest values of betweenness centrality, as they lie in a high proportion of shortest-path itineraries between other airports; hence, generating more opportunities for passengers to build attractive travel itineraries.

SUMMARY AND CONCLUSIONS

This study provided an analysis of airport connectivity based on supply and demand data, with particular focus on ranking the quantity and quality of hub connections provided by major airports in worldwide international markets. By using a set of quantitative indicators, the analysis tries to determine the evolution of the competitive position of global hubs, the rise of the Middle East hubs, and the potential for self-connectivity.

In terms of traffic generation and total number of destinations (direct and indirect) the most important airport in global international markets is London Heathrow. Yet, from the perspective of hub connectivity (i.e., market share of passenger connections), Dubai, followed closely by Frankfurt and Istanbul, are the most important airports. Moreover, Dubai, Doha, Istanbul, and to a lesser extent Abu Dhabi have been gaining market share in worldwide connecting markets at the expense of European hubs. This has been particularly observed in the market between North America and Asia-Pacific. Furthermore, Asian hubs seem to have lost their advantage in certain long-distance markets in which they have faced direct competition from the Middle East. Regarding the quality of airport connectivity, we have discussed the difference between having a good geographical location and showing a high geographical efficiency, which is measured in relation to the markets an airport actually serves. Results show that Dubai, Abu Dhabi and Doha are slightly less geographically efficient than the major European hubs since they participate in markets in which the connections provided do not follow the great circle distance. When the relative travel time detours are considered, the most time-efficient airports are the Asians (e.g., Singapore and Hong Kong) and the Europeans (London Heathrow, Amsterdam, Frankfurt, and Paris). Overall, we conclude that although Middle East hubs have become leaders in global international connectivity but they still lag behind their competitors in travel detours. Finally, our simple self-connectivity potential indicator shows that the major hubs in each region (e.g., Frankfurt, Atlanta) and the gateways between continents (e.g., Dubai) obtain the highest potential, proving that self-connectivity is not limited to low-cost airport bases.

These results should contribute to refocus the discussion about the rise of the Middle East hubs. While the discussion has mainly been focused on market shares, quantity, and size, our results indicate that the discussion should also focus on quality and efficiency. Firstly, US hubs seem to keep their position in a more competitive market. Secondly, European hubs seem to have problems related to their growth limits (e.g., curfews, airport capacity, hub specialization, planning limitations, etc.), which exacerbates the impact of the quick rise of Middle East hubs and the market leakage. Thirdly, Asian hubs seem to be impacted on certain particular markets, but otherwise resist well. Fourthly, quality and efficiency is the strength of European and Asian hubs, which they do not seem to be able to leverage in policy discussions, nor when it comes to marketing campaigns. In this regard, the increasing importance of the travel experience for the air traveler (e.g., Jiang & Zhang, 2016) is an area in which European and Asian airports should capitalize to generate increasing revenues. The debate on limited airport capacity, quality of service and increasing prices is highly linked to the discussion on the creation and impact of scarcity rents. Scarcity rents are out of the scope of this study and, in fact, there is limited literature on this topic. Yet, the generation of scarcity rents because of congestion could penalize the passengers in some European airports, and could redefine the discussion about the different forces acting in global connecting markets. With restricted access to an airport, the market processes cannot function, and the restricted capacity will lead to rising ticket prices to match passenger numbers to the seats available (ACI, 2017; Frontier Economics, 2014). In turn, this would place the airport in a weaker competitive position in the global connecting markets.

NOTES

1. Sixth freedom: the right of a carrier to transport passengers between foreign countries while stopping in the airline's own country.
2. Providing flight transfers has traditionally been considered incompatible with the low-cost business model. There are a few exceptions, airlines like Vueling, Air Berlin, Norwegian, or Southwest offer connecting services between some of their flights.
3. The degree centrality of a given airport represents the number of other airports to which it is connected by a non-stop flight. The betweenness centrality of an airport *i* is proportional to the number of shortest paths connecting any two other airports that involve a stopover at airport *i*.
4. The goal is to prevent all passengers from being allocated to the best weekly connection, which can lead to capacity problems.

5. The average number of indirect destinations generated by each direct destination is significantly higher for Heathrow (8.25) than for Dubai (5.68) and Frankfurt (5.31).

6. The Kangaroo Route traditionally refers to routes flown by Qantas between Australia and the United Kingdom via the Eastern Hemisphere. Although the term was coined by Qantas, it is used by others to refer to this type of routes.

7. These tables only include airports that have at least 50% the level of connectivity of Heathrow. This is done to compare only airports that have the largest connecting shares in worldwide international markets.

8. Figures 10–12 also provide information on the distribution of times for different capacity scenarios. The red solid line and the dark blue column provide the results considering capacity restrictions (i.e., when the aircraft for the best connection is full passengers are then allocated to the second best connection). The red dashed line and the light blue line provide the results without capacity restrictions, in other words, allocating all passengers to the best weekly connection. This provides indications for airports and airlines in terms of their capacity to improve their hub connectivity offerings in certain markets.

REFERENCES

ACI. (2017). *The impact of airport capacity constraints on air fares*. Airports Council International, SEO Amsterdam Economics and Cranfield University.

Airbus. (2012). Global Market Forecast 2012-2031, Airbus S.A.S., Toulouse, France.

Allroggen, F., Wittmann, D., & Malina, R. (2015). How air transport connects the world – A new metric of air connectivity and its evolution between 1990 and 2012. *Transportation Research Part E*, *80*, 184–201.

ARG. (2013). Atmosphere's global travel industry executive survey. Q3 2012. Retrieved from http://www.iata.org/whatwedo/stb/Documents/future-airline-distributionreport.pdf

Bel, G., & Fageda, X. (2008). Getting there fast: Globalization, intercontinental flights and location of headquarters. *Journal of Economic Geography*, *8*, 471–495.

Bel, G., & Fageda, X. (2010). Intercontinental flights from European airports: Towards hub concentration or not? *International Journal of Transport Economics*, *37*, 133–153.

Bowen, J. (2002). Network change, deregulation, and access in the global airline industry. *Economic Geography*, *78*, 425–439.

Bowen, J. T. (2010). *The economic geography of air transportation: Space, time, and the freedom of the sky*. New York, NY: Routledge.

Brueckner, J. K. (2003). Airline traffic and economic development. *Urban Studies*, *40*, 1455–1469.

Burghouwt, G. (2007). *Airline network developments in Europe and its implications for airport planning*. Aldershot: Ashgate.

Burghouwt, G. (2014). Long-haul specialization patterns in European multihub airline networks – An exploratory analysis. *Journal of Air Transport Management*, *34*, 30–41.

Burghouwt, G., & Redondi, R. (2013). Connectivity in air transport networks: An assessment of models and applications. *Journal of Transport Economics and Policy*, *47*, 35–53.

Burghouwt, G., & de Wit, J. (2005). Temporal configurations of European airline networks. *Journal of Air Transport Management*, *11*, 185–198.

Button, K. (2002). Debunking some common myths about airport hubs. *Journal of Air Transport Management*, *8*, 177–188.

Ciliberto, F., & Schenotne, C. (2012). Bankruptcy and product-market competition: Evidence from the airline industry. *International Journal of Industrial Organization*, *30*, 564–577.

De Poret, M., O'Connell, J., & Warnock-Smith, D. (2015). The economic viability of long-haul low cost operations: Evidence from the transatlantic market. *Journal of Air Transport Management*, *42*, 272–281.

De Wit, J. (2014). Unlevel playing field? A yes, you mean protectionism. *Journal of Air Transport Management*, *41*, 22–29.

Dijkstra, L., Garcilazo, E., & McCann, P. (2013). The economic performance of European cities and city regions: Myths and realities. *European Planning Studies*, *21*, 334–354.

Dobruszkes, F. (2006). An analysis of European low-cost airlines and their networks. *Journal of Transport Geography*, *14*, 249–264.

Dobruszkes, F. (2013). The geography of European low-cost airline networks: A contemporary analysis. *Journal of Transport Geography*, *28*, 75–88.

Doganis, R. (2002). *Flying off course*. London: Routledge.

Doganis, R. (2010). *Flying off course: Airline economics and marketing* (4th ed.). London: Routledge.

EC. (2014). Communication from the Commission – Guidelines on State aid to Airports and Airlines. Official Journal of the European Union 57. 04/04/2014.

Fageda, X., Suau-Sanchez, P., & Mason, K. (2015). The evolving low-cost business model: Network implications of fare bundling and connecting flights in Europe. *Journal of Air Transport Management*, *42*, 289–296.

Fichert, F., & Klophaus, R. (2016). Self-connecting, codesharing and hubbing among European LCCs: From point-to-point to connections? *Research in Transportation Business & Management*, doi:10.1016/j.rtbm.2016.07.001

Florida, R., Mellander, C., & Holgersson, T. (2015). Up in the air: The role of airports for regional economic development. *Annals of Regional Science*, *54*, 197–214.

Frontier Economics. (2014). *Impact of airport expansion options on competition and choice*. A report prepared for Heathrow Airport. London.

Goedeking, P. (2010). *Networks in aviation*. Heidelberg: Springer Verlag.

Goetz, A. R. (1992). Air passenger transportation and growth in the US urban system, 1950–1987. *Growth and Change*, *23*, 217–238.

Grether, J. M., & Mathys, N. A. (2010). Is the world's economic centre of gravity already in Asia? *Area*, *42*, 47–50.

Grimme, W. (2011). The growth of Arabian airlines from a German perspective – A study of the impacts of new air services to Asia. *Journal of Air Transport Management*, *17*, 333–338.

Grosche, T., & Klophaus, R. (2015). Hubs at risk: Exposure of Europe's largest hubs to competition on transfer city pairs. *Transport Policy*, *43*, 55–60.

Guimerà, R., Mossa, S., Turtschi, A., & Amaral, L. A. (2005). The worldwide air transport network: anomalous centrality, community structure and cities' global roles'. *Proceedings of the National Academy of Sciences*, *102*(22), 7794–7799.

Hess, S. (2007). Posterior analysis of random taste coefficients in air travel behaviour modelling. *Journal of Air Transport Management*, *13*, 203–212.

Hess, S., & Polak, J. W. (2005). Mixed logit modelling of airport choice in multi-airport regions. *Journal of Air Transport Management*, *11*, 59–68.

Hooper, P., Walker, S., Moor, C., & Al Zubaidi, Z. (2011). The development of the Gulf region's air transport networks – The first century. *Journal of Air Transport Management*, *17*, 325–332.

ICAO. (2014). List of low-cost carriers. Retrieved from http://www.icao.int/sustainability/Documents/LCC-list.pdf.

Jiang, H., & Zhang, Y. (2016). An assessment of passenger experience at Melbourne Airport. *Journal Air Transport Management*, *54*, 88–92.

Jimenez, E., Claro, J., & Pinho de Sousa, J. (2013). The airport business in a competitive environment. *European Journal of Transport Infrastructure Research*, *13*, 315–335.

Klophaus, R., Conrady, R., & Fichert, F. (2012). Low cost carriers going hybrid: Evidence from Europe. *Journal of Air Transport Management*, *23*, 54–58.

Maertens, S. (2010). Drivers for long haul flight supply at secondary airports in Europe. *Journal of Air Transport Management*, *16*, 239–243.

Maertens, S., Pabst, H., & Grimme, W. (2016). The scope for low-cost connecting services in Europe – Is self-hubbing only the beginning? *Research in Transportation Business & Management*, doi:10.1016/j.rtbm.2016.08.004

Malighetti, P., Paleari, S., & Redondi, R. (2008). Connectivity of the European airport network: "self-help hubbing" and business implications. *Journal of Air Transport Management, 14*, 53–65.

OAG. (2016). Self-connection: The rise and roadblocks of a growing travel booking strategy. OAG Reports.

O'Connell, J. F. (2011a). The rise of the Arabian Gulf carriers: An insight into the business model of Emirates Airline. *Journal of Air Transport Management, 17*, 339–346.

O'Connell, J. F. (2011b). An examination of the world's most profitable airline in 2009/10: the Emirates business model. In F. O'Connel & G. Williams (Eds.), *Air transport in the 21st century: Key strategic developments*. Farnham: Ashgate Publishing.

O'Connor, K. (2003). Global air travel: Toward concentration or dispersal? *Journal of Transport Geography, 11*, 83–92.

O'Connor, K., & Fuellhart, K. (2013). Change in air services at second rank cities. *Journal of Air Transport Management, 28*, 26–30.

Partnership for Open Fair Skies. (2015). Retrieved from http://www.openandfairskies.com/

Quah, D. (2011). The global economy's shifting centre of gravity. *Global Policy, 2*(1), 3–9.

Redondi, R., Malighetti, P., & Paleari, S. (2012). De-hubbing of airports and their recovery patterns. *Journal of Air Transport Management, 18*, 1–4.

Redondo, R., Malighetti, P., & Paleari, S. (2011). Hub competition and travel times in the world-wide network. *Journal of Transport Geography, 19*, 1260–1271.

Rodríguez-Déniz, H., Suau-Sanchez, P., & Voltes-Dorta, A. (2013). Classifying airports according to their hub dimensions: An application to the US domestic network. *Journal of Transport Geography, 33*, 188–195.

Seredyński, A., Rothlauf, F., & Grosche, T. (2014). An airline connection builder using maximum connection lag with greedy parameter selection. *Journal of Air Transport Management, 36*, 120–128.

Suau-Sanchez, P., Voltes-Dorta, A., & Rodríguez-Déniz, H. (2015). Regulatory airport classification in the US: The role of international markets. *Transport Policy, 37*, 157–166.

Suau-Sanchez, P., Voltes-Dorta, A., & Rodríguez-Déniz, H. (2016a). The role of London airports in providing connectivity for the UK: Regional dependence on foreign hubs. *Journal of Transport Geography, 50*, 94–104.

Suau-Sanchez, P., Voltes-Dorta, A., & Rodríguez-Déniz, H. (2016b). Measuring the potential for self-connectivity in global air transport markets: Implications for airports and airlines. *Journal of Transport Geography, 57*, 70–82.

Tembleque-Vilalta, M., & Suau-Sanchez, P. (2016). A model to analyse the profitability of long-haul network development involving non-hub airports: The case of the Barcelona-Asian market. *Case studies on Transport Policy, 4*, 188–197.

Van de Vijver, E., Derudder, B., & Witlox, F. (2014). Exploring causality in trade and air passenger travel relationships: The case of Asia-Pacific, 1980-2010. *Journal of Transport Geography, 34*, 142–150.

Veldhuis, J. (1997). The competitive position of airline networks. *Journal of Air Transport Management, 3*, 181–188.

INDEX

Printed in the United States
By Bookmasters